Multinational Enterprises and Host Country Development

World Scientific Studies in International Economics
(ISSN: 1793-3641)

Vol. 43 Farm Policies and World Markets: Monitoring and Disciplining the International Trade Impacts of Agricultural Policies
by Tim Josling (Stanford University, USA)

Vol. 44 Non-Tariff Barriers, Regionalism and Poverty: Essays in Applied International Trade Analysis
by L. Alan Winters (University of Sussex, UK)

Vol. 45 Trade Law, Domestic Regulation and Development
by Joel P. Trachtman (Tufts University, USA)

Vol. 46 The Political Economy of International Trade
by Edward D. Mansfield (University of Pennsylvania, USA)

Vol. 47 Trade-Related Agricultural Policy Analysis
by *David Orden (Virginia Polytechnic Institute and State University, USA)*

Vol. 48 The New International Financial System: Analyzing the Cumulative Impact of Regulatory Reform
edited by Douglas Evanoff (Federal Reserve Bank of Chicago, USA), Andrew G. Haldane (Bank of England, UK) & George Kaufman (Loyola University Chicago, USA)

Vol. 49 The Economics of International Migration
by Giovanni Peri (UC Davis)

Vol. 50 The Legal and Economic Analysis of the WTO/FTA System
by Dukgeun Ahn (Seoul National University, Korea)

Vol. 51 The Political Economy of Trade Policy: Theory, Evidence and Applications
by Devashish Mitra (Syracuse University, USA)

Vol. 52 Microeconometrics of International Trade
by Joachim Wagner (Leuphana University Lueneburg, Germany)

Vol. 53 Multinational Enterprises and Host Country Development
by Holger Görg (Kiel Institute for the World Economy, Germany)

The complete list of the published volumes in the series can be found at
http://www.worldscientific.com/series/wssie

53 World Scientific Studies in International Economics

Multinational Enterprises and Host Country Development

Holger Görg

Kiel Institute for the World Economy, Germany

World Scientific

NEW JERSEY • LONDON • SINGAPORE • BEIJING • SHANGHAI • HONG KONG • TAIPEI • CHENNAI • TOKYO

Published by

World Scientific Publishing Co. Pte. Ltd.
5 Toh Tuck Link, Singapore 596224
USA office: 27 Warren Street, Suite 401-402, Hackensack, NJ 07601
UK office: 57 Shelton Street, Covent Garden, London WC2H 9HE

British Library Cataloguing-in-Publication Data
A catalogue record for this book is available from the British Library.

World Scientific Studies in International Economics — Vol. 53
MULTINATIONAL ENTERPRISES AND HOST COUNTRY DEVELOPMENT

ISBN 978-981-4749-22-0

Desk Editor: Alisha Nguyen

Typeset by Stallion Press
Email: enquiries@stallionpress.com

About the Author

Holger Görg has been Professor of International Economics at the Kiel Institute for the World Economy, and the University of Kiel, Germany, since 2008. He is also affiliated with the Tuborg Research Centre for Globalisation and Firms, Aarhus University, the Centre for Research on Globalisation and Economic Policy at the University of Nottingham and IZA. Before joining Kiel he was on the staff at the University of Nottingham, the University of Ulster at Jordanstown and University College Cork. He completed a Ph.D. in Economics in 1999 at Trinity College Dublin. His research interests are in empirical international trade and industrial organisation focusing in particular on the activities of multinational companies, foreign direct investment, and international outsourcing. He has published widely in international journals, including the *Review of Economics and Statistics*, *Journal of International Economics*, *European Economic Review*, and *Economic Journal.* Prof. Görg has also worked as consultant for, among others, The World Bank, European Commission, UN Economic Commission for Africa, UN Industrial Development Organization, Inter-American Development Bank, and various governments.

Preface

All the papers in this volume are co-authored. I am very grateful to all of my co-authors for the very fruitful and stimulating collaborations we have had over the years. While I have very much enjoyed working with all of my co-authors, I would like to highlight three names in particular: Aoife Hanley, who is not only my co-author but, much more importantly, also my wife. And Sourafel Girma and Eric Strobl with both of whom I have worked very productively for more than a decade. Thanks to all of you!

I also wish to thank the publishers who have kindly given permissions for the use of copyright materials: Elsevier, John Wiley and Sons, Oxford University Press, and the Kiel Institute for the World Economy.

Acknowledgements

We would like to thank the following publishers and journals for granting their permissions to reproduce the articles in this volume:

Canadian Journal of Economics
Economic Inquiry
European Economic Review
Journal of Economic Behavior and Organization
Journal of International Economics
Review of International Economics
Review of World Economics/Weltwirtschaftliches Archiv
Scandinavian Journal of Economics
The Manchester School
World Bank Economic Review
World Bank Research Observer

Table of Contents

About the Author v

Preface vii

Acknowledgements ix

Introduction xv

Part I. Are Multinationals "Better" Than Domestic Firms? **1**

Chapter 1. Multinationals' productivity advantage: Scale or technology? 3

Chapter 2. Evaluating the foreign ownership wage premium using a difference-in-differences matching approach 17

Chapter 3. Why do foreign-owned firms pay more? The role of on-the-job training 33

Chapter 4. Foreign acquisitions, domestic multinationals, and R&D 53

Chapter 5. Foreign direct investment, access to finance, and innovation activity in Chinese enterprises 79

Chapter 6. 'Footloose' multinationals? 95

Chapter 7. Foreign acquisition, plant survival, and employment growth 115

Part II. Searching for Productivity Spillovers: The "Traditional Approach" 143

Chapter 8. Multinational companies and productivity spillovers: A meta-analysis 145

Chapter 9. Much ado about nothing? Do domestic firms really benefit from foreign direct investment? 163

Chapter 10. Exporting, linkages and productivity spillovers from foreign direct investment 191

Chapter 11. Spillovers through backward linkages from multinationals: Measurement matters! 213

Chapter 12. Estimating direct and indirect effects of foreign direct investment on firm productivity in the presence of interactions between firms 227

Part III. Alternative Ways of Looking for Spillovers 241

Chapter 13. Spillovers from foreign firms through worker mobility: An empirical investigation 243

Chapter 14. Creating backward linkages from multinationals: Is there a role for financial incentives? 261

Chapter 15. Suppliers of multinationals and the forced linkage effect: Evidence from firm level data 277

Chapter 16. Multinational companies, technology spillovers and plant survival 289

Chapter 17. Multinational companies and indigenous development: An empirical analysis 305

Chapter 18. Foreign direct investment, competition and industrial development in the host country 323

Introduction

Holger Görg[1]
Kiel Institute for the World Economy and Christian-Albrechts-University of Kiel, Germany

---

> *"If a prince bases the defence of his state on mercenaries he will never achieve stability or security. For mercenaries are disunited, thirsty for power, undisciplined, and disloyal; they are brave among their friends and cowards before the enemy; they have no fear of God, they do not keep faith with their fellow men; they avoid defeat just so long as they avoid battle; in peacetime you are despoiled by them, and in wartime by the enemy. The reason for all this is that there is no loyalty or inducement to keep them on the field apart from the little they are paid, and this is not enough to make them want to die for you. They are only too ready to serve in your army when you are not at war; but when war comes they either desert or disperse."*
>
> *Niccolò Machiavelli*: *The Prince* (*translated by George Bull, Penguin Publishers, 1995, p. 38*)

Foreign direct investment (FDI) by multinational enterprises (MNEs) is arguably one of the most visible and important aspects of economic globalisation. As the latest United Nations' *World Investment Report* shows, annual flows of FDI amounted to around $1.3 trillion in 2014 with the total stock rising to around $26 trillion. To put this in

[1]The author is also affiliated with the Tuborg Centre for Research on Globalisation and Firms at Aarhus University, the Centre for Research on Globalisation and Economic Policy at Nottingham University, and IZA. He is grateful to Aoife Hanley for helpful comments on an earlier draft.

perspective, FDI stocks stood at "merely" \$7.2 trillion in 2000 (UN 2015).

One may wonder whether multinationals behave like the mercenary troops described by Machiavelli. Are they as unreliable for host countries as mercenaries are for a prince? Many globalization critics may be prone to answer this question in the affirmative. Many governments, however, seem to contradict this negative view assuming that inward FDI can bestow large potential benefits to the economy. A fully satisfactory answer to this question would, of course, encompass detailed analyses of many economic, environmental, political and sociological issues, well beyond the scope of a single discipline, let alone this volume.

From an economic point of view, FDI by multinational enterprises channels not only new investment to the host country thus boosting national income. There is an additional important benefit, namely the inflow of new foreign knowledge and technology. This latter aspect of FDI may lead to spillovers to the local economy, resulting in higher productivity and thus accelerating overall economic development of the host country. These external effects from multinationals to domestic firms are generally referred to as "productivity spillovers" or "technology spillovers" (see Paper II.2 in this volume for a detailed review).[2] On the other hand, of course, multinationals may crowd out domestic entrepreneurship with potential negative effects for the economy.

Host country governments seem to assume that there are generally positive effects on economic development. This sanguine view of FDI is evidenced in the effort made by governments to actively attract multinational companies and encourage foreign direct investment into their economies. Policies applied by governments range from creating more liberal investment environments to providing substantial public subsidies. While it is difficult to obtain reliable data on such financial incentives, Girma et al. (2001) report that the UK

[2]There is a related literature which investigates whether inward FDI fosters economic growth using macro-level data. For example, Borensztein *et al.* (1998) and Alfaro *et al.* (2003) show that inward FDI can have positive growth effects if countries have a certain level of human capital or well developed financial markets.

government provided an estimated \$30,000 per employee to attract Samsung to the northeast of England in the late 1990s and \$50,000 per employee to attract the German multinationals Siemens. It seems reasonable to ask whether such policy intervention can be justified. Does the assumption that FDI brings with it growth and development enhancing spillovers really stand up to scrutiny?

This volume brings together a number of empirical studies showing that, contrary to Machiavelli's denunciation of mercenaries, multinational enterprises can indeed carry benefits to their host country.

Outlining the Issues

To orientate the reader, this review commences by presenting the basic intuitive framework as to why multinationals can be predicted to benefit host country firms or economic growth. In general, the availability of new foreign knowledge through inward FDI may benefit domestic firms as these can learn the technology from the multinationals, allowing them to upgrade their own production process and as a result to increase their productivity. The theoretical argument for why one may expect such productivity spillovers from multinationals is straightforward.

Given the foreign multinationals' limited knowledge of the local market, and the distance from their parent firm, they are generally at a disadvantage compared with local firms in the host country (Caves, 1996). Hence, multinationals will only be able to locate profitably abroad if they possess some sort of offsetting advantage. This takes the form of a "firm specific asset" (FSA), such as a superior production technique, know-how or management strategy. The impacts of FSAs are somewhat similar to those of a public good and the possession of such assets enables the firm to locate profitably abroad (Markusen, 2002). Most importantly, these FSA can be transferred at low or zero cost between subsidiaries of the same firm.[3]

[3]Examples of such firm specific assets are know-how, brand names or other intangible assets that have the characteristics of public goods, i.e., they can be easily transferred

The possibility of productivity spillovers then arises because multinationals may find it difficult to protect a leakage of the FSA in the host country, as other firms may somehow "learn" about, for example, the production technology or management strategy. They can then apply it in their own firm, thus allowing them to improve their technology and ultimately productivity. The public good characteristics imply that once the FSA is out in the open it can be used by other firms, due to its de facto non-rivalrous and non-excludable characteristics.[4]

The inability of the multinationals to protect these intangible assets is due to a number of reasons. Firstly, domestic firms may just imitate the multinationals in terms of products, production or management techniques. Secondly, labour may move from multinationals to domestic firms, taking with them some of the knowledge of the FSA. Thirdly, domestic firms supplying to or purchasing inputs from multinationals may be exposed to the superior technology and, hence, be able to upgrade their own production techniques. Fourthly, competition from multinationals may force domestic rivals to update production techniques to become more productive and competitive. This is frequently referred to as a "competition effect." As Aitken and Harrison (1999) point out, however, this competition effect may also reduce productivity in domestic firms, if multinationals siphon off demand from their domestic competitors, forcing domestic firms to reduce output and, hence, productivity.

---

within the firm, from the parent to subsidiaries abroad. The argument about FSA is in line with recent heterogeneous firms models which assume that multinationals face specific sunk costs and hence, only the most productive will choose to become multinationals, less productive firms export and the least productive ones serve purely the domestic market (Helpman *et al.*, 2004).

[4]This is the theoretical argument generally referred to in the literature. Markusen and Venables (1999) point out a different theoretical channel for spillovers. They highlight the role of pecuniary externalities, rather than technological externalities. The former do not affect the production function of the benefiting firm, rather they affect the profit function via cost reductions or increased revenues. In a nutshell, increases in output by multinationals lead to an expansion of demand for intermediate products supplied by domestic suppliers. This increase allows these suppliers to produce at a more efficient scale, thereby reducing average costs. This will ultimately reduce the price that multinationals and other domestically based final good producers pay for intermediates.

While this appears to be a very intuitive and plausible theoretical proposition, the question is whether it also stands up to empirical scrutiny. The first step in evaluating this is to start off by considering the importance of firm specific assets. If these are indeed crucial then one should observe that multinationals apply a comparatively "superior" technology *vis-à-vis* that applied by their domestic competitors. The use of technology is, of course, difficult to observe and measure, but it should arguably be correlated with a number of other measurable firm characteristics, and in particular with productivity. If a firm uses a superior technology one would, all other things equal, expect the firm to demonstrate higher levels of labour or total factor productivity than its rivals. The chapters in Part I look at this issue and consider productivity, technology and wages in multinational enterprises compared to purely domestic host country firms.

What we can take from this discussion thus far is that there are plausible theoretical reasons for why there may be spillovers from multinationals, and that the evidence generally also points to the prevalence of "superior characteristics" in multinationals — hence, the potential for spillovers should be taken as given. The next step is then to look for evidence that domestic firms do indeed appropriate productivity spillovers from multinationals.

When it comes to empirical analysis, it is important to point out that spillovers are difficult to measure since, as Krugman (1991) puts it, "knowledge flows [...] leave no paper trail by which they may be measured and tracked" (p. 53). The approach adopted in the empirical literature therefore largely avoids the (arguably difficult to answer) question as to how precisely productivity spillovers actually take place, but focuses on the simpler issue of whether or not the presence of multinationals affects productivity in domestic firms.

A large empirical literature has arisen that attempts to gauge the extent of spillovers (summarized in Papers II.1 and II.2 in this volume and, more recently in Iršová and Havránek, 2013 and Havránek and Iršová, 2011). Most econometric analyses are undertaken in a framework in which labour productivity or total factor productivity of domestic firms is regressed on a range of independent variables. To measure productivity spillovers from foreign multinationals a variable is included which proxies the extent of foreign firms' presence in the same or vertically related industries in order to gauge the importance of multinationals in the industry. This variable is usually calculated as the share of employment or sales in multinationals over total industry employment/sales in a given sector. If the regression analysis yields a positive and statistically significant coefficient on the foreign presence variable, this is taken as evidence that domestic firms have appropriated positive spillovers from multinationals. The papers collected in Part II of this volume present various approaches towards looking for spillovers using firm level data.

While most of the literature on host country effects of multinationals has focused on measuring productivity spillovers using this "traditional approach," there are also some attempts to explore other issues. Part III of this volume presents a number of papers that look specifically at the mechanisms through which spillovers may work, namely, worker movement and linkages at the micro level. Also, Part III contains papers presenting alternative ways of assessing the impact of multinationals on host country development, looking at the impact of multinationals on entry and survival of domestic firms.

We now provide a brief overview of the chapters included in this volume.

Part I — Are Multinationals "Better" Than Domestic Firms?

Part I includes chapters that attempt to evaluate whether affiliates of multinationals are indeed performing better than comparable domestic firms. One would expect this to be the case if the multinational possesses some sort of firm specific asset and, hence is able to apply a superior technology. The chapters in this section look at superior performance in terms of productivity, innovation, survival and wages.

An evaluation of such performance differences is not trivial. Quite to the contrary, there is a fundamental problem in identifying the performance difference that is attributable to a firm's multinationality status, per se. Multinationals may be attracted to more technology intensive industries. These technology intensive industries may be simultaneously more productive and also be associated with wage premia. It should therefore be evident that any regressions that attempt to explore performance differentials are subject to an endogeneity problem. Consequently, it is difficult to impute and interpret performance differentials between foreign and domestic firms. Controlling for some industry and firm characteristics might go some way towards reducing this bias, though the inclusion of all possible relevant control variables is a difficult, if not an impossible, task.

Chapter 1 attempts to overcome this problem by analyzing the effects of an acquisition of a domestic establishment by a foreign multinational enterprise on the resulting productivity growth in the acquisition target. Assuming that an acquisition does not change any of the main characteristics of the takeover target (at least in the short run) a possible effect of the foreign acquisition on productivity in the domestic target can be attributed to the change in ownership from domestic to foreign. The acquisition decision is unlikely to be random, however, which may again bias the estimated effect. In order to deal with this problem, the chapter uses a difference-in-differences propensity score matching approach to identify the average effect of foreign acquisitions on productivity growth in the domestic target.

Chapter 1 decomposes the possible productivity advantage into a technology and a scale effect. While the former represents the assumed technological advantage of a foreign multinational, the scale effect is due to the fact that, as output expands, workers and firms gain proficiency at producing particular products and are, consequently, able to improve their productivity. A distinction of these two effects is not only academically interesting but also highly policy relevant. Government policies are generally informed by the assumption that multinationals bring in new technologies. They are, hence, predicated on the existence of technical efficiency in multinationals. If, however, scale efficiency is the dominant component of foreign firms' productivity premia, such policies may be misguided.

The analysis uses establishment level data for the UK, focusing on selected manufacturing sectors over the period 1980 to 1994. He results of the econometric estimation indicate substantial sectoral heterogeneity but also clearly show that there is a positive impact of ownership change on productivity growth. This is predominantly due to changes in technical efficiency and not in scale effects. This finding underlines the importance of firm specific assets being transferred to the takeover target. The analysis also shows that the pre-acquisition TFP level of the takeover target plays a role in mediating the rate of technology transfer from the multinational parent companies. Furthermore, the estimated productivity growth effects are not merely limited to the year of acquisition but tend to persist through time.

Chapter 2 uses a similar identification strategy of analysing the effects of foreign acquisitions of domestic targets with a difference-in-differences propensity score matching approach. The focus of the paper is on the wage differential between foreign and domestic firms, however. Specifically, the paper estimates the impact of a foreign acquisition on average wages in the takeover target. The paper distinguishes the effects for the wages of skilled and unskilled workers, and allows for different effects of acquisitions depending on the nationality of the acquirer — namely, whether it is from the US, the EU or the rest of the world. The analysis is carried out using establishment level data for the UK, using data for the whole manufacturing sector over the period 1980 to 1994.

The econometric exercise shows robust and economically significant wage effects for both skilled and unskilled workers acquired by US multinationals. For skilled workers, the estimated wage effect is roughly 8 percent — i.e., the average wage for skilled workers increases by 8 percent as a result of an acquisition. The impact on unskilled wages is nearly 13 percent two years after the acquisition. In stark contrast, no evidence is found for any effect on wages, skilled or unskilled, following acquisition by EU based multinationals. Finally the paper also finds some evidence for positive effects on wages for unskilled workers (not for skilled workers) following acquisition by multinationals from the rest of the world. The estimated magnitudes are lower, however, than for US acquisitions.

Many papers in the literature document a wage premium for foreign owned multinationals. The causes of these premia are largely unexplored, however. Chapter 3 looks at a potential mechanism, arguing that differences in the provision of training by multinationals and domestic firms may explain wage differentials. Multinationals may have stronger incentives to provide training in order to equip workers with the necessary knowledge to implement the superior technology available in the firm.

In a simple theoretical model, the chapter shows that differences in the provision of training my lead to higher wage growth for workers in foreign compared to domestic firms, while starting wages of workers do not necessarily differ. The empirical analysis is carried out using a small linked employer-employee dataset for manufacturing firms in Ghana for the year 1998. The data was collected as part of the *Regional Programme for Enterprise Development* (*RPED*), an extensive data collection effort for a number of African countries, organised initially by the World Bank.

The empirical analysis shows that there are no statistically significant differences in starting wages of trained and untrained workers in foreign and domestic firms, once other individual and firm characteristics are controlled for. However, workers receiving on-the-job training in foreign firms experience higher wage growth than workers being trained in domestic firms. By contrast, there does not appear to be any difference in wage growth between workers not receiving training in either foreign or domestic firms. Training, hence, seems to be crucial for determining wage differences. This suggests that host country workers may benefit from the presence of foreign owned firms in terms of higher wages, particularly if the foreign multinationals provide training.

Chapter 4 looks at a more direct measure of technology, namely R&D expenditure by multinationals. This chapter investigates what happens to the R&D activity of firms in the host country once they are acquired by foreign multinationals. If foreign multinationals upgrade technology in the host country, one may expect a positive post-acquisition effect. However, it may also be the case that multinationals tend to siphon off R&D activity to their home country. In this case, there may be a negative effect on R&D activity in the host country. The chapter also considers whether the post-acquisition effect depends on whether the take-over target is itself a multinational firm, or whether it operates only on the host country market.

The empirical analysis is carried out using firm level data for Swedish manufacturing, a country that has a large number of domestic multinationals, many of which were taken over by foreign owners in recent decades. The data relates to the period 1993–2002. The empirical strategy is similar to that used in Chapters 1 and 2, combining propensity score matching and difference-in-differences in order to identify the effect of a foreign acquisition on R&D activity in the target firm.

The estimation results provide robust evidence that there are, on average, strong positive effects from foreign acquisitions on the R&D performance of Swedish acquisition targets. These effects are stronger for the acquisition of domestic non-MNEs than for Swedish MNEs. The point estimates show increases in R&D intensity by between 5 to 10 percent after a foreign acquisition. This suggests that foreign acquisitions may be an important way to generate new knowledge and to contribute to boosting the level of technology in the host economy.

Chapter 5 examines a different proxy for technology, measuring innovation output as the share of output due to new processes or technology in relation to total output. The aim of the paper is to establish whether this share is higher in firms with foreign ownership compared to domestic firms. Anticipating the ideas that will be further discussed in Part II of this volume, the paper also allows for spillovers from the presence of foreign multinationals in a sector/region on such innovation activity in firms. The estimation strategy is an instrumental variable Tobit model, allowing for the bounded nature of the dependent variable (output share lies between zero and one) and the possible endogeneity of the foreign ownership variables. The empirical estimation is implemented using firm level panel data for Chinese manufacturing, covering the period 1999 to 2005 — a period that witnessed a strong influx of foreign direct investment into the Chinese economy.

Results show that firms with foreign capital participation innovate more than others. This is in line with the idea that they have superior technology and a firm specific asset. Inward FDI at the sectoral level is positively associated with domestic innovative activity only if firms engage in their own R&D activities or have good access to domestic finance. These results again suggest that an influx of foreign multinationals may lead to technology upgrades in the host country.

If multinationals apply superior technology, they may also be expected to be better able to compete in the market. This, ceteris paribus, should enable them to have better survival prospects than competitors with lower technology levels (i.e., domestic firms). The corollary to this is that if one compares the survival probabilities of foreign and domestic firms in a host country, the former would be expected to exhibit higher survival probabilities. However, critics of multinationals frequently argue that these firms are inherently "footloose" and ready to move their facilities to other countries in the wake of an adverse shock. If this were true, one would expect the survival probabilities of foreign multinationals to be lower than those of comparable domestic firms. Chapter 6 looks at this question, using firm level data for manufacturing in the Republic of Ireland. The dataset is for the period 1973 to 1996. Given that the data covers virtually the whole population of establishments, firm entry, exit and survival can be measured quite precisely.

Chapter 6 conducts a survival analysis using Cox Proportional Hazard models. The results show that, controlling for a multitude of firm level characteristics, foreign firms have higher exit probabilities, i.e., lower rates of survival than comparable domestic firms. The point estimates suggest that the exit probability is about 40 percent higher for multinationals. While this suggests that multinationals may indeed be more 'footloose' than comparable domestic firms, an extension of the analysis shows that employment generated in surviving multinationals is more likely to persist than in domestic firms.

Since the identification strategy in Chapter 6 really only amounts to a simple comparison of survival rates between foreign and domestic firms, it cannot say much about a causal effect of foreign ownership. Chapter 7 digs somewhat deeper into this issue. It considers foreign acquisitions (i.e., a change in ownership) and estimates the effect of the foreign acquisition on the survival probability of the takeover target. Possible endogeneity of the acquisition decision is allowed for in an instrumental variables set up. The analysis is conducted using Swedish firm level data, similar to the data used in Chapter 4.

The estimation results show that foreign acquisition has an effect on plant survival only if the takeover target is a domestic exporter. If the target was not operating on international export markets, no effect can be estimated. One possible explanation for this is that firms that are already active on export markets use higher levels of technology and are more productive. Accordingly, domestic exporters are better able to absorb any new knowledge introduced by the foreign acquirer and improve their performance.

Depending on whether the acquisition is horizontal (i.e., within the same industry) or vertical, acquired exporters have a 20–30 percent or 6–8 percent higher survival probability, respectively, compared with plants of non-acquired firms. In an extension to the analysis, where the paper investigates the impact of the acquisition on employment growth, it is found that employment growth is also higher in takeover targets that were exporters prior to acquisition. There is no evidence of any negative effects for foreign acquisitions, neither on survival nor on growth. Accordingly, the evidence using the Swedish data demonstrates that fears for the sustainability of domestic industry with increasing foreign acquisition rates appear unfounded.

Taken together, the evidence in Part I of the volume indicates that multinationals can have positive direct effects for the host country. Multinationals tend to be more productive — hence, an influx of FDI may improve the host country's aggregate productivity performance. They also tend to pay higher wages than domestic firms, are more likely to conduct R&D and innovate, and may improve the survival and growth performance of domestic firms in the event of a takeover. All of this is in line with the theoretical idea that multinationals possess a firm specific asset, conferring an advantage vis-à-vis domestic competitors. Whether this firm specific asset confers further benefits for the host country through indirect "spillover" effects on domestic firms is an issue that is investigated in Part II of the volume.

Part II — Searching for Productivity Spillovers: The "Traditional Approach"

The empirical literature on measuring productivity spillovers from foreign direct investment started with Caves (1974), Globerman (1979) and Blomström and Persson (1983). They used cross section data for Australia, Canada and Mexico, respectively, and found positive associations between the presence of FDI in an industry and domestic firms' productivity in that industry. Since then, numerous studies have appeared that have refined and extended this "traditional approach," using mostly firm level data for different countries and time periods.

Chapter 8 presents an early meta-analysis of studies on productivity spillovers, including papers up to the late 1990s. The meta-analysis shows that papers based on cross-section data tend to find that FDI is positively associated with domestic productivity, while studies using panel data are less likely to find such evidence. A possible explanation is that cross section data do not allow researchers to adequately control for unobserved industry specific effects. A positive association between industry level FDI and domestic productivity in the sector may just be due to multinationals locating in high-productivity sectors (as would be expected given their firm specific assets) even in the absence of any productivity spillovers taking place. The use of panel data helps to mitigate this problem, by controlling for unobserved (time invariant) industry or firm characteristics.

A more traditional verbal review of the literature is supplied in Chapter 9 which also includes papers up to the early 2000s. The review also concludes that evidence for positive spillovers is, at best, mixed, and considers policy options that governments may use to foster spillovers.

A reason for not finding productivity spillovers in studies using panel data may be that they are searching for spillovers in the wrong place. The traditional approach is to look at intra-industry (horizontal) spillovers. In other words, the question is whether the productivity of domestic firms depends on FDI in the same sector. However, in the same sector, negative effects of competition may well outweigh any potentially positive spillover effects. It may be more fruitful to investigate whether the productivity of domestic firms is affected by multinationals in the context of a vertical linkage. Specifically, a linkage describes the case where multinationals buy intermediates from domestic firms or, alternatively, where multinationals sell intermediates to domestic firms. In other words, it may be important that there is a vertical linkage, either backward (if the local firm supplies to multinationals) or forward (if the local firm buys inputs from multinationals). These linkages have increasingly been investigated, starting with Driffield *et al.* (2002) and Javorcik (2004).

Chapter 10 conducts such a "traditional" spillover study, allowing for horizontal as well as vertical spillovers through FDI. In line with the literature, the latter are measured by the presence of multinationals in vertically related (backward and forward) industries. The chapter also considers two other issues. Firstly, it allows the effect of spillovers to differ across domestic firms by taking into account firms' absorptive capacity. This is measured as a firm's productivity relative to the industry leader, similar to the approach adopted by Girma (2005). It also distinguishes the effects of FDI on domestic exporters and non-exporters separately. The rationale for this distinction is the expectation that competition effects from multinationals are different for domestic firms in these two exporter categories. Secondly, the chapter allows for the heterogeneity of FDI by distinguishing spillovers from primarily export-oriented multinationals and those whose sales are aimed at local markets. Those "domestic market oriented multinationals" may pose stronger competition for local firms than their export-oriented counterparts.

The empirical analysis is based on firm level data for the United Kingdom and covers the years 1992 to 1999. Results point to the general conclusion that the export orientation of both domestic and foreign multinationals is relevant for productivity spillovers. Specifically, new insights are gained when one considers the export orientation of foreign MNEs. There is robust evidence for positive horizontal spillovers from export-oriented multinationals only. However, only domestic-market-oriented MNEs generate positive spillovers through backward linkages for both domestic exporters and non-exporters. In general, the evidence presented in the paper underlines the importance of buyer-supplier linkages for productivity spillovers.

The reliability of the evidence on spillovers from traditional spillovers studies, be they horizontal or vertical, crucially depends on the plausibility of the spillover proxies employed. The empirical strategy for measuring backward linkage spillovers has generally consisted of using foreign multinationals' output shares in each sector as a measure of the total multinational demand for inputs in that sector. Moreover, host country input–output tables can be used to proxy how this demand is distributed across sectors. Such a measure is based on a number of implicit assumptions, such as (i) that multinationals use domestically produced inputs in the same proportion as imported inputs, (ii) that foreign firms have the same input sourcing behaviour as domestic firms, (iii) that all MNEs have the same input sourcing behaviour irrespective of their origin, and (iv) that multinationals' demand for locally produced inputs is proportional to the share of output produced by MNEs in a given sector.

Chapter 11 discusses each of these assumptions — in particular their plausibility — and proposes alternative spillover proxies that do not rely on such strong assumptions. These alternative measures are then used in an analysis of spillovers from backward linkages using firm level panel data for Ireland over the period 1983–1998. The empirical results in the paper show clearly that the choice of backward linkage measure matters greatly in determining whether or not FDI is beneficial to the host economy. The preferred measure for backward linkages, which uses the input-output table for the multinational's home country rather than its host country, provides strong evidence for backward spillovers. No such evidence is found using the standard measure generally employed in the literature. The results are robust to controlling for the potential endogeneity of the spillover variables using instrumental variables/GMM techniques.

The results point to the conclusion that the discovery of spillovers from backward linkages is highly sensitive to assumptions made about the similarity of sourcing patterns for domestic and multinational firms. The assumption of perfect comparability in sourcing patterns goes against the very premises underlying the search for spillovers arising from FDI, namely that foreign multinationals, by virtue of their firm specific asset, differ from their domestic counterparts. Analogously, it is likely that results for other studies might also change once proxies of backward linkages are used that relax this strong assumption of similar sourcing patterns. After all, in any host country there are multinationals from different home countries with arguably different technologies and input sourcing behaviour. These differences may impinge on potential backward spillovers arising from FDI.

Chapter 12 links Part I and Part II by addressing two crucial problems related to the identification of direct effects and the traditional way of estimating spillovers. Firstly, from Part I we know that multinationals perform better than domestic firms. However, the identification strategies generally used in papers estimating such direct effects are usually based on the assumption that there are no indirect effects. In other words, when comparing domestic and foreign firms, estimation approaches typically assume that the presence of foreign firms exerts no indirect effects on domestic firms, and vice versa. Yet, Part II and the related literature reveal that indirect effects do matter. This casts some doubt on the identification strategies used when estimating direct effects. Secondly, the spillovers literature in Part II is generally quite silent about potential selection problems, i.e., the fact that multinationals select their location and that this location selection aspect might be correlated with the productivity of domestic firms.

Chapter 12 proposes and implements a unified framework to estimate direct and indirect effects from foreign ownership on firm level productivity. Specifically, the framework allows for interactions between foreign and domestic, and foreign and foreign firms. The approach follows recent econometric advances, such as Hudgens and Halloran (2008) and allows the consistent estimation of a number of different treatment effects, taking into account the problems mentioned in the previous paragraph. In particular, one direct effect of foreign ownership on firms in receipt of foreign capital (i.e., the topic of Part I) and two types of indirect effects, namely the indirect effects on other foreign and domestic firms. The latter comprises the topic of Part II. The estimated effects are all allowed to be moderated by the level of foreign ownership in an economic cluster.

This novel approach is illustrated using firm level data for Chinese manufacturing from the same source as the data used in Chapter 5. An important finding is that the direct effect of foreign ownership is not homogenous across industry-region clusters. It is generally positive and increases strongly with the overall level of foreign-owned firms in a cluster. The paper also finds consistently negative indirect effects of foreign-ownership on domestic firms, indicating negative spillovers from foreign presence on domestic firms. Spillovers are more pronouncedly negative with increasing presence of foreign firms up to a threshold of around 40 percent foreign presence in a sector, after which they become less negative.

Part III — Alternative Ways of Looking for Spillovers

An important drawback of the traditional spillover studies is that they treat the specific mechanisms by which the spillovers are supposed to occur as a "black box." As pointed out above, they usually regress total factor or labour productivity of domestic firms on a number of covariates, including a measure of the extent of multinational presence in an industry. A positive and statistically significant coefficient on that variable is then interpreted as evidence for positive productivity spillovers. The underlying mechanisms that empirically drive such correlations are generally not explored in the empirical analyses. The movement of workers from multinationals to domestic firms is one such potential mechanism, where workers take with them some of the knowledge about production or management processes (the firm specific asset) which can then be gainfully employed in the domestic firm and raise its productivity. This channel is also described in theoretical models such as Fosfuri *et al.* (2001).

Chapter 13 presents an early empirical study focusing on this particular channel. The paper exploits a small linked-employer employee dataset for Ghana from the same source as that used in Chapter 3. The data comprises five waves of an annual sample of Ghanaian manufacturing firms over the years 1991–1997. Information is provided on whether or not the entrepreneur, i.e. the owner or chairperson, of the domestic firms worked for a foreign multinational before joining or setting up his/her own domestic firm, and whether this work experience was gained in the same or in different industries. While the data do not provide information on all workers in a firm, they do relate to the entrepreneur, the main decision maker whose influence is particularly important for firm performance. Using these data, the paper investigates whether domestic firms employing entrepreneurs with foreign experience have a productivity advantage compared to other firms.

The empirical analysis proceeds in two steps. First, it is an estimation of production functions allowing for firm fixed effects. These are estimated separately for different industries. The residuals from these estimations are used as proxies for total factor productivity. TFP is then regressed on a number of firm level controls, including information pertaining to the entrepreneur. A potential criticism with this approach is that highly productive domestic firms may attract entrepreneurs that have gained experience in multinationals within the same industry. This criticism, however, would not apply if these domestic firms were established by the owners and were not already in existence prior to the owner having joined. Hence, an alternative estimation strategy only uses data on domestic firms that were newly established by the current owner.

Results show that firms whose entrepreneur worked in multinationals in the same industry are more productive than other domestic firms. No such evidence is found for firms run by entrepreneurs who worked for multinationals in other industries. This suggests that some of the multinationals' knowledge is industry specific and cannot be easily transferred to firms in other industries.

Another potential mechanism for spillovers that has been investigated in more detail is backward linkages. The traditional studies in the spirit of Driffield *et al.* (2002) and Javorcik (2004) — as in Chapters 10 and 11 — regress domestic firm productivity on the presence of multinationals in vertically related industries. There is no way of knowing, though, whether domestic firms actually do possess a linkage, i.e., whether they do actually supply multinationals. All the conventional approach allows one to do is to proxy whether there is a *potential* for backward linkages.

Chapter 14 looks directly at firm level evidence of actual backward linkages by multinationals. It discusses the policy focus on linkages and investigates the factors that determine the extent of multinationals' local sourcing using firm level panel data for Ireland for the period 1983 to 2002. The data base used provides firm level information on local purchases of intermediate inputs. The paper focuses on investigating whether the extent of such a local linkage is impacted upon by the amount of subsidies paid to the firm. The analysis is conducted using fixed effects estimation as well as a GMM estimator to account for endogeneity of subsidies received by firms.

The descriptive analysis in the paper shows that multinationals from different home countries, on average, source around 20 to 30 percent of their material inputs in Ireland. The main finding of the econometric analysis for the determinants of linkages, is that multinationals from the US and Europe develop backward linkages quite independently of government grants. This finding is most interesting from a policy perspective. By contrast, multinationals from the rest of the world respond positively to government subsidies in terms of linkage creation. It seems plausible that factors other than financial incentives override government efforts to influence linkages in the case of US and European multinationals.

Even if there are linkages, the mechanism through which backward linkages may generate positive effects for their suppliers is not clear. Do multinationals voluntarily share knowledge and cooperate with their suppliers or do they force their customers to adopt new practices — and punish suppliers if these new practices are not implemented to their satisfaction?

Chapter 15 tackles these issues by using firm level information on linkages, but focusing on the part of local suppliers. The first question to be addressed is whether domestic firms that supply multinationals are more productive than other domestic firms. The second question is then whether domestic firms gain more or less if they report that they experience "pressure from their customers to reduce production costs or create new products." The empirical analysis is carried out using firm level data for emerging market economies in Central and Eastern Europe and Central Asia, from the Business Environment and Enterprise Performance Survey (BEEPS) provided jointly by the World Bank and the European Bank for Reconstruction and Development. The paper combines data from the 2005 and 2002 surveys.

The difficulty is again posed when it comes to ascertaining the direction of causality. Is it the case that domestic firms improve their productivity if they supply multinationals (which is what the spillovers argument suggests) or is it simply the case that multinationals pick better performing firms as suppliers (Javorcik and Spatareanu, 2009)? In an attempt to deal with this problem, the estimation strategy adopted in the paper is to regress domestic firms' productivity growth between 2002 and 2005 on the supplier status in 2002, thus exploiting the panel dimension available in the data. This set up allows one to be more confident about identifying an effect of the supplier status on productivity growth. There is also an explicit test for the exogeneity of the supplier status, using an instrumental variables approach.

The empirical estimations show that productivity gains only materialize for suppliers of multinationals when they are pressured by their customers to reduce production costs or create new products. This adds a new angle to the literature. Most of the studies on spillovers through backward linkages, at least implicitly, are based on the assumption of a benevolent multinational that is willing to share knowledge voluntarily and instruct willing suppliers. While the evidence in the paper does not suggest otherwise, the results hints that the customer-supplier relationship may not always be so harmonious.

The remaining chapters in Part III move away from the standard approach of measuring spillovers on domestic firms' productivity. Rather, they are concerned with the implications of the presence of multinationals for domestic firms' entry, exit and survival. The approach used in Chapter 16 is based on the idea that an increase in productivity through spillovers will, *ceteris paribus*, reduce a host country firm's average cost of production and, hence, increase profitability. Profitability, in turn, has long been regarded as a main determinant of firm survival. Hence, technology spillovers from multinationals and the associated increase in productivity should lead to a higher probability of survival for host country firms.

This hypothesis is tested using establishment level data for Ireland covering virtually the entire population of manufacturing plants over the period 1973 to 1996 and is similar to the data used in Chapter 6. In the empirical analysis, using a Cox Proportional Hazard model, the paper finds that, controlling for other plant and sector specific effects, the presence of multinationals (measured as the foreign employment share) has a survival enhancing effect only on domestic plants operating in high technology sectors. This suggests that there may be productivity spillovers taking place in these industries. There is, however, no evidence for such effects on the survival of domestic plants in low technology industries. This may indicate a lack of absorptive capacity in such low tech domestic firms, hence, they are not able to benefit from spillovers.

Chapters 17 and 18 develop another alternative approach to gauge the effect of multinationals on the development of domestic plants. They apply and extend a theoretical approach implemented by Markusen and Venables (1999), which argues that multinationals, through developing backward linkages with domestic suppliers increase markets for these firms and, accordingly, increase their profits in the short run. This can lead to further entry of new domestic firms into supplier industries, a fact that both drives down the price of supplies and also increases the scope for the entry of new domestic firms into final good industries.

In line with this idea, Chapter 17 investigates econometrically whether the entry rate of domestic firms in an industry is positively related to the presence of multinationals (again measured as foreign employment share) in the same industry. Similar to Chapter 16, the study uses data on the population of manufacturing plants in Ireland from 1974 to 1995. In line with the theoretical expectation, the chapter reports evidence that the presence of multinationals indeed exerts a positive effect on the entry rate of domestic firms. This is taken to indicate that spillovers from multinationals encourage entrepreneurs to set up new firms, either in supplier or in final good industries.

Chapter 18 extends the Markusen and Venables (1999) model and allows for the interaction between MNEs and domestic firms to take place through several channels. The first channel works through factor markets. Multinationals lead to a capital inflow and modify the host country capital endowment. In addition, foreign affiliates use differentiated intermediate products which indirectly affect the production conditions for domestic firms. The second channel is a competition effect, whereby multinationals compete with local producers in their product markets as well as in the market for factors. The model shows that the evolution of the number of local firms as a function of the presence of foreign firms can be depicted as a u-shaped relationship where the competition effect first dominates but is gradually outweighed by positive externality effects. Empirical evidence, also based on the micro level data for Ireland, support this theoretical prediction.

Conclusion

The evidence amassed in the literature points towards the conclusion that multinationals can have positive effects on the economic development of the host country. Multinationals bring with them superior technology which manifests itself in multinationals having, on average, higher productivity and technology levels, and paying higher wages than comparable domestic firms. The evidence in Part I of this volume supports this conclusion. The superior technology of multinationals may spill over to domestic firms, a phenomenon that can increase the productivity performance of domestic firms as well as improving the survival and the development of local industry. These aspects are explored in Parts II and III.

There are still a number of remaining issues which the extant literature has not addressed satisfactorily. Do all domestic firms gain equally from multinationals, or are there certain characteristics that firms need to possess in order to reap these benefits? Do all multinationals have the same potential for spillovers? And, what precisely are the mechanisms through which spillovers arise and dissipate?

As regards the first question, a number of chapters, including Chapter 10 look at this and argue that domestic firms need some level of absorptive capacity. However, what exactly determines this absorptive capacity? Do firms need to perform their own R&D, export, employ skilled workers, or merely be highly productive? As these variables are all highly correlated, it is difficult to determine the factors critical for absorptive capacity. For policy makers it would be useful to know this, however, in order to be able to devise the right policies that can foster absorptive capacity.

Not only domestic firms differ from one another, but there is heterogeneity among multinationals as well. Some export, some do not, some are joint ventures while others are fully foreign owned. Moreover, foreign firms exhibit different levels of technology. Most of the literature however treats multinationals as a homogenous mass. But would one expect the same potential for spillovers from all of these different types of foreign firms?

Chapter 10 distinguishes export and domestic market oriented multinationals, Javorcik and Spatareanu (2008) divide multinationals into minority and majority owned foreign firms. Not surprisingly, spillovers differ. There is also an emerging literature that contrasts South-South and North-South FDI (e.g., Perez-Villar and Seric, 2015), with the latter assumed to apply higher levels of technology which may, however, not necessarily spill over into developing host economies. For policy makers it would be extremely useful to know which type of FDI is the "best" for maximising spillovers — while, at the same time, bearing in mind local economy characteristics.

We also still know too little about the actual mechanisms as to how knowledge moves from multinationals to domestic firms. Is it through workers moving from multinationals to domestic firms? How does knowledge flow within customer-supplier relationships? What is the role of "competitive pressure" and how precisely does it affect domestic enterprises? While there are a few examples of papers looking at these issues (e.g., Balsvik, 2011 on worker movements) many questions still remain unanswered. This seems to represent a very promising avenue for future research, as a good understanding of these mechanisms is not only academically exciting but also of immense policy interest.

References

Aitken, B.J. and Harrison, A.E. 1999. Do domestic firms benefit from direct foreign investment? Evidence from Venezuela. *American Economic Review* 89: 605–618.

Alfaro, L., A. Chanda, S. Kalemli-Ozcan, and S. Sayek. 2003. FDI and economic growth: The role of local financial markets. *Journal of International Economics* 64: 89–112.

Balsvik, R. 2011. "Is labor mobility a channel for spillovers from multinationals? Evidence from Norwegian manufacturing." *Review of Economics and Statistics* 93: 285–297.

Blomström, M. and H. Persson. 1983. "Foreign Investment and Spillover Efficiency in an Underdeveloped Economy: Evidence from the Mexican Manufacturing Industry." *World Development* 11: 493–501.

Borensztein, E., J. De Gregorio, and J.-W. Lee. 1998. "How Does Foreign Direct Investment Affect Economic Growth?" *Journal of International Economics* 45: 115–35.

Caves, R.E. 1974. "Multinational Firms, Competition, and Productivity in Host-Country Markets." *Economica* 41: 176–93.

Caves, R.E. 1996. *Multinational Enterprise and Economic Analysis.* Second Edition. Cambridge: Cambridge University Press.

Driffield, N., M. Munday, and A. Roberts. 2002. "Foreign Direct Investment, Transactions Linkages, and the Performance of the Domestic Sector." *International Journal of the Economics of Business* 9: 335–51.

Fosfuri, A., M. Motta, and T.s Rønde. 2001. "Foreign Direct Invesment and Spillovers through Workers' Mobility." *Journal of International Economics* 53: 205–22.

Girma, S. 2005. "Geographic Proximity, Absorptive Capacity and Productivity Spillovers from FDI: A Threshold Regression Analysis." *Oxford Bulletin of Economics and Statistics* 67: 281–306.

Globerman, S. 1979. "Foreign Direct Investment and 'Spillover' Efficiency Benefits in Canadian Manufacturing Industries." *Canadian Journal of Economics* 12: 42–56.

Havranek, T. and Irsova, Z., 2011. "Estimating vertical spillovers from FDI: Why results vary and what the true effect is." *Journal of International Economics* 85: 234–244.

Helpman, E., M.J. Meltiz and S.R. Yeaple. 2004. "Export versus FDI with heterogeneous firms."*American Economic Review* 94: 300–316.

Hudgens, M.G., and Halloran, M.E. 2008. "Toward Causal Inference With Interference." *Journal of the American Statistical Association* 103: 832–842.

Iršová, Z. and Havránek, T. 2013. "Determinants of Horizontal Spillovers from FDI: Evidence from a Large Meta-Analysis." *World Development* 42: 1–15.
Javorcik, B.S. 2004. "Does Foreign Direct Investment Increase the Productivity of Domestic Firms? In Search of Spillovers through Backward Linkages." *American Economic Review* 94: 605–627.
Javorcik, B.S. and M. Spatareanu 2008. "To Share or Not to Share: Does Local Participation Matter for Spillovers from FDI?" *Journal of Development Economics*, 85: 194–217.
Javorcik, B.S. and M. Spatareanu, 2009. "Tough Love: Do Czech Suppliers Learn from Their Relationships with Multinationals?" *Scandinavian Journal of Economics*, 111: 811–833.
Krugman, P.R. 1991. *Geography and Trade.* Cambridge, MA: MIT Press.
Markusen, J.R. 2002. *Multinational firms and the theory of international trade.* Cambridge, MA: MIT Press.
Markusen, J.R. and Venables, A.J. 1999. "Foreign Direct Investment as a Catalyst for Industrial Development." *European Economic Review* 43: 335–356.
Pérez-Villar, L., Seric, A. 2015. "Multinationals in Sub-Saharan Africa: Domestic Linkages and Institutional Distance." *International Economics* 142: 94–117.
United Nations 2015. *World Investment Report 2015: Reforming International Investment Governance.* Paris: United Nations.

PART I

Are Multinationals "Better" than Domestic Firms?

Chapter 1

MULTINATIONALS' PRODUCTIVITY ADVANTAGE: SCALE OR TECHNOLOGY?

SOURAFEL GIRMA and HOLGER GÖRG*

This study decomposes the productivity advantage of foreign multinationals into a technology and a scale effect and analyses the causal relationship between foreign ownership and these two components. This is done by analyzing the effects of an acquisition of a domestic establishment by a foreign multinational, using a combined propensity score matching and difference-in-differences estimation. The main results show that any positive impact of acquisition is predominantly due to changes in technical efficiency and not in scale and that the preacquisition productivity of the target plays a role in mediating the rate of technology transfer from the multinational. (*JEL* F23, L22)

I. INTRODUCTION

There is now a substantial body of empirical work that documents a robust and positive correlation between foreign ownership and firm or plant productivity growth across a number of countries.[1] The productivity advantage of foreign-owned firms is usually seen as reflecting multinationals' technological advantage vis-à-vis domestic firms. Multinationals are assumed to have a firm-specific asset, such as know-how, technology etc., which may be transferred easily across borders from the parent to subsidiaries abroad, as discussed by Markusen (2002). This allows them to be more productive than domestic firms.

However, high productivity growth is not exclusively derived from *technical progress*, at least in theory where the direct link between technology and productivity is only valid in a neoclassical production framework with perfect competition, long run equilibrium, and constant returns to scale. Specifically, the productivity analysis literature, such as Balk (2001), highlights the role of changes in scale economies for productivity growth. This is consistent with the notion of learning-by-doing effects as described by Lucas (1988). Intuitively, as output expands, workers and firms gain proficiency at producing particular products. Thus, changes in *scale efficiency* can also provide an explanation for the observed productivity advantage of foreign firms.

One aim of this study was to decompose the productivity advantage of foreign multinationals into two components: the technology and the scale effect. Apart from being of academic interest, this issue is highly policy relevant.

*This work contains statistical data from ONS, which is Crown copyright and reproduced with the permission of the controller of Her Majesty's Stationery Office and Queen's Printer for Scotland. The use of the ONS statistical data in this work does not imply the endorsement of the ONS in relation to the interpretation or analysis of the statistical data. The authors thank David Greenaway; Richard Harris; Jonathan Haskel; Pehr-Johan Norbäck; Steve Redding; Don Siegel: Eric Strobl; Dieter Urban; Frederic Warzynski; participants at seminars at LSE, IUI Stockholm, Berlin, Lausanne, Nottingham, Turin; and two anonymous referees for helpful comments and suggestions. All remaining errors are, of course, the authors'. Financial support from the European Commission Fifth Framework Programme (Grant HPSE-CT-1999-00017 and SERD-2002-00077) and the Leverhulme Trust (Grant F114/BF) is gratefully acknowledged.

Girma: Associate Professor/Reader, Nottingham University Business School, University of Nottingham, Jubilee Campus, Nottingham NG8 1BB, UK. Phone 44-115-8466656, Fax 44-115-8466667, E-mail sourafel.girma@nottingham.ac.uk

Görg: Associate Professor/Reader, Leverhulme Centre for Research on Globalisation and Economic Policy, and School of Economics, University of Nottingham, Nottingham NG7 2RD, UK. Phone 44-115-8466393, Fax 44-115-9514159, E-mail holger.gorg@nottingham.ac.uk

1. See, for example, Globerman, Ries, and Vertinsky (1994), Doms and Jensen (1998), and Girma, Greenaway, and Wakelin (2001).

ABBREVIATIONS

ARD: Annual Respondents Database
FDI: foreign direct investment
OECD: Organisation for Economic Co-operation and Development
ONS: Office for National Statistics
TFP: total factor productivity

Economic Inquiry
(ISSN 0095-2583)
Vol. 45, No. 2, April 2007, 350–362

doi:10.1111/j.1465-7295.2006.00008.x
Online Early publication November 27, 2006

Many governments around the world actively promote inward foreign direct investment (FDI) under the assumption that it may lead to an influx of new technology that will ultimately spill over into the domestic economy. Hence, these policies are predicated on technical efficiency in multinationals. If, however, scale efficiency is the dominant component of foreign firms productivity premium in a particular sector, such policies may be misguided. Unfortunately, FDI theory gives little guidance as to the relative importance of technological progress and scale efficiency in the productivity premium due to foreign ownership. The empirical literature also appears to have neglected the issue of decomposing the productivity effects of multinationality. Hence, this study aimed to uncover the sources of productivity growth in a panel of domestic and foreign plants.

The second objective of this study was to contribute to the ongoing debate about the causal relationship between foreign ownership and productivity growth. While a number of studies, as cited above, have established that foreign-owned firms may have higher productivity growth than their domestic counterparts, there remains a fundamental problem in identifying the performance difference that is attributable to multinationality per se. As Tybout (2000), for example, points out, multinationals may be attracted to more technology-intensive industries, which are also more productive and pay higher wages. Hence, there would be an endogeneity problem in the regressions, and the wage differential between foreign and domestic firms would be difficult to interpret. The inclusion of some observable industry and firm characteristics, as well as unobservable time invariant effects, might go some way toward reducing this bias, though the inclusion of all possible relevant control variables is a difficult if not impossible task.

In this study, we tried to overcome this problem by analyzing the effects of an acquisition of a domestic establishment by a foreign multinational enterprise on productivity growth, decomposed into technology and scale effects. Assuming that an acquisition does not change any of the main characteristics of the takeover target (at least in the short run), a possible effect of the foreign acquisition on productivity growth in the domestic target can be attributed to the change in ownership from domestic to foreign. We attempt to identify the causal effect of a foreign acquisition using a combined propensity score matching and difference-in-differences methodology, as, for example, discussed in a recent study by Blundell and Costa Dias (2000). To our knowledge, this is the first study to provide a decomposition of the causal effects of foreign acquisition on productivity growth.[2]

The empirical setting of the study was the UK manufacturing industry, where FDI is seen as an important device of technology transfer. Some half a billion pounds was paid in grants for internationally owned companies by the UK government between 1991 and 1995 under the Regional Selective Assistance scheme.[3] We used plant-level data, covering the period 1980–1994. We focused our analysis on establishments in the UK electronics and food industries.[4] We decided to examine in detail two sectors separately rather than pooling data for the whole manufacturing since recent empirical studies of firm-level productivity dynamics, such as Bartelsman and Doms (2000), have established that there is large and persistent heterogeneity across firms even within sectors, let alone across heterogeneous sectors. Concentrating on two fairly narrowly defined sectors should allow us to alleviate the problems associated with aggregating over heterogeneous units. The choice of these two sectors is based on two reasons: first, foreign-owned firms are important players in both sectors, accounting for about 19% of employment in electronics and 10% in the food industry in 1996 as shown by Griffith and Simpson (2004; Table 4); second, we may expect those sectors to be different in their technology usage; hence, there may be differences in the determinants of productivity for establishments in the two sectors.[5]

2. In a related study, we used a similar approach to investigate the effect of foreign acquisitions on wages, distinguishing the nationality of foreign acquirers; see Girma and Görg (2006). Arnold and Javorcik (2005) also applied a similar approach to investigate the effect of foreign acquisitions on plant performance in Indonesia.

3. For more detail, see the official report at http://www.dti.gov.uk/regional/evaluationRSA91-95.pdf.

4. More precisely, using SIC 1980 classification, SIC 33 (manufacture of office machinery and data processing equipment), SIC 34 (electrical and electronic engineering), and SIC 41/42 (food, drink, and tobacco).

5. According to an Organisation for Economic Co-operation and Development (OECD) classification, "electronics and communication" are classified as high-tech industries, while "food and beverages" are low-tech industries.

The study proceeds with section II where the productivity growth decomposition and the propensity score matching methodologies are discussed. Section III presents the data. Section IV compares the sources of productivity growth between foreign and domestic plants and decomposes the productivity growth effects of foreign acquisitions. Section V concludes.

II. EMPIRICAL STRATEGY

A. Decomposing Productivity Changes: The Analytical Framework

The productivity analysis literature abounds with productivity growth decomposition methodologies, ranging from nonparametric to fully parametric techniques. This study uses a parametric method of decomposing an *a Divisa* index of total factor productivity (TFP) growth based on the estimation of a translog production function.[6]

Let y, x_1, x_2, x_3, and x_4 denote output, skilled labor, unskilled labor, capital, and material inputs, respectively,[7] and let t index a time trend variable. For plant i at time t, the translog production function is expressed as

$$(1)\quad \ln y_{it} = \alpha_0 + \sum_{k=1}^{4} \alpha_k \ln x_k + \frac{1}{2}\sum_{k=1}^{4}\sum_{h=1}^{4} \alpha_{kh} \ln x_k \ln x_h^t + \psi_0 t + \frac{1}{2}\psi_{00} t^2 + \sum_{k=1}^{4} \xi_k t \ln x_k + \nu_{it}$$

where ν is a disturbance term that is potentially correlated with the inputs. Compared to a simple Cobb-Douglas production function, this approach has the major advantage of allowing for varying returns to scales across plants and time periods.

Defining an index of TFP growth as the difference between the rate of output growth and the rate of input growth, $\Delta TFP = \Delta \ln y - \Delta \ln x$, and totally differentiating equation (1), TFP growth can be decomposed as

$$(2)\quad \Delta TFP = \Delta T + (\varepsilon - 1)\sum_{k=1}^{n}(\varepsilon_k/\varepsilon)\Delta \ln x_k$$

where $\Delta T = \partial \ln y/\partial t$, $\varepsilon_k = \partial \ln y/\partial x_k$. $\varepsilon = \sum_{k=1}^{4} \varepsilon_k$ denotes returns to scale.

The first term on the right-hand side of equation (2) is the rate of technical change (the derivative of log output with respect to the time trend), while the second term captures the contribution of changes in scale efficiency. Note that scale efficiency at a point in time can be thought of as productivity relative to what is attainable under constant returns to scale.

To implement this decomposition empirically, we estimated equation (1) separately for each two-digit industry via instrumental variables methods to account for the potential endogeneity of inputs.[8] Furthermore, we allow for different factor elasticity coefficients for domestic- and foreign-owned plants in the estimation, by interacting all production function coefficient with a foreign ownership dummy. Thus, a foreign-acquired plant is allowed to have different coefficients in the production function before and after the acquisition year.[9]

B. Identifying the Causal Effects of Foreign Acquisition on Productivity Growth

Having decomposed productivity growth, the next step was to analyze whether there is a causal effect from an acquisition of a domestic establishment by a foreign owner on either or both of the components (technical change or scale efficiency). In other words, the empirical modeling problem is the evaluation of the causal effect of foreign acquisition on y, where y represents total productivity growth or one of its components in the domestic target.

Let $ACQ_{it} \in \{0,1\}$ be an indicator of whether a domestic plant i is acquired by a foreign establishment at time period t, and let

6. See, Färe et al. (1994) and Grifell and Lovell (1997) for examples of nonparametric; and Koop, Osiewalski, and Steel (1999), Balk (2001), and Orea (2002) for examples of fully parametric approaches. See also Heshmati (2003), for a review.

7. Output is defined as gross output. Skilled and unskilled labors are the number of nonproduction and production workers, respectively. Capital is defined as capital stock obtained using investment data (as described in Griffith 1999) and material as cost of materials and fuel used. All variables are in logs.

8. Twice lagged values of the factor inputs are used as instruments.

9. The point estimates of the production function are reported in Appendix 4 along with p values from the Sargan tests for the validity of the instrumental variable candidates.

y^1_{it+s} be the productivity growth at time $t + s$, $s \geq 0$, following acquisition. Also, denote by y^0_{it+s} the productivity growth of the plant *had it not been acquired.* The causal effect of foreign ownership for plant i at time period $t + s$ is defined as:

$$(3) \qquad y^1_{it+s} - y^0_{it+s}$$

The fundamental problem of causal inference is that the quantity y^0_{it+s} is unobservable for plants that have been acquired (i.e., for which we observed y^1_{it+s}). Thus, the analysis can be viewed as confronting a missing data problem. Following the microeconometric evaluation literature such as that by Heckman et al. (1997), we defined the *average* effect of acquisition on the acquired plants as

$$(4) \qquad E\{y^1_{t+s} - y^0_{t+s}|\mathrm{ACQ}_{it}=1\} = E\{y^1_{t+s}|\mathrm{ACQ}_{it} = 1\} - E\{y^0_{t+s}|\mathrm{ACQ}_{it}=1\}$$

Causal inference relies on the construction of the counterfactual for the last term in equation (4), which is the outcome the acquired plants would have experienced, on average, had they not been acquired. This is estimated by the average productivity growth (or its components) of the plants that remained in domestic hands, $E\{y^0_{it+s}|\mathrm{ACQ}_{it}=0\}$.

An important feature in this exercise is the selection of a valid control group. One way of doing so is by using matching techniques. The purpose of matching is to pair each foreign-acquired plant with a domestic plant that has not undergone any ownership change on the basis of some observable variables, in such a way that the control plants' productivity growth trajectories can be studied to generate the counterfactual for the acquired plant.

Since matching involves comparing acquired and nonacquired plants across a number of observable preacquisition characteristics (e.g., preacquisition productivity, size, and age), it would be difficult to determine along which dimension to match the plants or what type of weighing scheme to use. It is therefore desirable to perform the matching on the basis of a single index that captures all the information from those variables. In this study, we adopted the method of propensity score matching due to Rosenbaum and Rubin (1983), who suggest the use of the probability of receiving treatment (foreign acquisition in the present context) conditional on those characteristics, to reduce the dimensionality problem. Accordingly, we first identified the probability of being acquired (or "propensity score") using the following logit model

$$(5) \qquad P(\mathrm{ACQ}_{it}=1)=F(X_{it-1}, D_{it})$$

where D is the full set of industry and time dummies, and the vector X consists of the preacquisition level and growth of TFP, returns to scale (which is calculated from the instrumental variable translog production function estimates), plant size (proxied by log of fixed capital), age, and an indicator of whether the plant is located in an officially designated assisted area. The choice of these variables is motivated by the existing literature on ownership change, for example, Lichtenberg and Siegel (1987), McGuckin and Nguyen (1995), Conyon et al. (2002), Harris and Robinson (2002).

Now, let P_{it} denote the predicted probability of being acquired at time t for plant i (which is an actual takeover target). A nonacquired plant j, which is "closest" in terms of its propensity score (or probability of being a foreign takeover target) to an acquired plant, is then selected as a match for the latter using the "caliper" matching method.[10] The caliper method uses the nearest control plant whose propensity score falls within a prespecified radius as a match for an acquired plant. More formally, at time period t and for each newly acquired plant i, a domestic plant j is selected, such that[11]

$$(6) \qquad \lambda > |P_{it} - P_{jt}| = \min_{k\in\{\mathrm{domestic}\}} \{|P_i - P_j|\}$$

where λ is a prespecified scalar, which is set at 0.01 in our analysis. Furthermore, we impose the so-called common support condition in the matching algorithm. This involves dropping acquired plant observations whose propensity

10. The matching is performed in Stata Version 9 using the PSMATCH2 software provided by Leuven and Sianesi (2003).

11. A nonacquired g plant can be matched to more than one acquired plants. By the same token, it can happen that an acquired plant may not have a match.

score is higher than the maximum or less than the minimum propensity score of the control group plants.

Having constructed the comparison group (C) of plants that are similar to the acquired plants (A), we exploit the panel nature of our data and use a difference-in-differences estimator.[12] This is motivated by recent studies that argue that standard matching estimators are usually unsatisfactory but in combination with difference-in-differences, methodology can have the potential to "... improve the quality of non-experimental evaluation results significantly" (Blundell and Costa Dias 2000, 438).

At its simplest, the combined matching and difference-in-differences estimator we use can be described as follows. First, the difference between the average productivity before and after the change of ownership, say $\Delta^a y$, is calculated. Then, this difference is further differenced with respect to the before and after difference for the comparison control group, say $\Delta^c y$, to obtain the difference-in-differences estimator $\delta = \Delta^a y - \Delta^c y$. Defining ACQ as a vector of dummy variables for the postacquisition period, the regression

$$(7) \qquad \Delta y_{it} = \phi + \delta \text{ACQ}_{it} + u_{it}$$

on the matched sample of plants should produce a coefficient δ that can be interpreted as the average change in y that can be attributed to foreign acquisitions. In order to allow for differential acquisition effects across time, we considered two lags of the foreign acquisition dummy in addition to the contemporaneous effect. Furthermore, to control for possible observable factors that may be correlated with changes in TFP growth, we extended this basic framework by including a vector of regressors that consists of plant age and size and full sets of time and four-digit sectoral dummies.

It has been noted in the literature by, for example, Lapan and Bardhan (1973) and Wang and Blomström (1992) that the degree of technology transfer from parent company to new subsidiary is likely to be a function of the acquired plant's existing technological capability or absorptive capacity. Some threshold level of absorptive capacity or technological congruity might be needed for the acquired plants to benefit fully from their new association with multinationals. But it can also be argued that a domestic plant that operates near the technological frontier might have less to learn from their association with multinationals than otherwise equivalent plants. To explore the above conjectures, we also interacted the acquisition dummy variables with the preacquisition or initial level of TFP (ITFP). Our final estimating equation can then be expressed as

$$(8) \quad \Delta y_{it} = \phi + \beta_1 \text{age}_{it} + \beta_2 \text{size}_{it} + \sum_{s=0}^{2} (\delta_{1s} \text{ACQ}_{it-s} + \delta_{2s} \text{ACQ}_{it-s} \times \text{ITFP}_i) + D_t + D_{\text{sec}} + u_{it}$$

C. Testing the Reliability of the Propensity Score Matching Method

The propensity score matching method will provide a reliable and robust method for estimating the effects of foreign acquisitions if, conditional on the propensity score, the distribution of the preacquisition covariates is independent of the incidence of being acquired. This can be achieved by choosing a specification of the propensity score model (equation 5) that "balances" the preacquisition variables between the treatment and the control groups conditional on the propensity score. As emphasized by Rosenbaum and Rubin (1983), Dehejia and Wahba (2002), and Smith and Todd (2005a), among others, it is important to verify that this balancing condition is satisfied by the data.

In this study, we performed two tests to satisfy ourselves that the balancing conditions are not violated. The first is to conduct two sample t-tests of equality of the covariates between the treatment and the control groups. The second balancing test we explored is suggested by Smith and Todd (2005b) and it is cast within a regression framework. Let $\hat{P}(X)$ denote the estimated propensity score and let ACQ be a dummy variable assuming a value of 1 if a firm is foreign acquired. Then, for each variable included in the matching algorithm, the following regression function that is quartic

12. The simplest form of a matching estimator of the causal effect of foreign acquisition can be written as $\delta = \sum_{i \in A} (y_i - \sum_{j \in C} w(p_i, p_j) y_i)$ where the $w(p_i, p_j)$ are the weights placed on the comparison plant j, generated by the matching algorithm.

in $\hat{P}(X)$ is estimated (using the TFP variable as an example)

$$\text{(9)} \quad \text{TFP} = \beta_0 + \sum_{k=1}^{4} \beta_k \hat{P}(X)^k + \sum_{k=1}^{4} \gamma_k \text{ACQ}\hat{P}(X)^k + \varepsilon$$

and the joint significance of the coefficients on the terms involving the program participation dummy (that is the γs) is tested. As explained by Smith and Todd (2005b), if the propensity score satisfies the balancing condition, the treatment dummy (acquisition dummy in our case) should not provide any additional information and we should expect the γs to be jointly statistically insignificant.

III. DATABASE DESCRIPTION AND SAMPLE CHARACTERISTICS

We used confidential microdata from the Annual Respondents Database (ARD) provided by the Office for National Statistics (ONS) in the United Kingdom under controlled conditions. The data set consists of individual establishments' records underlying the annual census of production. As Barnes and Martin (2002) provide a very useful introduction to the data set, we only included a brief discussion of some of the features of the data that are relevant to the present work.

For each year, the ARD consists of two files. What is known as the "selected file" contains detailed information on a sample of establishments that are sent inquiry forms. The second file comprises the "nonselected" (nonsampled) establishments, and only basic information such as employment, location, industry grouping, and foreign ownership status is recorded. Some 14,000–19,000 establishments are selected each year, based on a stratified sampling scheme. The scheme tends to vary from year to year, but for the period under consideration, establishments with more than 100 employees were always sampled.

In the data, an establishment is defined as the smallest unit that is deemed capable of providing information on the Census questionnaire. Thus, a "parent" establishment reports for more than one plant (or "local unit" in the parlance of ARD). For selected multiplant establishments, we only have aggregate values for the constituent plants. Indicative information on the "children" is available in the nonselected file. In our sample period, about 95% of the establishments in these industries are single-plant firms. In the actual sample we used for the econometric estimation, this figure is around 80%. Hence, most of the data used are actually plant-level data, and we therefore tend to use the terms plant and establishment interchangeably.

This study uses data for two broad industries, electronics and food and drinks, spanning 49 four-digit SIC80 industries[13] over the period 1980–1994.[14] A consistently defined nationality indicator identifies whether an establishment is domestic or foreign owned. Table 1 gives the frequency distribution of plants by year and ownership in the two industries under consideration. We define the incidence of foreign acquisition in year t as an establishment that has been in domestic hands up to year t-1 and becomes a subsidiary of a foreign-based multinational, as identified by a change in its nationality indicator.[15] Since the matching process described in the previous section requires data on the preacquisition period, we considered foreign takeovers that took place between 1981 and 1994. Table 2 provides the frequency distribution of foreign acquisitions. It can be seen that most of these occurred in the electronics industry.

Table 3 reports some summary statistics of the main variables of interest, namely, TFP growth and its two components, technical change and scale effects. These variables are calculated from the instrumental variables translog production function estimates, as described in section II. Economically significant average productivity growth is observed in the office machinery and data processing equipment sector (SIC2 33) where technical progress accounts for most of this growth. Also, foreign plants enjoy a higher productivity growth and technical progress than domestic

13. These are SIC80 two-digit industries 33 and 34 (electronics) and 41 and 42 (food and drinks). We sometime refer to the latter as simply "food" throughout the manuscript. In the SIC80, the tobacco industry is also classified in the food sector. However, in our analysis, we do not consider tobacco manufacturing plants.

14. The motivation for concentrating on these two industries is discussed in the Introduction.

15. Establishments that appear to have experienced more than one change of ownership between 1980 and 1994 are excluded from the analysis. This is partly to avoid conflating the effects of different events and partly because we suspect the presence of measurement error problems.

TABLE 1
Frequency Distribution of Plants by Year and Ownership

	Electronics			Food		
Year	Foreign	Domestic	Total	Foreign	Domestic	Total
1980	172	830	1,002	63	1,103	1,166
1981	183	827	1,010	67	1,068	1,135
1982	170	866	1,036	62	1,074	1,136
1983	170	859	1,029	63	1,041	1,104
1984	186	1,168	1,354	67	1,439	1,506
1985	173	935	1,108	61	1,098	1,159
1986	170	936	1,106	55	1,066	1,121
1987	180	957	1,137	50	1,010	1,060
1988	187	985	1,172	55	1,046	1,101
1989	221	1,360	1,581	73	1,387	1,460
1990	197	1,031	1,228	69	1,067	1,136
1991	238	979	1,217	84	1,038	1,122
1992	261	979	1,240	70	1,014	1,084
1993	242	952	1,194	62	1,042	1,104
1994	226	804	1,030	58	737	795
Total	3,098	15,274	18,372	1,032	17,585	18,617

plants in this sector. By contrast, we found an average negative effect of technical change in both food sectors. This may at least be partly due to low innovation activity in that sector; for example, Morgan, Blake, and Poyago-Theotoky (2003) discuss the low R&D intensity in the food industry compared to other manufacturing sectors in the United Kingdom.[16]

IV. EMPIRICAL RESULTS

To investigate more closely whether there are productivity growth differentials between foreign and domestic plants, we started our econometric analysis by decomposing the productivity growth differentials for the two types of plants. These results are shown in Table 4. For each industry, we ran three sets of regressions separately: explaining TFP growth and its components technical change and scale effects. Our results show that, controlling for plant age, size, and four-digit industry and time effects, foreign-owned plants exhibit higher TFP growth in the electronics industry. However, there are some noteworthy differences between the two 2-digit sectors of this industry. In the office machinery and data processing equipment sector (SIC2 33), the TFP of foreign plants grows by 1.2% points faster than domestic plants, and this advantage is entirely due to their higher rates of technical change. By contrast, foreign plants in the electrical and electronic engineering sector (SIC2 34) enjoy a more modest productivity growth advantage over their domestic counterparts, at just above half a percentage point. It is worth noting that technical progress accounts for

16. They report that the R&D intensity in the food industry was 0.3% compared to a manufacturing average of 2.1% in 1997.

TABLE 2
Frequency of Foreign Acquisitions

Year	Electronics	Food
1981	11	3
1982	7	4
1983	6	9
1984	32	12
1985	10	1
1986	6	3
1987	15	5
1988	18	5
1989	30	14
1990	14	5
1991	41	15
1992	34	5
1993	24	10
1994	21	6
Total	269	97

TABLE 3
Summary Statistics for Productivity Growth

	SIC2 = 33				SIC2 = 34			
	Foreign		Domestic		Foreign		Domestic	
Variable	Mean	Standard Deviation	Mean	Standard Deviation	Mean	Standard Deviation	Mean	Standard Deviation
TFP growth	0.070	0.033	0.059	0.034	0.000	0.010	0.006	0.027
Technical change	0.071	0.012	0.055	0.011	0.000	0.006	0.002	0.009
Scale effect	−0.001	0.031	0.004	0.031	0.000	0.008	0.004	0.026

	SIC2 = 41				SIC2 = 42			
	Foreign		Domestic		Foreign		Domestic	
Variable	Mean	Standard Deviation	Mean	Standard Deviation	Mean	Standard Deviation	Mean	Standard Deviation
TFP growth	0.000	0.034	−0.011	0.007	−0.029	0.017	−0.016	0.021
Technical change	−0.001	0.019	−0.011	0.006	−0.028	0.006	−0.017	0.007
Scale effect	0.001	0.027	0.000	0.005	−0.001	0.016	0.001	0.020

just a third of this TFP growth differential, while scale effects appear to be a much more important component in this sector.

The picture that emerges from the food industry is more mixed. In the food manufacturing sector (SIC2 41), foreign plants have a 1.1% points productivity growth advantage, and this is entirely explained by technical efficiency. In sharp contrast, the TFP of domestic plants in the confectionary and drink manufacturing sector (SIC2 42) grew by more than 1.24% points faster than

TABLE 4
Decomposing Productivity Growth Differentials Between Foreign and Domestic Plants

	Electronics Sector		
	TFP Growth	Technical Change	Scale Effect
Foreign × SIC2 = 33	0.0121 (0.0038)***	0.0166 (0.0021)***	−0.0045 (0.0031)
Foreign × SIC2 = 34	0.0059 (0.0007)***	0.0020 (0.0005)***	0.0039 (0.0006)***
Size	−0.0002 (0.0001)**	−0.0003 (0.0000)***	0.0001 (0.0001)
Age	−0.0001 (0.0000)**	0.0001 (0.0000)***	−0.0002 (0.0000)***
Constant	0.0560 (0.0026)***	0.0538 (0.0018)***	0.0021 (0.0020)
Observations	12,038	12,038	12,038
R^2	0.45	0.83	0.03
	Food Sector		
	TFP Growth	Technical Change	Scale Effect
Foreign × SIC2 = 41	0.0109 (0.0031)***	0.0100 (0.0025)***	0.0009 (0.0017)
Foreign* SIC2 = 42	−0.0124 (0.0011)***	−0.0100 (0.0006)***	−0.0024 (0.0009)***
Size	−0.0002 (0.0001)*	−0.0003 (0.0001)***	0.0001 (0.0001)**
Age	−0.0001 (0.0001)	0.0001 (0.0000)**	−0.0002 (0.0001)***
Constant	−0.0036 (0.0014)**	0.0001 (0.0009)	−0.0037 (0.0011)***
Observations	12,178	12,178	12,178
R^2	0.12	0.40	0.02

Notes: Heteroscedasticity and within-plant serial correlation robust standard errors are given in parentheses. *significant at 10%, **significant at 5%, and ***significant at 1%. All regressions include the full set of time and four-digit industry dummies.

that of foreign plants. Interestingly, the contribution of scale efficiency to this TFP growth advantage is quite small, and faster technical progress appears to be the major factor responsible for this finding.

The above discussion focused on the importance of the various sources of productivity growth to the average domestic and foreign plants TFP differential. As discussed in the Introduction, it is inappropriate to draw any conclusions about causal relationships from this type of analysis. In what follows, we hence examine whether there is a more direct relationship between *ownership change* and the sources of productivity growth. To this end, we used the difference-in-differences estimator based on propensity score–matched plants described in section II.

Appendix 1 reports the marginal effects from logit regressions of the determinants of foreign acquisitions to illustrate the procedure used to calculate the propensity scores. Foreign multinationals appear to target older plants and plants with either lower level of productivity (in the electronics industry) or lower productivity growth (in the food industry). Furthermore, in the electronics sector, domestic plants with higher levels of returns to scale are more likely to be acquired.

Also, Appendices 2 and 3 summarize the results from the balancing tests for the propensity score matching method, and reassuringly, we found that the balancing conditions are met in both sectors. Thus, the tests give robust support for the soundness of the matching approach adopted in this study.

Table 5 provides a decomposition of the productivity growth effects of foreign acquisitions, and three broad patterns emerge: (i) any positive impact of ownership change is predominantly due to change in technical efficiency, (ii) the preacquisition TFP level of the erstwhile domestic plants play a role—positive or negative—in mediating the rate of technology transfer from the multinational parent companies, and (iii) the productivity growth effects are not confined to the year of acquisition and tend to persist through time. We provide a more detailed discussion of the results.[17]

Keeping the preacquisition level of productivity constant, ownership change brings a statistically and economically significant benefit to the acquired firms in the office machinery and data processing equipment sector (SIC2 33). Within 2 years of acquisition, technical efficiency is growing by about (0.0095 + 0.007 + 0.0085=) 2.5% points more than would otherwise be the case. Furthermore, we detected a negative and statistically significant initial TFP-acquisition interaction term 1 year after ownership change. This indicates that domestic plants that were further behind the technology frontier appear to benefit more from their new associations with multinationals. On the other hand, the impact of foreign acquisition in the electrical and electronic engineering sector (SIC2 34) is less pronounced. Within 2 years of ownership change, the average effect (holding initial TFP constant) on technical change is about 0.65% points. Also, domestic plants with lower or higher levels of initial TFP do not seem to derive any differential benefits from their new status as subsidiaries of multinationals. In both sectors, scale effects appear to play little or no role for overall productivity growth.

Focusing on the food sector, the unconditional TFP growth effect of foreign acquisitions in the food manufacturing sector (SIC2 41) appears to take place within a year of acquisition. On average, new foreign ownership is associated with a 1.88% points premium in the rate of technical change. However, conditioning on the preacquisition level of TFP, the higher this level of TFP, the less marked the rate of technology transfer appears to be. In sharp contrast, the results from the confectionery and drink manufacturing sector (SIC2 42) are quite different from the ones considered thus far. Ownership change is initially detrimental to the TFP growth trajectory of the acquired plants. Holding initial TFP constant, the rate of technical change is slower by 1.27% points within a year of acquisition, than would otherwise be the case. We also detected a decline in TFP growth due to a loss in scale efficiency a year into ownership change, and this loss is higher, the higher the level of initial TFP of the plant. However, we observed an unconditional positive effect of 1.02% points increase in the technical progress 2 years after acquisition. This suggests that while there may be losses in the short run, these seem to be significantly counteracted by positive effects 2 years after the acquisition.

17. Throughout, insignificant coefficients will be ignored when calculating the magnitudes of the acquisition effects.

TABLE 5
Decomposing the Productivity Growth Effects of Foreign Acquisitions

	Electronics Sector		
	TFP Growth	**Technical Change**	**Scale Effect**
SIC2 = 33			
Acquisition year	0.0114 (0.0055)**	0.0095 (0.0021)***	0.0001 (0.0060)
Acquisition year × initial TFP	0.0106 (0.0116)	−0.0043 (0.0044)	0.0162 (0.0124)
After 1 year	0.0056 (0.0066)	0.0070 (0.0025)***	−0.0029 (0.0070)
After 1 year × initial TFP	−0.0018 (0.0137)	−0.0104 (0.0052)**	0.0088 (0.0142)
After 2 years	0.0024 (0.0067)	0.0085 (0.0026)***	−0.0076 (0.0074)
After 2 years × initial TFP	0.0024 (0.0135)	−0.0001 (0.0051)	0.0034 (0.0142)
SIC2 = 34			
Acquisition year	0.0031 (0.0015)**	0.0024 (0.0006)***	0.0004 (0.0016)
Acquisition year × initial TFP	−0.0068 (0.0056)	0.0029 (0.0022)	−0.0102 (0.0059)*
After 1 year	0.0033 (0.0017)*	0.0025 (0.0006)***	0.0005 (0.0017)
After 1 year × initial TFP	−0.0026 (0.0063)	0.0025 (0.0024)	−0.0058 (0.0066)
After 2 years	0.0049 (0.0018)***	0.0016 (0.0007)**	0.0036 (0.0020)*
After 2 years × initial TFP	0.0035 (0.0069)	0.0038 (0.0027)	−0.0010 (0.0077)
Observations	2,226	2,226	2,226
R^2	0.35	0.79	0.03
	Food Sector		
	TFP Growth	**Technical Change**	**Scale Effect**
SIC2 = 41			
Acquisition year	0.0113 (0.0031)***	0.0077 (0.0019)***	0.0034 (0.0029)
Acquisition year × initial TFP	−0.0199 (0.0177)	−0.0398 (0.0109)***	0.0185 (0.0162)
After 1 year	0.0115 (0.0058)**	0.0111 (0.0036)***	0.0005 (0.0052)
After 1 year * Initial TFP	0.0618 (0.0495)	0.0052 (0.0303)	0.0577 (0.0442)
After 2 years	0.0965 (0.0685)	0.0671 (0.0419)	0.0465 (0.0698)
After 2 years × Initial TFP	−0.0025 (0.0035)	−0.0052 (0.0021)**	0.0029 (0.0032)
SIC2 = 42			
Acquisition year	−0.0077 (0.0031)**	−0.0067 (0.0019)***	−0.0013 (0.0028)
Acquisition year × initial TFP	−0.0148 (0.0138)	−0.0025 (0.0085)	−0.0129 (0.0129)
After 1 year	−0.0115 (0.0036)***	−0.0060 (0.0022)***	−0.0058 (0.0032)*
After 1 year × initial TFP	−0.0282 (0.0164)*	−0.0022 (0.0100)	−0.0271 (0.0145)*
After 2 years	0.0116 (0.0071)	0.0102 (0.0043)**	0.0037 (0.0078)
After 2 years × initial TFP	0.0012 (0.0162)	0.0015 (0.0099)	0.0009 (0.0146)
Observations	703	703	703
R^2	0.31	0.55	0.09

Notes: Heteroscedasticity and within-plant serial correlation robust standard errors are given in parentheses. *Significant at 10%, **significant at 5%, and ***significant at 1%. All regressions include the full set of time and four-digit industry dummies. The regressions also control for plant size and age, but the corresponding estimates are omitted to save space.

V. CONCLUDING REMARKS

This study had two objectives: first, to decompose the productivity advantage of foreign multinationals into two components: the technology and the scale effects—arguably a highly policy relevant issue that, however, has been neglected in academic research thus far; second, the study contributes to the ongoing debate about the causal relationship between foreign ownership and productivity growth. We do so by analyzing the effects of an acquisition of a domestic establishment by a foreign multinational enterprise on productivity growth, decomposed into technology and scale effects. In order to identify a causal effect, we used a combined propensity score matching and difference-in-differences estimation approach.

We analyzed separately plant-level data for the UK data for the electronics and food industries, which unearths substantial sectoral heterogeneity that would be lost if pooling data for the whole manufacturing industry. From our econometric investigation, we draw three major conclusions: (i) any positive impact of ownership change is predominantly due to change in technical efficiency and not in scale effects, (ii) the preacquisition TFP level of the erstwhile domestic plants play a role—positive or negative—in mediating the rate of technology transfer from the multinational parent companies, and (iii) the productivity growth effects are not confined to the year of acquisition and tend to persist through time.

APPENDIX 1

The Determinants of Foreign Acquisitions: Marginal Effects from the Logit Regressions

	Electronics		Food	
Age	0.008	0.001***	0.003	0.001*
Size	−0.001	0.001	0.000	0.000
TFP	−0.025	0.014*	0.002	0.002
TFP growth	−0.197	0.229	−0.336	0.130***
Return to scale	0.271	0.098*	0.021	0.014
Assisted area	0.002	0.008	−0.006	0.001
Observations	1,900		1,810	
Pseudo R^2	0.322		0.569	

Notes: Heteroscedasticity robust standard errors are given in parentheses. *Significant at 10%, **significant at 5%, and ***significant at 1%. All regressions include the full set of time dummies.

APPENDIX 2

Balancing Test Results: Electronics Sector

	Paired *t*-test		Regression-Based Test	
Variable	*t* value	$p > \|t\|$	*F* value	$p > \|F\|$
Age	0.84	0.404	0.36	0.843
Size	1.28	0.203	0.35	0.843
TFP	−1.88	0.062	0.19	0.941
TFP growth	−0.26	0.797	0.58	0.674
Return to scale	−1.06	0.289	0.33	0.857

APPENDIX 3

Balancing Test Results: Food Sector

	Paired *t*-test		Regression-Based Test	
Variable	*t* value	$p > \|t\|$	*F* value	$p > \|F\|$
Age	−0.03	0.973	1.08	0.377
Size	0.62	0.54	1.79	0.142
TFP	1.25	0.213	0.38	0.823
TFP growth	−1.53	0.13	0.95	0.441
Return to scale	−0.03	0.973	0.79	0.538

APPENDIX 4

Instrumental Variables Translog Production Function Estimates by Two-Digit Industry

	SIC80 Two-Digit Industry			
	33	**34**	**41**	**42**
x1	19.729 (1.17)	−12.637 (4.96)***	−5.078 (1.96)**	−3.313 (0.59)
x2	20.203 (1.66)*	7.136 (2.55)**	8.234 (4.13)***	10.030 (2.28)**
x3	−25.105 (1.55)	10.703 (3.20)***	−3.219 (2.00)**	4.292 (0.89)
x4	−3.613 (0.76)	0.924 (1.49)	1.244 (1.89)*	−1.935 (0.98)
x1x1	0.027 (0.36)	0.159 (9.96)***	0.093 (7.50)***	0.057 (2.18)**
x2x2	0.084 (2.15)**	0.052 (6.41)***	0.081 (11.77)***	−0.001 (0.03)
x3x3	0.167 (1.93)*	0.121 (5.68)***	0.114 (19.61)***	0.090 (4.51)***
x4x4	−0.005 (0.46)	−0.013 (6.21)***	−0.007 (8.99)***	−0.014 (5.18)***
x1x2	−0.033 (0.76)	−0.035 (4.69)***	−0.015 (1.89)*	0.017 (1.11)
x1x3	−0.054 (0.80)	−0.106 (5.99)***	−0.092 (14.02)***	−0.078 (4.23)***
x1x4	0.021 (1.56)	0.004 (1.67)*	0.000 (0.11)	0.017 (2.33)**
x1time	−0.010 (1.12)	0.007 (5.49)***	0.003 (2.44)**	0.002 (0.74)
x2x3	−0.048 (0.91)	−0.029 (3.38)***	−0.036 (8.38)***	−0.040 (3.15)***
x2x4	0.017 (1.65)*	−0.002 (1.10)	0.003 (1.67)*	0.005 (1.03)
x2time	−0.010 (1.60)	−0.003 (2.38)**	−0.004 (3.98)***	−0.005 (2.14)**
x3x4	−0.022 (1.49)	0.006 (2.71)***	0.005 (3.57)***	−0.005 (0.95)
x3time	0.012 (1.47)	−0.006 (3.51)***	0.001 (1.68)*	−0.002 (0.91)
x4time	0.002 (0.82)	−0.000 (1.32)	−0.001 (1.85)*	0.001 (1.10)
F*x1	0.000 (.)	0.000 (.)	−20.927 (3.18)***	0.000 (.)
F*x2	0.000 (.)	−21.512 (3.75)***	−6.327 (1.00)	0.000 (.)
F*x3	1.106 (0.37)	5.494 (2.19)**	0.000 (.)	0.000 (.)
F*x4	0.963 (0.24)	−2.208 (1.50)	−0.201 (0.15)	0.000 (.)
F*x1x1	−0.048 (0.41)	0.020 (0.42)	0.136 (1.31)	0.014 (0.12)
F*x2x2	−0.069 (0.74)	0.020 (0.89)	0.145 (3.81)***	0.100 (1.22)
F*x3x3	−0.090 (0.72)	0.165 (1.64)	0.046 (0.77)	−0.062 (0.43)
F*x4x4	0.039 (1.16)	−0.001 (0.22)	−0.044 (4.63)***	−0.077 (2.98)***
F*x1x2	0.081 (0.99)	0.045 (1.52)	−0.081 (1.52)	−0.021 (0.29)
F*x1x3	0.034 (0.42)	−0.081 (1.22)	−0.011 (0.17)	0.078 (0.61)
F*x1x4	−0.014 (0.34)	−0.006 (0.51)	0.060 (2.39)**	−0.051 (0.69)
F*x1time	−0.000 (0.39)	0.001 (1.13)	0.010 (2.95)***	−0.000 (0.34)
F*x2x3	0.001 (0.01)	−0.045 (1.18)	−0.083 (2.23)**	−0.135 (1.66)*
F*x2x4	0.026 (0.80)	0.000 (0.04)	0.013 (1.27)	0.088 (1.55)
F*x2time	−0.000 (0.68)	0.011 (3.87)***	0.004 (1.11)	0.000 (0.55)
F*x3x4	−0.046 (1.73)*	0.003 (0.20)	−0.056 (2.52)**	0.073 (1.26)
F*x3time	0.001 (0.30)	−0.004 (3.19)***	0.000 (0.37)	0.000 (0.18)
F*x4time	−0.000 (0.23)	0.001 (1.54)	0.001 (1.12)	−0.000 (0.29)
Time	1.587 (0.32)	−0.875 (1.01)	1.800 (2.44)**	−2.153 (1.18)
F*time	−0.029 (1.35)	0.026 (2.03)**	0.054 (3.16)***	0.008 (1.17)
Timetime	−0.001 (0.33)	0.000 (1.09)	−0.001 (2.45)**	0.001 (1.19)
F*timetime	0.000 (1.03)	−0.000 (1.62)	−0.000 (3.70)***	−0.000 (0.73)
Observations	538	8,834	6,288	3,462
Sargan test (*p* value)	0.134	0.213	0.121	0.176

Notes: Dependent variable is output and factor inputs are considered. These are skilled labor (x1), unskilled labor (x2), intermediate inputs (x3), and capital (x4). The prefix F* is used to denote interaction terms with the foreign ownership dummy. *Significant at 10%, **significant at 5%, and ***significant at 1%. Standard errors are given in parentheses.

REFERENCES

Arnold, J., and B. S. Javorcik. "Gifted Kids or Pushy Parents? Foreign Acquisitions and Plant Performance in Indonesia." CEPR Discussion Paper 5065, 2005.

Balk, B. M. "Scale Efficiency and Productivity Change." *Journal of Productivity Analysis*, 15, 2001, 159–83.

Barnes, M., and R. Martin. "Business Data Linking: An Introduction." *Economic Trends*, 581, 2002, 34–41.

Bartelsman, E. J., and M. Doms. "Understanding Productivity: Lessons from Longitudinal Microdata." *Journal of Economic Literature*, 38, 2000, 569–95.

Blundell, R., and M. Costa Dias. "Evaluation Methods for Non-Experimental Data." *Fiscal Studies*, 21, 2000, 427–68.

Conyon, M. J., S. Girma, S. Thompson, and P. W. Wright. "The Productivity and Wage Effects of Foreign Acquisition in the United Kingdom." *Journal of Industrial Economics*, 50, 2002, 85–102.

Dehejia, R., and S. Wahba. "Propensity Score Matching Methods for Non-Experimental Causal Studies." *Review of Economics and Statistics*, 84, 2002, 151–61.

Diewert, W. "Exact and Superlative Index Numbers." *Journal of Econometrics*, 4, 1976, 115–45.

Doms, M. E., and J. B. Jensen. "Comparing Wages, Skills, and Productivity between Domestically and Foreign-Owned Manufacturing Establishments in the United States," in *Geography and Ownership as Bases for Economic Accounting*, edited by R. Baldwin, R. Lipsey, and J. D. Richardson. Chicago: Chicago University Press, 1998, 235–55.

Färe, R., S. Grosskopt, M. Norris, and Z. Zhang. "Productivity Growth, Technical Progress and Efficiency Change in Industrialized Countries." *American Economic Review*, 84, 1994, 66–83.

Girma, S., and H. Görg. "Evaluating the Foreign Ownership Wage Premium Using a Difference-in-Differences Matching Approach." *Journal of International Economics*, (in press).

Girma, S., D. Greenaway, and K. Wakelin. "Who Benefits from Foreign Direct Investment in the UK?" *Scottish Journal of Political Economy*, 48, 2001, 119–33.

Globerman, S., J. C. Ries, and I. Vertinsky. "The Economic Performance of Foreign Affiliates in Canada." *Canadian Journal of Economics*, 27, 1994, 143–56.

Grifell, E., and C. A. K. Lovell. "The Sources of Productivity Change in Spanish Banking." *European Journal of Operational Research*, 98, 1997, 364–80.

Griffith, R. "Using the ARD Establishment Level Data to Look at Foreign Ownership and Productivity in the United Kingdom." *Economic Journal*, 109, 1999, F416–42.

Griffith, R., and H. Simpson. "Characteristics of Foreign-Owned Firms in British Manufacturing, " in *Creating a Premier League Economy*, edited by R. Blundell, D. Card, and R. Freeman. Chicago: Chicago University Press, 2004.

Harris, R., and C. Robinson. "The Impact of Foreign Acquisitions on Total Factor Productivity: Plant-level Evidence from UK manufacturing, 1987–1992." *Review of Economics and Statistics*, 84, 2002, 562–68.

Heckman, J., H. Ichimura, J. Smith, and P. Todd. "Matching as an Econometric Evaluation Estimator: Evidence from Evaluating a Job Training Programme." *Review of Economic Studies*, 64, 1997, 605–54.

Heshmati, A. "Productivity Growth, Efficiency and Outsourcing in Manufacturing and Service Industries." *Journal of Economic Surveys*, 7, 2003, 79–112.

Koop, G., J. Osiewalski, and M. F. J. Steel. "The Components of Output Growth: A Stochastic Frontier Analysis." *Oxford Bulletin of Economic and Statistics*, 61, 1999, 455–87.

Lapan, H., and P. Bardhan. "Localised Technical Progress and the Transfer of Technology and Economic Development." *Journal of Economic Theory*, 6, 1973, 585–95.

Leuven, E., and B. Sianesi. "PSMATCH2: Stata Module to Perform Full Mahalanobis and Propensity Score Matching, Common Support Graphing, and Covariate Imbalance Testing." 2003, http://ideas.repec.org/c/boc/bocode/s432001.html.

Lichtenberg, F., and D. Siegel. "Productivity and Changes in Ownership of Manufacturing Plants." *Brookings Papers on Economic Activity: Microeconomics*, 3, 1987, 643–73.

Lucas, R. E. "On the Mechanics of Economic Development." *Journal of Monetary Economics*, 22, 1988, 3–42.

Markusen, J. R. *Multinational Firms and the Theory of International Trade*. Cambridge, MA: MIT Press, 2002.

McGuckin, R. H., and S. V. Nguyen. "On Productivity and Plant Ownership Change: New Evidence from the Longitudinal Research Database." *Rand Journal of Economics*, 26, 1995, 257–76.

Morgan, C. W., A. Blake, and J. Poyago-Theotoky. "Managing Technological Change in the Food Industry: Some Case Studies." *International Journal of Biotechnology*, 5, 2003, 334–53.

Orea, L. "Parametric Decomposition of a Generalised Malmquist Productivity Index." *Journal of Productivity Analysis*, 18, 2002, 5–22.

Rosenbaum, P., and D. B. Rubin. "The Central Role of the Propensity Score in Observational Studies for Causal Effects." *Biometrika*, 70, 1983, 41–55.

Smith, J., and P. Todd. "Does Matching Overcome Ladonde's Critique of Nonexperimental Estimators?" *Journal of Econometrics*, 125, 2005a, 305–53.

———. "Rejoinder." *Journal of Econometrics*, 125, 2005b, 365–75.

Tybout, J. "Manufacturing Firms in Developing Countries: How Well Do They Do, and Why?" *Journal of Economic Literature*, 38, 2000, 11–44.

Wang, J.-Y., and M. Blomström. "Foreign Investment and Technology Transfer: A Simple Model." *European Economic Review*, 36, 1992, 137–55.

Chapter 2

Evaluating the foreign ownership wage premium using a difference-in-differences matching approach

Sourafel Girma [a], Holger Görg [b,*]

[a] University of Nottingham, UK
[b] GEP, University of Nottingham and CEPR, UK

Received 3 May 2005; received in revised form 20 February 2006; accepted 11 July 2006

Abstract

This paper seeks to identify the causal effect of foreign acquisitions on wages of skilled and unskilled workers, using difference-in-differences propensity score matching estimators. Our results suggest that there is substantial heterogeneity in the post-acquisition wage effect depending on the nationality of the foreign acquirer and the skill group of workers. We find sizable post acquisition wage effects on skilled and unskilled wages following an acquisition by a US firm. No such impacts result from acquisitions by EU multinationals. Also we discern some positive wage effects for unskilled workers resulting from acquisitions by multinationals from the rest of the world.

Keywords: Multinationals; Acquisitions; Wages; Difference-in-differences; Matching estimator

JEL classification: F23; J31

1. Introduction

It is by now almost accepted as a stylised fact that foreign multinational enterprises (MNEs) perform better than domestic firms for a number of indicators. In particular, recent analyses of micro level data commonly find that MNEs pay higher wages than their domestic counterparts.[1]

* Corresponding author. School of Economics, University of Nottingham, Nottingham NG7 2RD, UK. Tel.: +44 115 846 6393; fax: +44 115 951 4159.

E-mail address: holger.gorg@nottingham.ac.uk (H. Görg).

[1] See, for example, Feliciano and Lipsey (2006) for the US, Girma, Greenaway, and Wakelin (2001) for the UK and Lipsey and Sjöholm (2004) for Indonesia. These papers control for some observable firm and industry characteristics.

0022-1996/$ - see front matter
doi:10.1016/j.jinteco.2006.07.006

This is an important finding, as studying the implications of multinationals on domestic workers is arguably of great consequence to the economy, not least from a policy maker's perspective.[2]

However, even when controlling for observable and time invariant unobservable characteristics (e.g., in a fixed effects estimation), there remains a fundamental problem in identifying the performance difference that is attributable to multinationality *per se*. As Tybout (2000), for example, points out, multinationals may be attracted to more technology intensive industries, which are also more productive and pay higher wages. Hence, there would be an endogeneity problem in the regressions and the wage differential between foreign and domestic firms would be difficult to interpret. The inclusion of some industry and firm characteristics might go some way towards reducing this bias, though the inclusion of all possible relevant control variables is a difficult if not impossible task.

In this paper we try to overcome this problem by analyzing the effects of an acquisition of a domestic establishment by a foreign multinational enterprise on wages for skilled and unskilled workers using establishment level data for the UK. Assuming that an acquisition does not change any of the main characteristics of the takeover target (at least in the short run) a possible effect of the foreign acquisition on wages in the domestic target can be attributed to the change in ownership from domestic to foreign. We use a difference-in-differences propensity score matching approach to identify the average effect of foreign acquisitions (the treatment) on wages in the domestic target.

There have been a couple of earlier empirical studies which are related to our paper. Lipsey and Sjöholm (2002) study the wage premium following a foreign acquisition using plant level data for Indonesia. They relate the average wage in a plant to a number of ownership and plant characteristics and conclude that foreign takeovers are associated with higher wages even when controlling for firm and industry characteristics. However, this can only be interpreted as the causal effect of ownership change on wages if the foreign takeover is exogenous to unobserved shocks to plant level average wages. While the authors' control for unobserved time invariant plant level effects in the model, exogeneity is still a strong assumption as there are a number of time varying facts that are plausibly correlated with average wages.

Conyon et al. (2002) study the effect of foreign acquisitions on wages in the domestic target using company level data for UK manufacturing. They find that foreign acquired firms pay 3.4% higher wages than non-acquired firms, controlling for firm size as well as fixed firm and industry specific effects.[3] They acknowledge the potential endogeneity of the acquisition decision and identify the acquisition wage effect based on a simple instrumental variable estimation, using the probability of acquisition (conditional on, inter alia, lagged wages) as an instrument. This approach is only valid under the (arguably strong) assumption that the probability is uncorrelated with contemporaneous wages. It should also be noted that their data identify acquisitions of whole companies rather than plants. Furthermore, acquisitions cannot be observed directly in the data, but only indirectly as firms that change their ownership status from being "independent" to being a subsidiary of another firm. This, thus, excludes possible acquisitions of companies or plants that were subsidiaries of other enterprises prior to takeover.

[2] Of course, productivity effects of multinationals are also important to the economy. These have been the subject of many recent studies, see, for example, Girma and Görg (in press) and Doms and Jensen (1998). Another related, yet different, research question is whether multinationals increase the demand for skilled labour. See, for example, Slaughter (2000) and Figini and Görg (1999) for such studies.

[3] However, this differential disappears when labour productivity is added as a regressor, indicating that the wage difference can be wholly attributed to productivity differences between foreign and domestic firms.

We extend and improve upon these earlier papers in a number of ways. First, we use a non-parametric difference-in-differences propensity score matching approach to be able to identify the causal effect of the takeover on wages.[4] Matching estimators, in particular combined with the difference-in-differences technique, are arguably more appropriate compared to a simple instrumental variable approach as no strong exclusion restrictions are needed (e.g., Blundell and Costa Dias, 2000). Such an estimation approach is novel for the analysis of a foreign wage premium. In line with the recent statistical literature, we are also careful to assess the credibility of the matching procedure using a number of balancing tests.

Secondly, in contrast to earlier studies we allow for different effects of acquisitions by firms from different home countries, in particular from the US and the EU. As we discuss below, these distinctions bring up interesting differences in results for the two groups of workers and different firm nationalities. Thirdly, while Conyon et al. (2002) look at average wages per firm, our data set allows us to distinguish the effect of an acquisition on wages for skilled and unskilled workers separately, similar to Lipsey and Sjöholm (2002). Fourthly, our data set is at the establishment (mostly plant) level and allows us to identify takeovers directly in the raw data (in contrast to Conyon et al., 2002).

In the empirical analysis below we do find that foreign acquisitions lead to changes in domestic wages for skilled and unskilled workers, although there is substantial heterogeneity in the magnitude of the effects depending on skill group of workers and nationality of the acquirer. The remainder of the paper is structured as follows. In Section 2 we briefly outline the background for why we would expect an effect of foreign acquisition on wages. Section 3 describes the empirical methodology while Section 4 introduces the data set. Section 5 presents some balancing tests performed in order to ensure the reliability of the matching approach. Section 6 describes the results of the matching estimations and Section 7 concludes.

2. Background

Why would affiliates be expected to pay higher wages after having been acquired by a foreign-owned multinational? An explanation that is linked quite closely to the industrial organization theory of multinationals starts from the assumption that multinationals have access to some form of firm specific asset (Markusen, 2002). This can be a superior production technique, know-how, or management strategy, and has at least some of the characteristics of a public good and enables the firm to locate profitably abroad. This firm specific asset implies that multinationals use a "superior" level of technology and, hence, explains why they are usually expected to have higher levels of productivity compared to purely domestic firms.

If this implies that the foreign multinational has higher marginal productivity of homogeneous labour then, in a competitive labour market, it would be advantageous for the firm to expand output rather than increase wages. However, if one assumes that the efficient use of the firm specific asset requires "better" (in the sense of more productive) workers, then one may observe higher wages after the transfer of the firm specific asset to the takeover target. Another

[4] Subsequent to our analysis, Martins (2004) conducted a study using a propensity score matching approach to identify the link between foreign acquisition and wages. He uses linked firm-employee data for Portuguese manufacturing firms over the period 1991 to 1999. He finds negative effects of acquisitions on wage growth, while simple OLS estimations show a positive relationship between foreign ownership and wages. Our estimation approach may be considered more appropriate as we implement a combined difference-in-differences propensity score matching estimator. Also in contrast to Martins (2004) we are careful to explore the appropriateness of the matching procedures using a number of balancing tests.

explanation based on the firm specific asset idea that can be used to justify why multinationals pay higher wages to identical workers is that MNEs may want to minimize the amount of labour turnover in order to prevent the leakage of the firm specific asset. In order to do so they may pay higher wages to provide an incentive for workers not to quit.[5]

Apart from the possession and transfer of a firm specific asset, is there any reason to expect any additional effects of a foreign takeover on wages? The change in ownership may bring with it a change in industrial relations practices, which may have impacts on the wage structure. Budd et al. (2005) argue and provide evidence that multinationals share rents with workers across borders, i.e., the wage level in the foreign affiliate is linked to profits in the parent company. The implementation of these rent sharing arrangements may increase wages after the ownership change. Another industrial relations argument has been made by Carmichael (1992) who argues that US multinationals in the UK paid higher wages than domestic firms in order to "bribe" workers to avoid industrial relations disputes. Furthermore, Conyon et al. (2002) point out that multinationals, in particular from Japan, may actually bring with them successful work practices, industrial relations arrangements etc. which will be implemented in their foreign subsidiaries. In order to implement these new arrangements "peacefully" workers may be compensated with higher wages.

An interesting question to ask is whether takeovers by multinationals from different home countries should be expected to have different effects on post-acquisition wages. We may expect this for at least two reasons. First, in terms of technology as a firm specific asset, it is widely accepted that the US is the technological leader which gives the average US multinational a technological leadership vis-à-vis comparable UK companies (Criscuolo and Martin, 2004). Foreign firms from other EU countries may, however, have less of such a technological advantage compared with the average UK firm as they may be expected to have access to a fairly similar level of technology.[6] Hence a wage premium may be expected to be higher for affiliates taken over by US multinationals than by others.

On the other hand, considering industrial relations, we may expect less of a difference between US and UK firms, who have similar "Anglo-Saxon" industrial relations regimes, while firms from other continental EU countries (such as Germany and France) have very different labour market institutions (see, for example, Boeri et al., 2001). Hence, we may expect different effects also from that point of view between EU and US firms.

3. Empirical methodology

The aim of the paper is to analyse whether there is a causal effect from an acquisition of a domestic establishment by a foreign owner on wages in the domestic target. In other words, the empirical modelling problem is the evaluation of the causal effect of foreign acquisition on y, where y represents skilled or unskilled wages in the target establishment.

Let $ACQ_{it} \in \{0,1\}$ be an indicator of whether establishment i is acquired by a foreign MNE at time period t, and let y^1_{it+s} be wage at time $t+s$, $s \geq 0$, following acquisition. Also denote y^0_{it+s} as

[5] Lipsey (2004) provides a number of other reasons for why multinationals pay higher wages, in particular that workers may have an inherent preference to work for domestic firms and therefore need to be compensated, or that multinationals due to lack of knowledge of the local labour markets must pay higher wages to attract good workers. However, these reasons do not seem applicable for explaining relative short term changes in wages after a foreign acquisition of a domestic firm.

[6] This should not distract, however, from the general idea that foreign firms must have a technological advantage in order to operate successfully abroad.

the wage of the plant if it had not been acquired. The causal effect of foreign ownership for firm i at time period $t+s$ is then defined as:

$$y^1_{it+s} - y^0_{it+s}. \tag{1}$$

The fundamental problem of causal inference is that the quantity y^0_{it+s} is unobservable for plants that have been acquired (i.e., for which we observe y^1_{it+s}). Thus the analysis can be viewed as confronting a missing-data problem. Following the microeconometric evaluation literature (e.g. Heckman et al., 1997; Dehejia and Wahba, 2002), we define the *average* effect of acquisition on the acquired firms as

$$E\{y^1_{t+s} - y^0_{t+s} | \text{ACQ}_{it} = 1\} = E\{y^1_{t+s} | \text{ACQ}_{it} = 1\} - E\{y^0_{t+s} | \text{ACQ}_{it} = 1\} \tag{2}$$

where causal inference relies on the construction of the counterfactual for the last term in Eq. (2), which is the outcome the acquired establishments would have experienced, on average, had they not been acquired. This is estimated by the average wage of the plants that remained in domestic hands, $E\{y^0_{it+s} | \text{ACQ}_{it} = 0\}$.

This is, of course, only a valid approximation if there are no contemporaneous effects that are correlated with ACQ and that are not controlled for. If that is not the case then the empirical analysis is plagued with endogeneity and simultaneity bias. Hence, an important feature in the accurate construction of the counterfactual is the selection of a valid control group. The approach we take is to employ matching techniques. The purpose of matching is to pair each foreign acquired plant with a domestic establishment that has not undergone any ownership change on the basis of some observable variables, in such a way that the domestic establishments' wage dynamics can be studied to generate the counterfactual for the newly foreign owned plants.[7] This type of matching procedure is preferable to randomly or indiscriminately choosing the comparison group, because it is less likely to induce estimation bias by picking firms with markedly different characteristics.

Since matching involves comparing acquired and non-acquired establishments across a number of observable pre-acquisition characteristics (e.g., productivity, size, industry characteristics), it is desirable to perform the matching on the basis of a single index that captures all the information from those variables. We adopt the method of propensity score matching due to Rosenbaum and Rubin (1983), which suggests the use of the probability of receiving treatment (foreign acquisition in the present context) conditional on those characteristics, to reduce the dimensionality problem. Accordingly, we first identify the probability (or *propensity score*) of being acquired using a probit model

$$P(\text{ACQ}_{it} = 1) = F(X_{it-1}) \tag{3}$$

where X is a vector of covariates observed in the time period before acquisition. This vector consists of the pre-acquisition levels of establishment size (proxied here by capital stock), productivity, skilled and unskilled wages, as well as a dummy variable indicating whether or not a plant is located in an assisted area in the UK and a full set of time dummies.

The choice of covariates is influenced by the empirical literature on foreign acquisitions (e.g. Conyon et al., 2002; Harris and Robinson, 2002). Existing evidence suggests that establishment size

[7] Since the purpose of this paper is to compare foreign acquired with domestic plants any plant that remains in domestic hands is a valid control. This could also include domestic establishments that were taken over by other domestic owners, or that are likely to be targets for domestic takeovers. In our version of the ARD we are not able to adequately observe domestic acquisitions.

is an important determinant for acquisitions. Also, high productivity plants are commonly found to be more likely to be taken over, indicating that foreign firms may be "cherry picking" the best performing establishments. Wages by skill groups prior to acquisition are included to address the argument that foreign firms may take over high or low wage establishments (see Lipsey and Sjöholm, 2002).

Now let p_i denote the predicted probability of being acquired for plant i in the group of acquired plants (say group A) and let p_j denote the predicted probability of being acquired for plant j in the control group (say group C). A standard matching estimator of the causal effect of foreign acquisition can be written as

$$\mu = \sum_{i \in A} \left(y_i - \sum_{j \in C} g(p_i, p_j) y_i \right) \tag{4}$$

where g(.) is a function assigning the weights to be placed on the comparison firm j while constructing the counterfactual for acquired firm i. The different matching estimators proposed in the literature (such as nearest neighbour matching and kernel matching estimators) differ from each other in the choice of the weighting function they employ. For example, the Gaussian kernel function used in this paper is defined as follows:

$$g(p_i, p_j) = \frac{K\left[\frac{(p_i - p_j)}{h}\right]}{\sum_{k \in C} K\left[\frac{(p_i - p_k)}{h}\right]} \tag{5}$$

where $K(\mu) \propto \exp\left(\frac{-\mu^2}{2}\right)$ the Gaussian normal function, h is the bandwidth parameter and C denote the set of non-acquired plants.

Since we have longitudinal data, we do not employ this matching estimator in levels but rather use a difference-in-differences (DID) matching estimator on the matched plants instead. This is motivated by recent studies which argue that standard matching estimators are usually unsatisfactory (e.g., due to the strong assumption of "selection on observables"), but in combination with difference-in-differences methodology can have the potential to "...improve the quality of non-experimental evaluation results significantly" (Blundell and Costa Dias, 2000, p. 438). The difference-in-differences matching estimator has the additional advantage of eliminating unobserved time-invariant differences in wages between acquired and non-acquired firms that standard matching estimators fail to eliminate (Smith and Todd, 2005a).[8]

The DID matching estimator is defined as follows. Let Δy be the difference between the average wage before and after the change of ownership. Then following Heckman et al. (1997) the estimator can be expressed as:

$$\delta = \sum_{i \in A} \left(\Delta y_i - \sum_{j \in C} g(p_i, p_j) \Delta y_i \right). \tag{6}$$

We employ variants of this DID matching estimator for the empirical analysis below.[9]

[8] Hence, while the combined estimator still requires the assumption of "selection on observables", DID purges all unobserved time invariant plant characteristics.

[9] One caveat of this estimator is that to the extent that there are positive (negative) wage spillovers from acquisition FDI to the control group of domestic establishments, the difference-in-differences procedure is likely to underestimate (overestimate) the causal effects of international takeovers on the wages of acquisition targets.

4. Description of the data

We use data from the Annual Respondents Database (ARD), which is provided by the Office for National Statistics (ONS) in the UK under controlled conditions. The dataset consists of individual establishments' records underlying the Annual Census of Production and the data used cover the period 1980 to 1994. As Barnes and Martin (2002) provide a useful introduction to the data set, we only include a brief discussion of some of its features relevant to the present work.

In the period covered by our data, the ARD consists of two files. What is known as the 'selected file', contains detailed information on a sample of establishments that are sent inquiry forms. The second file comprises the 'non-selected' (non-sampled) establishments and only basic information such as employment, location, industry grouping and foreign ownership status is recorded. During our study period, some 14,000–19,000 establishments are selected each year, based on a stratified sampling scheme. The scheme tends to vary from year to year, but over the period under consideration establishments with more than 100 employees were always sampled.

In the data, an establishment is defined as the smallest unit that is deemed capable of providing information on the Census questionnaire. Thus a 'parent' establishment reports for more than one plant (or 'local unit' in the parlance of ARD). For selected multi-plant establishments, we only have aggregate values for the constituent plants. Indicative information on the 'children' is available in the 'non-selected' file. In the sample period considered in this paper over 95% of the establishment in both the electronics and food industries are single-plant firms. In the actual sample we used for the econometric estimation this figure is around 80% for both sectors. Thus most of the data we used is actually plant level data. As a result we tend to use the terms plant and establishment interchangeably.

In this paper we focus on two broad industries, namely electronics and food, rather than pooled data for the whole manufacturing industry.[10] In this way we avoid the potential problem of pooling plants that operate in very heterogeneous sectors and rather focus on relatively homogenous sets of plants within the two sectors. We focus on these two particular industries for two reasons. First, foreign-owned firms are important players in both sectors, accounting for about 19% of employment in electronics and 10% of employment in the food industry in 1996 (see Griffith and Simpson, 2003, Table 4). Second, we may expect the two sectors to be different in their technology usage, and hence, there may be differences in the determinants of foreign acquisition and its effects on skilled and unskilled wages.

We define skilled and unskilled workers in terms of non-production and production workers, respectively, in line with the recent literature (e.g., Machin and Van Reenen, 1998; Slaughter, 2000). While this could be considered a rough measure of skills we can take some support for this classification from the previous literature. Berman et al. (1994) show that the proportion of non-production workers matches quite closely over time with the proportion of white collar and more educated workers. Also, Head and Ries (2002) show that non-production workers are on average more skilled than production workers.

In the ARD a consistently defined nationality indicator identifies whether an establishment is domestic or foreign owned. Foreign acquisition is said to have occurred in year t when an establishment that has been in domestic hands up to year $t-1$ becomes a subsidiary of a foreign-

[10] More precisely, using SIC 1980 classification, SIC 33 (manufacture of office machinery and data processing equipment), SIC 34 (electrical and electronic engineering), and SIC 41/42 (food, drink and tobacco).

based multinational and changes its nationality indicator.[11] Since the matching process described in the previous section requires data on the pre-acquisition period, we consider foreign take-overs that took place between 1981 and 1994. Overall, there were 203 and 100 acquisitions in the electronics and food industries over that period, respectively, for which the necessary pre and post acquisition information is available.

Table A1 in the Appendix shows some summary statistics on the main variables used in the analysis, and the number of establishments in the data. The panel used is unbalanced. Table A2 shows the short run post-acquisition trajectories of employment for the two types of labour, and capital intensity in the acquired plants, by nationality of the acquirer. As is notable, there are only few statistically significant changes.

5. Testing the reliability of the propensity score matching method

5.1. Balancing and sensitivity tests

The propensity score matching method will provide a reliable and robust method for estimating the foreign acquisition effect if, conditional on the propensity score, the potential outcomes y^1 and y^0 are independent of the incidence of acquisition. Under the assumption of independence conditional on observables, the pre-acquisition variables should be balanced between the acquired and non-acquired groups. Lack of balance points to a possible mis-specification of the propensity score estimation. Hence, as emphasised by Rosenbaum and Rubin (1983) and Dehejia and Wahba (2002) it is important to verify that this balancing condition is satisfied by the data. In this paper we perform a number of balancing tests suggested in the recent literature (Dehejia, 2005; Smith and Todd, 2005b).

The first balancing test examines the standardised difference (or bias) for all variables in X (that is the vector of covariates used in the propensity score estimation) as described in Smith and Todd (2005b). For example, the standardised bias for the *size* variable is defined as the difference in means between the foreign acquired sample of firms (group A) and the appropriately matched comparison group of firms (group C) scaled by the average variances of the *size* variable in groups A and C. Based on *N* acquired firm this is given as

$$\mathrm{SDIFF}(\mathrm{size}) = \frac{100\frac{1}{N}\sum_{i\in \mathrm{A}}\left[size_i - \sum_{j\in \mathrm{C}} g(p_i, p_j) size_j\right]}{\sqrt{\frac{Var_{i\in \mathrm{A}}(\mathrm{size}) + Var_{j\in \mathrm{C}}(\mathrm{size})}{2}}}. \tag{7}$$

Note that the lower the standardised difference, the more balanced or similar the treatment and comparison groups will be in terms of the variable under consideration. Although there is no formal criterion as to how large a standardised bias should be for it to be considered serious, we follow Rosenbaum and Rubin (1985) and assume that a value of 20 is large. Furthermore, for each variable entering the propensity score model we perform a formal paired

[11] Establishments that appear to have experienced more than one change of ownership between 1980 and 1994 are excluded from the analysis. This is partly to avoid conflating the effects of different events, and partly because we suspect the presence of measurement error problems.

Table 1
Balancing tests from kernel matching

Variable	Mean		% Bias	% Bias reduction	*t*-test	Regression-based tests *F*-stat (*p*-value)
	Acquired	Control			*t*-stat (*p*-value)	
Skilled wage	8.9442	8.9287	4.5	93.6	1.29 (0.198)	0.26 (0.9347)
Unskilled wage	8.5177	8.4923	6.5	85.1	1.91 (0.056)	0.38 (0.8643)
Assisted area	0.36704	0.36612	0.2	98.9	0.06 (0.955)	0.40 (0.8479)
Productivity	10.5	10.459	4.9	82.3	1.43 (0.153)	0.54 (0.7466)
Size (capital)	15.361	15.152	6.9	78.7	1.84 (0.066)	0.20 (0.9630)
Year	1987.6	1987.4	7.1	93.5	1.97 (0.049)	0.18 (0.9699)

Definition of variables included in the matching: *Skilled wage*: log of average wage per employee for non-production workers, *Unskilled wage*: log of average wage per employee for production workers, *Assisted area*: Dummy = 1 if plant located in area specially designated as "assisted", *Productivity*: value added (total output − materials inputs) per employee. *Size*: log capital stock, *Year*: time trend.

t-test between acquired and matched comparison to satisfy ourselves that no significant differences exist.

Whereas the above balancing test calculates the cross-sample difference of each variable entering the probit model separately, there also exists a test that considers whether those differences can be taken as *jointly* insignificant. This test is known as the Hotelling's T-squared test and it has the flexibility of being based either on all observations or for separate segments of the sample defined by the propensity score estimates. In this study we divide the sample by propensity score quintile and conduct the Hotelling's T-squared test for each sub-sample.[12]

The third balancing test we explore is suggested by Smith and Todd (2005b) and it is cast within a regression framework. Let $\hat{P}(X)$ denote the estimated propensity score and let D be a dummy variable assuming a value of 1 if a plant is foreign acquired. Then for each variable included in the matching algorithm, the following regression function that is quartic in $\hat{P}(X)$ is estimated (again using the *size* variable as an example):

$$\text{SIZE} = \beta_0 + \sum_{k=1}^{4} \beta_k \hat{P}(X)^k + \sum_{k=1}^{4} \gamma_k D\hat{P}(X)^k + \varepsilon \tag{8}$$

and the joint significance of the coefficient on the terms involving the acquisition dummies (that is the γs) is tested. As explained by Todd and Smith (2005b), if the propensity score satisfies the balancing condition, D should not provide any additional information and we should expect the γs to be jointly statistically insignificant.

Following the suggestion of Dehejia (2005), a fourth diagnostic that we undertake regarding the propensity score method is to check the sensitivity of the matching estimates to minor changes in the propensity score model. If the results are not sensitive to such minor changes, the propensity score specification can be deemed robust and reliable.

[12] The extent of overlap between acquired and non-acquired plants on the propensity score is shown in Table A3 in the Appendix.

Table 2
Hotelling's T-squared tests by propensity score quintile

Quintile	T-squared statistics	F-test statistics	p-value
First	4.818	0.516	0.783
Second	6.179	0.772	0.604
Third	9.163	1.383	0.241
Fourth	6.720	1.073	0.383
Fifth	8.669	1.418	0.208

5.2. Evidence on balancing

Table 1 reports the balancing test results based on Gaussian kernel matching. The standardised differences between acquired and comparison sample are all less than 8% in the matched sample. The substantial bias reduction as a result of adopting the matching method is also apparent from the figures in Table 1.

The regression-based tests also corroborate the success of the propensity score-matching approach adopted in this paper. For all variables, we fail to reject the joint hypothesis that the γs are all equal to zero. It is thus comforting that both standardised differences and regression tests are doing very well, suggesting that the propensity score specification we have chosen is effective in accounting for factors that determine selection into the treatment (i.e. foreign acquisition). Table 2 summarises the results from the Hotelling test and reassuringly we find that the balancing conditions are satisfied within each propensity score quintile.

6. Difference-in-differences matching estimates

Having established that conditional on the propensity score, the comparison and treatment group of firms are comparable, we now present in Table 3 the difference-in-differences matching

Table 3
The impact of foreign acquisition on the log of skilled and unskilled wages

t	Skilled wage		Unskilled wage	
	Matching estimate	Standard error	Matching estimate	Standard error
Preferred propensity score model				
1	0.026	0.015**	0.054	0.017***
2	0.029	0.024	0.071	0.020***
3	0.030	0.023	0.075	0.028**
4	0.046	0.031	0.049	0.032
Modified propensity score model				
1	0.037	0.022*	0.044	0.020**
2	0.033	0.023	0.068	0.022***
3	0.061	0.050	0.071	0.030**
4	0.031	0.058	0.036	0.032

Notes:
(i) Significant at 10%; ** significant at 5%; *** significant at 1%.
(ii) Estimation is based on 336 foreign acquisitions.

estimates.[13] These give the causal effects of foreign ownership on (log) skilled and unskilled wages, and hence the figures in this table can be interpreted as percentage changes in wages. Throughout we impose the common support condition and confine our attention to the comparison group establishments that fall within the support of the propensity score distribution of the acquired plants.

The top half of Table 3 reports the foreign acquisition impact estimates based on the preferred propensity score specification — that is the specification that passed the balancing tests as described above. The post-acquisition period is given by t ranging from 1 (first year of foreign ownership) to 4. The estimates show that the average causal effect of foreign ownership on skilled wages is 2.6% in the first year of acquisition. The estimates turn, however, statistically insignificant in later years, indicating that the accuracy of our estimator falls with t. Interestingly, the impact on unskilled wages exhibits a different profile, with coefficients being statistically significant up to 3 years after the acquisition. The average impact is also higher compared with skilled wages: starting from 5.4% in the first year of acquisition and reaching 7.5% after 3 years. However, it is worth noting that the level of skilled wages is more than 40% higher than unskilled wages (see Table 1). Nonetheless this finding suggests that there is no evidence that FDI exacerbates income inequality, as unskilled wages appear to change by more than the average skilled wage.

The next step in the analysis is to check the sensitivity of the results by making a slight change to the propensity score specification suggested by Dehejia (2005). Here we add a quadratic size term to the original list of covariates, and the impact estimates are given in the lower half of Table 3.[14] It is clear that these are comparable to the ones discussed above, both in magnitude and statistical significance. This is further illustration of the appropriateness of propensity score specification.

6.1. In search of industry specific effects

The estimates reported in Table 3 are the average impact of the 303 foreign acquisitions, and as such may mask some interesting heterogeneity. Here we ask whether the wage effects are the same in the two broad sectors under consideration: the skill-intensive electronics sector in which 203 foreign takeovers are observed in our sample, and the low-tech food sector. The estimates presented in Table 4 shed some light on the issue. It seems that in both sectors unskilled workers receive on average higher wages as a result of their plant's newfound status as a subsidiary of a multinational company. The absence of a robust statistically significant effect of foreign ownership on skilled wages within both sectors may perhaps be due to lower test power when dividing the observations into subsamples. The absence of any strong apparent differences across sectors may suggest that industry specific effects perhaps do not capture the underlying technology. In the next subsection we explore whether the nationality of the foreign acquirer can shed more light on the issue.

6.2. Are there country specific effects?

As pointed out in Section 2, given the differences in technology and industrial relations institutions in different source countries, it is an interesting question to ask whether takeovers by

[13] These are based on the Gaussian Kernel matching as discussed above. We also considered the single nearest neighbour matching to check for robustness of our results to changes in the matching procedure. The results are very similar to the ones obtained using Kernel matching. Furthermore, we also compared our results with those obtained from a simple DID estimator. See Table A4 in the Appendix for some of these results. Further results are not reported here to save space, but can be obtained from the authors.

[14] This specification also passed the balancing tests. These are not reported here to save space.

Table 4
In search of industry-specific effects

t	Skilled wage		Unskilled wage	
	Matching estimate	Standard error	Matching estimate	Standard error
Electronics sector				
1	0.017	0.019	0.059	0.024**
2	0.021	0.026	0.072	0.027***
3	0.016	0.040	0.082	0.031**
4	0.029	0.035	0.042	0.042
Food sector				
1	0.036	0.034	0.037	0.019*
2	0.020	0.038	0.048	0.026*
3	0.010	0.043	0.058	0.120
4	0.022	0.055	0.047	0.118

Notes:
(i) Significant at 10%; ** significant at 5%; *** significant at 1%.
(ii) Estimation is based on 203 [100] foreign acquisitions in the electronics [food] sector.

multinationals from different countries have different effects on post-acquisition wages. In our data set we are able to distinguish three categories of nationalities, namely, US, EU and others. Overall, slightly more acquisitions were carried out by US multinationals (108) than by firms from the two other nationality categories (EU: 104, others: 91) over the time period analyzed. The

Table 5
Wage effects of acquisition FDI by country of origin

t	Skilled wage		Unskilled wage	
	Matching estimate	Standard error	Matching estimate	Standard error
USA				
1	0.036	0.024	0.085	0.041**
2	0.083	0.038**	0.090	0.041**
3	0.089	0.038**	0.129	0.059**
4	0.092	0.047**	0.067	0.058
EU				
1	0.011	0.022	−0.003	0.021
2	−0.016	0.020	0.030	0.027
3	−0.017	0.039	0.039	0.040
4	0.012	0.044	0.003	0.059
Others				
1	0.007	0.020	0.063	0.026**
2	−0.012	0.044	0.072	0.030**
3	−0.052	0.043	0.017	0.041
4	−0.030	0.039	0.014	0.034

Notes:
(i) Significant at 10%; ** significant at 5%; *** significant at 1%.
(ii) Estimation is based on 108 USA, 104 EU and 91 others acquisitions.

difference-in-differences matching estimates reported in Table 5 indeed reveal substantial differences across the nationality groups.

There is a robust and economically significant wage effect for both skilled and unskilled workers acquired by US multinationals. For skilled workers, this takes effect a period after acquisition and stands at more than 8%. The impact on unskilled wages is discernible at the period of acquisition and reaches nearly 13% after two years post-acquisition. In stark contrast, no evidence is found for any causal effect on wages, skilled or unskilled, following acquisition by EU based multinationals. Finally we document positive unskilled wage effects the first two years (4.4% and 6.8%) following acquisition by multinationals from the rest of the world.

To sum up the difference-in-differences matching estimates indicate that there is substantial heterogeneity in the post acquisition effects on wages of acquisitions by firms from different home countries. Hence, not taking account of this heterogeneity may miss out valuable information in the identification of the causal effect of foreign direct investment on wages.

7. Conclusions

This paper provides a systematic empirical analysis of wage differences between foreign multinationals and domestic firms. In order to identify adequately the effect of foreign ownership we investigate the impact on wages of the takeover of a domestic establishment by foreign owners. We pay particular attention to identifying the causal effect, using a difference-in-differences propensity score matching approach, and examine differences in post acquisition effects depending on the nationality of the acquirer.

Our results suggest that there is substantial heterogeneity in the post-acquisition wage effect depending on the nationality of the foreign acquirer, the industry in which the firms operate and the skill group of workers. In particular, we find that both skilled and unskilled workers, on average, experience a post acquisition increase in the wage rate following an acquisition by a US firm. However, no such effects are discernable following acquisitions by EU firms. The finding of substantial heterogeneity in the post acquisition effects suggests that studies that do not account for heterogeneity in worker types and nationality of ownership may be subject to considerable shortcomings.

An interesting remaining question to ask is whether the observed post acquisition wage premium, in particular for US acquisitions, is something desirable. This largely depends on the reason for the higher wage. If, as we assume, the higher wage reflects the fact that the firm specific asset is utilized efficiently and/or that some of the rents are shared between firm and workers, then this seems to be a desirable outcome. If, however, wages are higher because "better" workers are employed after the takeover, then there does not appear to be any particularly positive effect, even more so if the workers were poached from domestic firms who have to reallocate labour internally as a result of the poaching. A potential judgment about welfare implications becomes even more complicated if one takes into account the effects of a higher wage rate on domestic competitors, which may be priced out of the market. In order to address this question a full theoretical analysis would be necessary, which should then be backed up by detailed micro evidence on characteristics of workers and firms. This is a tall order that needs to be tackled in future research.

Acknowledgements

We are grateful to Bob Lipsey, Gordon Hanson, participants at workshops at IIIS Dublin, Aarhus School of Business, HWWA Hamburg and ONS London, and two anonymous referees for helpful comments. This work contains statistical data from ONS which is Crown copyright and reproduced with the permission of the controller of HMSO and Queen's Printer for Scotland. The use of the ONS statistical data in this work does not imply the endorsement of the ONS in relation to the interpretation or analysis of the statistical data. Financial support through the ESRC Grant Ref: RES-000-22-0468 (Girma) and the Leverhulme Trust Programme Grant F114/BF (Görg) is gratefully acknowledged.

Appendix A

Table A1
Some summary statistics

	Non-acquired Plants		Acquired plants	
	Mean	Standard deviation	Mean	Standard deviation
Log skilled labour	3.849	1.315	4.670	1.244
Log unskilled labour	4.828	1.186	5.256	1.198
Log skilled wage	8.811	0.350	8.933	0.313
Log unskilled wage	8.433	0.382	8.532	0.348
Log total output	15.606	1.406	16.308	1.338
Log capital stock	14.976	2.789	15.456	2.471
Log productivity	10.365	0.818	10.508	0.777
Number of plants	3200		303	
Total observations	22722		2974	
Unbalanced panel	Yes		Yes	

Table A2
Short run post-acquisition trajectories of labour and capital intensity

	USA acquisitions			EU acquisitions			Others acquisitions		
	Labour		Capital	Labour		Capital	Labour		Capital
Post-acquisition period	Skilled	Unskilled		Skilled	Unskilled		Skilled	Unskilled	
1	−0.109	−0.032	−0.500	−0.036	−0.006	0.317	0.048	−0.019	−0.661
	(2.76)***	(0.58)	(1.46)	(1.10)	(0.12)	(1.19)	(1.01)	(0.35)	(1.13)
2	−0.060	−0.034	−0.407	−0.075	0.051	0.485	0.046	−0.007	−0.703
	(1.39)	(0.67)	(1.38)	(2.40)**	(1.09)	(1.66)	(1.12)	(0.12)	(1.50)
3	−0.046	−0.056	−0.030	−0.090	0.079	0.032	−0.041	−0.092	−0.549
	(1.39)	(1.29)	(0.11)	(2.53)**	(0.91)	(0.11)	(1.02)	(2.07)**	(1.19)

Notes:
(i) All regressions include year dummies.
(ii) All variables are in log.
(iii) Robust t statistics in parentheses.
(iv) * significant at 10%; ** significant at 5%; *** significant at 1%.

Table A3
Frequency distribution of acquired and non-acquired plants by propensity score quintile

Quintile	Acquired plants	Non acquired plants
First	42	698
Second	16	761
Third	27	633
Fourth	60	560
Fifth	158	548
Total	303	3200

Table A4
The impact of foreign acquisition on skilled and unskilled wages: Further results

	Skilled wage		Unskilled wage	
t	Matching estimate	Standard error	Matching estimate	Standard error
Difference-in-differences combined with nearest neighbour matching estimates				
1	0.018	0.008**	0.065	0.017***
2	0.029	0.034	0.094	0.044***
3	0.051	0.043	0.081	0.044*
4	0.016	0.055	0.016	0.052
Simple difference-in-differences estimates				
1	0.007	0.014	0.041	0.019***
2	0.006	0.022	0.059	0.022***
3	−0.010	0.023	0.053	0.029*
4	0.002	0.028	0.019	0.032

Notes:
(i) Robust t statistics in parentheses.
(ii) * significant at 10%; ** significant at 5%; *** significant at 1%.

References

Barnes, M., Martin, R., 2002. Business data linking: an introduction. Economic Trends 581, 34–41.

Berman, E., Bound, J., Griliches, Z., 1994. Changes in the demand for skilled labor within manufacturing: evidence from the survey of manufacturers. Quarterly Journal of Economics 109, 367–398.

Blundell, R., Costa Dias, M., 2000. Evaluation methods for non-experimental data. Fiscal Studies 21, 427–468.

Boeri, T., Brugiavini, A., Calmfors, L., 2001. The Role of Unions in the 21st Century. Oxford University Press, Oxford.

Budd, J.W., Konings, J., Slaughter, M.J., 2005. International profit sharing in multinational firms. Review of Economics and Statistics 87, 73–84.

Carmichael, F., 1992. Multinational enterprises and strikes: theory and evidence. Scottish Journal of Political Economy 39, 52–68.

Conyon, M., Girma, S., Thompson, S., Wright, P., 2002. The impact of foreign acquisition on wages and productivity in the U.K. Journal of Industrial Economics 50, 85–102.

Criscuolo, C., Martin, R., 2004. Multinationals and US productivity leadership: evidence from Great Britain. CERIBA Discussion Paper. London.

Dehejia, R., 2005. Program evaluation as a decision problem. Journal of Econometrics 125, 141–173.

Dehejia, R., Wahba, S., 2002. Propensity score matching methods for non-experimental causal studies. Review of Economics and Statistics 84, 151–161.

Doms, M.E., Jensen, J.B., 1998. Comparing wages, skills, and productivity between domestically and foreign-owned manufacturing establishments in the United States. In: Baldwin, R., Lipsey, R., Richardson, J.D. (Eds.), Geography and Ownership as Bases for Economic Accounting. Chicago University Press, Chicago, pp. 235–255.

Feliciano, Z., Lipsey, R.E., 2006. Foreign ownership, wages, and wage changes in U.S. industries, 1987–92. Contemporary Economic Policy 24, 74–91.

Figini, P., Görg, H., 1999. Multinational companies and wage inequality in the host country: the case of Ireland. Weltwirtschaftliches Archiv 135, 594–612.

Girma, S., Görg, H., in press. Multinationals productivity advantage: Scale or technology? Economic Inquiry.

Girma, S., Greenaway, D., Wakelin, K., 2001. Who benefits from Foreign Direct Investment in the UK? Scottish Journal of Political Economy 48, 119–133.

Griffith, R., Simpson, H., 2003. Characteristics of Foreign-owned Firms in British Manufacturing. NBER Working Paper, vol. 9573.

Harris, R., Robinson, C., 2002. The effect of foreign acquisitions on total factor productivity: plant-level evidence from U.K manufacturing, 1987–1992. Review of Economics and Statistics 84, 562–568.

Head, K., Ries, J., 2002. Offshore production and skill upgrading by Japanese manufacturing firms. Journal of International Economics 58, 81–105.

Heckman, J., Ichimura, H., Smith, J., Todd, P., 1997. Matching as an econometric evaluation estimator: evidence from evaluating a job training programme. Review of Economic Studies 64, 605–654.
Lipsey, R.E., 2004. Home and host country effects of FDI. In: Baldwin, R.E., Winters, L.A. (Eds.), Challenges to Globalization. Chicago University Press, Chicago, pp. 333–379.
Lipsey, R.E., Sjöholm, F., 2002. Foreign Firms and Indonesian Manufacturing Wages: an Analysis with Panel Data. NBER Working Paper, vol. 9417.
Lipsey, R.E., Sjöholm, F., 2004. Foreign direct investment, education and wages in Indonesian manufacturing. Journal of Development Economics 73, 415–422.
Machin, S., Van Reenen, J., 1998. Technology and changes in skill structure: evidence from seven OECD countries. Quarterly Journal of Economics 113, 1215–1244.
Markusen, J.R., 2002. Multinational Firms and the Theory of International Trade. MIT Press, Cambridge MA.
Martins, P., 2004. Do Foreign Firms Really Pay Higher Wages? Evidence from Different Estimators. IZA Discussion Paper, vol. 1388. IZA Bonn.
Rosenbaum, P., Rubin, D.B., 1983. The central role of the propensity score in observational studies for causal effects. Biometrika 70, 41–55.
Rosenbaum, P., Rubin, D.B., 1985. Constructing a control group using a multivariate matched sampling method that incorporates. The Propensity Score. American Statistician 39, 33–38.
Slaughter, M.J., 2000. Production transfer within multinational enterprises and American wages. Journal of International Economics 50, 449–472.
Smith, J., Todd, P., 2005a. Does matching overcome Ladondes critique of nonexperimental estimators. Journal of Econometrics 125, 305–353.
Smith, J., Todd, P., 2005b. Rejoinder. Journal of Econometrics 125, 365–375.
Tybout, J., 2000. Manufacturing firms in developing countries: how well do they do, and why? Journal of Economic Literature 38, 11–44.

Chapter 3

Why Do Foreign-Owned Firms Pay More? The Role of On-the-Job Training

Holger Görg, Eric Strobl, and **Frank Walsh**

University of Nottingham; Ecole Polytechnique Paris; University College Dublin

Abstract: While foreign-owned firms have consistently been found to pay higher wages than domestic firms to what appear to be equally productive workers, the causes of this remain unresolved. In a two-period bargaining framework we show that if training is more productive and specific in foreign firms, foreign firm workers will have a steeper wage profile and thus acquire a premium over time. Using a rich employer-employee matched data set we verify that the foreign wage premium is only acquired by workers over time spent in the firm and only by those that receive on-the-job training, thus providing empirical support for a firm-specific human capital acquisition explanation. JEL no. F23, J24
Keywords: On-the-job training; foreign-owned firms; wages

1 Introduction

It appears to be widely accepted wisdom that foreign-owned firms pay higher wages than their domestic counterparts in the host country and a sizeable body of literature now provides evidence to substantiate this fact. Nevertheless, the causes of this differential are as of yet unresolved. For example, while the studies by Lim (1977) for Malaysian manufacturing, Aitken et al. (1996) for Mexico and Venezuela, Lipsey and Sjöholm (2004) for Indonesia, and te Velde and Morrisey (2003) for five African countries all find that part of the wage differential can be explained by worker and firm characteristics, a sizeable proportion remains unaccounted for. Similarly, the existence of an unexplained wage differential between foreign and domestic firms seems prevalent for developed countries; see Aitken et al.

Remark: We are particularly grateful to Francis Teal and the CSAE at Oxford for the provision of and advice on the data. Thanks are also due to Spiros Bougheas, Richard Upward and seminar participants at the Stockholm School of Economics and Nottingham University for helpful comments on an earlier draft. Holger Görg gratefully acknowledges financial support from the Leverhulme Trust (Programme Grant F114/BF). Please address correspondence to Eric Strobl, Department of Economics, Ecole Polytechnique, 91128 Palaiseau, France; e-mail: eric.strobl@shs.polythechnique.fr

DOI: 10.1007/s10290-007-0117-9

(1996) and Feliciano and Lipsey (2006) for the United States, Globerman et al. (1994) for Canada, and Griffith and Simpson (2004) for the United Kingdom.

There are several theoretical models that may explain why the wage premium in foreign-owned firms is acquired by workers over time through on-the-job training. It may be that training is more productive in foreign firms because foreign firms have access to firm-specific assets that give them a technological advantage over domestic firms in the same industry (see, Caves 1996), or foreign-owned firms having better access to capital which allows them to invest in better technology. If foreign firms choose a more training intensive outcome for one of the above reasons this may also lead to more able workers being chosen in the foreign sector which would also affect the wage profile. Yet another possibility is that monitoring is more difficult in foreign firms causing firms to pay efficiency wages. Such wage premia may induce the firms to engage in more specific training as in Acemoglu and Pischke (1999).

We investigate these possibilities empirically by using a rich employer-employee matched data set for manufacturing firms in Ghana, which allows us to control for a large variety of firm and worker level characteristics that could arguably be driving any wage differentials across nationality of ownership type. Distinguishing between those workers that have received on-the-job training from those that have not, our econometric estimations of wage regressions suggest that returns to on-the-job training explain the foreign firm wage premium. Specifically, we find that while there are no differences in starting wages between workers in domestic or foreign-owned firms, workers receiving on-the-job training in foreign firms experience higher wage growth than those working and receiving on the job training in domestic firms.

The remainder of the paper is structured as follows. Section 2 sets out the theoretical model. Section 3 discusses the data while Section 4 presents the results of the econometric estimations. Finally, Section 5 concludes.

2 Theoretical Framework

Traditionally the impact of firm-specific training on wages is analysed using Hashimoto's (1981) model where competition ensures that the contract maximizes expected joint surplus in an uncertain world. More recently, some authors have used two period bargaining models to solve for the pre and post training wage.[1] Accordingly, human capital acquisition is chosen in period one by the firm, firms make the choice of human capital acquisition anticipating a second period wage bargain which will condition on this, and the first period wage is determined by a participation condition.[2] Here, we follow in the spirit of the latter groups of models.

One might expect that if the difference in the level of firm provided training between foreign and domestic firms is the source for the foreign firm wage premium that the firms with training would have higher wage growth but lower starting wages. This is in fact not so. If foreign-owned firms train more because training is more productive for foreign firms we would expect starting wages to be lower in the foreign sector other things equal however if training is more specific in the foreign sector this will impact on the share of training workers are willing to pay for and prevent starting wages falling. If the efficiency wage model referred to earlier is relevant the efficiency wage acts as a wage floor and prevents the starting wage from falling (Acemoglu and Pischke 1999). We will see from our empirical results that while foreign firms have higher wage growth than domestic firms there is no statistically significant difference in starting wages. This is consistent with much of the empirical evidence in other studies which indicate that increased on-the-job training does not lower starting wages (see Barron et al. (1999) for a discussion).

As noted above there are a variety of models that may predict the different wage profiles for workers in foreign and domestic firms by making assumptions on differences in technologies, risk aversion, monitoring costs or worker ability across sectors. In the model below we assume foreign firms invest in training that is more productive and specific than domestic firms. In reality there may of course be other combinations of differences in technologies, separation rates or monitoring technologies which as outlined earlier are also consistent with the observed wage profile.[3]

---

[1] See Malcolmson (1999) for a discussion of these models or Acemoglu and Pischke (1999) for recent applications.

[2] Another implication of the bargaining model that has been used to analyse firm-specific capital accumulation is that because the surplus bargained over in the second period is not net of the costs of training, under-investment may occur (see Malcolmson 1999 for a discussion of the holdup problem).

[3] Given that we have extensive controls for worker ability in our regressions, we argue in the empirical section of the paper that this cannot be the explanation for the differing wage profiles.

2.1 The Model

There are two periods but the discount rate is set to zero for simplicity. Identical risk neutral workers have the utility function $u = w$ in each period where w is the wage. Firms have a per-worker production function $f(t)$, which is concave in training t. Output of each worker is assumed to be independent for simplicity. We assume training is partly specific so that workers have an outside wage which yields utility of $v(t)$ in each period and $v(t) < f(t)$ for all values of t. The cost of providing training is given by the convex function $c(t)$. There is free movement of workers across all firms. The exogenous turnover rate of firms is q and if the firm exits it gets a profit level of $\underline{\pi} = 0$. The wage in the first and second of the two periods are w_0 and w_1 respectively. A firm's expected profit function is thus:

$$\pi = (1 - q)[f(t) - w_1] - c(t) - w_0 \,. \tag{1}$$

If there is a separation the firm will get the alternative profit of zero in the second period. Profit is second period output less wage times the probability of no separation less the costs incurred in the first period. Workers have a given reservation utility level $\underline{u}$. To ensure worker participation a contract must satisfy:

$$\underline{u} \leq qv(t) + (1 - q)w_1(t) + w_0(t) \,. \tag{2}$$

Given that it is costless for workers to move across jobs (2) will hold with equality in all firms. This allows us to solve for the starting wage as:

$$w_0 = \underline{u} - qv - (1 - q)w_1 \,. \tag{3}$$

The bargaining solution to the second period wage is:[4]

$$w_1 = \beta f(t) \,. \tag{4}$$

Thus a clear prediction is that firms that train more would have higher second period wages. The first order condition for training after substituting (3) and (4) into (1) is:

$$\pi'(t) = (1 - q)f'(t) + v'(t) - c'(t) = 0 \,. \tag{5}$$

[4] We assume that the fallback options workers and firms would get during bargaining are zero. See Sutton (1986) or Malcolmson (1999) for a discussion on the outside option in bargaining models.

Our objective here is to illustrate in the simplest possible theoretical framework that while plausible differences in exogenous technological parameters are consistent with steeper wage profiles for workers in foreign firm's as we expect, starting wages for workers in foreign firm's need not be lower. The argument is that if a highly structured simplified model such as that outlined below makes no clear prediction on starting wages across firms then the same is true in a more general model. At this stage we assume that $c = \frac{t^2}{2}$, $f(t) = At$ and $v(t) = Bt$. The efficient level of training in this case is: $t = (1 - q)A + qB$. We will denote foreign firm values with * and assume that $\underline{u} = 1$, $c(t) = c^*(t)$, $A = 100$, $A^* = 150$, $B = 50$, $B^* = 0$ and $\beta = \beta^* = 0.8$. Substituting these values into (3) and (4) Figure 1 plots the first and second period wages at different separation rates.

Figure 1: *The Wage Profile for Foreign- and Domestic-Owned Firms*

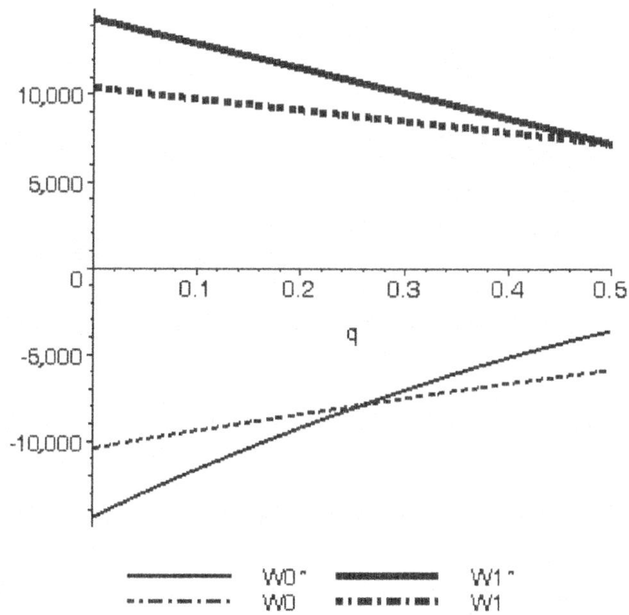

Figure 1 shows a range of separation rates where foreign-owned firms always have higher training and second period wages but starting wages move from being lower in the foreign firm to being higher at different separation rates. Firms with more training are expected to have higher second period wages while the starting wage may be higher or lower.

3 Data and Summary Statistics

In order to investigate whether the predictions of our theoretical model are consistent with what is observed empirically we utilize data for manufacturing firms in Ghana from the *Regional Programme for Enterprise Development* (RPED).[5] The data we use here are for the 1998 sample, i.e., the fifth annual wave, of Ghanaian manufacturing firms.[6] The initial wave of 200 firms in this survey was drawn from the 1987 Ghana Census of Manufacturing Activities, stratified by size, sector and location.[7] The sectors from which the firms were chosen are Food, Textiles and Garments, Wood, and Metal, which together comprise about 70 per cent of total manufacturing employment in Ghana.[8] When firms were closed down over the period they were replaced with firms in the same size, sector and location category.

The RPED data set is essentially an employer-employee matched data set in that, while each firm was interviewed for information at the firm level, additionally up to ten of its workers, representative of ten broad occupation categories, were interviewed. Firm level information used in this paper are the level of profit, total employment, value of capital stock, regional location, sector, incidence of state ownership, and, most importantly, the percentage of foreign ownership of each firm. Information from the worker surveys utilized include information concerning their current and previous year earnings and employment, starting earnings and employment, and their level of human capital.[9] In order to ensure that our sample size was consistent across estimation models we only used data for which we had

5 It is noteworthy that the Ghana data is also used by te Velde and Morrissey (2003) in their five country study, although an earlier wave with much less information than used here.

6 We use only the 1998 since this last wave provides the most information at the worker level. Unfortunately one cannot link workers across waves.

7 In the sampling large firms were oversampled. However, since there is no reliable source on the actual population of firms, we were not able to use weights for either our summary statistics our econometric estimation.

8 To be precise, the data set allows us to distinguish among ten sectors within these four main sectors.

9 All nominal variables were converted into 1998 prices using sectoral deflators.

all information at the worker and firm level that we used throughout the analysis. This left us with a sample of 144 firms and 1,365 workers.

Our variable of primary interest is the ownership of the firm. Most previous studies of the foreign wage premium simply distinguish between firms with no foreign ownership and those with at least some, but for the latter group do not distinguish between the degree of foreign ownership. In this paper we are careful to distinguish between the degree of foreign ownership within foreign-owned firms, as greater foreign ownership may also mean greater access to foreign capital and technology and better know-how. Also, greater foreign ownership may allow greater adoption of these advantages by the firm. An examination of the foreign-owned firms in our sample shows that the incidence of foreign ownership is quite dispersed; of the 144 firms in the sample 34 have some foreign ownership. Of those with at least some foreign ownership the mean, minimum, maximum and standard deviation of the degree of foreign ownership are 65, 20, 100 and 22 per cent, respectively. Thus allowing foreign ownership to vary among firms in a non-dichotomous manner allows us a more precise measure of the factors associated with foreign-owned firms if these depend on the degree of foreign ownership.

In Table 1 we present some summary statistics for workers in foreign- and domestic-owned firms. As can be seen the average wage rate in domestic firms is considerably lower than that for employees in foreign-owned firms.[10] This discrepancy already manifests itself in the starting wage of workers, and widens as workers spend more time in the firm. Part of the widening wedge is of course due to the fact that workers in foreign-owned firms stay on average longer in the same firm as is apparent from the tenure means. However, even when we calculate the average per year (spent in the firm) increase in the log real wage rate from these means, we find that the wage growth per year is still larger for workers employed by foreign-owned firms. The worker means, however, also show that workers in domestic firms are less educated—a factor which may, at least in part, be driving the difference in mean wages.

Examining some of the average characteristics of foreign- relative to domestic-owned firms, also given in Table 1, we find the two groups of firms differ in terms of these. Specifically, foreign-owned firms are found

---

[10] One should note that wages are measured as the complete compensation of the individual. In other words, earnings not only include explicit pay, but also the value of other allowances, bonuses and benefits.

Table 1: *Summary Statistics (Means)*

	Foreign	Domestic
Log(current wage)	1.56	1.05
Log(starting wage)	1.36	0.99
Wage growth	0.20	0.06
Tenure (years)	8.3	5.4
Years schooling	11.3	10.5
Employment (L)	244	54
Capital/L	0.11	0.03
Profit/L	0.009	0.002

Note: All nominal variables were converted to real values. Capital and profits in millions of CEDI.

to be substantially larger, enjoy greater profits, and have higher capital intensity than their domestic counterparts. In Table 2 we have calculated the sectoral distribution of firms by ownership in order to see whether foreign and indigenous firms operate in similar sectors. As can be seen, the Food Products, Metal Products, and Wood Products industries contain together over 60 per cent of total foreign firm population, the most dominant being the Food Products sector. In contrast, while Metal Products and Food Products are important industries for domestic firms, the most dominant sector are Furniture and Metal Products. Also, while no foreign plants are in the Bakery Goods industry, over 12 per cent of our domestic sample are categorized as mainly producing such products.

Table 2: *Sectoral Distribution (per cent)*

	Foreign across sectors	Indigenous across sectors	Share of foreign within sectors
Bakery Goods	0.0	12.4	0.0
Chemical Products	4.9	4.4	25.0
Food Products	24.4	13.9	34.5
Furniture	12.2	21.2	14.7
Garments	4.9	14.6	9.1
Machinery	4.9	2.9	33.3
Metal Products	19.5	21.2	21.6
Textile	9.8	1.5	66.7
Wood Products	19.5	8.0	42.1

Given the large differences in the means of employment, capital intensity, and profit per employee across type of ownership shown in Table 1, we also calculated the ownership differences of these aspects across sectors in Table 3. Accordingly, differences in the sectoral distribution are able to explain some of the results found in Table 1. For instance, for profit per employee, the difference in Food Products and Wood Products by ownership is exasperated by the larger foreign presence in these industries. Similarities in profits per employee, such as in Furniture and Metal Products, would have been of course aggregated away. Table 3 also shows that capital intensity is always larger for foreign firms except for in Machinery, although in many cases the discrepancy is not as large as in aggregate. In terms of the size of the workforce, foreign firms are always considerably larger except for in Chemical Products.

Table 3: *Sectoral Comparison of Profit, Capital Intensity and Size*

	Profit/L		Capital/L		L	
	I	F	I	F	I	F
Chemical Products	0.012	0.006	0.16	0.53	93	82
Food Products	0.005	0.025	0.05	0.13	108	214
Furniture	0.002	0.002	0.02	0.03	91	145
Garments	0.002	0.000	0.01	0.04	30	61
Machinery	0.000	0.011	0.08	0.05	18	66
Metal Products	0.005	0.005	0.02	0.07	42	252
Textile	0.001	0.004	0.08	0.13	35	583
Wood Products	0.001	0.011	0.06	0.09	149	261

Note: I = indigenous; F = foreign

Overall, one may conclude from these summary statistics there are clear differences between domestic- and foreign-owned firms. Clearly, some of these firm level features may be driving at least some of the wage premium. For instance, Strobl and Thornton (2004) have shown for an earlier wave of the data, that there was a large firm size wage premium—a factor that is commonly known as the employer size wage effect in the labour economics literature. Also some researchers have argued that the foreign wage premium may be associated with greater profit sharing (Budd and Konings 2005; te Velde and Morrissey 2003). Moreover, it is reasonable to suspect that if foreign-owned firms have greater or better quality capital they may need to hire more skilled workers, or, as we argue, train workers more intensely. The firm means provided at least tentatively suggest that these factors may also be linked to the foreign wage premium, since a simple correlation of these firm level variables, in aggregate and across sectors, suggest that they are all positively correlated with the degree of foreign ownership.

The differences across type of ownership may also be determining the decision to train in and of itself. For example, greater capital intensity in foreign-owned firms may require greater firm-specific skills, which induce the firm to seek more skilled and promising workers. Similarly, the on average larger workforce of foreign-owned firms may reflect a greater variety of more specialized skills, which in turn would increase the necessity to train. Another possibility is that the type of sectors that foreign-owned firms are more predominant in is a causal factor in the necessity to train. However, if one assumes that the more technology intensive sectors, i.e., Chemical Products, Machinery, and Metal Products, are the more likely to require firm-specific capital, then the relatively similar sectoral distribution with regard to these would suggest that sectoral differences are unlikely to be inducing foreign-owned firms on average to train more.

4 Econometric Evidence

4.1 Current Wages

The summary statistics confirm the general finding in the literature of a foreign wage premium for Ghanaian manufacturing. However, they also suggest that other human capital and firm characteristics that are usually associated with higher wages may be correlated with the degree of foreign ownership. We now turn to measuring the foreign wage premium controlling for other individual and firm-specific factors.

We first ran a simple OLS regression of determinants of the log of current hourly earnings only including foreign ownership as an explanatory variable as a our benchmark case, the results of which are given in the first column of Table 4. As can be seen, the ownership variable has a significant positive impact on the log hourly wage rate. At the mean of the hourly wage rate in levels, the coefficient implies that a one per cent increase of foreign ownership increases the log hourly wage rate by 0.65 per cent.

Using this initial specification as the benchmark case, we subsequently systematically added sets of explanatory variables to investigate how these may alter the foreign ownership wage premium. Firstly, the human capital model (see, e.g., Becker 1993) posits that differences in wages could be explained by differences in human capital. We thus included all available worker characteristics that may be related to the level of human capital in the regression, namely, education dummies (9), actual work experience at the start of the job and its value squared, Ghanaian language reading ability dummy, Ghanaian language writing ability dummy, English language speaking ability dummy, English language reading ability dummy, simple calculation ability dummy, gender dummy, marital status dummy, and African ethnicity dummy. The results of this exercise are given in the second column of Table 4. Accordingly, the size of the coefficient is reduced substantially from 0.65 to 0.46, although it is still highly significant.

We subsequently included characteristics pertaining to the job that the individual has performed, namely, tenure and its value squared, occupation dummies (19), and a set of dummies indicating whether the worker currently receives on-the-job training or received on-the-job training in the past, is a permanent employee, works part-time, and is a union member. As can be seen from the third column of Table 4, this set of dummies also reduces the coefficient on foreign ownership noticeably, although, again a significant and large wage premium remains.

Finally, we also included regional dummies (3), sectoral dummies (9), a state ownership dummy, profits per employee, capital intensity, and size (employment) to control for other differences across firms that may be driving the firm size wage premium. These may all arguably affect the wage rate and be possibly unevenly distributed across firm ownership type. In particular, the extensive literature on wage determination has shown that inter-industry wage differentials, the firm size wage effect, public ownership and regional labour markets can be important factors of wage determination (see, e.g., Strobl and Thornton 2004). Our inclusion of profits per employee also allows us to see whether rent sharing is an important feature of wage determination as is assumed in our theoretical model (see also Budd and Konings 2005). From the results in the fourth column of Table 4 it is reassuring to note that greater profits per employee increases the wage rate of workers significantly, indicating that indeed, as in our model, bargaining is an important feature of earnings. We also find that greater capital intensity of the workplace increases a worker's earnings. However, while the inclusion of all of these firm level variables does lower the size of the coefficient on foreign ownership by more than 50 per cent, it remains positive and significant. In other words, our results on the current wage rate suggest that

Table 4: *Current Wage*

	(1)	(2)	(3)	(4)	(5)	(6)
FOR	0.649***	0.458***	0.377***	0.085*	0.262**	0.072
	(0.071)	(0.050)	(0.048)	(0.047)	(0.131)	(0.051)
PROF/L	—	—	—	11.210***	14.070***	11.502***
				(1.539)	(3.175)	(1.762)
CAP/L	—	—	—	0.761***	0.671***	0.782***
				(0.135)	(0.234)	(0.169)
L	—	—	—	0.478***	0.162	0.588***
				(0.075)	(0.182)	(0.088)
Constant	1.089***	3.183***	2.641***	1.386***	−0.709	0.945***
	(0.025)	(0.131)	(0.256)	(0.309)	(0.551)	(0.248)
Human capital	No	Yes	Yes	Yes	Yes	Yes
Job charact.	No	No	Yes	Yes	Yes	Yes
Firm charact.	No	No	No	Yes	Yes	Yes
Sample	Total	Total	Total	Total	OJT	N-OJT
Observations	1364	1364	1364	1364	331	1033
$F(\beta_j = 0)$	93.9***	52.7***	39.2***	41.4***	12.9***	31.1***
R-squared	0.06	0.46	0.58	0.66	0.73	0.66

Note: Robust standard errors in parentheses. Dependent variable is the log of current wage rate. ***, **, and * signify 1, 5 and 10 per cent significance levels respectively. Human capital characteristics include: education dummies (9), actual work experience at the start of the job and its value squared, Ghanian language reading ability dummy, Ghanian language writing ability dummy, English language speaking ability dummy, English reading ability dummy, simple calculation ability dummy, gender dummy, marital status dummy, and African ethnicity dummy. Job characteristics include tenure and its value squared, occupation dummies (19), current on-the-job training dummy, past on-the-job training dummy, permanent worker dummy, and union status dummy. Firm characteristics include regional dummies (3), sectoral dummies (9), and state ownership dummy.

while controlling for observable human capital, job and firm characteristics across workers that there is some correlation between these and foreign ownership, they fail to explain fully the foreign ownership wage premium.[11]

Our discussion of the theoretical literature outlined why one might expect a foreign wage premium for workers that are engaged in on-the-job training, while for other workers this is unlikely to be (as) important.[12] We

[11] We also investigated whether the relationship may be non-linear by including higher order terms, but in all cases these were insignificant.

[12] Of course formal on-the-job training is not the only route through which workers acquire human capital in a firm. Informal training and/or learning may also be important. One may expect, however, that these forms of learning are highly correlated to formal training.

therefore divided our sample into those workers that currently received or have received on-the-job training (OJT) in the past and those that never had (N-OJT) and ran our OLS model of earnings determination including all our control variables for these separately, as given in the fifth and sixth column of Table 4 respectively.[13]

As can be seen, the coefficient for the N-OJT is smaller than for the overall sample and statistically insignificant, implying that these are not characterized by a foreign ownership premium. In contrast, as is in line with our theoretical model, workers with on-the-job training have higher earnings the higher the degree of foreign ownership as indicated by the large positive and significant coefficient on the foreign ownership. Specifically, each per cent increase in foreign ownership increases the hourly wage rate of workers with on-the-job training by 0.26 per cent. One should also note that when we ran similar specifications including all controls for the whole sample, or for the OJT and Non-OJT sub-samples, using a foreign ownership dummy this turned out to be insignificant, further suggesting the importance of accounting for different degrees of foreign ownership.[14]

4.2 Starting Wages

Our results on current earnings show that the foreign wage premium only exists for workers with on-the-job training, which is consistent with our theoretical model. As they spend time in the firm their wage profile will be steeper than that of their domestic firm counterparts. We next examine how foreign ownership affects the starting wage of workers. In doing so we are faced with one particular obstacle. Although we know when a worker started in the firm and at what wage and occupation, we only know the current degree of foreign ownership for our sample of workers.[15] We thus

[13] From the theoretical model one may expect that workers in foreign-owned firms may receive more training, hence it would be interesting to look at the duration of training received. Unfortunately, the data on the duration of on-the-job training are for the most part poor or missing.

[14] Detailed results available from the authors on request.

[15] Strictly speaking for a subset of workers, namely those that have started working the firm in years for which we can link firm level information on foreign ownership from previous waves, we can also find the degree of foreign ownership at the start of their job. However, given the number of firms that had been added since the start of the survey so that no previous information was available and the large number of missing values across the years on foreign ownership even for those firms that are continuously observed, our

make the assumption that foreign ownership has remained constant over time, at least in so far as the earliest starting wage is observed.[16] Using the information on workers' earnings at the start of their job in the firm, we regressed the real hourly wage rate on the degree of (current) foreign ownership first for workers who have received on-the-job training over time in the firm, as shown in the first three columns of Table 5. Accordingly, the foreign ownership wage premium without any controls is positive, but insignificant. As we add the human capital characteristics and subsequently job and firm level controls to the regression, shown in columns two and three, the size of the coefficient turns negative, but remains insignificant. As shown in the fourth and fifth column of Table 5, for the case of workers who do not receive on-the-job training we find a positive foreign wage premium, with and without including human capital controls. However, as soon as we add job and firm level controls the coefficient falls considerably in size and becomes insignificant. This suggests that once other factors are accounted for, workers in domestic-owned firms receive the same starting wage as those in foreign-owned firms if they do not receive on-the-job training in the future.

One should note that similar starting wages between foreign and indigenous workers who (will) receive on-the-job training are consistent with our theoretical model. This can arise because of the technological parameters in the production functions of firms. It may also be that since workers at the start of the contract only share in the cost of human capital acquired in the first period, that wage differences are just too low to be picked up statistically. One could also conjecture that in developing countries like Ghana credit constraints may prevent workers from falling below a certain wage level. Lower wage bounds like credit constraints, efficiency wages or minimum wages do not prevent on-the-job training and subsequent wage premium differences from taking place in our and other theoretical on-the-job training models although as Acemoglu and Pischke (1999) show they will lead to a more compressed wage distribution. The data in the empirical section indicates, however, that credit constraints are an unlikely explanation for foreign- and domestic-owned firms not having a statistically significant difference in their predicted starting wage. This can be easily seen from Table 1

sample size would have been reduced to less than a quarter of the size used for the current wage regressions.

[16] For the firms for which we had earlier information on foreign ownership, it appears to have changed very little, although we can only observe foreign ownership no earlier back than six years.

Table 5: *Starting Wage*

	(1)	(2)	(3)	(4)	(5)	(6)
FOR	0.212	−0.063	−0.165	0.304**	0.214*	0.096
	(0.294)	(0.295)	(0.330)	(0.123)	(0.114)	(0.124)
Constant	0.808***	6.916***	−0.150	1.291***	6.511***	11.141***
	(0.218)	(0.378)	(1.254)	(0.068)	(1.646)	(1.584)
Human capital	No	Yes	Yes	No	Yes	Yes
Job charact.	No	No	Yes	No	No	Yes
Firm charact.	No	No	Yes	No	No	Yes
Sample	OJT	OJT	OJT	N-OJT	N-OJT	N-OJT
Observations	331	331	331	1033	1033	1033
$F(\beta_j = 0)$	6.3***	5.5***	4.7***	6.1***	9.5***	8.0***
R^2	0.37	0.47	0.59	0.17	0.34	0.43

Note: Robust standard errors in parentheses. Dependent variable is the log of starting wage rate. ***, **, and * signify 1, 5 and 10 per cent significance levels respectively. We include year dummies for starting year. Human capital characteristics include: education dummies (9), actual work experience at the start of the job and its value squared, Ghanian language reading ability dummy, Ghanian language writing ability dummy, English language speaking ability dummy, English reading ability dummy, simple calculation ability dummy, gender dummy, marital status dummy, and African ethnicity dummy. Job characteristics include tenure and its value squared, starting occupation dummies (19), permanent worker dummy, and union status dummy. Firm characteristics include regional dummies (3), sectoral dummies (9), and a state ownership dummy.

where there are obvious differences in average starting wages between firm types, so that it is only when we control for personal and job characteristics that the difference becomes insignificant.

4.3 Wage Growth

The evidence presented thus far shows that workers with on-the-job training receive a higher wage premium the greater the degree of foreign ownership when considering their current wage, but not their starting wage. This suggests that the premium is acquired as the worker spends time and trains in the foreign-owned firm. In order to verify this we now examine how foreign ownership affects an individual's wage growth within a firm.

The information available to us allows us to calculate total wage growth experienced by workers since the start of the job. Clearly, workers who have spent longer time at a firm are more likely to have experienced greater wage growth for reasons such as seniority effects and greater bargaining power, amongst other things, so that this must be controlled for. One possibility is simply to calculate the average annual wage growth by dividing total wage growth by job tenure. This necessarily restricts the effects of tenure to be linear on wages, so that we instead rather use total wage growth as our dependent variable, but include tenure and its squared value as controls for time spent in the firm. Additionally, it must be pointed out that differences in tenure may also reflect differences in starting dates, and hence wage growth may capture different economic conditions at the time of the start of the job. We thus also included time dummies in all our wage growth regressions. Finally, one should note that by examining the determinants of wage growth we are able to purge any other unobservable, time invariant determinants of wages that we may have not been able to control for given the information in our data set from the regression.

The results of our wage growth regressions are given for workers with on-the-job training in the first column of Table 6. The positive and significant sign on the foreign ownership variable indicates that the higher the degree of foreign ownership of a firm, the greater the growth rate of a workers' wage. We subsequently also included our set of human capital, job and firm level controls to allow for greater wage growth due to these. For example, those with greater human capital may also be more likely to become more proficient at the task they perform and hence be rewarded with greater wage growth. If these higher ability individuals are also more likely to work for firms with greater foreign ownership then this could explain the greater wage growth associated with foreign ownership. However, as can be seen from the second column of Table 6, their inclusion does not significantly alter the conclusion that greater foreign ownership results in greater earnings growth if the worker receives on-the-job training.

We conducted the same exercise for our sample of workers who do not receive on-the-job training, the results of which are provided in columns three and four of Table 6. As can be seen, whether we include our human capital, job and firm controls or not, in no case does foreign ownership act to increase a worker's earnings growth. Our empirical findings are, hence, in line with the predictions of the model which suggests that workers receiving training will experience higher wage growth in foreign-owned firms, while there should be no such differential between workers in foreign- and domestic-owned firms that do not receive training.

Table 6: *Wage Growth*

	(1)	(2)	(3)	(4)
FOR	0.512*	0.546*	0.150	0.181
	(0.278)	(0.316)	(0.107)	(0.122)
Constant	−0.054	−3.670***	−8.174	−16.65***
	(0.148)	(1.083)	(5.367)	(5.394)
TIME	Yes	Yes	Yes	Yes
Human capital	No	Yes	No	Yes
Job & firm charact.	No	Yes	No	Yes
Sample	OJT	OJT	N-OJT	N-OJT
Observations	331	331	1033	1033
$F(\beta_j = 0)$	6.4***	3.3***	6.4***	3.9***
R-squared	0.38	0.56	0.18	0.30

Note: Robust standard errors in parantheses. Dependent variable is the wage growth rate. ***, **, and * signify 1, 5 and 10 per cent significance levels respectively. TIME are year dummies for starting year. Human capital characteristics include: education dummies (9), actual work experience at the start of the job and its value squared, Ghanian language reading ability dummy, Ghanian language writing ability dummy, English language speaking ability dummy, English reading ability dummy, simple calculation ability dummy, gender dummy, marital status dummy, and African ethnicity dummy. Job characteristics include tenure and its value squared, starting occupation dummies (19), current occupation dummies (19), permanent worker dummy, and union status dummy. Firm characteristics include regional dummies (3), sectoral dummies (9), and state ownership dummy.

5 Concluding Remarks

This paper shows theoretically that one explanation for the fact that foreign-owned firms pay higher wages than their domestic counterparts may be the provision of on-the-job training. A number of theoretical models predict that foreign-owned firms train more and have higher wage growth, while starting wages may be higher or lower. Our empirical analysis based on data for manufacturing firms in Ghana provides evidence that is in line with the theoretical predictions. While we find no statistically significant difference in starting wages of trained and untrained workers in foreign- and domestic-owned firms (once other individual and firm characteristics are controlled for) we find that workers receiving on-the-job training in foreign-owned firms experience higher wage growth than workers being trained in domestic-owned firms. By contrast, there does not appear to be any difference in wage growth between workers not receiving training in either foreign- or domestic-owned firms.

One more general conclusion to be drawn from our analysis is that host countries may benefit from the presence of foreign-owned firms, particularly if they encourage them to train their workers. Apart from leading to increases in wages to workers employed by multinationals, training directly increases the host country's level of absorptive capacity by improving its stock of human capital (see, e.g., Keller 1996). Also, movements of trained workers from foreign- to domestic-owned firms may cause indirect productivity spillovers to the domestic sector (see, e.g. Fosfuri et al. 2001), as workers apply their new skills in domestic-owned firms or set up their own business. Görg and Strobl (2005) provide evidence for such spillovers through worker mobility using the same data for Ghanaian manufacturing firms as used in this paper.

References

Acemoglu, D., and J. Pischke (1999). The Structure of Wages and Investment in General Training. *Journal of Political Economy* 107 (3): 539–572.

Aitken, B., A. Harrison, and R. Lipsey (1996). Wages and Foreign Ownership: A Comparative Study of Mexico, Venezuela, and the United States. *Journal of International Economics* 40 (3): 345–371.

Barron, J., M. Berger, and D. Black (1999). Replacing General with Specific Training: Why Restricting Alternatives Makes Sense. In S. Polachek and J. Robst (eds.), *Research in Labor Economics*. Amsterdam: JAI.

Becker, G. (1993). *Human Capital: A Theoretical and Empirical Analysis with Special Reference to Education*. Third edition. Chicago: Chicago University Press.

Budd, J. W., and J. Konings (2005). International Profit Sharing in Multinational Firms. *Review of Economics and Statistics* 87 (1): 73–84.

Caves, R. (1996). *Multinational Enterprise and Economic Analysis*. Second Edition. Cambridge: Cambridge University Press.

Feliciano, Z., and R. Lipsey (2006). Foreign Ownership, Wages, and Wage Changes in U.S. Industries, 1987–92. *Contemporary Economic Policy* 24 (1): 74–91.

Fosfuri, A., M. Motta, and T. Ronde (2001). Foreign Direct Investment and Spillovers Through Workers' Mobility. *Journal of International Economics* 53 (1): 205–222.

Globerman, S., J. Ries, and I. Vertinsky (1994). The Economic Performance of Foreign Affiliates in Canada. *Canadian Journal of Economics* 27 (1): 143–156

Görg, H., and E. Strobl (2005). Spillovers from Foreign Firms through Worker Mobility: An Empirical Investigation. *Scandinavian Journal of Economics* 107 (4): 693–709.

Griffith, R., and H. Simpson (2004). Characteristics of Foreign-Owned Firms in British Manufacturing. In R. Blundell, D. Card, and R. Freeman (eds.), *Creating a Premier League Economy*. Chicago: Chicago University Press.

Hashimoto, M. (1981). Firm Specific Human Capital as a Shared Investment. *American Economic Review* 71 (3): 475–482.

Keller, W. (1996). Absorptive Capacity: Understanding the Creation and Acquisition of Technology in Development. *Journal of Development Economics* 49 (1): 199–227.

Lim, D. (1977). Do Foreign Companies Pay Higher Wages Than Their Local Counterparts in Malaysian Manufacturing? *Journal of Development Economics* 4 (1): 55–66.

Lipsey, R., and F. Sjöholm (2004). Foreign Direct Investment, Education and Wages in Indonesian Manufacturing. *Journal of Development Economics* 73 (1): 415–422.

Malcolmson, J. (1999). Individual Employment Contracts. In O. Ashenfelter and D. Card (eds.), *Handbook of Labor Economics*. Volume 3B. Amsterdam: Elsevier Science.

Strobl, E., and R. Thornton (2004). Do Large Employers Pay More in Developing Countries? The Case of Five African Countries. *Journal of Economic Development* 29 (1): 139–161.

Sutton, J. (1986). Non-Cooperative Bargaining Theory: An Introduction. *Review of Economic Studies* 53 (5): 709–724.

Velde, D. te, and O. Morrissey (2003). Foreign Ownership and Wages: Evidence from Five African Countries. *Journal of African Economies* 12 (1): 41–73.

Chapter 4

Foreign Acquisitions, Domestic Multinationals, and R&D*

Roger Bandick

Aarhus University, 8210 Aarhus V, Denmark
roger@hih.au.dk

Holger Görg

Kiel Institute for the World Economy, DE-24105 Kiel, Germany
holger.goerg@ifw-kiel.de

Patrik Karpaty

Orebro University, SE-701 82 Orebro, Sweden
patrik.karpaty@oru.se

Abstract

Our aim in this paper is to evaluate the causal effect of foreign acquisition on research and development (R&D) intensity in targeted domestic firms. We are able to distinguish domestic multinational enterprises (MNEs) and non-MNEs, which allows us to investigate the fear that the change in ownership of domestic MNEs to foreign MNEs leads to a reduction in R&D activity in the country. Overall, our results give no support to the fears that foreign acquisition of domestic firms leads to a relocation of R&D activity in Swedish MNEs. Rather, in this paper, we find robust evidence that foreign acquisitions lead to increasing R&D intensity in acquired domestic MNEs and non-MNEs.

Keywords: Foreign acquisitions; multinational firms; R&D

JEL classification: *F*23; *L*10

I. Introduction

There is still a lively debate about the home country effects of multinational activity. While the popular media and the general public tend to associate outward investment by multinational enterprises (MNEs) necessarily with economic losses (in employment, wages, etc.), much economic research has found that this is not the case. Indeed, studies find that MNEs have an advantage over others in terms of efficiency and productivity, which can

*We would like to thank Linda Andersson, Daniela Andrén, Jakob Munch, Ingo Geishecker, Sourafel Girma, Aoife Hanley, Per-Johan Norbäck, Ignat Stepanok, and the anonymous referees for helpful comments. H. Görg is affiliated with the Tuborg Centre for Globalization and Firms, Aarhus University. He received financial support from the Seventh Framework Programme (Grant no. 244552).

be further exploited abroad. Even if they relocate activity abroad, they tend to concentrate on high value/high skill headquarter activities at home, and overall there is little evidence that they substitute employment in the host country for employment in the home country (e.g., Blomström *et al.*, 1997; Barba Navaretti *et al.*, 2009; Hijzen *et al.*, 2011).

The recent wave of cross-border mergers and acquisitions has added a new dimension to this debate. The following question is now discussed. What will happen to the domestic MNEs, and in particular their research and development (R&D) and other headquarter activities, once they are acquired by a foreign owner? In Sweden, the country to which our empirical analysis pertains, this has been an important issue. During the 1990s, a wave of foreign acquisitions of Swedish MNEs took place, and many headquarters were relocated abroad. Former flagship Swedish MNEs, such as Volvo, Saab, Asea, and Astra, were acquired by foreign owners. This raised national concerns against foreign firms exploiting the knowledge capital in Swedish firms or outsourcing domestic production to other countries.[1]

What happens to R&D activity once the domestic MNE is taken over by a foreign owner? Will the R&D of the firm be cut, depleting a country of its high skill activity? Or will the R&D location be maintained, and perhaps even extended, as a result of the foreign takeover? Also, how do these effects compare to the R&D effects of acquisitions of domestic non-MNE – is there a special "multinationality effect"? This is an important issue that is not only of academic interest, but also has strong policy implications. R&D is an activity that is likely to generate positive externalities; hence, the relocation of the R&D activity abroad might lead to potential welfare losses (Krugman, 1991).

The fear that R&D activity might be relocated can be explained in a simple theoretical set-up. Consider a firm that operates in a global technology market where R&D assets are important. The firm might wish to advance its market position through an international merger or acquisition (M&A). If the R&D performed in the acquired and acquiring firms is similar (i.e., substitutable), there is a risk that R&D in the acquired firm might be divested for cost minimization purposes (e.g., Veugelers, 2006). This can be especially important if the acquirer is more efficient at R&D. If there are economies of scale in R&D, the acquirer might find it profitable to concentrate R&D activities, even if R&D performed in the acquired and acquiring firms are complementing each other. In both cases, the acquirer has incentives to locate R&D close to the headquarters in the acquirers home country. This allows it to maintain better control over the long-term

[1] Braunerhjelm (2001) argues that the possible relocation of the headquarter activities of Swedish MNEs abroad might cause a "brain-drain" in the Swedish business sector.

direction of the R&D activity, and also limits communication costs between R&D activities and other headquarter services (Caves, 1996).[2]

Recent theoretical models suggest a more benevolent effect of foreign acquisitions, however. In the model by Ekholm and Hakkala (2007), firms locate production in large markets in order to access consumers, while R&D activities are attracted to countries that already have high R&D activities, in order to benefit from externalities. Such countries can be economies with small markets (where high skilled labor is relatively cheap, because of the absence of large production activities), which, through spillovers, generate an agglomeration of R&D activity. They argue that Sweden fits this pattern, because it is a country with a relatively small market potential but high agglomeration of R&D activity. While the model is strictly speaking about greenfield investment and not acquisitions, we can develop the intuition that, if these agglomeration forces are indeed strong, it can be expected that ownership changes might not lead to any changes in the pattern of location of R&D.

Bertrand *et al.* (2012) have developed a model that considers the relationship between the mode of foreign entry and R&D activity in the foreign affiliate. In their oligopolistic model, a MNE can acquire a foreign affiliate if the complementarity between the R&D assets of the parent and the foreign affiliate is sufficiently high.[3] This has two implications. First, the foreign acquirer has an incentive to increase R&D in the foreign affiliate post-acquisition, in order to prevent the expansion of domestic rivals. Second, the foreign acquirer tends to "cherry-pick" those affiliates with an initially high quality of the R&D asset, because this increases the profitability of the foreign MNE with respect to its domestic competitors. Hence, this model has clear empirically testable predictions: foreign acquisitions will tend to increase R&D activity in the acquisition target post-acquisition, and foreign acquirers tend to cherry-pick R&D active targets.

We look at the effects of foreign acquisitions on R&D in the target firm empirically and we use this theoretical discussion as a motivation for our empirical analysis. There are a number of earlier empirical studies to which our paper relates.[4] Some papers look at the relationship between

[2] For empirical evidence that firms locate R&D close to their headquarters at home, see UNCTAD (2005).

[3] In a review of the empirical literature, Veugelers (2006) has concluded that the probability of acquisitions increases with the R&D assets within target firms. This is especially important if there are complementarities in the R&D assets of the acquired and acquiring firms.

[4] Previous empirical literature using industry level data or a small number of firms found ambiguous effects on R&D activity in merged entities. Some explanations put forward for negative effects on R&D as a result of M&As were lower incentives because of larger market concentration caused by the M&A, and debt constraints because of costly M&As (Baysinger and Hoskisson, 1989; Hitt *et al.*, 1991). However, a large group of merged firms should

M&As in general, and foreign acquisitions in particular, on R&D in the host country (e.g., Cassiman *et al.*, 2005; Bertrand and Zuniga, 2006). However, this body of literature does not generally look at the effect on the target firm, but rather overall R&D, and also it does not specifically look at the experience of domestic MNEs. Bertrand (2009) has investigated empirically post-acquisition R&D performance in target firms using French data.[5] He has found that R&D activity increases post-acquisition. However, he does not distinguish targets into MNEs and non-MNEs. In a paper most closely related to our paper, Bertrand *et al.* (2012) have provided some empirical evidence from Swedish firm level data that acquisitions are associated with higher R&D intensity than greenfield investments. While this is consistent with their theoretical model, they are unable to investigate the relevance of cherry-picking with respect to post-acquisition increases in R&D. Our data allow us to do exactly this, and we specifically look at the post-acquisition R&D performance in the target firm, controlling for possible cherry-picking pre-acquisition.

We study in detail the acquisitions of domestic firms by foreign owners, and examine, in particular, the implications for R&D activity in the target. In the empirical analysis, we take particular account of the potential endogeneity of the acquisition decision by combining difference-in-differences (DID) with propensity score-matching (PSM) techniques.[6]

The analysis is based on unique detailed firm level data for Sweden, which allow us to investigate the extent of R&D undertaken in the Swedish firms before and after acquisition. We look at the timing of these effects, considering changes in R&D activity one, two, and three years after the acquisition took place. We also contrast the effect of acquisition on R&D for domestic MNEs and domestic non-MNEs.

---

more easily be able to raise finance for risky R&D investments not only internally but also on the capital market, because of more bargaining power (Hall, 2002). For a detailed review of this body of literature, see Bertrand (2009).

[5] There have also been studies with firm level data analyzing the effects of foreign acquisitions on productivity, employment, wages, or exit (e.g., Harris and Robinson, 2002; Girma and Görg, 2007; Huttunen, 2007; Bandick and Görg, 2010).

[6] The probability for a firm to be acquired is likely to be determined by information about the acquisition target, such as available R&D assets, human and real capital, etc. These factors might be unobservable to the researcher but not to the managers in the acquired and acquiring entities, and these can affect both R&D expenditures and the probability of acquisition. The decision to acquire a firm is thus endogenous. For example, in Table 5, we provide some evidence of persistent differences in R&D and capital and skill intensity between acquired and non-acquired firms. We control for these aspects in our econometric approach, assuming that the measured variables (including R&D, skill and capital intensity, as well as other firm level characteristics) are correlated with both the quantity and quality of R&D assets, and human and real capital. Unfortunately, we are not able to measure these indicators directly in our data.

From recent theoretical models of heterogeneous firms, we know that MNEs have "better" production technology than purely domestic firms (e.g., Helpman *et al.*, 2004). While theory assumes the productivity draws to be exogenous, in the real world, investment activities such as R&D clearly act to improve technology. Hence, R&D activities in MNEs generate firm-specific assets that are exploited when serving foreign markets (Markusen, 2002). R&D activities in purely domestic firms might be of a different nature, because evidently these activities do not allow the firm to generate the firm-specific asset that would allow it to become multinational.[7] Hence, the R&D activity in a MNE might be more complementary to the foreign acquirer, hence increasing the probability that the foreign acquirer will invest heavily in R&D post-acquisition. Moreover, from a policy point of view, given the fact that domestic MNEs tend to have higher R&D activities than purely domestic firms, there might be particular concern about the acquisition of such targets, because a relocation of R&D and other headquarter activities that generate externalities might lead to substantial welfare losses. To the best of our knowledge, we are the first to explore such potentially differential effects for domestic MNEs and non-MNEs in any detail.

To preview our results, we find robust evidence that there is, on average, no negative effect from acquisitions on R&D performance in Swedish firms. Rather, the evidence suggests that there are strong positive effects. These effects are stronger for the acquisition of domestic non-MNEs than for Swedish MNEs. However, it is important to stress that we do not find any evidence that foreign acquisitions of domestic MNEs lead to reductions of R&D in Sweden. Furthermore, our results suggest that there is cherry-picking, in that the R&D activity in the target firm pre-acquisition is strongly positively correlated with the probability of being acquired. These results are consistent with the theoretical model by Bertrand *et al.* (2012).

The rest of the paper is structured as follows. In Section II, we describe the dataset and present some preliminary empirics on the link between foreign acquisition and R&D. In Section III, we describe the empirical methodology. In Section IV, we discuss the first results from ordinary least-squares (OLS) and fixed effects estimations in order to provide initial correlations. In Section V, we focus on the DID PSM technique. We conclude in Section VI.

[7] This conjecture is in line with evidence on R&D activities in Ireland reported by Forfás (2011), which shows that domestic firms spend a large share (49 percent) of their R&D expenditure on licences and externally produced software. By contrast, MNEs spend 81 percent on instruments and equipment for own R&D activities. These latter activities are arguably more likely to generate firm-specific assets.

II. Data and Description

The data are from Statistics Sweden (SCB) and the Swedish Agency for Growth Policy Analysis, formerly the Swedish Institute for Growth Policy Studies (ITPS). The dataset covers all manufacturing firms operating in Sweden with at least 50 employees for the period 1993–2002. The register information used in this analysis was obtained from several sources and was merged using unique identification numbers. The Structural Business Statistics (SBS) gives us information by firm on sales, investments, R&D,[8] various inputs, and whether it is foreign- or domestic-owned. Foreign-owned firms (foreign MNEs) are firms where foreigners possess more than 50 percent of the voting rights. The data from the Agency from Growth Policy Analysis provides information on all Swedish controlled enterprise groups with subsidiaries abroad. Using these data, we are able to separate all domestically owned firms into Swedish MNEs and Swedish non-MNEs. A Swedish MNE is then a domestically owned firm that is part of an enterprise with affiliates abroad.[9] Non-MNEs are firms that are neither Swedish MNEs nor foreign MNEs.

By using the information on ownership status, we can define foreign acquisition of a domestic MNE as a change in ownership indicator from a domestic MNE to foreign, and foreign acquisition of a domestic non-MNE as a change in ownership indicator from a domestic non-MNE to foreign.[10] Hence, an acquisition implies that at least 50 percent of the voting rights are acquired by a foreign owner.[11]

[8] Unfortunately, we do not know whether R&D is internal or external R&D. In the SBS database, firms provide information on the actual level of R&D spending. If the level is less than 10 million SEK, the information is provided in specific intervals of SEK: 1–249,000, 250,000–999,000, 1–4.9 million, and 5–9.9 million. If the yearly R&D expenditures exceed 10 million SEK, the firms specify the exact amount. The R&D information covers firms that have a minimum of one employee who is active in any R&D activity at 50 percent of a full-time employment. Moreover, the SBS R&D statistics are retrieved annually and it is compulsory for firms to reply. For firms that provide information in intervals, we use the mid-point value in the analysis. Only 12 percent of all firms with R&D data provide the information in intervals, and thus we would not expect any severe bias in our estimation. To check the robustness, we also carry out a check where we estimate equation (2) using interval regression. The results, which are available upon request, are similar to those reported in Section IV

[9] The first year in which we can distinguish Swedish MNEs from non-MNEs is 1993. This explains why our analysis begins in 1993.

[10] Firms that switch between domestic and foreign ownership more than once over the period are not included in the sample. Also, firms that disappear from the sample one year and reappear in later years are excluded.

[11] We could argue that this includes takeovers by foreign financial investors. Unfortunately, we are not able to distinguish such cases from the genuine acquisition by a foreign company (with production facilities in other countries). However, our definition implies that foreign owners have at least 50 percent of the voting rights, not just 50 percent of the shares.

Because R&D data are only available for firms with at least 50 employees, we have to restrict the analysis to firms above this threshold.[12] However, the firms included in our sample cover more than three-quarters of total value added and employment in the manufacturing sector (Karpaty, 2006). Moreover, two-thirds of all private R&D is concentrated in the top ten R&D firms (see Karpaty and Tingvall, 2011). This should motivate an analysis based on larger firms only. Still, of course, our conclusions are conditional on large firms; we do not claim to be able to make general statements about the behavior of small manufacturing firms from this sample.

From Table 1, we see that the number of foreign MNEs and the employment shares in these firms have increased during the whole period in manufacturing industries. This seems to have been at the expense of Swedish MNEs. This pattern can be partly explained by the fact that several large Swedish MNEs have become foreign-owned because of acquisitions by foreign MNEs (e.g., Pharmacia and Upjohn 1995, Saab Automobile and General Motors 1998, Astra and Zeneca 1999, and Volvo Car Corporation and Ford 1999). The relative importance of Swedish non-MNEs remained fairly constant over the period, however.

Table 2 provides the distribution of the number of firms across 22 industries at the two-digit level in 1993 and 2002.[13] The distribution of foreign and domestic MNEs is characterized by large heterogeneity between different industries and over time. It appears that the presence of foreign firms decreased between 1993 and 2002 in only five out of 22 industries (in two other industries, there was no foreign presence at all). A different pattern is apparent for domestic MNEs whose share of firms fell in 11 out of 22 industries during the same period. Again, this reflects partly the extent of foreign acquisitions of domestic MNEs.

Table 3 shows differences in means for some firm characteristics between domestic and foreign-owned firms in 2002. We compare unweighted averages and use t-statistics for any possible difference between foreign and domestic firms for each variable. What seems to matter, in general, is not whether the firm is foreign-owned or domestically owned but whether the firm is multinational or not (see also Criscuolo and Martin, 2010). There

[12] Because R&D is only collected for firms with more than 50 employees, the analysis is restricted to firms that pass the threshold of 50 employees or more during the period. The observations in which the firms are not passing this threshold are excluded from the sample. This accounts for about 2 percent of the total observation per year. As a test of robustness, we have also excluded firms that have fewer than 50 employees, once or more. These results were similar to the results presented in Tables 6–10, and are thus not reported separately.

[13] The industry classification is based on SNI92, which is the Swedish standard for industrial classification (Svensk Näringsgrensgrensindelning). It corresponds to the two-digit European NACE Rev 1 classification system in 1993 and 2002.

Table 1. *Number of firms and employment shares in Swedish manufacturing, 1993–2002*

	Foreign MNEs		Swedish MNEs		Swedish non-MNEs	
Year	Firms (percent)	Empl. (percent)	Firms (percent)	Empl. (percent)	Firms (percent)	Empl. (percent)
1993	255 (20.5)	21.0	421 (33.8)	54.0	568 (45.7)	25.0
1994	275 (21.5)	22.0	436 (34.1)	56.6	567 (44.4)	21.4
1995	297 (22.2)	22.8	427 (31.8)	55.0	617 (46.0)	22.2
1996	342 (24.9)	26.7	402 (29.2)	51.1	631 (45.9)	22.2
1997	365 (26.2)	28.4	400 (28.7)	51.7	629 (45.1)	20.0
1998	396 (26.8)	29.8	396 (26.8)	49.2	683 (46.3)	20.9
1999	400 (27.6)	35.9	406 (28.1)	41.0	641 (44.3)	23.1
2000	426 (28.6)	41.1	415 (27.8)	36.6	651 (43.6)	22.3
2001	454 (30.5)	46.4	396 (26.6)	32.4	640 (43.0)	21.2
2002	464 (31.8)	47.3	396 (27.1)	33.6	601 (41.1)	19.0

Source: Statistics Sweden.
Notes: The sample is truncated at 50 employees. Foreign MNEs are firms where foreigners possess more than 50 percent of the voting rights. A Swedish MNE is a domestically owned firm that is part of an enterprise with affiliates abroad. Non-MNE firms are firms that are neither Swedish MNEs nor foreign MNEs.

is a statistically significant difference in all variables when we compare Swedish MNEs and non-MNEs. Hence, foreign and Swedish MNEs are more R&D intensive, larger, use more skilled labor, are more productive and pay higher wages than their non-MNE counterparts. This is in line with the idea that Swedish MNEs have more extensive headquarter activities in Sweden than purely domestic firms. Comparing Swedish and foreign MNEs, we find that there is no statistically significant difference in terms of employment, sales, labor productivity, and capital and skill intensity. However, it appears that foreign-owned firms invest more in R&D and pay higher wages than domestic MNEs.

In what follows, we investigate whether this higher R&D intensity, defined as the ratio of expenditures by a firm on R&D to the firm's sales, in foreign MNEs is a result of post-acquisition increases, or whether it can be explained by foreign firms targeting high R&D intensive domestic firms when choosing takeover targets. To see how important foreign acquisitions were in the Swedish manufacturing sector, Table 4 reports the

Table 2. *Development of MNEs and non-MNEs in Sweden by industry in percent for 1993 and 2002*

		1993			2002		
Industry	SNI 92 codes	Foreign MNEs	Swedish MNEs	Swedish non-MNEs	Foreign MNEs	Swedish MNEs	Swedish non-MNEs
Food and beverages	15	26.79	13.39	59.82	28.87	9.28	61.86
Tobacco products	16	0.00	100.00	0.00	0.00	100.00	0.00
Textiles	17	25.00	21.43	53.57	28.57	25.00	46.43
Apparel	18	11.11	44.44	44.44	0.00	100.00	0.00
Leather, footwear	19	0.00	100.00	0.00	0.00	0.00	100.00
Wood	20	3.64	27.27	69.09	17.50	13.33	69.17
Paper and pulp	21	18.75	47.92	33.33	42.86	34.92	22.22
Publishing, printing	22	9.62	17.31	73.08	13.19	21.53	65.28
Coke and petroleum	23	0.00	100.00	0.00	100.00	0.00	0.00
Chemicals	24	44.78	35.82	19.40	66.67	17.33	16.00
Rubber and plastic	25	25.93	46.30	27.78	34.21	46.05	19.74
Non-metallic mineral	26	19.30	52.63	28.07	55.81	13.95	30.23
Basic metals	27	24.44	46.67	28.89	53.06	22.45	24.49
Fabricated metal	28	11.67	34.17	54.17	17.87	29.47	52.66
Machinery, equipm.	29	23.12	46.24	30.64	32.38	36.67	30.95
Electrical and optical	30	62.50	12.50	25.00	9.09	27.27	63.64
Electrical machinery	31	45.10	15.69	39.22	42.86	28.57	28.57
Radio, TV	32	29.17	37.50	33.33	27.59	41.38	31.03
Medical instruments	33	25.71	57.14	17.14	53.33	31.11	15.56
Motor vehicles	34	18.00	40.00	42.00	32.94	40.00	27.06
Other transport eq.	35	34.62	34.62	30.77	29.03	25.81	45.16
Other manufacturing	36	10.77	33.85	55.38	21.79	34.62	43.59

Source: Statistics Sweden.
Notes: The sample is truncated at 50 employees.

Table 3. *Characteristics of MNEs (foreign and Swedish) and non-MNEs in Swedish manufacturing in 2002*

Variable	Foreign MNEs	Swedish MNEs	Non-MNEs	Difference[a] (t-ratio)	Difference[b] (t-ratio)
R&D intensity	28.5	23.4	8.8	5.1 (2.19)	14.6 (8.41)
Employment	408	334	125	74 (1.05)	209 (6.31)
Sales	711	536	151	175 (1.12)	385 (5.23)
Labor productivity	452	438	364	14 (0.68)	74 (5.45)
Capital–labor ratio	220	143	51	77 (1.43)	92 (3.51)
Skill intensity	20.1	18.7	14.2	1.4 (1.44)	4.5 (5.29)
Average wage	204	197	179	7 (2.73)	18 (7.33)

Source: Statistics Sweden.
Notes: [a]This is the difference between foreign MNEs and Swedish MNEs. [b]This is the difference between Swedish MNEs and non-MNEs. The sample is truncated at 50 employees. R&D intensity is defined as the ratio of R&D expenditure over firm sales. Labor productivity is measured as value added, deflated by the industry producer price index, per employee. Physical capital is here measured by the book value of machinery and buildings, per employee, and human capital intensity is measured by the proportion of employees with more than upper secondary education.

Table 4. *Frequency of foreign acquisitions by year 1993–2002*

Year	Acquired Swedish MNE	Acquired Swedish non-MNE	Total
1994	1	18	19
1995	5	16	21
1996	26	20	46
1997	3	11	14
1998	5	11	16
1999	10	14	24
2000	6	14	20
2001	3	39	42
2002	9	16	25
1994–2002	68	159	227

Source: Statistics Sweden.
Notes: The sample is truncated at 50 employees. We report a shift in ownership when a foreign firm acquires more than 50 percent of the votes in a Swedish firm.

number of foreign acquisitions in the sample used in the analysis for the period 1993–2002.[14]

In Table 5, we test the hypothesis that target and non-target Swedish firms have different characteristics before and after acquisitions using the sample of acquired and non-acquired firms (i.e., disregarding firms that are always foreign-owned). It appears that acquired firms invest more in R&D one year prior to an acquisition. There are also other important differences pre- and post-acquisition. Target firms are, in general, larger in terms of employment and sales, have higher capital and skill intensities, and are more productive than non-target firms. Most of these differences are maintained, or even strengthened, under the new ownership post-acquisition. Skill intensity does, however, decline in foreign-acquired firms post-acquisition. Overall, this suggests that foreign ownership does matter. In the next section, we go beyond these mean values and analyze more thoroughly the effects of foreign acquisition on R&D intensity post-acquisition.

[14] Recall that these are acquisitions rather than mergers. If the merger means that a new firm is created, it will not appear as an acquisition and will not be included in our analysis. However, if a foreign-owned firm and a Swedish-owned firm are merged, and the merged entity retains the same identifier as the Swedish firm, it will appear as a foreign acquisition. The main mode of market entry during the period 1993–2002 was acquisitions of Swedish firms (e.g., ITPS, 2002). Mergers constitute between 2 and 4 percent of the foreign-owned firms in Sweden. Our definition of an acquisition is that at least 50 percent of the voting rights are acquired by a foreign owner.

Table 5. *Pre- and post-acquisition differences in means between acquired and non-acquired firms*

Variable	$T-1$ Difference (t-ratio)	$T+1$ Difference (t-ratio)	$T+2$ Difference (t-ratio)	$T+3$ Difference (t-ratio)
R&D intensity	0.9	0.9	1.3	1.3
	(3.37)***	(2.73)***	(3.76)***	(3.45)***
Employment	314	401	416	422
	(2.94)***	(3.61)***	(3.69)***	(3.68)***
Sales	832	1086	743	713
	(3.12)***	(2.92)***	(1.75)*	(1.44)
Labor productivity	66	48	67	63
	(3.30)***	(2.26)**	(3.03)***	(2.49)**
Capital–labor ratio	268	369	357	373
	(5.27)***	(6.00)***	(5.31)***	(5.10)***
Skill intensity	3.5	2.8	2.7	2.4
	(3.09)***	(2.40)**	(2.23)**	(1.89)*
Observations of acquired firms	89	89	89	89
Observations of non-acquired firms	4,095	4,095	4,095	4,095

Source: Statistics Sweden.

Notes: The sample is truncated at 50 employees. Shipment is in million SEK. Capital–labor ratios and labor productivity, value added per employee, are in thousand SEK. R&D intensity (i.e., R&D expenditure over firm sales) and Skill intensity (i.e., share of employees with a post-secondary education) are in percent. ***, **, and * denote significance at the 1, 5, and 10 percent levels, respectively.

III. Methodology

Our aim in this paper is to evaluate the causal effect of foreign acquisition on R&D activity in a targeted domestic firm. Following Heckman *et al.* (1997), we define the average effect of acquisition on the acquired firms as

$$E\{y^1_{it+s} - y^0_{it+s} | AF_{it} = 1\} = E\{y^1_{it+s} | AF_{it} = 1\} - E\{y^0_{it+s} | AF_{it} = 1\} \quad (1)$$

where $AF_{it} \in \{0, 1\}$ is an indicator of whether domestic firm i is acquired by a foreign firm in time period t, and y^1_{it+s} denotes R&D activity s years after the acquisition year t given that the firm was acquired. Correspondingly, y^0_{it+s} denotes R&D activity in the firm in the absence of the treatment (acquisition). The problem is that y^0_{it+s} is, by definition, unobservable, because we cannot observe the counterfactual R&D activity for a treated firm in the absence of treatment. Hence, the counterfactual for the last term in equation (1) is estimated using the R&D activity of the domestic firms that were not acquired, $E\{y^0_{it+s} | AF_{it} = 0\}$.

In the empirical analysis, we first consider $s = 1$. Then, our first baseline estimation strategy is to regress the outcome variable on the acquisition dummy and a full set of time dummies,

$$y_{it+1} = \alpha_{it} + \beta AF_{it} + d_t + \varepsilon_{it}, \quad (2)$$

where AF_{it} is a dummy variable equal to 1 in the period when the firm is acquired, and 0 before this period.[15] It is also equal to zero throughout for non-acquired firms. Here, d_t is a vector of time dummies. We only include domestic firms in the control group. Firms that are foreign-owned at the beginning of the period under investigation are dropped from sample. We start by estimating this model using simple OLS and, alternatively an estimator with firm fixed effects. The coefficient β provides an unbiased estimate of the causal effect of AF on y under the assumption that there is no correlation between AF_{it} and ε_{it}.

However, this assumption is unlikely to hold. Time-varying differences in characteristics and performance between acquired and non-acquired firms in the years before acquisition might be correlated with foreign acquisition and might also affect post-acquisition performance. One example could be cherry-picking. If such cherries are firms that constantly outperform others, then this would be captured by the firm fixed effect in equation (2). However, if there are temporary firm-specific shocks to firm performance (e.g., through changing management), then firms that receive a positive shock would turn into cherries, would become likely targets for acquisitions, and would be likely to perform better after acquisition. Another example would be if firms receive early signs of being targets for acquisitions and, as a result of this, change their R&D activity. Both incidences would bias the estimates from equation (2).

To limit the influence of such effects, we use a second strategy – a DID PSM estimation (see Blundell and Costa Dias, 2000). The idea of the PSM approach is to find for every foreign-acquired firm, a similar firm that has remained in domestic hands, from which we can approximate the non-observed counterfactual event. Thus, the matching technique allows us to construct a sample of acquired and non-acquired firms with similar pre-acquisition characteristics.[16,17] This enables us to impose "common support" (i.e., we compare firms that are similar in terms of pre-treatment characteristics). DID eliminates the influence of unobserved firm-specific effects.

[15] Observations for post-acquisition periods where $s > 1$ are dropped. We have also experimented by defining the dummy = 1 in the period when the firm is acquired and in all post-acquisition periods. This produces similar results. These estimations are not reported here to save space, but can be obtained from the authors upon request.

[16] Because the purpose of this paper is to compare foreign-acquired firms with domestic firms, any firm that remains in domestic hands is a valid control. This could also include domestic establishments that have been taken over by other domestic owners, or that are likely to be targets for domestic takeovers. In our data, we are not able to adequately observe domestic acquisitions.

[17] Temporary shocks to firm performance would not invalidate this approach to the extent that these are correlated with the variables included in the propensity score estimation (observable pre-treatment characteristics) and uncorrelated with the treatment variable.

However, even this combined estimation approach leaves us with one potential problem concerning unobserved effects. Firms might be acquired based on their future potential. Our approach assumes that this potential is captured by our observed pre-acquisition characteristics, which are included in the propensity score estimation. Still, there might be time-varying unobserved (to the econometrician) effects that determine a firms future potential. If this is the case for both acquired and non-acquired firms (conditional on the estimated propensity score), then this should not cause a problem for our analysis. However, if firms with an unobserved good potential are more likely to be acquired, then our approach might overstate the positive effect of foreign acquisition. Unfortunately, we cannot completely rule out this possibility. Instead, we argue that our propensity score estimation, which includes pre-acquisition R&D and other firm variables, is rich enough so that it is unlikely that there are other time-varying unobservables that might be correlated with foreign acquisition and R&D.

The DID PSM proceeds in the following steps. Conditional on a set of firm characteristics, we estimate the propensity score of being acquired by a foreign firm using a probit model

$$P(AF_{it} = 1) = F(X_{it-1}, I_j, T_t), \tag{3}$$

where X_{it-1} is a vector of relevant firm-specific characteristics in year $t-1$, which might affect the firms probability of being acquired in year t. Here, I and T control for fixed industry and time effects, respectively.

Once the propensity scores are calculated, we can select the control firm that is closest in terms of its propensity score as a match for an acquired firm.[18] Moreover, we check whether the balancing condition is verified (i.e., whether each independent variable does not differ significantly between acquired and non-acquired firms). Another condition that must be fulfilled in the matching procedure is the so-called common support condition;[19] that is, firms with the same X values have a positive probability of being both target and control.[20]

[18] This is done using the nearest-neighbor matching method (i.e., a one-to-one matching). We match acquired and non-acquired firms using the PSMATCH2 routine in STATA, version 10 (Leuven and Sianesi, 2003).

[19] In determining the common support region, we use two methods. The first method is to compare the minima and maxima of the propensity score in both target and control groups. The second method is to estimate the density distribution in both groups. For a detailed review of these two methods, see Caliendo and Kopeinig (2008).

[20] Eventually, we end up with a sample (hereafter, the matched sample), which consists of 227 acquired firms and 2,842 non-acquired firms. Note that the difference can pertain to different calendar years for different firms. The propensity score estimation includes year dummies to take this into account.

The DID matching estimator, described by Blundell and Costa Dias (2000) and recently employed by, for example, Arnold and Javorcik (2009) and Girma and Görg (2007), can then be expressed as

$$\beta = \sum_{i \in A} \left[\Delta y_i - \sum_{j \in C} g(p_i, p_j) \Delta y_j \right] w_i. \tag{4}$$

Here, p_i denotes the predicted probability of being acquired (generated using equation (3)) for firm i in the group of acquired firms (A), p_j is the predicted probability of being acquired for firm j in the control group (C), and Δy is the log difference between the average R&D activity before and after the change of ownership. The function $g(\cdot)$ assigns the weights to be placed on the comparison firm j while constructing the counterfactual for acquired firm i. In the case of nearest-neighbor matching as employed in this paper, $g(\cdot) = 1$ for the pair with the minimum difference between p_i and p_j, and 0 for all other pairs. Here, w_i is the weight used in the construction of the outcome distribution for the treated sample ($1/N$ in the case of nearest-neighbor matching).

IV. Initial Estimations

We now turn to some first estimations, providing initial correlations on the link between foreign acquisition and R&D. We estimate equation (2) by measuring R&D activity as the log-level of R&D spending.[21] First, we present the results from a specification without firm-specific fixed effects in order to establish a benchmark. Then, we estimate the same equation using a fixed effects (FE) technique. The results are shown in Columns 1 and 2 of Table 6. These baseline results indicate that foreign-acquired firms had higher R&D spending in the year following takeover, compared to non-acquired firms.

In Columns 3 and 4, we estimate a similar model, but the dependent variable is now the log difference of R&D expenditures between $t-1$ and $t+1$, that is, ($\log \mathrm{R\&D}_{t+1} \log \mathrm{R\&D}_{t-1}$). Compared to the baseline model, the dependent variable in differences allows for unobserved time-invariant firm effects that are conditionally correlated with the acquisition decision and the growth of R&D activity (not levels as in the previous model). This estimation also shows positive effects of the acquisition on the growth of total R&D spending.

Columns 5 and 6 report estimations that have as the dependent variable, the log difference of R&D intensity (i.e., R&D spending over total sales). This also takes into account differences in R&D spending, depending on

[21] We use log-transformed variables in all regressions.

Table 6. *Post-acquisition effect on R&D OLS and fixed effect (FE) model*

	R&D$_{t+1}$		ΔR&D$_{t+1}$		ΔR&D intensity$_{t+1}$	
	OLS (1)	FE (2)	OLS (3)	FE (4)	OLS (5)	FE (6)
Foreign acquired	1.063	0.776	0.040	0.043	0.052	0.057
	(0.271)***	(0.122)***	(0.020)**	(0.020)**	(0.012)***	(0.012)***
Obs.	8,982	8,982	8,982	8,982	8,994	8,994
R^2	0.241	0.017	0.024	0.006	0.026	0.018

Source: Statistics Sweden.
Notes: The sample is truncated at 50 employees. Regressions include full sets of year and industry dummies. R&D activity is measured as the level of log R&D spending in Columns 1 and 2, as log difference of R&D expenditures between $t-1$ and $t+1$ in Columns 3 and 4, and as growth of log R&D intensity (i.e., R&D spending over total sales) in Columns 5 and 6. Industries are defined at the SNI 92 three-digit level (99 industries). Standard errors in parentheses. ***, **, and * denote significance at the 1, 5, and 10 percent levels, respectively.

the size of the firm. These results again underline the positive acquisition effect. From Columns 3–6, we can see that foreign acquisitions increase the growth of R&D activity by between 4 and 5 percent in the post-acquisition year.

These results provide initial evidence that fears about foreign acquisitions leading to less R&D activity in the target firms appear to be misplaced. The focus of the further analysis is to establish the robustness of a causal relationship between foreign acquisitions and R&D, using a PSM approach, and to investigate whether there are differences in effects depending on whether the target firm is itself multinational or not.

V. Difference-in-Differences Propensity Score Matching

Before turning to the estimation results, we look first at the propensity score. Table 7 presents the results of estimating the probit model in equation (3). The choice of variables included in the vector X is influenced by the empirical literature on foreign acquisitions (e.g., Conyon *et al.*, 2002; Harris and Robinson, 2002; Lipsey and Sjöholm, 2002; Girma and Görg, 2007). Such studies usually argue that establishment size and age are important determinants for acquisitions, and hence we include these in the probit. Also, high-productivity and capital- or skill-intensive firms are commonly found to be more likely to be taken over, indicating that foreign firms might be cherry-picking the best performing establishments. To control for sectoral effects, we include a full set of industry dummies and a measure of foreign presence in an industry, defined as the share of employment in foreign firms relative to total industry employment. Importantly, because we are interested in identifying an effect of foreign acquisition on R&D

Table 7. *Probit model: probability of foreign acquisition, 1993–2002*

Variable	Model 1	Model 2
R&D intensity	0.912	0.920
	(0.413)**	(0.414)**
Labor productivity	0.137	0.135
	(0.042)***	(0.042)***
Size	−0.003	−0.007
	(0.002)	(0.004)**
Skill intensity	0.887	0.900
	(0.137)***	(0.138)***
Age	−0.041	−0.041
	(0.009)***	(0.009)***
Age squared	0.001	0.001
	(0.000)***	(0.000)***
Capital intensity	0.121	0.124
	(0.012)***	(0.012)***
Size squared		0.001
		(0.001)
Foreign presence	0.133	0.130
	(0.017)***	(0.017)***
Industry dummies	Yes	Yes
Year dummies	Yes	Yes
Pseudo-R^2	0.043	0.043
LR chi^2	380.01	380.34
Observations	9,612	9,612

Source: Statistics Sweden.
Notes: The sample is truncated at 50 employees. Standard errors are given within parentheses. The explanatory variables are, apart from age and age squared, firm specific characteristics in year $t-1$. Firm size is firm employment relative to mean firm employment at the industry level. Labor productivity is value added per employee and skill intensity is the share of employees with post-secondary education at the firm level. R&D intensity is defined as R&D spending over total sales. The share of foreign employment at industry level (SNI 92 two-digit level) is used as a proxy for foreign presence. ***, **, and * denote significance at the 1, 5, and 10 percent levels, respectively.

post-acquisition, we include pre-acquisition ($t-1$) R&D intensity in the propensity score estimation. This also allows us to consider the particular cherry-picking hypothesis in Bertrand *et al.* (2012), where targets are picked depending on the quality of their R&D assets.

The results in Table 7 indicate that firms are more likely to be acquired by foreign owners, the more R&D active they are, which is in line with Bertrand *et al.* (2012).[22] Also, the acquisition probability of firms is higher, the more productive and skill-intensive they are, pre-acquisition. Moreover,

[22] We use R&D expenditures at $t-1$ as one of the conditioning variables, in an effort to even out all unobservables. Ideally, one would use a measure of R&D assets or human capital and shocks to these. As a test of robustness, we have replaced R&D expenditures at $t-1$ with the growth in R&D expenditures between $t-2$ and $t-1$. However, this did not significantly affect the results.

firms in industries with a large foreign presence are more likely to be taken over.

We also present the estimation of a slightly different model in Column 2. We use this model as a robustness check for the validity of our PSM. Dehejia (2005) suggests that one should check the sensitivity of the matching estimates to minor changes in the propensity score model. If the results are not sensitive to such minor changes, the propensity score specification can be deemed robust and reliable. In line with Girma and Görg (2007), who also estimated propensity scores for the probability of foreign acquisitions, we add a squared term of the size variable to the specification. While all our matching estimates reported in Table 7 are based on the first propensity score estimation in Column 1, the model in Column 2 produces very similar results, which we take as an indication that the matching procedure is reliable. These results are available upon request.

The PSM method will provide a reliable and robust method for estimating the foreign acquisition effect if, conditional on the propensity score, the potential outcomes for acquired and non-acquired firms are independent of the incidence of acquisition. Under this assumption of independence conditional on observables, the pre-acquisition variables should be balanced between the acquired and non-acquired groups. Therefore, we perform a number of balancing tests suggested in the recent literature (e.g., Smith and Todd, 2005).

The first balancing test examines the standardized difference (or bias) for all variables in the vector X. For example, the standardized bias for the skill intensity variable is defined as the difference in means between the foreign-acquired sample of firms (group A) and the appropriately matched comparison group of firms (group C) scaled by the average variances of the skill intensity variable in groups A and C. Note that the lower the standardized difference, the more balanced or similar the treatment and comparison groups will be in terms of the variable under consideration. Although there is no formal criterion as to how large a standardized bias should be for it to be considered serious, a value of 20 is generally considered large. Furthermore, for each variable entering the propensity score model, we perform a formal paired t-test between the acquired and matched comparison to satisfy ourselves that no significant differences exist.

Whereas the above balancing test calculates the cross-sample difference of each variable entering the probit model separately, there also exists a test that considers whether those differences can be taken as jointly insignificant. This test is known as the Hotelling T-squared test, and it has the flexibility of being based either on all observations or on separate segments of the sample defined by the propensity score estimates. In this study, we divide the sample by propensity score quintile and conduct the Hotelling T-squared test for each subsample.

Table 8. *Post-acquisition effect on R&D activity in foreign acquisitions: DID matching estimator*

				Observations		
					Untreated	
$y_{t+s} - y_{t-1}$		DID	Std error	Treated	On support	Off support
ΔR&D intensity	$s = 1$	0.064	(0.016)***	227	227	8,388
	$s = 2$	0.122	(0.024)***	227	227	7,013
	$s = 3$	0.063	(0.024)***	227	227	5,672
ΔR&D	$s = 1$	0.099	(0.021)***	227	227	8,015
	$s = 2$	0.113	(0.031)***	227	227	6,706
	$s = 3$	0.098	(0.032)***	227	227	5,431

Source: Statistics Sweden.
Notes: The sample is truncated at 50 employees. In the first three rows, the outcome variable is log R&D intensity before and after acquisition; in the last three rows, it is log R&D expenditures before and after acquisition. ***, **, and * denote significance at the 1, 5, and 10 percent levels, respectively.

The balancing tests are reported in Tables A1–A3 in the Appendix for both propensity score models. The standardized differences between the acquired and comparison samples are all less than 10 percent in the matched sample. There is also a substantial bias reduction as a result of adopting the matching method. Furthermore, the results from the Hotelling test indicate that the balancing conditions are satisfied within each propensity score quintile.

Having established that our PSM procedure appears to be reliable, we can now turn to the results of the DID PSM approach, as reported in Table 8. We look at both log R&D levels and log R&D intensity in the table. The first line, where $s = 1$, presents results that are comparable to the baseline estimates reported in the previous section. In this case, the outcome variable is calculated as $(y_{t+1} y_{t-1})$. We find significant positive post-acquisition effects for both R&D levels and intensity. The estimated coefficients suggest slightly larger effects than in Table 6. The incidence of foreign acquisition increases the growth of R&D activity by 6–10 percent in the post-acquisition year.

We then expand on the earlier analysis and consider longer time intervals in which the post-acquisition effect can take place. In the case of $s = 2$, the difference is calculated as $(y_{t+2} y_{t-1})$; that is, we look at the change in R&D activity two years after acquisition took place. Note that we find for both $s = 2$ and 3, still positive and statistically significant post-acquisition effects on R&D activity.[23]

[23] Of course, it might be the case that effects take more than three years to manifest themselves. If this is the case, our analysis would underestimate the true acquisition effects.

Overall, these results suggest that foreign acquisitions, in general, have positive effects on R&D activity in the target firm, in line with the theoretical predictions by Bertrand *et al.* (2012). We looked at the robustness of the results by using different matching estimators. Using kernel or radius matching does not change our results, and thus, in what follows, we report the results of nearest-neighbor matching.[24]

The analysis thus far is based on pooled data for the whole manufacturing sector. This hides potential industry heterogeneity. While being crucial for some industries, for other industries, R&D assets might be of minor importance. In order to look at this issue, we divide our sample into high- and low-tech sectors. This classification is based on R&D intensity in the sectors.[25] We find positive post-acquisition effects on R&D for both sectors in Table 9. However, judging by the magnitude of the coefficients, it appears that these effects are stronger in low-tech sectors. For example, the effects of foreign acquisition on the growth of R&D intensity in low-tech sectors for $s = 2$ and 3 are around 15 and 11 percent, respectively, while the corresponding figures for high-tech sectors are around 11 and 8 percent.[26]

In the policy debate, particular attention is paid to what happens to the headquarters, and in particular the R&D activity, of domestic MNEs if they are taken over by a foreign firm. As pointed out in the introduction, this might be an important issue given that MNEs can be expected to have more extensive R&D activities in Sweden. We now look at our data in more detail in order to investigate this. Specifically, to allow for different effects of foreign acquisitions on R&D intensity, depending on whether a Swedish

---

We do not expand our analysis further in time because the further we move away from the incidence of acquisition, the more difficult it becomes to establish causal links (i.e., to maintain the conditional independence assumption). Also, the ability to carry out long-term data analysis is heavily constrained by data availability, because we would need to be able to follow individual firms for more than three years.

[24] These results are available upon request. Another potential concern is that the analysis is based on continuing firms and, hence, does not capture the possibility that acquiring firms might close down the takeover target post-acquisition. Bandick and Görg (2010) focus on this question using a similar dataset. They show that for plants within acquired firms, the probability of surviving is higher than for plants within non-acquired firms in the Swedish manufacturing sectors. Hence, there is no evidence to expect that the probability of exit increases post-acquisition. Yet another potential concern is that the sample composition in Table 7 is not exactly the same for all possible outcomes ($s = 1$–3). However, we have estimated our regressions with a balanced sample (not reported in the paper to save space) and the results do not differ from those reported in Table 7.

[25] Following Hatzichronoglou (1997), sectors with R&D intensity lower than 5 percent are defined as low-tech sectors. This resulted in 10 low-tech sectors (SNI 92: 15–21, 23, 27, and 28 from Table 2) and 12 high-tech sectors.

[26] These differences, which are not reported here but can be obtained upon request, are significant at the 1 percent level.

Table 9. *Post-acquisition effect on R&D in low- and high-tech industries: DID matching estimator*

				Observations		
					Untreated	
$y_{t+s} - y_{t-1}$		DID	Std error	Treated	On support	Off support
Low-tech industries						
ΔR&D intensity	$s = 1$	0.061	(0.030)***	75	75	3,409
	$s = 2$	0.155	(0.037)***	75	75	2,855
	$s = 3$	0.111	(0.041)***	75	75	2,345
ΔR&D	$s = 1$	0.106	(0.034)***	75	75	3,257
	$s = 2$	0.114	(0.054)***	75	75	2,732
	$s = 3$	0.084	(0.018)***	75	75	2,240
High-tech industries						
ΔR&D intensity	$s = 1$	0.057	(0.022)***	152	152	4,979
	$s = 2$	0.107	(0.027)***	152	152	4,158
	$s = 3$	0.080	(0.029)***	152	152	3,327
ΔR&D	$s = 1$	0.107	(0.025)***	152	152	4,758
	$s = 2$	0.083	(0.042)*	152	152	3,974
	$s = 3$	0.079	(0.043)*	152	152	3,191

Source: Statistics Sweden.
Notes: See Table 8. Following Hatzichronoglou (1997), sectors with R&D intensity lower than 5 percent are defined as low-tech sectors. This resulted in 10 low-tech sectors (SNI 92: 15–21, 23, 27, and 28 from Table 2) and 12 high-tech sectors. ***, **, and * denote significance at the 1, 5, and 10 percent levels, respectively.

MNE or Swedish non-MNE is acquired, we split the sample accordingly. Table 10 shows the results of our estimations. These results indicate that compared to non-acquired firms, both targeted Swedish MNEs and non-MNEs have higher growth in R&D intensity, one, two, and three years after the takeover. However, these effects appear to be slightly stronger for non-MNEs than for Swedish MNEs.

While our overall findings that there are positive post-acquisition effects on R&D are in line with Bertrand *et al.* (2012), the results for the split samples are more difficult to interpret. While the model is not explicit on this, we can argue that firms in high-tech sectors, and those that are themselves MNEs, possess R&D assets that are of higher quality, and that might also be more complementary to those assets of the foreign acquirer. If this were the case, we would expect these firms to experience larger post-acquisition R&D increases. However, this is not what we find.

An alternative explanation for positive post-acquisition effects on R&D is that the foreign acquirer transfers technology to its foreign affiliate. This would enable the foreign affiliate to increase its own R&D activity as a result. However, the scope for technology transfer might be higher, the lower the quality of the targets own R&D activity. This is consistent with our summary statistics where we have found that Swedish MNEs are

Table 10. *Post-acquisition effect on R&D intensity in different targets: DID matching estimator*

				Observations		
					Untreated	
$y_{t+s} - y_{t-1}$		DID	Std error	Treated	On support	Off support
Acquired Swedish MNEs						
ΔR&D intensity	$s = 1$	0.032	(0.015)**	68	68	6,841
	$s = 2$	0.094	(0.037)***	68	68	5,355
	$s = 3$	0.093	(0.031)***	68	68	4,341
ΔR&D	$s = 1$	0.040	(0.018)**	68	68	6,565
	$s = 2$	0.098	(0.052)*	68	68	5,152
	$s = 3$	0.034	(0.051)	68	68	4,182
Acquired Swedish non-MNEs						
ΔR&D intensity	$s = 1$	0.094	(0.018)***	159	159	8,011
	$s = 2$	0.098	(0.025)***	159	159	6,075
	$s = 3$	0.136	(0.033)***	159	159	4,926
ΔR&D	$s = 1$	0.115	(0.029)***	159	159	8,010
	$s = 2$	0.107	(0.038)***	159	159	6,074
	$s = 3$	0.125	(0.043)***	159	159	4,924

Source: Statistics Sweden.
Notes: See Table 8. ***, **, and * denote significance at the 1, 5, and 10 percent levels, respectively.

similar to foreign MNEs, but both are different compared to Swedish non-MNEs. Hence, we would expect stronger post-acquisition effects for firms in low-tech sectors or firms that are non-MNEs.

VI. Conclusion

Overall, it would appear that the increased foreign presence in terms of foreign acquisitions of Swedish firms has had positive effects on the R&D activity in these firms. This is in line with the empirical study by Bertrand *et al.* (2012), who have also used Swedish data and have found a positive correlation between M&A and R&D. Compared to their paper, however, our methodology allows us to be more confident about causal effects, because we can distinguish pre-acquisition cherry-picking and post-acquisition R&D performance. We use different estimation strategies, based on combinations of PSM and DID estimations to control for selection bias in the evaluation of causal effects.

The point estimates from our DID PSM estimator suggest increases in R&D intensity by between 5 and 10 percent after a foreign acquisition. These effects are similar to those found for French firm level data by Bertrand (2009). However, our analysis exploits a further dimension in the data and shows that post-acquisition effects are stronger for the acquisition of domestic non-MNEs than for Swedish MNEs. However, it is important to stress that even for the acquisition of Swedish MNEs, the effect on R&D is generally positive, never negative. Hence, our results suggest that fears that the acquisition of large Swedish MNEs by foreign owners might lead to a relocation of R&D activities abroad appear to be unfounded.

Our findings are also policy relevant. The implication of our analysis is that foreign acquisitions can have beneficial effects for domestic R&D activity. Hence, there is no need to fear and therefore no need for policy-makers to start thinking about limiting international M&A activity. In contrast, foreign acquisitions might be an important way to generate new knowledge and to contribute to boosting the level of technology in the domestic economy. This result is based on data for Sweden, a country that is highly conducive to R&D, given its highly educated labor force and small size (Ekholm and Hakkala, 2007). Whether our results can be generalized to other country settings remains an important question for future research.

Appendix A: Details of the Propensity Score Matching

Table A1. *Balancing test for the matching sample: model 1*

		Mean		Standardized	Bias	*t*-test	
Variable	Sample	Treated	Control	bias	reduction	t	$p > \|t\|$
R&D intensity	Unmatched	0.017	0.009	20.0		3.33	0.001
	Matched	0.017	0.023	−7.2	14.3	1.28	0.200
Labor productivity	Unmatched	5.980	5.884	21.3		3.32	0.001
	Matched	5.980	5.995	−3.4	84.0	0.35	0.727
Size	Unmatched	5.774	5.504	3.1		0.46	0.643
	Matched	5.774	5.385	4.4	−44.1	0.50	0.617
Skill intensity	Unmatched	0.177	0.138	29.9		5.11	0.000
	Matched	0.177	0.181	−3.2	89.3	0.30	0.768
Age	Unmatched	13.035	15.838	−31.7		4.92	0.000
	Matched	13.035	14.044	−9.4	64.0	1.14	0.255
Age squared	Unmatched	254.700	322.270	−24.8		3.66	0.000
	Matched	254.700	289.380	−8.7	48.7	1.29	0.198
Foreign presence	Unmatched	8.783	8.613	19.8		2.81	0.005
	Matched	8.783	8.795	−1.4	93.0	0.15	0.881
Capital intensity	Unmatched	10.175	9.888	17.4		2.76	0.006
	Matched	10.175	10.197	−1.4	92.0	0.14	0.890

Source: Statistics Sweden.
Notes: The sample is truncated at 50 employees. Size is firm employment relative to mean firm employment at the industry level. Labor productivity is value added per employee, and skill intensity is the share of employees with post-secondary education at the firm level. R&D intensity is defined as R&D spending over total sales. The share of foreign employment at industry the level (SNI 92 two-digit level) is used as a proxy for foreign presence.

Table A2. *Balancing test for the matching sample: model 2*

		Mean		Standardized	Bias	*t*-test	
Variable	Sample	Treated	Control	bias	reduction	*t*	$p > \lvert t \rvert$
R&D intensity	Unmatched	0.017	0.009	20.0		3.33	0.001
	Matched	0.017	0.021	−8.9	45.8	0.86	0.200
Labor productivity	Unmatched	5.980	5.884	21.3		3.32	0.001
	Matched	5.980	5.971	1.9	91.2	0.18	0.727
Size	Unmatched	5.774	5.504	3.1		0.46	0.643
	Matched	5.774	6.183	−4.7	−51.8	0.48	0.617
Size squared	Unmatched	112.020	104.910	1.1		0.16	0.870
	Matched	112.020	122.120	−1.6	−42.1	0.18	0.854
Skill intensity	Unmatched	0.177	0.138	29.9		5.11	0.000
	Matched	0.177	0.183	−4.6	84.5	0.44	0.660
Age	Unmatched	13.035	15.838	−31.7		4.92	0.000
	Matched	13.035	133.097	−0.7	97.8	0.07	0.944
Age squared	Unmatched	254.700	322.270	−24.8		3.66	0.000
	Matched	254.700	262.250	−2.8	88.8	0.28	0.778
Foreign presence	Unmatched	8.783	8.613	19.8		2.81	0.005
	Matched	8.783	8.799	−1.9	90.3	0.21	0.836
Capital intensity	Unmatched	10.175	9.888	17.4		2.76	0.006
	Matched	10.175	10.093	4.9	71.7	0.50	0.616

Source: Statistics Sweden.
Notes: See Table A1.

Table A3. *Hotelling T-squared test for equality of means in different quintiles: models 1 and 2*

	Quintile 1		Quintile 2		Quintile 3		Quintile 4	
Variable	Treated	Untreated	Treated	Untreated	Treated	Untreated	Treated	Untreated
Model 1								
R&D intensity	0.002	0.002	0.002	0.007	0.012	0.009	0.022	0.020
Labor productivity	5.844	5.832	5.729	5.810	5.952	5.884	6.046	6.012
Size	5.854	5.342	4.587	5.414	5.001	5.851	6.152	5.400
Skill intensity	0.128	0.110	0.120	0.130	0.165	0.140	0.196	0.174
Age	21.520	19.000	15.040	16.880	16.460	15.010	10.180	12.360
Age squared	498.190	405.150	272.610	343.500	383.450	298.930	182.860	239.160
Foreign presence	8.588	8.329	8.816	8.577	8.740	8.727	8.817	8.822
Capital intensity	9.507	9.668	9.480	9.650	10.414	9.946	10.319	10.293
F-statistic	1.071		0.788		1.241		0.883	
P-value	0.381		0.613		0.271		0.506	
Model 2								
R&D intensity	0.002	0.002	0.002	0.007	0.012	0.009	0.022	0.020
Labor productivity	5.844	5.832	5.729	5.810	5.952	5.884	6.046	6.012
Size	5.854	5.342	4.587	5.414	5.001	5.851	6.152	5.400
Size squared	68.490	67.200	50.240	84.410	42.000	148.610	146.470	118.550
Skill intensity	0.128	0.110	0.120	0.130	0.165	0.140	0.196	0.174
Age	21.520	19.000	15.040	16.880	16.460	15.010	10.180	12.360
Age squared	498.190	405.150	272.610	343.500	383.450	298.930	182.860	239.160
Foreign presence	8.588	8.329	8.816	8.577	8.740	8.727	8.817	8.822

Table A3. *Continued.*

	Quintile 1		Quintile 2		Quintile 3		Quintile 4	
Variable	Treated	Untreated	Treated	Untreated	Treated	Untreated	Treated	Untreated
Capital intensity	9.507	9.668	9.480	9.650	10.414	9.946	10.319	10.293
F-statistic	1.133		0.707		1.103		0.826	
P-value	0.336		0.704		0.357		0.566	

Source: Statistics Sweden.
Notes: See Table A1.

References

Arnold, J. M. and Javorcik, B. S. (2009), Gifted Kids or Pushy Parents? Foreign Direct Investment and Plant Productivity in Indonesia, *Journal of International Economics 79*, 42–53.

Bandick, R. and Görg, H. (2010), Foreign Acquisition, Plant Survival and Employment Growth, *Canadian Journal of Economics 43*, 547–573.

Barba Navaretti, G., Castellani, D., and Disdier, A. (2009), How Does Investing in Cheap Labour Countries Affect Performance at Home? Firm Level Evidence from France and Italy, *Oxford Economic Papers 62*, 234–260.

Baysinger, B. and Hoskisson, R. E. (1989), Diversification Strategy and R&D Intensity in Multiproduct Firms, *The Academy of Management Journal 32*, 310–332.

Bertrand, O. (2009), Effects of Foreign Acquisitions on R&D Activity: Evidence from Firm-Level Data for France, *Research Policy 38*, 1021–1031.

Bertrand, O. and Zuniga, P. (2006), R&D and M&A: Are Cross-Border M&A Different? An Investigation on OECD Countries, *International Journal of Industrial Organization 24*, 401–423.

Bertrand, O., Hakkala, K. N., Norbäck, P.-J., and Persson, L. (2012), Should Countries Block Foreign Takeovers of R&D Champions and Promote Greenfield Entry?, *Canadian Journal of Economics 45*, 1083–1124.

Blomström, M., Fors, G., and Lipsey, R. E. (1997), Foreign Direct Investment and Employment: Home Country Experience in the United States and Sweden, *Economic Journal 107*, 1787–1797.

Blundell, R. and Costa Dias, M. (2000), Evaluation Methods for Non-Experimental Data, *Fiscal Studies 21*, 427–468.

Braunerhjelm, P. (2001), The Head Quarters are Moving Out, SNS Förlag, Stockholm.

Caliendo, M. and Kopeinig, S. (2008), Some Practical Guidance for the Implementation of Propensity Score Matching, *Journal of Economic Surveys 22*, 31–72.

Cassiman, B., Colombo, M. G., Gerrone, P., and Veugelers, R. (2005), The Impact of M&A on the R&D Process: An Empirical Analysis of the Role of Technological and Market Relatedness, *Research Policy 34*, 455–476.

Caves, R. E. (1996), Multinational Enterprise and Economic Analysis, Cambridge University Press, Cambridge.

Conyon, M. J., Girma, S., Thompson, S., and Wright, P. W. (2002), The Impact of Foreign Acquisition on Wages and Productivity in the UK, *Journal of Industrial Economics 50*, 85–102.

Criscuolo, C. and Martin, R. (2009), Multinationals and US Productivity Leadership: Evidence from Great Britain, *Review of Economics and Statistics 91*, 263–281.

Dehejia, R. H. (2005), Program Evaluation as a Decision Problem, *Journal of Econometrics 125*, 141–173.

Ekholm, K. and Hakkala, K. (2007), Location of R&D and High-Tech Production by Vertically Integrated Multinationals, *Economic Journal 117*, 512–543.

Forfás (2011), *Business Expenditure on Research and Development 2009/2010*, Stationary Office, Dublin.

Girma, S. and Görg, H. (2007), Evaluating the Foreign Ownership Wage Premium Using a Difference-in-Differences Matching Approach, *Journal of International Economics 72*, 97–112.

Hall, B. H. (2002), The Financing of Research and Development, *Oxford Review of Economic Policy 18*, 35–51.

Hatzichronoglou, T. (1997), Revision of the High-Technology Sector and Product Classification, *OECD Science*, Technology and Industry Working Paper 1997/02, OECD, Paris.

Harris, R. and Robinson, C. (2002), The Effect of Foreign Acquisitions on Total Factor Productivity: Plant-Level Evidence from UK Manufacturing, 1987–1992, *Review of Economics and Statistics 84*, 562–568.

Heckman, J. J., Ichimura, H., and Todd, P. E. (1997), Matching as an Econometric Evaluation Estimator: Evidence from Evaluating a Job Training Programme, *Review of Economic Studies 64*, 605–654.

Helpman, E., Melitz, M. J., and Yeaple, S. R. (2004), Export versus FDI with Heterogeneous Firms, *American Economic Review 94*(1), 300–316.

Hijzen, A., Jean, S., and Mayer, T. (2011), The Effects at Home of Initiating Production Abroad: Evidence from Matched French Firms, *Review of World Economics 147*, 457–483.

Hitt, M. A., Hoskisson, R. E., Ireland, R. D., and Harrison, J. S. (1991), Effects of Acquisitions on R&D Inputs and Outputs, *The Academy of Management Journal 34*, 693–706.

Huttunen, K. (2007), The Effect of Foreign Acquisition on Employment and Wages: Evidence from Finnish Establishments, *Review of Economics and Statistics 89*, 497–509.

ITPS (2002), Inward Investment – Impact on Swedish Economy, Swedish Institute for Growth Policy Studies, Stockholm.

Karpaty, P. (2006), Does Multinationality Matter? Evidence from Swedish Firm Data, *Applied Economics Quarterly 52*, 101–122.

Karpaty, P. and Tingvall, P. G. (2011), Competition and R&D, *Economics of Innovation and New Technology 20*, 63–88.

Krugman, P. (1991), Increasing Returns and Economic Geography, *Journal of Political Economy 99*, 483–499.

Leuven, E. and Sianesi, B. (2003), psmatch2: stata Module to Perform Full Mahalanobis and Propensity Score Matching, Common Support Graphing, and Covariate Imbalance Testing. Available at http://ideas.repec.org/c/boc/bocode/s432001.html.

Lipsey, R. E. and Sjöholm, F. (2002), Foreign Firms and Indonesian Manufacturing Wages: An Analysis with Panel Data, NBER Working Paper 9417.

Markusen, J. R. (2002), Multinational Firms and the Theory of International Trade, MIT Press, Cambridge, MA.

Smith, J. and Todd, P. (2005), Rejoinder, *Journal of Econometrics 125*, 365–375.

UNCTAD (2005), World Investment Report 2005: Transnational Corporations and the Internationalization of R&D. United Nations.

Veugelers, R. (2006), Literature Review on M&A and R&D, in B. Cassiman and M. G. Colombo (eds.), *Merger and Acquisitions – The Innovation Impact*, Edward Elgar, Cheltenham.

First version submitted January 2011;
final version received April 2013.

Chapter 5

Foreign Direct Investment, Access to Finance, and Innovation Activity in Chinese Enterprises

Sourafel Girma, Yundan Gong, and Holger Görg

A recent, comprehensive database is used to investigate the link between inward foreign direct investment (FDI) and innovation activity in China. The results of the analysis suggest that private and collectively owned firms with foreign capital participation and those with good access to domestic bank loans innovate more than other firms do. Among enterprises not owned by the state, inward FDI at the sectoral level is positively associated with domestic innovative activity only among firms that engage in their own research and development or that have good access to domestic finance. At the sector level the effect of inward FDI into technology transfer is distinguished from the effect on domestic credit opportunities. FDI affecting credit is of little significance for state-owned enterprises and is independent of their access to finance. In contrast, better access to credit is an important channel through which FDI affects the innovation of domestic private and collectively owned enterprises. JEL codes: O31, F23, G32

Since undergoing economic reforms beginning in 1979, China has emerged as a rapidly growing manufacturer and exporter. For economic development to continue apace, technological progress is crucial. In this regard, two features of the economy are notable. First, China has been an important location for research and development (R&D) and innovative activity by domestic enterprises since at least the mid-1990s (Jefferson and others 2006). Second, China

Sourafel Girma is a professor of industrial economics at the Nottingham University Business School and is a fellow at the Leverhulme Centre for Research on Globalisation and Economic Policy at the University of Nottingham; his email address is sourafel.girma@nottingham.ac.uk. Yundan Gong is a researcher at the Leverhulme Centre for Research on Globalisation and Economic Policy at the University of Nottingham; her email address is yundan.gong@nottingham.ac.uk. Holger Görg (corresponding author) is a professor of international economics at Christian-Albrechts-Universität and Institut für Weltwirtschaft, in Kiel, Germany, and an external fellow at the Leverhulme Centre for Research on Globalisation and Economic Policy at the University of Nottingham; his email address is holger.goerg@ifw-kiel.de. The authors are grateful to three anonymous referees and the journal editor for helpful comments on an earlier draft. Financial support from the Leverhulme Trust (Programme Grant F114/BF) and the Economic and Social Research Council under its National and International Aspects of Financial Development program is gratefully acknowledged.

THE WORLD BANK ECONOMIC REVIEW, VOL. 22, NO. 2, pp. 367–382 doi:10.1093/wber/lhn009
Advance Access Publication June 11, 2008

has become an important host country for inward foreign direct investment (FDI). Indeed, according to the Organisation for Economic Co-operation and Development (OECD 2004), in 2003 China overtook the United States as the world's largest recipient of FDI.[1]

This article examines whether there is a link between increased levels of inward FDI and innovation activity by Chinese domestic enterprises. It draws on a particularly rich and recent firm-level data set for 1999–2005 provided by the China National Bureau of Statistics (see China National Bureau of Statistics 2006, for a description) paying particular attention to the importance of domestic access to finance.

China is an interesting case to study because of the juxtaposition of an impressive record in attracting FDI with a highly inefficient and state-dominated domestic financial system. The Chinese financial system is widely regarded as inefficient and skewed toward providing financial resources for (also largely inefficient) state-owned enterprises (Huang 2003). It is therefore of considerable policy interest to investigate whether this skewed allocation of financing is related to the ability of domestic firms to benefit (or not) from the increased influx of FDI into the economy.

Increased FDI could affect product innovation by domestic enterprises through many channels. First, a domestic firm receiving an injection of foreign capital faces looser financial constraints—constraints that could hinder innovation (Harrison and McMillan 2003). Second, FDI may bring an inflow of technology. Multinational enterprises are assumed to have better technology than domestic firms (Markusen 2002); foreign capital inflow through acquisition, joint venture, or some other form of capital transfer may thus lead to the installation of foreign technology in the domestic firm. The superior knowledge injected into the economy through FDI may leak to domestic firms (through, for example, worker mobility and imitation), in the same way that productivity improvements spill over (Görg and Greenaway 2004). These firms may then be able to engage in more innovation activity.

A rich panel data set of 239,085 domestic enterprises in Chinese manufacturing industries for 1999–2005 is used to investigate these issues empirically. The analysis contributes to the literature on innovation and technology adoption in developing and transition economies. This literature, reviewed by Keller (2004) and Pack (2006), has amassed a large body of evidence on a number of countries. Econometric work, however, particularly on China, remains limited, despite the immense interest by policymakers and academics.

Using firm-level data for 1997–99 on some 20,000 enterprises, Jefferson and others (2006) model a knowledge production function to estimate

1. See Amiti and Javorcik (2008), Wei (2003), and Lemoine (2000) for analyses of the increased inflow of FDI and its determinants.

the determinants of innovation activity in Chinese enterprises.[2] They find that firm size and own R&D expenditure are important determinants of innovation.

This article expands on their analysis in a number of ways. First, it investigates the impact of inward FDI and the role of firm characteristics on innovation activity at the firm and industry level. This issue, which is not covered by Jefferson and others (2006), is of considerable policy interest. Second, the article addresses the role of access to finance for innovation and the link between such access and a firm's ability to benefit from positive spillovers from inward FDI. This issue has not, to the authors' knowledge, been investigated elsewhere. Third, unlike Jefferson and others (2006), who include dummy variables for different types of ownership, this article investigates whether the determinants of innovation activity, particularly the effect of inward FDI, differ across firms by type of ownership (privately owned, collectively owned, or state owned). Fourth, the data set used here covers more firms and a more recent time period than that used by Jefferson and others (2006).

The results show, not unexpectedly, that firms with foreign capital participation and good access to finance innovate more than others do and that inward FDI at the sectoral level is positively associated with domestic innovative activity only if firms engage in their own R&D activities or have good access to domestic finance. Following up on the suggestion of a possible adverse effect of domestic credit constraints on firms' ability to benefit from inward FDI, further analysis shows that finance constraints adversely affects private and collectively owned firms but not state-owned firms, which enjoy preferential access to domestic financial resources. Again, when the effects of sector-level inward FDI into technology transfer and FDI affecting domestic credit opportunities are distinguished, FDI affecting domestic credit opportunities is found to be of little significance for state enterprises and is independent of their access to finance. By contrast, it is an important channel through which FDI affects domestic private and collectively owned enterprises.

The article is structured as follows. Section I describes the empirical approach, and section II introduces the data set and provides some summary statistics. Section III discusses the econometric results. The final section provides some concluding comments.

2. Other, more loosely related articles should be noted. Hu, Jefferson, and Qian (2005) estimate the determinants of firm-level productivity using a data set similar to that used by Jefferson and others (2006). They focus on the role of own-firm R&D as well as technology purchased from foreign or domestic sources on firm-level productivity. Girma and Gong (forthcoming) use a Chinese data set to investigate the link between inward FDI spillovers and the productivity of state-owned enterprises. Berthelemy and Demurger (2000) use regional data to investigate the effect of inward FDI on regional growth in China.

I. EMPIRICAL APPROACH

In the empirical model a domestic firm (indexed by i) either innovates at time t ($S_{it} > 0$) or it does not ($S_{it} = 0$). A Tobit model is formulated in terms of a latent variable model to determine the relation between FDI and the rate of product innovation:

$$
\begin{aligned}
(1) \qquad S^*_{it} &= \alpha_1 FC_{it-1} + \alpha_2 FDI_{jt-1} + \alpha_3 FIN_{it-1} + \alpha_4 \mathbf{X}_{it-1} \\
&\quad + \alpha_5 FIN_{it-1}{}^{*}\mathbf{FDI}_{jt-1} + \alpha_6 RD_{it-1}{}^{*}FDI_{jt-1} + D_r + D_j + D_t + \varepsilon_{it}
\end{aligned}
$$

$$
\begin{aligned}
S_{it} &= 0 \quad && if\ S^*_{it} \leq 0 \\
S_{it} &= S^*_{it} \quad && if\ S^*_{it} > 0
\end{aligned}
$$

where the dependent variable S is defined as the share of innovation output products involving the use of new process innovation or novel technology in total output.[3] This variable, which measures the output of the innovation process, is a more suitable measure than R&D, which is an input into the innovation process (see Criscuolo, Haskel, and Slaughter 2005). The D variables in equation (1) are full sets of regional (r), industry (j), and time (t) dummy variables.

X is a vector of firm-level determinants of innovation. It includes R&D intensity, the ratio of employee training expenditure to the total wage bill, export intensity, subsidies, age, and the firm's market share within its three-digit industry. The choice of these firm-level covariates is guided by theoretical considerations as well as evidence from the empirical literature. R&D is an important input into the innovation process and thus is included in the model. Human capital is also an important determinant of innovation. One proxy for human capital is the amount of training provided by a firm, which is included in the empirical analysis. Criscuolo, Haskel, and Slaughter (2005) provide evidence that firms that are active on export markets are more innovative than others. The model here captures this notion by controlling for firms' export intensities. Because subsidies can help firms engage more in innovation (see Görg and Strobl 2007), a measure of the level of production-related grants is also included in the model. As Jefferson and others (2006) argue, the age of a firm may also be important in explaining innovation activity (as a proxy for a firm's experience) and hence the possibility for learning effects. Their approach is adopted here by including firm age in the equation. Aghion and others (2005) discuss the role of competition for innovation; Aitken and Harrison (1999) show that multinationals may affect the competitive landscape in the domestic economy, leading to an increase in competition for domestic firms.

3. Definitions of all variables, plus summary statistics, are provided in table 1, discussed in the next section.

To take account of these findings, the model includes a firm's market share as an indicator of its competitive position.

FIN is a measure of a firm's access to finance (measured by its ability to obtain loans from domestic banks). Financial constraints are a serious impediment to innovation activity (Hall 2002). This effect may be particularly pronounced in China, where the financial sector is highly regulated and inefficient, and lending is skewed toward inefficient state-owned enterprises (Huang 2003).

FC is a measure of foreign capital participation in firm *i*. It captures the central concern of this article—the impact of FDI on innovative activity in Chinese domestic firms. *FC* is included to allow for the fact that firms with some share of foreign capital may be more innovative than other firms, for the reasons discussed above.

FDI is a vector of industry-region-specific FDI indices. It captures the potential spillover or crowding-out effects of FDI at the industry level. The effect of **FDI** is allowed to vary based on a firm's R&D activity and access to finance by including two interaction terms in the empirical estimation of equation (1), namely **FDI** and R&D intensity and **FDI** and *FIN*. The interaction of **FDI** and R&D intensity captures the notion that firms with higher absorptive capacity are better able to benefit from the technology transferred by incoming FDI.[4] The interaction of **FDI** and *FIN* allows firms with better access to finance to benefit more from inward FDI; because they are less financially constrained, they may be better able to implement the new technology and less affected by reductions in the availability of domestic finance caused by demand for loans by foreign firms.

All covariates in the empirical model are lagged by one period to mitigate potential endogeneity concerns. Nevertheless, some firm-level variables in the specification may be endogenous. One is R&D intensity, which is a major input into the product innovation process. The choice of this input is likely to be correlated with factors that determine the firm's decision to innovate. Similar arguments can be made regarding the potential endogeneity of the other firm-level variables. To deal with this possible problem, all lagged firm-level variables except age are considered potentially endogenous. The instrumental variables technique for Tobit models developed by Smith and Blundell (1986) is used to estimate this model.[5]

4. See Girma (2005) for a discussion of the importance of absorptive capacity and an empirical illustration using firm-level data for the United Kingdom.

5. The estimation of Tobit models with endogenous regressors involves two steps. The first is to generate residual terms from linear regressions of each endogenous variable on the instrumental variables and all other exogenous regressors. The second is to estimate a standard Tobit model by including the residual terms from the first step in the list of covariates. The standard errors are bootstrapped to take account of the fact that residual terms are generated regressors. The residual terms are correction terms for the endogeneity problem; jointly statistically significant coefficients can be taken as evidence in favor of the hypothesis that instrumented variables are indeed endogenous. A one-step variant of this estimator involving stronger distributional assumptions is also available (Newey 1987). However, it fails to attain convergence in the data used here. This type of convergence problem is frequently encountered when there is more than one endogenous regressor.

Twice-lagged values of the potentially endogenous variables are used as instruments. The assumption is that conditional on the regressors, these variables are asymptotically uncorrelated with the error term of the model. Ultimately, of course, this is an empirical issue, tested using the Sargan–Hansen test for the validity of instrumental variables.

Additional instruments are also used. They include the share of state-owned enterprises in a region or industry, the share of loss-making state-owned enterprises in a region or industry, the level of regional financial development (bank loans to the private sector as a share of total loans), and whether the firm is politically affiliated with local, regional, or central governments. These instruments are designed to account for the endogeneity of sector-level FDI and access to finance. The share of the state sector, for example, is a proxy for state dominance in the region or industry; to the extent that access to finance is different for state-dominated sectors and regions, this is a reasonable instrument for firm-level access to finance. Similar arguments can be made for the share of loss-making state-owned enterprises and the level of regional financial development.

A large number of enterprises in China are affiliated with some level of government administration. The function of the relevant government body is to offer credit guarantees and political protection to the affiliated firms. This political affiliation variable is strongly related to firms' access to finance, because China's financial system remains dominated by the four large state banks. Different levels of political affiliation are used as instruments to reflect the realistic assumption that the main effect of political affiliation on innovation comes through its effects on finance. Ultimately, however, the relevance of the instruments is an empirical issue that is tested for in the estimation below.

II. Description of the Database and Construction of Variables

The econometric analysis draws on confidential micro data that underlie the *Annual Reports of Industrial Enterprise Statistics*, compiled by the China National Bureau of Statistics. The reports cover all firms with annual turnover of more than 5 million yuan (about $600,000). The firms in the data set account for an estimated 85–90 percent of total output in most industries.

The data set includes information on firm ownership structure, industry affiliation, geographic location, establishment year, employment, gross output, product innovation, R&D, value added, net fixed assets, exports, and employee training expenditures.[6] The whole sample (1.3 million observations from about 446,000 firms) is used to construct the variables of interest (such as the share of foreign firms in an industry or region or firms' market share).

6. Nominal values are deflated using industry-specific ex-factory price indices obtained from the *China Statistical Yearbook 2006* (China National Bureau of Statistics 2007).

The econometric work is confined to domestic-owned enterprises, the focus of this article.

The China National Bureau of Statistics assigns a categorical variable to each firm in the database indicating its ownership status. It is also possible to construct a continuous measure of ownership composition from the database by looking at the fraction of paid-in capital contributed by the state and by private (domestic and foreign) investors. This measure of ownership is used here. Firms are defined as state-owned, collectively owned, or privately owned based on majority ownership of the firm. The information necessary for the econometric estimation is available for 239,085 domestic firms (630,900 total observations).

The data set provides information on the extent of foreign capital participation at the level of the firm. This makes it possible to calculate the share of foreign ownership in the domestic enterprise and identify the direct effects of FDI on domestic firms' innovative activity. A different method is used to estimate the indirect (spillover) effect of FDI at the industry level. For each of the 171 three-digit industries and 31 provinces, the proportion of output accounted for by companies with foreign ownership in the industry and region is calculated.[7] Alternative measures of industry and region FDI are the proportion of new products accounted for by multinational companies (labeled FDI innovation), and the share of domestic bank loans extended to foreign multinationals (FDI loan).

The data reveal no substantial relation between firm ownership on the one hand and innovation activity or the level of R&D on the other (table 1). As expected, on average state-owned enterprises receive higher shares of bank loans and larger subsidies from the government. They are less export intensive and receive more modest inflows of foreign capital than privately or collectively owned firms.

The pattern of product innovation by state-owned enterprises across industries at the two-digit reveals three noteworthy points (table 2). First, the proportion of innovating firms rose over time in most sectors. In contrast, the share of new product sales in total sales, while generally significant, declined slightly in most sectors. Second, labor-intensive sectors (such as food manufacturing and paper products) have the lowest proportion of innovators. In contrast, export-competing labor-intensive sectors (such as textiles) exhibit a

7. Officially, foreign-owned multinationals are defined as enterprises with at least a 25 percent share of foreign capital. Domestically owned enterprises that have foreign capital participation of less than 25 percent are not considered in this definition. The richness of the data set is exploited by weighing the output of firms with foreign capital by the extent of their foreign participation, measured by the share of foreign capital at the firm level. Under this definition of sectoral FDI, firms classified as domestic but that have some foreign capital also contribute (proportionally) to the aggregate output of the foreign sector. The recent literature on productivity spillovers from FDI notes that domestic firms may benefit not only from horizontal but also from vertical spillovers through customer–supplier linkages (see Javorcik 2004). Vertical measures (backward and forward spillovers) were calculated by the authors but found not to be consistently statistically significant. They are therefore not included in the analysis that follows.

TABLE 1. Variable Definitions and Summary Statistics

Variable	Definition		State-owned enterprise		Private enterprise		Collective enterprise	
			Mean	Standard deviation	Mean	Standard deviation	Mean	Standard deviation
Product innovation	Share of output involving new process or product innovation		0.041	0.150	0.034	0.151	0.021	0.116
	Restricted sample of firms with nonzero product innovation		0.319	0.295	0.390	0.350	0.369	0.331
R&D	R&D expenditure divided by sales		0.002	0.021	0.002	0.013	0.001	0.007
	Restricted sample of firms with nonzero R&D expenditure		0.013	0.046	0.012	0.337	0.008	0.018
Labor training	Employee training expenditure per employee		0.007	0.027	0.008	0.035	0.008	0.037
	Restricted sample of firms with nonzero labor training outlay		0.015	0.037	0.021	0.053	0.037	0.053
Export intensity	Share of exports in total sales		0.043	0.164	0.127	0.298	0.110	0.281
	Restricted sample of exporters		0.307	0.328	0.580	0.380	0.594	0.374
Market shares	Firm's share of sales in total three-digit industry region sales		0.044	0.134	0.022	0.082	0.021	0.073
Domestic finance	Domestic bank loans normalized by total assets		1.806	2.519	0.825	1.874	0.876	1.886
Subsidy	Log of production subsidy from local and central governments		0.983	2.335	0.642	1.843	0.796	2.052
Age	Log of years since establishment		3.147	0.914	1.848	0.935	2.569	0.806
Foreign capital	Share of foreign multinationals capital in firm's total capital		0.002	0.033	0.004	0.050	0.006	0.060
FDI	Share of foreign multinationals' sales in three-digit industry-region total sales		0.143	0.181	0.194	0.191	0.175	0.182
FDI innovation	Share of multinationals' innovative output in *three*-digit industry-region total innovation		0.097	0.196	0.140	0.212	0.127	0.206
FDI loan	Share of multinationals' domestic bank loans over total domestic bank loans		0.099	0.161	0.168	0.198	0.148	0.184
Number of firms		239,085	34,549		148,694		55,842	
Number of observations		630,900	125,357		316,461		189,082	

Source: Authors' analysis based on data from China National Bureau of Statistics.

TABLE 2. Sectoral and Temporal Pattern of Product Innovation by State-Owned Enterprises (percent)

	Share of innovators		New product sales as share of total sales	
Two-digit industry classification	1999	2005	1999	2005
13: Food processing	2.0	10.1	32.3	16.6
14: Food production	4.3	11.6	29.2	23.9
15: Beverage industry	6.0	12.0	27.2	25.1
16: Tobacco processing	12.3	21.1	14.9	15.2
17: Textile Industry	17.3	17.2	30.7	29.6
18: Garments and other fiber products	3.5	6.5	45.0	45.3
19: Leather, furs, down and related products	4.1	8.1	49.4	39.7
20: Timber processing	2.8	6.8	46.2	23.0
21: Furniture manufacturing	4.2	10.0	36.0	21.4
22: Papermaking and paper products	4.0	7.2	37.1	19.0
23: Printing and record medium reproduction	1.8	5.9	37.5	35.0
24: Cultural, educational, and sports goods	9.4	9.2	33.5	38.9
25: Petroleum refining and coking	5.0	6.4	28.9	20.9
26: Raw chemical materials and chemical products	9.2	10.7	31.3	33.2
27: Medical and pharmaceutical products	24	25.2	35.8	37.2
28: Chemical fiber	14.0	10.4	26.7	39.4
29: Rubber products	12	9.8	32.0	30.5
30: Plastic products	9.1	10.2	38.2	33.9
31: Nonmetal mineral products	3.7	10.7	38.1	23.0
32: Smelting and pressing of ferrous metals	5.8	6.9	29.6	24.8
33: Smelting and pressing of nonferrous metals	6.0	9.7	32.9	335
34: Metal products	6.1	7.9	33.4	31.1
35: Ordinary machinery	14.2	13.2	29.5	320
36: Special purpose equipment	17.8	17.2	34.8	37.3
37: Transport equipment	14.1	15.5	35.5	34.7
39: Other electronic equipment	14.8	14.0	36.1	41.8
40: Electric equipment and machinery	26.8	23.2	47.6	53.3
41: Electronic and telecommunications	25.7	25.7	35.3	46.0
42: Instruments and meters	5.7	7.0	39.2	33.0

Source: Authors' analysis based on data from China National Bureau of Statistics.

relatively large number of innovators. Third, the intensity of product innovation is remarkably similar across labor-intensive, capital-intensive, and technology-intensive sectors.

III. DISCUSSION OF THE RESULTS

The benchmark Tobit model controls for firm heterogeneity by allowing for firm random effects (table 3, column 1). The model also includes two additional dummy variables for private and collectively owned firms.

The estimation shows that R&D intensity exerts a positive and significant influence on the rate of product innovation. This is as expected, given that

TABLE 3. Innovation Spillovers from FDI and Access to Finance: Results from Alternative Estimators

Variable	(1) Random effects Tobit model	(2) Tobit instrumental variables model	(3) Linear generalized method of moment model
R&D	2.312*** (30.4)	4.323*** (19.0)	2.118*** (10.8)
Labor training	0.481*** (11.5)	0.862*** (7.22)	0.700*** (3.65)
Export intensity	0.252*** (39.3)	0.238*** (24.4)	0.217*** (18.5)
Market share	0.576*** (41.6)	0.600*** (29.7)	0.901*** (21.0)
Finance	0.0413*** (46.9)	0.0696*** (35.6)	0.0684*** (23.8)
Subsidy	0.0271*** (38.8)	0.0313*** (24.7)	0.0399*** (18.3)
Age	0.0505*** (27.4)	0.0487*** (19.2)	0.00197*** (6.69)
Foreign capital	0.135*** (6.85)	0.217*** (5.54)	0.168*** (3.65)
FDI	−0.643*** (−45.8)	−0.797*** (−35.3)	−0.500*** (−23.5)
FDI × R&D	1.428*** (88.1)	1.881*** (54.2)	1.241*** (26.1)
FDI × finance	0.153*** (8.22)	0.0922** (2.21)	−0.00929 (−1.51)
Private firms	0.0463*** (9.39)	0.0634*** (10.8)	0.0389*** (12.4)
Collective firms	−0.110*** (−21.9)	−0.0686*** (−11.5)	−0.0800*** (−7.15)
Number of observations	630,900	390,352	390,352
p-value from Hansen's test of overidentification			0.179

***Significant at the 1 percent level; **significant at the 5 percent level; *significant at the 10 percent level.

Note: All specifications include time, regional, and industry fixed effects. Numbers in parentheses are *t*-statistics. All regressors are lagged by one period in all regressions. The use of twice-lagged variables as instruments in the Tobit instrumental variables and linear generalized method of moments (GMM) models sharply reduced the number of observations in the estimations. State-owned firms form the base group in all regressions.

Source: Authors analysis based on data from China National Bureau of Statistics.

R&D intensity is a major input in the product innovation process. Firms that invest in employee training have higher innovation intensity, suggesting possible complementarity between human capital investment and innovation, as suggested by Redding (1996). Production innovation and exporting are positively correlated, and firms that enjoy higher market shares in their industry are more likely to engage in product innovation activity. Firms' receipt of subsidies is also positively related to innovation. These findings are in line with the literature. The results also suggest that older firms are more likely to engage in product innovation than their younger counterparts, possibly indicating the importance of experience in the innovation process.[8]

The results indicate that firms with some foreign capital participation are more likely to engage in product innovation. This effect may reflect the influx

8. In an analysis of a smaller sample of Chinese firms, Jefferson and others (2006) find no statistically significant relation between age and innovation. The sample used here is much larger and the estimation controls for a much larger number of covariates than the earlier study did.

of new technology or the reduction in financial constraints associated with the capital injection (the data do not allow the two hypotheses to be tested separately).[9] Access to finance is also positively associated with innovation. The magnitude of the effect of firm-level foreign capital is economically significant. A doubling of the foreign ownership share, for example, is associated with a 13.5 percentage point change in the share of new products in total output, all else equal. The economic significance of access to domestic finance is noteworthy: a one standard deviation (2.5 from table 1) increase in this variable leads to a 10 percentage point increase in innovation intensity.

Firms benefit from inward FDI only if they are actively engaged in R&D or have good access to domestic finance in the form of bank loans. If the point estimates are taken at face value, firms with R&D intensities of at least 0.45 (and no domestic bank loans) and firms with a ratio of bank loans to assets of at least 4.2 (and no R&D) benefit from FDI. These two threshold values are well beyond the mean values in the sample (reported in table 1).

The results in column 1 treat all variables as exogenous. This may not be too heroic an assumption, considering that all covariates are lagged one period, dummy variables for private and collectively owned firms are added, and unobserved firm-level heterogeneity is allowed for by including firm random effects. There may still be a lingering concern about endogeneity, however. This problem is addressed more formally by estimating the model using the endogenous Tobit model (column 2 in table 3). Of course, the reliability of the endogenous Tobit hinges on the validity of the instruments used. To the authors' knowledge, there are no formal tests of the validity of instruments within the context of these endogenous Tobit specifications. The appropriateness of the instruments is gauged by estimating a linear instrumental variables model (using the same set of instruments as in the endogenous Tobit) and obtaining a Sargan test statistic of the implied overidentifying restrictions. The test result, reported in column 3, suggests the validity of the instrumental variables. Reassuringly, the results of the estimations in both columns 2 and 3 are very much in line with the baseline equation in column 1, in terms of both the statistical significance and the magnitude of the coefficients. In the rest of the discussion the focus is therefore on estimations using the Tobit estimator allowing for firm random effects (column 1).

This estimation allows for firm-level heterogeneity, but it constrains the coefficients of the independent variables to be the same for all types of firms. This may be an unrealistic assumption given the large performance differences between state-owned and other types of enterprises in China. The ownership dimension of the data set is exploited to address the sample, which is broken into state-owned, private, and collectively owned enterprises (table 4).

9. Another reason why foreign-owned firms may be more innovative is that they tend to employ more highly skilled workers. The estimation partly controls for this possibility by controlling for the quality of the workforce using a variable on labor training.

TABLE 4. Estimates of FDI Spillovers and Access to Finance from Panel Tobit Models with Firm-Specific Heterogeneity

Variable	(1) State-owned firms	(2) Private firms	(3) Collectively owned firms	(4) Loss-making firms	(5) Profit-making firms
R&D	1.100*** (12.3)	2.857*** (24.3)	6.591*** (19.5)	1.034*** (8.27)	3.213*** (32.8)
Labor training	0.552*** (6.40)	0.464*** (7.84)	0.415*** (4.56)	0.345*** (2.99)	0.449*** (9.90)
Export intensity	0.363*** (25.5)	0.232*** (26.2)	0.274*** (19.2)	0.267*** (15.6)	0.252*** (36.4)
Market share	0.487*** (29.7)	0.535*** (22.8)	0.497*** (11.5)	0.435*** (14.8)	0.625*** (39.7)
Finance	0.0085*** (31.7)	0.0384*** (26.8)	0.0406*** (18.9)	0.0372 (0.66)	0.0470*** (46.7)
Subsidy	0.0235*** (24.3)	0.0335*** (29.8)	0.0163*** (9.69)	0.0243*** (14.7)	0.0268*** (34.9)
Age	0.0478*** (15.0)	0.0465*** (17.9)	0.0806*** (17.1)	0.0218*** (5.93)	0.0409*** (21.6)
Foreign capital	0.333*** (7.73)	0.0978*** (3.35)	0.135*** (3.45)	0.0816* (1.68)	0.123*** (5.68)
FDI	−0.502*** (−19.4)	−0.631*** (−32.0)	−0.838*** (−25.1)	−0.358*** (−10.9)	−0.684*** (−43.9)
FDI × R&D	1.106*** (42.8)	1.474*** (62.6)	1.560*** (38.5)	1.178*** (30.7)	1.478*** (82.2)
FDI × finance	0.0975 (1.42)	0.0575* (1.93)	0.250*** (5.50)	0.128 (1.21)	0.112*** (5.29)
Number of observations	125,357	316,461	189,082	117,001	513,899

***Significant at the 1 percent level; **significant at the 5 percent level; *significant at the 10 percent level.

Note: All specifications include time, regional, and industry fixed effects. Numbers in parentheses are t-statistics. All regressors are lagged by one period in all regressions.

Source: Authors' analysis based on data from China National Bureau of Statistics.

TABLE 5. Access to Finance by FDI Firms and Innovation Spillovers to Domestic Firms

Variable	(1) State-owned firms	(2) Private firms	(3) Collectively owned firms	(4) Loss-making firms	(5) Profit-making firms
R&D	0.823*** (7.99)	2.914*** (36.1)	5.197*** (24.1)	1.134*** (13.2)	2.591*** (42.0)
Labor training	0.250** (2.32)	0.338*** (8.32)	0.300*** (5.20)	0.294*** (3.71)	0.309*** (10.6)
Export intensity	0.247*** (13.3)	0.105*** (17.8)	0.133*** (15.5)	0.144*** (13.0)	0.119*** (27.0)
Market share	0.350*** (16.0)	0.460*** (27.4)	0.282*** (10.4)	0.347*** (17.1)	0.431*** (40.1)
Finance	0.0011*** (19.1)	0.0289*** (27.8)	0.0281*** (19.6)	0.028 (1.21)	0.0311*** (44.9)
Subsidy	0.0172*** (14.0)	0.0234*** (29.6)	0.0117*** (10.8)	0.0159*** (14.0)	0.0181*** (35.5)
Age	0.0309*** (7.51)	0.0404*** (21.6)	0.0590*** (19.2)	0.0383*** (13.6)	0.0437*** (30.8)
Foreign capital	0.205*** (3.23)	0.0542*** (2.64)	0.0737*** (2.92)	0.0698** (2.09)	0.0757*** (5.26)
FDI innovation	−0.0345** (−2.35)	−0.110*** (−9.01)	−0.0452*** (−2.72)	−0.091* (−1.82)	−0.034*** (−10.4)
FDI innovation × R&D	0.384*** (8.74)	0.518*** (24.3)	0.314*** (9.82)	0.409*** (11.7)	0.443*** (30.1)
FDI innovation × finance	−0.0191 (−0.91)	0.0205** (2.22)	0.0490** (2.75)	−0.0067 (−1.19)	0.0677** (2.46)
FDI loan	−0.190 (−1.49)	−0.493*** (−35.2)	−0.475*** (−22.3)	−0.277*** (−12.0)	−0.433*** (−42.1)
FDI loan × R&D	0.653*** (11.2)	0.828*** (36.3)	0.864*** (24.5)	0.735*** (17.8)	0.764*** (47.5)
FDI loan × finance	0.0026 (0.90)	0.0115** (2.03)	0.0378** (2.47)	−0.00185 (−0.26)	0.059** (2.57)
Number of observations	125,357	316,461	189,082	117,001	513,899

***Significant at the 1 percent level; **significant at the 5 percent level; *significant at the 10 percent level.

Note: All specifications include time, regional, and industry fixed effects. Numbers in parentheses are *t*-statistics. All regressors are lagged by one period in all regressions.

Source: Authors' analysis based on data from China National Bureau of Statistics.

Several striking differences are apparent across the three ownership types. First, the relation between access to finance and innovation is strongest among private and collectively owned firms, which receive less favorable treatment from China's financial system than state-owned enterprises do. Second, the coefficient on foreign capital is largest for state enterprises, suggesting that injections of foreign capital are associated with the highest positive impact on innovation for this type of firm. This may reflect the fact these state-owned firms are more inefficient than other firms and therefore offer the greatest opportunities for improvement as a result of the influx of foreign capital.[10] Third, and perhaps most striking, the interaction term of FDI and access to finance is positive for private and collectively owned firms but statistically insignificant for state-owned enterprises. Access to domestic finance plays no role in generating spillovers to state-owned enterprises, which are largely inefficient but enjoy preferential access to domestic financial resources.

Profit-making firms can be distinguished from loss-making firms, most of which are owned by the state (columns 4 and 5 in table 4). The results are in line with expectations: access to finance has no effect on innovation in loss-making enterprises, and also does not matter for indirect effects from sector-level inward FDI.[11]

Sector-level FDI can affect domestic innovation by transferring technology to or creating credit opportunities for domestic firms. The next step of the analysis tries to distinguish these two channels by calculating two different FDI measures. The first measure is aggregate innovation by foreign multinationals, calculated as innovation output by foreign multinationals in a sector or region divided by total innovation output. The second measure is aggregate borrowing by foreign multinationals, calculated as the share of domestic bank loans in total bank loans in the sector or region.

The results in columns 1–3 of table 5 show that the effects of the two variables are broadly similar to those for private and collectively owned firms. FDI has a positive effect only if the firm is active in R&D and has access to bank loans. State-owned enterprises that invest in their own R&D also benefit more from technology transfer by multinationals than those that do not, but the firms' financial position does not mitigate the effect of FDI technology. The effect of FDI on credit opportunities has no statistically significant relation with state enterprises' ability to innovate. This result suggests that preferential access to domestic financial resources means that finance is not a constraint for state enterprises.

In alternative estimations in columns 4 and 5, the data are broken into loss-making and profit-making enterprises. Results for loss-makers closely resemble

10. This result is in line with the work by Bartel and Harrison (2005) that shows state-owned enterprises in Indonesia benefit greatly from foreign ownership in the enterprise.

11. As a robustness check, table 4 was reestimated using the endogenous Tobit estimator. The results are very similar and hence not reported here.

those for state-owned enterprises, suggesting that access to finance has little effect on innovation for such firms.[12]

IV. Conclusions

The econometric analysis conducted here shows that access to finance is an important issue for firms' innovation activity and their ability to benefit from inward FDI. This is mainly the case for private and collectively owned firms, however. It is far less important for state-owned firms, which receive preferential treatment under the current domestic financial system.

Firms with foreign capital participation and those with good access to domestic bank loans—that is, firms with less binding financial constraints—innovate more than others. Inward FDI at the sectoral level is positively associated with domestic innovative activity only if firms engage in their own R&D activities (that is, have some absorptive capacity) or have good access to domestic finance. This finding points to the possible adverse effect of domestic credit constraints on firms' ability to benefit from inward FDI. Grouping firms by ownership type reveals that access to finance plays a role only among firms that are not state owned. Although state-owned enterprises are largely inefficient, they enjoy preferential access to domestic financial resources; access to finance thus provides no bottleneck for them.

Sector-level inward FDI has two effects. It transfers technology and may increase domestic credit opportunities. The effect on credit is of very little significance for state-owned enterprises and is independent of their access to finance. In contrast, it is an important channel through which FDI affects the innovation of domestic private and collectively owned enterprises.

References

Aghion, Philippe, Nicholas Bloom, Richard Blundell, Rachel Griffith, and Peter Howitt. 2005. "Competition and Innovation: An Inverted-U Relationship." *Quarterly Journal of Economics* 120(2):701–28.

Aitken, Brian J., and Ann E. Harrison. 1999. "Do Domestic Firms Benefit from Direct Foreign Investment? Evidence from Venezuela." *American Economic Review* 89(3):605–18.

Amiti, Mary, and Beata S. Javorcik. 2008. "Trade Costs and Location of Foreign Firms in China." *Journal of Development Economics* 85(1–2):129–49.

Bartel, Ann P., and Ann E. Harrison. 2005. "Ownership versus Environment: Disentangling the Sources of Public-Sector Inefficiency." *Review of Economics and Statistics* 87(1):135–47.

Berthelemy, Jean-Claude, and Sylvie Demurger. 2000. "Foreign Direct Investment and Economic Growth: Theory and Application to China." *Review of Development Economics* 4(2):140–55.

China National Bureau of Statistics. 2006. *Annual Reports of Industrial Enterprise Statistics.* Beijing.

12. One other robustness check was conduced, which included squared terms of foreign capital, FDI innovation, and FDI loans in the estimations. The results, which are not reported here, are robust to this slight modification of the estimating equation.

———. 2007. *China Statistical Yearbook 2006*. Beijing: China Statistics Press.

Criscuolo, Chiara, Jonathan E. Haskel, and Matthew J. Slaughter. 2005. *Global Engagement and the Innovation Activities of Firms*. NBER Working Paper 11479. Cambridge, Mass.: National Bureau of Economic Research.

Girma, Sourafel. 2005. "Absorptive Capacity and Productivity Spillovers from FDI: A Threshold Regression Analysis." *Oxford Bulletin of Economics and Statistics* 67(3):281–306.

Girma, Sourafel, and Yundan Gong. Forthcoming. "FDI, Linkages and the Efficiency of State-Owned Enterprises in China." *Journal of Development Studies*.

Görg, Holger, and David Greenaway. 2004. "Much Ado about Nothing? Do Domestic Firms Really Benefit from Foreign Direct Investment?" *World Bank Research Observer* 19(2):171–97.

Görg, Holger, and Eric Strobl. 2007. "The Effect of R&D Subsidies on Private R&D." *Economica* 74(294):215–34.

Hall, Bronwyn H. 2002. "The Financing of Research and Development." *Oxford Review of Economic Policy* 18(1):35–51.

Harrison, Ann E., and Margaret S. McMillan. 2003. "Does Direct Foreign Investment Affect Domestic Credit Constraints?" *Journal of International Economics* 61(1):73–100.

Hu, Albert G. Z., Gary H. Jefferson, and Jinchang Qian. 2005. "R&D and Technology Transfer: Firm-Level Evidence from Chinese Industry." *Review of Economics and Statistics* 87(4):780–86.

Huang, Yasheng. 2003. *Selling China: Foreign Direct Investment during the Reform Era*. New York: Cambridge University Press.

Javorcik, Beata S. 2004. "Does Foreign Direct Investment Increase the Productivity of Domestic Firms? In Search of Spillovers through Backward Linkages." *American Economic Review* 94(3):605–27.

Jefferson, Gary H., Bai Huamao, Guan Xiaojing, and Yu Xiaoyun. 2006. "R&D Performance in Chinese Industry." *Economics of Innovation and New Technology* 15(4–5):345–36.

Keller, Wolfgang. 2004. "International Technology Diffusion." *Journal of Economic Literature* 42(3):752–82.

Lemoine, Françoise. 2000. "FDI and the Opening Up of China's Economy." CEPII Working Paper 2000-11. Centres d'Etudes Prospectives et d'Informations Internationales, Paris.

Markusen, James R. 2002. *Multinational Firms and the Theory of International Trade*. Cambridge, Mass.: MIT Press.

Newey, Whitney K. 1987. "Efficient Estimation of Limited Dependent Variables Models with Endogenous Explanatory Variables." *Journal of Econometrics* 36(3):231–50.

OECD (Organisation for Economic Co-operation and Development). 2004. *Trends and Recent Developments in Foreign Direct Investment*. Directorate for Financial, Fiscal and Enterprise Affairs, Paris.

Pack, Howard. 2006. "Econometric vs. Case Study Approaches to Technology Transfer." In Bernard M. Hoekman, and Beata S. Javorcik, eds., *Global Integration and Technology Transfer*. London, United Kingdom: Palgrave Macmillan and World Bank.

Redding, Stephen. 1996. "The Low-Skill, Low-Quality Trap: Strategic Complementarities between Human Capital and R&D." *Economic Journal* 106(March):458–70.

Smith, Richard J., and Richard W. Blundell. 1986. "An Exogeneity Test for a Simultaneous Equation Tobit Model with an Application to Labor Supply." *Econometrica* 54(4):679–86.

Wei, Yingqi. 2003. "Foreign Direct Investment in China." Working Paper 2003/002. Lancaster University Management School, United Kingdom.

Chapter 6

'FOOTLOOSE' MULTINATIONALS?*

by
HOLGER GÖRG
Leverhulme Centre for Research on Globalisation and Economic Policy, University of Nottingham
and
ERIC STROBL[†]
CORE, Université catholique de Louvain

We examine whether multinational companies are more footloose than their domestic counterparts in the host country, using data for the Irish manufacturing sector. First, we investigate whether plant survival rates differ between multinationals and indigenous plants. Second, we analyse whether employment is more unstable in multinationals. As regards the first aspect we find that multinationals are more likely to exit the market than indigenous plants when we control for other plant- and industry-specific characteristics. In terms of employment persistence we find that new jobs generated in multinational companies appear to be more persistent than jobs generated in indigenous plants. In contrast, they are not any more or less likely to reverse employment reductions, all other things being equal.

1 Introduction

It is frequently argued that multinational companies are inherently footloose, i.e. they can react almost instantaneously to adverse changes in the host country and shift their production facilities or parts thereof to another country if the present environment changes to their disadvantage (see Caves, 1996). This assumption of multinationals being footloose is based on the nature of multinationals, as only production processes that are easily transferable between countries can profitably be located abroad. This makes it easier for multinational companies to shift production from one host country to another than it is for the average indigenous firm in the host country to relocate production.

Flamm (1984) provides evidence for the footloose nature of US foreign direct investment in the semiconductor industry. His theoretical and empirical analysis shows that adjustments by US multinationals to changes in the

*Manuscript received 5.2.01; final version received 23.1.02.
[†]We are grateful to Katharine Wakelin, participants at a GEP Research Workshop at Nottingham and an anonymous referee for helpful comments on an earlier draft. All remaining errors are, of course, our own. Financial support through the European Commission Fifth Framework Programme (Grant HPSE-CT-1999-00017) and the Leverhulme Trust (Grant F114/BF) is gratefully acknowledged.

Published by Blackwell Publishers Ltd, 9600 Garsington Road, Oxford OX4 2DQ, and 350 Main Street, Malden, MA 02148, USA.

host country environment in terms of, for example, production costs or risks are 'extremely rapid' (p. 232). In discussing multinationals in the UK, Hood and Young (1997) argue that multinational companies may be more footloose than UK-owned firms due to their having only shallow roots in the host country economy. Cowling and Sugden (1999) also point to potential problems for host country development due to the footloose nature of multinationals' investment. Such multinationals may introduce an unstable element in the host economy by transferring production and/or production facilities out of the host country easily.

In this paper we analyse empirical evidence to investigate whether multinational companies located in the Republic of Ireland also show signs of being highly 'footloose'. Ireland is a particularly interesting case study given that its manufacturing industry is heavily dependent on foreign multinational companies. The importance of multinational companies for the Irish economy is now reflected in the fact that, in the manufacturing sector, foreign plants accounted for 47 per cent of employment, 77 per cent of net output produced and 83 per cent of total exports in Ireland in 1995 (Central Statistics Office, 1997).[1] Also, the official statistics show that about half of employment in foreign-owned plants is in US multinationals.

Our paper is somewhat related to an early study by McAleese and Counahan (1979). They analysed whether foreign multinationals in Ireland reduced employment during the recession in the early 1970s to a larger extent than indigenous plants, i.e. whether multinationals were faster to adjust employment levels following an adverse shock than were Irish-owned plants. Their evidence showed that employment adjustment in multinational companies during the recession did not appear to have been different from that of indigenous plants, while employment recovery after the recession was actually greater in multinational companies than in Irish-owned plants. Our paper investigates this issue further by taking two different angles. First we analyse, using a Cox proportional hazard model, whether survival rates for foreign and Irish-owned plants are different, i.e. whether foreign plants are more likely to exit than are domestic plants when we control for other plant- and industry-specific factors. Second, using a similar hazard model framework we examine whether jobs generated or destroyed in multinational companies are more persistent than jobs generated or destroyed in Irish-owned plants.

The paper is structured as follows. Section 2 describes the data used for the empirical analysis. Section 3 presents empirical results of the analysis of plant survival, estimating survival functions as well as a Cox proportional hazard model. Section 4 presents the empirical results of our analysis of differences in the persistence of employment changes between foreign and

[1]The effects of the large multinational presence on the Irish economy and, in particular, on the development of domestic plants have been analysed by Görg and Strobl (2002a, 2002b) and Barry and Bradley (1997).

indigenous plants. Our main results are summarized, and conclusions presented, in Section 5.

2 Description of the Data

In the empirical analysis we use data from the Employment Survey which is carried out annually by Forfás, the policy and advisory board for industrial development in Ireland. The survey has been undertaken since 1973 and data are available to us for the period 1973–96. The main advantages of the survey are that it covers virtually all known active manufacturing companies and that the response rate is generally over 99 per cent, thus providing a sample of over 15,000 plants. The unit of observation is the individual plant, for which nationality of ownership,[2] sector of location,[3] start-up year and the number of permanent full-time employed, amongst other things, are reported. This allows us to calculate annual net changes in employment levels at the level of the plant.

Given the nature of the survey we can interpret a plant's dropping out of the data as an exit. Each plant is identified by a unique plant number which is only changed if there is an actual change of ownership. This implies that we are not able to distinguish births and deaths from takeovers. While this may create some problems in terms of misrepresenting the importance of plant births and deaths, we suspect that, as a whole, takeovers would result in only negligible measurement errors in our calculations. This is because most foreign direct investment in Ireland has been in the form of greenfield investment, i.e. the setting up of entirely new plants, rather than takeovers of existing domestic plants (see Barry and Bradley, 1997).[4]

Table 1 provides summary measures of the foreign and indigenous subsectors of Irish manufacturing for the years 1973, 1984 and 1996. It should be noted that the foreign multinational sector has steadily increased its share of manufacturing employment from roughly 33 to 45 per cent. The number of foreign multinationals is substantially smaller than that of indigenous plants resulting in a considerably larger average size for foreign plants. Additionally, while there was a notable average age difference at the start of our sample period between indigenous and foreign plants, this has now largely disappeared.

[2]A plant is classified as being foreign-owned if 50 per cent or more of its shares are held by foreign owners.

[3]For the purpose of this paper we classify plants into the standard 68 subsectors of Irish manufacturing used by the Central Statistics Office over the period.

[4]We are also not able to identify takeovers by other domestic plants. However, consultation with the Irish Development Authority (IDA) leads us to believe that this was not a frequent occurrence in Irish manufacturing, especially since the IDA provided generous grants for indigenous start-ups but not for takeovers.

TABLE 1
DESCRIPTIVE STATISTICS

Ownership		*1973*	*1984*	*1996*
Indigenous	Employment	151741	126687	120728
	Plants	4039	6448	5830
	Age	21	17	19
	Size	38	20	21
Foreign	Employment	73827	80550	97559
	Plants	619	861	837
	Age	16	15	20
	Size	119	94	117

3 PLANT SURVIVAL

If multinationals are footloose they can be expected to be more likely to exit the host country following a negative shock than are domestic plants. We therefore examine the probabilities of plant survival, distinguishing foreign and Irish-owned plants in this section. As a first step in examining and comparing plant survival across the two nationality groups we calculate Kaplan–Meier survival functions, given by

$$S(t) = \prod_{j|t_j \le t} \left(\frac{n_j - d_j}{n_j} \right) \tag{1}$$

where n_t is the population alive and d_t is the number of failures respectively at time t. These are graphed in Fig. 1, comparing foreign and indigenous plants. A glance at the functions may suggest that these do not appear to be substantially different, with that of foreign plants lying marginally above that of their indigenous counterparts. However, a log rank test for the equality of survival functions can decisively reject the hypothesis that the two survival functions are equal (the χ^2 text statistic is 8.89, significant at the 1 per cent level). Based on this graph we may therefore conclude that foreign plants have higher survival rates than domestic plants, which is just the opposite of what we would have expected to find if multinationals were more footloose than their domestic counterparts. We thus find that, in a comparison of all domestic and foreign plants, multinationals do not appear to be more footloose than domestic plants.

Such an aggregated graph does not, of course, allow us to take into consideration other factors affecting plant survival that may be unequally distributed across foreign and indigenous plants. Therefore, in order to properly disentangle the role of other plant- and industry-specific factors from nationality on the survivability of plants we turn to a semiparametric modelling of plants' hazard rates. Following the related empirical literature (e.g. Mata and Portugal, 1994; Audretsch and Mahmood, 1995) we utilize a Cox proportional hazard model (Cox, 1972) for the empirical analysis of this issue.

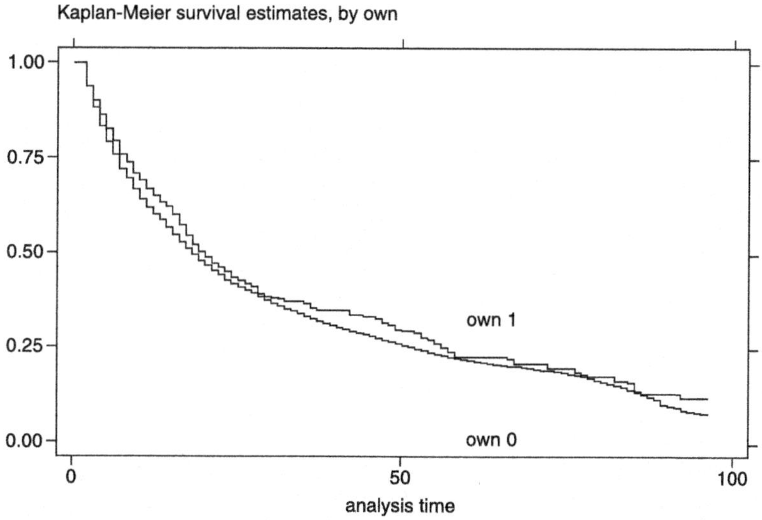

FIG. 1 Kaplan–Meier Plant Survival Functions by Nationality of Ownership
Note: own 1, foreign ownership; own 0, Irish ownership.

The Cox proportional hazard model specifies the hazard function $h(t)$, which is the rate at which plants exit at time t given that they have survived in $t-1$, to be

$$h(t) = h_0(t)\exp(\alpha\text{OWN} + \beta X + \gamma X * \text{OWN}) \qquad (2)$$

where h_0 is the baseline hazard function (the parametric form of which is not specified) when all of the covariates are set to zero. X is a vector of covariates assumed to capture the effect of plant and industry characteristics on survival by including a number of variables generally used in the literature and as available from our data set. In order to examine whether foreign plants' survival differs from that of domestic plants we include a dummy OWN which takes the value of one if the plant is foreign-owned and zero otherwise. If foreign firms are more footloose than domestic firms we would not only expect this dummy to indicate that foreign firms have a higher hazard of exiting than domestic firms but also expect that foreign firms are likely to react differently to changes in the other factors affecting plant survival. In order to capture the latter aspect of being footloose we include interaction terms of the ownership dummy with all covariates in X. This vector includes the following variables.[5]

[5]Equation (2) also includes time dummies to control for year-specific macroeconomic effects.

SIZE is the plant's size in terms of employment at time *t*. This variable is included as it can now be considered to be a stylized fact that small plants generally have lower probabilities of survival than large plants (see, for example, Dunne and Hughes, 1994; Audretsch and Mahmood, 1995). Also, Mata *et al.* (1995) find that current plant size is a better predictor of failure than initial size and we therefore include size at time *t* in our regression.

The minimum efficient scale of the industry, MES, is measured as the log of median employment size in sector *j* as in Sutton (1991).[6] Our *a priori* expectation as to the sign of the coefficient is ambiguous. On the one hand, one may expect plants entering industries with large MES to have lower probabilities of survival than plants entering other industries, as small entrants may find it difficult to attain the efficient level of production unless they experience sufficient growth in their infancy (Audretsch, 1991). On the other hand, as Audretsch (1991) points out, industries with high MES are usually also industries showing high price–cost margins, which should increase survival.

HERF denotes the Herfindahl index of sector *j*, which is found to be a significant explanatory variable in the study of plant survival in Portugal undertaken by Mata and Portugal (1994). Again, the expectation of the effect of market concentration on survival is not clear-cut. Higher market concentration may lead to higher price–cost margins in the industry which, *ceteris paribus*, should increase a plant's probability of survival. However, plants in highly concentrated markets may be subject to fierce aggressive behaviour by rivals which may reduce chances of survival.

SGROWTH is the net sectoral growth rate measured in terms of employment growth. Audretsch (1991) argues that industry growth may elevate the price above the long-run average cost, i.e. increase plants' price–cost margin, which, all other things equal, would affect survival rates positively. The sectoral growth rate also allows us to control for other sector-specific cyclical effects which may impact on plant survival.

Our results for estimating various specifications of equation (2) on our data set are given in Table 2. The log-likelihood and Wald tests do not indicate that our estimations suffer from misspecification. All estimations are stratified by sector, which allows for equal coefficients across strata (sectors) but baseline hazards unique to each stratum (sector).[7] It should be noted that, since the coefficients are those of a hazard model, a positive coefficient indicates that the respective covariate decreases the probability of survival

[6]In an alternative specification we defined MES as (the log of) average plant size in the industry. These results, which are not reported here but can be obtained from the authors upon request, yield similar results to the results obtained using average plant size. We are not able to calculate any additional alternative measures of MES due to lack of appropriate data.

[7]In effect, this is comparable to the inclusion of sectoral dummies in a standard ordinary least squares regression.

TABLE 2
DETERMINANTS OF PLANT SURVIVAL

	(i)	(ii)
SIZE	−0.007***	−0.009***
	(0.000)	(0.001)
MES	0.006	0.020
	(0.010)	(0.013)
HERF	0.001***	0.001***
	(0.000)	(0.000)
SGROWTH	−1.144***	−0.940***
	(0.172)	(0.181)
OWN	—	0.231***
		(0.059)
SIZE*OWN	—	0.003***
		(0.001)
MES*OWN	—	−0.025
		(0.017)
HERF*OWN	—	0.000
		(0.001)
SGROWTH*OWN	—	−1.703***
		(0.444)
Observations	144015	144015
LR test (RES vs UNRES)		75.4***
Log likelihood	−73242.97	−73182.42
Wald test	1419.22***	1540.31***

Notes: Standard errors in parentheses. LR, likelihood ratio; RES, restricted model; UNRES, unrestricted model.
*, **, *** denote statistical significance at the 10, 5, 1 per cent level respectively.

(increases the hazard of exiting) while a negative coefficient indicates a positive effect on survival, all other things being equal.

Column (i) presents the results of estimating equation (2) including only the vector of covariates X as an initial check to see how plant and industry characteristics affect plant survival in our sample. Plant size turns out to affect survival positively, i.e. small plants face a higher hazard of exit than do large plants. As pointed out above, this is a fairly standard finding in studies of firm survival. Our results also suggest that, the higher the level of concentration in the industry, the less likely a plant is to survive. This may indicate that plants in highly concentrated markets may be subject to fierce aggressive behaviour by rivals which reduces chances of survival. The coefficient of MES, another variable picking up industry characteristics, is statistically insignificant in the estimation, although, perhaps, the concentration variable may be capturing the effect of MES. As outlined above, one would expect that concentrated industries sustain higher price–cost margins; however, highly concentrated industries are also likely to be those with a high MES. Not surprisingly, we find that benevolent economic sectoral conditions, as measured by the sectoral growth rate, decrease the hazard of plant exit. In other words, fast growing markets appear to increase plant survival. This finding is in line with Mata and Portugal (1994) who also find that, for Portuguese firms, fast growing markets make survival easier for new entrants.

Given that the main focus of this paper is on differences across nationality of ownership we re-estimated equation (2) including OWN and terms interacting OWN with all other covariates. The dummy on its own measures whether foreign plants have different survival rates than indigenous plants after controlling for other explanatory factors, while the interaction terms allow for a different impact of the covariates on plant survival for foreign plants. It is first important to note that a likelihood ratio test of the equivalence of the unrestricted model (namely, that which allows for different intercept and slope coefficients across ownership type) versus the restricted model provides support for the unrestricted version. Based on the test statistic (75.4) we can reject the equivalence of the two models at the 1 per cent level. Thus, it is important to allow for different coefficients for foreign and indigenous plants when estimating plant survival.

Turning to the detailed results provided in the second column of Table 2, it should be noted that the coefficient on the ownership dummy is statistically significant and positive, suggesting that foreign plants have a lower rate of survival than domestic plants. In order to be able to interpret the magnitude of this coefficient we can calculate the hazard ratio by calculating the exponentiated coefficient. For the case of a dummy variable covariate, equation (2) shows that calculating the exponential of the coefficient α generates the increase in the hazard ratio for the case when OWN equals 1, holding everything else constant. Thus calculating the hazard ratio for the coefficient on OWN yields 1.36, indicating that the hazard of exiting is approximately 1.4 times higher for foreign than for domestic plants. Hence, while the Kaplan–Meier survival functions above suggested that foreign plants have higher survival rates our regression results indicate that, once we control for other factors, foreign plants have a higher chance of exiting than their indigenous counterparts. In the context of our discussion in this paper this indicates that foreign plants are more footloose than indigenous plants. This may be due to the fact that, all other things being equal, a foreign multinational company may find it easier to transfer production facilities from one country to another than a comparable indigenous plant.

From the interaction terms we also find that two of the covariates, namely SIZE and SGROWTH, have different effects on the survival of foreign and domestic plants. The statistically significant negative coefficient on SIZE*OWN indicates that the size effect (i.e. the increase in survival probability as the plant becomes larger) is less for foreign plants than for their domestic counterparts. Again, this provides evidence that it is easier for foreign plants to move their production facility abroad, irrespective of the size of the plant. On the other hand, the positive effect of a growing sector on plant survival is even stronger for foreign plants than for domestic ones.

This implies that foreign plants in a declining industry are more likely to exit than domestic plants in the same industry. We may also interpret this as a sign that foreign firms are more footloose, as they appear more likely to leave if sectoral conditions change adversely.

4 Employment Persistence

Having established that multinationals are more likely to exit than domestic plants, *ceteris paribus*, we examine whether there are differences between foreign and indigenous plants in the persistence of employment generated or destroyed as a second step in assessing whether multinational companies are more footloose than their domestic counterparts. Given that multinational companies are more likely to exit than domestic plants one might also expect that employment adjustments in multinationals are less persistent.

However, in forming priors as to whether multinationals are more likely to adjust employment temporarily one could also appeal to human capital theory (as outlined by, for example, Parsons, 1986), which stresses that plants and workers may find it advantageous to invest in the development of plant-specific human capital. This is because higher skilled labour provides returns to both the worker (in terms of higher wages) and the plant (in terms of higher productivity). Consequently the rate of separation between employer and employee should be lower for high skilled workers than for low skilled workers, i.e. jobs are more persistent in the case of the former. This, in turn, has implications for employment persistence in multinational companies since multinationals, due to their plant-specific assets (Caves, 1996), can be expected to use a higher level of technology than indigenous plants. Since the use of a higher technology necessitates the presence of more skilled labour, multinationals will find it profitable to make an organizational capital investment in order to provide training for workers to develop their human capital and use it efficiently in the plant. This human capital investment will increase workers' productivity. Hence, there will be lower separation rates, and higher costs of labour adjustment, for multinationals than for indigenous plants (which use lower levels of technology). This implies higher persistence of jobs in multinationals.

To investigate the issue of employment persistence empirically we make use of the fact that our data set allows us to identify net changes in the level of employment in a plant between two years. We can thus identify positive and negative net employment changes at the plant level and track whether these adjustments persist over time. In evaluating these we are faced with a number of obstacles, however. First, our data set only allows us to identify the level of employment, but not the underlying job types. Thus even though, for example, an increase in employment of 10 may still persist at some future point, we are unable to identify whether the actual structure of employment has changed, i.e. whether these 10 jobs that persist until $t + s$ are the same as those created at time t. For the purposes here we assume that jobs are homogeneous within plants so that changes in the level are equivalent to changes in jobs.

Second, in order to evaluate persistence in employment changes analogously to our study of plant survival in the previous section, i.e. using a hazard model, we need to identify a reversal of an employment adjustment as either occurring or not occurring. A plant, however, may only partially reverse its original employment decision. We thus first treat even a partial reversal as the outcome 'reversal of the original decision'. In order to check whether this biases our results we subsequently consider only a complete reversal of the original change as a reversal. This provides a more stringent definition of reversal, namely that only if all employment gained (lost) is subsequently re-lost (re-gained) is the original adjustment reversed. For example, if a plant increases employment from 10 to 20 at time t, then if at time $t + 1$ employment is any less than 20 our approach is to consider the original decision reversed under the first more flexible definition. In contrast, we only consider the original decision reversed if employment at time $t + 1$ falls below 10 under the more stringent definition. Finally, given that our plant survival analysis in the previous section already deals with plant entry and subsequent exit, we only consider employment adjustments and their (potential) reversal in continuing plants.[8]

We first calculated simple Kaplan–Meier functions of the persistence of employment creation and destruction in foreign and domestic plants using equation (1) for the case where a partial re-gain (re-loss) is considered a 'reversal', i.e. the more flexible definition of reversal. These functions are depicted in Figs 2 and 3, respectively. As can be seen, employment creation persistence is clearly higher for foreign plants one year after the adjustment. The difference increases until about five years after the event and then remains fairly stable although overall the survival rates are decreasing at a decreasing rate. The difference in these survivor functions is also supported by a log rank test of equivalence (the χ^2 statistic is 129.7, significant at the 1 per cent level). In contrast, the difference between the survivor function of employment losses is much smaller, with that of foreign plants being marginally higher. As matter of fact, a log rank test of equivalence (χ^2 statistic 2.5) does not allow one to conclude that these are significantly different.

In Figs 4 and 5 we also graphed the Kaplan–Meier survival function for the case of the more stringent definition of employment change reversal. As

[8]This means that we do not take account of jobs created due to plant birth and death and also that non-reversed employment adjustments are considered truncated from the sample once a plant exits. As pointed out by Davis and Haltiwanger (1992) for the USA, and supported by Strobl (1996) for Ireland, plant exit only comprises a small proportion of total employment loss in any period. Rather, most of the employment adjustment observed at the micro-level is due to continuing plants continuously readjusting their employment level to aggregate, sectoral and idiosyncratic temporary and permanent shocks.

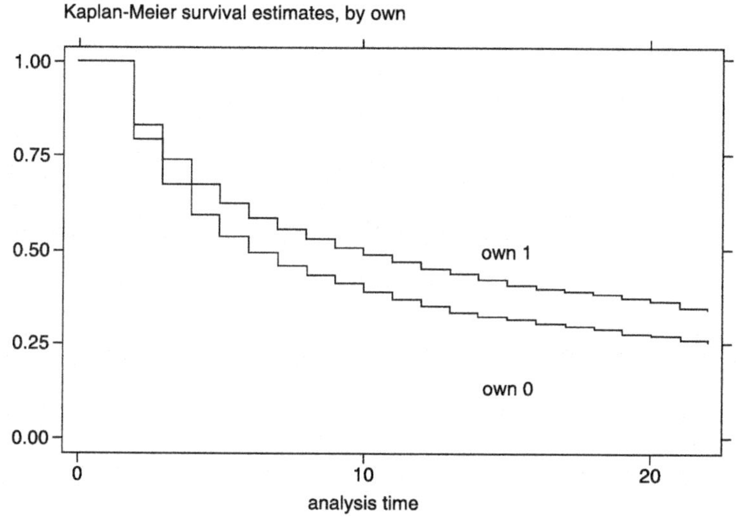

FIG. 2 Kaplan–Meier Survival Functions of Employment Creation Persistence by Nationality of Ownership (Partial Reversal)
Note: own 1, foreign ownership; own 0, Irish ownership.

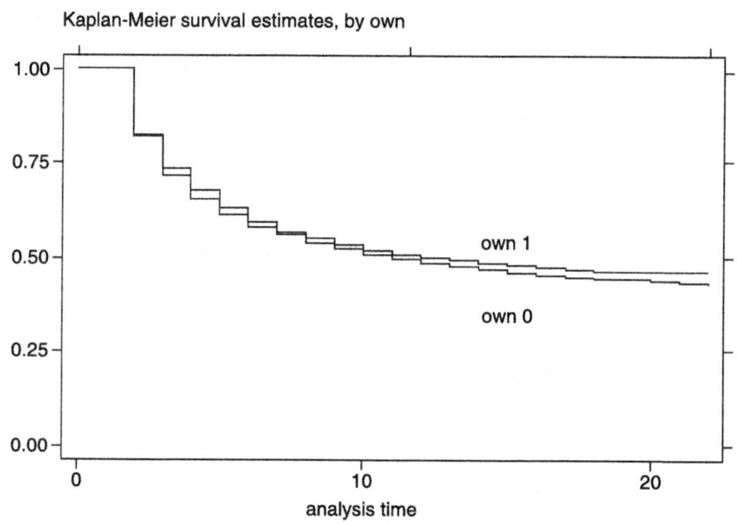

FIG. 3 Kaplan–Meier Survival Functions of Employment Destruction Persistence by Nationality of Ownership (Partial Reversal)
Note: own 1, foreign ownership; own 0, Irish ownership.

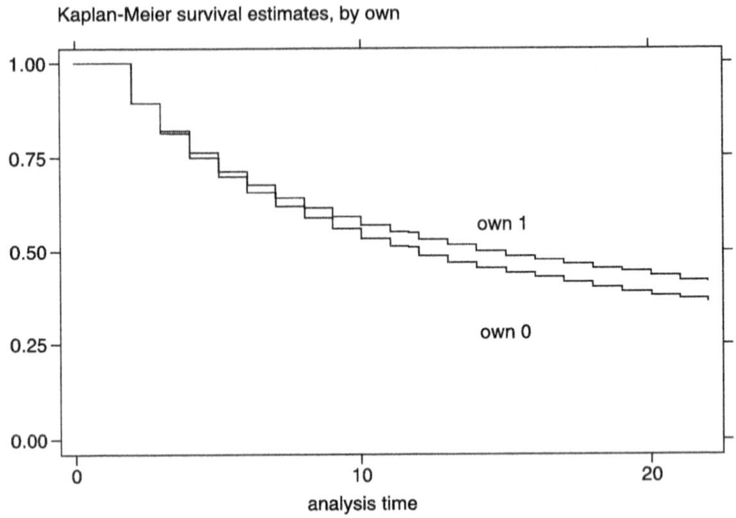

FIG. 4 Kaplan–Meier Survival Functions of Employment Creation Persistence by Nationality of Ownership (Complete Reversal)
Note: own 1, foreign ownership; own 0, Irish ownership.

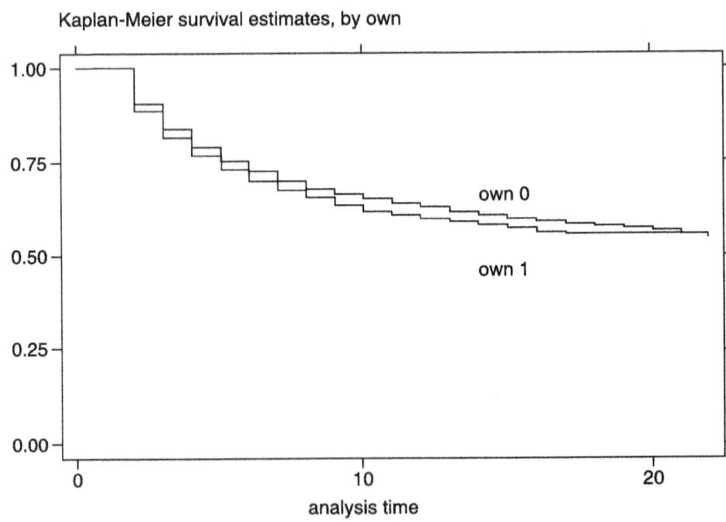

FIG. 5 Kaplan–Meier Survival Functions of Employment Destruction Persistence by Nationality of Ownership (Complete Reversal)
Note: own 1, foreign ownership; own 0, Irish ownership.

would be expected given the more stringent condition for reversal, here the survival rates are higher for both employment creation and destruction. For employment creation the difference in the series is not as pronounced as in the earlier graph, and only really becomes apparent after five years and seems to be slowly increasing thereafter. Nevertheless, a log rank test ($\chi^2 = 18.2$, significant at the 1 per cent level) indicates that, as with our more relaxed definition, the survivor functions for foreign and domestic plants are not identical. For the case of employment destruction, we now find that the survival rate of employment losses is higher for domestic plants, suggesting that foreign plants are more likely to recover from negative shocks to employment. This is supported by a log rank test of equivalence which rejects the hypothesis that the two functions are identical (the χ^2 statistic is 10.7, significant at the 1 per cent level).

Thus, without controlling for other factors, these graphs suggest that jobs created in foreign firms appear more likely to persist than those created in domestic plants, irrespective of whether we consider total or only partial reversals of job creations. On the other hand, when to consider a reduction in employment as being reversed may be important in terms of considering whether foreign plants are more or less likely to recover lost jobs. While there does not appear to be a perceptible difference in the persistence of jobs lost in domestic or foreign plants under the flexible definition (i.e. considering partial reversal) foreign plants seem more likely to recover all or more jobs lost in a previous period. This may suggest that when one considers re-gaining lost employment, foreign plants are more likely to re-gain all jobs lost previously.

As with plant survival, there are, of course, likely to be other factors affecting the persistence of employment changes and it is important to control for these as they may be correlated with the type of ownership of the plant. Thus, analogously to the investigation of differences in plant survival, we estimated a Cox proportional hazard model as in equation (2). In estimating equation (2) for employment creation and employment destruction persistence we similarly used the same explanatory variables, except that we also included plant age and RATE, a variable defined as the (absolute value) of the employment change relative to level of employment at the time of the adjustment. The latter variable is intended to control for the importance of the employment change undertaken relative to the size of the plant and hence can serve as an indicator of the size of the shock which induced the change and the adjustment costs involved. Plant size and age as well as the sectoral variables described above are included in the estimation since Davis *et al.* (1996) show that job persistence may differ between firms with different sizes and ages, and between sectors. We therefore chose to control for these factors in our analysis also.

Table 3 presents the results of estimating the Cox proportional hazard model for employment creation persistence. In line with the analysis of plant

TABLE 3
DETERMINANTS OF EMPLOYMENT CREATION PERSISTENCE

	(i) Partial reversal	*(ii) Complete reversal*	*(iii) Partial reversal*	*(iv) Complete reversal*
SIZE	–0.002***	–0.003***	–0.004***	–0.004***
	(0.000)	(0.000)	(0.000)	(0.000)
AGE	0.008***	0.008***	0.009***	0.008***
	(0.000)	(0.000)	(0.000)	(0.000)
RATE	–0.575***	-3.236***	–0.525***	-3.271***
	(0.056)	(0.072)	(0.063)	(0.080)
MES	–0.000	–0.003	0.005	0.003
	(0.005)	(0.005)	(0.007)	(0.006)
HERF	0.686*	0.589*	0.681*	0.544
	(0.353)	(0.351)	(0.358)	(0.357)
SGROWTH	-1.696***	-2.157***	-1.564***	-2.109***
	(0.146)	(0.148)	(0.159)	(0.161)
OWN	—	—	–0.095*	–0.132**
			(0.055)	(0.056)
SIZE*OWN	—	—	0.002***	0.002***
			(0.000)	(0.000)
AGE*OWN	—	—	0.002	0.003**
			(0.001)	(0.001)
RATE*OWN	—	—	–0.530***	–0.200
			(0.145)	(0.190)
MES*OWN	—	—	–0.007	–0.008
			(0.007)	(0.006)
HERF*OWN	—	—	0.693*	0.658*
			(0.365)	(0.348)
SGROWTH*OWN	—	—	–0.602*	–0.166
			(0.308)	(0.302)
Observations	144015	218311	144015	218311
LR test (RES vs UNRES)			121.1***	109.8***
Log likelihood	–73242.97	–74137.73	–73182.42	–74082.82
Wald test	1419.22***	4197.55***	1540.31***	4307.36

Notes: Standard errors in parentheses.
*, **, *** denote statistical significance at the 10, 5, 1 per cent level respectively.

survival we first estimated the model without allowing for ownership differences. These results are given in columns (i) and (ii) of the table for partial and complete reversals respectively. It should be noted that the results are very similar, in terms of magnitude and statistical significance, in both estimations. Job gains are more likely to persist in larger plants than in smaller ones. In contrast, the relationship between persistence and age is negative, with older plants being more likely to increase employment only temporarily. The significance on RATE shows that it is important to control for the relative importance of the change, and suggests that the larger the adjustment the more likely it is permanent. We also find that plants that are in more concentrated sectors are more likely to undertake temporary employment increases, i.e. are more likely to reverse newly created jobs. Finally, the significant coefficient on SGROWTH shows that benevolent sectoral conditions act to make job gains more permanent.

Including the ownership dummy and interacting it with the covariates, as shown in the third and fourth columns of Table 3, does not change any of the aforementioned conclusions. The less restricted models (including OWN and interaction terms) are supported by likelihood ratio tests of equivalence of the restricted and unrestricted models which allow us to reject the equivalence of the two models (with test statistics of 121.1 and 109.8 respectively). The results of the unrestricted models show, in line with the Kaplan–Meier survivor functions, that foreign plants are less likely than domestic ones to reverse increases in employment, as indicated by the statistically significant and negative ownership dummy. These coefficients are similar for both the cases of partial and complete reversals of jobs created. Calculating hazard ratios from these coefficients yields 0.91 and 0.88 respectively indicating that the hazard of reversing the employment decision is about 10 per cent lower for foreign than for comparable domestic plants.

For both definitions of reversals we also find that the interaction terms indicate that, while plant size in general acts to make job gains more permanent, this effect is less so for foreign plants. There is therefore less difference between large and small foreign plants in terms of employment creation persistence. Also, the finding that plants in highly concentrated sectors are more likely to reverse employment creation decisions is stronger for foreign firms, as indicated by the sign and statistical significance of the coefficient on the interaction term HERF*OWN.

The impacts of the other interaction terms, however, are different for the two definitions of employment decision reversal. Considering partial reversals, we find that larger employment adjustments, as measured by RATE, are more likely to lead to persistence of employment creation in foreign plants than in domestic ones. Also, the benevolent effect of locating in a growing sector on persistence has a larger effect on foreign plants. These two factors do not appear to be important, however, when considering complete reversals only. In that case, rather, we find that under the more stringent definition the age effect is more pronounced for foreign plants, i.e. old foreign plants are more likely to reverse completely their employment decisions than their old domestic counterparts. Thus, foreign plants are likely to react differently to changes in some of the determinants of reversing employment decisions than are domestic plants.

We turn to analysing the persistence of negative employment changes next. The results of the hazard model for employment destruction persistence are reported in Table 4. As in the previous table we distinguish estimations based on the less stringent (i.e. partial) and more stringent (i.e. complete) definition of the employment decision. Results for the restricted hazard model for both definitions are given in the first and second columns

Table 4
Determinants of Employment Destruction Persistence

	(i) Partial reversal	*(ii) Complete reversal*	*(iii) Partial reversal*	*(iv) Complete reversal*
SIZE	0.0004***	0.001***	0.001***	0.001***
	(0.000)	(0.000)	(0.000)	(0.000)
AGE	–0.006***	–0.009***	–0.006***	–0.009***
	(0.001)	(0.001)	(0.001)	(0.001)
RATE	0.003	–0.488***	0.003	–0.471***
	(0.003)	(0.032)	(0.003)	(0.033)
MES	0.004	0.005	0.007	0.007
	(0.006)	(0.006)	(0.006)	(0.007)
HERF	–0.622	–0.888*	–0.765*	–1.134**
	(0.442)	(0.464)	(0.453)	(0.481)
SGROWTH	1.626***	1.925***	1.696***	1.991***
	(0.180)	(0.186)	(0.197)	(0.204)
OWN	—	—	–0.003	0.110
			(0.062)	(0.067)
SIZE*OWN	—	—	–0.000	–0.001***
			(0.000)	(0.000)
AGE*OWN	—	—	–0.004**	–0.006***
			(0.002)	(0.002)
RATE*OWN	—	—	0.002	–0.133
			(0.049)	(0.112)
MES*OWN	—	—	–0.005	–0.004
			(0.007)	(0.008)
HERF*OWN	—	—	0.662	0.865*
			(0.437)	(0.446)
SGROWTH*OWN	—	—	–0.373	–0.322
			(0.376)	(0.375)
Observations	109330	170775	109330	170775
LR test (RES vs UNRES)			15.5***	43.2***
Log likelihood	–44365.44	–44054.00	–44357.67	–44032.39
Wald test	530.29***	1119.90***	545.83***	1163.13***

Notes: Standard errors in parentheses.
*, **, *** denote statistical significance at the 10, 5, 1 per cent level respectively.

of Table 4, respectively. Accordingly, larger and younger plants and plants with low employment adjustments are more likely to re-gain lost jobs (although the last result only holds when considering complete reversals). In terms of the sectoral variables we find that in more concentrated industries employment losses are more likely to be persistent and that, as would be expected, employment destruction reversal is positively related to sectoral conditions.

Columns (iii) and (iv) of Table 4 depict the results of the unrestricted model, including OWN and interaction terms, of employment destruction persistence for the two definitions of reversal. The likelihood ratio tests support in both cases the preference of the unrestricted model. In these estimations we find no statistically significant difference in job destruction persistence for foreign plants irrespective of the definition of the incidence of employment reversal. Thus, in contrast to the Kaplan–Meier survival functions, once we control for other plant- and industry-specific effects we find no difference in the employment destruction persistence between foreign and domestic plants.

Even though foreign plants are no more likely to recover or maintain a reduction in employment than domestic plants *per se*, various other factors are more pronounced for foreign plants. Specifically, we find in both cases that there is a different age effect for foreign and for domestic plants with the effect being more pronounced for the former. That is, the positive relationship between plant age and probability of persistence is stronger for foreign plants. For the case of complete reversals we find additionally that the size effect, i.e. that larger plants are more likely to recover lost jobs, is less so for multinational companies. Also, an industry's concentration is less likely to make employment losses persistent for foreign plants.

5 Discussion and Conclusions

We investigate the claim that affiliates of multinational companies are more footloose than domestic plants in the host country. We look at two different facets of this issue by examining plant survival as well as the persistence of employment changes (positive or negative) at the level of the plant over time. We address both questions using the framework of a Cox proportional hazard model.

Estimating the determinants of plant survival we find that plants belonging to multinational companies located in Ireland have lower survival rates than indigenous plants, all other things being equal. Also, we find that foreign plants react differently to changes in some of the factors determining survival, such as plant size or sectoral conditions. Taken together we interpret these findings as evidence that multinational companies are more footloose than domestic plants, *ceteris paribus*.

It is a different question, however, whether this higher probability of exiting the host country also means that employment in multinationals is more unstable than employment in indigenous plants. Focusing only on continuing plants we analyse the factors determining whether employment changes at the plant level persist over time. Estimating a hazard model for the persistence of new jobs created in foreign and domestic plants we find that jobs created in the former are, *ceteris paribus*, more likely to persist than those created in the latter. Furthermore, we find no evidence that jobs destroyed in foreign plants are more or less likely to be recovered than those destroyed in domestic plants. These results do not lend support to the claim that employment is more unstable in multinational companies than in indigenous plants due to the footloose nature of multinationals. We do find evidence, however, that some of the determinants of employment persistence differ between foreign and domestic plants, i.e. foreign plants react differently to changes in some of the factors impacting on employment persistence.

As a tentative conclusion, our results may suggest that employment decisions in multinationals are made with a longer time horizon in mind than in domestic plants. Multinationals seem to be more likely to create new jobs only if they expect those jobs to last in the long run while domestic plants base job creation decisions more on a short-term basis. This process possibly reflects the fact that multinationals in general are at a disadvantage compared to domestic plants when setting up abroad (Hymer, 1976).[9] On the one hand, these disadvantages may imply that foreign multinationals are more likely to leave the host country if they are unable to overcome these difficulties. On the other hand, however, the existence of such obstacles also suggests that affiliates of multinationals have stronger incentives to plan carefully their investment decisions and expansion strategies, over a long-term horizon. Also, it may indicate that multinationals have superior management expertise, allowing them to predict market fluctuations and plan responses well in advance. This seems to be borne out by our findings regarding the persistence of positive employment changes.

References

Audretsch, D. B. (1991). 'New-firm Survival and the Technological Regime', *Review of Economics and Statistics*, Vol. 60, pp. 441–450.

Audretsch, D. B. and Mahmood, T. (1995). 'New-firm Survival: New Results Using a Hazard Function', *Review of Economics and Statistics*, Vol. 77, pp. 97–103.

Barry, F. and Bradley, J. (1997). 'FDI and Trade: the Irish Host-country Experience', *Economic Journal*, Vol. 107, pp. 1798–1811.

Caves, R. E. (1996). *Multinational Enterprise and Economic Analysis*, 2nd edn, Cambridge, Cambridge University Press.

Central Statistics Office (1997). *Census of Industrial Production 1995*, Dublin, Stationary Office.

Cowling, K. and Sugden, R. (1999). 'The Wealth of Localities, Regions and Nations: Developing Multinational Economies', *New Political Economy*, Vol. 4, pp. 361–378.

Cox, D. R. (1972). 'Regression Models and Life Tables', *Journal of the Royal Statistical Society, Series B*, Vol. 34, pp. 187–220.

Davis, S. J. and Haltiwanger, J. (1992). 'Gross Job Creation, Gross Job Destruction and Job Reallocation', *Quarterly Journal of Economics*, Vol. 107, pp. 819–864.

Davis, S. J., Haltiwanger, J. C. and Schuh, S. (1996). *Job Creation and Destruction*, Cambridge, MA, MIT Press.

Dunne, P. and Hughes, A. (1994). 'Age, Size, Growth and Survival: UK Companies in the 1980s', *Journal of Industrial Economics*, Vol. 42, pp. 115–140.

Flamm, K. (1984). 'The Volatility of Offshore Investment', *Journal of Development Economics*, Vol. 16, pp. 231–248.

[9]Zaheer (1995) provides empirical evidence that affiliates of multinational companies indeed face such difficulties.

Görg, H. and Strobl, E. (2002a). 'Multinational Companies and Indigenous Development: an Empirical Analysis', *European Economic Review*, Vol. 46, pp. 1305–1322.

Görg, H. and Strobl, E. (2002b). 'Multinational Companies and Entrant Start-up Size: Evidence from Quantile Regressions', *Review of Industrial Organization*, Vol. 20, pp. 15–31.

Hood, N. and Young, S. (1997). 'The United Kingdom', in J. H. Dunning (ed.), *Governments, Globalization and International Business*, Oxford, Oxford University Press.

Hymer, S. H. (1976). *The International Operations of National Firms: A Study of Direct Foreign Investment*, Cambridge, MA, MIT Press.

Mata, J. and Portugal, P. (1994). 'Life Duration of New Firms', *Journal of Industrial Economics*, Vol. 42, pp. 227–245.

Mata, J., Portugal, P. and Guimaraes, P. (1995). 'The Survival of New Plants: Start-up Conditions and Post-entry Evolution', *International Journal of Industrial Organization*, Vol. 13, pp. 459–482.

McAleese, D. and Counahan, M. (1979). '"Stickers" or "Snatchers"? Employment in Multinational Corporations during the Recession', *Oxford Bulletin of Economics and Statistics*, Vol. 41, pp. 345–358.

Parsons, D. O. (1986). 'The Employment Relationship: Job Attachment, Work Effort, and the Nature of Contracts', in O. C. Ashenfelter and R. Layard (eds), *Handbook of Labor Economics*, Vol. 2, New York, North-Holland.

Strobl, E. A. (1996). 'Essays on Labour Market Dynamics in Ireland', *PhD Thesis*, Trinity College, Dublin, unpublished.

Sutton, J. (1991). *Sunk Costs and Market Structure*, Cambridge, MA, MIT Press.

Zaheer, S. (1995). 'Overcoming the Liability of Foreignness', *Academy of Management Journal*, Vol. 38, pp. 341–363.

Chapter 7

Foreign acquisition, plant survival, and employment growth

Roger Bandick *Department of Economics, Aarhus School of Business, Denmark*
Holger Görg *Kiel Institute for the World Economy, University of Kiel, Germany*

Abstract. This paper analyzes the effect of foreign acquisition on survival and employment growth of targets using data on Swedish manufacturing plants. We separate targeted plants into those within Swedish MNEs, Swedish exporting non-MNEs, and purely domestic firms. The results, controlling for possible endogeneity of acquisition using IV and propensity score matching approaches suggest that acquisition by foreign owners increases the lifetime of the acquired plants only if the plant was an exporter. The effect is robust to controlling for domestic acquisitions and differs between horizontal and vertical acquisitions. We find robust positive employment growth effects only for exporters and only if the takeover is vertical. JEL classification: F23, L23

Acquisition par l'étranger, survie de l'établissement et croissance de l'emploi. Ce mémoire analyze l'effet d'une acquisition étrangère sur la survie et sur la croissance de l'emploi dans les firmes ciblées à l'aide de données sur les établissements manufacturiers suédois. On sépare les établissements ciblés en trois groupes: ceux qui sont parties d'un multinationale suédoise, ceux qui sont des établissements suédois qui exportent mais ne sont pas des multinationales, et les entreprises purement domestiques. Contrôlant pour une possible endogénéité de l'acquisition, les résultats suggèrent que l'acquisition par des propriétaires étrangers accroît la vie des établissements acquis seulement si c'était un établissement exportateur. L'effet est robuste si on contrôle pour les acquisitions domestiques, et est différent selon que l'acquisition est horizontale ou verticale. On trouve des effets positifs robustes sur la croissance de l'emploi seulement pour les exportateurs, et seulement si l'acquisition est verticale.

Holger Görg is also affiliated with CEPR, IZA, and GEP Nottingham. Roger Bandick is also affiliated with the Department of Economics, Swedish Business School, Örebro University. We thank two anonymous referees and Werner Antweiler for very helpful comments on an earlier draft. Financial support from the Touborg Foundation is gratefully acknowledged. Email: rbandick@asb.dk; goerg@economics.uni-kiel.de

Canadian Journal of Economics / Revue canadienne d'Economique, Vol. 43, No. 2
May / mai 2010. Printed in Canada / Imprimé au Canada

0008-4085 / 10 / 547–573 / © Canadian Economics Association

1. Introduction

Foreign direct investment (FDI) is one of the main aspects of current-day globalization. The total volume of world-wide FDI has increased tremendously in the last two decades. UNCTAD (2007) shows that, in 2006, total FDI flows amounted to 1.3 trillion USD, contributing to a total worldwide FDI stock of roughly 12 trillion USD – equivalent to about 25% of world GDP. At the same time it is well known that the majority of FDI flows are due to international mergers and acquisitions (M&A) rather than setting up new projects abroad (greenfield). Again, UNCTAD (2007) shows that in 2006 the total value of worldwide cross-border M&As was roughly 0.9 trillion USD, amounting to about 70% of total FDI flows.[1] These trends have brought international mergers into the academic debate, with recent literature attempting to model these activities theoretically and providing empirical evidence on their determinants (e.g., Neary 2007; Hijzen et al. 2008; Head and Ries 2008). Moreover, the growing importance of M&As has given rise to policy concerns as to the impact of such cross-border mergers for domestic economies. From the point of view of the host country, a potential downside is that a foreign multinational acquiring a domestic firm may shut down the plant or part thereof completely after acquisition, or reduce employment.[2] On the positive side, however, a foreign acquisition may bring new technology and market access opportunities and thus strengthen the overall competitiveness and survival prospects of the takeover target.

In this paper we study in detail the implications of foreign acquisitions for the survival and employment growth prospects of the target plants. We investigate, firstly, plant closures as the adjustment along the extensive margin, as they are an important aspect of industry dynamics, shaping industry productivity and forming the competitive landscape in an economy.[3] However, we also consider the intensive margin of adjustment by examining what happens to employment growth in surviving firms after acquisitions. We use recent, unique, detailed plant-level data (which also provide some information at the firm level) for Sweden to investigate survival probabilities in the context of a hazard model. We take particular account of the potential endogeneity of the acquisition decision (e.g., due to 'cherry picking') by implementing an instrumental variables approach.

1 Strictly speaking the UNCTAD data on FDI and M&A are not fully comparable, as they come from different sources. Still, they give a good indication of the importance of M&A.

2 Recall, for example, the public debate surrounding the Vodafone takeover of the German company Mannesmann in 1999/2000: http://www.eurofound.europa.eu/eiro/1999/11/feature/de9911220f.htm (accessed on 7 August 2008).

3 It is also one aspect of plant outcomes that is still under-researched. By contrast, productivity and wage effects of foreign acquisitions have received far higher attention in the literature. See, for example, papers by Arnold and Javorcik (2005), Girma and Görg (2007a,b), Harris and Robinson (2002), Petkova (2007), and Fukao et al. (2006). A related literature also considers the effect of changes in managerial ownership and firm performance, for example, Harris, Siegel, and Wright (2005) and Coles, Leman, and Meschke (2007).

Furthermore, we check the robustness of the IV approach with estimations on a matched sample of firms based on propensity score matching.

Sweden is an interesting case to analyze in this context. Over the last two decades Sweden has introduced a considerable number of liberalization reforms in order to promote foreign ownership. However, it was not until 1995 that, in connection with Swedish membership in the European Union (EU), the business climate improved considerably and Swedish firms became more attractive targets for foreign investors. Ever since then, Sweden has witnessed a rapid increase of inward FDI, mainly through mergers and acquisitions. Well-known former Swedish-owned multinational enterprises, such as Astra, Pharmacia, Volvo Car, and Saab Automobile, changed ownership in the 1990s and are now foreign owned. At the beginning of the 2000s, the employment share in foreign owned firms in manufacturing was among the highest in OECD.[4]

The empirical evidence on the impact of foreign acquisitions on survival probabilities is rather limited. A few studies, for example, Bernard and Sjöholm (2003) for Indonesia, and van Beveren (2007) for Belgium, document differences in survival rates between foreign multinationals and domestic plants (the latter paper distinguishing domestic multinationals from purely domestic plants).[5] These studies indicate that the probability of shutdown is larger for plants that are part of a multinational, at least when controlling for other factors related to plant survival. As for studying the effect of a foreign acquisition on survival, one of the few papers to have looked at this is Girma and Görg (2004). They find evidence that foreign acquisition reduces the lifetime of acquired UK plants in electronics and food industries.

There is a somewhat richer literature on employment effects of acquisition, but this is by no means exhaustive. For example, Conyon et al. (2002), using firm-level data for the UK, find that labour demand of the typical firm decreased somewhat in the years following foreign acquisition. Huttunen (2007) and Almeida (2007), using data for Finland and Portugal, respectively, focus on employment by skill groups. Huttunen finds that foreign acquisition decreases the share of high-skilled workers in targets, while Almeida finds no significant effects on relative employment of skills in Portugal.

We extend and improve upon these earlier papers in a number of ways. First, we examine acquisitions by foreign multinationals and use different econometric approaches to be able to identify the causal effect of takeovers on exit probability and employment growth changes of a plant. Second, using the detailed and unique data for Sweden, we are able to link our empirical work to the recent literature on firm heterogeneity in international trade (e.g, Helpman, Melitz, and

4 Compared with 21 other OECD countries in 2002, only Ireland, Luxembourg, and Hungary had larger employment shares than Sweden in foreign owned firms in manufacturing (Hansson et al. 2007).

5 Another related study is by Bernard and Jensen (2007), who focus on differences in plant survival rates in US manufacturing between plants within domestic US multinationals and other plants. They do not distinguish the takeover by a foreign firm.

Yeaple 2004). Specifically, we are able to categorize all domestic firms into being either (i) a domestic firm with affiliates abroad, (ii) a domestic firm with export sales (and no foreign affiliates), and (iii) a purely domestic firm with no involvement on foreign markets. We refer to (i) and (ii) as domestic multinationals and domestic exporters, respectively, in what follows. Theoretical heterogeneous firm models would predict that these types of plants are intrinsically different. We therefore analyze whether the extent of global engagement of the plant (multinational, exporting, none) impacts on plant survival through mediating the impact of foreign acquisition on the target.

The quality of our data also allows further novelties in our research design. Firstly, we can use our data to identify domestic acquisitions. This allows us to investigate whether our foreign acquisition effect merely reflects a 'pure acquisition effect' that would be similar for domestic acquisitions also, or whether there is a particular 'foreign effect.' Owing to data limitations, not many studies that have investigated foreign acquisitions have been able to take this into account. Secondly, we investigate whether the effect of acquisitions is different depending on whether the acquisition is horizontal or vertical. To the best of our knowledge, this has not been investigated in earlier studies.[6] Finally, our data combine plant-level with firm-level information and is therefore able to control for the role of firm attributes in plant survival. Bernard and Jensen (2007) is one of the few other papers in the literature that is able to do so. They include a dummy for plants that are part of a multiplant firm. We not only do this but also are able to investigate whether plants' probability of exit is influenced by whether or not other plants within the same firm failed in the same period.

To preview our results, we find, after controlling for the possible endogeneity of the acquisition dummy and also controlling for a number of plant and firm specific characteristics, that foreign acquisition has an effect on plant survival only for domestic exporters. Depending on whether the acquisition is horizontal (i.e., within the same industry) or vertical, acquired exporters have 20–30% or 6–8% higher survival probabilities, respectively, compared with plants of non-acquired firms. We also find that employment growth is higher in takeover targets that were exporters prior to acquisition.

The remainder of the paper is structured as follows. Section 2 discusses some background to motivate our empirical analysis. Section 3 presents the data and illustrates the increased importance of foreign ownership in Swedish manufacturing in the 1990s. Section 4 discusses the analytical framework and empirical results for the effect of foreign acquisitions on plant survival, while section 5 focuses on employment growth effects. Section 6 concludes.

6 Moreover, unlike some of the earlier studies, our data allow us to be confident that we observe true exits in our data set; these are not a result of plants disappearing from the data due to mergers and acquisitions or because they drop in size below a certain cut-off level. The former is a potential issue in Mata and Portugal (2002), while the latter problem potentially affects the study by Van Beveren (2007).

2. Theoretical and empirical motivation

Conceptually, the effect of a foreign acquisition on the survival and employment growth prospects in the target plant are not unambiguous. In the standard models of multinationals, these types of firms are generally assumed to have some sort of firm specific asset or efficiency advantage that enables them to operate abroad successfully (Markusen 2002; Helpman, Melitz, and Yeaple 2003). If a foreign multinational then takes over a domestic plant, it may be likely that some of the firm specific asset is transferred to the takeover target in terms of technology, know-how, skills, and so on. This, in turn, may increase survival prospects and raise employment growth (and other aspects of firm performance) in the acquired target. One may call this a benevolent view of the actions of the acquirer.

A different view may be that multinationals, owing to their advantages, may use foreign acquisitions in order to gain market access and eliminate competition by taking over a rival and closing it down afterwards or reducing substantially the scale of operations and therefore reducing employment (e.g., Thompson 1999). In this case, the expected effects of a foreign acquisition on survival and growth would clearly be negative.

An argument with similar predicted outcomes can be constructed around the empirical observation that foreign-owned multinationals are generally more 'footloose' than domestic firms in the host country (e.g., Bernard and Sjöholm 2003). This is attributed to their possibilities of relocating production and employment among their affiliates in different countries and, hence, their ability to respond more quickly to changes in the business environment in alternative host countries. If this is the case, then the change in ownership may lead to lower survival probabilities and employment growth in the takeover target, as the multinational owner may be quicker to shut down or reduce employment in the plant once it is part of the multinational firm structure.

The effects of foreign acquisitions may still be ambiguous a priori even when we are distinguishing acquisitions motivated by either horizontal or vertical motives. For the former, firms acquire plants abroad in order to gain market access. If the aim of the market access is to eliminate competition and consolidate the industry, then it is likely that it may lead to plant closures and plant downsizing. On the other hand, the acquisition may be designed to open new markets by using the already existing facilities owned by other firms in the foreign markets; that is, the acquirer intends to 'grow by acquisition.' Then the acquirer is likely to maintain the plant network that is already available and improve them through technology transfers in order to suit its own needs. In this case, the prospects for the acquired target would be positive in terms of both survival and employment growth.

This may be different for non-horizontal, in particular vertical, acquisitions. If the motive is to acquire plants at different stages of the production process, then it is likely that this is done with a view to integrating them into the multinational company structure. In this case, the acquirer may transfer technology and improve quality in the acquisition target, leading to improvements in survival and employment prospects.

For acquisitions that are not related through input-output linkages or horizontal motives, foreign acquirers may use the acquisition as a device to acquire access to the country, technology, skills, and so on through the acquisition, even if it is not immediately linked into the production process. Once these resources have been ingested, the acquiring firm may divest itself of the acquired establishment and source its requirements from its plants elsewhere (Thompson 1999). Hence, in this case, there would be clear negative effects on survival probabilities in the takeover target after foreign acquisition.

Another consideration when formulating expectations concerning the post-acquisition effects relates to the characteristics of the acquisition target. Since plants of globally engaged firms tend to be a priori 'better' along a line of observable and (to the econometrician) unobservable characteristics, they may be able to experience different effects if they are acquired. As established in the recent literature on heterogeneous firms in international trade, there is theoretical justification and empirical evidence for the findings that multinationals tend to be the most productive firms, followed by exporters that are not multinationals, and that firms without any foreign involvement are the least productive. This may have implications for their post-acquisition expectations.

In particular, 'better' targets are likely to be able to absorb technology transfers from the foreign acquirer more easily. However, since plants of domestic multinationals are already at a level of technology similar to that of foreign multinationals (Criscuolo and Martin 2008), we may not expect that foreign acquisitions improve their survival prospects or employment growth. Furthermore, since domestic multinationals are already highly footloose (similar to foreign multinationals), we would not necessarily expect that foreign acquisition substantially increases their exit probabilities. Hence, if foreign acquisitions are accompanied by technology transfers, we expect these to be most effective for targets that are exporting plants, but not necessarily multinational plants, compared with targets in purely domestic firms. This is because the evidence shows that exporters are more productive than purely domestic firms (Wagner 2007), while domestic multinationals outperform exporters (Greenaway and Kneller 2007) and are more similar to foreign multinationals (Criscuolo and Martin 2008). We therefore expect to see larger positive effects of foreign acquisitions on plant survival and employment growth for targets that were already exporters.

3. A first look at the data

The data used in this paper are uniquely assembled and combine data from Statistics Sweden (SCB) and the Swedish Institute for Growth Policy Studies (ITPS). The data consist of three register-based data sets where information at the plant and firm levels are linked together by a unique identification code. Our period of observation covers 1993 to 2002.

Statistics Sweden provided two data sets, the Regional Labour Market Statistics (RAMS) and Financial Statistics (FC). The former contains information at the plant level *for the population of manufacturing plants* on variables such as total employment, the number of employees with post-secondary education, and the age of the plant.[7] Each plant is identified by a unique plant identifier. The appearance of a new identification number implies necessarily that a new plant has entered; the disappearance of a previous number means that this plant has exited. If the number remains unchanged in subsequent years, the plant has survived. Furthermore, RAMS reports firm and industry codes for each plant.

The firm code attached to each plant enables us to match data from Financial Statistics (FC) including information at the firm level such as labour productivity, capital-labour ratio, exports, whether a firm is a multi- or single plant, and ownership status (foreign or domestic). A firm is foreign if foreign owners posses more than 50% of the voting rights. Using this data, we define a foreign acquisition as a change in the ownership indicator from domestic to foreign.[8] The firm-level variables are available from the year 1993 onwards only for larger firms, that is, firms with 50 employees and more.

The database provided by ITPS is a register of all Swedish firms that are multinational enterprises (MNE).[9] By merging the three databases using the firm identifier of plants, we can assign the firm level information to the plant-level data. In that way we can also separate plants into those within foreign MNEs, those part of a Swedish MNE, those part of an exporting (non-MNE) firm, and those that operate purely domestically. A Swedish MNE is defined as a domestically owned firm that is part of an enterprise group with affiliates abroad.

The clear distinction into different types of MNEs and exporting activities is a distinct advantage of our data over the previous literature. This is an important dimension to the analysis, since the prospect of survival and employment growth may differ between ownership structures, owing to their ex ante different characteristics, as highlighted by, for example, Helpman, Melitz, and Yeaple (2004). Moreover, with our data we can be confident, given that it covers the whole population of plants, that we observe true exits and do not confound them with (i) disappearance of a plant code due to mergers and acquisitions, or (ii) a plant's dropping out of a sample due to size thresholds for inclusion in the sample.[10]

7 We have access to plant-level data from 1986 onwards. For plants entering after 1986 we are able to calculate the exact plant age, while older plants are improperly assigned to enter in 1986.

8 Plants within firms that switched between domestic and foreign ownership more than once over the period are not included in the sample. Also, plants in firms that disappear from the sample in one year and reappear in later years are also excluded.

9 The fact that the first year we can distinguish Swedish MNEs from non-MNEs is 1993 explains why our analysis begins in 1993.

10 Our data, owing to the restrictions of the FC database, include only firms with 50 employees or more. However, since we use plant-level data for the population of plants from RAMS, we still

TABLE 1
Foreign MNEs, Swedish MNEs, and exporting non-MNEs: number of plants and employment shares, 1993–2002

	Foreign MNEs		Swedish MNEs		Exporting non-MNEs	
Year	Plants (%)	Employment %	Plants (%)	Employment %	Plants (%)	Employment %
1993	1,402 (25.8)	21.5	1,722 (31.6)	53.3	1,141 (21.0)	16.1
1994	1,476 (27.4)	21.1	1,911 (35.5)	57.3	1,141 (21.2)	14.8
1995	1,534 (29.1)	22.0	1,618 (30.6)	55.1	1,156 (21.9)	15.3
1996	1,624 (31.5)	27.4	1,495 (29.0)	50.4	1,238 (24.0)	14.9
1997	1,490 (28.9)	27.8	1,761 (34.2)	51.8	1,044 (20.3)	14.7
1998	1,686 (31.8)	30.8	1,536 (29.0)	48.4	1,077 (20.3)	15.3
1999	1,774 (37.7)	34.9	1,180 (25.1)	43.6	943 (20.1)	16.1
2000	1,837 (37.3)	41.1	1,385 (28.1)	38.8	958 (19.4)	14.7
2001	2,051 (41.6)	46.8	1,216 (24.6)	32.2	954 (19.3)	16.0
2002	1,815 (40.5)	48.3	1,123 (25.1)	32.3	850 (19.0)	13.1
1993–2002	16,689 (32.9)	32.2	14,947 (29.5)	46.3	10,502 (20.7)	15.1
	Number of unique plants					
1993–2002	4,305 (29.5)		4,684 (32.1)		3,047 (20.9)	

Furthermore, our data cover the 1990s and early 2000s, which is a particularly interesting period to study, given recent increases in international merger activity.

During the 1990s, Sweden went through a period of liberalization reforms in order to promote foreign ownership. Since then, foreign ownership increased rapidly and the trend seems to have been more pronounced in Sweden than in other OECD countries (see Hansson et al. 2007). Table 1 shows that in the 1990s the employment share in plants within foreign MNEs increased by almost 27 percentage points. This trend seems to have evolved at the expense of Swedish MNEs, whose employment share dropped by 21 percentage points. The table also shows that over the period 1993 to 2002, the share of plants within foreign MNEs increased from 26% to 41%, whereas the share of plants within Swedish MNEs has fallen by almost 7 percentage points. However, the employment and plant shares for Swedish exporters remained fairly constant over the period.

During the 1990s several large Swedish multinationals have become foreign owned, owing to acquisitions by foreign MNEs, for example, Pharmacia and Upjohn 1995, Saab Automobile and General Motors 1998, Astra and Zeneca 1999, and Ford and Volvo Car Corporation 1999. Table 2 reports, by year, the frequencies of plant acquisitions by foreign firms. On average 33% of plants acquired were part of Swedish MNEs before foreign takeover, and almost 58% were plants of Swedish exporters. Table 2 also shows that more than 90% of

can observe all the plants that are within a firm, even if that firm drops below the threshold size value. Hence, contrary to some papers in the literature, we do not mix sample exit with true exit.

TABLE 2
Frequency of foreign acquisitions: number of plants and employment shares

	Swedish MNEs to foreign MNEs		Exporting non-MNEs to foreign MNEs		Non-exporting non-MNEs to foreign MNEs	
Year	Plants (%)	Employment share*	Plants (%)	Employment share*	Plants (%)	Employment share*
1994	7 (9.2)	19.4	51 (67.1)	66.7	18 (23.7)	13.9
1995	19 (20.0)	30.0	74 (77.9)	68.8	2 (2.1)	1.2
1996	161 (55.5)	72.1	123 (42.4)	26.1	6 (2.1)	1.8
1997	8 (18.2)	26.0	23 (52.3)	57.8	13 (29.5)	16.2
1998	25 (41.7)	74.8	34 (56.7)	19.4	1 (1.7)	5.9
1999	78 (72.2)	77.3	23 (21.3)	15.3	7 (6.5)	7.4
2000	20 (41.7)	88.0	14 (29.2)	10.6	14 (29.2)	1.4
2001	5 (1.9)	4.0	217 (82.8)	85.0	40 (15.3)	11.0
2002	13 (26.0)	26.9	34 (68.0)	65.8	3 (6.0)	7.3
1993–2002	336 (32.5)	46.5	593 (57.4)	46.2	04 (10.1)	7.3

*Share of total employment in plants within acquired firms

the employees in the takeover targets were employed in plants that were part of Swedish MNEs or Swedish exporters before foreign acquisition.[11]

Table 3 shows that in the years before acquisition, plants within acquired firms are larger in terms of employment and are younger than plants of non-acquired firms. Moreover, the acquired firms seem to have higher skill and R&D intensity, higher labour productivity and capital-labour ratios, and are more export intensive than non-acquired firms in the pre-acquisition years. Table 3 also provides us with some evidence of 'cherry picking,' that is, that firms that perform 'well' and have plants with 'good' characteristics are more likely to be acquired by foreigners.

Differences in characteristics and performance between acquired and non-acquired plants in the years before acquisition could bias the estimates of the causal effect of foreign acquisition on plant survival or employment growth. To overcome this problem, we use various econometric methods, which we discuss in detail in the following sections. We examine first the impact of foreign acquisition on plant survival, that is, adjustment after acquisition along the extensive margin.

11 In the working paper version (Bandick and Görg 2009) we show the distribution of acquisitions by plant and firm across manufacturing sectors. Over the period studied, 12% of all manufacturing firms were acquired by foreign firms (Recall that firm level information is only available for firms with 50 or more employees.) Over the same period, 7% of all plants were acquired. Moreover, the shares of foreign acquisitions are more pronounced in sectors with a high degree of product differentiation and high R&D intensity, such as chemicals, metals and motor vehicles.

TABLE 3
Mean variable differences between acquired and non-acquired firms in the pre-acquisition period, whole sample

	T = 0	T = −1	T = −2
Plant variables			
Employment	22 (2.48)***	35 (3.71)***	52 (4.69)***
Age	−1.82 (9.27)***	−1.11 (5.47)***	−1.01 (4.26)***
Skill intensity	−0.07 (1.09)	−0.01 (0.16)	−0.13 (1.57)
Obs. target/non-target	907/28,490	808/27,411	572/26,784
Firm variables			
Employment	170 (2.54)**	175 (2.52)**	156 (2.05)**
Skill intensity	3.1 (3.66)***	2.5 (2.93)***	2.7 (2.97)***
R&D intensity	0.7 (2.52)**	0.8 (2.98)***	0.7 (2.61)***
Capital-labour ratio	39.6 (0.64)	75.5 (2.22)**	39.0 (1.06)
Shipment	451 (1.76)*	444 (1.90)*	389 (1.68)*
Export intensity	8.2 (3.72)***	8.1 (3.60)***	6.0 (2.48)**
Productivity	22.60 (1.32)	39.2 (2.41)**	42.0 (2.44)**
Obs. target/non-target	207/7,456	198/6,932	168/6,425

4. Foreign acquisition and plant survival

4.1. Methodology

To establish whether the acquisition of a plant by foreign owners changes its survival prospects compared with other plants, we model the determinants of plant survival and check whether the incidence of acquisition is a statistically significant determinant of a plant's hazard of exiting. We use a complementary log-log model (cloglog) for the empirical estimations.[12] The underlying assumption of the proportional hazard model is that the hazard ratio depends only on time at risk, $\theta_0(t)$ (the so-called baseline hazard) and on explanatory variables affecting the hazard independently of time, exp $(\beta' X)$. The hazard ratio is then

12 The related empirical IO literature (e.g., Audretsch and Mahmood 1995; Disney, Haskel, and Heden 2003) generally uses a Cox proportional hazard model for this type of analysis. Given that our data are collected on a yearly basis, the cloglog model is more appropriate. Essentially, it is equivalent to the discrete time version of the proportional hazard model. The cloglog model has the same assumptions on the coefficient vector β as the continuous-time version of the proportional hazard model (Prentice and Gloeckler 1978).

given by

$$\theta(t, X) = \theta_0(t) \exp(\beta' X). \tag{1}$$

More specifically, the discrete-time hazard function takes the following form:

$$h(j, X) = 1 - \exp[-\exp(\beta' X + \gamma_j)], \tag{2}$$

where $h(j, X)$ shows the interval hazard for the period between the beginning and the end of the jth year after the first appearance of the plant and $\gamma_j = \log \int_{a_{j-1}}^{a_j} \theta_0(t)dt$ capture, within each interval, period-specific effects on the hazard. The β parameters show the effects of the explanatory variables X (at the plant and firm levels) on the hazard rate.[13]

The main interest in our analysis is a dummy variable showing whether a plant is part of a Swedish firm that has been acquired by a foreign MNE (*Foreign Acquired*). The dummy switches to one in the year that the firm changes its ownership status from domestic to foreign and is zero if ownership status is domestic.

To be able to identify the acquisition effect we need to control for other plant-level variables that are potentially correlated with it and that also affect plant survival. The literature generally finds that plant size and age are important determinants of plant survival. We therefore include both variables in the vector X. Size is measured as log employment size and plant age as years of operations. Furthermore, we calculate a measure of skill intensity of a plant's production process. This is defined as the percentage of employees with post-secondary education in a plant relative to the industry mean skill intensity.

We also take into account variables at the firm level. We include a dummy capturing whether or not a firm is a multi-plant operation. This has been shown by Bernard and Jensen (2007) as an important determinant of firm survival. We also go further than this and check whether restructuring within the firm affects plant survival. To do so, we calculate a dummy variable that is equal to one if another plant in the same firm exited, either as a result of the foreign acquisition or for other reasons. Furthermore, we control for R&D intensity, capital intensity, and labour productivity at the firm level.

The final baseline hazard model can then be written as

$$h(j, X) = 1 - \exp\begin{bmatrix} -\exp(\beta_0 + \beta_1 Acquired + \beta_2 plant\_controls \\ + \beta_3 firm\_controls + \gamma_j) \end{bmatrix}. \tag{3}$$

13 The cloglog model does not allow for unobserved plant heterogeneity. To do so we use the random-effects version of complementary log-log model as a robustness check. As these estimations produce results that are largely comparable with the simple cloglog model, we report estimations of the preferred specifications using this alternative estimator only in the working paper version (Bandick and Görg 2009), to save space.

TABLE 4
Kaplan-Meier survival function, indigenous plants by firm type

	Whole sample		
Time	Non-exporter	Exporter	Swedish MNE
1	93.1 (0.005)	89.2 (0.006)	86.5 (0.005)
2	80.3 (0.008)	78.8 (0.008)	78.8 (0.006)
3	71.2 (0.010)	73.0 (0.008)	70.1 (0.007)
4	64.1 (0.010)	68.6 (0.009)	60.0 (0.007)
5	53.0 (0.026)	58.1 (0.010)	47.8 (0.008)
6	48.2 (0.011)	50.4 (0.010)	42.2 (0.008)
7	39.6 (0.011)	46.0 (0.010)	34.6 (0.007)
8	30.4 (0.010)	35.6 (0.010)	28.3 (0.007)
9	30.4 (0.010)	35.6 (0.009)	28.2 (0.007)

NOTES: Standard errors are within parentheses.

We expand on this baseline model in the empirical analysis in a number of ways. First, we include a dummy variable for domestic acquisitions in order to identify whether the variable captures a general acquisition effect or some specifically foreign effect. Second, we allow the effects of foreign acquisitions to differ for horizontal and vertical acquisitions (the definitions of these are discussed below). Third, we allow the acquisition effect to differ across plants depending on whether they are within globally engaged firms, that is, Swedish MNEs and exporting non-MNEs or purely domestic firms before foreign takeover. This accounts for an important aspect of firm heterogeneity highlighted in the recent theoretical and empirical literature, namely, that there is a clear ordering of firm types, with the 'best' becoming outward investors, the next exporters, and the least-equipped firms remaining in the domestic market (Helpman, Melitz, and Yeaple 2004). This can have implications for the post-acquisition survival prospects.

In table 4 we calculate simple Kaplan-Meier survival functions to compare survival probabilities of the three different types of firms. As the table shows, Swedish multinationals have the lowest survival probabilities; that is, they are the most footloose of the type. This is in line with the empirical finding that foreign multinationals have higher exit probabilities than purely domestic firms (e.g., Bernard and Sjöholm 2003) – that is, domestic multinationals are similar to foreign multinationals in this respect.[14] By contrast, there is no clear difference in survival probabilities between purely domestic plants and exporters; the functions cross at time $t = 3$.

Before proceeding to the estimation results, we need to describe in more detail our identification strategy. In equation (3) identification of the coefficient β_1 on the acquisition dummy rests on the assumption that, conditional on the plant and firm controls included, acquisition is exogenous. This is, arguably, a strong assumption. If it does not hold, then the stochastic dependence between the acquisition dummy and the error term may bias our estimates. In order to take account of this possible endogeneity we use two approaches: instrumental variables estimation and selection of a control group based on propensity score matching.

For the first approach we construct an instrumental variable as the probability of a firm being taken over by foreign owners. This instrumental variable is calculated as the predicted value of the dependent variable from a probit regression for the probability of foreign takeover.[15] The probit model is

$$p\,(Acquisition_{it} = 1) = F\left(X_{it-1}, D_j, D_t\right), \tag{4}$$

where X is a vector of firm and plant characteristics in $t-1$. This vector includes, in the first instance, labour productivity in firm i, plant age, age-squared, current employment size (relative to the industry mean), R&D and skill intensity, export intensity, and a measure of foreign presence in the industry. The latter measure captures potential spillover effects in an industry. D_j and D_t control for fixed industry and time effects. In a robustness check we also investigate how robust results are to changes in the variables that are included in the probit.

The results of estimating equation (4) are reported in table 5. The estimation results suggest that more productive, skill-intensive, and export-oriented plants are more likely to be acquired. Furthermore, firms located in industries with higher foreign presence are more likely to become acquisition targets. We also estimated alternative specifications of equation (4), including additional variables in the probit estimation, to check whether our results depend on the process by which the instrument was generated. These results are reported in columns (ii) and (iii) of the table. The estimation of the hazard models below is robust to this change in the instrument-generating specification.

14 This mirrors recent contributions to the literature on productivity differences between multinationals and domestic firms which show that it is multinationality per se, and not foreign ownership, which is correlated with a productivity premium vis-à-vis domestic firms. In other words, domestic and foreign multinationals are more productive than purely domestic firms. See, for example, Criscuolo and Martin (2008), who use UK data.

15 A similar approach was taken by McGuckin and Nguyen (2001), who analyze the effect of acquisitions on plant exit in the US, and Hujer, Maurer, and Wellner (1999) in a non-linear hazard model for the analysis of the effect of training on unemployment duration in Germany. Conyon et al. (2002) also use this approach in modelling the wage effects of foreign acquisitions. Note that, in order to get accurate standard errors for the estimators using generated IV we compute bootstrapped standard errors.

TABLE 5
Probability of foreign acquisition: the Probit model

Variables	(i)	(ii)	(iii)
Export intensity	0.296	0.276	0.419
	(3.42)***	(3.17)***	(8.25)***
R&D intensity	0.524	0.524	0.524
	(0.94)	(0.94)	(0.94)
Relative employment	0.003	0.004	0.003
	(1.01)	(0.12)	(1.48)
Labour productivity	0.127	0.065	0.207
	(2.11)**	(0.98)	(5.22)***
Skill intensity	0.077	0.087	0.160
	(1.88)*	(2.17)**	(7.56)***
Age	−0.077	−0.076	−0.048
	(5.42)***	(5.35)***	(5.75)***
(Age)^2	0.002	0.002	0.001
	(4.35)***	(4.21)***	(5.52)***
Foreign presence	0.064	0.059	0.127
	(2.14)**	(1.95)*	(7.33)***
Capital intensity		0.042	
		(2.11)**	
Sales			0.016
			(2.98)***
Year dummies	Yes	Yes	Yes
Pseudo R^2	0.050	0.052	0.054
LR Chi^2 (16)	112.24	114.89	118.53
Observations	9.716	9.716	9.716

NOTES: Z-statistics are within parentheses. Relative employment is the firm's employment relative to the industry mean employment. Apart from age and (age)^2, all other variables are lagged one period. The share of foreign employment at industry level (SNI92 2-digit level) is used as a proxy for foreign presence. ***, **, and * indicate significance at the 1%, 5%, and 10% levels, respectively.

In an alternative approach we use propensity score matching to establish a valid counterfactual of non-acquired firms that have pre-acquisition characteristics similar to those of the acquired firms. Under the matching assumption, conditional on the propensity score, acquisition is random. We then carefully construct a sample of acquired plants and matched non-acquired plants and estimate equation (3) on this matched sample.[16]

The idea of the propensity score-matching method is to find, for every foreign acquired firm, a similar firm that has remained in domestic hands and from which we can approximate the non-observed counterfactual event. Thus, the matching technique enables us to construct a sample of acquired and non-acquired firms with similar pre-acquisition characteristics X, for example, productivity, wages,

16 A similar approach of using matching to establish a control group was employed by Greenaway and Kneller (2008). See also Arnold and Javorcik (2005), Girma and Görg (2007a), and Petkova (2007) for recent applications of propensity score matching, and descriptions of the assumptions and tests, in the context of identifying the effects of foreign acquisitions on target firms.

and size. Conditional on these characteristics, we estimate the probability (or propensity score) of being acquired by a foreign firm using the same probit model as in equation (4). Once the propensity scores are calculated, we can (using the 'caliper'-matching method) select the nearest control firms in which the propensity score falls within a pre-specified radius as a match for an acquired firm.[17] Moreover, we check whether the balancing condition is verified; that is, each independent variable does not differ significantly between acquired and non-acquired firms.

Another condition that must be fulfilled in the matching procedure is the so-called common support condition. This criterion implies that at each point in time, a newly acquired firm is matched with non-acquired firms with propensity scores only slightly larger or smaller than the target firm. Note that some acquired firms may be matched with more than one non-acquired firm, while acquired firms not matched with a non-acquired firm are excluded. Eventually, we end up with a sample, henceforth denoted the matched sample, which consists of 207 acquired firms with 907 plants and 2,372 non-acquired firms with 10,776 plants.

Since the aim of the matching is to find a group of acquired and non-acquired firms with similar characteristics, we once more report, in appendix table A1, mean variable differences between the two groups of firms that were successfully matched together. The matching procedure has substantially reduced the firm-level differences between acquired and non-acquired firms. Regarding the plant-level characteristics, the differences are slightly reduced, compared with the unmatched sample in table 3. However, there still are significant differences between plants of acquired firms and plants of non-acquired firms. Hence, in the estimation of the hazard model we control for variations among the plants with respect to size, age, and skill intensities. Finally, from appendix table A2 it is clear that the matching procedure also has been successful in constructing a sample with the same structure of ownership changes as in the unmatched sample.

4.2. Empirical results

To examine whether survival prospects differ across foreign-acquired and non-acquired plants, we estimate different specifications of the hazard model described in equation (3). We report the hazard ratios (exponentiated coefficients) that allow a straightforward interpretation of the coefficient size. For example, a ratio β less than one on a dummy variable implies that changing the dummy from 0 to 1 reduces the hazard rate of exiting (or increases the probability of survival) by $(1 - \beta) * 100\%$, ceteris paribus.

Table 6 presents the main estimation results. In the first four columns we report the result from estimating equation (3) for the whole sample, that is, Swedish manufacturing plants in firms with 50 employees or more between 1993

17 The procedure we utilize to match acquired and non-acquired firms is the PSMATCH2 routine in Stata version 10 described in Leuven and Sianesi (2003). In our analysis, the prespecified radius is set to 0.01.

TABLE 6
Result of Cox Hazard model. Foreign and domestic acquisition of plants of all Swedish manufacturing firms

	Exogenous acquisition (i)	IV 1 (ii)	IV 2 (iii)	IV 3 (iv)	Matched sample (v)
Foreign acquisition	0.689	0.914	0.904	0.888	0.786
	(8.91)***	(0.94)	(1.13)	(1.78)*	(5.38)***
Plant-level controls					
Age	0.249	0.251	0.251	0.251	0.267
	(77.90)***	(79.65)***	(69.19)***	(74.63)***	(58.30)***
Size	0.817	0.818	0.818	0.818	0.825
	(15.64)***	(15.47)***	(15.00)***	(13.92)***	(12.51)***
Skill intensity	0.986	0.986	0.986	0.986	0.997
	(2.57)***	(2.50)**	(2.76)***	(2.43)**	(0.38)
Firm-level controls					
Multiplant	0.905	0.921	0.921	0.921	1.711
	(1.22)	(0.94)	(1.02)	(0.94)	(4.83)***
Failed other plant	0.537	0.533	0.533	0.533	0.826
	(16.32)***	(16.03)***	(16.55)***	(16.15)***	(4.34)***
Capital intensity	1.100	1.086	1.087	1.087	1.082
	(9.61)***	(7.87)***	(8.63)***	(8.38)***	(6.52)***
R&D intensity	0.728	0.761	0.764	0.771	0.437
	(0.86)	(0.70)	(0.84)	(0.70)	(2.01)**
Labour productivity	0.658	0.657	0.657	0.657	0.722
	(11.81)***	(11.11)***	(11.68)***	(13.48)***	(7.45)***
Observations	31,047	31,047	31,047	31,047	19,784
Wald Chi^2	10,627	14,535	9,343	15,121	6,910
Hausman test (p-value)		0.002	0.002	0.002	
Linktest (hatsq)	0.009	0.006	0.010	0.005	−0.004
	(1.25)	(1.07)	(1.38)	(0.97)	(0.40)

NOTES: Estimations are stratified by industry and year. Industries are defined at the SNI92 2-digit level (22 industries). Standard errors in parentheses. ***, **, and * indicate significance at the 1%, 5%, and 10% levels, respectively. Only plants in firms with 50 employees or more are included.

and 2002. The results in column (i) are based on estimation of the hazard model assuming that foreign acquisitions are exogenous conditional on the control variables. The column reveals that plants of acquired firms are more likely to survive than plants of non-acquired firms. Controlling for plant and firm level characteristics, acquisition by foreign owners increases a plant's probability of survival by roughly 30%.

In terms of the control variables, it is reassuring to note that their results are largely as expected. In line with the large IO literature on firm survival, we find that older, larger, and more skill-intensive plants have lower exit hazards. We do not find that plants that are part of a multiplant firm per se are more or less likely to exit than other plants. However, we do find evidence that a plant's exit probability is reduced if another plant in the same firm failed. Furthermore, plants in firms with higher labour productivity and lower capital intensities are more likely to survive.

Returning to the effect of acquisition on survival, our results thus far suggest that this is positive. However, this may be purely due to foreign acquirers choosing targets with a priori positive characteristics, a practice known as 'cherry picking,' as illustrated above in tables 3 and 5. These characteristics may also account for the higher survival probabilities of such plants after acquisition. To some extent, this is already accounted for by the large number of relevant firm and plant characteristics that we include in our empirical model. However, we also explicitly correct for the possible endogeneity of the foreign acquisition dummy. To this end we first estimate a variant of the hazard model in equation (3), which instruments for the acquisition dummy using the probability of foreign acquisition (as in table 5) as an instrument. As an alternative, we use a propensity score-matching approach in column (v).

The results based on the three alternative instrumental variables are reported in columns (ii) to (iv). Unfortunately, there is, to the best of our knowledge, no formal method of choosing between the standard and the IV estimation in the context of a hazard model. Hence, preference for the IV model would be predicated on the assumption of endogenous acquisitions, which is, strictly speaking, not reliably testable. However, we may use a standard Hausman test to get a rough indicator of whether or not the assumption of exogeneity holds. These tests, which are reported at the bottom of table 6, provide evidence that in all cases we can reject the assumption of exogeneity of the acquisition dummy.

These results show that the point estimate of the effect of acquisition on exit is reduced (the coefficient is higher) and it is statistically significant in only one case in column (iv). The reliability of the IV approach hinges on the relevance and validity of the instruments used. While the relevance is to some extent shown in the IV-generating probit in table 5, there is, to the best of our knowledge, no test of instrument validity in the context of this non-linear hazard estimation. Hence, our results are reliable under the assumption of instrument validity, which cannot be tested.

We therefore use an approach which does not depend on such an assumption. We implement a propensity score-matching procedure to generate a sample of acquired and non-acquired (matched) firms that can serve as a valid counterfactual. We then estimate equation (3) on this matched sample of firms, similar to the approach of Greenaway and Kneller (2007). The results are reported in column (v). Note that the acquisition effect is now statistically significant and positive. The point estimate suggests that the probability of surviving in plants within acquired firms is around 20% higher than in plants within non-acquired firms.

We now consider various extensions to the baseline model. The first extension is concerned with the acquisition effect as such. The foreign acquisition effect we identify in the baseline estimation arguably includes two distinct components. First, acquisitions may affect plant survival independent of whether the acquirer is foreign or domestic. This may be termed a 'pure acquisition effect.' Second, there may be a differential effect of foreign and domestic acquisitions, which may be considered as a 'foreign effect.' The analysis in the baseline model bundles these two effects. This is a common problem in the literature (e.g., Arnold and Javorcik 2005; Girma and Görg 2007a; Petkova 2007) and is usually difficult to address, owing to data limitations.

With our Swedish data we can make some progress on this issue. While, as in many other data sets, we do not observe domestic acquisitions directly, we exploit the firm and plant dimension in our data. Specifically, plant and firm identifiers are linked so we can follow the entity along both dimensions. If a plant remains within the same firm, both plant and firm identifier stay the same. If we observe a firm in $t-1$ but not in t, and observe its plants in both years, the plants will have a constant plant identifier but different 'old' and 'new' firm identifiers in $t-1$ and t, respectively. We may then conclude from the data that the firm was acquired and that the new firm identifier relates to the acquiring firm. If this firm is not foreign, then we define this as a domestic takeover. In this way we identify 625 domestic acquisitions over the time period analyzed in our data.

Another issue concerns the nature of the foreign acquisition. The literature broadly distinguishes foreign direct investments into horizontal and vertical (e.g, Alfaro and Charlton 2009). There may arguably be different effects of foreign acquisitions on targets, depending on these two motives. For example, horizontal acquisitions may involve substantial transfers of technology from the parent to the target, which may increase survival. However, it may also be about trying to eliminate rivals or consolidate the number of plants, leading to negative effects on survival probabilities. By contrast, acquisitions of vertically related suppliers may more likely lead to transfer of technology to improve or sustain quality, and hence may lead to strong positive effects on survival.

This is an issue that has not been investigated in the literature thus far, mainly owing to data availability. We use our data and check the industry classification for the acquired firm before and after acquisition. If the 2-digit industry code remains constant, we define the acquisition as horizontal. If it is changed, it is instead regarded as vertical. Using this definition, we classify about 11% of all foreign acquisitions in our sample as 'vertical.' This is not an ideal measure by any means. In particular, it is likely that our vertical group includes both 'true' vertical acquisitions of, say, supplier firms, and also conglomerate mergers where the target and acquirer are in unrelated industries. Unfortunately, we do not have sufficient information to establish industry linkages. Still, the measure allows us to compare horizontal and other types of acquisitions. In order to do so we allow for separate acquisition effects for horizontal and vertical acquisitions. This is done by interacting a dummy for horizontal acquisitions and the foreign acquisition dummy, and similarly for vertical acquisitions.

The results of estimating equation (3) with these two modifications are reported in table 7. Columns (i) to (iii) show the IV estimations. We use instruments for both foreign and domestic acquisition dummies. The instrument for the latter

TABLE 7
Result of Cox Hazard model. Foreign and domestic acquisition of plants of all Swedish manufacturing firms

	IV (i)	IV 2 (ii)	IV 3 (iii)	Matched sample (iv)	Matched sample (v)	Matched sample (vi)
Vertical acquisition	0.362	0.347	0.403	0.736	0.786	
	(2.88)***	(3.02)***	(2.92)***	(6.81)***	(4.67)***	
Horizontal acquisition	0.815	0.862	0.704	0.852	0.889	
	(0.09)	(0.15)	(1.07)	(0.99)	(0.81)	
Domestic acquisition	0.176	0.188	0.166	0.466		0.424
	(8.51)***	(8.76)***	(9.33)***	(7.79)***		(7.09)***
Plan- level controls						
Age	0.264	0.247	0.246	0.278	0.261	0.267
	(75.22)***	(75.22)***	(74.84)***	(56.01)***	(46.71)***	(36.63)***
Size	0.822	0.825	0.823	0.836	0.822	0.845
	(15.29)***	(15.32)***	(15.21)***	(11.54)***	(10.17)***	(7.54)***
Skill intensity	0.982	0.982	0.982	0.996	1.005	0.997
	(3.22)***	(3.21)***	(3.22)***	(0.64)	(0.57)	(0.31)
Firm-level controls						
Multiplant	0.878	0.875	0.886	1.812	1.900	1.547
	(1.79)*	(1.85)*	(1.67)*	(5.28)***	(4.72)***	(2.18)**
Failed other plant	0.545	0.543	0.543	0.831	0.663	1.349
	(14.95)***	(14.99)***	(14.98)***	(4.17)***	(7.35)***	(4.23)***
Capital intensity	1.081	1.089	1.087	1.078	1.062	1.158
	(7.63)***	(8.47)***	(8.18)***	(6.18)***	(3.79)***	(8.50)***
R&D intensity	0.901	0.875	0.875	0.439	0.302	0.212
	(0.28)	(0.36)	(0.36)	(1.99)**	(2.83)***	(2.01)**
Labour productivity	0.621	0.619	0.615	0.701	0.743	0.539
	(13.43)***	(13.56)***	(13.60)***	(8.24)***	(5.26)***	(11.39)***
Observations	31,047	31,047	31,047	,784	13,395	9,394
Wald Chi^2	13,549	13,664	13,467	6,731	4,734	2,902
Hausman test (p-value)	0.001	0.001	0.002			
	0.006	0.008	0.004	0.001	0.021	−0.014
Linktest (hatsq)	(1.06)	(1.13)	(1.06)	(0.05)	(2.15)**	(1.19)

NOTES: Estimations are stratified by industry and year. Industries are defined at the SNI92 2-digit level (22 industries). Standard errors in parentheses. ***, **, and * indicate significance at the 1%, 5%, and 10% levels, respectively. Only plants in firms with 50 employees or more are included. In column (v) plants within firms taken over by other domestic firms are excluded, and in column (vi) plants within firms taken over by foreign MNEs are excluded.

is constructed also using a probit equation of the probability of domestic acquisition, similar to equation (4). However, this probit model does not include the presence of foreign firms in the industry as regressor. From the IV estimations we find statistically significant positive effects from vertical acquisitions, while there is no evidence for an acquisition effect from horizontal takeovers. We also find that domestic acquisitions lead to improvements in the survival probabilities of the domestic plants, and these effects appear to be stronger than for foreign acquisitions. This conclusion also holds in the matching approach in column (iv), although the magnitude of the effects is reduced.

In column (iv) the matching is done using a probit modelling the determinants of the probability of acquisition, not distinguishing foreign and domestic. If the determinants are different for these two types of acquisitions, the matching procedure is not correct. We therefore provide two alternative estimations. In the first we look only at foreign acquisitions. We match using the probit model as described above and exclude from the sample all firms that are acquired by domestic firms. The results are reported in column (v). In the second approach we match only domestic acquisitions, excluding foreign acquisitions from the sample. The results are reported in column (vi). Both columns show results that are consistent with what we found in column (iv).

In table 2 we observed that, on average, almost 90% of the plants that are within foreign acquired firms were plants of globally engaged firms, that is, Swedish MNEs and exporting non-MNEs, before acquisition. We may expect that the survival prospect after foreign takeover differs, depending on whether the plants were within targeted Swedish MNEs, exporting non-MNEs, or purely domestic firms. The recent literature on firm-level heterogeneity makes the point that these firms have, a priori, differences in their characteristics (Helpman, Melitz, and Yeaple 2004). This may affect not only their likelihood of being a takeover target but also the post-acquisition effects on survival, as discussed above.

To investigate whether there are indeed differences, we replace our foreign acquisition dummies in equation (3) with dummies showing the ownership status before foreign takeover; *Acquired Swedish MNE*, *Acquired Swedish exporter*, and *Acquired Swedish domestic*. The first dummy equals one if the plants were within Swedish MNEs before foreign takeover and zero if the plants are within non-acquired firms. The second dummy takes the value of one if the plants were within exporters (non-MNEs) before foreign takeover and the last dummy shows whether the plants were within purely domestic firms before foreign takeover. We again allow the coefficients to be different for horizontal and vertical acquisitions.

Table 8 shows the results, which indicate that plants that are within targeted Swedish exporters have higher survival ratios after foreign takeover compared with plants within non-acquired firms. These results are similar in direction for horizontal and vertical acquisitions, but stronger in magnitude for the latter. These findings are also robust to the estimation strategy. The most conservative estimates in columns (iv) and (v) suggest the survival ratio for acquired exporters improves by between 17% and 34% after foreign takeover for vertical and 6% and 8% for horizontal acquisitions. However, there is no robust evidence that acquisition impacts the survival probabilities of either Swedish MNEs or purely domestic firms. This indicates that just looking at the acquisition effect without considering heterogeneity in the impact depending on firm characteristics may

TABLE 8
Result of Cox Hazard model. Foreign acquisition of Swedish MNE plants and plants of exporting and non-exporting firms

	(i) IV 1	(ii) IV 2	(iii) IV 3	(iv) Matched sample	(v) Matched sample
Vertical acquired	0.643	0.775	1.387	0.866	1.014
Swedish MNE	(1.94)**	(1.78)*	(0.63)	(1.69)*	(0.11)
Vertical acquired	0.221	0.235	0.309	0.658	0.824
Swedish exporter	(4.53)***	(4.70)***	(3.80)***	(3.67)***	(1.98)**
Vertical acquired	1.187	1.578	0.808	1.594	1.620
Swedish domestic	(0.33)	(1.01)	(0.27)	(1.54)	(1.53)
Horizontal acquired	0.985	1.057	1.301	1.220	1.471
Swedish MNE	(0.21)	(0.46)	(0.74)	(0.32)	(0.98)
Horizontal acquired	0.700	0.750	0.701	0.920	0.934
Swedish exporter	(2.35)**	(2.29)***	(2.75)***	(2.08)***	(2.12)***
Horizontal acquired	1.352	2.162	1.750	2.645	1.061
Swedish domestic	(0.55)	(0.96)	(0.96)	(1.22)	(0.88)
Domestic acquisition	0.186	0.191	0.157	0.467	
	(7.77)***	(8.58)***	(9.09)***	(7.74)***	
Multiplant	0.891	0.890	0.897	1.854	1.974
(plant level)	(1.29)	(1.50)	(1.36)	(5.49)***	(5.04)***
Failed other plant	0.541	0.540	0.541	0.826	0.671
(plant level)	(14.80)***	(15.79)***	(15.78)***	(4.33)***	(7.31)***
Labour productivity	0.613	0.610	0.608	0.700	0.778
(firm level)	(13.85)***	(13.50)***	(13.42)***	(8.19)***	(4.37)***
Plant controls	Yes	Yes	Yes	Yes	Yes
Firm controls	Yes	Yes	Yes	Yes	Yes
Observation	31,047	31,047	31,047	19,784	13,395
Wald Chi^2	11,996	12,314	12,641	6,875	4,864
Hausman test (p-value)	0.002	0.001	0.002		
Linktest (hatsq)	0.010	0.007	0.007	−0.001	0.021
	(0.98)	(0.90)	(0.90)	(0.18)	(2.22)***

NOTES: Estimations are stratified by industry and year. Industries are defined at the SNI92 2-digit level (22 industries). Standard errors in parentheses. ***, **, and * indicate significance at the 1%, 5%, and 10% levels, respectively. Only plants in firms with 50 employees or more are included. In column (v) plants within firms taken over by other domestic firms are excluded.

lead to biased conclusions. We show that only exporters experience increases in their survival prospects, and that it matters whether the acquisition is horizontal or non-horizontal.

Why do we not find any effects for acquired MNEs or purely domestic firms? The former may be quite similar to their acquirer and, hence, have little to learn in terms of new technology coming in. This ties in with recent empirical work on productivity differences between firms, which shows that multinationals, regardless of whether they are domestic or foreign owned, have a productivity premium compared with purely domestic firms (Criscuolo and Martin 2008). By contrast, purely domestic firms may be quite different from the acquirer in terms of their pre-acquisition characteristics. In fact, they may be too different to absorb the new knowledge and hence are not able to improve their survival chances significantly. Only exporters, which have a certain level of 'absorptive capacity,' may be able to use the new knowledge that comes in with the foreign acquirer.

5. Employment effects

Thus far we have considered the extensive margin of adjustment, namely, the survival of the plants. Plant closure is, of course, not the only mechanism of adjustment after foreign acquisition. The acquisition may also lead to adjustment along the intensive margin for surviving plants, whereby the scale of the operations may be reduced or increased. Here we look at employment adjustment, as this is one of the most policy-relevant plant performance measures, as it directly relates to concerns about job losses following foreign takeovers of previous national firms.

In order to estimate the impact of ownership change on employment growth in acquired plants we adopt a differences-in-differences methodology. The first step proceeds by comparing the average employment growth $\dot{E}$ before acquisition with its post-acquisition counterpart. However, the resulting quantity, say, $\Delta^a \dot{E}$, is a biased estimator of the impact of the ownership change on employment growth, since it is likely to be affected by other factors that are contemporaneous with the acquisition. Now consider the changes in employment growth of the control plants corresponding to the pre- and post-acquisitions periods, say, $\Delta^c \dot{E}$. If exogenous shocks that are contemporaneous with the acquisitions affect the acquired and control firms in more or less similar fashions, the differences-in-differences estimator, which is defined as $\delta = \Delta^a \dot{E} - \Delta^c \dot{E}$, would purge the effects of common shocks and provide an unbiased estimator of the impact of ownership change.

To implement the above methodology within a regression framework, one can estimate the following equation, using the sample of acquired plants plus the control group:

$$\dot{E}_{it} = \alpha + \delta \, Acquisition_i + \varepsilon_{it}. \tag{5}$$

Here i and t index plants and time periods, respectively, and *Acquisition* is, as before, a dummy equal to one if the plant is acquired by a foreign owner. In equation (5) the estimator for δ yields the average percentage point change in the growth rate of employment that can be attributed to foreign acquisitions.

In our empirical implementation, we extend the basic regression framework in several directions. Firstly, we allow for different effects of foreign acquisitions of Swedish MNEs, exporters, and purely domestic firms, as in the hazard model in table 8. We also include interaction terms for vertical acquisitions, and include a dummy for domestic acquisitions in the control group in order to identify a 'foreign acquisition' effect. Furthermore, year dummies and industry-specific effects are included to capture aggregate shocks and permanent differences in the trend of employment growth across sectors, respectively. A vector of plant and firm characteristics is also included to control for observable changes that are potentially correlated with employment changes. This vector consists of the growth of labour productivity, capital intensity and R&D intensity, plant age, employment level in $t - 1$, plants skill intensity relative to the industry mean skill intensity, a dummy capturing whether the plant belongs to a multi-plant firm, and a dummy variable that is equal to one if another plant in the same firm exited.

The above methodology assumes that foreign acquisitions are exogenous to the process underlying the process of employment dynamics of the acquired plants. However, if employment growth plays some role in driving acquisitions, then it is possible that the acquisition indicators may be endogenous to equation (5). As above, possible endogeneity may be allowed for by using the estimate of the probability of foreign acquisition as an instrument or selecting a control group based on propensity score matching.[18]

The results of the estimation of equation (5) using IV estimation as well as estimation of the model using a matched sample are reported in table 9. What is notable is that adjustment along the intensive margin of employment is somewhat different from adjustment along the extensive margin of plant survival. While we found that both vertical and horizontal foreign acquisitions raise the survival probabilities of domestic exporters (not MNEs) only, employment growth is higher after vertical acquisitions in Swedish exporters. Based on the matched sample in column (iv), a foreign acquisition leads to an increase in employment growth by roughly 4–5% for Swedish exporters. Furthermore, we find that the effect of domestic acquisitions is also positive, but only statistically significant in two out of four cases. As before, we still find, however, that there are no foreign acquisition effects if the target is a purely domestic firm. The post-acquisitions effects for Swedish MNE are positive, but not robust across different estimation techniques.

18 Vella and Verbeek (1999) have shown that this type of instrumental variables (IV) approach generates estimates comparable to Heckman's (1978) well-known endogeneity bias corrected OLS estimator.

TABLE 9
Foreign and domestic acquisition of all Swedish manufacturing plants (growth in employment as dependent variable)

	(i) IV	(ii) IV 2	(iii) IV 3	(iv) Matched sample	(v) Matched sample	(vi) Matched sample
Vertical acquired Swedish MNE	0.088 (1.90)**	0.078 (1.84)*	0.052 (1.63)	0.021 (1.67)*	0.025 (1.71)*	
Vertical acquired Swedish exporter	0.112 (2.49)***	0.124 (2.63)***	0.117 (2.62)***	0.049 (2.20)***	0.046 (1.97)**	
Vertical acquired Swedish domestic	0.066 (1.49)	0.068 (1.69)*	0.023 (1.27)	0.011 (1.03)	0.014 (1.10)	
Horizontal acquired Swedish MNE	−0.033 (0.31)	−0.053 (0.55)	0.009 (0.14)	−0.002 (0.04)	0.012 (0.22)	
Horizontal acquired Swedish exporter	0.027 (0.44)	0.023 (0.11)	0.010 (0.15)	0.013 (1.17)	0.013 (0.73)	
Horizontal acquired Swedish domestic	−0.048 (1.55)	−0.022 (0.93)	−0.013 (0.54)	−0.009 (0.21)	0.012 (0.50)	
Domestic acquisition	0.062 (1.70)*	0.060 (1.61)	0.026 (0.63)	0.021 (2.79)***		0.038 (3.54)***
Multiplant (plant level)	−0.079 (13.63)***	−0.080 (12.98)***	−0.080 (12.88)***	−0.090 (12.35)***	−0.091 (10.69)***	−0.110 (8.92)***
Failed other plant (plant level)	−0.010 (1.75)*	−0.010 (1.88)*	−0.010 (1.63)	−0.018 (2.18)**	−0.005 (0.50)	−0.024 (2.01)**
Growth in labour productivity (firm level)	0.018 (2.11)**	0.019 (2.15)**	0.018 (2.00)**	0.014 (1.14)	0.019 (1.25)	−0.015 (0.65)
Plant controls	Yes	Yes	Yes	Yes	Yes	Yes
Firm controls	Yes	Yes	Yes	Yes	Yes	Yes
Observations	23,730	23,730	23,730	16,128	13,399	9,394
Adjusted R^2	0.02	0.02	0.02	0.03	0.03	0.03
Hausman test (p-value)	0.002	0.002	0.001			

NOTES: All regressions contain year and 2-digit industry dummies. Standard errors in parentheses. ***, **, and * indicate significance at the 1%, 5%, and 10% levels, respectively. Only plants in firms with 50 employees or more are included. In column (v), plants within firms taken over by other domestic firms are excluded.

6. Conclusions

This paper has investigated the effect of foreign acquisition on plant survival and employment growth in Swedish manufacturing during the 1990s. To this end we have used a unique data set where firm- and plant-level information is linked. This means that we are able to use firm information as well as characteristics at the plant level.

When we control for possible endogeneity of the acquisition dummy by using an instrumental variable approach and a matched sample and also control for other plant- and firm-specific characteristics, the result reveals that survival ratio for acquired exporters, but not other types of firms, improves post-acquisition.

Depending on whether the acquisition is in the same industry (horizontal) or not (vertical), the point estimates suggest that survival increases by between 17% and 34% after foreign takeover for vertical and 6% and 8% for horizontal acquisitions. We also find that employment growth is higher in takeover targets that were exporters prior to acquisition.

There are important implications of this finding for researchers and policy makers. Firstly, foreign acquisition appears to have overall positive or neutral effects on survival and employment growth of targets. There is no evidence of negative effects. Hence, strong fears as to the sustainability of domestic industry in the light of increasing foreign acquisitions appear unfounded. Secondly, when judging the magnitude of these effects, it is important to take into account aspects of firm-level heterogeneity, as not all types of firms benefit equally in terms of higher survival prospects or employment growth from foreign acquisition.

Appendix A

TABLE A1
Mean variable differences between acquired and non-acquired firms in the pre-acquisition period, matched sample

	T = 0	T = −1	T = −2
Plant variables			
Employment	20	33	49
	(1.83)*	(2.88)***	(3.67)***
Age	−1.40	−0.7	−0.61
	(6.85)***	(3.49)***	(2.58)***
Skill intensity	−0.10	−0.05	−0.19
	(1.55)	(0.77)	(2.21)**
Obs. target/non-target	907/10,776	808/10,387	572/10,121
Firm variables			
Employment	78	76	46
	(0.88)	(0.81)	(0.44)
Skill intensity	0.9	0.3	0.6
	(0.86)	(0.32)	(0.55)
R&D intensity	0.1	0.2	0.1
	(0.37)	(0.67)	(0.36)
Capital-labour ratio	23.6	50.0	16.3
	(0.68)	(1.37)	(0.43)
Shipment	285	252	172
	(1.13)	(0.95)	(0.60)
Export intensity	4.3	4.3	2.2
	(1.84)*	(1.82)*	(0.87)
Productivity	5.57	25.4	31.2
	(0.32)	(1.52)	(1.82)*
Obs. target/non-target	207/2,372	198/2,240	168/2,114

TABLE A2
The share of total number of firm and plant acquired by foreign MNEs (whole and matched sample)

	Whole sample					
	Swedish MNEs		Exporting non-MNEs		Non-exporting non-MNEs	
	Firms	Plants	Firms	Plants	Firms	Plants
1993–2002	30.6	31.5	56.6	56.0	12.8	12.5
	Matched sample					
	Swedish MNE		Exporter		Non-exporter	
	Firms	Plants	Firms	Plants	Firms	Plants
1993–2002	29.6	30.3	57.5	57.0	12.9	12.7

References

Alfaro, L., and A. Charlton (2009) 'Intra-industry foreign direct investment,' *American Economic Review*, forthcoming

Almeida, R.K. (2007) 'The effects of foreign owned firms on the labour market,' *Journal of International Economics* 71, 75–96

Arnold, J., and B.S. Javorcik (2005) 'Gifted kids or pushy parents? Foreign acquisitions and plant performance in Indonesia,' CEPR Discussion Paper 5065

Audretsch, D.B., and Mahmood, T. (1995) 'New-firm survival: new results using a hazard function,' *Review of Economics and Statistics* 77, 97–103

Bandick, R., and H. Görg (2009) 'Foreign acquisition, plant survival, and employment growth,' Kiel Working Paper 1525, Kiel Institute for the World Economy

Bernard, A., and B. Jensen (2007) 'Firm structure, multinationals and manufacturing plant deaths,' *Review of Economics and Statistics* 89, 193–204

Bernard, A., and F. Sjöholm (2003) 'Foreign owners and plant survival,' NBER Working Paper No. 10039

Coles, J., M. Lemon, and F. Meschke (2007), 'Structural models and endogeneity in corporate finance: the link between managerial ownership and corporate performance,' mimeo

Conyon, M.J., S. Girma, S. Thompson, and P.W. Wright (2002) 'The impact of foreign acquisition on wages and productivity in the United Kingdom,' *Journal of Industrial Economics* 50, 85–102

Criscuolo, C., and R. Martin (2008) 'Multinationals and the US productivity leadership: evidence from Britain,' *Review of Economics and Statistics*, forthcoming

Disney, R., J. Haskel, and Y. Heden (2003) 'Entry, exit and establishment survival in UK manufacturing,' *Journal of Industrial Economics* 51, 91–112

Fukao, K., K. Ito, H. Kwon, and M. Takizawa (2006) 'Cross border acquisitions and target firm performance: evidence from Japanese firm level data,' NBER Working Paper No. 12422

Girma, S. and Görg, H. (2004) 'Blessing or Curse? Domestic plants survival and employment prospects after foreign acquisition,' *Applied Economics Quarterly* 50, 89–110

— (2007a) 'Evaluating the foreign ownership wage premium using a difference-in-differences matching approach,' *Journal of International Economics* 72, 97–112
— (2007b) 'Multinationals' productivity advantage: scale or technology?' *Economic Inquiry* 45, 350–62
Greenaway, D., and R. Kneller (2007) 'Firm heterogeneity, exporting and foreign direct investment,' *Economic Journal* 117, F134–61
— (2008) 'Exporting, productivity and agglomeration,' *European Economic Review* 52, 919–39
Hansson, P., P. Karpaty, M. Lindvert, L. Lundberg, A. Poldahl, and L. Yun (2007) 'Svenskt näringsliv i en globaliserad värld,' ITPS A2007:4.
Harris, R., and C. Robinson (2002) 'The effect of foreign acquisitions on total factor productivity: plant-level evidence from U.K.manufacturing, 1987–1992,' *Review of Economics and Statistics* 84, 562–8
Harris, R., D. Siegel, and M. Wright (2005) 'Assessing the impact of management buyouts on economic efficiency: plant-level evidence from the United Kingdom,' *Review of Economics and Statistics* 87, 148–53
Head, K., and J. Ries (2008), 'FDI as an outcome of the market for corporate control: theory and evidence,' *Journal of International Economics* 74, 2–20
Heckman, J.J. (1978) 'Dummy endogenous variables in a simultaneous equation system,' *Econometrica* 46, 931–59
Helpman, E., M. Melitz, and S. Yeaple (2004) 'Export versus FDI with heterogeneous firms,' *American Economic Review* 94, 300–16
Hijzen, A., H. Görg, and M. Manchin (2008) 'Cross-border mergers and acquisitions and the role of trade costs,' *European Economic Review* 52, 849–66
Hujer, R., K. Maurer and M. Wellner (1999), 'Estimating the effect of vocational training on unemployment duration in West Germany – a discrete hazard-rate model with instrumental variables,' *Jahrbücher für Nationalökonomie und Statistik* 218, 619–46
Huttunen, K. (2007) 'The effect of foreign acquisition on employment and wages: evidence from Finnish establishments,' *Review of Economics and Statistics* 89, 497–509
Leuven, E., and B. Sianesi (2003) PSMATCH2: 'Stata module to perform full Mahalanobis and propensity score matching, common support graphing, and covariate imbalance testing.' Available at http://ideas.repec.org/c/boc/bocode/s432001.html
Mata, J., and P. Portugal (2002) 'The survival of new domestic and foreign-owned firms,' *Strategic Management Journal* 23, 323–43
McGuckin, R.H., and S.V. Nguyen (2001) 'The impact of ownership changes: a view from labour markets,' *International Journal of Industrial Organization* 19, 739–62
Neary, J.P. (2007) 'Cross-border mergers as instruments of comparative advantage,' *Review of Economic Studies* 74, 1229–57
Petkova, N. (2007) 'Does foreign ownership lead to higher productivity?' mimeo, University of Michigan
Prentice, R.L., and L.A. Gloeckler (1978) 'Regression analysis of grouped survival data with application to breast cancer data,' *Biometrics* 34, 57–67
Thompson, S. (1999) 'Takeovers, joint ventures and the acquisition of resources for diversification,' *Scottish Journal of Political Economy* 46, 303–18
UNCTAD (2007) *World Investment Report 2007* (New York: United Nations)
Van Beveren, I. (2007) 'Footloose multinationals in Belgium?' *Review of World Economics* 143(3)
Vella, F., and M. Verbeek (1999) 'Estimating and interpreting models with endogenous treatment effects,' *Journal of Business and Economic Statistics* 17, 473–8
Wagner, Joachim (2007) 'Exports and productivity: a survey of the evidence from firm-level data,' *World Economy* 30, 60–82

PART II

Searching for Productivity Spillovers: The “Traditional Approach”

Chapter 8

MULTINATIONAL COMPANIES AND PRODUCTIVITY SPILLOVERS: A META-ANALYSIS*

Holger Görg and Eric Strobl

This paper presents a meta-analysis of the literature on multinational companies and productivity spillovers. By collecting information from a sample of published and unpublished papers on the impact of multinational presence on domestic productivity, we investigate whether certain aspects of the study design affect the results, and whether there is publication bias in the literature. Our findings show that some aspects of the empirical methods used, namely, how the presence of multinationals is defined, and whether cross-section or panel analysis is employed, may have an effect on the results. We also discover some evidence that there may be publication bias.

The increasing importance of multinational companies (MNCs) and associated foreign direct investment (FDI) for international production has prompted considerable interest in the effects of MNCs on host countries.[1] One of the most frequently referred to positive effect is the presence of technological externalities, which can lead to productivity spillovers from MNCs to domestic firms in the host country. Since MNCs use a higher level of technology, and technology, or knowledge, has certain characteristics of public goods (Caves, 1996, Markusen, 1995), there is scope for technological externalities and indigenous firms may benefit through spillovers from MNCs. If there are productivity spillovers, the presence of MNCs leads to productivity increases in domestic firms, allowing them to become more efficient.[2]

Such spillovers can occur through three main channels (Blomström and Kokko, 1998). First, if there are movements of highly skilled staff from MNCs to domestic firms, these employees may take with them knowledge which may be usefully applied in the domestic firm. Second, there may be so-called 'demonstration effects' if there are arm's-length relationships between MNCs and domestic firms and domestic firms learn superior production technologies from MNCs. Third, competition from MNCs may force domestic rivals to update production technologies and techniques to become more productive. This is frequently referred to as a 'competition effect'. As Aitken and Harrison (1999) point out, however, this competition effect may also reduce productivity in domestic firms, if MNCs attract away demand from their domestic competitors.

* We are grateful to Salvador Barrios, Sourafel Girma, Steve Machin (the editor) and four anonymous referees for helpful comments and suggestions. Any remaining errors are, of course, our own. Financial support through the European Commission Fifth Framework Programme (Grant No. HPSE-CT-1999-00017) and the Leverhulme Trust (Programme Grant F114/BF) is gratefully acknowledged.

[1] There is also a literature concerned with examining the effects of MNCs on home countries, see, for example Blomström *et al.* (1997). As this is not the focus of our paper, we do not review these issues herein.

[2] See Blomström and Kokko (1998) and Pack and Saggi (1997) for recent concise reviews of the literature on host country effects, in particular, productivity spillovers and technology flows, of MNCs.

Productivity spillovers are difficult to measure, since, as Krugman (1991, p. 53) points out, 'knowledge flows ... leave no paper trail by which they may be measured and tracked'. The approach adopted in the empirical literature therefore largely avoids the (arguably difficult to answer) question as to how productivity spillovers actually take place, but focuses on the simpler issue of whether the presence of MNCs affects productivity in domestic firms. This is usually done in the framework of an econometric analysis in which labour productivity or total factor productivity in domestic firms is regressed on a number of covariates assumed to have an effect on productivity, one of which is the presence of foreign firms. If the estimate of the coefficient on the foreign presence variable turns out to have a positive and statistically significant sign, this is taken as evidence that spillovers have taken place from MNCs to domestic firms.

The empirical results on the presence of spillovers are mixed. In the first empirical study of this kind, Caves (1974), using cross-sectional data for Australia, finds evidence of positive spillovers. His initial approach has been refined and extended subsequently by, for example, Globerman (1979) for Canada, and Blomström and Persson (1983), Blomström (1986), Blomström and Wolff (1994) and Kokko (1994, 1996) using data for Mexico. These studies, all of which use cross-sectional data, also find statistically significant positive effects of the presence of MNCs on productivity in domestic firms. Haddad and Harrison (1993) appears to be the first paper which benefits from the availability of firm level data for several years, and newly developed panel data econometric techniques to analyse productivity spillovers from MNCs in Morocco. Using such highly disaggregated data and the appropriate estimation techniques, they find evidence for negative spillover effects of multinationals, ie *ceteris paribus,* the presence of MNCs in Morocco reduces productivity in domestic firms.

Table 1 lists the results of our literature search, described in more detail in section 1, on papers on productivity spillovers from MNCs. It is apparent that, while there have been a number of spillover studies since Caves (1974), recent years have seen a surge of such studies. This reflects, on the one hand, the growing interest, not least from policy makers, in the effects of MNCs on host countries in order to justify policy incentives aimed at attracting MNCs. On the other hand, it also bears testimony to the fact that disaggregated data over longer time periods and estimation techniques for the analysis of such data allowing the investigation of this issue have become widely available to researchers. One should note from the table that, since Kokko *et al.* (1996), all but two studies listed had available firm level data. Also, the table shows that all but one study using panel data find statistically significant negative or statistically insignificant effects of MNC presence on domestic productivity, while all but one cross-sectional study find statistically significant positive effects. This suggests that the availability of longitudinal firm level data, and the appropriate statistical techniques for analysing them, have had profound effects on the results obtained in spillover studies.

Various explanations are put forward in the literature to explain statistically

Table 1

Papers on productivity spillovers included in the meta-analysis

Author(s)	Country	Year	Data	Aggreg.	MNC Measure	Obs.	t-stat	Result
Caves (1974)	Australia	1966	cs	industry	empl	22	3.2	+
Globerman (1979)	Canada	1972	cs	industry	output	42	1.5	+
Blomström and Persson (1983)	Mexico	1970	cs	industry	empl	215	3.1	+
Blomström (1986)	Mexico	1970/75	cs	industry	empl	145	3.1	+
Haddad and Harrison (1993)	Morocco	1985–89	panel	firm & ind.	assets	11,772/440	−0.1/−5.9	−
Blomström and Wolff (1994)	Mexico	1970/75	cs	industry	empl	20	4.1	+
Kokko (1994)	Mexico	1970	cs	industry	empl	216	3.5	+
Kokko (1996)	Mexico	1970	cs	industry	empl	156	2.4	+
Kokko *et al.* (1996)	Uruguay	1970	cs	firm	output	159	0.9	?
Aitken and Harrison (1999)	Venezuela	1976–89	panel	firm	assets	32,521	−3.6	−
Blomström and Sjöholm (1999)	Indonesia	1991	cs	firm	output	13,663	4.4	+
Chuang and Lin (1999)	Taiwan	1991	cs	firm	assets	8846	27.7	+
Sjöholm (1999*a*)	Indonesia	1980–91	cs	firm	output	15,670/7,760/2,892	19.7/4.9/3.0	+
Sjöholm (1999*b*)	Indonesia	1980–91	cs	firm	output	2,892	3.2	+
Djankov and Hoekman (2000)	Czech Rep.	1993–96	panel	firm	assets	340	−3.1	−
Kathuria (2000)	India	1976–89	panel	firm	sales	108	−4.7	−
Liu *et al.* (2000)	UK	1991–95	panel	industry	empl	240	2.1	+
Driffield (2001)	UK	1989–92	cs	industry	sales	103	1.3	+
Girma *et al.* (2001)	UK	1991–96	panel	firm	empl	11,406	0.3/−1.1	?
Barrios (2000)	Spain	1990–94	panel	firm	output	3,073	−1.0	?
Flores *et al.* (2000)	Portugal	1992–95	panel	firm	output	36	1.7	?

insignificant or negative results. For example, the presence of foreign firms can reduce productivity of domestic firms, as pointed out by Aitken and Harrison (1999). Since foreign firms can frequently be assumed to posses some sort of firm-specific assets (Caves, 1996) which allow them to use a superior production technology, they have lower marginal cost than a domestic competitor and can attract demand away from domestic firms. Thus, productivity in domestic firms falls, at least in the short run, because of competition with MNCs.

It is also argued in the literature that positive spillovers only affect a certain group of firms and aggregate studies may, therefore, underestimate the true significance of such effects. Kokko *et al.* (1996) find evidence for productivity spillovers only to domestic firms with moderate technology gaps *vis-à-vis* foreign firms, ie domestic firms with at least some capability of being able to make use of the spillover effects. They do not find evidence for spillovers from MNCs to domestic firms which use considerably lower levels of technology. Aitken and Harrison (1999) find that productivity in small Venezuelan firms (with less than 50 employees) has increased following the presence of MNCs, while there does not appear to be a similar effect on large domestic firms.

The question remains unanswered, however, as to why some studies find positive, while others find negative or no spillover effects from MNCs, and why the magnitude of regression coefficients differs across studies. As argued above, differences in research design, methodology and data may have an impact on the results obtained. In this paper, we try to shed some light on this issue by performing a meta-analysis of the literature on productivity spillovers. Meta-analysis can be used to summarise, and to explain variations in results of a number of similar empirical studies concerned with one research topic (Stanley and Jarrell, 1989). While meta-analysis has been frequently applied in educational, psychological and medical research,[3] its application in economics has been limited to a relatively small number of studies. For example, Phillips (1994) examines the effect of education and farmers' efficiency, Phillips and Gross's (1995) analysis focuses on the impact of taxes on economic development, Smith and Huang (1995) examine the relationship between willingness to pay for reductions in air pollution, and the level thereof, while Stanley (1998) uses meta-analysis to investigate empirical studies of the Ricardian equivalence theorem. Meta-analysis can also be used to test for publication bias in the literature, that is the tendency in academic journals to publish results which are statistically significant. Such analyses were recently carried out by Card and Krueger (1995) for minimum-wage studies, and Ashenfelter *et al.* (1999) for papers on the estimates of returns to schooling.

One of the possible reasons why meta-analysis has not been used more frequently in economics may be that the nature of the data used in economic research is, in most cases, non-experimental, while data in the fields of education, psychology or medicine are mainly based on experiments. It may there-

[3] See Glass *et al.* (1981), Hunter *et al.* (1982) and Egger and Smith (1997) for introductions to meta-analysis in the three respective fields.

fore be difficult to transfer many of the methods used in those fields into economics, as results obtained in different economic studies of one topic may be dependent on each other. As Stanley and Jarrell (1989) argue, however, the problem of dependence of observations is likely to be no more important (or unimportant) for meta-analyses than for primary econometric studies, as those are not the result of controlled experiments either.

Be that as it may, meta-analysis, despite its limitations, can provide a useful tool to analyse the literature on productivity spillovers. Specifically, it allows one to quantify and disentangle certain trends in the empirical results that would be difficult to gauge from simple eyeballing. We acknowledge, however, that there are potential problems which ought to be kept in mind when interpreting the results of this paper.

Following Card and Krueger (1995), we employ meta-analysis in the following fashion: for a sample of studies of productivity spillovers, we collect the different coefficients on the foreign presence variable found in the different studies, and their associated values of the *t*-statistic. We then regress the *t*-statistics on a number of meta-independent study characteristics, such as sample size, variable definitions used, etc.; a technique named by Stanley and Jarrell (1989) as 'meta-regression analysis'. Some of these study characteristics, namely, whether it is a cross-section or panel analysis, and variable definitions have an effect on the size of the coefficient found in the productivity studies. Thus, our analysis suggests that the research design is crucial for a proper analysis of productivity spillovers. Estimating a different specification of the meta-regression, we also find evidence that there may be publication bias in the literature on productivity spillovers.

The remainder of this paper is structured as follows. Section 1 presents the sample of studies used and section 2 provides the results of the meta-regression analysis. In section 3, we describe the results of an analysis of publication bias, and section 4 summarises our main results and presents some concluding comments.

1. Description of the Sample

The sample of papers from the productivity spillovers literature analysed in our paper consists of 21 studies, 18 of which are published in academic journals, one is a contribution to an edited volume, and two are unpublished manuscripts; see Table 1 for a listing of studies included. The papers were obtained from inspection of the recent concise survey of the literature of the wider area of technology spillovers by Blomström and Kokko (1998) as well as an EconLit search for the key words 'productivity spillovers'.[4] Furthermore, we searched through recent issues of appropriate journals and conducted internet searches for unpublished papers. There may, no doubt, be further published

[4] The EconLit search produced 171 references, most of which, however, were concerned with the related, yet distinct, issue of R&D spillovers and growth. See, for example, Griliches (1998) for a discussion. Also, we only included papers written in English in our meta analysis.

and unpublished papers, and especially dissertations which we were not able to take account of in this study. Of the papers included, nine are concerned with measuring productivity spillovers in developed countries (three for the UK, one for Australia, Canada, Czech Republic, Portugal, Spain, and Taiwan). The remaining papers deal with developing countries, five of which examine the Mexican case. All studies relate to manufacturing industries.

In terms of the research design, most studies analyse data for one year, or one specified time period, using one particular definition of the dependent variable and varying the number and definition of explanatory variables reported in the regression results. For such studies, we included in our sample the most preferred specification, either by examining the highest R^2 value or by the comparability of the variable definitions to the other studies included. There are, however, three papers for which we include more than one regression result in the sample. From Sjöholm (1999*a*), we include three results because he examines different time periods and uses different definitions of the dependent variable and, from Haddad and Harrison (1993) and Girma *et al.* (2001), we include two results each to account for their different dependent variable definition. This leads to a total of 25 observations to be used in our meta-analysis.

Fourteen observations (from 12 papers) are obtained from studies which used plant level data, while 11 observations relate to industry level data (at varying levels of aggregation). Panel data were only used in eight papers, from which we obtained ten observations, while the remaining studies are based on cross-section data. In terms of the variable definitions, nine observations relate to foreign presence being measured as employment share in foreign owned firms, nine measure foreign presence as output (or value added) share while the other seven use other related measures. Haddad and Harrison (1993), Chuang and Lin (1999) and Djankov and Hoekman (2000) measure foreign presence as the share of assets held by foreign firms, Aitken and Harrison (1999) use the share of foreign equity participation, while Kathuria (2000) uses the share of sales of foreign firms. Driffield (2001) calculates the growth of sales in foreign-owned firms as a measure of foreign presence.

Of the observations included in our sample, 14 out of the 25 cases define the dependent variable as labour productivity (ie output or value added per worker), while output growth is used in nine cases. Blomström (1986) calculates a different measure, namely, an efficiency index $e_i = \bar{y}_i / y_i^+$ where y_i^+ is value added per employee in firms in a size class with the highest value added per employee within an industry i, and $\bar{y}_i$ is the industry average. Thus, this index calculates the distance of the industry average from the 'best practice' or 'efficiency frontier' in the industry. Kathuria (2000) uses a similar measure in his study of productivity spillovers in India.[5]

[5] In some of their specifications, Aitken and Harrison (1999) also use a different dependent variable definition, namely the log of output. In that case, however, both the dependent and the foreign presence variable are defined differently and we therefore do not include this result in our meta-analysis.

2. Meta-Regression Analysis

To attempt an explanation of the variations in results across the sample of studies of productivity spillovers, we follow Stanley and Jarrell (1989) who suggest estimating an equation as follows:

$$Y_j = \beta_0 + \sum_{k=1}^{K} \beta_k Z_{jk} + e_j \qquad j = 1, 2, \ldots N \tag{1}$$

where Y_j is the reported estimate in study j from a total of N studies, and Z_{jk} are meta-independent variables which proxy characteristics of the empirical studies in the sample so as to explain the variation in $Y_j s$ across studies.

It must be pointed out that an analysis of the differences in the effect of spillovers across studies is hampered by the fact that the foreign presence variable is measured in different units in the different studies. For example, Globerman (1979) measures value-added per worker in thousands of Canadian dollars, while Flores *et al.* (2000) use millions of Portuguese escudos. Of course, these differences in measurement will affect the magnitude of the coefficients on foreign presence. We, therefore, decided to use a dimensionless variable, namely the *t*-statistic (which can take on positive as well as negative values) as the dependent variable in our meta-analysis, as suggested by Stanley and Jarrell (1989). The *t*-statistic provides us with a standardised measure of the effect of the foreign presence variable on the dependent variable which allows a cross-study comparison.

In terms of the choice of explanatory variables to be included in the estimation of (1), we are confronted with two main problems: first, there is no economic theory to guide us for our empirical specification, and, second, we are constrained to use a small number of explanatory variables due to a small number of degrees of freedom. Given these constraints, there are a number of characteristics of individual studies which we feel may, *a priori*, impact on the size of the *t*-statistic. For example, results may differ because of differences in numbers of observations used in the papers. In our sample, the smallest number of observations was available to Blomström and Wolff (1994) with only 20 observations, while Aitken and Harrison (1999), on the other side of the scale, can avail themselves of 32,521 observations. *Ceteris paribus*, an increase in the sample size should raise the (absolute value of the) *t*-ratio. To take account of differing sample sizes, we include the square root of the degrees of freedom in our meta-analysis, as in Card and Krueger (1995). As we discuss in more detail below, this variable also allows us to conduct a simple test for publication bias in the studies on productivity spillovers.

We also control for differences in the time periods used in the studies by including the average year of the study period. We take account of the nature of the data used by including dummies to control for whether data are industry or plant level, and whether they are cross-section or panel data. Furthermore, we calculate a set of dummies to take account of different definitions of the foreign presence variable (measured as either employment share, output share, or other) and of the dependent variable (output per worker, growth of output, or other). Ideally, we would also like to include country specific dummies; however, given our sample size, this was not feasible. To control for differences across host countries we, instead, include a dummy variable equal to one if a country is a developing country and zero if it is developed.

Furthermore, without constraints, it would appear reasonable to include a variable to control for the nature of the different explanatory variables included in the different studies. Again, however, the small size of our sample prevents the inclusion of additional dummy variables to control for this. Suffice it to say that most studies include additional sectoral characteristics as explanatory variables, such as measures of market concentration (Blomström, 1986), average capital–labour ratio in domestic firms (Kokko *et al.*, 1996), measures of labour quality (Globerman, 1979) or measures of labour and capital inputs in estimations of total output growth (Haddad and Harrison, 1993).

The results of the meta-regression, using OLS are reported in Table 2. As Stanley and Jarrell (1989) point out, since the dependent variables are drawn from studies with widely different characteristics, it is highly likely that the error terms of the meta-regression are not homoscedastic. Furthermore, we use multiple estimates from three papers, so the error terms from observations taken from the same papers will most likely be correlated. To take account of this, we calculate standard errors which allow for heteroscedasticity and a non-specified correlation between observations from the same group (ie paper).[6] Columns (1)–(4) present estimation results for the total sample, while columns (5)–(8) produce results based on a sample in which we excluded two spillover results that appear to be outliers. We eliminated these two observations, namely one of the results reported by Sjöholm (1999*a*) and the result by Chuang and Lin (1999), from our sample because they have what appear to be excessively high *t*-statistics compared to the other studies.

Our results suggest that studies which use cross-sectional data tend to have, on average, higher *t*-ratios than panel studies. In other words, the effect of productivity spillovers appears to be higher in cross-sectional studies. Although we already pointed out above that none of the cross-sectional studies finds a negative result, while most panel data studies do not find positive results, it is interesting to note that this finding is also true when controlling for other characteristics of the research design.

This difference across data set types may arise because of problems associated with unobserved time invariant effects. Specifically, if there are time-invariant effects across the individual units (either industry or firms) that are not captured in the explanatory variables but which are correlated with the foreign presence variable then the cross-sectional studies may produce biased and inconsistent estimates of the effect arising from spillovers. Such time-invariant effects may, however, be purged from panel data studies if, for

[6] We refer to these as heteroscedasticity-autocorrelation consistent standard errors. See Newey and West (1987) for a discussion on the calculation of a covariance matrix with such properties.

Table 2
Results of Meta-regression

Dependent variable: t-statistic

Variable	Including outliers				Excluding outliers			
	(1)	(2)	(3)	(4)	(5)	(6)	(7)	(8)
Square root of degrees of freedom	0.030	0.052	0.034	0.039	−0.014	0.003	−0.011	−0.004
	(0.037)	(0.037)	(0.035)	(0.038)	(0.012)	(0.016)	(0.013)	(0.019)
Dummy = 1 if data are industry level		0.619		−2.051	–	−0.344	–	−0.922
		(3.417)		(4.895)		(2.020)		(2.297)
Dummy = 1 if data are cross-section		11.169		12.422	–	5.047	–	4.067
		(3.692)***		(4.612)**		(1.479)***		(1.399)***
Dummy = 1 if data are for developing country		−4.511		−4.304	–	−1.891	–	−0.912
		(3.050)		(2.777)		(1.187)		(0.969)
Average year of study period		0.229		0.291	–	0.043	–	0.064
		(0.182)		(0.205)		(0.090)		(0.067)
Dummy = 1 if dependent variable is output growth			−4.474	−3.962	–	–	1.262	0.590
			(3.862)	(2.973)			(1.378)	(1.085)
Dummy = 1 if dependent variable is other definition			−4.973	−1.333	–	–	−1.063	−0.976
			(5.301)	(2.290)			(1.628)	(1.410)
Dummy = 1 if foreign presence measured as output share			0.806	−3.465	–	–	−0.343	−1.606
			(2.193)	(3.117)			(1.046)	(1.418)
Dummy = 1 if foreign presence measured as other definition			0.601	1.221	–	–	−4.376	−3.100
			(5.514)	(3.759)			(1.584)***	(1.278)**
Constant	1.627	−457.614	3.012	−577.099	1.996	−86.048	2.708	−125.963
	(1.175)	(363.216)	(1.686)*	(409.476)	(0.752)**	(179.265)	(0.581)***	(132.312)
no. of obs.	25	25	25	25	23	23	23	23
F	0.67	2.74	0.90	4.07	1.33	4.11	6.76	11.81
R^2	0.05	0.53	0.16	0.63	0.05	0.55	0.49	0.69

Notes: heteroscedasticity-autocorrelation consistent standard errors in parentheses.
***, **, * denote statistical significance at the 1%, 5%, 10% level respectively

example, a fixed or random effects estimation technique is used (Baltagi, 1995).[7] Of course, there may be other aspects of the studies, such as misspecified dynamics or time variant unobservable variables that differ across the cross-sectional and panel studies that we are failing to control for. However, despite meticulous checking, no such pattern became apparent.

In terms of variable definitions, it does not appear to make a difference how the dependent variable is defined: whether it is output per worker, output growth, or another measure. Our results suggest, however, that the choice of foreign presence proxy may be an important determinant of differences across studies. Including separate dummy variables for whether a study used foreign output share or some other variable to proxy foreign presence, we find that the latter proxy produces lower results relative to our base-line category of foreign employment share. The coefficient on that variables is, however, only statistically significant if we exclude the two outlying observations (ie columns (5) to (8)). This may suggest that a proper definition of the variable which is supposed to capture the spillover effect is important. As pointed out above, most studies use either the share of employment in foreign-owned firms, or the share of output produced by these firms, as a proxy to capture this effect. Some studies, however, use other measures and our results show that these studies find lower spillover effects than others, *ceteris paribus.* This raises the question for empirical studies of how to measure foreign presence properly.

Our findings suggest that it does not appear to matter whether a study uses industry or plant level data, whether a study is concerned with a developing or developed country, and whether the data are recent. In a simple correlation analysis we do, however, find statistically significant (at the 5% and 10% level respectively) negative correlations between the average year of the study and the dummy for use of cross-section data (−0.52), and the year and the dummy for use of industry level data (−0.35). This suggests that studies using older data tend to be those which use cross-section and industry level data, which may be due to the availability of better and more disaggregated data for more recent research, as discussed above. There is no statistically significant correlation between the use of industry level and cross-section data, however, indicating that the availability of more disaggregated data does not necessarily imply that these data are available in longitudinal format. Thus, in terms of the data available, what appears to be important is the question of whether the data are available over a period of time, rather than just a cross-section. The availability of more disaggregated data at a firm level does not seem to affect the result of productivity spillover studies.

[7] Related to this point is the argument put forward by Aitken and Harrison (1999) that, if foreign multinationals gravitate towards more productive sectors there may be a positive association between sectoral productivity and the presence of foreign firms even without spillovers taking place. They find in their study of a panel of Venezuelan firms that including industry dummies changes a positive and statistically significant coefficient into being negative and significant. However, this lack of industry dummies cannot explain the differences in the results for the sample of observations we use, as we have collected results for econometric specifications without dummies for all but one (Blomström and Sjöholm, 1999) study.

3. Testing for Publication Bias

At least since De Long and Lang (1992) economists have recognised that there may be a tendency among editors of academic journals to publish papers preferably if they reject their null hypothesis, ie if they produce statistically significant results. This is frequently referred to as publication bias and has attracted growing interest in the recent economics literature (Card and Krueger, 1995; Neumark and Washer, 1996; Ashenfelter *et al.*, 1999). As these papers argue, a meta-analysis provides an opportunity to test for publication bias using the results available from the literature.

Such tests are usually based on the idea that, if there were no publication bias, the *t*-statistic on the coefficient in question should be positively related to the size of the sample used in the analysis (Begg and Berlin, 1988). In the case of studies of productivity spillovers, for example, we would therefore expect that studies based on only a small number of observations should be more likely to find a statistically insignificant spillover effect than studies using large numbers of observations. If there were publication bias present, however, we would see that the *t*-ratio was independent of sample size, since studies based on small samples would be equally likely to produce statistically significant effects. As Begg and Berlin (1988) point out, however, this effect of publication bias is based on the assumption that the true spillover effect in the various studies is unrelated to sample size. While this seems intuitively plausible in the case of a single fixed spillover effect, ie if the spillover effect were assumed to be the same across countries and time periods, the assumption of a fixed effect is clearly not appropriate for our analysis, and, indeed, for most studies in economics. The papers included in our meta-analysis are concerned with a variety of host countries with widely different characteristics, and different time periods. It does, therefore, not appear reasonable to expect the true spillover effect to be fixed across the different studies included; rather, we should assume that the effect is randomly distributed. If that is the case, we need to consider whether we would still expect the random effects to have a distribution which is independent of sample size. Following Begg and Berlin's (1988) arguments, we would expect that that is indeed the case. In economic analyses, sample sizes are usually not planned (as they are, for example, in medical research); instead, they depend mainly on the availability of data and computing power. Therefore, as argued by Begg and Berlin (1988), it may be reasonable to assume that the sample size is determined without any meaningful association to the underlying true random effect.

This assumption then allows us to investigate for publication bias by analysing whether there is indeed no meaningful relationship between sample size and spillover effect. We utilise the test proposed by Card and Krueger (1995), which is a simple yet intuitive test of publication bias. As pointed out above, basic sample theory suggests that, loosely speaking, studies with larger numbers of observations should also produce higher *t*-ratios. More precisely, as Card and Krueger (1995) point out, the coefficient of a regression of the log of the absolute value of the *t*-ratio on the log of the square root of the degrees of freedom should be equal to 1. This suggests a straightforward test for publication bias, namely, estimate the said regression and examine the size of the coefficient. This is what we set out to do in this section.

We use the same data set as used for the meta-analysis in section 2, excluding the two unpublished studies. Fig. 1 shows the relationship between the absolute value of the estimated *t*-statistics and the square root of degrees of freedom (srdf) in the included studies. We would expect a positive relationship between the estimated *t*-statistics and degrees of freedom, which does not appear to be the case for the data displayed in the graph. It is not obvious from Fig. 1 whether there is any relationship, the scatter of points appears to be most closely fitted by a horizontal line. Note that this graph clearly shows the two results which are outliers in our sample and which may blur the overall relationship. To take account of this, we also graphed the observations excluding the two outliers in Fig. 2. Again now clear-cut relationship is apparent.

To examine this issue in more detail, we regress the log of the absolute value of the *t*-statistics on the log of the square root of degrees of freedom (lsrdf), controlling for other meta-independent characteristics as above. We then perform a simple *t*-test on the coefficient on lsrdf to check whether the hypothesis that the coefficient is equal to 1 can be rejected. The results of different specifications of this regression are reported in Table 3. As in the estimations in the previous sections, we present results for the total sample in Columns (1)–(4) and for the sample excluding the two outliers in columns (5)–(8).

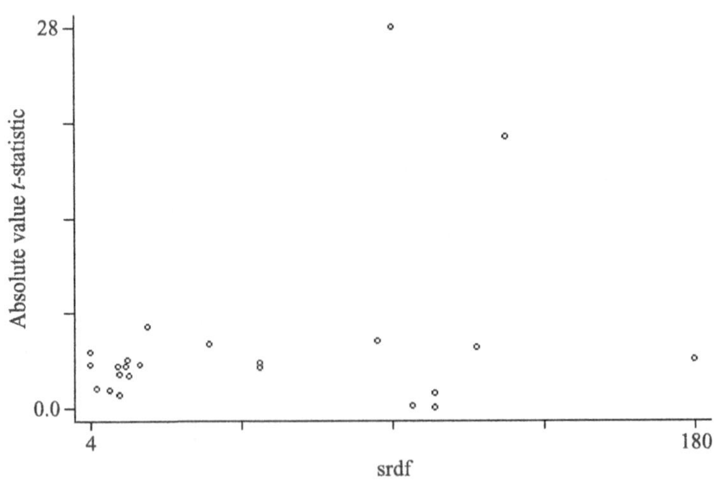

Fig. 1. *Relation of t-statistics to log of degrees of freedom (including outliers)*

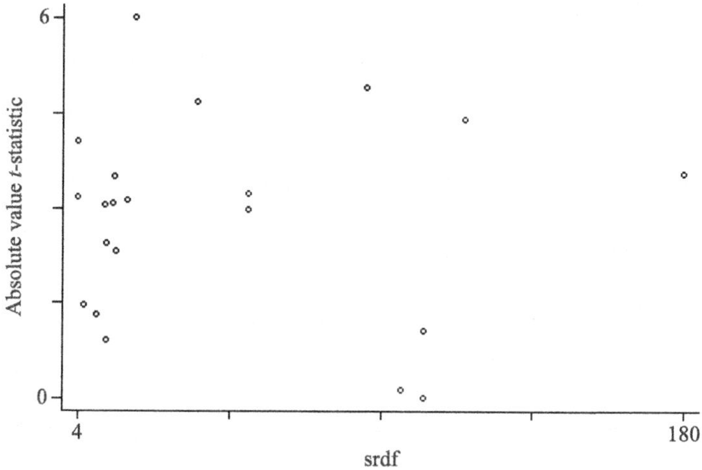

Fig. 2. *Relation of t-statistics to log of degrees of freedom (excluding outliers)*

Inspection of the *t*-statistics reported in the table shows that we can reject the hypothesis of the coefficient on lsrdf being equal to 1 for two out of four specifications of the estimations reported in columns (1)–(4), and for all estimations presented in columns (5)–(8). Thus, our analysis provides at least some evidence that publication bias may be present, ie that studies of productivity spillovers are more likely to become published if they report statistically significant effects of foreign presence on productivity in domestic firms.

Card and Krueger (1995) also suggest that a regression of the coefficient in question on its standard error may provide evidence as to whether publication bias is present. In theory, one would expect no systematic relationship between these two variables but if publication bias is present, a *t*-ratio will have to exceed (roughly) 2 in absolute value, in which case there may be a positive relationship between the coefficient and the standard error (since $t = b/\mathrm{SE}$). Performing this regression on all observations in our sample yields the following regression (heteroscedasticity-autocorrelation consistent standard errors in parentheses):[8]

$$b_j = \underset{(0.101)}{-0.051} + \underset{(0.090)}{3.134}\, SE_j \qquad (2)$$

where the coefficient on *SE* is statistically significant at the 1% level and the R^2 equals 0.78.

Arguably, as Card and Krueger (1995) point out, the above equation may

[8] Exclusion of the two outlying observations yields qualitatively and quantitatively similar results.

Table 3

Results of Meta-Regression to Test for Publication Bias

Dependent variable: log of absolute values of t-statistic

Variable	Including outliers				Excluding outliers			
	(1)	(2)	(3)	(4)	(5)	(6)	(7)	(8)
Log of square root of degrees of freedom	−0.077 (0.330)	0.174 (0.529)	−0.215 (0.403)	0.232 (0.485)	−0.326 (0.311)	−0.293 (0.484)	−0.439 (0.392)	−0.135 (0.435)
Dummy = 1 if data are industry level		0.514 (1.096)		0.727 (1.506)		0.232 (0.901)		1.217 (1.375)
Dummy = 1 if data are cross-section		1.222 (0.794)		1.615 (1.035)		0.180 (0.612)		−0.398 (1.142)
Dummy = 1 if data are for developing country		0.506 (0.863)		0.322 (0.621)		1.124 (0.617)*		0.843 (0.671)
Average year of study period		0.016 (0.040)		0.006 (0.052)		−0.003 (0.033)		−0.027 (0.053)
Dummy = 1 if dependent variable is output growth			−0.546 (0.746)	−0.317 (0.966)			0.146 (0.733)	0.562 (1.026)
Dummy = 1 if dependent variable is other definition			0.379 (0.589)	0.440 (0.822)			0.911 (0.567)	0.778 (0.860)
Dummy = 1 if foreign presence measured as output share			1.100 (1.023)	0.447 (0.961)			0.955 (0.889)	1.449 (1.402)
Dummy = 1 if foreign presence measured as other definition			1.023 (0.823)	1.434 (0.824)			0.505 (0.525)	0.560 (0.577)
Constant	1.119 (0.817)	−31.975 (79.413)	1.097 (0.829)	−13.564 (103.085)	1.702 (0.784)**	6.280 (64.764)	1.510 (0.810)	52.092 (104.836)
No. of obs.	23	23	23	23	21	21	21	21
t-stat (h_0: $\beta = 1$)	−3.26	−1.56	−3.01	−1.58	−4.27	−2.67	−3.67	−2.61
F	0.05	0.71	1.31	3.76	1.10	0.97	1.37	7.93
R^2	0.01	0.19	0.14	0.34	0.08	0.27	0.19	0.38

Notes: heteroskedasticity-autocorrelation consistent standard errors in parentheses.
**, *, denote statistical significance at the 5%, 10% level respectively

not be appropriate because different studies estimate different functional forms and the coefficients and standard errors obtained may therefore not be comparable. To overcome this problem, they estimate elasticities based on the regression coefficients and sample means. Unfortunately, we are not able to do the same because the majority of studies of productivity spillovers do not provide information on sample means of productivity and foreign presence. To take account of the above problem, we therefore decided to split our sample into papers using linear and those using log specifications and estimate regression (2) separately for both samples. Only five studies, however, use a log specification which does not allow us to run a meaningful regression on that sample. Estimating the regression on the sample including the 12 remaining published papers which use linear specifications (yielding 16 observations) gives the result[9]

$$b_j^{\text{lin}} = \underset{(0.129)}{0.029} + \underset{(0.096)}{3.098}\ SE_j \tag{3}$$

with an R^2 of 0.82.

Thus, while these results have to be interpreted with some caution, they may lend further credence to the claim that there is indeed evidence of publication bias in the literature on productivity spillovers which we have included in our sample.

4. Conclusion

A substantial body of literature analysing whether there are productivity spillovers from the presence of multinational companies to domestic firms in host countries has developed over the past 25 years, but these studies produce mixed empirical results. Our meta-analysis of the results published or circulated in a number of studies in this area shows that some aspects of the research design may affect the results of that study. We find that, on average, cross-sectional studies report higher coefficients of the effect of foreign presence than panel data studies, and that the definition of the foreign presence variable included in the studies seems to affect the results obtained. We also find some evidence that suggests there may be publication bias in the studies that we reviewed.

Our analysis has implications for future analyses of spillover studies. As pointed out above, these have become more ubiquitous in the last decade, possibly because of the greater availability and quality of data to study such effects. Our meta-regression analysis suggests that the results of productivity spillover studies do not seem to be affected by whether the studies use sector or firm level data, but that it is important whether the data used are cross-sectional or panel data. Specifically, cross-sectional studies may overstate the spillover effects of MNCs on domestic productivity because they do not allow for other time-invariant firm or sector specific effects, which may impact on

[9] Again, excluding the two outliers does not change the result qualitatively or quantitatively.

the relationship between MNCs and productivity, but for which the researcher does not have any information. For example, high productivity sectors or firms may attract the location of MNCs in the same sector yielding a positive relationship between these even without spillovers taking place. Panel data would allow the researcher to control for such factors.

Also, our findings point to the need for researchers to take care in defining foreign presence in a sector, as different measures may yield different evidence as to whether productivity spillovers from MNCs take place. Assuming that data are available, it seems to be preferable to use alternative measures of foreign presence before concluding on whether indigenous firms benefit from their foreign counterparts through spillovers.

Finally, the possibility of publication bias in the literature suggests that studies of productivity spillovers are more likely to be published if they find statistically significant results for the presence of either positive or negative spillovers. This implies that the currently available published literature may not be completely representative of what may have thus far been found on the topic. An implication is that some studies, if they find statistically insignificant results and are unlikely to be published, may never make it to the scrutiny of the public eye.

University of Nottingham
University College Dublin

References

Aitken, B. J. and Harrison, A. E. (1999). 'Do domestic firms benefit from direct foreign investment? Evidence from Venezuela', *American Economic Review*, vol. 89, pp. 605–18.

Ashenfelter, O., Harmon, C. and Oosterbeek, H. (1999). 'A review of estimates of the schooling/earnings relationship, with tests for publication bias', *Labour Economics*, vol. 6, pp. 453–70.

Baltagi, B. H. (1995). *Econometric Analysis of Panel Data*, Chichester: John Wiley and Sons.

Barrios, S. (2000). 'Foreign direct investment and productivity spillovers: evidence from the Spanish experience (1990–1994)', Working Paper 2000-19, Fundación de Estudios de Economía Aplicada, Madrid.

Begg, C. B. and Berlin, J. A. (1988). 'Publication bias: a problem in interpreting medical data', *Journal of the Royal Statistical Society. Series A (Statistics in Society)*, vol. 151, pp. 419–45.

Blomström, M. (1986). 'Foreign investment and productive efficiency: the case of Mexico', *Journal of Industrial Economics*, vol. 35, pp. 97–112.

Blomström, M. and Kokko, A. (1998). 'Multinational corporations and spillovers', *Journal of Economic Surveys*, vol. 12, pp. 247–77.

Blomström, M. and Persson, H. (1983). 'Foreign investment and spillover efficiency in an underdeveloped economy: evidence from the Mexican manufacturing industry', *World Development*, vol. 11, pp. 493–501.

Blomström, M. and Sjöholm, F. (1999). 'Technology transfer and spillovers: does local participation with multinationals matter?' *European Economic Review*, vol. 43, pp. 915–23.

Blomström, M. and Wolff, E. N. (1994). 'Multinational corporations and productive convergence in Mexico', in (W. J. Baumol, R. R. Nelson and E. N. Wolff, eds) *Convergence of Productivity: Cross National Studies and Historical Evidence*, pp. 263–83. Oxford: Oxford University Press.

Blomström, M., Fors, G. and Lipsey, R. E. (1997). 'Foreign direct investment and employment: home country experience in the United States and Sweden', ECONOMIC JOURNAL, vol. 107, pp. 1787–97.

Card, D. and Krueger, A. B. (1995). 'Time-series minimum-wage studies: a meta-analysis', *American Economic Review*, vol. 85, pp. 238–43.

Caves, R. E. (1974). 'Multinational firms, competition, and productivity in host-country markets', *Economica*, vol. 41, pp. 176–93.

Caves, R. E. (1996). Multinational Enterprise and Economic Analysis, second edition. Cambridge: Cambridge University Press.

Chuang, Y. and Lin, C. (1999). 'Foreign direct investment, R&D and spillover efficiency: evidence from Taiwan's manufacturing firms', *Journal of Development Studies*, vol. 35, pp. 117–37.

De Long, B. J. and Lang, K. (1992). 'Are all economic hypotheses false?' *Journal of Political Economy*, vol. 100, pp. 1257–72.

Djankov, S. and Hoekman, B. (2000). 'Foreign investment and productivity growth in Czech enterprises', *World Bank Economic Review*, vol. 14, pp. 49–64.

Driffield, N. (2001). 'The impact on domestic productivity of inward investment in the UK', *Manchester School*, vol. 69, pp. 103–19.

Egger, M. and Smith, G. D. (1997). 'Meta-analysis: potentials and promise', *British Medical Journal*, vol. 315, pp. 1371–4.

Flores, R. G., Fontoura, M. P. and Santos, R. G. (2000). 'Foreign direct investment spillovers: what can we learn from Portuguese data?' Working Paper 4/2000, Universidade Tecnica de Lisboa.

Girma, S., Greenaway, D. and Wakelin, K. (2001). 'Who benefits from foreign direct investment in the UK?' *Scottish Journal of Political Economy*, forthcoming.

Glass, G. V., McGaw, B. and Smith, M. L. (1981). *Meta-Analysis in Social Research.* London: Sage Publications.

Globerman, S. (1979). 'Foreign direct investment and "spillover" efficiency benefits in Canadian manufacturing industries', *Canadian Journal of Economics*, vol. 12, pp. 42–56.

Griliches, Z. (1998). *R&D and Productivity: The Econometric Evidence*, Chicago: University of Chicago Press.

Haddad, M. and Harrison, A. (1993). 'Are there positive spillovers from direct foreign investment? Evidence from panel data for Morocco', *Journal of Development Economics*, vol. 42, pp. 51–74.

Hunter, J. E., Schmidt, F. L. and Jackson, G. B. (1982). *Meta-Analysis: Cumulating Research Findings Across Studies*, London: Sage Publications.

Kathuria, V. (2000). 'Productivity spillovers from technology transfer to Indian manufacturing firms', *Journal of International Development*, vol. 12, pp. 343–69.

Kokko, A. (1994). 'Technology, market characteristics, and spillovers', *Journal of Development Economics*, vol. 43, p. 279–93.

Kokko, A. (1996). 'Productivity spillovers from competition between local firms and foreign affiliates', *Journal of International Development*, vol. 8, pp. 517–30.

Kokko, A., Tansini, R. and Zejan, M. C. (1996). 'Local technological capability and productivity spillovers from FDI in the Uruguayan manufacturing sector', *Journal of Development Studies*, vol. 32, pp. 602–11.

Krugman, P. R. (1991). *Geography and Trade*, Cambridge, MA: MIT Press.

Liu, X., Siler, P., Wang, C. and Wei, Y. (2000). 'Productivity spillovers from foreign direct investment: evidence from UK industry level panel data', *Journal of International Business Studies*, vol. 31, pp. 407–25.

Markusen, J. R. (1995). 'The boundaries of multinational enterprises and the theory of international trade', *Journal of Economic Perspectives*, vol. 9, pp. 169–89.

Neumark, D. and Wascher, W. (1996). 'Is the time-series evidence on minimum wage effects contaminated by publication bias?' NBER Working Paper No. 5631.

Newey, W. K. and West, K. D. (1987). 'A simple, positive semi-definite, heteroskedasticity and autocorrelation consistent covariance matrix', *Econometrica*, vol. 55, pp. 703–8.

Pack, H. and Saggi, K. (1997). 'Inflows of foreign technology and indigenous technological development', *Review of Development Economics*, vol. 1, pp. 81–98.

Phillips, J. M. (1994). 'Farmer education and farmer efficiency: a meta-analysis', *Economic Development and Cultural Change*, vol. 43, pp. 149–65.

Phillips, J. M. and Gross, E. P. (1995). 'The effect of state and local taxes on economic development: a meta-analysis', *Southern Economic Journal*, vol. 62, pp. 320–33.

Sjöholm, F. (1999*a*). 'Technology gap, competition and spillovers from direct foreign investment: evidence from establishment data', *Journal of Development Studies*, vol. 36, pp. 53–73.

Sjöholm, F. (1999*b*). 'Productivity growth in Indonesia: the role of regional characteristics and direct foreign investment', *Economic Development and Cultural Change*, vol. 47, pp. 559–84.

Smith, V. K. and Huang, J. (1995). 'Can markets value air quality? A meta-analysis of hedonic property value models', *Journal of Political Economy*, vol. 103, pp. 209–27.

Stanley, T. D. (1998). 'New wine in old bottles: a meta-analysis of Ricardian equivalence', *Southern Economic Journal*, vol. 64, pp. 713–27.

Stanley, T. D. and Jarrell, S. B. (1989). 'Meta-regression analysis: a quantitative method of literature surveys', *Journal of Economic Surveys*, vol. 3, pp. 161–70.

Chapter 9

Much Ado about Nothing? Do Domestic Firms Really Benefit from Foreign Direct Investment?

Holger Görg • David Greenaway

Governments the world over offer significant inducements to attract investment, motivated by the expectation of spillover benefits to augment the primary benefits of a boost to national income from new investment. There are several possible sources of induced spillovers from foreign direct investment. This article evaluates the empirical evidence on productivity, wage, and export spillovers in developing, developed, and transition economies. Although theory can identify a range of possible spillover channels, robust empirical support for positive spillovers is at best mixed. The article explores the reasons and concludes with a review of policy aspects.

Of all the drivers of globalization—arm's length trade, migration of workers, and cross-border investment—the last is probably the most visible. This is probably why public anxiety about globalization often manifests itself as hostility toward multinational firms (see Deardorff 2003 for a recent appraisal of such anxieties). From an economic standpoint, cross-border investment may also be at the margin the most important manifestation of globalization. Annual flows of foreign direct investment (FDI) now exceed $700 billion, and the total stock exceeds $6 billion. Over the past decade FDI flows have grown at least twice as fast as trade.

As with arm's length trade, the FDI environment is policy distorted, but it is gradually becoming more liberalized. Of 145 regulatory changes made by 60 countries in 1998, 94 percent created more favorable conditions for FDI (UN 1999). In many cases interventions have extended beyond creating a more liberal environment to providing substantial public subsidies. For example, Head (1998) reports that the government of Alabama paid the equivalent of $150,000 per employee to Mercedes for locating its new plant in the state in 1994. Across the Atlantic the UK government

The World Bank Research Observer, vol. 19, no. 2,

doi:10.1093/wbro/lkh019 19:171–197

provided an estimated $30,000 per employee to attract Samsung to the northeast of England in the late 1990s and $50,000 per employee to attract Siemens (Girma and others 2001). Some countries also provide tax incentives. For example, Ireland offers a corporate tax rate of 12.5 percent to all manufacturing firms locating there.

There seems to be a widely held assumption that foreign firms more than pay their way, bringing not only new investment that boosts national income but also secondary spillovers, resulting in productivity growth or higher export growth. Much econometric work has been done in this area, but the results on the importance of spillovers are mixed at best. There is some evidence from case studies of spillover benefits to domestic firms (see Moran 2001), but even at that level there is disagreement in particular instances.[1]

The failure of econometric work to find unambiguously positive effects could be due to a number of factors. Despite theoretical arguments supporting spillovers, they may simply be unimportant in reality. Multinational corporations may be effective at ensuring that firm-specific assets and advantages do not spill over. Another possibility is that spillovers exist and make up some part of the residual that appears in all growth equations, but current statistical methods and data sets are unable to identify them. Furthermore, there may be much heterogeneity in spillovers, and aggregate studies may therefore fail to detect them. Moreover, the lack of good-quality, comprehensive firm- and plant-level data sets is a serious impediment to research.

This article examines in detail the evidence for intraindustry productivity spillovers in theory and in econometric analyses, taking essentially a microeconomic and microeconometric view.[2] It updates earlier surveys, such as Blomström and Kokko (1998) and Lipsey (2002) and highlights methodological issues and the scope for policymakers to enhance potential spillover effects. The review is more focused on spillovers from FDI than are related studies by Keller (2001) or Saggi (2002), who discuss the scope and evidence for international technology diffusion more generally, without much detail on FDI.

This article looks first at what guidance theory can give, on two counts: the possible channels for transmission of spillover benefits and whether host country characteristics are likely to make a difference in the extent or speed with which spillovers occur. It examines the empirical evidence on spillovers in developed, developing, and transition economies and then draws some implications for policy. Should governments intervene, and if so, how? Does policy make any difference?

What Does Theory Tell Us?

A well-developed and extensively surveyed (see Caves 1996; Markusen 1995) body of literature tries to explain why multinational corporations set up overseas rather than export directly or license their product or technology. The most persuasive explanations emphasize the coexistence of proprietary knowledge and market failures in protecting that knowledge. Thus the firm internalizes certain transactions to protect its brand, technology, and marketing advantages. These motives are taken as given, in particular, the existence of some kind of firm-specific asset, usually some kind of technological advantage, including innovative management and organizational processes as well as new production methods and technologies.

The first question, then, is having chosen a particular location, how might any advantages spill over to the local economy through firms in the same industry? Then, with potential transmission channels identified, are there particular host economy characteristics that make benefits from spillovers more or less likely?

Spillover Channels

When a firm sets up a plant overseas or acquires a foreign plant, it does so in the expectation of realizing a higher rate of return than a given home country firm with an equivalent investment. The source of the higher return is the technological advantage alluded to. Whatever its source, the only way domestic firms can gain from external benefits is if some form of indirect technology transfer takes place—multinational firms will not simply hand over the source of their advantage. The theoretical literature identifies four channels through which spillovers might boost productivity in the host country: imitation, skills acquisition, competition, and exports (table 1).

Imitation. Imitation is the classic transmission mechanism for new products and processes. One mechanism commonly alluded to in the theoretical literature on technology transfer from developed to developing economies is reverse engineering (Das 1987; Wang and Blomström 1992). Its scope depends on the complexity of products and processes, with simple manufactures and processes easier to imitate than more complex ones. The same principle applies to managerial and organizational innovations, although these are thought to be easier to imitate. Imitation is, of course, not the same as replication, and it would be surprising if the rents accruing

Table 1. Potential Channels for Spillover from Foreign Direct Investment

Driver	*Sources of productivity gain*
Imitation	Adoption of new production methods. Adoption of new management practices.
Skills acquisition	Increased productivity of complementary labor. Tacit knowledge.
Competition	Reduction in X-inefficiency. Faster adoption of new technology.
Exports	Scale economies. Exposure to technology frontier.

Source: Authors' compilation; see text for details.

to multinational firms were entirely dissipated by the process. However, any upgrading to local technology deriving from imitation could result in a spillover, with consequent benefits for the productivity of local firms.

Skills Acquisition. Adoption of new technology can also occur through the acquisition of human capital. Even when the locational pull for FDI is relatively low wages, multinational firms tend to demand relatively skilled labor. Generally, they will invest in training, and it is impossible to lock in such resources completely. (This inability to fully protect investment in human capital has long been an argument for infant industry protection as a response to potential first-mover disadvantages; see Baldwin 1969.) The movement of labor from multinational firms to other existing or new firms can generate productivity improvements through two mechanisms: through a direct spillover to complementary workers and through knowledge carried by workers who move to another firm. Haacker (1999) and Fosfuri and others (2001) argue that the knowledge that workers bring with them is the most important channel for spillovers, and some empirical work supports this (Djankov and Hoekmann 1999; Görg and Strobl 2002c).

Competition. Many models emphasize the role of competition (Wang and Blomström 1992; Glass and Saggi 2002). Unless an incoming firm is offered monopoly status, it will produce in competition with indigenous firms. Even if indigenous firms are unable to imitate the multinational's technology and production processes, entry of the multinational firm puts pressure on them to use existing technology more efficiently, yielding productivity gains. Greater competition leading to a reduction in X-inefficiency is analogous to one of the standard gains from arm's length trade and is frequently identified as one of the major sources of gain. In addition, competition may increase the speed of adoption of new technology.

Exports. A further indirect source of productivity gain might be through exports. Crudely, domestic firms can learn to export from multinationals (Aitken and others 1997; Barrios and others 2003; Greenaway and others forthcoming). Exporting generally involves fixed costs to establish distribution networks, create transport infrastructure, and learn about consumers' tastes, regulatory arrangements, and so on in overseas markets. Multinational firms generally come already armed with such information and exploit it to export from the new host country. Through collaboration, or more likely imitation, domestic firms can learn how to penetrate export markets. There is a growing body of literature that links exporting and productivity. Recent work on Germany, Mexico, Morocco, Spain, the United Kingdom, the United States, and Venezuela suggests that productivity levels are higher in exporting firms than in nonexporting firms (Clerides and others 1998; Bernard and

Jensen 1999; Bernard and Wagner 1997; Delgado and others 2003; and Girma and others forthcoming). Central to this literature is whether firms self-select into exporting or increase their productivity after entering export markets.

Host Country Characteristics and Spillovers

The literature on the determinants of FDI emphasizes locational characteristics as important factors in multinationals' decisions on where to invest (Wheeler and Mody 1992; Brainard 1997; Görg 2002). The focus here, however, is on whether there are locational characteristics that affect the speed of adoption of new technology and the spillover of productivity gains.

In a pioneering contribution Findlay (1978) emphasizes the importance of relative backwardness and contagion. Findlay's model suggests that the greater is the distance between two economies in terms of development, the greater the backlog of available opportunities to exploit in the less advanced economy, and so the greater the pressure for change and the more rapid the uptake of new technology. Speed of adoption is also a function of contagion or the extent to which the activities of the foreign firm pervade the local economy. Thus technology transfer will be more rapid if the multinational firm quickly establishes upstream and downstream networks, because domestic firms involved in supply and distribution chains gain exposure to new technology, promoting its diffusion.

Glass and Saggi (1998) also see a role for technological distance between the host and home country, but a different one from Findlay's. Any technology gap signals something to the multinational firm about absorptive capacity. The bigger the gap, the less likely the host is to have the human capital, physical infrastructure, and distribution networks to support inward investment. This influences not only the decision to invest but also what kind of technology to transfer. Specifically, the bigger the gap, the lower the quality of technology transferred and the lower the potential for spillovers. This seems more plausible than Findlay's notion of a lack of absorptive capacity as the driver. Clearly, technological distance will be directly related to the potential gains from spillovers, but it is also likely to be inversely related to the probability that domestic firms are actually able to access them.

Summary

Economic theory gives some guidance on what to expect from cross-border investment and spillovers. In general, multinational firms have firm-specific advantages that might be related to the production methods they use, the way they organize their activities, the way they market their products and services, and so on. Once a multinational has set up a subsidiary, it may be unable to prevent some of the benefits of these advantages from spilling over to indigenous firms through imitation, labor mobility, competition, or export. Such spillovers have the potential to raise productivity, and exploitation of these potential channels of spillovers might be related to the structural characteristics of the host economy, in particular its absorptive capacity.

What Does the Evidence Tell Us?

Empirical studies on spillovers from FDI were pioneered by Caves for Australia (1974), Globerman for Canada (1979), and Blomström for Mexico (1986). Since then, their empirical models have been extended and refined, although the basic approach remains. Most econometric analyses use a framework that regresses the labor productivity or total factor productivity of domestic firms on a range of independent variables. To measure productivity spillovers from multinational firms, a variable is included that proxies the extent of foreign firms' penetration, usually calculated as the multinational's share of total employment or sales in a given sector.[3] In other words, the regression allows for an effect of FDI on the productivity of domestic firms in the same industry. If the regression analysis yields a positive and statistically significant coefficient on the foreign presence variable, this is taken as evidence that spillovers have occurred from multinational firms to domestic firms.[4] Most studies use either the contemporaneous level of foreign penetration or relatively short lags (most often one year) as their explanatory variables. If anything, therefore, these studies usually measure short-run effects of foreign presence on domestic productivity.

Table 2 sets out details of 40 studies of horizontal productivity spillovers in manufacturing industries in developing, developed, and transition economies. Of those, 22 report unambiguously positive and statistically significant horizontal spillover effects (2 of which find positive and significant effects for only one of several countries studied). All but eight of those reporting unambiguously positive spillovers use cross-sectional data, which may lead to biased results.

Görg and Strobl (2001) argue that panel data using firm-level data are the most appropriate estimating framework for two reasons. First, they permit investigation of the development of domestic firms' productivity over a longer time period, rather than at one point in time. Second, they allow investigation of spillovers after controlling for other factors. Cross-section data, particularly if aggregated at the sectoral level, fail to control for time-invariant differences in productivity across sectors that might be correlated with foreign presence without being caused by it. Thus coefficients on cross-section estimates are likely to be biased. For example, if productivity is higher in the electronics sector than in the food sector, multinationals may be attracted to the electronics sector. Cross-sectional data would show a positive and statistically significant relationship between the level of foreign investment and productivity consistent with spillovers, even though foreign investment did not cause high levels of productivity but rather was attracted by them.

Table 2. Papers on Intraindustry Productivity Spillovers

	Author	*Country*	*Period*	*Data*	*Aggregation level*[a]	*Result*[b]
	Developing economies					
1	Blomström and Persson (1983)	Mexico	1970	Cross-sectional	Industry	+
2	Blomström (1986)	Mexico	1970/1975	Cross-sectional	Industry	+
3	Blomström and Wolff (1994)	Mexico	1970/1975	Cross-sectional	Industry	+
4	Kokko (1994)	Mexico	1970	Cross-sectional	Industry	+
5	Kokko (1996)	Mexico	1970	Cross-sectional	Industry	+
6	Haddad and Harrison (1993)	Morocco	1985–89	Panel	Micro and industry	?
7	Kokko and others (1996)	Uruguay	1990	Cross-sectional	Micro	?
8	Blomström and Sjöholm (1999)	Indonesia	1991	Cross-sectional	Micro	+
9	Sjöholm (1999a)	Indonesia	1980–91	Cross-sectional	Micro	+
10	Sjöholm (1999b)	Indonesia	1980–91	Cross-sectional	Micro	+
11	Chuang and Lin (1999)	Taiwan	1991	Cross-sectional	Micro	+
12	Aitken and Harrison (1999)	Venezuela	1976–89	Panel	Micro	–
13	Kathuria (2000)	India	1976–89	Panel	Micro	?
14	Kokko and others (2001)	Uruguay	1988	Cross-sectional	Micro	?
15	Kugler (2001)	Colombia	1974–98	Panel	Industry	?
16	López-Córdova (2002)	Mexico	1993–99	Panel	Micro	–, ?
17	Görg and Strobl (2002c)	Ghana	1991–97	Panel	Micro	+
	Developed countries					
18	Caves (1974)	Australia	1966	Cross-sectional	Industry	+
19	Globerman (1979)	Canada	1972	Cross-sectional	Industry	+
20	Liu and others (2000)	United Kingdom	1991–95	Panel	Industry	+
21	Driffield (2001)	United Kingdom	1989–92	Cross-sectional	Industry	+
22	Girma and others (2001)	United Kingdom	1991–96	Panel	Micro	?
23	Girma and Wakelin (2001)	United Kingdom	1980–92	Panel	Micro	?
24	Harris and Robinson (2004)	United Kingdom	1974–95	Panel	Micro	?
25	Girma and Wakelin (2002)	United Kingdom	1988–96	Panel	Micro	?

(Continued)

Table 2. (Continued)

Author	*Country*	*Period*	*Data*	*Aggregation level*[a]	*Result*[b]
26 Haskel and others (2002)	United Kingdom	1973–92	Panel	Micro	+
27 Girma (2002)	United Kingdom	1989–99	Panel	Micro	?
28 Girma and Görg (2002)	United Kingdom	1980–92	Panel	Micro	?
29 Ruane and Ugur (2002)	Ireland	1991–98	Panel	Micro	+
28 Barrios and Strobl (2002)	Spain	1990–94	Panel	Micro	?
29 Dimelis and Louri (2002)	Greece	1997	Cross-sectional	Micro	+
30 Castellani and Zanfei (2002b)	France, Italy, Spain	1992–97	Panel	Micro	+ for Italy; – for Spain; ? for France
31 Keller and Yeaple (2003)	United States	1987–96	Panel	Micro	+
32 Görg and Strobl (2003)	Ireland	1973–96	Panel	Micro	+
Transition economies					
33 Djankov and Hoekman (2000)	Czech Republic	1993–96	Panel	Micro	–
34 Kinoshita (2001)	Czech Republic	1995–98	Panel	Micro	?
35 Bosco (2001)	Hungary	1993–97	Panel	Micro	?
36 Konings (2001)	Bulgaria	1993–97	Panel	Micro	–
	Poland	1994–97			?
	Romania	1993–97			–
37 Damijan and others (2001)	Bulgaria, Czech Republic, Estonia, Hungary, Poland, Romania, Slovakia, Slovenia	1994–1998	Panel	Micro	? or – + only for Romania
38 Li and others (2001)	China	1995	Cross-sectional	Industry	+
39 Smarzynska-Javorcik (forthcoming)	Lithuania	1996–2000	Panel	Micro	?
40 Zukowska-Gagelmann (2000)	Poland	1993–97	Panel	Micro	–

[a]Micro data are at the firm, plant, or establishment level.

[b]A + indicates positive and statistically significant, – indicates negative and statistically significant, and ? indicates mixed or statistically insignificant results on the foreign presence variable for the aggregate sample.

Taking this into consideration, the evidence on positive horizontal spillovers is much weaker. There are only eight studies employing panel data that find unambiguously positive evidence in the aggregate, and almost all of these are for developed economies: Liu and others (2000) and Haskel and others (2002) for the United Kingdom, Castellani and Zanfei (2002b) for Italy, Keller and Yeaple (2003) for the United States, Ruane and Ugur (2002) and Görg and Strobl (2003) for Ireland, Damijan and others (2001) for Romania, and Görg and Strobl (2002c) for Ghana. Liu and others (2000), however, use industry-level data that aggregates over heterogeneous firms, which may lead to biased results.[5] This leaves only seven studies using appropriate data and estimation techniques that report positive evidence for aggregate spillovers.

Several studies using firm-level panel data find some evidence of negative effects of the presence of multinationals on domestic firms in the aggregate. These include Aitken and Harrison (1999) for Venezuela, López-Córdova (2002) for Mexico, Castellani and Zanfei (2002b) for Spain, Djankov and Hoekman (2000) for the Czech Republic, Konings (2001) for Bulgaria, Zukowska-Gagelmann (2000) for Poland, and Damijan and others (2001) for seven countries in Central and Eastern Europe. Many studies on transition economies find at least some evidence of negative results. Nineteen of the studies find no statistically significant effects on average of multinationals on domestic productivity.[6]

What Explains the Negative or Neutral Effects?

There have been several explanations for the negative results found by some studies. The most plausible is that foreign firms reduce the productivity of domestic firms through competition effects, as suggested by Aitken and Harrison (1999) and Konings (2001). They argue that multinationals have lower marginal costs due to some firm-specific advantage, which allows them to attract demand away from domestic firms, thus forcing the domestic firms to reduce production and move up their (given) average cost curve.

This argument is not necessarily inconsistent with the theoretical discussion in the previous section, which presented competition as one of the channels through which positive spillovers are transmitted. Some firms may experience negative competition effects in the short run (moving up a given average cost curve), whereas other firms may improve efficiency (shifting down their average cost curve) because of increased competition in the short run as well as the long run. Evidence for positive effects of competition are found by Kokko (1996) for Mexico and Driffield (2001) for the United Kingdom.

There are also other explanations for a failure to find evidence of positive aggregate spillovers in the short run. There may be lags in domestic firms' learning from multinationals, which short-run analyses do not pick up. Multinational firms may be able to guard their firm-specific advantages closely, preventing leakages to domestic firms and therefore spillovers as well. Positive spillovers may affect only a subset of firms, so that aggregate studies underestimate the true significance of such effects. Spillovers may occur not horizontally (intraindustry) but vertically through relationships that are missed in conventional spillover studies.

The first two explanations are straightforward and plausible and require little comment. More detailed discussion is warranted for the last two explanations.

Absorptive Capacity. As discussed, the theoretical literature suggests that not all firms would be expected to benefit equally from knowledge spillovers from multinationals. Whether a firm benefits depends on its relative backwardness and its capacity for assimilating knowledge—its absorptive capacity. Some of the empirical literature has also considered these issues.

Kokko (1994) advances the idea that spillovers depend on the complexity of the technology transferred by multinationals and on the technology gap between domestic firms and multinational firms. Using cross-section industry-level data for Mexico, he finds no evidence for spillovers in industries in which multinationals use highly complex technologies (as proxied by large payments on patents or high capital intensity). A large technology gap on its own does not appear to hinder technology spillovers on average, although industries with large gaps and a high foreign presence experience lower spillovers than others. Expanding on Kokko (1994), Kokko and others (1996) hypothesize that domestic firms can benefit only if the technology gap is not too wide so that domestic firms can absorb the knowledge available from the multinational—an argument similar to that of Glass and Saggi (1998). Thus domestic firms using very backward production technologies and low skilled workers may be unable to learn from multinationals. Using a cross-section of firm-level data for Uruguay, Kokko and others find evidence for productivity spillovers to domestic firms with moderate technology gaps (measured as the difference between the domestic firm's labor productivity and the average labor productivity in foreign firms) but not for firms that use considerably lower levels of technology.[7]

Girma and others (2001), using firm-level panel data, find no evidence of productivity spillovers in UK manufacturing on average—under the assumption that spillovers are homogeneous across different types of domestic firms. There is evidence for spillovers to firms with a small gap between their productivity level and the industry frontier productivity level (called the technology gap). Productivity appears to increase with increasing foreign presence for firms with a technology gap of 10 percent or less, whereas it appears to diminish in firms with larger gaps. Girma (2002) uses threshold regression techniques to quantify the significance of absorptive capacity, and Girma and Görg (2002) use conditional quantile regression techniques to allow for different effects of FDI on establishments at different quantiles of the productivity distribution. Both studies find support for the hypothesis that only firms with some minimum level of absorptive capacity benefit from productivity spillovers.

In a similar vein, Barrios and Strobl (2002), in firm-level panel data for Spanish manufacturing, find little evidence for any aggregate horizontal spillovers from multinational firms. There is evidence for positive spillovers from foreign presence to domestic exporters but not to nonexporters, which they interpret as evidence that absorptive capacity matters. They argue that exporting firms are more exposed to international competition and therefore are more likely to use more advanced technologies and to benefit from positive spillovers than are nonexporters. Kinoshita (2001), using firm-level panel data for the Czech Republic, also finds no evidence of spillovers on average but finds positive spillovers for local firms that are research and development (R&D) intensive. She interprets this as evidence that absorptive capacity is important.

Damijan and others (2001) also define absorptive capacity in terms of local firms' R&D activities. In their firm-level panel data for a number of Central and Eastern European transition economies, they fail to detect evidence of productivity spillovers affecting the average firm. Taking into account absorptive capacity, by interacting the foreign presence variable with a firm's R&D expenditure, they find evidence of negative spillovers for the Czech Republic and Poland but positive spillovers for Romania, and no evidence for all other countries.

Regional Dimensions. Because human capital acquisition and imitation are considered important channels for knowledge spillovers, domestic firms located near multinationals may be more likely to benefit than other firms. For example, Audretsch (1998:21) argues that geographic proximity is necessary to facilitate knowledge spillovers because "knowledge is vague, difficult to codify, and often only serendipitously recognized." Therefore, transmission costs are assumed to increase with distance.

Several studies have investigated the geographic dimension of horizontal spillovers. Calculating proxies for foreign presence at the regional level and using cross-sectional data for Indonesia, Sjöholm (1999a) fails to find evidence of a regional component. Aitken and Harrison (1999), using firm-level panel data for Venezuela, also fail to find positive spillovers from multinationals to domestic firms in the same region, though they find negative spillovers from multinationals in the same sector in any region in the country. From firm-level panel Girma and Wakelin (2002) find evidence for positive spillovers from FDI in the same region and sector as domestic firms in the United Kingdom, but the results are significant only for firms that have a low technology gap vis-à-vis multinationals.

Importance of vertical linkages. If multinationals prevent the transfer of their firm-specific knowledge to domestic competitors in the same industry, there is no scope for intraindustry knowledge spillovers. It is possible, however, that multinational firms voluntarily or involuntarily help increase the efficiency of domestic suppliers or customers through vertical input-output linkages. Multinationals may provide technical assistance to suppliers to help them raise the quality of the intermediate products they produce (Moran 2001), or they may simply insist on high quality standards for local inputs, providing incentives for local suppliers to upgrade their technology. Multinationals may also provide active assistance or passive guidelines to domestic customers on the most effective way to use the products the firms supply.

Several recent studies have empirically investigated vertical spillovers (table 3).[8] Kugler (2001) worked with industry-level panel data for 10 Colombian manufacturing industries during 1974–98, using an estimation framework that distinguishes intraindustry and interindustry spillovers. He finds widespread evidence for positive interindustry spillovers, but finds evidence for intraindustry spillovers only in one sector (machinery equipment). However, his framework does not distinguish spillovers through backward or forward linkages. Smarzynska-Javorcik (forthcoming) uses firm-level panel data for Lithuania for 1996–2000 to consider spillovers through backward linkages. Although she found no evidence for aggregate horizontal spillovers, she does find productivity spillovers through backward linkages. Blalock and Gertler (2003) also find results suggesting positive productivity spillovers through backward linkages in their analysis of Indonesian plant-level panel data. They do not find evidence for horizontal spillovers, however.

Driffield and others (2002) allow for spillovers through horizontal, backward, and forward relationships. They examine the relative importance of each using industry-level panel data for UK manufacturing during 1984–92. Their econometric estimations show evidence for positive spillovers through forward linkages but not of statistically significant spillovers through backward linkages. The results for horizontal spillovers are inconclusive. In a further study for the United Kingdom, Harris and Robinson (2004) use plant-level panel data to estimate productivity equations for 20 manufacturing sectors separately. Like Kugler (2001), they distinguish only horizontal and vertical spillovers; they do not separate vertical spillovers into backward or forward linkages. Their results suggest that interindustry spillovers are much more prevalent than intraindustry spillovers. None of the spillovers are always positive, however, and there is evidence of negative spillovers in many sectors. Girma and others (2003), using UK firm-level data, also find substantial differences in whether domestic firms benefit from vertical linkages, depending on their export activities.

Wage Spillovers

If there are positive productivity spillovers from multinational firms to domestic firms and if some of these spillovers are due to increasing labor productivity, domestic firms will pay higher wages in competitive labor markets. Another field of empirical

Table 3. Studies on Vertical Spillovers

Author	*Country*	*Period*	*Data*	*Aggregation level*[a]	*Result*[b]		
					Horizontal	*Backward*	*Forward*
1 Kugler (2001)[c]	Colombia	1974–98	Panel	Industry	?	Many +	NA
2 Smarzynska-Javorcik (forthcoming)	Lithuania	1996–2000	Panel	Micro	?	+	NA
3 Driffield and others (2002)	United Kingdom	1984–92	Panel	Industry	?	?	+
4 Harris and Robinson (2002)[c]	United Kingdom	1974–95	Panel	Micro	?	?	?
5 Blalock and Gertler (2003)	Indonesia	1988–96	Panel	Micro	?	+	NA

[a]Micro data are at the firm, plant, or establishment level.

[b]A + indicates positive and statistically significant, – indicates negative and statistically significant, and ? indicates mixed or statistically insignificant results on the foreign presence variable for the aggregate sample. NA = not applicable.

[c]Do not distinguish backward and forward spillovers.

Table 4. Studies on Wage Spillovers

Author	Country	Period	Data	Aggregation level[a]	Result[b]
1 Aitken and others (1996)	Mexico	1984–90	Panel	Industry	–
	Venezuela	1977–89	Panel	Industry	–
	United States	1987	Cross-sectional	Industry	+
2 Lipsey and Sjöholm (2001)	Indonesia	1996	Cross-sectional	Micro	+
3 Girma and others (2001)	United Kingdom	1991–96	Panel	Micro	?
4 Driffield and Girma (2003)	United Kingdom	1980–92	Panel	Micro	?

[a]Micro data are at the firm, plant, or establishment level.

[b]A + indicates positive and statistically significant, – indicates negative and statistically significant, and ? indicates mixed or statistically insignificant results on the foreign presence variable for the aggregate sample.

research focuses on this connection, emphasizing horizontal spillovers (table 4).[9] Productivity spillovers are not the only channel for such wage spillovers, however. Multinationals often pay higher wages, even after controlling for size and other firm and sectoral characteristics (Girma and others 2001; Lipsey and Sjöholm 2001; Görg and others 2003). This is attributed to the multinational firms' ownership of firm-specific assets, implying that they use higher levels of technology than domestic firms. If multinationals and domestic firms compete in the same labor market, domestic firms have to pay higher wages to attract workers. Wage spillovers can also be negative, however, if there are negative productivity spillovers from multinationals.

As with productivity, identifying wage spillovers usually involves estimating the determinants of wages in domestic firms and including a measure of foreign presence (multinationals' share of total employment) in the industry as a covariate. Aitken and others (1996) use industry-level data for manufacturing industries for Mexico (1984–90), Venezuela (1977–89), and the United States (1987). They find positive effects in the United States, but negative effects in Mexico and Venezuela. As with productivity spillovers, the result for the United States should be treated with caution because the study uses cross-sectional data. Lipsey and Sjöholm (2001) study the same effect for the Indonesian manufacturing sector using plant-level cross-sectional data for 1996 and find that higher foreign presence in a sector leads to higher wages in domestic firms in the same sector. Girma and others (2001), using firm-level panel data for UK manufacturing for 1991–96, find no effect on average of multinationals in a sector on the wage level in domestic firms but weak evidence of a negative effect on wage growth.

Export Spillovers

A third strand in the literature focuses on whether multinationals spread their knowledge of global markets to domestic firms, thus enabling them to become more successful exporters. Domestic firms can be affected through three primary channels. First, if multinationals have better access to information about foreign markets, this can spill over through their export activities. Second, domestic firms can learn the multinationals' superior production or management techniques through observation (demonstration effects), enabling the domestic firms to compete more successfully in export markets. Third, competition with multinational firms at home and in foreign markets can induce domestic firms to improve their export performance.

Several studies have examined export spillovers (table 5). Aitken and others (1997) estimate a probit model using export activity by multinationals in the industry and region as a proxy for export information externalities. Using plant-level cross-section data for Mexican manufacturing industries for 1986 and 1989, they find that export activities by multinational firms in a sector positively affect the probability of a firm in the same sector, foreign or domestic, being an exporter.

Using firm-level panel data for the United Kingdom for 1992–96, Greenaway and others (forthcoming) also investigate whether spillovers affect a firm's probability of exporting but extend the analysis to examine what affects a firm's export ratio. In a two-step Heckman selection model, they first estimate the probability of exporting and then estimate the factors that affect a firm's export ratio. They include three measures of multinational presence to capture the three spillover channels.

Their results suggest that multinational firms' exports have a positive effect on domestic firms' probability of exporting but do not affect their export ratio. They also find that R&D spillovers from multinationals to domestic firms and the presence of multinational firms in the sector positively affect the decision to export and the export ratio. Thus, export information externalities appear to matter only for the decision of whether to export. This is not surprising because these externalities can be expected to aid domestic firms in overcoming the sunk costs of exporting, which should affect their probability of exporting but not their export ratio.

Table 5. Papers on Export Spillovers

Author(s)	*Country*	*Period*	*Data*	*Aggregation level*[a]	*Result*[b]
1 Aitken and others (1997)	Mexico	1986/1989	Cross-sectional	Micro	+
2 Kokko and others (2001)	Uruguay	1998	Cross-sectional	Micro	?
3 Greenaway and others (forthcoming)	United Kingdom	1992–96	Panel	Micro	+
4 Banga (2003)	India	1994–2000	Panel	Micro/industry	+
5 Barrios and others (2003)	Spain	1990–98	Panel	Micro	?

[a]Micro data are at the firm, plant, or establishment level.

[b]A + indicates positive and statistically significant, – indicates negative and statistically significant, and ? indicates mixed or statistically insignificant results on the foreign presence variable for the aggregate sample.

Barrios and others (2003) also focus on export information externalities and on demonstration effects through R&D spillovers. Using firm-level panel data for Spanish manufacturing for 1990–98, they estimate a probit model to explain why firms export and a tobit model to estimate what determines the firm's export ratio. They find no evidence that either R&D activity or export activity by multinationals in a sector affects the probability that domestic firms export, although they find spillovers from both types of activity on other foreign-owned firms. The tobit estimations, however, find evidence for positive effects of multinationals' R&D activity on domestic firms' export ratios, but no spillovers from multinationals' export activities on domestic firms. The export ratios of other foreign firms again benefit from both types of spillovers. In an extension Barrios and colleagues (2003) discover that R&D spillovers increase domestic firms' exports only to other developed economies, which are generally markets with a superior technological capability.

Kokko and others (2001) investigate the decision to export by domestic firms in Uruguay using cross-sectional firm-level data for 1998. They include only a simple measure of the presence of multinational firms—their output share in an industry, not their export activity—and it is thus not clear which channel leads to spillovers. However, they distinguish between the presence of multinational firms in import-substituting and export-orientated industries and find evidence only for spillovers from export-oriented multinationals. This suggests that the trade regime within which multinationals operate may determine their potential for generating positive export spillovers.

Summary

An extensive array of empirical studies have searched for productivity spillovers from multinationals of various forms. Much of this work has relied on cross-section methods. With the growing availability of longitudinal data at the plant and firm level, however, more analysts are using panel techniques. This is a helpful development for two reasons: first because the plant or firm is the most appropriate level of scrutiny, and second because there are methodological shortcomings associated with applying cross-section techniques.

Much of the work fails to find positive horizontal spillovers on aggregate, with some studies reporting negative effects of multinational presence on domestic productivity. Evidence on horizontal effects on wages and export spillovers is also mixed. However, studies that further disaggregate data into more homogeneous groups of firms or plants find more encouraging results. In particular, there is evidence that the absorptive capacity of domestic firms and their geographic proximity to multinationals are important determinants of whether domestic firms benefit from FDI in the same sector. This suggests that spillovers may not affect all firms equally but may benefit only firms with high levels of absorptive capacity or close proximity to multinationals. Furthermore, the few studies that have looked at the potential for vertical (interindustry) spillovers find evidence suggesting that vertical spillovers may be a more important channel for knowledge externalities than horizontal spillovers (see also Moran 2001).

Is There a Role for Policy?

In general, most governments see FDI as having greater potential to improve total factor productivity than an equivalent amount of domestic investment. This would be taken as axiomatic in developing and transition economies and, depending on the origin of the multinational firm, in at least some developed economies. Add to this the potential spillovers from multinational firms to domestic firms that are believed to raise their productivity, yielding a second growth bonus, and it becomes clear why attracting inward investment figures prominently in the policy priorities of so many governments. This leads naturally to three questions: Can active policy intervention influence the level and composition of inward investment? Can particular policies maximize the potential for spillovers, both by encouraging multinationals to transfer technologies and by improving the absorptive capacity of domestic firms? Do targeted policies yield net benefits?

Policy and the Level and Composition of FDI

The role of policy in influencing the level and composition of FDI has been reviewed extensively (see, for example, Balasubramanyam and Salisu 2001; Pain 2000; Hanson 2001). Most work relates to developing economies because policy interventions there have in general been more active, though a growing volume of research relates to industrial countries, where most FDI originates.

Several key points emerge from this work.

- Trade policy is relevant. In general, economies with more open trade regimes have done better at attracting FDI and benefiting from it than countries with inward-oriented regimes (Balasubramanyam and others 1996).
- Although there is some evidence that investment incentives can affect the location choice of multinationals, the effect appears to be small (Coughlin and others 1991; Head and others 2000). Head and colleagues (2000) even argue that competition between potential host governments may render incentives ineffective as they offset each other. Also, this form of competition for FDI may have

affected the distribution of incentives and is likely to have redistributed income from host countries to multinational firms (Haaland and Wooton 1999).

- Trade-related investment measures (TRIMS), such as local content requirements and minimum export requirements, are often introduced to recapture some of the rents that accrue to multinational firms. Although these measures can have positive welfare effects on the host country, the evidence does not point to major effects on levels of inward investment in developing economies (Greenaway 1992).
- The quality of local infrastructure is vitally important, in particular communication and transportation facilities, both in attracting initial investments and in sustaining clusters (Coughlin and others 1991; Coughlin and Segev 2000).
- The availability of relatively skilled labor is an important magnet (Coughlin and Segev 2000) as well as a key driver of agglomeration (Ottaviano and Puga 1998). It has also been argued that host countries are more likely to benefit from spillovers if they have a large supply of skilled labor (Keller 1996) and if domestic firms have a high level of technological capacity (Glass and Saggi 1998).

Overall the evidence seems to suggest that interventions should strive largely to provide a supportive economic environment. More specifically, this flags a role for education and training policies aimed at upgrading general skills, technology policies aimed at developing clusters, and public investment policies aimed at developing efficient and reliable transportation and communication networks.

Policy and Spillovers

The evidence on spillovers reported here is mixed at best. There are no clear results that domestic firms always and unambiguously gain from the presence of multinational firms. Several factors could be at play. Under the optimistic view that spillovers occur but measurement instruments are not fine enough to identify them, the question is whether governments can implement policies to maximize the prospects for extracting benefits from multinational firms. General policies—designed to change the environment within which multinationals operate—include industrial policy, infrastructure development, trade policy, exchange rate policy, and so on. There is evidence to suggest that such policies are related to the overall level of inward investment into an economy over a period of time. General policies may turn out to be the most effective means of boosting the probability of positive spillovers. If, for example, absorptive capacity is the critical driver, education and training policy is likely to be key to facilitating spillovers.

As for specific policies, many TRIMS are targeted at encouraging spillovers (table 6). Local content requirements, which have been widely used, are intended to raise the share of local value added in subsidiary production and in the process encourage

Table 6. TRIMS Targeted at Spillovers

Instrument	*Intended effect*
Input TRIMS	
Local content requirements	Specify that some proportion of value added or intermediate inputs is locally sourced.
Local equity participation	Specifies that some proportion of the equity must be held locally.
Local hiring targets	Ensure specified employment targets are hit.
Expatriate quotas	Specify a maximum number of expatriate staff.
National participation in management	Specifies that certain staff must be nationals or sets a schedule for the 'indigenisation' of the management.
R&D requirements	Commit multinationals to investment in research and development.
Technology transfer	Commits multinationals to local use of specified foreign technology.
Output TRIMS	
Export controls	Specify that certain products may not be exported.
Licensing requirements	Oblige the investor to license production of output in the host country.
Technology transfer	Commits multinationals to a specified embodied technology.

Source: Derived from Greenaway (1992).

upstream development, with the intention of stimulating interindustry spillovers. Because one can argue that spillovers are more likely if there is some local ownership, local equity requirements are geared to that end. Local hiring targets and expatriate quotas are intended to raise the share of employment accounted for locally, with a view to encouraging spillovers through the transfer of human capital. R&D and technology transfer requirements are intended to make multinational firms commit to some minimum level of R&D expenditures or transfer technology to local firms.[10]

The economics of TRIMS is not straightforward. In general they are second-best measures. For example, analytically a local content requirement is equivalent to an input tariff, though less efficient. What little work has so far been completed on TRIMS has failed to establish a direct link between them and the transfer of useful technologies (Blomström and others 1994; Greenaway 1992). This appears to be because many of the measures are difficult to specify precisely and to monitor. But it is also because the more general policies referred to are in practice rather more important.

Conclusions

FDI is a key driver of economic growth and development. Most governments consider attracting FDI a priority, particularly in developing and transition economies. It is given this emphasis not just because it boosts capital formation but also because it can enhance the quality of the capital stock. The reason is that multinationals are assumed to bring with them best practice or, as a minimum, better practice technology and management. Moreover, it is possible (even probable) that a given multinational firm will not be able to protect its superior technology or management fully to prevent some elements from being absorbed by indigenous firms. If spillovers occur, they provide an external benefit from FDI, one that governments are hoping to secure when they offer inducements.

Theory points to reasons why spillovers might arise, but finding robust empirical evidence to support their existence is more difficult. This could indicate that the benefits are in fact illusory, in that multinational firms are effective in protecting their assets. But it could as well be that researchers are looking in the wrong place and with the wrong lens. Many studies focus on the industry rather than the firm or plant. The growing availability of survey data at the firm and plant level makes such study increasingly feasible. Most studies use cross-section data when panel data are required for proper analysis.

Because research on disaggregated data with both cross-sectional and longitudinal variation is still limited, the message is clear: More systematic research is needed. More discriminating work is also required, analysis that probes what really matters—form of entry (greenfield or acquisition), ownership characteristics, corporate governance, absorptive capacity of domestic firms, and so on.

The consensus in the policy literature is also clear: General policies aimed at altering the fundamentals are more important than specific policies aimed at attracting particular investments. Such specific policies seem to affect primarily the distribution of rents. Governments compete in offering investment incentives and in the process create rents for multinational firms. They then use (at least some) TRIMS to try to reclaim some of those rents.

Both econometric evidence and survey and case study work suggest that the characteristics of the economic environment are generally much more important: infrastructure, local labor market conditions, reliability of communications systems, and so on, as well as the overall macroeconomic and trade policy climate. That, of course, does not mean that selective interventions will cease to be extensively deployed. Governments will no doubt continue to see opportunities for targeted measures, and multinational firms will stand ready to accept them. This is another area for future work. Very little is known about the comparative impact of different instruments.

Notes

Holger Görg is lecturer in the School of Economics and a research fellow at the Leverhulme Centre for Research on Globalisation and Economic Policy, University of Nottingham. He is also affiliated with the German Institute of Economic Research, Berlin; his e-mail address is holger.gorg@nottingham.ac.uk.

David Greenway is professor of economics and director of the Leverhulme Centre for Research on Globalisation and Economic Policy, School of Economics, University of Nottingham; his e-mail address is david.greenaway@nottingham.ac.uk. Earlier versions of the article were presented at a UN Economic Commission for Europe/European Bank for Reconstruction and Development meeting in Geneva, a UN Economic Commission for Latin America and the Caribbean conference in Mexico City, an Inter-American Development Bank/World Bank conference in Washington, D.C., and a Centre for Economic Policy Research meeting in Turin. The authors wish to thank in particular Wolfgang Keller, Bob Lipsey, Mauricio Mesquita Moreira, Andres Rodríguez-Claré, and Ian Wooton for helpful comments. In addition, reports from four anonymous referees and the managing editors of the journal were extremely helpful. Financial support from the Leverhulme Trust under Programme Grant F114/BF and the European Commission under grant no. SERD-2002–00077 is gratefully acknowledged.

1. For example, Larrain and others (2000) conclude that the location of Intel in Costa Rica has had positive effects on the local economy. Hanson (2001) argues that there is little evidence for spillovers from Intel on domestic firms. He also argues that Ford and General Motors plants in Brazil have failed to show the expected spillover benefits.

2. A related body of literature examines the macro effect of inward FDI on growth in the framework of cross-country growth regressions. See, for example, Balasubramanyam and others (1996), Borensztein and others (1998), and Alfaro and others (forthcoming) for recent evidence. DeMello (1997) provides a review of that literature.

3. Castellani and Zanfei (2002a) argue for the use of the absolute level of foreign activity in the sector rather than foreign activity as a proportion of total activity, because changes of the same magnitude in foreign and aggregate activities within a sector would have no effect on the dependent variable. Although this is an interesting econometric argument, it is not clear what the economic rationale for using absolute rather than relative FDI penetration would be.

4. Interpretation of this coefficient of course hinges on the assumption that the FDI variable does not merely pick up the effect of other correlated factors on productivity—it assumes that a full vector of productivity-augmenting activities is included in the empirical model. Although this may be problematic in some of the studies reviewed herein, it is beyond the scope of this article to discuss this in detail. The article therefore assumes that the estimated FDI coefficient adequately reflects spillovers.

5. Dunne and others (1989) note this for the case of measuring the growth performance of manufacturing plants in the United States.

6. The magnitude of the coefficients, which indicates the strengths of the spillovers, also differs across studies. Görg and Strobl (2001) attempt to explain the differences in magnitude in a meta-regression analysis, using characteristics of the studies (such as data, variables used, countries covered) as explanatory variables.

7. By contrast, Sjöholm (1999b), using cross-sectional data for Indonesian manufacturing firms, finds that productivity spillovers from foreign to domestic firms are larger the larger the technology gap (also defined in terms of differences in labor productivity) and the higher the degree of competition in the industry.

8. Related theoretical models by Rodríguez-Claré (1996) and Markusen and Venables (1999) show that multinationals can have positive effects on the development of domestic firms through vertical input-output linkages. Görg and Strobl (2002a, b) show empirical evidence that the presence of multinational firms has fostered the entry and development of domestic firms in the Republic of Ireland. Alfaro and Rodríguez-Claré (forthcoming) point out that the Rodríguez-Claré (1996) model makes a case for expecting horizontal (intraindustry) rather than vertical spillovers.

9. A related issue is whether FDI contributes to the shift in labor demand toward skilled labor in the host country. See, for example, Feenstra and Hanson (1997) for empirical analysis for Mexico, Figini and Görg (1999) for Ireland, Blonigen and Slaughter (2001) for the United States, and Taylor and Driffield (forthcoming) for the United Kingdom.

10. The Uruguay Round obligated countries to phase out certain TRIMS (those that violate Articles III and XI of the General Agreement on Trade and Tarrifs), with local content requirements being the most prominent. The key issue here, however, is whether they work.

References

Aitken, Brian J., and Ann E. Harrison. 1999. "Do Domestic Firms Benefit from Direct Foreign Investment? Evidence from Venezuela." *American Economic Review* 89(3):605–18.

Aitken, Brian, Gordon H. Hanson, and Ann E. Harrison. 1997. "Spillovers, Foreign Investment, and Export Behavior." *Journal of International Economics* 43(1–2):103–32.

Aitken, Brian, Ann Harrison, and Robert E. Lipsey. 1996. "Wages and Foreign Ownership: A Comparative Study of Mexico, Venezuela, and the United States." *Journal of International Economics* 40(3–4):345–71.

Alfaro, Laura, and Andres Rodríguez-Claré. Forthcoming. "Multinationals and Linkages: An Empirical Investigation." *Economia*.

Alfaro, Laura, Areendam Chanda, Sebnem Kalemli-Ozcan, and Selin Sayek. Forthcoming. "FDI and Economic Growth: The Role of Local Financial Markets." *Journal of International Economics*.

Audretsch, David B. 1998. "Agglomeration and the Location of Innovative Activity." *Oxford Review of Economic Policy* 14(2):18–29.

Balasubramanyam, V. N., and Mohammed Salisu. 2001. "Foreign Direct Investment and Globalisation." In S. Lahiri, ed., *Regionalism and Globalisation*. London: Routledge.

Balasubramanyam, V. N., Mohammed Salisu, and David Sapsford. 1996. "Foreign Direct Investment and Growth in EP and IS Countries." *Economic Journal* 106(434):92–105.

Baldwin, Robert. 1969 "The Case against Infant Industry Protection." *Journal of Political Economy* 77:295–305.

Banga, Rashmi. 2003. "The Differential Impact of Japanese and U.S. Foreign Direct Investments on Exports of Indian Manufacturing." Working paper, Delhi School of Economics, India.

Barrios, Salvador, and Eric Strobl. 2002. "Foreign Direct Investment and Productivity Spillovers: Evidence from the Spanish Experience." *Weltwirtschaftliches Archiv* 138:459–81.

Barrios, Salvador, Holger Görg, and Eric Strobl. 2003. "Explaining Firms' Export Behaviour: R&D, Spillovers and the Destination Market." *Oxford Bulletin of Economics and Statistics* 65(4):475–96.

Bernard, Andrew, and J. Bradford Jensen. 1999. "Exceptional Exporter Performance: Cause, Effect or Both?" *Journal of International Economics* 47(1):1–26.

Bernard, Andrew, and Joachim Wagner. 1997. "Exports and Success in German Manufacturing." *Weltwirtschaftliches Archiv* 133:134–57.

Blalock, Garrick, and Paul Gertler. 2003. "Technology from Foreign Direct Investment and Welfare Gains through the Supply Chain." Working paper, Cornell University, Ithaca, N.Y.

Blomström, Magnus. 1986. "Foreign Investment and Productive Efficiency: The Case of Mexico." *Journal of Industrial Economics* 35(1):97–112.

Blomström, Magnus, and Ari Kokko. 1998. "Multinational Corporations and Spillovers." *Journal of Economic Surveys* 12(3):247–77.

Blomström, Magnus, and Håkan Persson. 1983. "Foreign Investment and Spillover Efficiency in an Underdeveloped Economy: Evidence from the Mexican Manufacturing Industry." *World Development* 11(6):493–501.

Blomström, Magnus, and Fredrik Sjöholm. 1999. "Technology Transfer and Spillovers: Does Local Participation with Multinationals Matter?" *European Economic Review* 43(4–6):915–23.

Blomström, Magnus, and Edward N. Wolff. 1994. "Multinational Corporations and Productive Convergence in Mexico." In William J. Baumol, Richard R. Nelson, and Edward N. Wolff, eds., *Convergence of Productivity: Cross National Studies and Historical Evidence*. Oxford: Oxford University Press.

Blomström, Magnus, Ari Kokko, and Mario Zejan. 1994. "Host Country Competition, Labor Skills, and Technology Transfer by Multinationals." *Weltwirtschaftliches Archiv* 130:521–33.

Blonigen, Bruce A., and Matthew J. Slaughter. 2001. "Foreign-Affiliate Activity and U.S. Skill Upgrading." *Review of Economics and Statistics* 83(2):362–76.

Borensztein, E., J. De Gregorio, and J.-W. Lee. 1998. "How Does Foreign Direct Investment Affect Economic Growth?" *Journal of International Economics* 45(1):115–35.

Bosco, Maria Giovanna. 2001. "Does FDI Contribute to Technological Spillovers and Growth? A Panel Data Analysis of Hungarian Firms" *Transnational Corporations* 10(1):43–68.

Brainard, S. Lael. 1997. "An Empirical Assessment of the Proximity-Concentration Trade-Off between Multinational Sales and Trade." *American Economic Review* 87(4):520–44.

Castellani, Davide, and Antonello Zanfei. 2002a. "Multinational Companies and Productivity Spillovers: Is there a Specification Error?" Working paper, University of Urbino, Italy.

———. 2002b. "Technology Gaps, Absorptive Capacity and the Impact of Inward Investments on Productivity of European Firms." Working paper, University of Urbino, Italy.

Caves, Richard E. 1974. "Multinational Firms, Competition, and Productivity in Host-Country Markets." *Economica* 41(162):176–93.

———. 1996. *Multinational Enterprise and Economic Analysis*, 2nd ed. Cambridge: Cambridge University Press.

Chuang, Yih-Chyi, and Chi-Mei Lin. 1999. "Foreign Direct Investment, R&D and Spillover Efficiency: Evidence from Taiwan's Manufacturing Firms." *Journal of Development Studies* 35(4):117–37.

Clerides, S. K., S. Lach, and J. R. Tybout. 1998. "Is Learning by Exporting Important? Micro-Dynamic Evidence from Colombia, Mexico, and Morocco." *Quarterly Journal of Economics* 113(3):903–48.

Coughlin, Cletus C., and Eran Segev. 2000. "Location Determinants of New Foreign-Owned Manufacturing Plants." *Journal of Regional Science* 40(2):323–51.

Coughlin, Cletus C., Joseph V. Terza, and Vachira Arromdee. 1991. "State Characteristics and the Location of Foreign Direct Investment within the United States." *Review of Economics and Statistics* 73(4):675–83.

Damijan, Joze P., Boris Majcen, Mark Knell, and Matija Rojec. 2001. "The Role of FDI, Absorptive Capacity and Trade in Transferring Technology to Transition Countries: Evidence from Firm Panel Data for Eight Transition Countries." UN Economic Commission for Europe, Geneva.

Das, Sanghamitra. 1987. "Externalitites, and Technology Transfer through Multinational Corporations: A Theoretical Analysis." *Journal of International Economics* 22(1–2):171–82.

Deardorff, Alan. 2003. "What Might Globalisation's Critics Believe?" *World Economy* 26(5):639–58.

Delgado, M., J. Fariñas, and S. Ruano. 2002. "Firm Productivity and Export Markets: A Non-Parametric Approach." *Journal of International Economics* 57(2):397–422.

DeMello, Luiz R. 1997. "Foreign Direct Investment in Developing Countries and Growth: A Selective Survey." *Journal of Development Studies* 34(1):1–34.

Dimelis, Sophia, and Helen Louri. 2002. "Foreign Direct Investment and Efficiency Benefits: A Conditional Quantile Analysis." *Oxford Economic Papers* 54:449–69.

Djankov, Simeon, and Bernard Hoekman. 2000. "Foreign Investment and Productivity Growth in Czech Enterprises." *World Bank Economic Review* 14(1):49–64.

Driffield, Nigel. 2001. "The Impact on Domestic Productivity of Inward Investment in the UK." *Manchester School* 69(1):103–19.

Driffield, Nigel, and Sourafel Girma. 2003. "Regional Foreign Direct Investment and Wage Spillovers: Plant Level Evidence from the Electronics Industry." *Oxford Bulletin of Economics and Statistics*: 65(4):453–74.

Driffield, Nigel, Max Munday, and Annette Roberts. 2002. "Foreign Direct Investment, Transactions Linkages, and the Performance of the Domestic Sector." *International Journal of the Economics of Business* 9(3):335–51.

Dunne, Timothy, Mark J. Roberts, and Larry Samuelson. 1989. "The Growth and Failure of U.S. Manufacturing Plants." *Quarterly Journal of Economics* 104(4):671–98.

Feenstra, Robert C., and Gordon H. Hanson. 1997. "Foreign Direct Investment and Relative Wages: Evidence from Mexico's Maquiladoras." *Journal of International Economics* 42(3–4):371–93.

Figini, Paolo, and Holger Görg. 1999. "Multinational Companies and Wage Inequality in the Host Country: The Case of Ireland." *Weltwirtschaftliches Archiv* 135:594–612.

Findlay, Ronald. 1978. "Relative Backwardness, Direct Foreign Investment, and the Transfer of Technology: A Simple Dynamic Model." *Quarterly Journal of Economics* 92(1):1–16.

Fosfuri, Andrea, Massimo Motta, and Thomas Rønde. 2001. "Foreign Direct Invesment and Spillovers through Workers' Mobility." *Journal of International Economics* 53(1):205–22.

Girma, Sourafel. 2002. "Geographic Proximity, Absorptive Capacity and Productivity Spillovers from FDI: A Threshold Regression Analysis." GEP Research Paper 02/06. University of Nottingham, UK.

Girma, Sourafel, and Holger Görg. 2002. "Foreign Direct Investment, Spillovers and Absorptive Capacity: Evidence from Quantile Regressions." GEP Research Paper 02/14. University of Nottingham, UK.

Girma, Sourafel, and Katharine Wakelin. 2002. "Are There Regional Spillovers from FDI in the UK?" In David Greenaway, Richard Upward, and Katharine Wakelin, eds., *Trade, Investment, Migration and Labour Markets*. Basingstoke, UK: Macmillan.

Girma, Sourafel, David Greenaway, and Katharine Wakelin. 2001. "Who Benefits from Foreign Direct Investment in the UK?" *Scottish Journal of Political Economy* 48(2):119–33.

Girma, Sourafel, Holger Görg, and Mauro Pisu. 2003. "The Role of Exports and Foreign Linkages for FDI Productivity Spillovers." Working paper, University of Nottingham, United Kingdom.

Girma, Sourafel, David Greenaway, and Richard Kneller. Forthcoming. "Entry to Export Markets and Productivity: A Microeconometric Analysis of Matched Firms." *Review of International Economics*.

Glass, Amy, and Kamal Saggi. 1998. "International Technology Transfer and the Technology Gap." *Journal of Development Economics* 55(2):369–98.

———. 2002. "Multinational Firms and Technology Transfer." *Scandinavian Journal of Economics* 104(4):495–514.

Globerman, Steven. 1979. "Foreign Direct Investment and 'Spillover' Efficiency Benefits in Canadian Manufacturing Industries." *Canadian Journal of Economics* 12(4):42–56.

Görg, Holger. 2002. "Fancy a Stay at the 'Hotel California'? Foreign Direct Investment, Taxation and Exit Costs." GEP Research Paper 02/28. University of Nottingham, UK.

Görg, Holger, and Eric Strobl. 2001. "Multinational Companies and Productivity Spillovers: A Meta-Analysis." *Economic Journal* 111(473):F723–39.

———. 2002a. "Multinational Companies and Entrant Start-up Size: Evidence from Quantile Regressions." *Review of Industrial Organization* 20(1):15–31.

———. 2002b. "Multinational Companies and Indigenous Development: An Empirical Analysis." *European Economic Review* 46(7):1305–22.

———. 2002c. "Spillovers from Foreign Firms through Worker Mobility: An Empirical Investigation." GEP Research Paper 02/13. University of Nottingham, UK.

———. 2003. "Multinational Companies, Technology Spillovers and Plant Survival." *Scandinavian Journal of Economics* 105(4):581–95.

Görg, Holger, Eric Strobl, and Frank Walsh. 2003. "Why Do Foreign Firms Pay More? The Role of On-the-job Training." GEP Research Paper 02/15. University of Nottingham, UK.

Greenaway, David. 1992. "Trade Related Investment Measures and Development Strategy." *Kyklos* 45(2):139–60.

Greenaway, David, Nuno Sousa, and Katharine Wakelin. Forthcoming. "Do Domestic Firms Learn to Export from Multinationals?" *European Journal of Political Economy*.

Haacker, Marcus. 1999. "Spillovers from Foreign Direct Investment through Labour Turnover: The Supply of Management Skills." CEP Discussion Paper. London School of Economics.

Haaland, Jan I., and Ian Wooton. 1999. "International Competition for Multinational Investment." *Scandinavian Journal of Economics* 101(4):631–49.

Haddad, Mona, and Ann Harrison. 1993. "Are There Positive Spillovers from Direct Foreign Investment? Evidence from Panel Data for Morocco." *Journal of Development Economics* 42(1):51–74.

Hanson, Gordon H. 2001. "Should Countries Promote Foreign Direct Investment?" G-24 Discussion Paper 9. UNCTAD, Geneva.

Harris, Richard, and Catherine Robinson. 2004. "Productivity Impacts and Spillovers from Foreign Ownership in the United Kingdom." *National Institute Economic Review* 187:58–75.

Haskel, Jonathan E., Sonia C. Pereira, and Matthew J. Slaughter. 2002. "Does Inward Foreign Direct Investment boost the Productivity of Domestic Firms?" NBER Working Paper 8724. Cambridge, Mass.

Head, Keith. 1998. "Comment on 'Comparing Wages, Skills, and Productivity between Domestically and Foreign-Owned Manufacturing Establishments in the United States.' " In R. Baldwin, R. Lipsey, and J. D. Richardson, eds., *Geography and Ownership as Bases for Economic Accounting*. Chicago: Chicago University Press.

Head, Keith C., John C. Ries, and Deborah L. Swenson. 2000. "Attracting Foreign Manufacturing: Investment Promotion and Agglomeration." *Regional Science and Urban Economics* 29(2):197–218.

Kathuria, Vinish. 2000. "Productivity Spillovers from Technology Transfer to Indian Manufacturing Firms." *Journal of International Development* 12(2):343–69.

Keller, Wolfgang. 1996 "Absorptive Capacity: Understanding the Creation and Acquisition of Technology in Development." *Journal of Development Economics* 49:199–227.

———. 2001. "International Technology Diffusion." NBER Working Paper 8573. Cambridge, Mass.

Keller, Wolfgang, and Stephen Yeaple. 2003. "Multinational Enterprises, International Trade, and Productivity Growth: Firm-Level Evidence from the United States." GEP Research Paper 03/03. University of Nottingham, UK.

Kinoshita, Yuko. 2001. "R&D and Technology Spillovers through FDI: Innovation and Absorptive Capacity. CEPR Discussion Paper DP2775. Centre for Economic Policy Research, London.

Kokko, Ari. 1994. "Technology, Market Characteristics, and Spillovers." *Journal of Development Economics* 43(2):279–93.

———. 1996. "Productivity Spillovers from Competition between Local Firms and Foreign Affiliates." *Journal of International Development* 8(4):517–30.

Kokko, Ari, Ruben Tansini, and Mario C. Zejan. 1996. "Local Technological Capability and Productivity Spillovers from FDI in the Uruguayan Manufacturing Sector." *Journal of Development Studies* 32:602–11.

Kokko, Ari, Mario Zejan, and Ruben Tansini. 2001. "Trade Regimes and Spillover Effects of FDI: Evidence from Uruguay." *Weltwirtschaftliches Archiv* 137:124–49.

Konings, Jozef. 2001. "The Effects of Foreign Direct Investment on Domestic Firms: Evidence from Firm Level Panel Data in Emerging Economies." *Economics of Transition* 9(3):619–33.

Kugler, Maurice. 2001. "The Diffusion of Externalities from Foreign Direct Investment: The Sectoral Pattern of Technological Spillovers." Working paper, University of Southampton, UKm.

Larrain, Felipe B., Luis F. Lopez-Calva, and Andres Rodriguez-Claré. 2000. "Intel: A Case Study of Foreign Direct Investment in Central America." Center for International Development Working Paper 58. Harvard University, Cambridge, Mass.

Li, Xiaoying, Xiaming Liu, and David Parker. 2001. "Foreign Direct Investment and Productivity Spillovers in the Chinese Manufacturing Sector." *Economic Systems* 25(4):305–21.

Lipsey, Robert E. 2002. "Home and Host Country Effects of FDI." NBER Working Paper 9293. Cambridge, Mass.

Lipsey, Robert E., and Fredrik Sjöholm. 2001. "Foreign Direct Investment and Wages in Indonesian Manufacturing." NBER Working Paper 8299. Cambridge, Mass.

Liu, Xiaming, Pamela Siler, Chengqi Wang, and Yingqi Wei. 2000. "Productivity Spillovers from Foreign Direct Investment: Evidence from UK Industry Level Panel Data." *Journal of International Business Studies* 31(3):407–25.

López-Córdova, J. Ernesto. 2002. "NAFTA and Mexico's Manufacturing Productivity: An Empirical Investigation Using Micro-Level Data." Working paper, Inter-American Development Bank, Washington, D.C.

Markusen, James R. 1995. "The Boundaries of Multinational Enterprises and the Theory of International Trade." *Journal of Economic Perspectives* 9(2):169–89.

Markusen, James R., and Anthony J. Venables. 1999. "Foreign Direct Investment as a Catalyst for Industrial Development." *European Economic Review* 43(2):335–56.

McCullogh, Neil, Alan Witners, and Xavier Cirera. 2001. "Trade Liberalisation and Poverty: A Handbook." Working paper, Centre for Economic Policy Research, London.

Moran, Theodore. 2001. *Parental Supervision: The New Paradigm for Foreign Direct Investment and Development*. Washington, D.C.: Institute for International Economics.

Ottaviano, Gianmarco I. P., and Diego Puga. 1999. "Agglomeration in the Global Economy: A Survey of the New Economic Geography." *World Economy* 21(6):707–31.

Pain, Nigel, ed. 2000. *Inward Investment Technological Change and Growth*, London: Palgrave.

Rodríguez-Claré, Andres. 1996. "Multinationals, Linkages, and Economic Development." *American Economic Review* 86(4):852–73.

Ruane, Frances, and Ali Ugur. 2002. "Foreign Direct Investment and Productivity Spillovers in Irish Manufacturing Industry: Evidence from Firm Level Panel Data." Trinity Economic Papers 02/06. Trinity College, Dublin.

Saggi, Kamal. 2002. "Trade, Foreign Direct Investment, and International Technology Transfer: A Survey." *World Bank Research Observer* 17(2):191–235.

Sjöholm, Fredrik. 1999a. "Technology Gap, Competition and Spillovers from Direct Foreign Investment: Evidence from Establishment Data." *Journal of Development Studies* 36(1):53–73.

———. 1999b. "Productivity Growth in Indonesia: The Role of Regional Characteristics and Direct Foreign Investment." *Economic Development and Cultural Change* 47(3):559–84.

Smarzynska-Javorcik, Beata K. Forthcoming. "Does Foreign Direct Investment Increase the Productivity of Domestic Firms? In Search of Spillovers through Backward Linkages." *American Economic Review*.

Taylor, Karl, and Nigel Driffield. Forthcoming. "Wage Inequality and the Role of Multinationals: Evidence from UK Panel Data." *Labour Economics*.

UN (United Nations). 1999. World Investment Report. Geneva: United Nations.

Wang, Jian-Ye, and Magnus Blomström. 1992. "Foreign Investment and Technology Transfer: A Simple Model." *European Economic Review* 36(1):137–55.

Wheeler, David, and Ashoka Mody. 1992. "International Investment Location Decisions: The Case of U.S. Firms." *Journal of International Economics* 33(1–2):57–76.

Zukowska-Gagelmann, Katarzyna. 2000. "Productivity Spillovers from Foreign Direct Investment in Poland." *Economic Systems* 24(3):223–56.

Chapter 10

Exporting, linkages and productivity spillovers from foreign direct investment

Sourafel Girma *Nottingham University Business School, University of Nottingham*
Holger Görg *Institut für Weltwirtschaft and Christian-Albrechts-Universität, Kiel*
Mauro Pisu *National Bank of Belgium*

Abstract. In this paper we analyse productivity spillovers from foreign direct investment using firm-level panel data for U.K. manufacturing industries from 1992 to 1999. We investigate spillovers through horizontal, backward, and forward linkages; distinguish spillovers from export-oriented vs domestic-market-oriented FDI; and allow for differing effects, depending on domestic firms' export activities. The results suggest that the mechanisms through which spillovers affect domestic firms are very complex and that there are substantial differences in spillover benefits for domestic exporters and non-exporters, and from different types of inward investment. JEL classification: F1, F2

Exportation, effets d'entraînement, et effets externes de productivité en provenance de l'investissement direct de l'étranger. Dans ce mémoire, on analyse les effets externes de productivité en provenance de l'investissement direct de l'étranger en utilisant des données de panel pour les industries manufacturières au Royaume Uni entre 1992 et 1999. On examine les effets externes dans leurs effets d'entraînement en amont, en aval et d'une manière horizontale, tout en distinguant les effets externes découlant des investissements étrangers destinés à produire pour l'exportation par opposition à une production pour le marché domestique. On note aussi les effets différents sur les entreprises domestiques selon l'intensité de leurs activités à l'exportation. Les résultats suggèrent que les mécanismes à travers lesquels se transmettent les effets de débordement sur les entreprises domestiques sont très complexes, qu'il y a des différences significatives dans ces effets pour les entreprises exportatrices et non exportatrices et selon le type d'investissement étranger.

Görg is also affiliated with GEP, University of Nottingham; Pisu is also affiliated with GEP, University of Nottingham. The authors are grateful to Nigel Driffield, Wolfgang Keller, Ted Moran, Beata Javorcik, and two anonymous referees for helpful comments. Of course, the usual disclaimer applies. The authors gratefully acknowledge financial support from the European Commission (Grant No. SERD-2002–00077) and the Leverhulme Trust (Grant No. F114/BF).
Email: holger.gorg@nottingham.ac.uk

Canadian Journal of Economics / Revue canadienne d'Economique, Vol. 41, No. 1
February / février 2008. Printed in Canada / Imprimé au Canada

0008-4085 / 08 / 320–340 / © Canadian Economics Association

1. Introduction

Foreign direct investment (FDI) is often seen as an engine to economic growth and development, an assumption that has led many governments around the globe to try to attract multinationals by offering generous financial incentives. For example, in the late 1990s the Government of the United Kingdom provided an estimated $30,000 and $50,000 per employee to attract Samsung and Siemens, respectively, to northeast England (Girma, Greenaway, and Wakelin 2001). One of the main rationales for these policy interventions is the belief that domestic firms can benefit from the presence of foreign multinationals through positive spillovers, thus allowing them to improve their productivity. The argument, in a nutshell, is that foreign firms have a technological advantage vis-à-vis domestic firms and, hence, domestic firms can learn from them.

While this is easy to believe for developing countries, one may argue that there is less of an a priori reason why this should also hold true in developed economies. However, continuing with the example of the U.K., we note that recent studies show that foreign firms are more productive than the average domestic firm (e.g., Girma and Görg 2007), and that, in particular, U.S. multinationals are more productive than the headquarters of British firms that have operations abroad (Criscuolo and Martin 2004). Therefore, there is a potential for spillovers from multinationals to domestic firms even in developed countries.

These spillovers can work through a number of channels. First, domestic firms can benefit from the presence of multinationals in the same industry, leading to intra-industry or *horizontal* spillovers through the movement of workers within industries, demonstration effects, competition effects, and so on. Second, there may be spillovers from multinationals operating in other industries, leading to *vertical* spillovers. The latter type of external effect is usually attributed to buyer-supplier linkages and therefore may be towards downstream industries (forward spillovers) and/or towards upstream industries (backward spillovers).[1]

While some case studies provide evidence suggestive of positive spillover effects (e.g., Moran 2001), the results from econometric analyses are mixed (e.g., Görg and Strobl 2001). However, Girma, Greenaway, and Wakelin (2001), Haskel, Pereira, and Slaughter (2002), and Keller and Yeaple (2003) are recent studies using firm-level panel data, which find positive spillover effects for the U.K. and the U.S. As a counterbalance, a large number of studies, such as Aitken and Harrison (1999) and Djankov and Hoekman (2000) for Venezuela and the Czech Republic, respectively, find negative spillovers in micro panel data.[2] The frequently given explanation for such negative effects is that multinationals compete with domestic firms and 'steal business' from them. This forces domestic firms up their average cost curves and reduces measured productivity.

1 See Blomström and Kokko (1998) for more detailed discussion of the channels for spillovers.

2 Lipsey and Sjöholm (2005) argue that these mixed results can be explained as reflecting different firms' and countries' characteristics in the different data sets used.

However, the literature to date is subject to a number of shortcomings, which can perhaps also explain at least part of the failure to detect any significant spillover effects on domestic firms. First, most papers restrict themselves to attempts to detect *horizontal* spillovers by, say, relating the productivity (growth or level) of firm *i* in industry *j* to the presence of foreign multinationals in the same industry *j*, defined using the standard 2-, 3-, or 4-digit classification. This largely neglects the possibility of gains for domestic firms from *vertical* linkages with multinationals, even though arguably some of these links will be between industries within the same 2- or 3-digit classification. However, the importance of more appropriately investigating vertical spillovers has been stressed by, for example, Keller (2001) and has been taken up in a number of recent papers: Driffield, Munday, and Roberts (2002), Blalock and Gertler (2003), and Javorcik (2004) argue and provide evidence that what may be more important are *vertical* rather than horizontal spillovers.

Secondly, in many studies the coefficient indicating spillovers is constrained to be the same for all firms; that is, all domestic firms are assumed to benefit equally from FDI. This has been recognized in some recent work stressing the importance of domestic firms' absorptive capacity in order to benefit from spillovers (see, e.g., Kokko, Tansini, and Zejan 1996; Kinoshita 2001; Girma 2005). Arguably, it is also important when the negative business-stealing effect is considered, as different types of firms may be more or less likely to be in competition with multinationals. Thirdly, it is usually assumed that FDI is homogeneous and therefore that the potential spillover effect is the same for all types of FDI. However, as Moran (2001) shows in a number of case studies, multinational investment is quite heterogeneous with respect to its relationship with local firms, which can be assumed to have implications for any spillovers.[3]

In this paper we take all three of these issues into account, using firm-level panel data for U.K. manufacturing industries from 1992 to 1999. First, we investigate the importance of both horizontal and vertical spillovers, where the latter are identified through backward and forward linkages from input-output tables.[4] Secondly, we allow the effect of spillovers to differ across domestic firms in two ways. We take into account firms' absorptive capacity, similar to the approach of Girma (2005), but we also distinguish the effects of FDI on domestic exporters and non-exporters separately. The rationale for this distinction is the expectation that competition effects are different between these two types of firms and multinationals. Thirdly, we allow for the heterogeneity of FDI by distinguishing spillovers from primarily export-oriented and domestic-market-oriented

3 One way to describe this heterogeneity is by looking at the degree of ownership of foreign firms. For example, Javorcik and Spatareanu (2007) find that there are positive horizontal spillovers from fully owned foreign affiliates but not from partially owned affiliates in their firm-level data for Romania. The opposite is true for vertical spillovers. We consider a different aspect of heterogeneity in this paper.

4 Driffield, Munday, and Roberts (2002) look also at vertical spillovers but use industry-level data. Our firm-level data are an improvement over that study.

multinationals. Considering the export orientation of domestic and foreign firms goes some way towards distinguishing competition effects from pure knowledge spillovers. To the best of our knowledge, our paper is the first to take account of all three of these issues in a consistent way.

The remainder of the paper is organized as follows: the next section outlines the main sources of productivity spillovers from FDI. Section 3 discusses the methodology employed to detect such externalities. The description of the data set is in section 4, while the estimation results are presented in section 5. Section 6 provides a summary and conclusions.

2. Spillovers from FDI

The theoretical argument for why one may expect productivity spillovers from foreign multinationals is straightforward. Multinationals are expected to have access to some form of firm-specific asset (FSA), such as a superior production technique, know-how, or management strategy, which has at least some of the characteristics of a public good and enables the firm to locate profitably abroad (Caves 1996). These firm-specific assets can be transferred at low or zero cost between subsidiaries of the same firm.

The possibility for positive spillovers arises because multinationals may find it difficult to protect a leakage of this FSA to other firms in the host country. The public good characteristics imply that once the FSA is out on the external market it can be used by other firms as well, owing to its being at least to some extent non-rival and non-excludable. The inability of multinationals to protect the asset is due to labour mobility between firms (Fosfuri, Motta, and Ronde 2001; Görg and Strobl 2005), but is also due to contacts between domestic suppliers or domestic customers and multinationals (Javorcik 2004). These spillover channels have been described extensively in the recent literature (see, e.g., Blomström and Kokko 1998).

As pointed out in the introduction, most of the literature to date has focused on measuring *horizontal* spillovers, that is, the beneficial effects from multinationals on domestic firms operating in the same industry (e.g., Aitken and Harrison 1999; Girma, Greenaway, and Wakelin 2001; Keller and Yeaple 2003). However, the knowledge transfers between domestic suppliers or customers and multinationals cannot, or can to a very limited degree, be captured by horizontal contacts alone, as there are *vertical* backward and forward relationships between firms in different industries. Such vertical relationships have been investigated theoretically by Rodríguez-Clare (1996), while Driffield, Munday, and Roberts (2002), Blalock and Gertler (2003), and Javorcik (2004) provide empirical evidence. The importance of vertical linkages has also been recognized in the recent *UN World Investment Report 2001* (UNCTAD 2001), which, however, focuses on backward linkages.

The first contribution of this paper is that we consider all the possible directions through which positive spillovers may occur. We distinguish spillover effects due to the presence of MNEs in the same industry as the domestic firms (i.e., horizontal spillovers) from effects due to vertical, (i.e., buyer-supplier) relationships, considering both forward and backward linkages. Domestic producers buying inputs from or supplying inputs to multinationals are potentially in an ideal position to appropriate some of multinationals' FSA because of knowledge transfer that business-to-business relationships could entail.

On the one hand, contacts between foreign producers and domestic suppliers may improve the technical competencies of the latter through reverse engineering, improved product design, and market information. This may lead to productivity gains. On the other hand, foreign companies supplying inputs to domestic enterprises could generate positive spillovers through the superior proprietary asset, knowledge, and technology embodied in their inputs and through the training provided to employ them appropriately.

However, negative externalities may offset the potentially positive effects of both horizontal and vertical spillovers. Horizontal spillovers might be mitigated by the increased competition generated by foreign companies. Indeed, a situation may be envisaged where some firms may be forced to improve efficiency in order to be able to compete successfully with multinationals. As Aitken and Harrison (1999) argue, this competition effect may actually result in negative effects on domestic firms' productivity if multinationals 'steal business' from domestic firms and force them up their average cost curve.

To tackle this issue we consider the export orientation of both domestic and foreign firms.[5] This is the second main contribution of our investigation. The idea is that domestic exporters may eschew the competition of multinationals whose output serves the domestic market. By the same token, export-oriented multinationals may exert less competitive pressure on domestic companies than host-country market-oriented ones. Hence, this distinction goes some way towards distinguishing spillovers due to competition from those due to pure knowledge transfers.

As regards vertical linkages between domestic firms and MNEs, a potentially important reason why these might lead to negative spillovers is asymmetries in bargaining power. More specifically, foreign multinationals may be expected to have much more bargaining power than domestic companies, owing to their size and international operations. In this circumstance it is unlikely that indigenous firms are able to experience productivity gains fully, as these may be appropriated by the more powerful contractual partner, that is, the multinational (e.g., Klein, Crawford, and Alchian 1978; Graham, Thorpe, and Hogan 1999). The larger bargaining power of foreign firms may lead to un-favouring contractual

5 Apart from exporting, it would be interesting to consider the degree of import activity of multinationals as well. Import behaviour could be assumed to be a major determinant of the potential for vertical linkages, as only those multinationals that source inputs from the local market can be expected to yield vertical spillovers. However, such data are not available to us, unfortunately.

agreements towards domestic enterprises. This squeezes profits for domestic suppliers, thus reducing measured productivity.

Another explanation of negative backward spillovers is put forward by Rodriguez-Clare (1996). In his theoretical model foreign firms buying inputs from local supplier will generate positive productivity spillovers towards them only if they use intermediate inputs intensively and when the variety of intermediate inputs produced by domestic suppliers is not too different. If these conditions are not satisfied, then negative backward productivity spillovers may arise.

The export orientation of multinationals is likely to be relevant to vertical spillovers also, since it contributes to determining the degree of contact foreign affiliates have with domestic firms (in upstream and downstream industries). As regards forward spillovers, indigenous companies necessarily establish business-to-business contacts with non-exporting foreign suppliers but not with export-oriented ones. Therefore, they may reap the productivity benefit of the advanced know-how and technology embedded in inputs provided by host-market-oriented MNEs.

Also, the export intensity of foreign companies could affect the extent of backward linkages, although ambiguously. On the one hand, exporting foreign firms are probably more isolated from the rest of the domestic economy than non-exporting ones. Hence, they may be operating in enclave sectors (Kokko, Zejan, and Tansini 2001) with few contacts with local suppliers. On the other hand, Moran (2001), drawing evidence from several case studies, suggests that multinational affiliates, being part of tightly integrated networks of production (viz., those serving as export platforms), develop more durable and relevant contacts with domestic suppliers.[6]

To disentangle the effect on productivity spillovers from FDI due to absorptive capacity and that due to the nature of competition between domestic and foreign firms (and captured by their export activities) in the empirical specification we also explicitly consider the absorptive capacity of firms. Recent FDI productivity spillovers studies have reported that absorptive capacity is important (i.e., spillovers differ according to how much domestic firms are distant from the technological frontier; see Kokko, Tansini, and Zejan 1996; Kinoshita 2001; Girma 2005). We take account of absorptive capacity by allowing the effect of spillovers to vary depending on host country firms' 'technology gap,' that is, the distance between the firms' productivity and that of the industry leader. All other things being equal, we would expect that firms with higher relative productivity are more able to learn from multinationals.

6 One should keep in mind, however, that Moran's (2001) case studies relate to multinationals located in developing countries. More specifically, his argument highlights two dimensions of linkages: First, the number of linkages is likely to be smaller if the multinational is part of an international network, as the network likely provides a relatively large share of inputs. On the other hand, those linkages that do exist are likely to be stronger, since the domestic supplier will, in effect, be part of the international network.

3. Methodology

In line with the literature, we investigate productivity spillovers from FDI by regressing firm level productivity on measures of foreign presence in related industries, controlling for a number of other covariates. To do so we proceed in two steps. First, we estimate a Cobb-Douglas production function,

$$\ln y_{it} = \beta_0 + \beta_l \ln l_{it} + \beta_k \ln k_{it} + \beta_m \ln m_{it} + \beta_f for + \ln\text{TFP}_{it}, \qquad (1)$$

where y is output and l, k, m, and *for* are labour, capital, material inputs, and an indicator of foreign ownership, respectively, to obtain total factor productivity (TFP) estimates for firm i as residual.[7] Secondly, TFP of domestic firms is regressed on foreign presence indices and other controls.

One concern with estimating equation (1) is that firms may observe TFP at least partly and that this may influence the choice of factor input combinations in the same period. Hence, there would be a correlation between TFP and the contemporaneous covariates, leading to biased estimates of the coefficients. This is usually referred to as a simultaneity problem. In order to deal with this we use the Olley and Pakes (1996) methodology, which suggests overcoming the simultaneity problem by using investment as proxy variables for the unobserved productivity component. In order to take into account sectoral heterogeneity we estimate equation (1) separately for each 2-digit industry. In this stage we include data for all firms, both domestic and foreign owned.

The second stage involves regressing (log) TFP for domestic firms only on the foreign presence indices. We allow the spillover effect to vary across domestic firms according to their level of the absorptive capacity (ABC). Our assumption is that plants with higher levels of ABC are able to reap greater benefits from foreign direct investment, as they have the necessary technological ability to assimilate the knowledge available from foreign multinationals. As additional controls, we include the R&D intensity and the level of competition (measured by the Herfindahl index) in the respective industry in order to capture other sectoral variables that may be correlated with firm-level TFP.

The fully specified equation is

$$\ln(\text{TFP}_{it}) = \beta' X_{jt} + \gamma_1 \text{FDI}_{jt} + \gamma_2 \text{FDI}_{jt} * \text{ABC}_{it} + d_t + d_j + \varepsilon_{it}, \qquad (2)$$

where X is the vector of control variables for industry j, d_t, and d_j are time and industry dummies, respectively, FDI is the vector of foreign presence variables, which are defined in the following section, and ABC is the measure of absorptive capacity of domestic firm i.

7 Ideally, we would like to include the share of capital held by foreign owners. However, this is unfortunately not available in our data.

We follow Girma (2005) and compute absorptive capacity as

$$\mathrm{ABC}_{it} = \ln(\mathrm{TFP}_i/\mathrm{TFP}_{\max}), \tag{3}$$

where $\mathrm{TFP}_{\max}$ is the maximum TFP level (i.e., the technological frontier) in the industry of firm i. A high level of relative efficiency is supposed to indicate technological congruity with industry leaders.[8]

4. Data and variables

The data set used covers the period 1992 to 1999 and is constructed from two main sources, namely, the *OneSource* firm-level panel data base for the U.K., supplemented by the U.K. Input-Output Supply and Use Tables. The *OneSource* database includes information on all public limited companies, all companies of more than 50 employees, and the top companies based on turnover, net worth, total assets, or shareholders funds (whichever is largest) up to a maximum of 110,000 companies.[9] The database includes only private companies that were in operation in 1999 and therefore excludes companies that exited prior to that year. Companies that were dissolved or in the process of liquidation in 1999 are excluded. In this paper we concentrate on manufacturing firms from this data source.

This firm-level data set is one of the few U.K. firm-level data sets to contain both foreign ownership indicators as well as information on the export status of the firm. The nationality indicators are for the latest year alone, so that it is not possible to identify when a firm became a subsidiary of a foreign multinational. To track the dynamics of ownership, we matched the population of manufacturing firms in the database to a list of U.K. firms acquired by foreign multinationals.[10]

OneSource provides information on employment, physical capital, output, and cost of goods sold, in a consistent way both across firms and across time. The data were screened to select those firms for which there are complete sets of information about the value of output, factors of production, and exports. Given that there is entry in the data, this left an unbalanced sample of approximately 18,000 observations containing information for around 4,600 firms. Nominal aggregates were deflated using 5-digit-level industry deflators obtained from the U.K. Office for National Statistics (ONS).

The inputs in the production function are labour, materials, and capital. The labour input is the number of employees and material is the cost of goods sold.

8 We caution, however, that TFP is only a noisy measure of a firm's technological level, as there may, for instance, be temporary shocks that affect TFP but do not at the same time change a firms' technological capability. If anything, this should cause estimated spillover effects to be downward biased.

9 For this study we used the *OneSource* CD-ROM (licensed to the University of Nottingham) entitled 'UK companies, Vol. 1,' for October 2000.

10 This information is confidential and is obtained from the Office of National Statistics upon special request.

The capital stock was computed using data on investment, with the perpetual inventory method assuming a depreciation rate of 8% and deflated using the GDP deflator of capital formation.

The information to construct the backward and forward linkage indices at SIC92 2-digit level was obtained from the annual U.K. Input-Output Supply and Use Tables. These provide information on the value of output each industry of the economy supplies as input to each other industry.[11] However, these figures contain the value of imported inputs besides the factors procured in the U.K. This is problematic, since the latter do not link to domestic sectors. To construct indices measuring the upstream and downstream connections between domestic firms and foreign multinationals based in the U.K., only semi-finished products produced in the U.K. and used in other production processes in the U.K. are relevant.

For this reason we estimated the value of the factor of industry j produced in a foreign country and used by industry i in the U.K. (for any $I \neq j$ and $I = j$) for every year. The values of the thus estimated imported inputs were subtracted from the I-O table's figures in order to obtain the values of input j produced in the U.K. and used by any other U.K. industry. Further details on this procedure can be found in appendix B.

The foreign presence indicators were computed as follows: The horizontal measurement (*Hor*) is

$$Hor_{jt} = Y^f_{jt} \Big/ Y_{jt}, \tag{4}$$

where the numerator is the total production of foreign firms operating in the U.K. in sector j and time t and the denominator is total output (i.e., output of foreign and domestic firms) of the same sector in the same year. Then, the value of this index simply represents the proportion of the total output of a given industry in a given year that has been produced by foreign firms. This is the measure most commonly employed in spillover studies.

The backward measure (*Back*) was computed as

$$Back_{jt} = \sum_k \alpha_{kjt} \mathrm{Hor}_{kt} \quad for\, k \neq j, \tag{5}$$

where α_{kjt} is the proportion of the output of sector k supplied to industry j; that is,

$$\alpha_{kjt} = Y_{kjt} \big/ Y_{kt}. \tag{6}$$

In the formula above, Y_{kjt} is the output of industry k provided to industry j. Hence, the greater the proportion of output supplied to an industry with foreign

11 The input-output tables use an industry classification different from the SIC92 classification of the *OneSource* database. Nonetheless, the tables provide the correspondence with the SIC92 classification at the 2-, 3-, or 4-digit level. We aggregated the input-output tables' data at the SIC92 2-digit level.

multinational presence and the greater the foreign firms' activities in the sector receiving intermediates from industry k, the greater the backward index. This index has this name because the spillovers, if they exist, are expected to be towards upstream industries.

We also compute a forward measure in a similar fashion. The difference is that instead of α_{kjt} we have β_{jht}, which represents the proportion of sector h inputs that are provided by sector j. Hence,

$$For_{jt} = \sum_h \beta_{jht} Hor_{ht}. \tag{7}$$

Thus, the greater the proportion of the output supplied by an industry with foreign multinational presence and the larger the proportion of the output of supplying industries produced by foreign firms, the higher the value of this index. The name of this index is derived from the expected direction of spillovers, which is downstream in this case.

As pointed out above, a novel feature of this paper is that we also consider the export orientation of foreign multinationals. This is likely to be an important determinant of productivity externalities. Hence, for the horizontal and backward indices we calculate two measures each, namely, *Hor-Dom*, *Hor-Exp*, *Back-Dom*, and *Back-Exp*. The indices with the *Dom* suffix were computed considering the output of foreign firms sold in the U.K., whereas those with the *Exp* suffix take the output of the same firms that is exported. Such a distinction is not appropriate for the forward measure, as exporting multinationals by definition do not have any downstream linkages with domestic firms.

Summary statistics for employment, TFP, and wages are reported in table 1 for foreign and domestic firms separately.[12] As can be seen, foreign firms perform better for all three measures. The difference between foreign and domestic companies is statistically significant in nearly all years.[13] Hence, it seems to be that foreign firms may appear to be the source of productivity spillovers towards domestic enterprises, since they are more productive and employ a more skilled workforce than the former.

5. Empirical results

Table 2 shows the estimates of equation (2) based on the TFP measure calculated using the Olley and Pakes (1996) method. Since we are interested in the productivity spillovers from foreign firms towards domestic companies, these regressions

12 The 2-digit industry production function estimates used to calculate TFP are given in appendix A.

13 Note that to make meaningful comparisons between domestic and foreign companies in different years and industries the wage, employment, and productivity values of table 1 are computed as logarithmic deviations from the yearly and 2-digit industry mean.

consider only the latter type of firms. Column (1) is based on pooling data for all domestic firms, while columns (2) and (3) distinguish domestic exporters and non-exporters, respectively.

The coefficients reported in the table show evidence of significant horizontal spillovers from export-oriented multinationals to domestic exporters, but not to non-exporters. This effect is increasing with improvements in exporters' absorptive capacity. The point estimates in column (2), for example, suggest that an exporter with a median level of absorptive capacity experiences a 1.2% increase in productivity following a 1 percentage point increase in horizontal export-oriented FDI.[14] No such effects are observable for domestic non-exporters. The different results for exporters and non-exporters are likely to reflect the fact that exporters are generally 'better' than non-exporters (e.g., Bernard and Jensen 1999). Whether this depends on management abilities, organizational structure, or other factors that are likely to be internal to the firm is impossible to say in this study because of lack of data. We limit ourselves to observe that horizontal spillovers differ between exporters and non-exporters because the former are able to turn the superior technology available from foreign firms into higher productivity levels. The absence of any positive spillovers from domestic-market-oriented multinationals suggests that this type of FDI increases competition on the domestic market, and, hence, any possible positive externalities are outweighed by negative business-stealing effects.

As regards backward linkages, we find that there are effects from domestic-market-oriented FDI on domestic exporters and non-exporters.[15] Again, this spillover is increasing in the domestic firms' level of absorptive capacity and is higher for domestic exporters. This provides strong evidence that multinationals can affect their suppliers' productivity, in line with the evidence provided by Javorcik (2004) for Lithuania.

However, in contrast to this result for backward linkages from domestic-market-oriented multinationals, we find that export-oriented FDI impacts negatively on their domestic supplier's productivity. This may perhaps be due to export-oriented multinationals operating in enclave sectors without significant backward linkages to the domestic economy (Kokko, Zejan, and Tansini 2001), or may be explained by the fact that domestic firms do not provide the variety of inputs foreign exporters require (Rodriguez-Clare 1996). In addition, it may indicate that multinationals have greater bargaining power than their local suppliers (Graham and Thorpe 1999). Hence, while multinationals may teach their suppliers to be more efficient, in return they may demand a lower price for the intermediate inputs and, hence, negate any increase in output and measured

14 Calculated as $(0.085 + 0.062 * -1.18 = 0.012)$. The median of log ABC is -1.18.

15 While exporters sell a proportion of their output abroad, they generally do not export all of it. Hence, the share of output sold on the domestic market can be supplied to multinationals, which would create a linkage.

TABLE 1
Summary statistics for foreign and domestic firms

	Productivity			Employment			Wages		
	Domestic	Foreign	Difference	Domestic	Foreign	Difference	Domestic	Foreign	Difference
1990	−0.007	0.020	0.027	−0.057	0.160	0.217**	−0.077	0.216	0.294**
	(0.524)	(0.578)	(0.018)	(1.212)	(1.3590	(0.042)	(1.240)	(1.422)	(0.043)
1991	−0.006	0.017	0.023	−0.073	0.194	0.267**	−0.095	0.252	0.347**
	(0.528)	(0.616)	(0.017)	(1.213)	(1.359)	(0.039)	(1.251)	(1.432)	(0.041)
1992	−0.010	0.024	0.034*	−0.079	0.192	0.271**	−0.106	0.260	0.366**
	(0.524)	(0.585)	(0.016)	(1.201)	(1.335)	(0.037)	(1.242)	(1.404)	(0.038)
1993	−0.012	0.030	0.042**	−0.078	0.186	0.265**	−0.109	0.260	0.369**
	(0.517)	(0.575)	(0.015)	(1.183)	(1.342)	(0.035)	(1.224)	(1.412)	(0.036)
1994	−0.017	0.038	0.055**	−0.078	0.172	0.250**	−0.110	0.243	0.353**
	(0.500)	(0.569)	(0.014)	(1.171)	(1.327)	(0.032)	(1.210)	(1.383)	(0.034)
1995	−0.023	0.048	0.071**	−0.093	0.194	0.287**	−0.130	0.271	0.401**
	(0.498)	(0.603)	(0.013)	(1.149)	(1.308)	(0.032)	(1.190)	(1.357)	(0.031)
1996	−0.029	0.060	0.089**	−0.104	0.211	0.315**	−0.139	0.284	0.423**
	(0.470)	(0.599)	(0.012)	(1.131)	(1.310)	(0.030)	(1.160)	(1.369)	(0.028)
1997	−0.018	0.008	0.026**	−0.074	0.035	0.109**	−0.097	0.046	0.143**
	(0.518)	(0.592)	(0.014)	(1.250)	(1.388)	(0.029)	(1.287)	(1.420)	(0.033)
1998	−0.013	0.006	0.019**	−0.105	0.049	0.155**	−0.121	0.057	0.177**
	(0.489)	(0.579)	(0.014)	(1.220)	(1.376)	(0.032)	(1.244)	(1.404)	(0.032)
1999	−0.012	0.006	0.017**	−0.101	0.049	0.150**	−0.120	0.058	0.179**
	(0.482)	(0.573)	(0.015)	(1.206)	(1.372)	(0.032)	(1.229)	(1.387)	(0.035)

NOTES: 1. Values in the table are log deviation from industry (UK SIC 92 2-digit) and yearly mean.
2. Standard errors are in parentheses.
3. + significant at 10%, * significant at 5%, ** significant at 1%.

TABLE 2
Heterogeneous FDI and the productivity growth of domestic firms

	All firms (1)	Exporters (2)	Non-exporters (3)
Hor-Dom FDI	−0.038	−0.048	−0.036
	(1.15)	(1.45)	(0.41)
Hor-Dom FDI ∗ ABC	−0.066	−0.067	−0.075
	(0.47)	(0.68)	(0.96)
Hor-Exp FDI	0.073	0.085	0.059
	(3.67)***	(3.35)***	(0.80)
Hor-Exp FDI ∗ ABC	0.064	0.062	0.043
	(2.35)**	(2.19)**	(0.76)
For FDI	−0.063	−0.125	0.129
	(0.73)	(1.19)	(0.90)
For FDI ∗ ABC	0.144	0.149	0.147
	(0.68)	(1.15)	(1.04)
Back-Dom FDI	0.059	0.063	0.057
	(7.61)***	(6.89)***	(3.94)***
Back-Dom FDI ∗ ABC	0.053	0.044	0.078
	(5.24)***	(6.32)***	(2.39)**
Back-Exp FDI	−0.015	−0.019	−0.039
	(2.32)**	(2.23)**	(1.80)*
Back-Exp. FDI ∗ ABC	−0.018	−0.007	−0.023
	(2.29)**	(2.03)**	(1.07)
Herfindhal index	0.003	−0.004	−0.027
	(0.60)	(0.93)	(1.82)*
R&D intensity	0.014	0.017	0.010
	(2.97)***	(2.30)**	(2.02)**
Constant	−0.036	0.017	0.059
	(6.35)***	(3.59)***	(5.40)***
Observations	22726	14845	7881

NOTES: The dependent variable is the Olley-Pakes TFP measure.
The regression includes a constant and a full set of time and 2-digit industry dummies. Robust cluster corrected t-statistics are in parentheses.
*significant at 10%; **significant at 5%; ***significant at 1%.

productivity.[16] Unfortunately, owing to data limitations, we are unable to investigate the reasons for this negative effect in any further detail.

With a view to forward linkages, we do not find any robust statistically significant effects, either for domestic exporters or non-exporters. Again, this is in line with Javorcik (2004), who fails to establish any robust evidence for spillovers through forward linkages using micro data from Lithuania.

Examining the remaining regressors, we find that the Herfindahl index is negative and statistically significant for the sample of non-exporters only. The

16 Unfortunately, with the data at hand it is impossible to distinguish this price from a true efficiency effect. Ideally, detailed price data are necessary to tackle this issue. Katayama, Lu, and Tybout (2003) suggest an interesting and different approach to solving this problem, which, however, is based on some strong assumptions about firm and industry characteristics and therefore is not applicable to a study such as ours that uses data on a variety of sectors.

industry-level R&D intensity is positive, however, and is statistically significant in all specifications. This indicates that that there are general technological spillovers generated by the R&D activities conducted by other firms operating in the same sector.

In estimating equation (2) using data for all manufacturing industries, we implicitly assume that the effect of the explanatory variables is uniform across different industries. This is arguably a quite restrictive assumption, given that we pool firms operating in sectors with different levels of FDI and export orientation. If some unobserved industry characteristic is correlated with export activity of multinationals, then it would be difficult to attribute our results to the FDI type rather than the industry type. Arguably, the inclusion of sectoral dummies in the regression mitigates this concern to a large extent, as does the inclusion of the Herfindahl index and the R&D intensity, which capture some time-varying industry characteristics. However, in order to dig deeper into this issue we separate the industries in our data into those with high growth of domestic-oriented FDI and those with high growth of export-oriented FDI.[17]

The results of estimating equation (2) on this split dataset are reported in table 3. They show that, indeed, there are a number of noteworthy sectoral differences. First, we find that industries that are characterized by a high growth of domestic-oriented FDI also show evidence of positive horizontal spillovers from domestic-market-oriented FDI. In other words, domestic firms in industries in which this segment of FDI grows over-proportionally are able to benefit from domestic-market-oriented FDI. Perhaps in these industries inward investors are competing with each other rather than with the local competitors, hence enabling them to learn the new technology brought into the economy.

Another important difference between the two types of industries is that only in sectors that show high growth of export-oriented FDI do we find evidence for negative spillovers through backward linkages from export-oriented FDI. This strengthens the earlier explanation that either export-oriented FDI is not linked well into the domestic economy, hence providing little potential for positive spillovers, and/or that domestic firms do not provide the required inputs and hence lose from contacts with their multinational customers at least in the short run while they are attempting to readjust production to satisfy their customers.

In both types of sectors we find that there are positive spillovers from horizontal export-oriented FDI to domestic exporters, as found in table 2, and that they are of roughly similar magnitude. Furthermore, backward linkages from domestic-oriented FDI exert positive effects on productivity of both domestic exporters and non-exporters, again underlining the results provided earlier.

Hence, while the positive effects from horizontal domestic-oriented FDI and the negative backward linkage effects from export-oriented FDI seem to be sector

17 An industry is defined to be a 'high domestic-oriented FDI growth sector' if the growth rate of domestic-oriented FDI exceeds that for export-oriented FDI in the industry over the sample period and vice versa for 'high export-oriented FDI growth sectors.'

TABLE 3
Heterogeneous FDI and the productivity growth of domestic firms: are there sectoral differences?

	High domestic-oriented FDI growth sectors			High export-oriented FDI growth sectors		
	All firms	Exporters	Non-exporters	All firms	Exporters	Non-exporters
Hor-Dom FDI	0.047	0.035	0.061	−0.049	−0.052	−0.392
	(2.22)**	(2.87)***	(3.09)***	(0.81)	(0.35)	(1.16)
Hor-Dom FDI ∗ ABC	0.027	0.036	0.125	−0.096	−0.077	−0.026
	(1.92)**	(0.93)	(2.52)**	(0.64)	(1.10)	(1.62)
Hor-Exp FDI	0.042	0.068	0.024	0.088	0.073	0.094
	(3.61)***	(3.12)***	(2.03)**	(7.63)***	(7.17)***	(6.72)***
Hor-Exp FDI ∗ ABC	0.017	0.011	0.020	0.026	0.018	0.037
	(2.95)***	(2.14)**	(1.94)*	(2.41)**	(2.99)***	(2.48)**
For FDI	−0.042	−0.062	0.012	−0.042	−0.212	0.424
	(1.10)	(1.37)	(0.18)	(0.41)	(2.70)***	(1.31)
For FDI ∗ ABC	−0.043	−0.042	−0.032	0.015	−0.019	0.091
	(1.84)*	(1.43)	(0.82)	(0.59)	(0.58)	(1.67)*
Back-Dom FDI	0.069	0.073	0.055	0.086	0.093	0.088
	(2.79)***	(1.94)*	(2.17)*	(3.63)***	(3.47)***	(4.78)***
Back-Dom FDI ∗ ABC	0.035	0.033	0.038	0.024	0.026	0.016
	(7.05)***	(5.53)***	(4.46)***	(4.45)***	(9.15)***	(5.58)***
Back-Exp. FDI	−0.010	−0.068	−0.096	−0.029	−0.004	−0.067
	(1.30)	(0.69)	(1.39)	(5.12)***	(8.64)***	(5.34)***
Back-Exp FDI ∗ ABC	−0.010	−0.016	0.070	0.051	−0.046	−0.030
	(1.26)	(1.57)*	(1.15)	(1.13)	(1.00)	(0.49)
Herfindhal index	0.009	−0.001	−0.035	0.018	0.007	−0.006
	(1.12)	(0.12)	(2.41)**	(1.49)	(0.68)	(2.53)**
R&D intensity	0.017	0.028	0.006	0.020	0.032	0.009
	(2.21)**	(2.75)***	(2.55)**	(2.21)**	(2.42)**	(2.39)**
Constant	0.026	0.026	−0.038	0.041	−0.208	−0.212
	(4.75)***	(4.04)***	(4.18)***	(3.33)***	(11.28)***	(5.89)***
Observations	17632	11171	6461	5094	3674	1420

NOTES: The dependent variable is the Olley-Pakes TFP measure. The regression includes a constant and a full set of time and 2-digit industry dummies. Robust cluster corrected t-statistics are in parentheses. *significant at 10%; **significant at 5%; ***significant at 1%.

specific, the positive results on horizontal export FDI and backward domestic-oriented FDI are robust to the definition of sector. Thus, from the results discussed so far it is apparent that there are both intra-industry (i.e., horizontal) and inter-industry (i.e., vertical) spillovers through backward linkages. However, the sign of vertical spillovers through backward linkages depends on the nature of the operations of the multinational, that is, whether it is export oriented or not.

The U.K. government is actively aiming policies at attracting inward foreign direct investment. One aim of the policy is to secure, in particular, inward investment in 'knowledge driven' industries (UK Trade & Investment 2005). Hence, there is arguably a slight bias in policy towards attracting the location of what may broadly be defined as 'high technology' multinationals into the country. This

TABLE 4
Heterogeneous FDI and the productivity growth of domestic firms: are there high-tech/low-tech sector differentials?

	High-tech sectors			Low-tech sectors		
	All firms	Exporters	Non-exporters	All firms	Exporters	Non-exporters
Hor-Dom FDI	−0.029	−0.024	−0.046	0.061	0.063	0.046
	(2.96)***	(2.42)**	(2.07)**	(1.22)	(1.02)	(0.58)
Hor-Dom FDI ∗ ABC	0.017	0.032	−0.038	0.012	0.011	0.107
	(0.40)	(0.65)	(0.49)	(1.28)	(1.11)	(1.36)
Hor-Exp FDI	0.047	0.972	0.031	0.028	0.031	0.010
	(3.00)***	(2.65)***	(1.45)	(1.78)*	(2.32)**	(1.91)*
Hor-Exp FDI ∗ ABC	0.025	0.026	0.018	0.049	0.082	0.26
	(2.30)**	(2.13)**	(0.19)	(1.54)	(0.98)	(1.50)
For FDI	−0.049	−0.060	−0.021	0.068	−0.061	0.080
	(1.07)	(1.11)	(0.05)	(0.63)	(1.72)*	(1.39)
For FDI ∗ ABC	−0.068	−0.155	0.186	0.085	0.144	0.042
	(0.57)	(0.97)	(1.40)	(0.79)	(1.43)	(0.17)
Back-Dom FDI	0.151	0.134	−0.165	0.126	0.109	0.049
	(1.92)*	(2.06)**	(0.18)	(1.86)*	(2.44)**	(0.15)
Back-Dom FDI ∗ ABC	0.030	0.037	0.026	0.018	0.024	0.082
	(2.25)**	(1.82)*	(0.07)	(2.12)**	(2.21)**	(0.64)
Back-Exp FDI	−0.067	0.057	0.020	0.063	−0.094	−0.092
	(1.62)	(1.19)	(1.32)	(1.51)	(0.23)	(0.40)
Back-Exp FDI ∗ ABC	−0.038	−0.066	0.027	0.015	0.010	−0.082
	(1.73)*	(1.91)*	(1.31)	(0.75)	(1.18)	(0.57)
Herfindahl index	−0.005	−0.005	−0.012	0.013	−0.009	−0.019
	(0.87)	(0.65)	(1.00)	(1.96)*	(2.05)**	(0.23)
R&D intensity	0.045	0.044	0.039	0.016	0.017	0.022
	(2.31)**	(0.28)	(2.73)***	(2.80)***	(1.69)*	(2.38)**
Constant	0.005	0.008	0.013	−0.014	−0.014	−0.011
	(0.73)	(0.90)	(1.29)	(2.51)**	(3.17)***	(1.14)
Observations	8575	6642	1933	14151	8203	5948

NOTES: The dependent variable is the Olley-Pakes TFP measure. The regression includes a constant and a full set of time and 2-digit industry dummies. Robust cluster corrected t-statistics are in parentheses. *significant at 10%; **significant at 5%; ***significant at 1%.

is partly based on the assumption that 'high-tech' firms have a greater potential for spillovers to the domestic economy. In order to investigate the implications of this for spillovers we split our sample into 'high-tech' and 'low-tech' sectors and estimate equation (2) separately on the two samples.[18]

The results, reported in table 4, show that our main findings of positive spillovers from horizontal export-oriented FDI and from backward domestic-oriented FDI carry through in both sectors, although the magnitude of the effects is different in both. There are, however, some differences compared with the earlier

18 We use the OECD classification to define high-tech and low-tech. See appendix D for a list of industry classifications.

results. We now find evidence of negative effects of horizontal domestic-oriented FDI on firms in high-tech sectors, and this effect is larger for non-exporters. This is likely to indicate the strong competition effect in this sector, where, broadly speaking, domestic firms may be more similar to multinationals than in low-tech sectors.

6. Conclusion

Using a panel data set of U.K. companies from 1992 to 1999, we investigate whether or not there exist productivity spillovers from foreign direct investment. This is done considering the possibility not only of horizontal but also of vertical spillovers and controlling for the export orientation of both domestic companies and foreign multinationals. Our findings point to the general conclusion that the export orientation of domestic and foreign multinationals alike is relevant to productivity spillovers.

Taking into account the export orientation of foreign MNEs yields interesting insights. We find robust evidence for positive horizontal spillovers only from export-oriented multinationals. However, only domestic-market-oriented MNEs generate positive spillovers through backward linkages for both domestic exporters and non-exporters. In general, our evidence underlines the importance of buyer-supplier linkages for productivity spillovers as emphasized by the UNCTAD (2001) report, which also stresses backward linkages as a conduit for positive productivity spillovers from foreign direct investment.

Appendix A

TABLE A1
Production function estimates by 2-digit SIC industry

	SIC2 = 15	SIC2 = 16	SIC2 = 17	SIC2 = 18	SIC2 = 19	SIC2 = 20	SIC2 = 21	SIC2 = 22
Employment	0.078	0.154	0.314	0.161	0.157	0.081	0.167	0.174
	(20.22)***	(3.68)***	(6.91)***	(17.93)***	(16.01)***	(5.21)***	(21.79)***	(11.78)***
Capital	0.075	0.055	0.138	0.011	0.035	0.045	0.054	0.059
	(17.36)***	(1.61)	(5.20)***	(1.54)	(5.05)***	(8.06)***	(11.10)***	(12.78)***
Material	0.845	0.805	0.460	0.805	0.810	0.882	0.780	0.751
	(233.10)***	(29.20)***	(5.28)***	(71.95)***	(75.04)***	(54.36)***	(113.80)***	(69.73)***
Foreign	0.014	−0.093	0.253	0.086	0.042	0.116	0.049	0.031
	(1.27)	(0.96)	(4.17)***	(3.82)***	(1.43)	(3.44)***	(3.61)***	(1.71)*
Constant	0.381	0.714	1.827	1.130	0.837	0.446	0.885	1.119
	(15.99)***	(3.43)***	(7.48)***	(15.26)***	(20.76)***	(5.77)***	(25.98)***	(17.28)***

	SIC2 = 23	SIC2 = 24	SIC2 = 25	SIC2 = 26	SIC2 = 27	SIC2 = 28	SIC2 = 29	SIC2 = 30
Employment	0.013	0.106	0.169	0.213	0.162	0.265	0.216	0.087
	(0.60)	(12.51)***	(34.17)***	(28.39)***	(26.31)***	(38.80)***	(34.22)***	(3.48)***
Capital	0.099	0.070	0.049	0.064	0.030	0.048	0.031	0.053
	(4.35)***	(11.28)***	(14.87)***	(10.11)***	(5.00)***	(16.09)***	(12.81)***	(3.20)***
Material	0.846	0.814	0.783	0.721	0.801	0.678	0.746	0.863
	(41.76)***	(69.97)***	(158.27)***	(67.58)***	(127.17)***	(121.70)***	(131.07)***	(31.31)***
Foreign	0.130	0.039	0.033	−0.009	0.035	−0.001	0.005	0.180
	(2.16)**	(2.10)**	(3.05)***	(0.55)	(2.37)**	(0.01)	(0.63)	(4.01)***
Constant	0.581	0.648	0.837	1.041	0.986	1.348	1.216	0.601
	(6.20)***	(16.52)***	(33.00)***	(28.02)***	(36.38)***	(49.06)***	(48.35)***	(6.14)***

	SIC2 = 31	SIC2 = 32	SIC2 = 33	SIC2 = 34	SIC2 = 35	SIC2 = 36
Employment	0.183	0.136	0.240	0.182	0.115	0.183
	(22.12)***	(6.20)***	(27.10)***	(19.05)***	(4.17)***	(31.68)***
Capital	0.046	0.063	0.021	0.034	0.078	0.031
	(8.92)***	(4.10)***	(5.10)***	(7.47)***	(4.60)***	(10.99)***
Material	0.768	0.788	0.748	0.784	0.823	0.795
	(99.51)***	(46.34)***	(87.28)***	(103.24)***	(25.64)***	(144.60)***
Foreign	0.031	0.053	−0.010	0.015	0.200	0.062
	(1.96)*	(2.51)**	(0.66)	(2.04)**	(5.61)***	(4.14)***
Constant	0.986	0.915	1.234	0.976	0.555	0.891
	(26.50)***	(11.53)***	(30.23)***	(32.91)***	(4.60)***	(29.33)***

NOTES: Robust t-statistics are in parentheses. *significant at 10%; **significant at 5%; *** significant at 1%.

Appendix B: Computation of imported inputs

The imported inputs were estimated in the following fashion. First, we calculated for each year a proxy of the value of total imports of good j (M_j) that was used as intermediate (MX_j). This was calculated as: $MX_j = (X_j/Y_j)M_j$, where X_j is the U.K. intermediate demand of product j, viz., the value of the product j that was used as factor of production by all U.K. industries and Y_j is the total domestic demand of the same product, that is, U.K. intermediate demand plus U.K. consumption demand. When this methodology is used, it is implicit that the assumption that the share of the total U.K. demand of good j used as input (X_i/Y_i) is equal to the share of the value of imports of the same item employed as intermediate (MX_j/M_j). Secondly, we allocated a certain fraction of MX_j to each industry. More specifically, the value of the imported intermediate j used in any other industry i was estimated. This was calculated as $Mx_{ij} = (x_{ji}/X_j)MX_j$ where x_{ji} is the value of the intermediate produced by industry j and employed in industry i.

Appendix C

TABLE A2
Correlation matrix of foreign presence indices

	Hor-Dom FDI	*Hor-Exp* FDI	*For* FDI	*Back-Dom* FDI	*Back-Exp* FDI
Hor-Dom FDI	1				
Hor-Exp FDI	0.4447	1			
For FDI	0.1091	0.3676	1		
Back-Dom FDI	0.0773	0.1505	0.2654	1	
Back-Exp FDI	0.0704	0.2539	0.2983	0.8864	1

Appendix D: Definition of high- and low-tech industries

High-technology industries
Aircraft and spacecraft
Pharmaceuticals
Office, accounting, and computing machinery
Radio, TV, and communications equipment
Medical, precision, and optical instruments

Medium-high-technology industries
Electrical machinery and apparatus, n.e.c.
Motor vehicles, trailers, and semi-trailers

Chemicals excluding pharmaceuticals
Railroad equipment and transport equipment, n.e.c.
Machinery and equipment, n.e.c.

Medium-low-technology industries
Building and repairing of ships and boats
Rubber and plastics products
Coke, refined petroleum products and nuclear fuel
Other non-metallic mineral products
Basic metals and fabricated metal products

Low-technology industries
Manufacturing, n.e.c.; Recycling
Wood, pulp, paper, paper products, printing, and publishing
Food products, beverages, and tobacco
Textiles, textile products, leather, and footwear
(Note: high tech is defined as high- and medium-high tech. Source: OECD: www1.oecd.org/publications/e-book/92–2003-04–1-7294/annex-1.htm)

References

Aitken, Brian J., and Ann E. Harrison (1999) 'Do domestic firms benefit from direct foreign investment? Evidence from Venezuela,' *American Economic Review* 89, 605–18

Bernard, Andrew B., and J. Bradford Jensen (1999) 'Exceptional exporter performance: cause, effect, or both?' *Journal of International Economics* 47, 1–25

Blalock, Garrick, and Paul Gertler (2003) 'Technology from foreign direct investment and welfare gains through the supply chain,' mimeo, Cornell University

Blomström, Magnus, and Ari Kokko (1998) 'Multinational corporations and spillovers,' *Journal of Economic Surveys* 12, 247–277.

Caves, Richard E. (1996) *Multinational Enterprise and Economic Analysis*, 2nd ed. (Cambridge: Cambridge University Press).

Criscuolo, Chiara, and Ralf Martin (2004) 'Multinationals and US productivity leadership: evidence from Great Britain,' CEP Discussion Paper 0672, London School of Economics

Djankov, Simeon, and Bernard Hoekman (2000) 'Foreign investment and productivity growth in Czech enterprises,' *World Bank Economic Review* 14, 49–64

Driffield, Nigel, Max Munday, and Annette Roberts (2002) 'Foreign direct investment, transactions linkages, and the performance of the domestic sector,' *International Journal of the Economics of Business* 9, 335–51

Fosfuri, Andrea, Massimo Motta, and Thomas Rønde (2001) 'Foreign direct investment and spillovers through workers' mobility,' *Journal of International Economics* 53, 205–22

Girma, Sourafel (2005) 'Absorptive capacity and productivity spillovers from FDI: a threshold regression analysis,' *Oxford Bulletin of Economics and Statistics* 67, 281–306

Girma, Sourafel, and Holger Görg (2007) 'Multinationals' productivity advantage: scale or technology?' *Economic Inquiry* 45, 350–62

Girma, Sourafel, David Greenaway, and Katharine Wakelin (2001) 'Who benefits from foreign direct investment in the UK?' *Scottish Journal of Political Economy* 48, 119–33
Görg, Holger, and Eric Strobl (2001) 'Multinational companies and productivity spillovers: a meta-analysis,' *Economic Journal* 111, F723–F739
— (2001) 'Spillovers from foreign firms through worker mobility: an empirical investigation,' *Scandinavian Journal of Economics* 107, 693–709
Graham, Paul, Sally Thorpe, and L. Hogan (1999) 'Non-competitive market behaviour in the international Cokery coal market,' *Energy Economics* 21, 195–212
Haskel, Jonathan E., Sonia C. Pereira, and Matthew J. Slaughter (2002) 'Does inward foreign direct investment boost the productivity of domestic firms?' NBER Working Paper No. 8724
Javorcik, Beata Smarzynska (2004) 'Does foreign direct investment increase the productivity of domestic firms? In search of Sspillovers through backward linkages,' *American Economic Review* 94, 605–27
Javorcik, Beata Smarzynska, and Mariana Spatareanu (2007) 'To share or not to share: does local participation matter for spillovers from foreign direct investment?' *Journal of Development Economics*, forthcoming
Katayama, Hajime, Shihua Lu, and James R. Tybout (2003) 'Firm-level productivity studies: illusions and a solution,' NBER Working Paper No. 9617
Keller, Wolfgang (2001) 'International technology diffusion,' NBER Working Paper 8573
Keller, Wolfgang, and Stephen Yeaple (2003) 'Multinational enterprises, international trade, and productivity growth: firm-level evidence from the United States,' NBER Working Paper
Kinoshita, Yuko (2001) 'R&D and technology spillovers through FDI: innovation and absorptive capacity,' CEPR Discussion Paper DP2775
Klein, Benjamin, Robert G. Crawford, and Armen A. Alchian (1978) 'Vertical integration, appropriable rents, and the competitive contracting process,' *Journal of Law and Economics* 21, 297–326
Kokko, Ari, Ruben Tansini, and Mario C. Zejan (1996) 'Local technological capability and productivity spillovers from FDI in the Uruguayan manufacturing sector,' *Journal of Development Studies* 32, 602–11
Kokko, Ari, Mario Zejan, and Ruben Tansini (2001) 'Trade regimes and spillover effects of FDI: Evidence from Uruguay,' *Weltwirtschaftliches Archiv* 137, 124–49
Lipsey, Robert E., and Fredrik Sjöholm (2005) 'Host country impacts of inward FDI: why such different answers?' In *The Impact of Foreign Direct Investment on Development*, ed. Magnus Blomström, Edward Graham, and Theodore Moran (Washington, DC: Institute for International Economics)
Moran, Theodore (2001) *Parental Supervision: The New Paradigm for Foreign Direct Investment and Development* (Washington, DC: Institute for International Economics)
Rodríguez-Clare, Andres (1996) 'Multinationals, linkages, and economic development,' *American Economic Review* 86, 852–73
Olley, Steven, and Ariel Pakes (1996) 'The dynamics of productivity in the telecommunications equipment industry,' *Econometrica* 64, 1263–97
UK Trade & Investment (2005) *Departmental Report 2005* (London: HMSO)
UNCTAD (2001) *World Investment Report 2001: Promoting Linkages* (New York: United Nations)

Chapter 11

Spillovers through backward linkages from multinationals: Measurement matters!

Salvador Barrios [a], Holger Görg [b,c], Eric Strobl [d,e,*]

[a] Institute for Prospective Technological Studies, Joint Research Centre, European Commission, Spain
[b] Kiel Institute for the World Economy, University of Kiel, Germany
[c] CEPR, UK
[d] Department of Economics, Ecole Polytechnique, Paris, France
[e] SALISES, Trinidad and Tobago

ARTICLE INFO

Article history:
Received 25 November 2009
Accepted 4 October 2010
Available online 23 October 2010

JEL Classification:
F23
L22

Keywords:
Multinationals
Backward spillovers
Productivity spillovers
Linkages

ABSTRACT

We argue that the measures of backward linkages used in recent papers on spillovers from multinational companies are potentially problematic, as they depend on a number of restrictive assumptions, namely that (i) multinationals use domestically produced inputs in the same proportion as imported inputs, (ii) multinationals have the same input sourcing behaviour as domestic firms, irrespective of their country of origin, and (iii) the demand for locally produced inputs by multinationals is proportional to their share of locally produced output. We discuss why these assumptions are likely to be violated in practice, and provide alternative measures that overcome these drawbacks. Our results, using plant level data for Ireland, clearly show that the choice of backward linkage measure and thus, the assumptions behind it, matters greatly in order to draw possible conclusions regarding the existence of foreign direct investment (FDI)-related spillovers. Using the standard measure employed in the literature we fail to find robust evidence for spillovers through backward linkages. However, when we use alternative measures of backward linkages that relax assumptions (i)–(iii), we find robust evidence for positive FDI backward spillover effects.

1. Introduction

The first paper on productivity spillovers to host country firms from multinational companies (MNCs) was published more than 30 years ago (Caves, 1974). Even so, the search for these effects continues.[1] In theory, the potential productivity benefits for local firms from inward foreign direct investment (FDI) have important implications for economic policy. However, the empirical evidence of such benefits thus far has been conclusive. Much of the literature has (with limited success) searched only for horizontal spillovers, i.e., benefits to domestic firms operating in the same industry as the MNCs. However, several theoretical contributions showed that spillovers through backward linkages, i.e., benefits to domestic firms that operate in sectors that supply inputs to multinationals, could be another important channel (see, for instance, Rodríguez-Claré, 1996; Markusen and Venables, 1999). Additionally, a number of anecdotes and case studies also suggested that many multinationals play an important role in actively assisting their suppliers in host countries to improve their quality and

* Corresponding author at: Department of Economics, Ecole Polytechnique, Paris, France.
E-mail address: eric.strobl@polytechnique.edu (E. Strobl).

[1] There is a large and still growing literature on this. Recent published papers include Javorcik and Spatareanu (2008), Girma and Wakelin (2007), Keller and Yeaple (forthcoming). Görg and Strobl (2001) and Keller (2004) provide comprehensive overviews of this literature.

0014-2921/$ - see front matter © 2010 Elsevier B.V. All rights reserved.
doi:10.1016/j.euroecorev.2010.10.002

efficiency (e.g., Moran, 2001). Several recent empirical studies using large firm level data sets seem to have confirmed the importance of such positive vertical spillover effects (e.g., Javorcik, 2004; Gorodnichenko et al., 2007, Blalock and Gertler, 2008). This is seen as providing an answer as to why much of the literature on horizontal spillovers failed to find a beneficial role of multinationals in the host economy.

The reliability of evidence in support of the existence of spillovers, whether of a horizontal or vertical nature, depends crucially on the plausibility of their proxies employed. The empirical strategy in capturing the importance of backward linkage spillovers has essentially exclusively consisted of using the share of foreign multinational output in each sector as a measure of their total demand of inputs in that sector, and input–output tables of the host country to proxy how this demand was distributed across sectors. However, measuring backward linkages in such a way relies on a number of underlying assumptions about the nature of input demand of foreign multinationals. In a nutshell, these are that (i) multinationals use domestically produced inputs in the same proportion as imported inputs, (ii) that foreign firms have the same input sourcing behaviour as domestic firms, and all MNCs have the same inputs sourcing behaviour irrespective of their origin, and (iii) that multinationals' demand for locally produced inputs is proportional to the share of output produced by MNCs in a given sector.

In this paper we explicitly address the plausibility of these assumptions—an aspect previously neglected in the literature. We clearly spell out the assumptions, discuss why these are likely to be violated in practice, and provide alternatives that attempt to at least partly overcome these limitations. We then illustrate the importance of using the alternative proxies of backward linkages with manufacturing plant level data for the Republic of Ireland. This case study is particularly relevant as FDI in Ireland is well known to have played an important role for economic growth over the last three decades. We focus on FDI in manufacturing sectors as these are in general more prone to benefit local producers via backward linkages compared to other sectors of activity (see the seminal contribution by Hirschman, 1958).

Our results show clearly that the choice of backward linkage measure matters greatly in determining whether or not FDI is beneficial to the host economy. For instance, using the standard measure employed in the literature we fail to find any robust evidence for spillovers through backward linkages. In contrast, measures of backward linkages relaxing assumptions (i)–(iii) produce positive spillover effects. This result is robust to controlling for any potential endogeneity of the spillover variables. In order to tackle the endogeneity issue we use instrumental variables/GMM techniques.

We also show that our preferred measure of backward linkages, which uses the input–output table for the home country of multinationals rather than the host country, produce results that are unlikely to be generated by chance. To show this we compare our results to that of hypothetical linkages based on randomly assigned input–output (I–O) coefficients. Hence, we conduct a Monte Carlo experiment where we assign randomly chosen I–O coefficients to firm nationalities, and repeat this experiment 500 times. We show that the results we get using our preferred measure of backward linkages (but not that obtained using the standard measure!) differ from this hypothetical pattern. We take this to indicate that our approach provides useful information and does not just reflect a random process.

The remainder of the paper is structured as follows. Section 2 discusses the proxies for horizontal and backward spillovers used in the literature, and identifies the assumptions and their drawbacks implicit in the latter and proposes alternatives that overcome these arguably unrealistic assumptions. Section 3 describes the plant level data used in the econometric analysis, which is described in Section 4. Section 5 presents some conclusions.

2. Proxies of horizontal and vertical spillovers

As noted earlier, traditionally the literature estimating spillovers from FDI has focused on horizontal, i.e., within industry, spillovers, and only recently turned its attention to spillovers due to vertical linkages, related to the input–output structure of the economy. The standard measure used to proxy horizontal spillovers is

$$HORIZONTAL_{jt} = Y^{f}_{jt}/Y_{jt} \tag{1}$$

where the numerator is the total production of foreign affiliates f in industry j at time t and the denominator is total output (i.e., output of foreign and domestic plants) of the same industry in the same year. In other words, this index represents the proportion of the total output of a given industry in a given year produced by all foreign affiliates.[2] As a measure of foreign presence in the industry this variable was used in the initial spillover study (Caves, 1974) and in many papers since.

The measurement of backward linkages was brought to the fore by Javorcik (2004). The main idea is to calculate a variable which captures the effect that the greater the proportion of output supplied by domestic firm i to foreign multinationals, the higher the potential spillovers through backward linkages. To measure this Javorcik (2004) used the following proxy:

$$BACKWARD\_IO_{jt} = \sum_{k} \alpha^{IO}_{kj} HORIZONTAL_{kt} \quad \text{for } k \neq j \tag{2}$$

[2] This measure was also used by Javorcik (2004). Alternative measures are based on employment shares (e.g., Haskel et al., 2009, Kosova, forthcoming) or capital shares (Djankov and Hoekman, 2000). In a meta-analysis of the productivity spillover literature, Görg and Strobl (2001) conclude that estimates of spillovers tend to be lower if capital shares are used, compared to output or employment shares. However, the use of employment shares or output shares does not appear to produce different results.

864 S. Barrios et al. / European Economic Review 55 (2011) 862–875

where $HORIZONTAL_{kt}$ is defined as above. α_{kj}^{IO} is the proportion of the output of sector j supplied to industry k, i.e. $\alpha_{kj}=Y_{kj}/Y_k$, such that Y_{kj} is industry j's output provided to industry k.[3] To approximate α_{kj}^{IO} the approach by Javorcik (2004) and subsequent papers thus far has been to use the input–output coefficients from the host country's input–output (I–O) tables. These coefficients are calculated excluding products supplied for final consumption but including imports of intermediate goods.[4]

Importantly, it needs to be made clear that defining *HORIZONTAL* and the α_{kj}^{IO}'s in such a measure of backward linkages implicitly assumes the following conditions to hold:

*A*1: Domestically produced inputs are used in the same proportion as imported inputs.

*A*2: Foreign multinationals have the same input sourcing behaviour as domestic firms, and multinationals from different nationalities have the same input sourcing behaviour.

*A*3: The share of total output by foreign multinationals in a sector is reflective of their demand for locally produced inputs.

*A*1 and *A*2 follow directly from using input demand coefficients for intermediate products from total I–O tables of the host country, while *A*3 is a result of using *HORIZONTAL* as a proxy for input demand of foreign multinationals within a sector.

However, it can be easily argued that these assumptions are in reality likely to be violated. For example, with regard to *A*1 the recent literature on international outsourcing of intermediate inputs suggests that firms are likely to outsource different stages of production abroad. Hence, they tend to import different types of inputs than they source in the domestic economy.[5] Nevertheless, it must be noted that this assumption is not imposed in all papers on vertical spillovers. For example, Gorodnichenko et al. (2007), Girma et al. (2008) and Ayyagari and Kosova (2010) exclude imported inputs from their measure.[6] In some other studies, for example, Blalock and Gertler (2008) it is not clear whether the analysis is based on I–O tables including or excluding imported inputs.

As regards *A*2, it is arguably unlikely that foreign multinationals have the same input sourcing behaviour as domestic firm. The same input sourcing behaviour would implicitly mean that foreign multinationals have the same production technology as indigenous establishments. This would, however, contradict the basic idea behind the possibility of FDI spillovers, namely, that foreign multinationals have superior technology and knowledge from which the host economy can learn (e.g., Markusen, 2002). Moreover, the extent of local input sourcing may differ across foreign nationalities. In this context, Rodríguez-Clare (1996) shows that the decision of whether or not to source inputs locally is likely to depend on distance, with multinationals from neighbouring countries being more likely to source inputs from home due to relatively low transport costs.

There is some case study evidence that arguably supports our criticism of this assumption. For instance, Japanese multinationals tend to buy intermediate inputs from other Japanese multinationals (or SMEs) belonging to the same Keiretsu which in turn influence their overseas affiliates' demand for local intermediates inputs, see for instance Belderbos et al. (2001). The latter is especially true if Japanese multinationals also tend to locate in the same (or neighbouring) countries, see Head and Mayer (2004). Hence, these firms are likely to have the same sourcing strategies at home and abroad. Moran (2001) also provides case study evidence for the automotive, computer/electronics and other sectors that shows that foreign firms in a large majority of cases introduce state-of-the art technology and business practices in the host economy. In other words, the production technology used in the host is similar to that used at home, which suggests that sourcing strategies are also likely to be similar to those used at home. More generally, the business literature has provided extensive evidence showing that the sourcing policy of a multinational company is the result of firm decisions which are largely influenced by the firm's nationality of ownership and national networks. These may translate into intense backward–forward linkages within firms and also between firms sharing the same nationality (for example, Buckley and Pearce, 1979).

Finally, one can also argue that assumption *A*3 is unlikely to hold in reality. First, nothing guarantees that the proportion of locally sourced inputs to locally produced outputs is constant within and across broadly defined sectors. In other words, the underlying production technology may differ across producers of different products in the same broad sector of activity. Additionally, the extent of local input sourcing may differ across foreign nationalities and this may not be proportional to differences in output across nationalities if their technologies and/or their tendency to import are strongly influenced by home-country specific characteristics.

All of the criticisms stated above could arguably lead to biased measures of backward linkages and hence to biased estimates of their impact on productivity. Moreover, it is not *a priori* clear whether these would lead to an upward or downward bias in the estimates. The purpose of this paper is thus to explicitly investigate the extent of the potential problems in estimates of spillovers through backward linkages using the case study of Ireland. In particular, our data allow us to consider the following issues.

First, the Irish I–O tables, which we use here, allow the distinction between imported and domestically sourced inputs. Hence, our first alternative measure uses I–O coefficients, α_{kj}^{NIMP} (where NIMP stands for "no imported inputs") calculated

[3] One may want to note that these coefficients are generally from a single year since I–O tables tend to be available only over long time intervals. This, however, may not be too much of a problem as input–output relationships only change slowly over time. Our data similarly also only provides us with I–O coefficients for one year.

[4] This definition of backward spillovers may not necessarily reflect the fact that researchers believe this to be the most appropriate definition, but may be due to data availability.

[5] For example, the studies by Görg et al. (2008), Amiti and Wei (2009) and McCann (forthcoming) suggest that the use of internationally outsourced materials or services affects productivity differently than using domestic inputs. Also, Munch and Skagsten (2009) show that internationally outsourced and domestically sourced inputs have different effects on wages for workers, suggesting that they are different types of inputs.

[6] In fact, Ayyagari and Kosova (2010) exclude imports as well as exports and final consumption.

using only domestically sourced inputs

$$BACKWARD\_NIMP_{jt} = \sum_k \alpha_{kj}^{NIMP} HORIZONTAL_{kt} \quad \text{for } k \neq j \tag{3}$$

This allows us to examine the validity of *A*1, assuming that *A*2 and *A*3 hold. Second, we make use of input–output tables for a large number of different countries in order to calculate the α's separately for multinationals from the I–O table of their own home country rather than that of the host country. The measure of backward linkages using the home-country I–O table can be defined as follows:

$$BACKWARD\_HOME_{jt} = \sum_k \sum_n \alpha_{knj}^{HOME} HORIZONTAL_{knt} \quad \text{for } k \neq j \tag{4}$$

where *n* refers to the nationality origin of the foreign multinational types. This measure, hence, allows for different input-sourcing behaviour according to the home country of the multinationals, rather than constraining all foreign firms to share the same technology.[7] It thus addresses potential problems inherent in *A*2, assuming that *A*1 and *A*3 are true.[8] In particular, it allows us to examine whether the assumption that foreign multinationals' input sourcing behaviour is more like that found in its origin country rather than in the host country, might alter any conclusion regarding spillovers from backward linkages.

In order to address *A*3 we take advantage of the fact that the Irish data also include information on the total amount of inputs a multinational sources in the domestic economy. Unfortunately, we do not know from which industries these inputs are purchased, and thus need to proxy for this. In order to examine *A*3 assuming that *A*1 and *A*2 hold, we thus start out first using the simple I–O tables, as in the original backward linkages measure described in Eq. (2) and combine it with information on domestic inputs used by multinationals

$$ALTERNATIVE\_IO_{jt} = \sum_k \alpha_{kj}^{IO} \frac{\sum_n M_{nkt}^D}{\sum_n M_{nkt}} \quad \text{for } k \neq j \tag{5}$$

where M^D is the amount of material inputs sourced domestically by a given multinational *n* and *M* is the total amount of material inputs used by *n*. We also experiment by combining the same information with the measure described in Eq. (3)

$$ALTNERNATIVE\_NIMP_{jt} = \sum_k \alpha_{kj}^{NIMP} \frac{\sum_n M_{nkt}^D}{\sum_n M_{nkt}} \quad \text{for } k \neq j \tag{6}$$

The measure proposed in Eq. (6) lets us investigate how jointly relaxing *A*1 and *A*2, but assuming that *A*3 still holds, affects any vertical spillover estimation. Viewed in conjunction with the results from using Eqs. (3) and (5), this allows us to then get a feel for whether the restriction inherent in *A*1 or that in *A*2, assuming that *A*3 still holds, plays a greater role in determining results.

Finally we propose a measure that relaxes all three assumptions. More specifically, we calculate the amount of inputs demanded by other sectors (*k*) from sector *j* by combining the firm specific measure of multinational's demand for locally sourced inputs and the home country's foreign I–O table

$$ALTERNATIVE\_HOME_{jt} = \sum_k \alpha_{kj}^{\text{home}} \frac{\sum_n M_{nkt}^D}{\sum_n M_{nkt}} \quad \text{for } k \neq j \tag{7}$$

Of all of our proposed alternative proxies for backward linkages, this is the least restrictive. Arguably this measure is the most preferable, as it only imposes the assumption that foreign multinationals have the same sourcing behaviour as their sectoral counterparts in their country of origin. This begs the question whether the latter is a realistic assumption.

In this regard it is important to point out that there is plenty of case-study evidence which shows that foreign affiliates implement technology in the host country that is state-of-the-art and similar to that employed in the home country parent. For instance, Moran (2001, 2005) provides examples for the automobile and, more relevant for Ireland, computer and electronics industries. Recent evidence from a unique and large firm level database of multinationals around the world by Alfaro and Charlton (2009) also shows that parents of multinationals choose to own affiliates abroad that are in stages of the production process that are very close to their own (in terms of 4 digit industry classification). If the affiliates use similar technology to the parent, then they are also likely to source inputs from different supplier industries in a way similar to the parent. Furthermore, there are also plenty of studies on the sourcing behaviour of multinationals that show that foreign multinationals are likely to source fewer of their inputs in the host economy than comparable domestic firms.[9]

[7] While this allows for different input sourcing behaviour depending on the home country, the assumption that input sourcing of foreign affiliates in the host country is the same as in the home country is also not without criticism. One may argue that foreign affiliates have different input sourcing behaviour from that of the home and host countries. Unfortunately, the nature of our data does not allow either to refute or to support this possibility. We therefore use our analysis to establish essentially two benchmark cases: (1) assuming that input sourcing behaviour is as in the host country (as in the literature) and (2) that it is as in the home country and examine whether this has implications for estimates of backward spillovers.

[8] The foreign I–O tables do not allow us to purge imported inputs. We are thus essentially assuming that *A1* holds but within the foreign multinationals' origin country context.

[9] For Ireland, this has been documented by, e.g., Ruane (2001) and Barry and Bradley (1997).

866 S. Barrios et al. / European Economic Review 55 (2011) 862–875

More generally, this suggests that a given foreign affiliate follows the organisation mode of its parent, which would allow the latter to compete successfully with its domestic counterparts abroad. This indicates that using I–O tables from foreign multinationals' origin country is likely to provide a closer approximation of foreign multinational sourcing behaviour than employing the host country's I–O table.

Besides horizontal and backward spillovers, Javorcik (2004) also calculates a measure of forward linkages

$$FORWARD\_IO_{jt} = \sum_k \beta_{kj}^{IO} HORIZONTAL_{kt} \quad \text{for } k \neq j \tag{8}$$

where β_{kj}^{IO} is the share of inputs of sector *j* purchased from industry *k*. Hence, this variable gives an indication of the availability of intermediate inputs supplied by foreign multinationals that are available to domestic firms in industry *j*.

We also calculate a forward linkage measure similar to Eq. (8) but using β_{kj}^{NIMP}, i.e., excluding imports of goods. This allows us to deal with assumption *A*1. As regards the other assumptions, as we are now looking at domestic firms sourcing inputs from foreign multinationals, the domestic I–O table can be assumed to describe adequately their sourcing behaviour; hence assumption *A*2 is not relevant. In terms of assumption *A*3 this may similarly apply to domestic firms, but, unfortunately, we do not have detailed data on input sourcing by domestic firms from foreign multinationals that would allow us to relax this assumption. Hence, in what follows, we use the measure of forward linkages $FORWARD\_NIMP_{jt}$ to examine the impact of for forward linkages.[10]

3. Data and summary statistics

The data for our empirical investigation are taken from the *Irish Economy Expenditure Survey* (IEE), undertaken annually over the period 1983–1998 by Forfás, the government agency with responsibility for enterprise development, science and technology. This is an annual survey of larger plants in Irish manufacturing with at least 20 employees, although a plant, once it is included, is generally still surveyed even if its employment level falls below the 20 employee cut-off point. The response rate to this survey is generally estimated to be between 60 and 80 percent of the targeted plant population. Hence, while our data can be regarded as representative of the targeted population of plants, it does not generally include plants with less than 20 employees.

The survey provides plant level information needed to calculate productivity performance including, *inter alia*, output (measured in terms of sales), value added (sales minus intermediate inputs), employment, wages, capital employed, and nationality of ownership. Additionally, we have details on plants' expenditure on raw materials and components (which we refer to as materials) and the proportion of these sourced abroad.[11] However, information on the capital stock is only available from 1990 onwards, and hence, since we focus on total factor productivity, our sample period consists of the years 1990–1998.

A plant is defined by Forfás as foreign owned if at least 50 percent of its shares are held by foreign owners. This definition relates to the last year in the data and is time invariant. Note that the dataset only provides us with an indicator variable for foreign ownership, not the actual ownership share. Our selection of Irish-owned plants is thus based on plants with less than 50% foreign ownership in 1998. While this may leave out plants with minority foreign ownership, Irish researchers generally assert that it has been the case in Ireland, certainly over the period covered, that most, if not all FDI was in the form of new wholly foreign-owned greenfield investment (see, e.g., Barry and Bradley, 1997, Ruane and Ugur, 2005).

Neither Forfás nor the Irish Central Statistics Office, which uses the same definition of foreign ownership, provides any information of actual ownership shares and, hence, these claims are difficult to evaluate. However, data from the US Bureau of Economic Analysis provides some hard facts that provide empirical support. The 2004 benchmark survey of US direct investment abroad shows that there were 516 non-bank foreign affiliates of non-bank US multinationals in Ireland in 2004. 510 of those, that is, 99 percent of those, were majority owned.[12] Given that more than half of the foreign-owned firms are from the US, this may be considered as a good indicator of the prevalence of majority ownership. Hence, we are reasonably confident that the focus on majority foreign-owned firms should not be too problematic for our analysis.

Our plant level data is combined with the input–output table for Ireland and input output tables taken from the OECD database on I–O tables. Those tables are not available for the same year across all countries such that we used in each case the

[10] While, from a general policy perspective, vertical spillovers from both backward and forward linkages are important, a number of countries seem to clearly favour backward linkages. For example, the Irish strategy, summarized by Ruane (2001) very much focused on creating backward linkages between multinationals and domestic firms. Formally, this policy focus manifested itself through a National Linkages Programme (NLP) which was established in 1985. The aim of this was "to increase the ability of Irish suppliers to serve the MNC market in Ireland—in effect to build backward linkages between MNCs and LCs" (Ruane, 2001). Given this policy focus we also look mainly at backward linkages in this paper, and treat forward linkages as a control variable. Moreover, the literature on productivity spillovers generally finds that forward spillovers are statistically insignificant (Javorcik, 2004; Görg and Greenaway, 2004). Ayyagari and Kosova (2010) are an exception, though they look at entry of domestic firms, rather than productivity effects for existing firms. We also experimented re-running all of our models below excluding the forward linkages variables; this does not affect our main conclusion on the backward spillover variables.

[11] Materials not sourced abroad may have been purchased from foreign affiliates of multinationals located in Ireland rather than just from purely domestic firms. Unfortunately, the dataset does not allow us to distinguish these two sources for domestically purchased inputs. Also, the dataset does not provide information on the source country or industry of the inputs.

[12] Statistics available at http://www.bea.gov/international/usdia2004f.html (accessed 26 July 2010).

Table 1
Share of output by nationality of foreign owner.
Sources: Irish Economy Expenditure Survey, Forfás and authors' calculations.

Nationality	Code	Share (%)	$Input_{local}/Input_{total}$
Canada	CA	2.6	0.23
Germany	DE	6.0	0.20
Denmark	DK	0.6	0.25
Spain	ES	0.1	0.38
Finland	FI	0.3	0.25
France	FR	3.4	0.27
Greece	GR	0.2	0.98
Italy	IT	1.0	0.26
Japan	JP	5.6	0.15
Netherlands	NL	2.5	0.31
Norway	NO	0.1	0.22
United Kingdom	UK	12.9	0.25
United States	US	61.8	0.27
Korea	KO	0.1	0.71
China	CH	0.1	0.66
India	IN	0.1	0.33
Switzerland	SZ	1.7	0.32
Australia	AU	0.5	0.36
Austria	AT	0.1	0.37

Table 2
Correlations of I–O tables.
Sources: Irish Economy Expenditure Survey, Forfás and authors' calculations.

Sector	Sector #	Corr. of I–O's	Corr(M^{D}_{nkt}/M_{nkt}, Y^{F}_{jt}/Y_{jt})
Mining and quarrying	1	−0.18	0.10
Food, beverages, and tobacco	2	−0.23	−0.26
Textiles, clothing, and leather	3	−0.06	−0.22
Wood and wood products	4	−0.02	0.74
Paper and printing	5	−0.04	−0.63
Coke and petroleum pr.	6	—	0.99
Chemicals	7	0.29	0.54
Rubber and plastics	8	—	-0.39
Other non-metallic minerals	9	0.67	0.54
Basic metals	10	0.41	0.63
Fabricated metals	11	—	−0.77
Machinery and equipment	12	−0.12	0.28
Office and computing machinery	13	0.11	−0.89
Electrical and electronic	14	0.16	0.17
Radio, television, and Communication	15	0.14	−0.09
Medical, precision, and optical	16	−0.19	−0.65
Motor vehicles	17	−0.19	0.05
Other transport equipment	18	0.02	0.32
Other	19	—	0.52

year that matched most closely the period available in the Irish data for the following foreign countries (the year of the I–O being indicated in parentheses): Canada (1997), Germany (1995), Denmark (1997), Spain (1995), Finland (1995), France (1995), Greece (1994), Italy (1992), Japan (1997), Netherlands (1998), Norway (1997), United Kingdom (1998), United States (1997), Korea (2000), China (2000), India (1995), Switzerland (2001), Austria (1995), and Australia (1998). The lack of foreign input–output tables for any remaining multinationals in the IEE data meant their exclusion. Those from the countries listed above constituted in any year well over 98 percent of total foreign output and over 97 percent of total foreign employment located in Irish manufacturing. The share of total foreign output by nationality group is given in Table 1.

In choosing an industry classification we settled on the one that allowed us to combine all datasets, roughly equivalent to the ISIC Rev.3 classification at the two digit level. This left us with a total of 19 sectors, which are listed in Table 2. All nominal variables are deflated using Irish sectoral prices from the EU KLEMS database.[13] Overall our econometric analysis allows the estimation of productivity determinants for 1037 domestic Irish-owned plants over our sample period.

To first investigate whether the use of imported inputs versus locally produced ones differs, we calculated the correlation of the α's for imported and locally produced inputs (i.e., α^{NIMP}_{kj} and α^{IO}_{kj}) within our 19 sectors in the third column of Table 2.

[13] The database is available at www.euklems.net

868 S. Barrios et al. / European Economic Review 55 (2011) 862–875

In this regard it is important to note that for three of these sectors we were not able to calculate correlation coefficients since no inputs were imported. Of those where at least some inputs were imported, the results of Table 2 suggest that there is little evidence that the sectoral structure of locally sourced inputs is correlated with that of imported inputs.

We also calculated the correlation of the I–O coefficients from the Irish I–O (total) with their foreign equivalents for each sector, as depicted in Fig. 1. Accordingly, in some sectors, namely Food, beverages, and tobacco; textiles, clothing, and leather; wood and wood products; and paper and printing (i.e. sectors 2–5 in Table 2) the assumption that the local I–O tables serve as good proxies for foreign multinational input use appears to be a reasonable assumption as the correlation for most nationalities with the Irish coefficients is close to 1. However, it is clear that for the majority of industries this is not the case.

In the last column in Table 2 we additionally provide the correlation between the foreign share of output in a sector and the share of locally sourced relative to total inputs by foreign multinationals. In other words, this is the correlation between the standard proxy of *horizontal* as in Eq. (1) and M_{nt}^{D}/M_{nt}. As can be seen, there is a wide range of correlation across sectors with no clear detectable pattern. We also calculated the average M_{nt}^{D}/M_{nt} by nationality, reported in Column 2 of Table 1. There is a large variation across country of origin. While this could be due to the different sectoral allocation of production by nationality, further investigation did not provide much evidence in support of this. For example, US plants sourced on average 27 percent of their inputs locally, while the equivalent figures for Chinese multinationals was over double this.

Finally, Table 3 provides the raw correlations of the various measures of backward spillovers. It is notable that the correlations between the different measures are less than perfect, even though the correlation is positive and statistically significant in almost all cases. An exception is the correlation between the standard backward and the alternative measure based on the I–O tables excluding imports. In particular, the correlation is quite high between the standard backward and the alternative measure based on the home country I–O table, perhaps suggesting that the standard practice may not be too

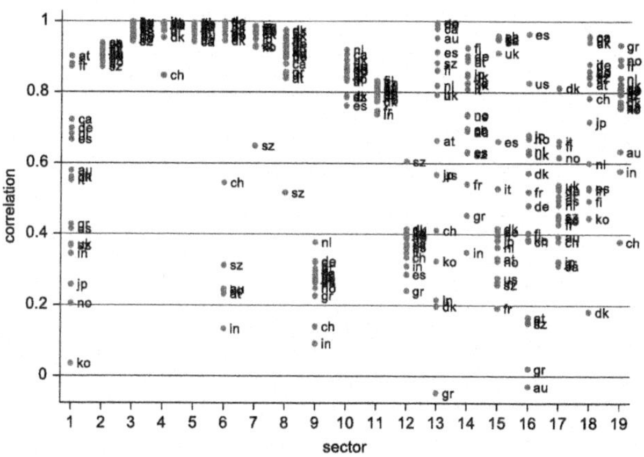

Fig. 1. Correlations by sector and country. *Note*: Sectors' codes are given in Table 2.

Table 3
Pair-wise correlations of backward spillover variables.

	Backward_IO	*Backward_NIMP*	*Backward_HOME*	*Alternative_IO*	*Alternative_NIMP*
Backward_NIMP	0.0223				
	0.0000				
Backward__HOME	0.4393	0.5722			
	0.0000	0.0000			
Alternative_IO	0.8488	0.0743	0.4263		
	0.0000	0.0000	0.0000		
Alternative_NIMP	−0.0563	0.9599	0.4778	0.0180	
	0.0000	0.0000	0.0000	0.0000	
Alternative_HOME	0.4710	0.5669	0.9822	0.4798	0.4719
	0.0000	0.0000	0.0000	0.0000	0.0000

Note: correlation coefficient and *p*-values.

problematic. However, these are, of course, unconditional correlations and in order to see whether they produce similar estimates of backward linkages, we need to turn to an econometric investigation.

4. Specification and estimation results

With the standard and our alternative measures of backward linkages at hand the next task is to investigate how these may produce differing results in terms of their impact on domestic plant productivity. Early studies of productivity spillovers generally estimate an augmented Cobb–Douglas production function in conjunction with standard OLS techniques. However, using panel data, Aitken and Harrison (1999) demonstrate that not controlling for firm fixed effects is likely to bias any conclusion regarding spillovers arising from FDI, so that now panel data have become the standard. A problem with using simple fixed effects in production function estimation is, however, that factor inputs should be considered potentially endogenous in the production function. This is the case because the contemporaneous level of TFP may affect the current choice of variable input factors, in which case inputs would be correlated with the error term (e.g., Levinsohn and Petrin, 2003).

The popular approach to deal with this sort of simultaneity is to implement estimators proposed by Levinsohn and Petrin (2003) or Olley and Pakes (1996), which are derived from a structural model. These can be employed to estimate productivity consistently. Then one can use the derived proxy within a fixed effects framework to control for firm specific time invariant unobservables. One should note that the Levinsohn and Petrin approach was recently implemented by, e.g., Javorcik and Spatareanu (2008) and Keller and Yeaple (forthcoming) in the FDI spillovers literature. We follow these examples and employ a Levinsohn and Petrin (2003) type productivity measure controlling for plant specific fixed effects.[14] Thus our benchmark specification for measuring spillovers arising from foreign direct investment and potentially affecting domestic plants' productivity levels is

$$\ln LP_{it} = \beta_1 HORIZONTAL_{jt} + \beta_2 FORWARD_{jt} + \beta_3 BACKWARD_{jt} + \beta_4 ind\_growth + d_t + \mu_i + \varepsilon_{it} \tag{9}$$

where *LP* is the Levinsohn and Petrin (2003) measure calculated using only data for domestic firms. The industry growth rate (measured using output at the two digit level) is included in order to control for industry specific demand shocks which may drive the spillover measures. Hence, if not controlled for, this would lead to biased estimates of the coefficients. d_t is a full set of time dummies, μ_i is a plant specific time invariant error term and ε_{it} is the remaining error term, clustered at the two digit industry level.[15] The μ_i are purged from Eq. (9) by implementing a fixed effects estimator. Below we also use an alternative approach, estimating an augmented production function for domestic firms using system GMM, to check the robustness of our results.

Estimation of Eq. (9) only allowing for horizontal spillovers is presented in the first column of Table 4 to establish a benchmark. This variable returns a negative but statistically insignificant coefficient. This is analogous to the findings in the literature that have spurned the search for spillovers through backward linkages. We next include the simple standard measure of backward linkages that has been used in the literature in the equation as reported in the second column. The estimation returns a positive sign as in Javorcik (2004), although the estimate is statistically insignificant in our case.

How robust is this result to changes in the measurement of the backward spillovers variable that allow relaxing the assumptions spelled out above? In order to investigate this, we start off by using the *BACKWARD_NIMP* measure, as given in Eq. (3) and shown in the third column of Table 4. The size of the coefficient changes relative to the standard one but it remains statistically insignificant. This would thus suggest that relaxing the assumption that domestically produced inputs are used in the same proportion as imported ones using an I–O table that distinguishes domestic supplies and imports does make some difference for judging the importance of spillovers. However, most importantly these two results suggest that using the measures of backward linkages used in the literature (either including or excluding imported inputs) does not suggest any evidence for backward spillovers in our data.

In the next regression we employ *BACKWARD_HOME* as in Eq. (4), where we employ input–output tables from the multinationals' home countries instead of the host country's I–O table. Now we find that the coefficient is statistically significant and positive, suggesting that backward linkages indeed produce productivity spillovers to domestic plants.

We subsequently re-estimated Eq. (9) but using *ALTERNATIVE_IO*, i.e., using an actual measure of local input used by foreign multinationals and using the host country's I–O table, including imported inputs. We find that the results suggest statistically significant negative spillovers, i.e., that inputs demanded by foreign multinationals from domestic plants reduce domestic plant's productivity. Excluding imports from this, however, renders the coefficient statistically insignificant, while still negative (*ALTERNATIVE_NIMP*).

In the last column of Table 4 we employ our final measure of the extent of backward linkages, namely *ALTERNATIVE_HOME*. This uses information on actual input use of foreign multinationals in Ireland and proxies how the purchase of these is distributed across sectors via the foreign multinationals' home country I–O weights. As discussed in Section 2, this is our preferred measure for a number of reasons. This variable produces a positive and significant coefficient on the linkages

[14] We implement their methodology, using plant level energy consumption as proxy and then generate total factor productivity as the residual from that regression. We do not use the Olley and Pakes approach for two reasons. First, the approach has been criticised for the use of lumpy investment data as proxy for the unobserved productivity shock (Levinsohn and Petrin, 2003). Second, we do not have information on actual investment and, hence, are unable to implement this approach empirically.

[15] Note that we do not include a full set of industry dummies as these are captured by the plant specific effect. Industry information refers to the latest year in the data and is, hence, time invariant.

870 *S. Barrios et al. / European Economic Review 55 (2011) 862–875*

Table 4
Estimates of horizontal and backward spillovers.

	(1)	(2)	(3)	(4)	(5)	(6)	(7)
Horizontal	−0.115	1.408	1.054	1.296	1.615	0.856	1.212
	(0.116)	(2.019)	(1.971)	(1.921)	(1.871)	(1.970)	(1.919)
Forward		−1.775	−1.211	−1.424	−1.730	−1.045	−1.354
		(2.132)	(2.025)	(1.967)	(1.907)	(2.028)	(1.965)
Backward_JO		0.917					
		(0.587)					
Backward_NIMP			0.132				
			(0.577)				
Backward_HOME				0.662			
				(0.273)**			
Alternative_JO					−1.965		
					(1.008)*		
Alternative_NIMP						−4.010	
						(3.990)	
Alternative_HOME							1.446
							(0.795)*
Industry growth	−0.008	−0.007	−0.008	−0.008	−0.008	−0.008	−0.008
	(0.001)***	(0.001)***	(0.001)***	(0.001)***	(0.001)***	(0.001)***	(0.001)***
Observations	4750	4750	4750	4750	4750	4750	4750
Number of plants	1025	1025	1025	1025	1025	1025	1025
R-squared	0.01	0.01	0.01	0.01	0.01	0.01	0.01

Notes: Dependent variable is log TFP estimated using the Levinsohn and Petrin (2003) approach. Estimation with plant fixed effects and full set of time dummies. Constant included standard errors clustered at the two digit level in parentheses.
* Significant at 10%.
** Significant at 5%.
*** Significant at 1%.

variable, thus suggesting the existence of vertical FDI spillovers in Ireland. By contrast, the coefficients on horizontal and forward spillovers are in all cases statistically insignificant.

The next issue to be tackled is the potential endogeneity of the spillover variables themselves. If multinationals are prone to locate in high productivity industries, then our finding of a positive relationship between the backward spillover variable and productivity of domestic firm may be biased due to this reverse causality. Assuming that industry productivity does not change much over time, a fixed effects estimator alleviates this problem (Aitken and Harrison, 1999). However, time variation in industry productivity may be an issue and then fixed effects estimation would not be sufficient. To address this issue partly, we also control for industry output growth, which may pick up some of this correlation. However, in order to deal with this problem more fully we, firstly, lag the two spillover variables, reporting the results in Table 5.

The results show that we now only find statistically significant positive backward spillovers effects in the last column, where we use our preferred measure. Note, also, that the size and statistical significance of the positive backward spillover variable in column (6) is now higher than before.

Lagging the variables may not be sufficient if there is, as may be expected, persistence in the variables. Hence, we now turn to an alternative approach, instrumenting for the spillover variables. In the search for valid instruments we make use of a particular feature of Irish industrial policy, namely, its financial support to foreign multinational companies (i.e., those that are majority owned by foreign shareholders). Financial incentives in Ireland were not only used to attract multinationals into the economy, but also to encourage them to generate links with the domestic economy.[16] We have access to a unique Forfas dataset which provides exhaustive annual plant-level information on all grant payments that have been made to plants in Irish manufacturing. We use this data and calculate the level of government grants given to foreign firms in a four-digit industry, which we use as instrument for the linkage variables.

This variable is, thus, likely to be highly correlated with the presence of multinationals in a given sector. However, as it only includes information on grant payments to the foreign-owned firms and not to domestic firms, it is likely to be uncorrelated with the error term of the equation modelling the productivity of domestic firms, conditional on other exogenous regressors. These are the key conditions required by credible instruments. As additional instruments we use twice lagged levels and growth of the spillover variables.

[16] As pointed out above, the National Linkage Programme was set up to foster backward linkages between multinationals and domestic firms. In tandem with the NLP, grants were awarded to foreign firms on the basis of linking them into the local economy. One qualifying reason for grant support was that the project could tap into skill-intensive indigenous supplier firms, reflecting the aim that the supported multinational should aid to create or maintain employment in the economy "that would not be maintained without assistance and will increase output and value added within the economy" (KPMG, 2003). This, hence, reflects the objective of linkage creation between multinationals and domestic suppliers. Görg et al. (forthcoming) present empirical evidence based on Irish micro data that grant support has had a positive effect on linkage creation by foreign multinationals. See also Ruane (2001) for a detailed discussion of Irish policy towards linkage generation.

Table 5
Robustness check: lagged spillover variables.

	(1)	(2)	(3)	(4)	(5)	(6)
Horizontal	1.101	1.037	1.191	1.271	1.087	1.172
	(1.980)	(1.932)	(1.894)	(1.872)	(1.891)	(1.793)
Forward	−1.435	−1.357	−1.500	−1.507	−1.410	−1.466
	(1.977)	(1.974)	(1.926)	(1.894)	(1.929)	(1.821)
Backward_JO	0.059					
	(0.722)					
Backward_NIMP		−0.870				
		(0.494)*				
Backward_HOME			0.400			
			(0.429)			
Alternative_JO				−1.839		
				(1.472)		
Alternative_NIMP					−3.979	
					(2.861)	
Alternative_HOME						2.253
						(1.032)**
Industry growth	−0.002	−0.002	−0.002	−0.002	−0.002	−0.002
	(0.004)	(0.002)	(0.002)	(0.002)	(0.002)	(0.002)
Observations	4434	4434	4434	4434	4434	4434
Number of plants	1020	1020	1020	1020	1020	1020
R-squared	0.01	0.01	0.01	0.01	0.01	0.02

Notes: Dependent variable is log TFP estimated using the Levinsohn and Petrin (2003) approach. Estimation with plant fixed effects and full set of time dummies. Constant included. All right-hand-side variables are lagged one period.
Standard errors clustered at the two digit level in parentheses.

***Significant at 1%.
* Significant at 10%.
** Significant at 5%.

Table 6
Robustness check: IV/GMM.

	(1)	(2)	(3)	(4)	(5)	(6)
Horizontal	−2.107	4.813	1.558	0.204	4.529	5.696
	(6.778)	(3.642)	(5.494)	(5.310)	(2.942)	(4.510)
Forward	0.829	−5.942	0.479	2.052	−4.403	−5.906
	(5.300)	(5.069)	(6.829)	(7.736)	(2.943)	(5.452)
Backward_JO	6.135					
	(3.833)					
Backward_NIMP		0.966				
		(1.898)				
Backward_HOME			1.192			
			(0.492)**			
Alternative_JO				−0.091		
				(4.124)		
Alternative_NIMP					1.969	
					(4.382)	
Alternative_HOME						5.484
						(1.853)***
Industry growth	−0.002	−0.013	0.002	0.003	−0.007	−0.009
	(0.007)	(0.010)	(0.010)	(0.014)	(0.003)***	(0.008)
Observations	2717	2717	2717	2717	2717	2717
Number of plants	555	555	555	555	555	555
Partial *R*2 horizontal (*p*-value)	0.09	0.04	0.02	0.03	0.08	0.03
F test forward (*p*-value)	0.09	0.03	0.02	0.02	0.08	0.02
F test backward/alternative (*p*-value)	0.24	0.34	0.14	0.16	0.37	0.21
Hansen *J* (*p*-value)	0.66	0.38	0.91	0.81	0.85	0.36

Notes: Dependent variable is log TFP estimated using the Levinsohn and Petrin (2003) approach. Instrumental variables GMM estimation with plant fixed effects and full set of time dummies. Constant included.
Standard errors clustered at the two digit level in parentheses.

*Significant at 10%.
** Significant at 5%.
*** Significant at 1%.

Table 7
Spillovers in augmented production function using IV/GMM.

	(1)	(2)	(3)	(4)	(5)	(6)
ln(*k*)	0.189	0.183	0.176	0.200	0.180	0.169
	(0.042)***	(0.028)***	(0.025)***	(0.037)***	(0.038)***	(0.039)***
ln(*l*)	0.194	0.234	0.256	0.164	0.203	0.189
	(0.099)**	(0.060)***	(0.096)***	(0.079)**	(0.123)*	(0.099)*
ln(*m*)	0.513	0.514	0.506	0.527	0.535	0.515
	(0.037)***	(0.030)***	(0.037)***	(0.036)***	(0.038)***	(0.036)***
Horizontal	−0.093	−1.700	−1.879	1.304	0.509	−0.358
	(3.657)	(1.241)	(4.456)	(1.923)	(5.239)	(3.619)
Forward	0.641	1.620	1.662	−1.051	−0.567	0.293
	(3.372)	(1.149)	(3.785)	(1.632)	(4.477)	(3.064)
Backward_IO	−1.117					
	(0.953)					
Backward_NIMP		−0.960				
		(0.262)***				
Backward_HOME			−0.910			
			(0.396)**			
Alternative_IO				1.747		
				(1.113)		
Alternative_NIMP					1.383	
					(7.003)	
Alternative_HOME						3.357
						(1.437)**
Industry growth	0.052	0.014	0.003	0.043	0.027	0.025
	(0.046)	(0.018)	(0.062)	(0.033)	(0.077)	(0.055)
Observations	1902	1902	1902	1902	1902	1902
Number of plants	460	460	460	460	460	460
Hansen *J* (*p*-value)	0.84	0.72	0.81	0.82	0.59	0.25

Notes: Dependent variable is log output. Estimation with system GMM estimator including full sets of industry and time dummies. Constant included. Standard errors clustered at the two digit level in parentheses.
* Significant at 10%.
** Significant at 5%.
*** Significant at 1%.

The estimation is carried out using an IV-GMM estimator, controlling for firm fixed effects. The results are reported in Table 6. First, note that the instruments used are relevant in all cases as indicated by the first stage *R*-squared for the excluded instruments. The Hansen *J* statistic also indicates that the instruments are valid.

Based on these estimations we can conclude that the positive effect of backward linkages is robust in column (6) where we use our preferred measure. There is also evidence of a positive backward spillover effect in column (3) when using the home country I–O tables. However, all other backward linkage measures return statistically insignificant coefficients. As before, the coefficient on the standard measure of backward linkages is statistically insignificant. Furthermore, there is no evidence for horizontal or forward spillovers in any of the regressions.

We now investigate how sensitive our results are to the method of estimating productivity. Thus far we have used the Levinsohn–Petrin approach as this has been used in the literature and thus allows us to compare our results with previous papers. We now use an alternative method of estimating productivity. Rather than proceeding in two steps, i.e., estimating TFP as a residual and then regressing it on the spillover variables we estimate an augmented production function of the form

$$\ln y_{it} = \alpha_1 \ln k + \alpha_2 \ln l + \alpha_3 \ln m + \beta_1 HORIZONTAL_{jt} + \beta_2 FORWARD_{jt} + \beta_3 BACKWARD_{jt} + d_t + \mu_i + v_{it} \quad (10)$$

where *y*, *k*, *l*, *m* are log output, capital, labour, and materials, respectively. As pointed out above, estimating this model using OLS would be biased due to simultaneity of input choices. We therefore treat the factor inputs, as well as the spillover variables as endogeneous and estimate the model using an instrumental variables/GMM estimator as before, using twice lagged differences and thrice lagged levels of the endogenous variables as instruments.

The results of these estimations are reported in Table 7. This shows the robustness of our results thus far. We fail to find statistically significant positive backward spillover effects using the standard measure, but find positive spillovers only when using the alternative measure we propose.

We discuss in Section 2 why we put forward our alternative measure of backward linkages, using the home country input–output table, as preferred measure. In order to support these arguments further, we, as a final robustness check, randomly assign I–O tables to foreign firms from a given country.[17] If we get the same results based on these hypothetical distributions of I–O coefficients, then

[17] This is somewhat akin to Keller (1998) who randomly assigned import shares as weights to R&D stocks in order to measure trade-related R&D spillovers.

Table 8
Randomization of the I–O table.

	(1)
	Alternative_HOME
FE estimator	0.003
	(0.155)
IV estimator	0.011
	(1.658)
GMM estimator	−0.011
	(0.058)

Notes: Table reports average coefficient and standard errors on *Alternative_HOME* from regression models as in Tables 2, 4 and 5. The I–O tables are randomly assigned. Estimations are based on 500 replications.
*Significant at 10%.
**significant at 5%.
***significant at 1%.

we should conclude that the positive results we get on the *Alternative_HOME* measure is just generated by chance. If, however, the results differ, then this suggests that our approach provides useful information on the importance of backward linkages.

In order to check for this, we conduct a Monte Carlo experiment where we assign a randomly chosen I–O table to a firm nationality. We then estimate the empirical model using FE, IV and GMM estimators. We repeat this experiment 500 times. Table 8 reports the average coefficients and standard errors obtained from these regressions with the "randomized" *Alternative_HOME* measure. The coefficients are statistically insignificant in all three estimation approaches. Hence, using a random assignment of the I–O tables to firm nationalities actually produces the same statistically insignificant result as using the standard backward linkages measure using the host country I–O table. By contrast, our result of positive backward spillovers using the home country I–O table for foreign firms produces a result that does not appear to be generated "by chance".

Taking the results thus far in conjunction with each other, one can now draw a general picture about how and whether assumptions *A*1, *A*2, and *A*3 underlying the standard measure are likely to affect results in estimating spillovers due to backward linkages. In particular it becomes obvious that using the host country's I–O tables, whether including imported inputs or not, may fail to capture vertical spillovers, once potential endogeneity of the spillovers variables is corrected for. More precisely, assuming that foreign multinational input sourcing behaviour is similar to that of their domestic counterparts, and hence that one can simply use the host country's I–O tables which includes inputs' usage by both groups, may be inappropriate for the task at hand. Rather multinationals are more likely to source inputs as they do at home. One can also conclude that proxying the intensity of input demand by foreign multinationals is important. In terms of our terminology employed in Section 2, it appears that *A*2 and *A*3 are particularly critical assumptions in determining whether backward spillovers are found.

Having established the robustness of our result we now move from statistical to economic significance. One point to note is that the coefficient on backward linkages has increased in size from around 1.4 in the regression in Column (7) of Table 4 – which assume the variable in contemporaneous levels to be exogenous – to 2.2 in Column (6) of Table 5, about 5.4 in the estimation using IV/GMM in Column (6) of Table 6, and 3.4 in the final IV/GMM estimation in Table 7 (column 6). These results imply that increasing the backward linkage measure by one percentage point leads to an improvement in TFP by between 1 and 5 percent. To set this in context, the mean of the backward linkage measure is 0.043, i.e., 4.3 percent. Mean TFP is 2.81. The standard deviation around the mean of the backward linkage measure is 0.0369 which can be decomposed into a between (i.e. across plants) standard deviation of 0.0367 and a within (i.e., in the time series variation) component of 0.0054. Hence, increasing the backward linkage measure by 1 percentage point is roughly equal to an increase by two standard deviations in the time series dimension; i.e., a very substantial increase. This would, on average, increase TFP by between 0.03 and 0.15, i.e., from 2.81 to between 2.84 and 2.96.

5. Conclusions

The recent literature on spillovers to domestic firms from backward linkages of multinationals has in a number of cases provided evidence of such positive effects. We make explicit assumptions used to calculate such measures of backward spillovers and argue that these are unlikely to hold in practice. These assumptions implicitly consider that (i) multinationals use domestically produced inputs in the same proportion as imported inputs, (ii) multinationals have the same input sourcing behaviour as domestic firms, irrespective of their country of origin, and (iii) the demand for locally produced inputs by multinationals is proportional to their share of locally produced output. We then provide alternative measures that relax these.

Our empirical analysis shows that results change greatly depending on the measure of backward linkages used and thus on their implicit assumption regarding (i)–(iii). In particular, in our case we do not find robust evidence of spillovers through backward linkages when using the standard measure used in the literature. However, when we use our preferred measure which relaxes the arguably unrealistic assumptions we find statistically significant positive effects. This result is robust to different specifications, in particular to controlling for potential endogeneity of the backward spillover variable.

Our results lead us to a few general conclusions. First, it seems that whether one assumes that foreign multinationals have input sourcing behaviour identical to that of domestic firms is crucial in terms of finding backward linkages spillovers. Given that this assumption goes against the very premises underlying the search for spillovers arising from FDI, namely that foreign multinationals are different from their domestic counterparts in production organisation mode, it is likely that results for other studies might also change once proxies of backward linkages relaxing this assumption are used. After all, in any host country there are multinationals from different home countries with arguably different technologies and input sourcing behaviour. Our results suggest that these differences impinge on potential backward spillovers arising from FDI.

It is difficult to infer that our finding for the case of Ireland is a general result. Hence, it is not *a priori* clear that other studies necessarily suffer from the same problem. For example, since Ireland is a developed country it may be the case that multinationals in developed countries tend to behave as in their home countries – but that their behaviour may be different in developing or transition host countries. In particular the fact that some developing countries impose local content requirements may alter multinationals' sourcing strategies. These are highly policy relevant questions for further research.

Still, based on our analysis it is not *a priori* to be taken that other studies *do not* encounter the same problem of measuring appropriately vertical spillovers, without doing a careful analysis with alternative measures. Few countries may have similar data that one would wish to have in order to perform a similar exercise. This may be especially the case in developing countries, where potential spillovers from multinationals are arguably even more relevant. However, our paper suggests that it may be worthwhile to think about how one may work around existing data limitations in order to produce robust results that allow one to adequately inform policy makers.

Acknowledgements

The authors are grateful to Beata Javorcik, Wolfgang Keller, Bob Lipsey, Selin Sayek, Fredrik Sjöholm, seminar participants at Bilkent, Kiel, Nijmegen and the ETSG meeting at Rome, and anonymous referees for very helpful comments on earlier drafts. Holger Görg is also affiliated with GlobID at Aarhus School of Business/University of Aarhus, and he gratefully acknowledges financial support from the Tuborg Foundation. The views expressed by the authors are not necessarily those of the institutions they are affiliated with. Any errors remain the authors' alone.

References

Aitken, Brian J., Harrison, Ann E., 1999. Do domestic firms benefit from direct foreign investment? Evidence from Venezuela. American Economic Review 89 (3), 605–618.

Alfaro, L., Charlton, A., 2009. Intra-industry foreign direct investment. American Economic Review 99, 2096–2119.

Amiti, M., Wei, S.J., 2009. Service offshoring and productivity: evidence from the US. The World Economy 32, 203–220.

Ayyagari, M., Kosova, R., 2010. Does FDI facilitate domestic entry? Evidence from the Czech Republic. Review of International Economics 18, 14–29.

Barry, F., Bradley, J., 1997. FDI and trade: the Irish host-country experience. Economic Journal 107, 1798–1811.

Belderbos, R., Capannelli, G., Fukao, K., 2001. Backward vertical linkages of foreign manufacturing affiliates: evidence from Japanese multinationals. World Development 29 (1), 189–208.

Blalock, G., Gertler, P.J., 2008. Welfare gains from foreign direct investment through technology transfer to local suppliers. Journal of International Economics 74, 402–421.

Buckley, P., Pearce, R.D., 1979. Overseas production and exporting by the world's largest enterprises: a study in sourcing policy. Journal of International Business Studies 10 (1), 9–20.

Caves, Richard E., 1974. Multinational firms, competition, and productivity in host-country markets. Economica 41 (162), 176–193.

Djankov, S., Hoekman, B., 2000. Foreign investment and productivity growth in Czech enterprises. World Bank Economic Review 14, 49–64.

Girma, S., Görg, H., Pisu, M., 2008. Exporting, linkages and productivity spillovers from foreign direct investment. Canadian Journal of Economics 41, 320–340.

Girma, S., Wakelin, K., 2007. Local productivity spillovers from foreign direct investment in the U.K. electronics industry. Regional Science and Urban Economics 37, 399–412.

Gorodnichenko, Y., Svejnar, J., Terrell, K., 2007. When does FDI have positive spillovers? Evidence from 17 Emerging Market Economies, IZA Discussion Paper 3079.

Görg, H., Greenaway, D., 2004. Much ado about nothing? Do domestic firms really benefit from foreign direct investment? World Bank Research Observer 19, 171–197.

Görg, H., Hanley, A., Strobl, E., 2008. Productivity effects of international outsourcing: evidence from plant level data. Canadian Journal of Economics 41, 670–688.

Görg, H., Hanley, A., Strobl E. Creating backward linkages from multinationals: Is there a role for financial incentives, Review of International Economics, forthcoming.

Görg, H., Strobl, E., 2001. Multinational companies and productivity spillovers: a meta-analysis. Economic Journal 111 (475), F723–F739.

Haskel, J., Pereira, S.C., Slaughter, M.J., 2009. Does inward foreign direct investment boost the productivity of domestic firms? Review of Economics and Statistics 89, 482–496

Head, K., Mayer, T., 2004. Market potential and the location of Japanese firms in the European Union. Review of Economics and Statistics 86 (4), 959–972.

Hirschman, A., 1958. The Strategy of Economic Development. Yale University Press, New Haven.

Javorcik, B.S., 2004. Does foreign direct investment increase the productivity of domestic firms? In search of spillovers through backward linkages. American Economic Review 94, 605–627.

Javorcik, B.S., Spatareanu, M., 2008. To share or not to share: does local participation matter for spillovers from foreign direct investment? Journal of Development Economics 85.

Keller, W., 1998. Are international R&D spillovers trade-related? Analyzing spillovers among randomly matched trade partners. European Economics Review 42, 1469–1481.

Keller, W., 2004. International technology diffusion. Journal of Economic Literature 42, 752–782.
Keller, W., Yeaple, S. Multinational enterprises, international trade, and technology diffusion: a firm-level analysis of the productivity effects of foreign competition in the United States, Review of Economics and Statistics, forthcoming.
Kosova, R. Do foreign firms crowd out domestic firms? Evidence from the Czech Republic, Review of Economics and Statistics, forthcoming.
KPMG, 2003, Investment in Ireland, KPMG Publications Limited, Dublin (available at 〈http://www.kpmg.ie/inv_irl/Pubs/Investment.pdf〉, accessed 20-09-07).
Levinsohn, J., Petrin, A., 2003. Estimating production functions using inputs to control for observables. Review of Economic Studies 70, 317–341.
Markusen, J.R., 2002. Multinational Firms and the Theory of International Trade. MIT Press.
Markusen, J.R., Venables, A.J., 1999. Foreign direct investment as a catalyst for industrial development. European Economic Review 43, 335–356.
McCann, F. The heterogeneous effect of international outsourcing on firm productivity, Review of World Economics, forthcoming.
Moran, Theodore, 2001. Parental Supervision: The New Paradigm for Foreign Direct Investment and Development. Institute for International Economics, Washington, D.C.
Moran, Theodore, 2005. How does FDI affect host country development? Using industry case studies to make reliable generalizations. In: Moran, T., Graham, E., Blomström, M. (Eds.), Does Foreign Direct Investment Promote Development? Institute for International Economics, Washington DC, pp. 281–314.
Munch, J.R., Skagsten, J.R., 2009. Specialization, outsourcing and wages. Review of World Economics 145, 57–73.
Olley, S., Pakes, A., 1996. The dynamics of productivity in the telecommunications equipment industry. Econometrica 64, 1263–1298.
Rodríguez-Claré, Andres, 1996. Multinationals, linkages, and economic development. American Economic Review 86, 852–873.
Ruane, F., 2001. Reflections on linkage policy in Irish manufacturing—policy chasing a moving target? Available at 〈http://www.unece.org/ead/misc/ffd2001/ruane.doc〉, accessed 03-07-08.
Ruane, F., Ugur, A., 2005. Labour productivity and foreign direct investment in Irish manufacturing industry—A decomposition analysis. Economic and Social Review 36 (1), 19–43.

Chapter 12

Estimating direct and indirect effects of foreign direct investment on firm productivity in the presence of interactions between firms

Sourafel Girma [a], Yundan Gong [b], Holger Görg [c,*], Sandra Lancheros [d]

[a] University of Nottingham and GEP
[b] Aston Business School
[c] Kiel Institute for the World Economy, University of Kiel, Aarhus University, and IZA
[d] University of Nottingham Ningbo China and GEP

ARTICLE INFO

Article history:
Received 25 September 2013
Received in revised form 17 September 2014
Accepted 10 November 2014
Available online 17 November 2014

Keywords:
Multinational
Companiestreatment
Effectsspillovers

ABSTRACT

We implement a method to estimate the direct effects of foreign-ownership on foreign firms' productivity and the indirect effects (or spillovers) from the presence of foreign-owned firms on other foreign and domestic firms' productivity in a unifying framework, taking interactions between firms into account. To do so, we relax a fundamental assumption made in empirical studies examining a direct causal effect of foreign ownership on firm productivity, namely that of no interactions between firms. Based on our approach, we are able to combine direct and indirect effects of foreign ownership and calculate the total effect of foreign firms on local productivity. Our results show that all these effects vary with the level of foreign presence within a cluster, an important finding for the academic literature and policy debate on the benefits of attracting foreign owned firms.

1. Introduction

When considering the impact of inward foreign direct investment on host country productivity, researchers and policy makers generally think about two aspects. The first is the direct effect of foreign ownership, boiling down to the question as to whether affiliates of foreign multinationals in a host country are more productive than comparable domestic firms. The second aspect is "spillovers", i.e., whether there is any effect from the presence of foreign firms on the productivity of domestic or other foreign-owned firms. These two questions have been pursued in, for the most part, two separate literatures.

One research strand (e.g., Harris and Robinson, 2002; Girma and Görg, 2007a; Arnold and Javorcik, 2009) implements methods from microeconometric programme evaluation to estimate the direct treatment effects for firms receiving the "treatment" of being foreign compared to non-treated domestic firms (without considering "spillovers"). This literature appeals to theoretical models of multinationals, either in the tradition of the knowledge capital model as in Markusen (2001), or the more recent models of heterogeneous firms (e.g., Helpman et al., 2004), which assume that foreign owned multinationals have firm specific assets which translate into a productivity advantage. The second research strand (e.g., Aitken and Harrison, 1999; Haskel et al., 2007; Keller and Yeaple, 2009) looks at indirect effects through productivity "spillovers" (while largely neglecting direct treatment effects). The theoretical intuition is that domestic firms can learn from the presence of foreign multinationals in their vicinity, e.g., because workers move from a foreign firm to a domestic competitor (e.g., Fosfuri et al., 2001).

Examining direct effects and spillovers in isolation leads to potentially biased estimates and policy conclusions, however. When evaluating the direct treatment effect of foreign ownership, the econometric approaches assume that the productivity of the control group is independent of foreign ownership – an assumption in contrast with the idea of spillovers.[1] In the "spillovers literature", identification of the effects of foreign ownership at the industry level on domestic firm productivity is problematic because of endogeneity concerns – there are industry or region specific shocks that positively affect domestic firms' productivity and raise the attractiveness of the location for foreign multinationals.

In this paper, we bring the two strands of literature together and propose and implement a unified framework to estimate direct and indirect effects from foreign ownership on firm level productivity which allows for interaction between foreign and domestic, and foreign and foreign firms. Our approach, detailed in the following sections, allows us to estimate consistently a number of different treatment effects. In particular, we can distinguish the direct effect of foreign ownership on the treated firms and two types of indirect effects of the treatment, namely the indirect effects on treated and non-treated firms. These indirect effects, thus, capture externalities or learning effects from foreign

* Corresponding author at: Kiel Institute for the World Economy, Kiellinie 66, 24105 Kiel, Germany.
E-mail address: holger.goerg@ifw-kiel.de (H. Görg).

[1] This is known as the Stable Unit Treatment Value Assumption (SUTVA), which states that an individual outcome does not depend on the treatment status of others.

http://dx.doi.org/10.1016/j.jinteco.2014.11.007
0022-1996/© 2014 Elsevier B.V. All rights reserved.

firms on other foreign (i.e., treated) or domestic firms (i.e., non-treated). Furthermore, combining the direct and indirect effects we can calculate a total effect of foreign firms on local productivity.

Distinguishing these effects is not only of academic merit but also highly policy relevant, as it allows us to provide much richer and sharper insights on the nexus between foreign ownership, proximity to foreign-owned firms, and firm productivity. Hence, the approach suggested here provides a very useful tool for policymakers to understand better the benefits of encouraging foreign direct investment.[2]

We implement our econometric framework using firm level data for Chinese manufacturing. Following, Hudgens and Halloran (2008) our approach to take into account the role of interactions among firms when evaluating the effects of foreign ownership on firms' productivity is to use the proportion of foreign firms within well-defined clusters at the industry-region level. Thus, the potential outcomes depend not only on the firm's treatment status, but also on the fraction of foreign firms in a particular cluster.

Our empirical results show that the direct effect of the treatment on the treated firms is not homogenous across industry-region clusters, but rather differs strongly across such clusters. In particular, we find that the direct effect of foreign-ownership on the treated (i.e. foreign-owned) firms is positive and increases strongly with the overall level of foreign-owned firms in a cluster. This suggests that the standard approach of estimating direct treatment effects, which neglects interactions between firms, fails to uncover potentially important heterogeneity in the effect across clusters.

We also find a consistently negative indirect effect of foreign-ownership on non-treated firms, indicating negative "spillovers" from foreign presence on domestic firms. Also, in contrast to much of the literature on spillovers cited above, our approach shows that the strength of this negative spillover is not constant but differs significantly with the level of foreign ownership in a cluster. Spillovers are more negative with increasing presence of foreign firms up to a threshold of around 40 percent foreign-owned firms, after which they become less negative.

In terms of the indirect impact of foreign ownership on the treated (i.e. the spillovers from the presence of foreign firms on other foreign firms in the same cluster), we also find a negative effect up to a level of 40 percent foreign-owned firms in a cluster. However, after reaching this threshold these effects turn positive. This has important implications for arguments favouring the agglomeration of foreign-owned firms in a cluster, as this shows that the benefits from such agglomerations might only become positive once a certain threshold is reached.

The remainder of the paper is structured as follows. Section 2 presents the theoretical motivation of the paper. Section 3 discusses our identification strategy and introduces the different types of effects we aim to estimate. Section 4 presents the data set that we use to illustrate our arguments, while Section 5 gives a detailed explanation of the empirical implementation of our econometric approach. Section 6 discusses the main findings of the paper, and Section 7 concludes.

2. Theoretical motivation

In this section we sketch out a simple theoretical framework in order to motivate the empirical analysis. The model is closely related to Guadalupe et al. (2012) (GKT), who look at the impact of foreign investment on firms' innovation activities in a model of firm heterogeneity. They, however, only look at a direct causal effect of foreign acquisition, implicitly assuming no spillover effects. To capture such spillovers, our theoretical sketch essentially re-interprets their model for a case in which firms' productivity enhancing activities also depend on the presence of other foreign firms in a cluster and the capacity of foreign and domestic firms to absorb spillovers from FDI.

As in GKT we work with a model with heterogeneous firms in a monopolistic competition setting and a CES demand function. Firm i has an initial productivity level of φ_i and it can make a productivity enhancing investment, γ_i. In GKT this investment is considered to be innovation. We take a broader view and consider this to be any activity that is productivity-increasing at the firm level, and that will lead to a measurable increase in productivity as a result of firm level foreign investment.

Firm i profits are given by

$$\pi_i = B_i \tau_i \phi_i \tag{1}$$

where $B_i = A_i\left(\frac{1-\rho}{\rho}\right)\rho^{\sigma}$ with A being market size and ρ defining the elasticity of substitution between varieties $\sigma = 1/(1-\rho)$.[3] For ease of exposition we define $\tau_i = (\gamma_i)^{\sigma-1}$ and $\phi_i = \varphi_i^{\sigma-1}$ which are transformed measures of productivity-enhancing investments and initial productivity, respectively. Firms must engage in costly investments in order to increase their productivity level. As in GKT we assume that the cost of such investments (C_i) include a fixed and a variable component, as follows:

$$C_i = a_i + \frac{b_i}{\alpha_i N_r} f(\tau_i) \tag{2}$$

with f denoting a general positive function of τ_i without specific assumptions about its functional form.

In GKT, foreign ownership impacts innovation only by affecting the parameters a_i and b_i. We follow their approach and assume that these parameters are positive and lower for foreign (F) than for domestic firms (D): $0 \le b_F < b_D$ and $0 \le a_F < a_D$. This reflects the foreign multinational's access to better technology, or lower costs of financing, which imply that the firm has lower costs for implementing productivity enhancing investments. We interpret this as the *direct effect* of foreign ownership on firms' productivity, which we attempt to identify in our empirical analysis.

To capture the *indirect effects* from other foreign firms, we extend GKT by allowing the variable cost of productivity enhancing investment also to depend on: i) the number of foreign firms in a cluster (N_r), and ii) a firm specific constant, capturing its capacity to absorb spillovers from foreign firms (α_i). The assumption that the cost of productivity enhancing technologies depends on the number of foreign firms (N_r) captures the notion of spillovers. These are generally expected to be positive due to learning effects. While we do not model the exact underlying mechanism (which we also cannot measure in our data), one reasonable interpretation for such positive effects is worker movements. As discussed by Fosfuri et al. (2001), domestic workers may be hired by foreign firms (which possess superior technology) and then trained to be able to use the up-to-date technology.[4] After a period of training, they may then either remain in the foreign-owned firm or move to a domestic competitor. In the latter case, they take with them some knowledge about technology, which then makes it easier for the domestic firm to implement this new technology. A domestic firm without a foreign-trained worker is not able to do so. Hence, the costs of improving technology are, in this case, lower for the domestic firm with foreign-trained worker than for the domestic firm without. We assume that the chance

[2] We outline the main reasons why a simple linear model where the direct and indirect effects of FDI are estimated within a single framework is unlikely to be an adequate empirical tool in Appendix D.

[3] Guadalupe et al. (2012) allow the parameter A to vary across foreign and domestic firms. Their idea is that foreign firms may have access to larger markets than domestic firms. We simplify this model and abstract from this market size effect in order to be able to focus on the effect we find more relevant, namely, the effects of foreign ownership on the cost of productivity enhancing investments.

[4] Görg and Strobl (2005) provide empirical evidence from firm level data for Ghana.

of being able to employ such a foreign-trained worker is increasing in the number of foreign-owned firms.[5]

However, the empirical literature shows that spillovers may also be negative, see for example Aitken and Harrison (1999). This is generally attributed to competition effects. Multinationals have lower marginal costs due to some firm-specific advantage, which allows them to attract demand away from domestic firms, thus forcing the domestic firms to reduce production and move up their (given) average cost curve. This leads to lower productivity. Whether the spillover effect is positive or negative is, hence, an empirical issue.

The second innovation in our model is the inclusion of the firm specific term, α_i, which measures the strength with which spillovers affect firm i. This captures the idea that spillover effects may not be uniform across firms but may differ depending on some firm specific characteristic. Görg and Greenaway (2004), for example, argue that whether a firm benefits from spillovers may depend on its relative backwardness and its capacity for assimilating knowledge. In particular, foreign firms with access to superior technology are likely to benefit more from the presence of other foreign firms in the cluster. To capture the notion of heterogeneity in the spillover effects we allow the parameter α_i to be different for domestic and foreign firms. In particular we assume $\alpha_F > \alpha_D$, indicating the superiority of foreign firms to absorb positive foreign spillovers. We can identify these two different indirect effects on foreign and domestic firms in our empirical work.

Given the operating profits and the cost of improvements in productivity, the value of a firm i is given by

$$V_i = B_i \tau_i \phi_i - a_i - \frac{b_i}{\alpha_i N_r} f(\tau_i) \tag{3}$$

To determine the level of investment in productivity enhancing technology that maximizes the value of the firm we set the first derivative $(dV_i / d\tau_i)$ equal to zero and obtain

$$\alpha_i N_r B_i \phi_i = b_i f'(\tau_i^*) \tag{4}$$

Eq. (4) implies that productivity enhancing investment is higher (i) the lower is b_i, (ii) the higher is the spillover effect from the number of foreign firms ($\alpha_i N_r$) and (iii) the higher is initial productivity ϕ_i. In other words, as in GKT, there is a direct effect of foreign ownership on productivity enhancing investment as foreign firms have lower b_i. Moreover, expanding on GKT, there is also an indirect effect through the number of foreign firms in the cluster (N_r) and this indirect effect is different for foreign and domestic firms (which have different α_i). Finally, the First Order Condition (FOC) given by Eq. (4) also suggests that initial productivity plays a role for firms' investments in productivity enhancing technology.

An important insight from equation (4) is that a lower marginal cost of investing in productivity enhancing technology (i.e., b_i) and stronger indirect effects (through $\alpha_i N_r$) have the same effect on the optimal choice of τi. In other words, the two cannot be separately identified. Not taking into account the impact of $\alpha_i N_r$ in an empirical estimation of the direct effect of foreign ownership (due to b_i) would imply that the estimated direct effect might be biased. Depending on the specific assumption about the expected effect of $\alpha_i N_r$ it would be either over- or underestimated. In our empirical framework, we can separate these effects and obtain an unbiased estimate of the direct causal effect due to b_i and also estimate the indirect effects of foreign ownership on foreign and domestic firms.

[5] There may also be other channels for spillovers from multinationals to domestic firms, such as learning externalities or vertical linkages. See Keller (2010) for a discussion.

We can also say something about the acquisition decision, which is unlikely to be random. In order to see whether an acquisition is profitable, we can compare the value of a firm (given in Eq. (3)) under foreign and domestic ownership. Specifically, given the different characteristics of firms according to their ownership structure, the difference in value, at the optimal level of investment in new technology τ_i^*, between a foreign and domestic firm is given by

$$V_i^{F*} - V_i^{D*} = \left(\tau_i^{F*} - \tau_i^{D*}\right) B_i \phi_i - (a_F - a_D) - \left(\frac{b_F}{\alpha_F N_r} f\left(\tau_i^{F*}\right) - \frac{b_D}{\alpha_D N_r} f\left(\tau_i^{D*}\right)\right) \tag{5}$$

Differentiating this with respect to ϕ_i yields a positive expression, indicating that the difference in value is increasing in initial productivity.

$$d\left(V_i^{F*} - V_i^{D*}\right) / d\phi_i = \left(\tau_i^{F*} - \tau_i^{D*}\right) B_i \tag{6}$$

Hence, the value enhancing benefits from foreign acquisitions are more pronounced for firms with high initial productivity, or, in other words, foreign acquired targets in the host country are likely to be more productive prior to acquisition. This result arises from the assumption that any investment in productivity is more valuable under foreign control. For our empirical implementation this implies that we need to control for initial productivity when attempting to identify the direct effect of foreign ownership, which we do in a propensity score framework.

In our set up we can also look at how the acquisition incentives change with the number of existing foreign firms in the cluster (N_r). The sign of the partial derivative

$$d\left(V_i^{F*} - V_i^{D*}\right) / dN_r = \frac{b_F}{\alpha_F N_r^2} f\left(\tau_i^{F*}\right) + \frac{b_D}{\alpha_D N_r^2} f\left(\tau_i^{D*}\right) \tag{7}$$

depends on the sign of the parameters α_F and α_D. For example, in the case where $\alpha_F > \alpha_D > 0$ (that is, assuming that foreign firms have relatively higher absorptive capacity) expression 7 is unambiguously positive, indicating that the incremental value of the firm under foreign ownership is increasing in the number of foreign firms in the cluster. Thus, acquisition is more likely in clusters with a high presence of foreign firms. We control for this also in our empirical estimation.

To sum up, our theoretical discussion provides a basis for expecting a positive *direct* effect of foreign ownership on productivity enhancing investments in a firm. There are also potentially different *indirect* effects of foreign ownership on foreign and domestic firms, and these need to be taken into account in order to obtain an unbiased estimate of the direct effect. Furthermore, the acquisition decision is not random, but may be related to firms' initial productivity and the number of foreign firms in a cluster. We now turn to the empirical analysis.

3. Identification strategy

The estimation of direct and indirect effects of foreign ownership on productivity is rendered difficult because of an important assumption in the commonly used micro-econometric approaches for estimating direct effects – the Stable Unit Treatment Value Assumption (SUTVA). This assumption essentially states that an individual outcome does not depend on the treatment status of others. Or, in other words, there are no indirect effects (or spillovers) from all treated individuals on the outcome for an individual. Translated into the specifics of the FDI and productivity debate, the assumption implies that the average productivity of a firm (foreign or domestic) is not influenced by the presence of other treated (i.e., foreign-owned) firms. This assumption is, thus, in direct contrast to the notion of productivity spillovers. This implies that it is likely that SUTVA is violated in studies looking at productivity differences between foreign and domestic firms using standard micro-econometric evaluation techniques.

Our approach to estimating consistently direct and indirect effects of foreign ownership is based on recent work in the statistical and econometric literature that has sought to relax SUTVA.[6] According to this literature, treatment externalities (or spillovers) occur when an individual's potential outcome is affected by other individuals' treatment status within a group. The approach we take, following Hudgens and Halloran (2008), is to use the *proportion* of treated firms within a group as a measure of interaction between individual firms.[7] The potential outcomes are thus expressed as a function of the firm's treatment status and the fraction of foreign firms in a particular group or cluster.

Suppose we have $r = 1 \ldots R$ sufficiently heterogeneous economic clusters, which for the purpose of this application we define in terms of broad industry groups and geographical areas as industry-region clusters. A key identifying assumption is the so-called *partial interference assumption* where SUTVA holds across clusters but not within clusters. In other words, we only allow interactions between firms in the same industry and geographic area. We use this definition of clusters as it is in line with the finding in much of the empirical work that "spillovers" from FDI appear strongest if they happen in the same broad industry and region (e.g., Girma and Wakelin, 2007; Xu and Sheng, 2012).[8] Also, this definition (instead of using clusters based solely on, say, industry classification, or regions) provides us with a sufficiently large number of clusters.

For ease of exposition we assume that there are $i = 1 \ldots N$ firms in each cluster and N_r of these receive the treatment, i.e., in our case, have some amount of foreign ownership. Hence, the proportion of treated firms is $p_r = \frac{N_r}{N}$, $r = 1, \ldots, R$. Restricting ourselves to a binary treatment variable ($d_{ir} = 1$ if firm i in cluster r has foreign ownership and $d_{ir} = 0$ if not), we have $p_r = \frac{N_r}{N} = \frac{\sum_i^N d_{ir}}{N}$.

Letting y be the outcome variable (i.e. firm productivity) there are two potential outcomes, y^0 and y^1, corresponding to the two treatment states. Only one of those can be observed for any one firm. If SUTVA holds within clusters, an individual's potential outcomes are only a function of its own treatment status:

$$E(y_{ir}|d_{ir}) \equiv y_{ir}^d = y_{ir}^d(d_{ir}); \; d = 0, 1. \tag{8}$$

If SUTVA does not hold, one can think of the extreme case of unrestricted interactions between all individuals within a cluster, in which case potential outcomes are not only functions of the individual's treatment status, but also of all 2^N combinations of treatments, say $d_{\bar{ir}}$: $y_{ir}^d = y_{ir}^d(d_{ir}, d_{\bar{ir}})$; $d = 0,1$. Following Hudgens and Halloran (2008), it makes practical sense to think in terms of the distribution of the treatment variable within a cluster, rather than of all possible treatment combinations.

A natural starting point is to consider the proportion of treated firms in the cluster, $p_r = \frac{N_r}{N}$. The potential outcomes under the two treatment states can then be expressed as a function of the individual's treatment status and p_r:

$$y_{ir}^d \equiv y_{ir}^d(p_r); d = 0, 1 \text{ and } p_r \in [0, 1]. \tag{9}$$

Now we define the average (across independent clusters) *potential* outcomes corresponding to the two treatment states as a function of the proportion of treated individuals (i.e. share of firms with foreign ownership in a cluster) as follows:

$$\overline{y}_p^d = E_r\left[\overline{y}_r^d(p_r)\right]; d = 0, 1 \text{ and } p_r \in [0, 1] \tag{10}$$

If $\frac{\partial \overline{y}_p^d}{\partial p} \neq 0$ for any $\boldsymbol{d}$, then SUTVA would not be supported by the data. This is intuitive as an individual's potential outcomes should be independent of other individuals' treatment status for the assumption of no treatment externalities to hold in the data.

Once the average potential outcomes $\overline{y}_p^d$ are constructed for $d = 0, 1$ and all possible relevant values $p_r \in [0, 1]$, various treatment effect parameters can be defined and estimated. Like all causal effect estimators, these are defined as differences between two average potential outcomes. As discussed by Hudgens and Halloran (2008), four causal treatment effect parameters may be of particular interest:

i. The *direct causal effect* of the treatment (Eq. (11)), which compares average potential outcomes for a firm with foreign ownership with the potential outcome for that firm without FDI, keeping the cluster-specific treatment level constant at $\boldsymbol{p}$ (i.e. keeping possible interactions fixed).

$$\overline{y}_{pp}^{10} = \overline{y}_p^1 - \overline{y}_p^0 \tag{11}$$

ii. The *indirect effect* on the non-treated (Eq. (12)), which in this literature is generally referred to as an FDI "spillover" on domestic firms. This estimator is defined as the change in the potential outcome of non-foreign-owned firms resulting from increasing the cluster-specific proportion of foreign firms from 0 to $\boldsymbol{p}$.

$$\overline{y}_{p0}^{00} = \overline{y}_p^0 - \overline{y}_0^0 \tag{12}$$

iii. The *total treatment* effect (Eq. (13)), which captures the change in the potential outcome of foreign firms when the proportion of foreign firms in the cluster is $\boldsymbol{p} > 0$ compared to the no-treatment outcome that would occur if $\boldsymbol{p} = 0$ (i.e., no foreign firms in the cluster).

$$\overline{y}_{p0}^{10} = \overline{y}_p^1 - \overline{y}_0^0 \tag{13}$$

As shown by Hudgens and Halloran (2008), the total treatment effect can be decomposed into direct and indirect effects, that is $\overline{y}_{p0}^{10} = \overline{y}_{pp}^{10} + \overline{y}_{p0}^{00}$.

iv. The *marginal treatment effect* on the treated - or *indirect effect* on the treated- (Eq. (14)), which measures the marginal change in the potential outcome for foreign-owned firms when the proportion of foreign firms goes from 0 to $\boldsymbol{p}$ (Hudgens and Halloran (2008). In other words, this captures a "spillover" of FDI activity on foreign-owned firms themselves.

$$\overline{y}_{p0}^{11} = \overline{y}_p^1 - \overline{y}_0^1 \tag{14}$$

Next we turn to the discussion of the data used in our empirical analysis.[9]

4. Data description

We implement the empirical analysis using firm level data from the Chinese manufacturing industry. The dataset is based on the Annual

[6] Seminal theoretical papers on "causal inference with interactions" include Sobel (2006); Rosenbaum (2007); Hudgens and Halloran (2008) and Manski (2013). Building on these works Ferracci et al. (forthcoming) provide a comprehensive study of the impacts of training programmes on unemployment duration in the presence of interactions in the local labour markets. Angelucci and de Giorgi (2009) employ village-level randomisation to assess the indirect impact of cash transfer program in Mexico.

[7] The most general (extreme) case of interactions are "unrestricted interactions" between all individuals within a group, in which case potential outcomes are not only functions of the individual's treatment status, but also of all possible combinations of treatments. With unrestricted interactions, calculating the number of potential outcomes might become impracticable if the population size is large. Hence, in order to be able to implement this approach, we follow Hudgens and Halloran (2008) and place some restrictions on the possible interactions.

[8] Note that we do not see this definition as excluding spillovers from vertical linkages, as highlighted by Javorcik (2004), as our industrial classification (see Appendix A) is sufficiently broad to also include vertical links. Moreover, our approach may be seen as offering a new alternative way of estimating intra-cluster spillovers.

[9] It is worth noting that the benchmark treatment level in Eqs. (11)–(14) need not be 0: comparisons can be made between any two treatment levels. For example, if interest lies in estimating the indirect effects of increasing the proportion of FDI firms from 20% to 30% we would compute $\overline{y}_{0.30,0.20}^{00} = \overline{y}_{0.30}^0 - \overline{y}_{0.20}^0$.

Table 1
Summary statistics of some firm level variables of interest.

	Mean	Standard deviation	Min	Max
Domestic firms				
Log productivity (2004)	3.993	1.284	−6.050	11.374
Log productivity (2006)	4.149	1.080	−4.901	9.600
Log wages (2004)	2.418	0.505	−3.135	8.440
Exporting intensity (2004)	0.118	0.288	0.000	1.000
Size (log of assets, 2004)	8.183	1.661	−0.026	17.666
Log of age (2004)	1.970	0.936	0.000	4.605
Log of number of foreign firms in region (2004)	7.678	1.494	2.485	9.357
Number of firms	133,010			
Foreign firms				
Log productivity (2004)	4.055	1.345	−4.723	11.613
Log productivity (2006)	4.343	1.268	−3.724	11.875
Log wages (2004)	2.737	0.612	−0.665	7.140
Exporting intensity 2004)	0.452	0.438	0.000	1.000
Size (log of assets, 2004)	8.939	1.724	−0.026	16.685
Log of age (2004)	1.842	0.727	0.000	4.554
Log of number of foreign firms in region (2004)	8.360	1.073	2.485	9.357
Number of firms	42085			

Table 2
Summary statistics of some cluster level variables.

	Mean	Standard deviation	Min	Max	Inter-quartile range
Proportion of FDI firms (2005)	0.208	0.119	0.043	0.553	0.172
Average wage (thousand RMB) (2004)	7.183	0.323	6.390	8.179	0.465
Average productivity (2004)	4.269	0.372	3.380	5.418	0.470
Average export intensity (2004)	0.235	0.127	0.029	0.610	0.168
Share of SOEs (2004)	0.093	0.062	0.006	0.247	0.096
Average size (log of assets, 2004)	8.520	0.439	7.788	10.041	0.450
Average age (2004)	2.006	0.175	1.218	2.510	0.191
Average log number of FDI firms (2004)	5.077	1.209	2.303	8.148	1.648
Number of clusters	127				

Reports of Industrial Enterprise Statistics, compiled by the China National Bureau of Statistics. The dataset covers all firms in China with an annual turnover of more than 5 million Renminbi (about $800,000). These companies account for an estimated 85–90 percent of total output in most industries. For the purpose of this analysis, we have more than 147,000 firms over the period 2004–2006. Our "treatment" is defined as a firm having foreign investment in 2005.[10]

Table 1 gives some summary statistics of variables of interest by foreign ownership status. These include pre-treatment (i.e. in 2004) firm characteristics and the pre and post treatment values (2004 and 2006) of the outcome variable, which is the log of labour productivity defined as value added per worker.[11] As one might expect, there are substantial differences between domestic and foreign firms vindicating the adoption of a treatment effects evaluation framework. The raw data suggest that on average foreign and domestic firms recorded approximately a 30% and 15% cumulative growth in productivity respectively between 2004 and 2006. Using a relatively naïve difference-in-differences estimator, one would have concluded that the causal effect of foreign ownership is to the tune of 15%.

As discussed in the previous section, our identification strategy invokes the partial *interference assumption* where firm interaction is freely allowed within well-defined clusters. In this paper we classify firms into clusters based on 11 geographic areas and 13 broadly defined industries.[12] This gives us 127 clusters, half of which comprise of at least 768 firms.[13] Table 2 reports some summary statistics of cluster level variables. The average proportion of firms with foreign ownership in a cluster is about 21 percent. It is also apparent from the various measures of dispersion given in Table 2 that clusters are quite heterogeneous in terms of average characteristics. Table 3 reports the number of foreign firms and proportion of foreign (treated) firms by cluster.

[10] A firm is deemed to have foreign ownership if foreign investment accounts for at least 10% of firms' paid-up capital.

[11] Value added per worker is deflated by the consumer price index. Since our main objective is to suggest a framework for estimating the direct and indirect effects of FDI in a unified way, we want to abstract from the various well-documented econometric issues plaguing the estimation of TFP, and concentrate rather on value added per worker (which in any case is found to be highly correlated with TFP in most countries' micro data). However, below we also provide a robustness check and report results based on TFP estimated following Levinsohn and Petrin (2003).

[12] See Appendix A for a list of geographic areas and industries.

[13] We impose the condition that at least 4% of firms in a cluster should be foreign-invested and the total number of firms should not be less than 100. For this reason we have to leave out 17 clusters from the analysis.

As can be seen, there is substantial heterogeneity across clusters. Furthermore, Table 4 shows that the proportion of foreign firms in a cluster exhibits significant correlation with average cluster-specific characteristics.

The next section discusses the econometric implementation of the approach outlined in Section 3, which proceeds in two steps.

5. Empirical implementation

5.1. Estimation of potential outcomes

In the first step we focus on the estimation of potential or counterfactual outcomes (Eq. (10)) as this is a key ingredient for estimating the treatment effect parameters (Eqs. (11)–(14)) which are defined as differences between average potential outcomes. Accordingly, for each of the 127 clusters, we estimate the average potential outcomes $\overline{y}_r^1$ and $\overline{y}_r^0$ under FDI and no FDI scenarios respectively [see Eq. (10)], where y denotes the outcome variable, labour productivity.

In order to deal with selection and unobserved heterogeneity in this estimation we apply the conditional independence assumption (CIA) as in the propensity-score matching literature (Rubin, 1974). This involves estimating the propensity of a firm receiving treatment (i.e., being foreign owned) by conditioning the treatment dummy variable (which is equal to one if a firm has foreign ownership and zero otherwise) on a vector of the following pre-treatment firm characteristics: *wages (level and growth), productivity (level and growth), size (log of total assets), age, export intensity,* and motivated by the theoretical discussion in Section 2, *the number of foreign firms in the firm's region.* To account for firm-level unobserved heterogeneity, we combine CIA with difference-in-differences (cf., Girma and Görg, 2007b) by considering the change in the outcome variables between post (2006) and pre-treatment (2004) periods. However, for ease of exposition, we maintain the y notation for the outcome variables.

In the empirical implementation we identify the expected individual outcomes per cluster by estimating the outcome equation using inverse propensity-score weighted regression also controlling for the pre-treatment covariates (Hirano et al., 2003).[14] For each cluster, this involves:

[14] Before implementing this approach, we carry out a standard propensity score matching combined with difference in differences analysis for comparison. This standard PSM, of course, relies on SUTVA. Applying this technique we find that foreign ownership has a positive causal effect on productivity with a magnitude of around 15 percent. The PSM estimation is based on nearest neighbour matching as applied in Girma and Görg (2007b), with successful balancing tests and imposing common support. Details are not provided here to save space, but can be obtained from the authors upon request.

Table 3
Number of foreign firms and proportion of foreign (treated) firms by cluster.

Cluster	NF	PF	Cluster	NF	PF	Cluster	NF	PF	Cluster	NF	PF
1	177	0.31	**33**	79	0.16	**65**	275	0.12	**97**	802	0.36
2	211	0.49	**34**	132	0.28	**66**	526	0.18	**98**	73	0.12
3	984	0.23	**35**	407	0.42	**67**	414	0.21	**99**	15	0.07
4	247	0.2	**36**	302	0.19	**68**	603	0.38	**100**	37	0.04
5	543	0.26	**37**	418	0.3	**69**	64	0.06	**101**	141	0.25
6	458	0.35	**38**	630	0.21	**70**	19	0.07	**102**	442	0.4
7	126	0.1	**39**	1180	0.48	**71**	40	0.07	**103**	297	0.12
8	84	0.11	**40**	60	0.14	**72**	133	0.05	**104**	446	0.15
9	74	0.1	**41**	21	0.14	**73**	90	0.1	**105**	558	0.17
10	301	0.07	**42**	48	0.18	**74**	52	0.22	**106**	315	0.32
11	122	0.08	**43**	67	0.07	**75**	54	0.27	**107**	65	0.08
12	240	0.32	**44**	45	0.14	**76**	87	0.18	**108**	23	0.07
13	776	0.44	**45**	43	0.18	**77**	90	0.26	**109**	125	0.31
14	1065	0.28	**46**	62	0.34	**78**	77	0.18	**110**	290	0.47
15	1689	0.26	**47**	103	0.11	**79**	99	0.3	**111**	132	0.09
16	3234	0.31	**48**	218	0.15	**80**	36	0.17	**112**	299	0.2
17	2592	0.55	**49**	138	0.13	**81**	31	0.14	**113**	229	0.2
18	188	0.16	**50**	162	0.25	**82**	29	0.11	**114**	341	0.41
19	25	0.16	**51**	10	0.09	**83**	87	0.11	**115**	34	0.09
20	142	0.17	**52**	555	0.36	**84**	55	0.14	**116**	16	0.12
21	212	0.1	**53**	898	0.47	**85**	94	0.19	**117**	145	0.32
22	35	0.08	**54**	828	0.31	**86**	175	0.34	**118**	190	0.32
23	137	0.2	**55**	1390	0.38	**87**	301	0.1	**119**	182	0.21
24	321	0.38	**56**	1714	0.28	**88**	263	0.19	**120**	300	0.25
25	385	0.18	**57**	3456	0.53	**89**	444	0.2	**121**	310	0.17
26	288	0.19	**58**	73	0.13	**90**	412	0.26	**122**	268	0.43
27	589	0.18	**59**	13	0.09	**91**	69	0.06	**123**	38	0.12
28	954	0.34	**60**	99	0.17	**92**	120	0.17	**124**	43	0.17
29	50	0.09	**61**	179	0.1	**93**	279	0.28	**125**	29	0.14
30	64	0.13	**62**	75	0.13	**94**	188	0.17	**126**	87	0.09
31	52	0.08	**63**	136	0.19	**95**	294	0.17	**127**	70	0.09
32	133	0.06	**64**	348	0.42	**96**	362	0.18			

Note: Cluster = Cluster (region-sector) number; NF = Number of foreign firms; PF = Proportion of foreign (treated firms).

a. Generating the propensity-score (ρ) of being treated via a logistic regression with $\boldsymbol{X}$ as covariates.[15]
b. Estimating the following outcome equation (after imposing the common support condition) via inverse probability weighted regression, with treated firms getting weight of $1/\rho$ and non-treated firms getting weight of $1/1-\rho$,

$$y_{ir} = \alpha + \beta d_{ir} + \delta X + error; i = 1 \ldots N. \tag{15}$$

c. Finally computing the cluster specific potential outcomes based on the estimated regressions as[16]

$$\bar{y}_r^1 = \frac{1}{N}\sum_{i=1}^{N} \hat{\alpha} + \hat{\beta} + \hat{\delta}X \text{ and } \bar{y}_r^0 = \frac{1}{N}\sum_{i=1}^{N} \hat{\alpha} + \hat{\delta}X \tag{16}$$

5.2. Calculating treatment effects

In the second step, we use the estimated cluster-specific potential outcomes to estimate the direct and indirect effects of FDI on firms' productivity in the presence of interaction between firms. To this end, we use the proportion of foreign firms in the cluster as a measure of firms' interactions. Hence, we treat the cluster level average potential outcomes under foreign ownership and no foreign ownership, $\bar{y}_r^1$ and $\bar{y}_r^0$, (estimated in the first step) as our "outcome" variables and the proportion of foreign firms in each cluster as our (continuous) "treatment" variable. In other words, once the average potential outcomes $\bar{y}_p^d$ are constructed for $d = 0, 1$ and all relevant values p the various treatment effect parameters can be estimated. We do this using a causal inference approach for continuous treatments, specifically a generalised propensity score (GPS) technique. This step involves working with cluster level variables and conditioning on the general propensity score for the proportion of foreign firms in a cluster (see Appendix C for details).

5.3. Does SUTVA hold?

Before commencing with this estimation we briefly consider the validity of SUTVA in our data. We do so by firstly checking whether there is a correlation between the cluster-specific ATEs estimated using Eqs. (15) and (16) and the observed proportion of foreign owned firms in the cluster. Fig. 1 presents a scatter plot as well as a regression line from a nonparametric regression of the ATE on the proportion of treated firms in the cluster. Taken at face value, this indicates fairly heterogeneous behaviour across treatment clusters, suggesting that SUTVA is unlikely to be satisfied by the data (i.e., a firm's potential outcome is not independent of the treatment level per cluster).

However, as shown in Table 4, clusters also differ along a line of other characteristics. Hence, to further test the validity of SUTVA, we investigate more formally the existence of a causal link between potential outcomes and the proportion of foreign firms in a cluster using the GPS approach outlined in Step 2. Our results, presented in Fig. C1 (Appendix C), show that the potential outcomes (for treated and untreated firms) vary systematically with the treatment level in the cluster, suggesting that SUTVA does not hold.

Hence, the standard PSM approach masks substantial cross cluster heterogeneity, as is obvious from Figs. 1 and C1. Our novel approach, as explained in the previous sections, arguably provides a more appropriate way of estimating the causal effect of foreign ownership

[15] See Appendix B for a summary of the estimated coefficients from the cluster-specific logit model. Covariate balancing tests, which consist of testing for difference (at 10% level or lower) between the average values of the covariates in treatment and control groups, conditional on the propensity score, are given in the last column of the table in Appendix B.

[16] Note that under SUTVA, the difference between these two potential outcomes $(\hat{\beta})$ would give a consistent estimator of the average treatment effect (ATE) in each cluster.

Table 4
Correlation matrix of cluster level variables.

	Proportion of FDI firm	Average wage	Average productivity	Average export intensity	Average export intensity	Average size	Average age	Log number FDI firms
Proportion of FDI firms	1							
Average wage	0.503***	1						
Average productivity	0.222*	−0.186*	1					
Average export intensity	0.657***	0.425***	−0.145	1				
Share of SOEs	−0.415***	0.0968	−0.172	−0.529***	1			
Average size	−0.175*	0.341***	0.0395	−0.348***	0.402***	1		
Average age	−0.0969	0.404***	−0.223*	−0.258**	0.606***	0.486***	1	
Log number of FDI firms	0.654***	0.147	0.0871	0.736***	−0.642***	−0.409***	−0.312***	1

Notes: * $p < 0.05$, ** $p < 0.01$, *** $p < 0.001$.

on productivity. In the next Section we, therefore, turn to calculating the direct, indirect, total and marginal treatment productivity effects (defined in Section 3) by varying the proportion of treated firms in a cluster.

6. Treatment effects with interactions: main findings

For ease of presentation, we plot the estimated effects along with their 95% confidence intervals.[17] It is apparent from Fig. 2 that the proportion of foreign-owned firms in a cluster matters significantly, both statistically and economically.

Our first finding is that the direct average treatment effects, i.e., the productivity premium due to having foreign ownership differs strongly as one varies the proportion of foreign firms in the cluster. While they are positive irrespective of the proportion of foreign firms in the cluster, it is apparent from Fig. 2 that the share of foreign firms matters significantly for any conclusion one can draw from the data. This is in line with our motivating discussion in Section 2, where we argue that foreign owned firms have higher investments in productivity enhancing activities and that such investments may be higher (in the presence of positive spillovers) the more prevalent are foreign firms in the cluster

We can see, for example, that the direct effect is smaller for a cluster with a 10 percent share of foreign owned firms than for a cluster with insignificant foreign presence. After the 10 percent mark we see strong increases in the direct effect with increasing proportions of foreign-owned firms. For example, the direct productivity effects of foreign ownership would be 20% and 35% when the proportions of foreign firms in the cluster are 20% and 50% respectively.

In contrast, we uncover significant negative indirect effects on non-treated (i.e. domestic owned) firms. In the context of the literature on FDI, we can interpret this as evidence for negative productivity spillovers. This is not unusual in the literature on spillovers, which in many cases finds negative effects of the presence of FDI on productivity of domestic firms (see Görg and Greenaway, 2004) and is generally regarded as indicating negative competition or market-stealing effects from multinationals. Interestingly, we document evidence that this effect varies with the proportion of foreign owned firms; it seems to be most negative around the 40% mark. This is a novel finding, as the literature generally only estimates a constant spillover effect that does not vary with the level of the proportion of foreign owned firms.

From the combination of direct and indirect effect we can calculate the total effect of the treatment. Note that, while these total effects on productivity are uniformly positive, they do not increase monotonically with the share of foreign owned firms. Rather, we find that the total effect declines when the proportion of foreign owned firms in a cluster moves from 0 to about 20. This is due to the negative indirect effects which outweigh the direct effects. Only after reaching this 20 percent threshold do we see further increases in the total effect with increasing shares of foreign firms in the cluster. Still, we find that even though we have strong evidence for negative spillovers (indirect effect), the total effect of the treatment (i.e., foreign ownership) is generally positive.

The non-monotonic relationship between the proportion of foreign firms in a cluster and the total treatment effect is further illustrated when one studies the marginal average treatment effects on the treated. Recall that this gives the marginal change in the potential outcome for treated firms when the proportion of treated firms changes from 0 to p. These marginal effects become increasingly negative up to a threshold of 20 percent. They only start turning positive after the 40% mark. Hence, this result indicates that low proportions of foreign ownership in a cluster are not optimal from the perspective of treated (i.e., foreign owned) firms. Instead, it seems to be the case that a "critical mass" of foreign owned firms in a cluster (with the critical mass point being in the region of 40%) is necessary in order to stimulate productivity in foreign owned firms. This evidence thus suggests that foreign firms thrive in clusters with a high presence of other foreign firms. This is in line with arguments by Lee et al. (2013), Chen (2009) and Henderson (2003) who find that agglomerations of firms (in particular foreign owned) can be important for firm level productivity and development. Our evidence, however, shows that this is not necessarily a monotonically positive relationship, but that the positive effects only kick in after reaching a certain level of foreign presence in a cluster.

As our results thus far rely on labour productivity as outcome variable, we now provide a robustness check where we measure total factor productivity (TFP) using the Levinsohn and Petrin (2003) methodology. The results are presented in Fig. 3. Note that the patterns of results look very similar to the patterns observed using labour productivity. The

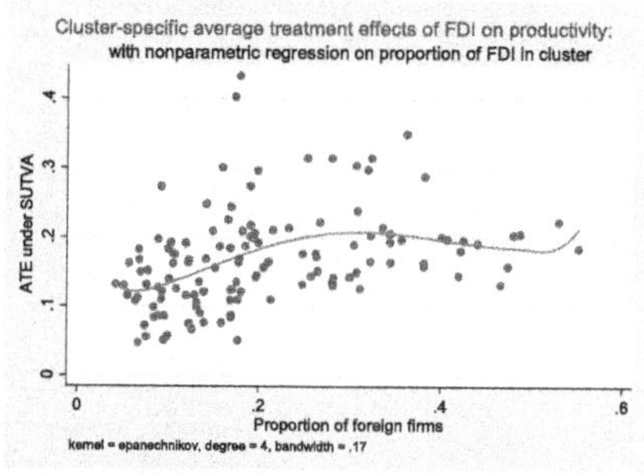

Fig. 1. Cluster-specific average treatment effects of FDI on productivity: with nonparametric regression on proportion of FDI in cluster.

[17] The calculation of standard errors is outlined in Appendix C.

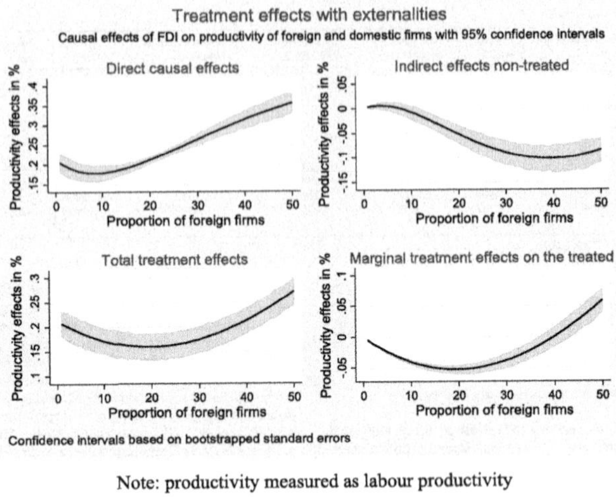

Fig. 2. Treatment effects with externalities. Causal effects of FDI on productivity of foreign and domestic firms with 95% confidence intervals. Note: productivity measured as labour productivity.

main difference is that the effects based on TFP have turning points at lower percentage shares of foreign firms. For example, we can see that the marginal treatment effects start to pick up at around 10 per cent of foreign owned firms in a cluster and become positive after reaching about 30 percent when using TFP. When using labour productivity, they only become positive after reaching around 40 percent of foreign owned firms in a cluster.

7. Conclusions

This paper offers a causal analysis of the direct and indirect effects of foreign ownership on firm level productivity of treated (i.e., foreign) and non-treated (i.e., domestic) firms. The approach we follow in this paper enables us to estimate, in a unified framework, the direct effect of foreign-ownership on the productivity of foreign firms, as well as

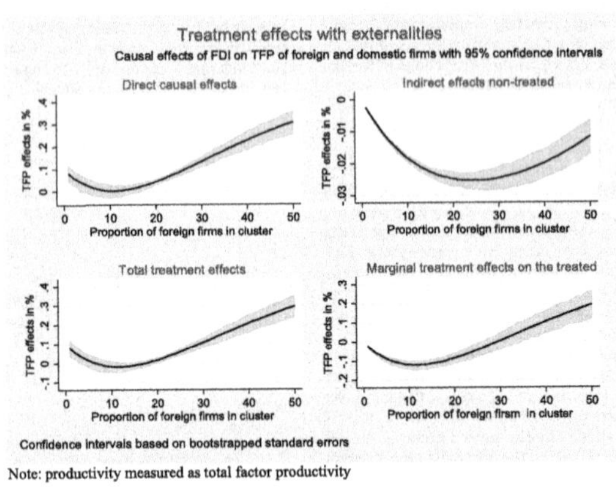

Fig. 3. Treatment effects with externalities. Causal effects of FDI on TFP of foreign and domestic firms with 95% confidence intervals. Note: productivity measured as total factor productivity.

two types of indirect effects, namely on domestic and foreign firms. These latter two effects provide estimates of "spillovers" from the presence of foreign-owned firms on foreign and domestic firms. Combining direct and indirect effects we can also calculate a total effect of foreign firms. Our approach thus allows us to distinguish between different types of treatment effects, which are not only academically interesting but also highly policy relevant.

Importantly, we provide empirical evidence that not only the direct effects vary systematically with the proportion of foreign firms in the cluster, but also the spillover effects differ strongly across such clusters. Specifically, the analysis shows that for our Chinese data spillovers on domestic firms become more negative with increasing presence of foreign-invested firms up to a threshold of around 40 percent foreign ownership in a cluster. After this threshold they become less negative.

For spillovers on other foreign firms we find that these are negative up to a threshold of 40 percent foreign ownership in a cluster. After this value they turn positive, however. This latter result provides an important finding for the academic literature and policy debate on the benefits from "agglomerations" of foreign owned firms, showing that these benefits are not uniform but depend strongly on the level of foreign ownership in a well-defined cluster.

Combining our treatment effects we find a total effect that is positive but initially declines with low shares of foreign firms in a cluster. However, after reaching about 20 percent of foreign firms the total effect increases with increasing shares of foreign firms in the cluster. Hence, for policymakers, this might suggest that they might aim to encourage concentrations of foreign firms above these thresholds in a cluster.

Overall, our research suggests that estimating the various treatment effects described in this paper is a rewarding exercise as it sheds much needed light on the various mechanisms through which the proportion of foreign firms affects potential outcomes of foreign and non-foreign firms. In so doing, our paper provides important inputs into the policy debate on the benefits from inward foreign direct investment for host country firms.

Appendix A. Geographic classification used in this paper

AREA	PROVINCES	Share of foreign ownership
1	Beijing and Tianjin	0.25
2	Shanghai	0.39
3	Liaoning and Shandong	0.21
4	Jiangsu	0.24
5	Fujian and Zhejiang	0.23
6	Guangdong and Hainan	0.44
7	Inner Mongolia, Hebei and Shanxi	0.10
8	Jilin, Heilongjiang	0.12
9	Jiangxi, Anhui	0.12
10	Qinghai, Henan, Gansu, Shaanxi, Hunan, Ningxia, Hubei, Guangxi and Xinjiang	0.08
11	Guizhou, Yunnan, Sichuan and Chongqing	0.09

Industrial classification used in this paper

Industry group	Industry name	Share of foreign ownership
1	Food processing	0.16
1	Food production	0.25
1	Beverages	0.18
2	Textiles	0.23
2	Garments and other fibre products	0.44
2	Leather, furs, down related products	0.42
3	Timber processing	0.20
3	Furniture manufacturing	0.35
3	Papermaking and paper products	0.17
3	Printing and record medium reproduction	0.14
4	Rubber products	0.26
4	Plastic products	0.29
5	Smelting and pressing of ferrous metals	0.11
5	Smelting and pressing of nonferrous metals	0.16
6	Electric equipment and machinery	0.25
6	Electronic and telecommunications	0.54
6	Instruments and meters	0.36
6	Other electronic equipment	0.38
7	Raw chemical materials and chemical products	0.17
8	Medical and pharmaceutical products	0.19
9	Non-metal mineral products	0.17
10	Metal products	0.22
11	Ordinary machinery	0.18
12	Special purpose equipment	0.24
13	Transport equipment	0.19

Appendix .B Summary statistics of estimated coefficients from the first stage cluster-specific Logit model (N = 127):

Pre-treatment covariates (in 2004)	Mean	Average St. error	Min	Max	Proportion of clusters with significant coefficients	Proportion of clusters with balanced covariates
Log productivity	.0890319	.1203289	-.2622438	.597029	.2755906	0.976
Log wages	1.187789	.2782815	−1.787512	2.724028	.8976378	0.984
Wages growth	-.5439145	.3858767	−8.982675	.4646787	.488189	0.992
Productivity growth	-.0824834	.1951044	−1.312997	2.76314	.2519685	0.984
Exporting intensity	2.701552	.576253	−3.520742	11.78326	.9606299	0.961
Size	.295387	.0829834	-.1505758	.6941422	.7874016	0.976
Age	-.3614924	.1539911	-.9862373	.1851604	.6692913	0.976
Log of number of foreign firms in region	.4355861	1.043163	−10.30238	23.77369	.6141732	0.835

Notes:

1. Estimated coefficients from binary logit models can be interpreted as the effects of the covariates on the log odd-ratio of foreign ownership.
2. The penultimate column gives the proportion of *individually* statistically significant coefficients at 10% level or lower. In all cases the coefficients are jointly statistically significant.
3. The last column gives the results from the covariate balancing test which consists of testing (at 10% level or lower) for difference in the means of the covariates in treatment and control groups, conditional on the estimated propensity score.

Appendix C. Calculating treatment effects

We investigate the existence of causal links between potential outcomes and the proportion of treated firms in a cluster. For this purpose, we treat the cluster level average potential outcomes $\bar{y}_r^1$ *and* $\bar{y}_r^0$ as the "outcome" variables and the corresponding proportion of foreign-owned firms, p_r, as the "treatment" variable.

Since we now have a continuous treatment variable rather than a binary one, we employ the causal inference approach for continuous treatments (Hirano and Imbens, 2004; Imai and van Dyk, 2004).[18] A key result from this literature is that causal inference can be conducted by conditioning on the generalised propensity score (GPS), which is the conditional density of the treatment given some pre-treatment variables. Hence, this can be seen as an extension of the conditional independence assumption (CIA) to the case of a continuous treatment variable. Since our assumption is that of "no interaction across clusters", SUTVA holds for the cluster level analysis.

Since the treatment variable is a proportion between 0 and 1, we estimate the determinants of treatment using the fractional logit model due to Papke and Wooldrige (1996). In the empirical implementation, we condition p_r on a vector $\boldsymbol{Z}$ of observable pre-treatment cluster characteristics which include *average wages, productivity, size, age and the proportion of exporting, state-owned and the number of foreign owned firms in the region.*. The econometric estimates and corresponding marginal effects from this fractional logit model, and balancing test results are reported in Tables C1 and C2.

Letting $\hat{\lambda}$ be the vector of estimated coefficients from the fractional logit model, the GPS conditional on $\boldsymbol{Z}$ and p_r can then be obtained as

$$\hat{G}_r = \left[\frac{e^{Z_i\hat{\lambda}}}{1+e^{Z_i\hat{\lambda}}}\right]^{p_r}\left[1-\frac{e^{Z_i\hat{\lambda}}}{1+e^{Z_i\hat{\lambda}}}\right]^{1-p_r} \tag{C1}$$

We then estimate the expected values of each of the two potential outcomes ($\bar{y}_r^1$ and $\bar{y}_r^0$) at cluster level conditional on $\hat{G}_r$ and p_r. These expected values are unknown and can be estimated using a polynomial approximation (Hirano and Imbens, 2004) such as the following quadratic form which is often found to be adequate: [19]

$$Ey_r^d \big| \hat{G}_r, p_r = \beta_0 + \beta_1\hat{G}_r + \beta_2 p_r + \beta_3\hat{G}_r^2 + \beta_4 p_r^2 + \beta_5\hat{G}_r p_r \tag{2}$$

with sample counterpart

$$\frac{1}{R}\sum_{r=1}^{127}\hat{\beta}_0 + \hat{\beta}_1\hat{G}_r + \hat{\beta}_2 p_r + \hat{\beta}_3\hat{G}_r^2 + \hat{\beta}_4 p_r^2 + \hat{\beta}_5\hat{G}_r p_r \tag{C3}$$

In Fig. C1, we plot the 95% confidence regions of the two potential outcomes $\bar{y}_r^1$ *and* $\bar{y}_r^0$ against p_r (based on bootstrapped standard errors) over the practically feasible range of 0 to 50%.[20] This clearly shows that the potential outcomes for productivity (for treated and untreated firms) vary systematically with the treatment level in the cluster. Given our econometric approach, we can interpret this as a causal relationship, i.e., changes in the treatment level per cluster lead to changes in potential outcomes. This indicates that SUTVA does not hold in our analysis.

The thus calculated potential outcomes for different levels of p_r are then used to calculate the treatment effects described in Eqs. (11) to (14).

[18] See Du and Girma (2009), and Fryges and Wagner (2008) for international trade applications of GPS matching techniques.

[19] Note that the parameters of such parametric approximation do not have any behavioural interpretation (Hirano and Imbens, 2004). These are used to obtain an unbiased estimator of the population mean.

[20] In our data, the proportion of foreign owned firms is less than 50% in 98% of the clusters.

Table C1
Estimated coefficients and marginal effects from the fractional logit model: Dependent variable: proportion of FDI firms in cluster.

	Estimated coefficients	Marginal effects
Wages	1.024***	0.158***
	(0.1660)	(0.0258)
Productivity	0.695***	0.107***
	(0.1155)	(0.0181)
Export intensity	0.985*	0.152*
	(0.5659)	(0.0871)
SOE share	−1.200	−0.186
	(0.9849)	(0.1523)
Log of number of FDI Firms	0.218***	0.034***
	(0.0496)	(0.0077)
Size	−0.242**	−0.037**
	(0.0997)	(0.0155)
Age	0.414	0.064
	(0.2888)	(0.0448)
Observations	127	

Notes:
(i) Standard errors are given in parenthesis
(ii) * $p < 0.10$, ** $p < 0.05$, *** $p < 0.01$

Table C2
Balancing tests second stage estimation.

Covariate (pre-treatment period)	Quartile 2	Quartile 3	Quartile 4
Wages	0.30	0.16	0.37
Productivity	0.29	0.70	0.42
Export intensity	0.44	0.75	0.92
SOE share	0.72	0.52	0.93
Number of FDI firms	0.14	0.05	0.08
Size	0.55	0.68	0.89
Age	0.28	0.45	0.45

Note: Since the treatment is continuous we divided the observations into four groups by treatment quartiles and conditional on the generalised propensity score, we tested for equality of means of each of the covariates across all quartiles (using Quartile 1 as the base group). We did not reject the null hypothesis of equality of means in any of the tests whose p-value are reported below.

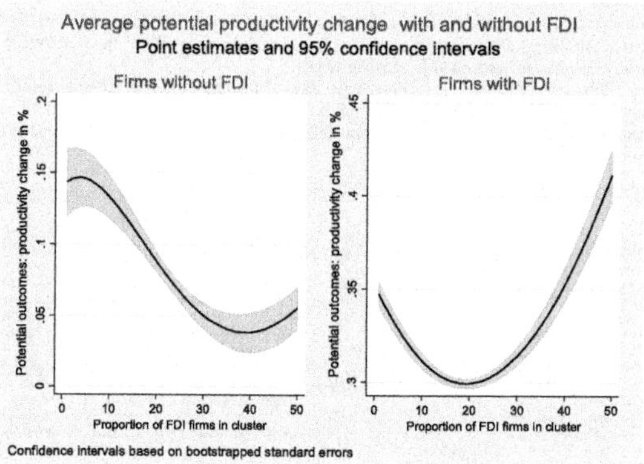

Fig. C1. Average potential productivity change with and without FDI Point estimates and 95% confidence intervals.

Calculating standard errors

To illustrate how the bootstrapped standard errors are calculated, we take the example of estimating the indirect effects of FDI using the formula given in Eq. (12). This estimator is defined as the change in the potential outcome of non-foreign-owned firms resulting from increasing the cluster-specific proportion of foreign firms from 0 to p ∈ {0, 1}

$$\bar{\gamma}_{p0}^{00} = \bar{y}_p^0 - \bar{y}_0^0$$

The average treatment effect based on our 127 clusters (indexed by c below) is naturally estimated as

$$\bar{\gamma}_{p0}^{00} = \frac{1}{127}\sum_{c=1}^{127} y_{pr}^0 - y_{0r}^0$$

Recall that the ys in the above equation are potential outcomes based on the inverse probability-weighted regression (Eq. (15)). The issue here is that standard formula for calculation the standard errors of means will be inadequate due the need of accounting for the fact the propensity score are estimated. Accordingly we compute bootstrapped standard errors via resampling with replacement. In our practical estimation we implemented 200 bootstraps (indexed by B below) and used the following formula:

$$s.e\left(\bar{\gamma}_{p0}^{00}\right) = \sqrt{\frac{1}{200}\sum_{B=1}^{200}\left(\bar{\gamma}_{p0,B}^{00} - \bar{\gamma}_{B}^{00}\right)^2}$$

with $\bar{\gamma}_{B}^{00} = \frac{1}{200}\sum_{B=1}^{200}\bar{\gamma}_{p0,B}^{00}$

Appendix D

Following the very helpful suggestion of a referee, we outline the main reasons why a simple linear model where the direct and indirect effects of FDI are estimated within a single framework is unlikely to be an adequate empirical tool.

Suppose we aim to estimate the direct and indirect effects of FDI on an outcome variable *y*:

$$y_{ir} = \alpha + \sum\nolimits_{r=1}^{R} \beta_r d_{ir} + \gamma p_r + \delta p_r * d_{ir} + \varepsilon_{ir} \tag{D1}$$

In the above equation r = 1. … R indexes clusters and i = 1. … N denotes firms within clusters, where for simplicity we assume each cluster has the same number of firms N.

We define d = 1 if the firm is foreign owned, and 0 else. Thus the β's would capture cluster-specific direct effects of FDI. $p_r = \frac{1}{N}\sum_{i=1}^{N} d_{ir}$ is the average foreign presence in cluster r. Thus γ would measure FDI spillovers to domestic firms, whereas γ + δ would identify FDI spillovers to foreign firms. The estimation of this simple yet attractive empirical model is fraught with difficulties, however. Firstly, since there is selection at both firm and cluster level (as argued in the main body of this paper), identification would involve estimating two (generalised) propensity scores, one at firm level (say $P1_i$) and one at cluster level (say $P2_i$). However, to the best our knowledge, there is no available estimator which can deal, within a single equation, with two propensity-scores estimated at two different levels. So it would not suffice to estimate Eq. (D1) by inverse probability weighted regression, with treated firms getting weight of 1/p1 and non-treated firms getting weight of 1/1-p1, as we would still have $E(\varepsilon_{ir}|p_r) \neq 0$ rendering the resulting estimator inconsistent.

The above problem notwithstanding, the second issue associated with estimating Eq. (D1) has to do with the fact that it does not, unlike the estimation approach advocated in this paper, allow for a richer counterfactual analysis. For example the relationship between y and p_r is essentially linear restricting spillovers to be a monotonic function of foreign presence.

The third problem with the estimation of Eq. (D1), especially the inclusion of the term capturing FDI spillovers to foreign firms, is a variant of the well-known reflection problem in social interaction models (see Manski, 1993). To be more precise, foreign firm i contributes 1/N to p_r (the FDI variable). Consequently it is conceptually difficult to isolate direct from indirect effects in this setup, again the problem of dealing with two propensity scores estimated at two different levels notwithstanding.

References

Aitken, Brian J., Harrison, Ann E., 1999. Do Domestic Firms Benefit from Foreign Direct Investment? Evidence from Venezuela. Am. Econ. Rev. 605–618.

Angelucci, M., De Giorgi, G., 2009. Indirect Effects of an Aid Program: The Case of Progresa and Consumption. Am. Econ. Rev. 99, 486–508.

Arnold, J., Javorcik, B.S., 2009. Gifted kids or pushy parents? Foreign direct investment and plant productivity in Indonesia. J. Int. Econ. 79 (1), 42–53.

Chen, Y., 2009. Agglomeration and location of foreign direct investment: The case of China. China Econ. Rev. 20, 549–557.

Du, J., Girma, S., 2009. The effects of foreign acquisitions on domestic and export markets dynamics in China. World Econ. 32 (164–177), 2009.

Ferracci, Marc, Jolivet, Grégory, van den Berg, Gerard, 2014. Evidence of treatment spillovers within markets. Rev. Econ. Stat. (forthcoming).

Fosfuri, A., Motta, M., Rønde, T., 2001. Foreign Direct Investment and Spillovers Through Workers' Mobility. J. Int. Econ. 53, 205–222.

Fryges, H., Wagner, J., 2008. Exports and Productivity Growth: First Evidence from a Continuous Treatment Approach. Rev. World Econ. 144, 695–722.

Girma, S., Görg, H., 2007a. Multinationals productivity advantage: Scale or technology? Econ. Inq. 45 (2), 350–362.

Girma, S., Görg, H., 2007b. Evaluating the foreign ownership wage premium using a difference-in-differences matching approach. J. Int. Econ. 72, 97–112.

Girma, S., Wakelin, K., 2007. Local productivity spillovers from foreign direct investment in the U.K. electronics industry. Reg. Sci. Urban Econ. 37 (3), 399–412.

Görg, H., Greenaway, D., 2004. Much ado about nothing? Do domestic firms really benefit from foreign direct investment?'. World Bank Res. Obs. 19, 171–197.

Görg, H., Strobl, E., 2005. Spillovers from Foreign Firms through Worker Mobility: An Empirical Investigation. Scand. J. Econ. 107, 693–709.

Guadalupe, M., Kuzmina, Olga, Thomas, C., 2012. Innovation and Foreign Ownership. Am. Econ. Rev. 102 (7), 3594–3627.

Harris, R., Robinson, C., 2002. The effect of foreign acquisitions on total factor productivity: Plant-level evidence from UK manufacturing. Rev. Econ. Stat. 84, 562–568.

Haskel, Jonathan E., Pereira, Sonia C., Slaughter, Matthew J., 2007. Does Inward Foreign Direct Investment boost the Productivity of Domestic Firms? Rev. Econ. Stat. 89 (3), 482–496.

Helpman, E., Melitz, M., Yeaple, S., 2004. Exports versus FDI with Heterogeneous Firms. Am. Econ. Rev. 94, 300–316.

S. Girma et al. / Journal of International Economics 95 (2015) 157–169 169

Henderson, J.V., 2003. Marshall's scale economies. J. Urban Econ. 53, 1–28.

Hirano, K., Imbens, G.W., 2004. The propensity score with continuous treatments. In: Gelman, Andrew, Meng, Xiao-Li (Eds.), Applied Bayesian Modeling and Causal Inference from Incomplete-Data Perspectives. Wiley.

Hirano, K., Imbens, G., Ridder, G., 2003. Efficient Estimation of Average Treatment Effects Using the Estimated Propensity Score. Econometrica 71, 1161–1189.

Hudgens, M.G., Halloran, M.E., 2008. Toward Causal Inference With Interference. J. Am. Stat. Assoc. 103, 832–842.

Imai, K., van Dyk, D.A., 2004. Causal inference with general treatment regimes: Generalizing the propensity score. J. Am. Stat. Assoc. 99, 854–866.

Javorcik, B.S., 2004. Does Foreign Direct Investment Increase the Productivity of Domestic Firms? In Search of Spillovers through Backward Linkages. Am. Econ. Rev. 94, 605–627.

Keller, W., 2010. International Trade, Foreign Direct Investment, and Technology Spillovers, Chapter 19. In: Hall, B., Rosenberg, N. (Eds.), Handbook of the Economics of Innovation. Elsevier, North-Holland.

Keller, W., Yeaple, S., 2009. Multinational Enterprises, International Trade, and Productivity Growth: Firm-Level Evidence from the United States. Rev. Econ. Stat. 91 (4), 821–831.

Lee, Y., Chyi, Yih-Luan, Lin, Eric S., Shih-Ying, Wu., 2013. Do local industrial agglomeration and foreign direct investment to China enhance the productivity of Taiwanese firms? J. Int. Trade Econ. Dev. 22 (6), 839–865.

Levinsohn, J., Petrin, A., 2003. Estimating Production Functions Using Inputs to Control for Observables. Rev. Econ. Stud. 70 (2), 317–341.

Manski, C., 1993. Identification of Endogenous Social Effects: The Reflection Problem. Rev. Econ. Stud. 60 (3), 531–542.

Manski, C., 2013. Identification of treatment response with social interactions. Econ. J. 16 (6), S1–S23.

Markusen, J.R., 2001. Multinational firms and the theory of international trade. MIT Press.

Papke, E., Wooldrige, J., 1996. Econometric methods for fractional response variables with an application to 401(k) plan participation rates. J. Appl. Econ. 11, 619–632.

Rosenbaum, P.R., 2007. Interference between Units in Randomized Experiments. J. Am. Stat. Assoc. 102, 191–200.

Rubin, D.B., 1974. Estimating Causal Effects of Treatments in Randomized and Nonrandomized Studies. J. Educ. Psychol. 66, 688–701.

Sobel, M., 2006. What Do Randomized Studies of Housing Mobility Demonstrate? Causal Inference in the Face of Interference. J. Am. Stat. Assoc. 101, 1398–1407.

Xu, X., Sheng, Y., 2012. Are FDI spillovers regional? Firm-level evidence from China. J. Asian Econ. 23, 244–258.

PART III

Alternative Ways of Looking for Spillovers

Chapter 13

Spillovers from Foreign Firms through Worker Mobility: An Empirical Investigation*

Holger Görg

University of Nottingham, Nottingham NG7 2RD, England
holger.gorg@nottingham.ac.uk

Eric Strobl

Ecole Polytechnique Paris, 91128 Palaiseau Cedex, France
eric.strobl@shs.polytechnique.fr

Abstract

While there is a large empirical literature on productivity spillovers from multinationals, this literature treats the channels through which these spillover effects work as a black box. The new approach in this paper is to investigate whether spillovers occur via worker mobility. We use data on whether or not the owner of a domestic firm has previous experience in a multinational, and relate this information to firm-level productivity. Our results suggest that firms which are run by owners who worked for multinationals in the same industry immediately prior to opening up their own firm are more productive than other domestic firms.

Keywords: Foreign direct investment; spillovers; worker mobility; training

JEL classification: *F*21; *F*23; *J*61

I. Introduction

Over the last decades, foreign direct investment (FDI) has become increasingly important in the world economy. Developing countries, in particular, have witnessed significant increases in the importance of FDI, with their

* We are particularly grateful to the Centre for the Study of African Economies (CSAE) at Oxford University for providing the data and to Francis Teal for advice on the data and useful discussions. Earlier versions of the paper were presented at the Mid-West International Economics meeting at Notre Dame, the Development Economics Study Group (DESG) conference in Nottingham, a workshop at the Institute for International Integration Studies (IIIS) in Dublin and a seminar at the University of Leicester. Thanks are due to Laurie-Ann Agama, Salvador Barrios, Carl Davidson, David Fielding, Sourafel Girma, David Greenaway, Keith Head, Philip Lane, Bob Lipsey, Fanis Mamuneas, Ray Riezman, Mark Schaffer, Beata Smarzynska Javorcik, Dirk te Velde and two anonymous referees for helpful comments. Görg gratefully acknowledges financial support from the Leverhulme Trust (Programme Grant F114/BF).

inward FDI having risen from about 4 percent of GDP in 1980 to almost 16 percent in 1996; cf. UN (1998). This has gone hand-in-hand with a shift in emphasis among policymakers towards actively attracting FDI. Many host countries now encourage the inflow of FDI by providing generous investment and/or tax incentives. While the expected potential benefits include employment creation, capital formation and export promotion, one of the most frequent reasons for attracting FDI is the prospect of acquiring new technology which may spill over to the host country and allow domestic firms to improve their performance. This may be a particularly important potential mechanism for developing countries to catch-up with the industrialised world.

More specifically, multinational companies are expected to have access to some sort of firm-specific asset, manifesting itself as a superior knowledge base, production technology, or marketing and management technique; see Caves (1996) and Markusen (2002). By inviting multinationals into the country, host country governments expect that at least some of this firm-specific asset will be transferred to domestic firms, thus enabling them to improve their performance in terms of productivity, skills or export performance. This knowledge transfer can be either voluntary through technology transfer arrangements or involuntary through knowledge spillovers.

Over the last three decades or so, a large microeconomic literature has developed to address such knowledge, or productivity, spillovers.[1] These are assumed to occur through three main channels. First, there are "demonstration effects", i.e., domestic firms learn through imitation from multinationals. Second, there is a "competition effect" whereby domestic firms face competition from more productive multinationals and have to improve their own performance to compete successfully. Third, spillovers may occur through movement of labour, whereby workers trained by or working in multinationals decide to leave and join an existing domestic firm or open up a new enterprise. In the process, they take with them some or all of the firm-specific knowledge of the multinational.

Many empirical studies have set out to measure the magnitude of productivity spillovers at the micro level for both developing and developed countries; see e.g. Kokko (1994), Aitken and Harrison (1999), Blomström and Sjöholm (1999), Keller and Yeaple (2003) and Smarzynska-Javorcik (2004).[2] However, the evidence is mixed. For example, using plant-level

[1] See Blomström and Kokko (1998) and Görg and Greenaway (2004) for reviews of this literature.

[2] There are also a number of papers which try to assess the macro effect of FDI on GDP growth; see, for example, Balasubramanyam, Sapsford and Salisu (1996), Borensztein, De Gregorio and Lee (1998) and Alfaro, Chanda, Kalemli-Ozcan and Sayek (2004). These studies find positive growth effects for a certain group of countries.

panel data for Venezuela, Aitken and Harrison (1999) find no evidence for productivity improvements in host country firms due to foreign presence. In fact, they find that some firms even experience negative effects from FDI in the same industry. By contrast, using firm-level data for the US, Keller and Yeaple (2003) find that domestic firms are able to benefit from intra-industry FDI. Furthermore, Smarzynska-Javorcik (2004) shows that domestic firms in Lithuania benefit from vertical (inter-industry) rather than horizontal (intra-industry) spillovers from multinationals. These mixed results have been explained by Lipsey and Sjöholm (2005) as reflecting different firm and country characteristics in the datasets used, whereas Görg and Strobl (2001) attribute them to different estimation techniques.

One of the drawbacks of these studies is that they treat the specific mechanisms by which the spillovers are supposed to occur as a "black box". As such they usually regress total factor or labour productivity of domestic firms on a number of covariates, including a measure of the extent of multinational presence in an industry. A positive and statistically significant coefficient on that variable is then interpreted to indicate the existence of positive productivity spillovers.

While empirical studies do not, by and large, examine the mechanisms through which spillovers may occur, the recent theoretical literature has focused on one particular channel, namely the movement of workers from foreign to domestic firms; see Fosfuri, Motta and Rønde (2001) and Glass and Saggi (2002). To the best of our knowledge, no empirical studies have examined the effect of worker movements on the performance of domestic firms. The new approach of our paper is, therefore, to offer a detailed analysis of this issue at the empirical level. Worker movements may be particularly important in developing countries, where skilled labour is usually scarce and there is thus a large potential for domestic workers to receive training and experience in multinational companies. Acquired knowledge can then, of course, increase the knowledge stock in domestic firms if workers from foreign firms join them.

We have access to detailed firm-level data for a sample of manufacturing firms in Ghana which allow us to tackle the issue at hand. Specifically, we have information on whether or not the entrepreneur, i.e., the owner or chairman, of the domestic firms in the sample worked for a foreign multinational before joining or setting up his/her own domestic firm and we can determine whether this experience was gained in the same or in other industries. Furthermore, the data allow us to identify whether or not he/she received training by a multinational firm at any point during the sample period. Thus, while the data do not provide information on all workers in a firm, they do relate to the entrepreneur, the main decision maker whose influence is particularly important for firm performance. Using these data, we investigate whether domestic firms which have entrepreneurs with foreign training and/or experience have a productivity advantage compared to other firms.[3]

Our econometric results show that firms whose entrepreneur worked in multinationals in the same industry are more productive than other domestic firms. No such evidence is found for firms run by entrepreneurs who worked for multinationals in other industries. This suggests that some of the multinationals' knowledge is industry specific and cannot be transferred to firms in other industries. Moreover, explicit training received in multinationals does not appear to affect the firm's performance.

The remainder of the paper is structured as follows. In Section II we briefly discuss why spillovers may be expected through movements of workers. The dataset is described in Section III, while Section IV contains the results of the econometric estimations. Section V summarises our findings and concludes.

II. Spillovers through Worker Mobility

Spillovers can arise when workers receive training or accumulate experience while working for multinationals, and then move to domestic firms or set up their own enterprise. When moving, they may take with them some of the knowledge acquired in the multinational, which can be usefully applied in the domestic firm and help improve its performance. This channel for spillovers has recently been investigated theoretically by Fosfuri *et al.* (2001) who examine the conditions under which such spillovers occur. Glass and Saggi (2002) also provide a formal representation of the movement of trained workers from multinationals to domestic firms as a channel for spillovers.

Empirical work in this area is scarce, however. There is some evidence that multinationals are important providers of training activities in developing countries; cf. ILO (1981) and Lindsey (1986). Some studies find that in a comparison of domestic firms and multinationals, the latter provide more training than the former. Gershenberg (1987) provides such evidence from a survey of 72 managers in manufacturing firms in Kenya.[4] He also finds some evidence for movements of managers from

[3] It should be noted that we treat the decision of the entrepreneur to move from a foreign to a domestic firm as exogenous. The related literature argues that employees may decide to become entrepreneurs if the expected earnings are higher than the expected wage when remaining in paid employment; see, for example, Evans and Jovanovic (1989) and Evans and Leighton (1989).

[4] This finding is only true in a comparison of multinationals and purely domestic private firms. Multinationals do not appear to provide more training than joint ventures or publicly owned Kenyan companies.

multinationals to domestic firms.[5] Djankov and Hoekman (1999) analyse enterprise-level panel data for the Czech Republic. In their summary statistics they show that multinationals provide higher levels of training than domestic firms.

Sousa (2001) appears to provide the most comprehensive analysis of training activities of multinationals. Using detailed data on workplaces in the UK, he finds that multinationals are more likely to provide training, as well as higher intensities of training, than domestic firms, while controlling for a number of workplace and sector-specific characteristics. Using a matched firm and worker-level dataset for Ghanaian manufacturing firms, Görg, Strobl and Walsh (2002) find that workers who are employed by and receive training in foreign firms experience more rapid wage growth than workers trained in domestic firms. This is consistent with their theoretical model, according to which training provided by foreign firms is more productive than that of domestic firms and, hence, workers trained in foreign firms have steeper wage profiles.

The aforementioned studies hint at the potential for spillovers through the movement of highly trained and experienced workers from multinationals to domestic firms. Other empirical studies show that inward FDI increases wages paid by domestic firms; see e.g. Aitken, Harrison and Lipsey (1996), Girma, Greenaway and Wakelin (2001) and Lipsey and Sjöholm (2004). Under certain assumptions, such findings may be interpreted as providing indirect evidence for spillovers through labour mobility, thereby leading to higher wages in domestic firms. However, as far as we can tell, no study to date has attempted to determine whether the domestic firms that receive the new workers actually benefit from spillovers.

III. Description of the Data

The data used in this paper are drawn from a firm-level survey of manufacturing firms in Ghana. The survey is part of the Regional Programme for Enterprise Development (RPED), an extensive data collection effort for a number of African countries, organised initially by the World Bank.[6] The data consist of five waves of an annual sample of Ghanaian manufacturing firms in the food processing, bakeries, textiles and garments, wood products, furniture, metal and machinery sectors, covering the years 1991–1997.[7]

[5] Pack (2001) similarly refers to evidence for Taiwan that managers from multinationals leave to set up their own business.

[6] Collection of the data for Ghana was carried out by a team from the Centre for the Study of African Economies (CSAE), University of Oxford, the University of Ghana, Legon, and the Ghana Statistical Office; it was funded by the Overseas Development Administration in the UK.

[7] The last two waves were conducted two years apart so that information for the prior year was collected retrospectively.

These sectors comprise about 70 percent of total manufacturing employment in Ghana.[8] As is standard for most firm-level panel data, the dataset includes information on the level of output, total expenditures on wages, the replacement value of the capital stock, the level of value added, and the level of employment.[9]

In order to measure spillovers through worker mobility one would, in an ideal world, like to have data on the history of all workers in firms so as to trace whether they have had any work experience in, or have been trained by, multinational companies before joining the current firm. Using such data, one would then be able to determine whether a firm that employs such workers becomes more technology intensive, uses better technology and, ultimately, is more efficient and productive. Unsurprisingly, neither our data, nor data for other countries of which we are aware, provide such information.

However, the Ghana data do provide specific information on characteristics of the owners/chairmen (also referred to as entrepreneurs) of private domestic firms. This allows us to investigate whether domestic firms benefit from their entrepreneur having received training or gained work experience in a foreign firm. Specifically, we can identify three distinct types of previous contact with foreign firms: first, whether the owner/chairman has received any explicit training by foreign firms in the past; second, whether the owners' immediate previous experience was in a foreign firm within the same industry as that of their current firm; or, third, whether the owner worked for a foreign firm in some other industry. Furthermore, we are able to ascertain whether the owners had any previous experience working in the same industry in general.[10] For our purposes, we are interested in investigating whether training and/or experience of the owner/chairman in a foreign firm affects firm-level productivity. We create zero–one-type dummy variables to indicate this contact.

The RPED data also include information on the schooling of the owner/chairman. In some waves, there is information on the age at which the individual left school and what qualification he/she achieved; in other waves, only information on the former is available. Where possible we use

[8] An initial sample of 200 firms was drawn from the 1987 Ghana Census of Manufacturing Activities, stratified by size, sector and location. It should be noted that in the sampling, large firms were oversampled. When firms closed down over the period they were replaced with firms in the same size, sector and location category.

[9] Nominal values are deflated using sectoral output price deflators.

[10] These questions were re-asked if the firm changed ownership/chairmanship. Given that the information on actual employment by a foreign employer only pertains to the experience immediately prior to becoming owner/chairman of the firm questioned, we are unable to identify those who may have worked for a foreign firm, although not immediately prior to becoming the owner/chairman of their current firm.

both types of information to construct years of schooling. We explicitly use this variable to proxy for the level of human capital, excluding foreign training and experience, of the individual in question.

The dataset includes information on a total of 278 domestic manufacturing firms. After dropping observations with missing values for output, capital, material inputs, employment, or for indicators of foreign experience/training, we ended up with data on 228 firms. Of these, 32 had owners with training or work experience in foreign firms. In particular, the owners of 12 firms had immediate prior experience working in foreign firms in the same industry, nine had immediate prior experience working with foreign firms in different industries, and 13 had undergone training provided by foreign firms. Only two had owners who both worked for and received training from a foreign multinational.

Table 1 reports some summary statistics on the percentages of firms with owners with foreign training/experience (FT/E) compared to firms with owners without FT/E. The first column shows the distribution of firms with FT/E across manufacturing sectors, the second shows the equivalent sectoral distribution for firms without FT/E. It should be noted that firms with owners with FT/E are more prevalent in the furniture and metals sectors, which are arguably the most technology-intensive (broad) sectoral categories. The third column reports the share of firms in a sector with FT/E relative to the total number of firms in the sector. Again, this indicates the importance of the metals and furniture sectors where 18.6 and 20.4 percent of firms, respectively, are run by entrepreneurs with FT/E.

Some further summary statistics over the entire period, 1991–1997, for domestic firms by the incidence of FT/E are provided in Table 2. These are: total factor productivity (*tfp*),[11] output (q), value added (*vad*), total

Table 1. *Percentages of firms with and without foreign training/experience*

	Sectoral distribution of firms		Firms with FT/E as % of total
	With FT/E	Without FT/E	
Food processing	6.3	11.7	8.0
Bakeries	0.0	11.2	0.0
Textiles	18.8	24.5	11.1
Wood products	9.4	8.2	15.8
Furniture	31.3	19.9	20.4
Metals and machinery	34.4	24.5	18.6
Total	100.0	100.0	14.0
Total number of firms	32	196	

[11] See Section IV for a description of how TFP is calculated.

Table 2. *Summary statistics by ownership with and without foreign training/experience, mean and standard deviation*

	Without		With		
	Mean	Std. dev.	Mean	Std. dev.	Diff.
log(*tfp*)	−0.389	1.548	0.296	1.698	***
log(*q*)	10.989	2.410	13.064	2.654	***
log(*vad*)	9.690	2.537	11.770	2.688	***
log (*l*)	2.642	1.205	3.871	1.469	***
log(*k/l*)	7.812	2.044	9.309	2.245	***
log(*m/l*)	7.748	1.890	8.516	1.924	***

Note: ***difference statistically significant at 1%.

employment (l), capital per worker (k/l), and material inputs per worker (m/l). All variables are expressed in logs. First of all, there is substantial variation in the data, as indicated by the standard deviations. As can also be seen, domestic firms owned or run by entrepreneurs with experience and/or training in foreign firms are significantly larger, in terms of output, value added or employment than other domestic firms. In addition, they are more intensive in both capital and labour usage and have higher total factor productivity. These differences are all statistically significant at the 1 percent level.

These descriptive statistics provide preliminary evidence in support of the idea that managers who moved from multinationals to domestic firms run enterprises that are "better" than others. This may indicate that such individuals bring some of the knowledge from their previous experience with them, which then "spills over" to the new firm. The figures are, of course, averages over fairly heterogeneous firms and the summary statistics may confound the effects of different sector, firm or owner characteristics. We therefore turn to an econometric analysis in order to disentangle the effect of foreign experience/training from other variables impacting on firm productivity.

IV. Econometric Analysis

In order to examine more precisely the existence of spillovers through the movement of individuals from foreign multinationals to domestic firms, we model econometrically the effect of entrepreneurs' characteristics on firm-level productivity. We start off with a Cobb–Douglas-type production function similar to, for example, Aitken and Harrison (1999) and Smarzynska-Javorcik (2004). It is written in log values as

$$y_{it} = \beta_0 + \beta_1 k_{it} + \beta_2 l_{it} + u_i + e_{it}, \qquad (1)$$

where y is the log of value added (calculated as total output minus materials) for firm i, and k and l are log values of capital and labour inputs. u_i is an unobserved firm-specific time-invariant effect that may impact on total factor productivity (such as unobserved managerial ability, or industrial sector) and e_{it} is the remaining white noise error term. We use this to obtain estimates of the factor elasticities and derive (log) total factor productivity (TFP) as the firm- and period-specific residual ($u_i + e_{it}$) using a fixed effects estimator. In order to take heterogeneity across sectors into account, we estimated equation (1) for each of the industries available in our sample separately.[12]

Using these TFP estimates we then proceed to examine the effect of entrepreneurs' characteristics on productivity by estimating a regression[13]

$$tfp_{it} = \gamma_0 + \gamma_1 FT_i + \gamma_2 FE_{ij} + \gamma_3 FE_{ih} + \gamma_4 s_i + \gamma_5 E_{ij} + \gamma_6 D_j + \gamma_7 T_t + v_{it}, \tag{2}$$

where *tfp* is the log value of total factor productivity derived from equation (1), D_j and T_t are full sets of industry and time dummies, respectively, and v_{it} is a white noise error term. The first three variables are the dummy variables included to capture any spillovers arising from work experience or training in multinationals. FT_i is equal to one if the owner underwent training by a multinational. FE_{ij} is a dummy equal to one if the owner of the firm had gained experience working for a multinational within the same industry j prior to starting in the domestic firm. FE_{ih} is equal to one if previous experience was gained in a multinational in a different industry $h \neq j$. If all or part of the knowledge accumulated by workers is industry specific, experience gained in multinationals in the same industry would be expected to allow the entrepreneur to improve the performance of the domestic firm, while this effect would be less if experience were gained outside the industry.

We also include two available proxies for the entrepreneur's ability: years of schooling (s_i) and a dummy equal to one if he/she has had any previous experience in the same industry (E_{ij}). If we did not include these variables, our analysis would be subject to a number of criticisms. First, foreign firms may be more likely to hire or provide training to more skilled workers as such employees may already have more and better human capital. In that case, our foreign experience/training variables might only indicate that the

[12] These estimates are provided in the Appendix. As can be seen, the individual coefficients on the inputs seem reasonable. Nevertheless, differences across sectors demonstrate that it is important to take sectoral heterogeneity into account when considering TFP measures.

[13] Given the time-invariant nature of our foreign firm experience/training indicator variables, the estimation of an augmented production function, incorporating the independent variables from equation (2) in equation (1), would not have been possible using a fixed effects estimator.

entrepreneur is of higher ability. In other words, while foreign experience or training may seem to increase productivity, this may only be due to the fact that the owner is better educated and/or more able *a priori*. It may also be the case that better (i.e., more productive) firms can attract better managers. In that case, again, the observed relationship between foreign experience and productivity growth may not be due to a causal relationship between the two variables if we did not control for entrepreneurs' ability. Furthermore, without including E_{ij}, it may be argued that FE_{ij} only captures the effect of experience gained in the industry *per se*, but does not represent an effect particular to experience gained in foreign firms. Of course, these two variables are only imperfect but we would regard them as reasonable proxies to address these issues.[14]

Table 3 reports the results of estimating different specifications of equation (2). Columns (1)–(3) use TFP as the dependent variable. In the initial regression in column (1) we distinguish training received and experience gained in foreign firms. In column (2) we distinguish the latter into experience gained in foreign firms in the same industry (FE_{ij}) and experience gained in foreign firms in other industries (FE_{ih}). From these regressions we find that FE_{ij} has a positive effect on firm-level productivity but that the coefficient on this is statistically insignificant. By contrast, FT and FE_{ih} return negative coefficients. We consider a possible explanation for this result below.

In column (3) we interact the schooling variable with the three foreign experience/training variables (FT, FE_{ij}, FE_{ih}) as well as the dummy for general industry experience (E_{ij}). This allows us to capture the effect whereby employees with higher skills may benefit differently from foreign experience/training or general industry experience than less skilled individuals. Inclusion of the interaction terms leads to some interesting changes in the significance of the spillover variables. For within-industry experience (FE_{ij}) we now find a positive and statistically significant coefficient, suggesting that owners who gained experience in multinationals in the same industry indeed run more productive firms. Thus, this provides evidence in support of the idea that there are spillovers through worker movements, where domestic entrepreneurs bring with them knowledge accumulated in the multinationals and put it to use in the domestic firm. The negative coefficient on the interaction term also suggests that the least skilled entrepreneurs (in terms of years of schooling) can gain more from experience in multinationals. Hence, prior human capital and training received in foreign firms are not necessarily

[14] Due to data limitations we are not able to include any other variables for owners' ability. However, we are reassured by the fact that years of schooling is widely used in the labour economics literature to proxy individuals' ability; see Willis (1987) for a review of empirical estimates of the human capital earnings function.

Table 3. *Basic regression results*

	(1) TFP	(2) TFP	(3) TFP	(4) Lab. prod.	(5) Output	(6) Value added
FT_i	−0.606	−0.725	0.437	2.239	−1.042	−0.436
	(0.314)*	(0.323)**	(1.540)	(1.343)*	(1.772)	(1.700)
FE_i	0.163					
	(0.744)					
FE_{ij}		0.665	4.977	4.885	6.408	6.072
		(0.834)	(2.285)**	(2.494)*	(2.509)**	(2.564)**
FE_{ih}		−1.915	−1.374	−0.490	−1.816	−2.417
		(0.980)*	(0.681)**	(0.688)	(1.016)*	(1.160)**
$FT_i * s_i$			−0.101	−0.253	0.020	−0.024
			(0.138)	(0.120)**	(0.151)	(0.143)
$FE_{ij} * s_i$			−0.430	−0.448	−0.555	−0.531
			(0.226)*	(0.246)*	(0.241)**	(0.251)**
$FE_{ih} * s_i$			0.122	−0.009	0.128	0.151
			(0.057)**	(0.057)	(0.082)	(0.091)
s_i	0.068	0.061	0.204	0.181	0.247	0.261
	(0.025)***	(0.025)**	(0.049)***	(0.040)***	(0.075)***	(0.085)***
E_{ij}	−0.391	−0.486	1.582	1.129	1.712	1.721
	(0.281)	(0.285)*	(0.703)**	(0.630)*	(1.056)	(1.209)
$E_{ij} * s_i$			−0.171	−0.122	−0.202	−0.196
			(0.055)***	(0.046)***	(0.085)**	(0.094)**
Constant	−1.341	−1.252	−2.781	5.151	8.588	8.539
	(0.329)***	(0.329)***	(0.621)***	(0.694)***	(1.049)***	(1.158)***
Observations	725	725	725	751	763	751
R-squared	0.13	0.14	0.21	0.39	0.41	0.42

Notes: Robust standard errors in parentheses, clustered around firm identifier. *Statistically significant at 10%; **significant at 5%; ***significant at 1%. Regressions include sectoral and time dummies.

complements. Entrepreneurs' individual human capital may benefit most from additional learning in multinationals compared to well-educated domestic entrepreneurs who may gain only little additional knowledge. Specifically, the point estimates of the coefficient on the interaction term suggest that the positive effect from experience gained in foreign firms vanishes for individuals with more than 11 years of schooling.[15]

Yet there is also evidence that gaining experience in multinationals outside an entrepreneur's own industry has a negative effect on productivity. Again, however, we find that this effect is lower, the more skilled the entrepreneur. One possible explanation for this is that the knowledge obtained in multinationals is largely industry specific and cannot be easily

[15] The mean value of schooling is 10.8, with a median of 10. This also explains why FE_{ij} is not significantly different from zero in column (2), as the mean/median value is close to the value of s for which the effect of FE_{ij} is equal to zero.

transferred to businesses in different industries. It appears that, at least in the short run, these entrepreneurs run firms that are less productive than the average domestic firms. This may, perhaps, be due to their having to spend time building up or improving their industry-specific knowledge. Another possible reason is that the skills acquired in foreign firms may be even more industry specific than those acquired in domestic firms. However, a further, not mutually exclusive explanation is that work experience in foreign firms in other sectors is likely to be negatively correlated with the degree of general experience in the same industry. If the dummy for general industry experience (E_{ij}) and its interaction with schooling are unable to capture all of the differences in the degree of same-industry experience, then the lack of such experience may in part be captured by FE_{ih}.

The coefficient on training provided by multinationals is now positive with a negative interaction term, although both coefficients are statistically insignificant. This suggests that training does not appear to be an important channel for spillovers.

In terms of the other two control variables included, the years of schooling variable on its own shows consistently positive coefficients in all specifications, which suggests that more able individuals run more productive firms, as expected. Previous experience in the industry is positively related to TFP in column (3), although the negative interaction term indicates that experience is less valuable for more skilled entrepreneurs.

Although TFP is arguably the most appropriate measure for capturing knowledge spillovers resulting from labour mobility, it is also insightful to examine other proxies of firm performance. Thus columns (4)–(6) display results for estimations similar to those reported above, but here we use log values of labour productivity (value added per employee), total output and total value added, respectively, as dependent variables. In terms of total output and total value added, the results are remarkably similar to the TFP estimations in column (3), both in terms of statistical significance levels and the magnitude of the coefficients. In contrast, there are some differences in terms of the labour productivity estimation. Specifically, training in foreign multinationals now has a statistically significant positive effect on firm performance, although this decreases with the level of schooling of the entrepreneur, as indicated by the significantly negative interaction term. Moreover, we now find that foreign firm experience in other sectors has no statistically significant effect. Nevertheless, our previous result of a significant positive—although decreasing with schooling—impact of experience in a foreign firm in the same industry still holds for the labour productivity estimation.

But does the positive effect of experience gained in foreign firms in the same industry merely reflect the fact that highly productive firms attract entrepreneurs who have gained experience in multinationals in the same industry? These firms may provide a highly attractive working environment for the new entrepreneur. In that case the spillover dummies would, of course, be endogenous. But this criticism would not apply if these domestic firms were established by the owners and did not have a history of existence before the owner joined. Fortunately, our dataset allows us to determine whether an owner established a firm himself and whether the business had been run by the owners' family. By focusing on these two groups of firms we should be able to avoid possible bias arising from situations where productive firms attract experienced high-ability entrepreneurs.

Table 4, therefore, shows the results of estimating the same specifications as in Table 3 using data only for firms that were founded by the current owner or that were run by the owners' family before he/she took over ownership. Reassuringly, the results for TFP remain very similar to the results in Table 3 in terms of magnitude and statistical significance.

Table 4. *Alternative regression results for firms established by owner or family*

	(1) TFP	(2) TFP	(3) TFP	(4) Lab. prod.	(5) Output	(6) Value added
FT_i	−0.559	−0.673	0.351	2.068	−1.123	−0.542
	(0.308)*	(0.323)**	(1.465)	(1.305)	(1.675)	(1.602)
FE_i	0.123					
	(0.770)					
FE_{ij}		0.589	5.058	5.033	6.393	6.071
		(0.897)	(2.445)**	(2.528)**	(2.761)**	(2.841)**
FE_{ih}		−1.737	−0.984	−0.256	−1.147	−1.634
		(0.952)*	(0.775)	(0.846)	(1.141)	(1.276)
$FT_i * s_i$			−0.089	−0.236	0.036	−0.005
			(0.130)	(0.114)**	(0.143)	(0.133)
$FE_{ij} * s_i$			−0.447	−0.461	−0.570	−0.550
			(0.239)*	(0.248)*	(0.262)**	(0.274)**
$FE_{ih} * s_i$			0.097	−0.023	0.086	0.100
			(0.064)	(0.070)	(0.091)	(0.099)
s_i	0.075	0.068	0.219	0.192	0.270	0.286
	(0.025)***	(0.025)***	(0.051)***	(0.042)***	(0.080)***	(0.091)***
E_{ij}	−0.262	−0.364	1.842	1.329	2.138	2.195
	(0.274)	(0.282)	(0.725)**	(0.646)**	(1.113)*	(1.278)*
$E_{ij} * s_i$			−0.181	−0.130	−0.219	−0.215
			(0.057)***	(0.048)***	(0.090)**	(0.100)**
Constant	−2.311	−1.908	−3.687	4.914	9.163	7.765
	(0.641)***	(0.512)***	(0.775)***	(0.846)***	(1.137)***	(1.269)***
Observations	697	697	697	721	731	721
R-squared	0.13	0.14	0.21	0.41	0.42	0.43

Notes: Robust standard errors in parentheses, clustered around firm identifier. *Statistically significant at 10%; **significant at 5%; ***significant at 1%. Regressions include sectoral and time dummies.

The only difference is that the impact of experience in foreign firms in other industries is no longer statistically significant. In terms of the other performance measures we find, importantly, that all results for TFP hold. The only exception is that for labour productivity there is no longer a positive impact of training in foreign firms. This suggests that the positive effect of training on labour productivity reported in Table 3 is not robust to ensuring that entrepreneurs are not simply hired by more productive firms.

Taken together, our analysis provides consistent evidence that domestic firms, run by entrepreneurs who gained experience while working for multinationals in the same industry before running their own firms, are more productive than other firms.[16] This effect diminishes, however, for more skilled (in terms of years of schooling) entrepreneurs. This may be interpreted as a sign that the knowledge accumulated by entrepreneurs while employed in multinationals can be usefully applied in the new domestic firm in the same industry.[17] The fact that there is no consistent positive effect if the entrepreneur gained his/her experience in multinationals in a different industry suggests that the knowledge obtained in multinationals is largely industry specific and therefore cannot be easily transferred to businesses in different industries. In some specifications there is indeed evidence that these entrepreneurs run firms which are less productive than the average domestic firms, although this is not robust to different specifications. One explanation for such negative results might be that such entrepreneurs have to spend time building up or improving their industry-specific knowledge since the skills acquired in foreign firms may be even more industry specific than those acquired in domestic firms.[18]

While these results concerning experience gained in foreign firms provide some evidence that there are spillovers from worker mobility, there is

[16] We also carried out a number of further robustness checks. First, we dropped the foreign training variable as it did not provide a consistently significant effect across alternative specifications. We also ran regressions excluding the schooling variable, as well as excluding jointly the schooling variable and the dummy variable capturing general industry experience. These regressions were also estimated only on the sample of firms that were founded by the current owner or were run by the owners' family. The results suggest the robustness of our previous findings. These additional results are not reported here, but can be obtained from the authors on request.

[17] Thus, our findings provide a counterbalance to Smarzynska-Javorcik (2004) who argues and provides evidence for Lithuania that domestic firms only benefit from inter-industry but not from intra-industry spillovers from multinationals.

[18] However, another possible and not mutually exclusive explanation is that our proxy for own-industry experience, a simple zero–one-type dummy variable, does not fully capture the impact of own-industry experience, so that the proxy for experience in a multinational in other industries in part captures the lack of own-industry experience.

no consistent evidence to suggest that firms also benefit if their owners receive only training in multinationals. As the training variable only captures explicit training provided by multinationals it may, however, be the case that we are not able to measure adequately other types of more informal acquisitions of human capital and/or that explicit training only constitutes a small proportion of total human capital acquired in a foreign-owned firm.

V. Conclusions

While there is a large empirical literature on productivity spillovers from foreign to domestic firms, it treats the channels through which these spillover effects work as a black box. Some theoretical work has recently stressed the importance of the movement of workers from foreign to domestic firms as a channel for spillovers. To date, however, there are no empirical studies which examine this issue in detail. This paper constitutes an attempt to fill this gap in the literature.

While our results focus solely on one possible mechanism for spillovers through worker mobility, namely the movement of the owner/chairman of the firm, they suggest that firms which are run by owners who worked for multinationals in the same industry immediately prior to opening up their own firm have higher productivity levels than other firms. This implies that these entrepreneurs bring with them some of the knowledge accumulated in the multinational which can be usefully applied in the new domestic firm. In contrast, we do not find any consistent positive effects on firm performance if the owner had experience in multinationals in other industries, or received only training by multinationals.

Our analysis treats the decision of the entrepreneur to move from a foreign to a domestic firm as exogenous. In a sense this is quite limiting; it may therefore be of interest to endogenise the decision by specifying and estimating an equation that describes it. Although this is beyond the scope of the current paper, it provides an interesting avenue for future research.

Appendix

Table A1. *TFP estimation results*

	(1) Food processing	(2) Bakeries	(3) Textiles	(4) Wood products	(5) Furniture	(6) Metals and machinery
k	0.182	0.101	0.323	0.118	0.125	0.123
	(0.122)	(0.123)	(0.103)***	(0.070)*	(0.076)	(0.064)*
l	0.818	0.310	0.483	0.552	0.243	0.571
	(0.227)***	(0.253)	(0.164)***	(0.291)*	(0.190)	(0.199)***
Constant	7.380	9.113	5.909	10.011	8.961	8.391
	(1.747)***	(1.305)***	(0.920)***	(1.748)***	(1.083)***	(1.054)***
Observations	156	115	269	94	237	310
Number of firms	33	22	56	22	50	72
R-squared	0.34	0.76	0.56	0.29	0.24	0.18

Notes: Fixed effect estimation, standard errors in parentheses. *Statistically significant at 10%; **significant at 5%; ***significant at 1%. Regressions include time dummies.

References

Aitken, B. J. and Harrison, A. E. (1999), Do Domestic Firms Benefit from Direct Foreign Investment? Evidence from Venezuela, *American Economic Review 89*, 605–618.

Aitken, B., Harrison, A. and Lipsey, R. E. (1996), Wages and Foreign Ownership: A Comparative Study of Mexico, Venezuela, and the United States, *Journal of International Economics 40*, 345–371.

Alfaro, L., Chanda, A., Kalemli-Ozcan, S. and Sayek, S. (2004), FDI and Economic Growth: The Role of Local Financial Markets, *Journal of International Economics 64*, 89–112.

Balasubramanyam, V. N., Sapsford, D. and Salisu, M. (1996), Foreign Direct Investment and Growth in EP and IS Countries, *Economic Journal 106*, 92–105.

Blomström, M. and Kokko, A. (1998), Multinational Corporations and Spillovers, *Journal of Economic Surveys 12*, 247–277.

Blomström, M. and Sjöholm, F. (1999), Technology Transfer and Spillovers: Does Local Participation with Multinationals Matter?, *European Economic Review 43*, 915–923.

Borensztein, E., De Gregorio, J. and Lee, J. W. (1998), How Does Foreign Direct Investment Affect Economic Growth?, *Journal of International Economics 45*, 115–135.

Caves, R. E. (1996), *Multinational Enterprise and Economic Analysis*, Cambridge University Press, Cambridge.

Djankov, S. and Hoekman, B. (1999), Foreign Investment and Productivity Growth in Czech Enterprises, *World Bank Economic Review 14*, 49–64.

Evans, D. S. and Jovanovic, B. (1989), An Estimated Model of Entrepreneurial Choice under Liquidity Constraints, *Journal of Political Economy 97*, 808–827.

Evans, D. S. and Leighton, L. S. (1989), Some Empirical Aspects of Entrepreneurship, *American Economic Review 79*, 519–535.

Fosfuri, A., Motta, M. and Rønde, T. (2001), Foreign Direct Investment and Spillovers through Workers' Mobility, *Journal of International Economics 53*, 205–222.

Gershenberg, I. (1987), The Training and Spread of Managerial Know-how: A Comparative Analysis of Multinational and other Firms in Kenya, *World Development 15*, 931–939.

Girma, S., Greenaway, D. and Wakelin, K. (2001), Who Benefits from Foreign Direct Investment in the UK?, *Scottish Journal of Political Economy 48*, 119–133.

Glass, A. J. and Saggi, K. (2002), Multinational Firms and Technology Transfer, *Scandinavian Journal of Economics 104*, 495–513.

Görg, H. and Greenaway, D. (2004), Much Ado About Nothing? Do Domestic Firms Really Benefit from Foreign Direct Investment?, *World Bank Research Observer 19*, 171–197.

Görg, H. and Strobl, E. (2001), Multinational Companies and Productivity Spillovers: A Meta-analysis, *Economic Journal 111*, F723–F739.

Görg, H., Strobl, E. and Walsh, F. (2002), Why Do Foreign Firms Pay More? The Role of On-the-Job Training, Discussion Paper no. 590, IZA, Bonn.

ILO (1981), *Multinationals' Training Practices and Developments*, International Labour Office, Geneva.

Keller, W. and Yeaple, S. (2003), Multinational Enterprises, International Trade, and Productivity Growth: Firm-level Evidence from the United States, NBER Working Paper no. 9504.

Kokko, A. (1994), Technology, Market Characteristics, and Spillovers, *Journal of Development Economics 43*, 279–293.

Lindsey, C. W. (1986), Transfer of Technology to the ASEAN Region by US Transnational Corporations, *ASEAN Economic Bulletin 3*, 225–247.

Lipsey, R. E. and Sjöholm, F. (2004), FDI and Wage Spillovers in Indonesian Manufacturing, *Review of World Economics/Weltwirtschaftliches Archiv 134*, 321–332.

Lipsey, R. E. and Sjöholm, F. (2005), Host Country Impacts of Inward FDI: Why Such Different Answers?, in M. Blomström, E. Graham and T. Moran (eds.), *The Impact of Foreign Direct Investment on Development*, Institute for International Economics, Washington, DC.

Markusen, J. R. (2002), *Multinational Firms and the Theory of International Trade*, MIT Press, Cambridge, MA.

Pack, H. (2001), The Role of Foreign Technology Acquisition in Taiwanese Growth, *Industrial and Corporate Change 10*, 713–734.

Smarzynska-Javorcik, B. (2004), Does Foreign Direct Investment Increase the Productivity of Domestic Firms? In Search of Spillovers through Backward Linkages, *American Economic Review 94*, 605–627.

Sousa, N. (2001), Multinationals and Technology Transfer through Labour Training, paper presented at CEPR Workshop on Labour Market Effects of European Foreign Investments, Dublin, July 2001.

UN (1998), *World Investment Report 1998*, United Nations, Geneva.

Willis, R. J. (1987), Wage Determinants: A Survey and Reinterpretation of Human Capital Earnings Functions, in O. Ashenfelter, P. Layard and R. Layard (eds.), *Handbook of Labor Economics, Vol. 1*, North-Holland, Amsterdam.

First version submitted January 2004;
final version received July 2004.

Chapter 14

Creating Backward Linkages from Multinationals: Is there a Role for Financial Incentives?

*Holger Görg, Aoife Hanley, and Eric Strobl**

Abstract

We investigate whether government subsidies encourage foreign multinationals to create linkages with domestic suppliers. To this end we use a unique panel dataset of foreign multinationals located in Ireland for which we have exhaustive information on grant receipt. Our results indicate that while European and US foreign plants develop backward linkages independently of grant receipt, multinationals from other parts of the world respond positively to government support. Our results hold even when controlling for the possible endogeneity of grants and the boundedness of the linkage variable. We conclude that governments should not apply a "one-size-fits-all" approach to incentivizing foreign multinationals.

1. Introduction

There is consensus in the international economics literature that backward linkages between multinational enterprises (MNEs) and domestic suppliers can be good for the domestic economy. These benefits arise for a number of reasons. First, linkages may induce increased demand for inputs inducing employment and growth in domestic upstream firms (see Markusen and Venables, 1999).

Related to this, Rodríguez-Clare (1996) argues that MNEs typically produce more complex products than domestic firms, acting as a further spur to local suppliers to upgrade their own technology base.[1] Second, although MNEs are likely to displace some local domestic firms, as shown by Alfaro and Rodríguez-Clare (2004, AR hereafter), their ability to create employment for local suppliers, often more than offsets this displacement loss.[2] Finally, evidence from Javorcik (2004), Blalock and Gertler (2008), and Girma et al. (2008) for various countries suggests that linkages stimulate the upgrading of domestic suppliers where demand for highly specialized inputs increases, opening up the potential for knowledge spillovers from multinationals.[3]

While backward linkages may have these positive effects on domestic firms, such effects do not arise automatically. Indeed, research shows that linkages are created and produce benefits, only when certain conditions are met (Rodríguez-Clare, 1996; Larraín et al., 2000; Belderbos et al., 2001 (BCK hereafter); Alfaro et al., 2006). For example, local suppliers need to be able to manufacture inputs to a sufficiently high capacity before securing the custom of foreign MNEs. Others such as Kwon and Chun (2009) and Yaşar and Morrison Paul (2009) point out that local suppliers have to be technologically advanced to absorb knowledge spillovers and deal with the demand for

* Görg: Kiel Institute for the World Economy and University of Kiel, Hindenburgufer 66 24105, Kiel, Germany. Tel: +49 431 8814 258; E-mail: goerg@economics.uni-kiel.de; also CEPR and GlobID (Aarhus School of Business). Hanley: Kiel Institute for the World Economy and University of Kiel, Hindenburgufer 66 24105, Kiel, Germany. Tel: +49 431 8814 339; E-mail: hanley@economics.uni-kiel.de. Strobl: Ecole Polytechnique, Département d'Economie, 91128 Palaiseau, France. Tel: +33 169 333416; E-mail: eric.strobl@polytechnique.edu. We are grateful to Beata Javorcik, Ted Moran, participants at a workshop at the Kiel Institute, and anonymous referees for helpful comments on earlier drafts.

specialized inputs. This latter reason is why backward linkages are more often a feature of FDI from industrialized home countries to industrialized host countries. In this case, local procurement markets are well developed. Similarly, industrialized countries usually possess well-functioning capital markets enabling domestic upstream firms to set up, expand, and upgrade their operations as suppliers of inputs to foreign MNEs (Alfaro et al., 2006).

The above points make it clear that, from a policy perspective, governments interested in maximizing the value of linkages need to understand why and how MNEs form backward linkages. This has been the subject of recent research (see, for example, Görg and Ruane, 2000 (hereafter GR); BCK, 2001; AR, 2004; Kiyota et al., 2008). Yet, despite growing interest in the subject, questions remain.

Particularly under-researched is the extent to which foreign MNEs respond to government incentives by setting up backward linkages with domestic suppliers—a highly important question from a government perspective. The aim of this paper is to fill this literature gap. We explore how MNE affiliates respond to host government grants by creating linkages, using the case study of Ireland. To our knowledge, this question has not been tackled in formal econometric work.[4]

Another novel aspect of our paper is to establish whether foreign plants respond differently to grants depending on the MNE's country of origin. The Rodríguez-Clare (1996) model predicts that MNEs are more likely to generate linkages and impact the host economy as the cultural and/or geographic distance increases. Accordingly, the anticipated effect of grants in motivating linkages with domestic industry differs according to the FDI source.

We look at these issues using two empirical approaches. The first, similar to, among others, BCK (2001) and AR (2004), regresses a measure of local linkages on firm characteristics, exploring the importance of firm heterogeneity for linkage creation. The second approach, in line with Kiyota et al. (2008) estimates the relative demand for locally procured inputs based on a translog cost function. Reassuringly, both approaches provide similar results, indicating the robustness of our findings. Furthermore, we control for the possible endogeneity of grant receipt and allow for the bounded nature of our dependent variable using an endogenous tobit estimation approach.

Our analysis using unique plant-level data for Irish manufacturing firms (1983 to 2000) was created by linking information from an official plant-level survey (providing data on input sourcing, among others) with exhaustive plant-level information on government subsidies provided in Ireland. Arguably, Ireland is a good case study: the steady stream of FDI (the mid-1980s to early 1990s) preceded an increase in domestic supplier sales of 83%, a productivity increase of 36% and employment of 33%. Some Irish suppliers went on to become international subcontractors (Condron, 2007).

The main finding, and most interesting from a policy perspective, is that Rest of the World (ROW) multinationals, respond positively to government subsidies in terms of linkage creation, whereas US and European MNEs in Ireland develop backward linkages quite independently of government grants. It could be conjectured that different factors other than financial incentives override government efforts to influence linkages.

The policy implications of our findings are two-fold. First, our results suggest that governments should not apply a "one-size-fits-all" approach to incentivizing foreign MNEs. Only in the case of ROW firms can it be said that grants deliver value in generating linkages. Second, linkage formation is influenced by factors other than financial incentives. Particularly, there is a negative relationship between an MNE's export intensity and linkage creation.

Our paper is structured as follows. The first section supplies background on the Irish grant system and the role of foreign linkages. Then follows a description of the data used followed by a section detailing our two econometric approaches and presenting results. Concluding remarks are provided in the final section.

2. Foreign Firms in Ireland and Domestic Suppliers

Ireland is a country which has prospered from having attracted FDI from flagship companies in various export oriented sectors; for example, Intel and Dell (ICT sector). But Ireland has only relatively recently maximized its benefits from FDI by shaping and reshaping policy on the basis of experience.

In the early 1980s, Irish policymakers conceded that Irish suppliers were failing to make the most of their potential to supply affiliates of foreign firms (NESC, 1982). The National Linkage Programme sponsored by the Industrial Development Agency (IDA) was introduced to make more of these opportunities.[5] This program focused in its initial phase on the purchase of raw materials and other inputs (backward linkages) and on the sales of intermediate goods (forward linkages) between indigenous firms and foreign affiliates.

The program targeted potential purchasers and sub-suppliers in the most promising export-oriented sectors and identified potential "winners." It created a better environment for MNE input suppliers, assisting them in upgrading technology. Understandably, the presence of reliable and skilled suppliers is only one criterion for linkage creation. In the absence of strong local suppliers, grant aid is of little use in stimulating linkages (Rodríguez-Clare, 1996; BCK, 2001).

While the National Linkage Programme mostly targeted domestic suppliers, the Irish government also targeted financial incentives towards multinationals. Although employment generation has been key to awarding grants, there have also been other objectives. Indeed, grants were awarded in Ireland on the basis of linking foreign firms into the local economy. One qualifying reason for grant support was that the project could tap into skill-intensive indigenous suppliers, reflecting the policy goal that supported MNEs create or maintain employment, "that would not be maintained without assistance and will increase output and value added within the economy" (KPMG, 2003).

Note, however, grants are production-related subsidies, rather than incentives awarded to create linkages, so why should linkages arise? First, linkage creation is one explicit goal of grant support.[6] Second, in our analysis we control for other factors in addition to potential endogeneity of grant receipt. Hence, assuming the validity of our empirical approach, the identification of any effect of subsidies on linkages suggests a causal relationship. Although firms may also use grants for other purposes, they are at least in part used to create linkages.

Accordingly, we investigate whether grants impact linkage creation. Specifically, we look at grants administered by the Irish Industrial Development Agency (IDA) which promotes foreign firms. Despite some changes in grant provision over time, awards made within the period captured by our data can be summarized as follows: grant recipients were involved in the production of goods with an export bias, were technologically advanced, or exhibited linkages with skilled Irish suppliers. Additionally, grants could be extended to sectors facing stiff international competition (see KPMG, 2003). Total grant levels were negotiated bilaterally between the company and IDA but did not generally exceed certain capital cost thresholds, usually between 45% and 60%.[7]

3. Data Description

For our analysis, we use two datasets covering the years 1983 to 2002, and collected by Forfás, the Irish policy and advisory board. The first source is the Irish Economy Expenditure (IEE) survey (more recently, the Annual Business Survey (ABS)). It comprises an annual survey of manufacturers in Ireland with at least 20 employees, extending to over 80% of the MNE population.

The data provide information on intermediates (both domestic and imported). Also included are sales (an output measure), employment, exports, plant age, nationality, and a three-digit sector of production.[8] The foreign ownership information relates to the last year in the data and therefore is time invariant. However, this is not an issue as most FDI takes the form of greenfield investment where ownership is time invariant anyway. Importantly for our research question, Forfás also holds exhaustive annual data on all grants paid to manufacturing plants since 1972 which are linked via a firm-level identifier. Specifically, our analysis focuses on foreign MNE affiliates in Ireland (1069 plants in all).

It is worth mentioning that Irish industry is dominated by large MNEs which account for much of the overall output and exports (Lane and Ruane, 2006) and are highly active in a small number of knowledge-intensive, export-oriented manufacturing sectors.

We can calculate a linkage indicator in line with the literature, as based on Hirschman (1958), as the ratio of materials and/or components sourced locally over total inputs (see e.g. Cohen, 1973; Wilson, 1992; GR, 2000; AR, 2004).[9]

Table 1 gives an initial breakdown of key variables in the data by ownership status. Clearly, the vast majority of plants are either European or US. Among these MNEs, US plants are the largest (on employment and sales measures). They receive the lion's share of grants (in absolute terms and when measured relative to turnover). Interestingly, all MNE groupings have a similar mean linkage ratio, defined as domestically sourced materials relative to total material inputs, where plants typically procure 29–30% of their total inputs on domestic markets.

Figures 1 and 2 show the simple relationship between grant receipt and linkages.[10] The kernel density plots in Figure 1 show how the distribution of linkages varies according to whether plants receive grant assistance. Plot 1 includes plants which do not receive such grants. For firms receiving grants, one can observe the distribution of linkages based on whether grant assistance is classified as medium (plot 2) or high (plot 3). All plots bear a striking similarity to each other. They are U-shaped as most plants have no, or very low, linkages with domestic upstream plants. On the basis of Figure 1, the tendency for plants to conduct comparatively little procurement from domestic suppliers does not appear to be influenced by grant assistance. Figure 2 further controls for the different nationalities of foreign plants, viz. European, US, or ROW. Again we observe a U-shaped distribution with the majority of plants conducting little or no local procurement.

To visualize the extent to which the origin of FDI matters for linkages, we estimate several simple regressions with FDI origin dummies, where the baseline category is European FDI (Table 2). There are no significant differences across the FDI categories, leading us to conclude that European, US, and ROW plants in Ireland conduct similar levels of local procurement. This negligible effect is robust to the technique used.

4. Econometric Analysis

In order to control for other covariates we now turn to a more formal modeling of the determinants of linkages, paying particular attention to grant receipt and FDI origin.

Table 1. Breakdown of Key Variables for Foreign Firms, by Nationality

EU	*Mean*	*Median*	*SD*	*N*
Number of employees	158	88	216	3917
Sales turnover (€000's)	23,428	8426	44,673	3917
Age of firm (*age*)	28	18	26	3917
Material linkage	28.7	15.0	31.4	3917
Ratio of grants to turnover	1.5	0	9.5	3917
Grant amount (€000's)	127.1	0	396.4	3917
US				
Number of employees	223	109	356	3815
Sales turnover (€000's)	89,612	13,848	404,899	3815
Age of firm (*age*)	19	17	13	3815
Material linkage	29.3	20.0	28.9	3815
Ratio of grants to turnover	17.6	0	708.8	3815
Grant amount (€000's)	415.0	0	1988.2	3815
ROW				
Number of employees	182	128	161	963
Sales turnover (€000's)	40,034	13,972	73,154	963
Age of firm (*age*)	23	17	22	963
Material linkage	29.9	20.0	29.1	963
Ratio of grants to turnover	7.6	0	181.6	963
Grant amount (€000's)	249.8	0	1002.6	963

To do so we use two approaches. The first investigates the determinants of linkages calculated as locally sourced inputs over total inputs, by relating the linkages measure to a number of firm characteristics, building on work by GR (2000) and BCK (2001). The second approach estimates relative demand for locally produced inputs from a translog cost function (see Kiyota et al., 2008).

Determinants of Linkages

Implementing the first approach, we estimate the impact of grants on the amount of local procurement by foreign plants using equations of the following form:

$$linkage_{it} = \beta_1 grants_{it} + \beta_2 X_{it} + d_t + d_s + \mu_i + \varepsilon_{it}, \tag{1}$$

where the dependent variable is the linkage ratio of plant i at time t, as defined above in section 3. The right-hand-side variables reflect the costs of establishing linkages. This includes, in our baseline specification, *grants ratio*, defined as the value of grants received in time t relative to the annual turnover of the plant.[11] Subsidies are expected to reduce MNE search costs for local suppliers.

Further variables are included in vector X, in line with similar work. Employment controls for firm size. Large plants are expected to have lower linkages, scale economies making them more self-sufficient than smaller plants (GR, 2000). Several papers support the inclusion of "length of time the MNE operates in the host market" as a

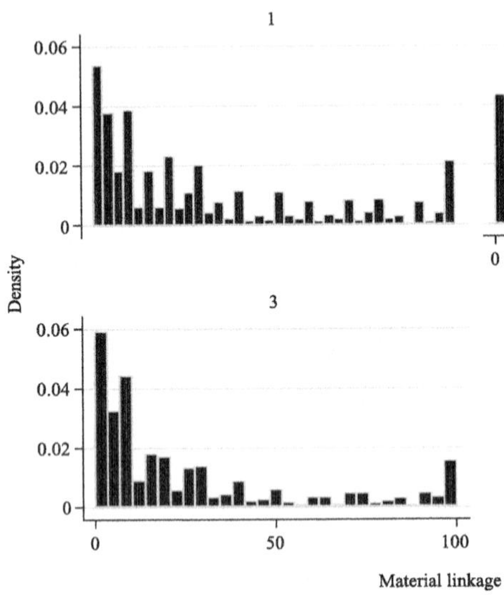

Figure 1. Material Linkage and Grant Receipt

Note: Grant group 1: low grant (grant ratio = 0); grant group 2: medium grant (grant ratio < 3.48 [90th percentile]), grant group 3: high grant (grant ratio > 3.48).

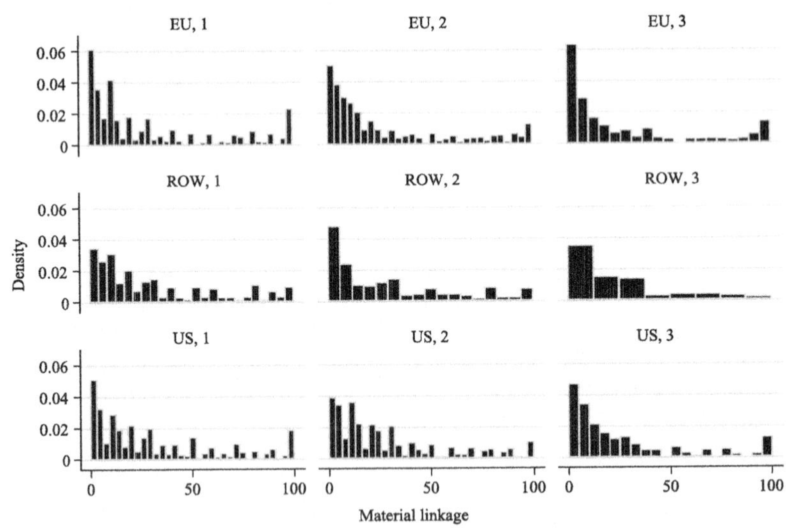

Figure 2. Material Linkage, Nationality, and Grant Receipt

Table 2. Nationality Premia

	OLS	*RE*	*RE Tobit*
US	0.334 (0.684)	0.884 (1.976)	0.702 (0.575)
ROW	1.050 (1.079)	−2.093 (3.066)	−3.154 (1.128)***
Constant	28.054 (1.752)***	29.420 (1.650)***	30.780 (1.050)***
Observations	8695	8695	8695
R-squared	0.01	0.01	
Number of plants	1069	1069	1069

Notes: Bracketed SE; ** and *** significant at 5% and 1%; constant included, year and two-digit sector dummies; dependent variable is ratio of domestic purchased to total inputs; base category European firms.

covariate, where affiliate age exerts a positive effect on linkages (GR, 2000; BCK, 2001; AR, 2004). This expectation is in line with Rauch and Watson (2003), who argue that firms may start with low levels of local sourcing in an unfamiliar environment, but that this may increase over time as customers learn about the quality and reliability of domestic suppliers. Specifically, we include the variable *age*, i.e. age of the MNE affiliate in Ireland.

Foreign plant productivity is another model covariate. Girma and Görg (2004) find that more productive establishments have a higher ratio of purchased inputs (either sourced locally or abroad) to value-added. On this basis, highly productive foreign plants may have a differing capacity to outsource locally than their less productive counterparts. Accordingly, we include MNE productivity (defined as sales per employee), *productivity*.[12]

The export orientation of multinationals may also matter for linkage creation. Specifically, Moran (2001) notes that linkages are likely to be smaller if the MNE affiliate is part of an international network, as inputs are procured through the network at lower cost. Given the fact that much FDI in Ireland is export oriented we control for exports by including the foreign plant export ratio (defined as exports over total turnover), *exports*. Finally, the estimation includes a full set of time and sector dummies (d_t and d_s) as well as a plant-specific effect (μ_i).[13]

Table 3 shows the results for our baseline estimations of equation (1) which are implemented using a fixed effect (within-transformation) panel estimator. Importantly, the grant ratio has no effect on linkages (columns (1) and (3)). This result is robust to defining plant size either in terms of employment (column (1)) or sales (column (3)). Likewise, the alternative definition of the grant variable as the absolute value of a grant does not produce any statistically significant coefficient (column (2)).

In terms of the other covariates, the fixed effects estimations which produce positive elasticities on the size variable suggest that foreign plant growth leads to higher linkages, although the effect is only statistically significant in column (2). Consistent with other work, the positive sign on the MNE affiliate *age* shows greater procurement from local upstream firms over time (GR, 2000; BCK, 2001; AR, 2004). Perhaps somewhat surprisingly, productivity improvements are not associated with more local procurement. Finally, we find a negative association between the export ratio and the extent of local linkages, in line with expectation, although this coefficient is statistically insignificant.

Arguably, our failure to see an effect of grants on linkages happens because grants take time to affect linkages. In order to test for the delayed effects of grants we apply

Table 3. Determinants of Linkages, Basic Specification Using FE Estimator

	(1)	*(2)*	*(3)*	*(4)*	*(5)*
grant ratio	–0.000 (0.00)		–0.000 (0.00)	0.000 (0.00)	
grants		–0.118 (0.076)			–0.072 (0.079)
employment	0.779 (0.41)	0.841 (0.41)**		0.698 (0.47)	0.741 (0.48)
age	0.217 (0.07)***	0.193 (0.07)***	0.217 (0.07)***	0.321 (0.07)***	0.307 (0.07)***
productivity	–1.187 (0.44)***	–1.146 (0.42)***	–1.970 (0.60)***	–1.496 (0.50)***	–1.502 (0.50)***
export ratio sales	–0.011 (0.02)	–0.011 (0.02)	–0.010 (0.02)	0.005 (0.02)	0.005 (0.02)
			0.781 (0.418)		
Observations	8695	8695	8695	7214	7214
No. plants	1069	1069	1069	1004	1004
R-squared	0.01	0.01	0.01	0.04	0.04

Notes: Bracketed SE; ** and *** significant at 5% and 1%; constant included, year and two-digit sector dummies.

Table 4. Separate Regressions, FE

	US	*EU*	*ROW*
employment	1.543 (0.59)***	–0.591 (0.69)	(1.18)
age	0.304 (0.11)***	0.161 (0.10)*	–0.010 (0.18)
productivity	–2.123 (0.60)***	–1.170 (0.84)	2.293 (1.06)**
export ratio	0.040 (0.03)	–0.014 (0.02)	–0.166 (0.04)***
grant ratio	–0.000 (0.00)	–0.032 (0.03)	0.010 (0.00)***
Observations	3815	3917	963
No. plants	477	468	124
R-squared	0.02	0.00	0.07

Notes: Bracketed SE; ** and *** significant at 5% and 1%; constant included, year and two-digit sector dummies.

lagged grant variables in columns (4) and (5). This does not change our results, although we lose a large number of observations due to lagging. Hence, in what follows we use the full panel with the contemporaneous grant levels. Additionally, further on below, we instrument properly for the grant variable using lagged values.[14]

In Table 3 we constrained the effects of grants on linkages to be uniform over the source of the FDI. However, we recall the Rodríguez-Clare (1996) prediction that the origin of FDI matters for responsiveness of linkages to grants. Accordingly, we split up the sample into the three nationality categories, EU, US, and ROW (see Table 4).

We now observe a significantly positive effect of grants on backward linkages, but only for ROW plants. Examining the other covariates shows that growing and/or maturing US firms develop higher linkages. This positive effect is also exhibited by maturing EU plants. Productivity increases only induce higher linkages for ROW plants. For US plants the opposite is true. Finally, the export-platform conjecture only seems to hold true for ROW plants, while this effect is statistically insignificant for other plants.[15]

Up to now, we have considered the explanatory variables as exogenous in the fixed effects estimation. This may not be a reasonable assumption if grant receipt and linkages are jointly determined by a third variable, and if the thus introduced correlation with the error term varies over time, i.e. is not captured by the fixed effect. Furthermore, productivity, size, and the export ratio are also arguably endogenous. To deal with this potential problem, we employ a system GMM estimator (Blundell and Bond, 1998) which essentially uses a stacked system of first-differenced and level versions of equation (1), where for the former appropriately lagged values and for the latter appropriately lagged differences of the endogenous variables (grants, productivity, size, exports) can serve as valid instruments. The validity of these instruments is tested using a Hansen J-test.

The results of the system GMM estimations are reported in Table 5. Note, first, that we fail to reject the null of instrument validity for the US and ROW sample, but not for the European plants, and hence that we need to treat the results for European plants with caution. The main result is encouraging, as it is in line with previous results: we find a positive effect of grants on linkages only for ROW MNEs, not for US or EU plants.

Another potential criticism of our estimation thus far is that we do not take into account the nature of our dependent variable, which is bounded between zero and one. Hence, the issue of biased linear estimators comes to the fore. To address this, while simultaneously controlling for the potential endogeneity of regressors, we now employ

Table 5. Separate Regressions, System GMM

	US	*EU*	*ROW*
employment	0.354 (1.84)	0.953 (2.02)	–4.813 (2.29)**
age	0.262 (0.24)	–0.176 (0.174)	0.071 (0.270)
productivity	–0.283 (1.78)	–2.923 (2.14)	0.466 (2.42)
export ratio	0.049 (0.07)	–0.031 (0.08)	0.079 (0.08)
grant ratio	–0.000 (0.00)	0.076 (0.03)***	0.007 (0.00)***
Hansen J-test (*p*-value)	1.00	0.00	1.00
AR(2) (*p*-value)	0.82	0.29	0.15
Observations	3815	3917	963
No. plants	477	468	124

Notes: Bracketed SE; ** and *** significant at 5% and 1%; constant included, year and two-digit sector dummies.

Table 6. Separate Regressions, Endogenous Tobit

	US	*EU*	*ROW*
employment	–0.699 (0.55)	–1.534 (0.70)**	–4.529 (1.38)***
age	0.048 (0.05)	0.351 (0.03)***	0.432 (0.05)***
productivity	1.386 (0.75)*	3.179 (0.94)***	5.032 (1.26)***
export ratio	–0.077 (0.03)***	–0.170 (0.02)***	–0.048 (0.04)
grant ratio	–1.209 (0.90)	0.628 (0.56)	2.148 (1.03)**
Observations	2580	2642	644

Notes: Bracketed SE; ** and *** significant at 5% and 1%; constant included, year and two-digit sector dummies.

an instrumental variables technique for tobit models attributed to Smith and Blundell (1986). Similar to the GMM estimation, we use lagged values of the potentially endogenous variables (grants, productivity, size, exports) as instruments.[16] The estimation of tobit models with endogenous regressors essentially involves two steps:[17] (i) generate residual terms from linear regressions of each endogenous variable on the instrumental variables and all other exogenous regressors, and (ii) estimate a standard tobit model by including the residual terms from step (i) in the list of covariates. The residual terms are correction terms for the endogeneity problem, and jointly statistically significant coefficients support the hypothesis that instrumented variables are indeed endogenous.

Reassuringly, the result (see Table 6) for the grant variable is consistent with results from the previous estimations: higher grant intensities to ROW plants lead to higher linkages. Interestingly, the signs of all the other covariates are invariant across the different FDI origin countries. Also reassuring and in line with existing work is the result for age: plants with longer establishment histories in the host market have higher linkages with domestic suppliers (e.g. AR, 2004). Similar to GR (2000), we see that smaller plants are most linked with local suppliers on the likely basis that smaller suppliers are less able to produce inputs internally. We now can discern that *ex ante* more productive plants are those that opt for higher levels of linkages with domestic firms, a result consistent across the different FDI origin categories. The negative result we have evidenced in previous estimations for the export ratio is also reported here: exporters exhibit low linkage ratios.

Relative Demand for Local Inputs

Estimating equations like (1) allows for plant-level heterogeneity along a number of observed and unobserved variables, as in other work (see Wilson, 1992; BCK, 2001; AR, 2004). Arguably, the approach is somewhat ad hoc and is not much theoretically motivated. By contrast, Kiyota et al. (2008) estimate MNE demand for local inputs using a translog cost function, a technique we apply as a robustness check.[18] Accordingly, we assume that a firm minimizes costs described by a translog cost function for firm i at time t which in general form is:

$$C_{it} = f(\log(w_{it}), \log(r_{it}), \log(p^D_{it}), \log(p^M_{it}), \log(Y_{it}), \log(Z_{it})), \tag{2}$$

where C is the cost function, w, r, p^D, and p^M the prices of the variable factors of production labor, capital, locally sourced intermediates, and imported intermediates, respectively. Y is plant output and Z captures other potential control variables.

Differentiating the translog cost function in its proper functional form with respect to p^D yields

$$S_{it} = \varphi_i + \beta_1 \log(w_{it}) + \beta_2 \log(r_{it}) + \beta_3 \log(p^D_{it}) + \beta_4 \log(p^M_{it}) + \beta_5 Y_{it} + \beta_6 Z_{it}, \tag{3}$$

where $S = (\delta C/\delta p^D) * (p^D/C)$ is the share of locally sourced inputs in total cost. The latter is measured as the sum of intermediate input purchases and wage costs.[19] The price of labor w is measured as the average wage paid by firm i. As in Kiyota et al. (2008), the firm-level factor prices r, p^D, and p^M are unobservable in our data. To proceed we assume common factor prices in the same three-digit industry, but possibly variant over time. We thus capture the effect of these variables using a full set of three-digit industry-specific time dummies in our estimation. Output Y is measured as foreign MNE plant sales. Additional control variables Z include those also used in equation (1), namely, *age*, *productivity*, and a plant's *export* ratio.[20] Lastly, our most important variable, *grants ratio* is also included.

Table 7 presents the results of estimating equation (3) separately for US, EU, and ROW plants, using an endogenous tobit estimator. These estimations help shore up our previous findings where the grant ratio is a statistically significant and positive driver of linkages demand only for plants from ROW countries. The effects of plant-level *productivity*, *age*, and *export* intensity are also roughly similar to what we obtained before.

Table 7. Relative Demand Estimation, Endogenous Tobit

	US	*EU*	*ROW*
ln (w_{it})	−7.867 (1.07)***	−12.045 (1.20)***	−10.946 (2.24)***
ln (y_{it})	0.122 (0.30)	−0.296 (0.36)	−4.872 (0.81)***
grant ratio	−0.561 (0.49)	−0.653 (0.28)**	1.310 (0.63)**
age	0.077 (0.03)***	−0.150 (0.02)***	0.097 (0.04)**
productivity	1.543 (0.54)***	6.823 (0.72)***	11.107 (1.10)***
export ratio	−5.986 (1.24)***	−7.740 (0.98)***	11.435 (2.55)***
Observations	2471	2600	631

Notes: Bracketed SE; ** and *** significant at 5% and 1%; constant included, year and two-digit sector dummies.

5. Conclusion

A clear message from our analysis as regards policies towards multinationals to increase linkages is to avoid a "one-size-fits-all" policy when subsidizing foreign affiliates. We have shown that in certain cases grants to foreign MNEs do succeed in forming linkages with suppliers. However, European and US MNEs seem insensitive to grant aid. We conclude that applying a uniform policy towards foreign MNEs may be less beneficial than a tailored approach. We stress the importance of more hands-off policies (not related to financial incentives) to encourage linkage creation; for example, the provision of information to foreign plants about prospective local suppliers. Linkage creation is largely an issue of searching and finding suitable partner firms, as evidenced by the strong showing of the "length of time the MNE operates in the host market" variable.

In the light of our findings, policies need to take stock of underlying knowledge gaps between potential upstream input suppliers and downstream MNEs before awarding grants. Such gaps have implications for technology transfer to upstream local firms and the overall efficiency of production within the linkage. Policymakers should work towards making linkages with local suppliers attractive to MNEs (e.g. through helping indigenous firms to upgrade production, as under the Irish National Linkage Programme). In sum, linkages grow organically and cannot be manufactured.

Another implication of our analysis is the extent to which competing policy goals can be conflicting and the need to distinguish primary from secondary goals. We find strong evidence that the plants with the highest export intensities are not those most deeply embedded in the local economy. Hence, attracting export-oriented foreign multinationals to the economy may come at the expense of the development of linkages, a point also stressed by Moran (2001). However, one may want to qualify this pessimistic finding: it may not be the *quantity* of inputs supplied from local producers that matters so much (linkage intensity) as the *quality* of the linkage, and if foreign firms with the strongest export bias foster better quality linkages, this problem disappears.[21]

References

Alfaro, Laura and Andrés Rodríguez-Clare, "Multinationals and Linkages: An Empirical Investigation," *Economia* 4 (2004):113–69.

Alfaro, Laura, Areendam Chanda, Sebem Kalemli-Ozcan, and Selin Sayek, "How Does Foreign Direct Investment Promote Economic Growth? Exploring the Effects of Financial Markets on Linkages," NBER working paper 12522 (2006).

Belderbos, René, Giovanni Capannelli, and Kyoji Fukao, "Backward Vertical Linkages or Foreign Manufacturing Affiliates: Evidence from Japanese Multinationals," *World Development* 29 (2001):189–208.

Blalock, Garrick and Paul Gertler, "Welfare Gains from Foreign Direct Investment through Technology Transfer to Local Suppliers," *Journal of International Economics* 74 (2008):402–21.

Blundell, Richard and Stephen Bond, "Initial Conditions and Moment Restrictions in Dynamic Panel Data Models," *Journal of Econometrics* 87 (1998):115–37.

Bobonis, Gustavo and Howard Shatz, "Agglomeration, Adjustment, and State Policies in the Location of Foreign Direct Investment in the United States," *Review of Economics and Statistics* 89 (2007):30–43.

Cieślik, Andrzej, "Multinational Firms, International Knowledge Flows, and Dual Labor Markets in Developing Economies," *Review of Development Economics* 12 (2008):160–79.

Cohen, Benjamin, "Comparative Behaviour of Foreign and Domestic Export Firms in a Developing Economy," *Review of Economics and Statistics* 55 (1973):190–97.

Condron, Barry, "Building linkage between FDI and domestic companies—the Irish experience?", Presentation to the OECD Working Group on Investment Promotion, Antwerp. Available at https://www.oecd.org/dataoecd/54/30/38869496.ppt (2007).

Girma, Sourafel and Holger Görg, "Outsourcing, Foreign Ownership, and Productivity: Evidence from UK Establishment-Level Data," *Review of International Economics* 12 (2004):817–32.

Görg, Holger and Frances Ruane, "An Analysis of Backward Linkages in the Irish Electronics Sector," *Economic and Social Review* 31 (2000):215–35.

Görg, Holger and Eric Strobl, "Multinational Companies and Indigenous Development: An Empirical Analysis," *European Economic Review* 46 (2002):1305–22.

Girma, Sourafel, Holger Görg, and Mauro Pisu, "Exporting, Linkages and Productivity Spillovers from Foreign Direct Investment," *Canadian Journal of Economics* 41 (2008):320–40.

Hanson, Gordon, Raymond Mataloni, and Matthew Slaughter, "Vertical Production Networks in Multinational Firms," *Review of Economics and Statistics* 87 (2005):664–78.

Harding, Torfinn and Beata Javorcik, "Developing Economies and International Investors: Do Investment Promotion Agencies Bring Them Together?" CEPR discussion paper 6418 (2007).

Hirschman, Albert, *The Strategy of Economic Development*, New Haven CT: Yale University Press (1958).

Javorcik, Beata, "Does Foreign Direct Investment increase the Productivity of Domestic Firms? In Search of Spillovers through Backward Linkages," *American Economic Review* 94 (2004):605–27.

Kiyota, Kozo, Toshiyuki Matsuura, Shujiro Urata, and Yuhong Wei, "Reconsidering the Backward Vertical Linkages of Foreign Affiliates: Evidence from Japanese Multinationals," *World Development* 36 (2008):1398–414.

KPMG, *Investment in Ireland*, Dublin: KPMG Publications Ltd (2003). Available at http://www.kpmg.ie/.

Kwon, Chul-Woo and Bong Chun, "Local Content Requirement under Vertical Technology Diffusion," *Review of Development Economics* 13 (2009):111–24.

Lane, Philip and Frances Ruane, *Globalisation and the Irish Economy*, IIIS Occasional Paper No. 1, Dublin: Institute for International Integration Studies (2006).

Larraín, Felipe, Luis Lopez-Calva, and Andrés Rodriguez-Clare, "Intel: A Case Study of Foreign Direct Investment in Central America," CID working paper 58, Harvard University (2000).

Markusen, James and Anthony Venables, "Foreign Direct Investment as a Catalyst for Industrial Development," *European Economic Review* 43 (1999):335–56.

Meyler, Aidan and Eric Strobl, "Regional Industrial Policy and Job Generation in Ireland," *Economic and Social Review* 31 (2000):111–28.

Moran, Theodore, *Parental Supervision: The New Paradigm for Foreign Direct Investment and Development*, Washington, DC: Institute for International Economics (2001).

NESC, *A Review of Industrial Policy*, Dublin: National Economic and Social Council (1982).

Newey, Whitney, "Efficient Estimation of Limited Dependent Variables Models with Endogenous Explanatory Variables," *Journal of Econometrics* 36 (1987):231–50.

Rauch, James and Joel Watson, "Starting Small in an Unfamiliar Environment," *International Journal of Industrial Organization* 21 (2003):1021–42.

Rodriguez-Clare, Andrés, "Multinationals, Linkages and Economic Development," *American Economic Review* 86 (1996):852–73.

Ruane, Frances, "Reflections on Linkage Policy in Irish Manufacturing—Policy Chasing a Moving Target?" mimeo. Available at www.unece.org/ead/ (2001).

Smith, Richard and Richard Blundell, "An Exogeneity Test for a Simultaneous Equation Tobit Model with an Application to Labor Supply," *Econometrica* 54 (1986):679–86.

Wilson, Patricia, *Exports and Local Development: Mexico's New Maquiladoras*. Austin, TX: University of Texas Press (1992).

Yaşar, Mahmut and Catherine Morrison Paul, "Size and Foreign Ownership Effects on Productivity and Efficiency: An Analysis of Turkish Motor Vehicle and Parts Plants," *Review of Development Economics* 13 (2009):576–91.

Notes

1. An example of a spur to domestic firms is cited in Larraín et al. (2000) who conclude that Intel's decision to locate in Costa Rica in 1997 meant that; "... the development of local producers has been fast and ambitious, thanks to a coordinated effort by the government" (p. 32). Görg and Strobl (2002) report that the entry of new domestic firms is positively influenced by the influx of multinationals in Ireland.
2. One concern is that domestic firms suffer from foreign firm entry if increased demand for local inputs bids up their price. Larraín et al. (2000), based on their discussions with local Costa Rican firms, conclude that any negative general-equilibrium effects were perceived as short run as supply readjusted.
3. Moran (2001) provides interesting case studies further showing potential localized benefit of FDI.
4. In related work, Belderbos et al. (2001) investigate *inter alia* the impact of local content requirements (LCRs) for Japanese overseas linkages and find a moderately positive effect. Also, Kwon and Chun's (2009) model analyzing effects of LCRs predicts that if LCRs are set too high, foreign MNEs can switch to local in-house production, thus killing off technical transfer to indigenous firms via linkages (although positive employment effects can still arise, as argued by Cieślik (2008). Also, a more general literature looks at the government's role in attracting FDI (see Bobonis and Shatz, 2007; Harding and Javorcik, 2007).
5. See Ruane (2001) and Condron (2007) for a description of Irish linkage policy.
6. Similar but not as restrictive as some LCRs, i.e. in UK's 70% LCR from Japanese MNEs (see Kwon and Chun, 2009). In Ireland, linkages represent a grant criterion but the LCR percentage is not made explicit.
7. See Meyler and Strobl (2000) for a more detailed discussion of grant provision in Ireland.
8. Forfás defines foreign plants as those majority-owned by foreign shareholders, i.e. at least 50 foreign owned. While, arguably, plants with lower foreign shares should also be considered, this is not really a problem since most inward FDI to Ireland has been greenfield. Note that our data only provide a dummy based on this definition rather than a percentage of ownership.
9. Locally sourced inputs include both inputs sourced from domestic plants and inputs bought from foreign plants located in Ireland. Unfortunately, we are unable to distinguish these two input types, a fact which should be borne in mind when interpreting the estimates.
10. The raw correlation between linkages and grants is very low as cross-correlations (not reported) reveal.
11. Because the grants awarded by the IDA in Ireland are paid in pre-specified and successive installments subject to periodic reviews, it helps that we have a fairly long panel (almost two decades) charting impacts of grants on formation of backward linkages.
12. We do not have reliable capital data allowing a calculation of more sophisticated measures of TFP.
13. The plant-level fixed effect also controls for sectoral heterogeneity, as the sector data are time invariant (relating to the last year in the sample).
14. Note that these regressions include two time-invariant country dummies for plants from the US and ROW showing that, *ceteris paribus*, US firms have higher linkages than other multinationals.
15. We should make it clear that this result is unlikely to be due to sectoral heterogeneity between ROW and US/EU plants. Our FE approach controls for this, as sectoral information is time invariant.
16. To our knowledge there are no formal tests of instrument validity within the context of this endogenous tobit specification. To gauge the instrument appropriateness we use lagged values which exhibit instrument validity in the linear context of the GMM model (see Table 5).
17. A one-step variant of this estimator involving stronger distributional assumptions is also available (see Newey, 1987). However, convergence is not achieved. We therefore replaced the time dummies with a time trend. This problem often arises with more than one endogenous regressor.

18. In doing so, they adapt an approach by Hanson et al. (2005), who model the demand for imported intermediates. Yaşar and Morrison Paul (2009) similarly apply a translog function to their input vector (although their outcome variable is productivity and not linkages) because this functional form allows for differential plant production structures and scale economies.
19. Ideally, total cost should also include interest, rent, and depreciation (see Kiyota et al., 2008). However, such data are not available to us. Assuming similar capital costs capital for firms within the same three-digit industry, such differences are captured by industry dummies.
20. Belderbos et al. (2001) and Kiyota et al. (2008) include parent firm variables for foreign plants. Unfortunately, we do not have data for this. However, running separate estimations for US, EU, and ROW plants, controls for common time-invariant differences in parent characteristics within country groupings.
21. In the same context, Javorcik (2004) notes that spillovers to upstream firms through linkages arise when both supplier and buyer cooperate on the product. Not all linkages have this feature of close cooperation, and therefore it is the quality of a linkage that matters.

Chapter 15

Suppliers of multinationals and the forced linkage effect: Evidence from firm level data

Olivier N. Godart[a,*], Holger Görg[b]

[a] Kiel Institute for the World Economy and University of Kiel, Germany
[b] Kiel Institute for the World Economy, University of Kiel and CEPR, Germany

ARTICLE INFO

Article history:
Received 2 November 2011
Received in revised form 2 November 2012
Accepted 21 January 2013
Available online 29 January 2013

JEL classification:
F23
O12

Keywords:
Backward linkages
Multinational customers
Suppliers
Forced linkage

ABSTRACT

Using information on more than 1000 firms in a number of emerging countries, we find quantitative evidence that suppliers of multinationals that are pressured by their customers to reduce production costs or develop new products have higher productivity growth than other firms, including other host country suppliers of multinationals. These findings provide first empirical support for a "forced linkage effect" from supplying multinational companies. Our findings hold controlling for other factors within and outside the supplier–customer relationship and when endogeneity concerns are taken into consideration.

1. Introduction

The search for positive productivity effects (commonly termed "spillovers") from multinational companies to host country firms has attracted considerable interest in the academic literature. While the earlier literature looked specifically for within-industry "horizontal spillovers", the consensus is now that much stronger effects should be expected from vertical and in particular backward linkages between multinationals and their local suppliers.[1] Somewhat inspired by these empirical findings, many countries have attracted actively foreign direct investment (FDI) with fiscal incentives, hoping that in return indigenous suppliers will learn through their business relationship with multinational customers.[2]

While the available empirical literature produces encouraging results, it suffers from one main conceptual shortcoming. The traditional backward spillovers studies, such as Javorcik (2004), measure linkages between multinationals and domestic firms only at the industry level. Specifically, productivity in domestic firms is linked to a measure of the importance of multinationals in downstream industries, calculated using aggregate input–output tables. This does not allow the researcher

* Corresponding author. Tel.: +0049 4318807415; fax: +0049 4318807415.
E-mail address: olivier.godart@ifw-kiel.de (O.N. Godart).

[1] The most widely cited example of a study on horizontal spillovers is probably Aitken and Harrison (1999), see also Haskel et al. (2007) and Keller and Yeaple (2009). The importance of backward linkages has been shown in theoretical models (Rodriguez-Clare, 1996; Markusen and Venables, 1999) as well as recent econometric studies (Javorcik, 2004; Liu, 2008; Girma et al., 2008). There are also studies that point to a potential for negative spillovers through backward linkages, due to potential hold up problems between supplier and multinational customer (e.g. Driffield et al., 2002; Blalock and Gertler, 2008). Görg and Greenaway (2004) and Havranek and Irsova (2011) provide comprehensive reviews of this literature.

[2] Harrison and Rodriguez-Clare (2009) argue that China's emphasis on domestic content requirement to foreign multinationals has been, inter alia, motivated by empirical evidence on productivity spillovers from foreign direct investment to supplying industries.

0167-2681/$ – see front matter
http://dx.doi.org/10.1016/j.jebo.2013.01.007

to identify the exact channels through which domestic firms in upstream industries are expected to benefit – is it a supplier effect, a competition effect, or something else entirely?[3]

Javorcik and Spatareanu (2009) and Gorodnichenko et al. (2007) are among the first to confront this limitation. Javorcik and Spatareanu (2009) use firm level data for the Czech Republic, including information on whether a domestic firm is a supplier to a multinational. They show that suppliers are indeed more productive than non-suppliers. Gorodnichenko et al. (2007) use data for 17 Eastern European and Central Asian countries. They exploit firm level information on the share of output supplied by domestic firms to multinationals and find that a higher share is correlated with higher productivity growth. These papers, however, are silent on the actual mechanism that is at work and that causes productivity to increase. We, therefore, expand on these papers by examining one potential mechanism through which suppliers may improve their productivity. We refer to this as a "forced linkage effect".

While many authors interpret the above results as suggesting that there is learning from multinationals, whereby multinationals voluntarily share knowledge and cooperate with their suppliers (backed up by some case study evidence, such as Moran, 2001), this may be a somewhat overly benevolent view of how multinationals manage their suppliers in emerging economies. An alternative interpretation is that multinationals force their customers to adopt new practices – and may punish if these are not implemented to their satisfaction. Blomström and Kokko (1998), also based on case study evidence, point out that such "forced linkage effects" may be an important mechanism through which domestic suppliers can improve their performance.

To the best of our knowledge, no one has explored empirically the existence of such a "forced linkage" mechanism thus far. This paper attempts to fill this gap in the literature. We investigate empirically whether this is an important channel through which multinationals increase the productivity of their suppliers. In order to do so, we use a rich source of firm level data for emerging market economies in Central and Eastern Europe and Central Asia. This data comes from the Business Environment and Enterprise Performance Survey (BEEPS) provided jointly by the World Bank and the European Bank for Reconstruction and Development (EBRD). We use the 2005 survey, complemented with some information from the 2002 survey. Our dataset provides unique information, at the firm level, on whether a firm supplies multinationals (and how much) and also on whether a firm perceives to be subject to pressure from customers to reduce production costs or to create new products. The combination of these two variables is central to our measurement of the forced linkage effect.

What exactly do we mean by a "forced linkage effect"? We conceptualize this idea in the following way. First, multinationals require that their suppliers meet their higher standards on product features, delivery schedules, quality control, inventory holding and accommodate continuously their demanding business procedures. Second, such requirements have a potential productivity enhancing effect on host country suppliers because multinationals have gathered their own experience and best practices with similar products in their main country. Third, and this is the main difference from a mere cooperation effect, suppliers are forced by their multinational customers to meet those requirements.[4] Multinationals, due to their extensive experience with international production networks, are in a position to evaluate the performance of host country suppliers accurately. This enables them to "punish" local suppliers, e.g. through switching supplier sources or forcing price reductions, if the required standards are not met.

While the concept of a "forced linkage" is not firmly grounded in the existing theoretical literature, recent theoretical developments on imperfect contracts and bargaining may provide some guidance for a better understanding of frictions between customers and suppliers in general and the forced linkage effect in particular. In the "property rights" view of the firm, as applied to international sourcing decisions by, e.g. Antràs (2003) and Antràs and Helpman (2004, 2008), a final good producer and its one supplier are engaged in generalized Nash bargaining on the total surplus generated from the relationship. In this set up, one interpretation of "pressure" from the customer is that it shifts the bargaining weight in favor of the customer. Normally, we would expect that this would reduce the incentives for the independent supplier and thus lead to an underinvestment in terms of effort, i.e. lower productivity for the supplier.

However, the situation of a multinational company and its supplier is likely to be somewhat different than assumed in this stylized model. Firstly, the multinational has access to superior technology, which it may transfer to the supplier. This may either be done voluntarily, or it may come with pressure to fulfill some tough requirements or else be punished. The latter would correspond to our notion of a "forced linkage". In our empirical analysis, we attempt to distinguish the simple technology transfer effect from a forced linkage effect. Another important difference from the theoretical model is that it is unlikely to be the case that one supplier exclusively supplies one multinational firm. Rather, independent suppliers have the option of working for additional customers.[5] In this case, the benefits of responding to pressure by multinationals might

[3] There are also methodological problems related to the assumptions implicit in the use of aggregate input–output tables, see Barrios et al. (2011) for a discussion.

[4] For example, Javorcik (2008) provides some evidence for the Czech Republic that multinationals require suppliers to improve quality assurance, acquire ISO 9000 certification or improve the timeliness of delivery.

[5] Grossman and Helpman (2002) allow the produced good to be valuable for other producers on a secondary market in cases in which the bargaining breaks down. This offers a positive outside option for the supplier at the bargaining stage. Note that the commitment given by the multinational to keep the supplier as a separate legal entity (i.e. not to "integrate" the supplier) is that the customer gives up a valuable outside option at the bargaining stage (see Antràs and Helpman, 2004). In Grossman and Helpman (2004) a customer can give its supplier a higher stake in the relationship when he cannot monitor its independent supplier. While this creates incentive for the supplier to provide more effort, it might also as well bind the supplier to this specific customer when the supplier uses its option to serve other customers.

have additional positive effects for the output sold to other firms. These two aspects are likely to overcome the disincentive to provide effort when pressured by the customer, and provide higher overall productivity gains when supplying pressuring multinationals.

Our paper is, to the best of our knowledge, the first to investigate whether knowledge is transferred through a forced linkage or through a more cooperative channel. Thereby we add to the existing studies on productivity spillovers from multinational companies, providing one further step toward understanding the mechanisms at work. Indeed, the existence of a forced linkage effect might help explain an ambivalence often found in surveys on suppliers of multinationals: they complain occasionally about their multinational clients but at the same time they are eager to develop or extend business relationships with multinationals.[6] The forced linkage effect highlights a possibly more frictional customer–supplier relationship than one in which multinationals share their proprietary knowledge freely.[7]

The paper by Gorodnichenko et al. (2007) is closest to us as it also uses data from the 2005 BEEPS survey and uses information on supplies to multinationals at the firm level. However, they do not consider the "forced linkage" as a channel through which productivity may be boosted in local suppliers but only ask whether suppliers experience higher productivity growth. As we show below, it is however crucially important to distinguish the effect of supplying to multinationals for firms that experience "pressure from their customers" from those that do not. Furthermore, the identification of a causal effect from supplier status to productivity growth is difficult in the Gorodnichenko et al. (2007) study. They regress productivity growth between 2002 and 2005 on the supplier status of a firm in 2005. Hence, it is difficult to judge whether they estimate the effect of supplying on productivity growth, or whether they pick up the fact that highly productive firms are more likely to become suppliers. Our research design is different in that we use data on productivity growth between 2002 and 2005 and regress this on the supplier status in 2002, exploiting the panel dimension available in the BEEPS data. This set up allows us to be more confident about identification of an effect of the supplier status of the firm on productivity growth. We also combine our approach with an explicit test for exogeneity, using instrumental variables available in the BEEPS data.[8,9]

To preview our results, we find evidence for a productivity gain of being a supplier only if the supplier status is interacted with a variable indicating that there is pressure from customers. We interpret this as evidence that there is a forced linkage at work and that spillovers do not seem to materialize in the absence of such pressure. This result is robust to various specifications of the empirical model.

In Section 2 we develop our empirical strategy, while Section 3 discusses the data used and presents summary statistics. The econometric analysis is presented in Section 4. Section 5 provides some concluding comments.

2. Empirical framework

In our empirical analysis we investigate whether there are positive productivity effects from supplying multinationals, and whether these may be due to a "forced linkage". In order to do so we examine the relationship between productivity growth of a host country firm and its status of whether it is a supplier to a multinational.

More specifically, we estimate the determinants of productivity growth using an augmented Cobb–Douglas production function, which in its most basic form looks as follows[10]

$$\Delta Y_i = \alpha^M \Delta x_i^M + \alpha^K \Delta x_i^K + \alpha^L \Delta x_i^L + \beta_1 s_i^{MNE} + \beta_2 p_i^{CUST} + \beta_3 (p_i^{CUST} \times s_i^{MNE}) + \beta_3 C_i + \mu_j + \nu_c + \sigma_i \quad (1)$$

where ΔY_i, Δx_i^M, Δx_i^K and Δx_i^L, are respectively measures of percentage changes (growth rates) in output, material, capital and labor inputs for firm i over the three year period from the end of 2002 to the end of 2005. We use growth rates of these variables in order to purge any unobserved firm level effects that may impact productivity *levels*. We include a vector of firm level controls C (size dummies and a foreign ownership dummy), and μ_j and ν_c which are industry and country dummy

[6] Javorcik (2008) shows using a survey on Czech suppliers of multinationals that 37.5% of multinationals mandatory scheduled regular price cuts to their suppliers which might lead to complaints from suppliers. She also shows that more than 35% of suppliers report to undertake improvements to satisfy their multinational clients.

[7] This does not contradict the findings that suppliers might on some occasions receive some effective assistance from their multinational clients as, for example, illustrated by Liker and Choi (2004).

[8] Another difference is that Gorodnichenko et al. (2007) only use data for 17 countries (due to availability of input–output tables) while we use firm level data for 25 Eastern European and Central Asian countries.

[9] Our use of panel data implies, however, that our sample size is smaller than if we used the full cross section for 2005. However, in this trade-off between larger sample size and more precise identification of the estimated effects we opt for the latter. Reassuringly, Gorodnichenko et al. (2007) as well as the companion paper Gorodnichenko et al. (2010) both compare the cross-section results with the smaller set of panel results. They do not find any major differences in results, apart from the fact that coefficients appear less statistically significant in the panel. Hence, if anything, it is likely that we would underestimate any effects.

[10] The production function estimation allows us to estimate the determinants of productivity growth, i.e. the variation in the change of output that is not explained by variations in the growth of inputs. The setup of a one-step production function has been used extensively for analyzing the effect of foreign direct investment on productivity; see, for example, Javorcik (2004). An alternative would be a two-step approach, were one retrieves TFP as the error term of a simple production function and in a second step regresses TFP on the spillover variables. We do not follow such an approach mainly for two reasons. Firstly, it is less efficient than the one step estimation. Second, while the two step approach allows the researcher to better deal with potential simultaneity in the production function (see Levinsohn and Petrin, 2003) we cannot implement such an approach due to data limitations.

variables that control for any shock that could occur along these aggregates. The remaining error term σ_i is assumed to be white noise.[11]

The focus of our study is on whether being a supplier to a multinational firm matters for productivity growth. In order to capture this, we include s_i^{MNE}, a dummy variable indicating whether a firm sells to multinationals or not. This variable is constructed using the following survey question:

"What percent of your domestic sales are to: Multinationals located in your country...?"

We set s_i^{MNE} equal to 1 for any firm that sells part of its output to multinational firms in 2002 and zero otherwise. As an alternative variable we also use the actual share of sales to multinationals in a different specification of the empirical model. We use information relating to 2002 as this is prior to the measurement of the dependent variable. This allows us to attenuate potential endogeneity problems between productivity growth and the supplier status.

The next important variable, p_i^{CUST}, captures whether firms receive pressure from customers to reduce production costs or to create new products based on the following questions in the BEEPS survey:

"How would you rate the importance of [PRESSURE FROM CUSTOMERS] on key decisions about your business with respect to "reducing the production costs of existing products and services"? or "creating new goods and services and new markets by customers"?"

Respondents had to rate the magnitude of such pressure according to a Likert-type scale from 1 (not at all important) to 4 (very important). We use the information available in 2002 in order to generate p_i^{CUST} for each firm. We set p_i^{CUST} equal to one if the respondent answered "very important" to either the question on reducing costs or creating new products. It is zero otherwise.

Following the arguments set out in the introduction, the expected sign for p_i^{CUST} is ambiguous. On the one hand, the underinvestment problem of the supplier becomes more severe when the balance of power is shifted in favor of the customer. In this case, "pressure" is likely to exacerbate the underinvestment problem, reduce the incentives for the supplier and thus lead to less effort, i.e. lower productivity for the supplier.[12] However if a supplier has more than one customer, pressure by one customer to reduce inefficiency may positively affect also output sold to other customers, thus leading to productivity growth.

The main variable of interest is our proxy for "forced linkages". To generate this, we interact ($p_i^{CUST} \times s_i^{MNE}$). This interacted variable allows us to test whether the effect of supplying a multinational is different depending on whether there is pressure from customers or not.[13] If there is a forced linkage mechanism, we expect a positive association between firm's productivity growth and pressure from customers in firms supplying multinational customers. Note that this variable is also measured in 2002 in order to alleviate endogeneity concerns.

This set up allows us to distinguish a simple technology transfer between multinational and its customer from the forced linkage effect, where the technology transfer is accompanied by tough demands. The coefficient β_1, if statistically significant and positive, represents any productivity enhancing effect while β_3 would only be positive and significant if pressure is applied by the multinational.

In order to identify the forced linkage effect more precisely we also introduce, in extensions to Eq. (1) an additional variable that measures pressure from competitors to reduce production costs p_i^{COMPET} and add also its interaction term ($p_i^{COMPET} \times s_i^{MNE}$).[14] The survey question used to construct p_i^{COMPET} has an identical design to p_i^{CUST} and allows generating a dummy exactly the same way as for p_i^{CUST}: p_i^{COMPET} is equal to 1 if important pressure is reported by a firm in 2002.

One way pressure from competition might be related to higher supplier productivity is provided by Horn et al. (1995). They analyze the design of optimal incentive contracts in an environment with international trade in which a principal cannot monitor the actions undertaken by its supplying agent. In their framework, openness to trade increases competition on product markets through a general equilibrium effect and contributes to higher levels of managerial effort provided by the supplier, and thus improved internal efficiency (i.e. reduced X-inefficiency). If "pressure by competitors to reduce production costs" is a good proxy for how increased competition impact firms in this framework, then we would expect that

[11] Details of the data source are provided in the next section and variable definitions in Appendix 1. All firms are classified according to a broad industry classification: mining and quarrying, construction, manufacturing, transport storage and communication, real estate, renting and business service and other service activities. Compared to studies of backward spillovers where the aggregation of industries is very important, our study does not rely on the aggregation of industries because we use precise information about firms and their business relationship with multinational customers.

[12] Alternatively, firms might report pressure from their customers because of the risk to be let down at short notice or because customers switch their supply sources often. As a result, suppliers are confronted with uncertainty about future demand conditions which is likely to slow down productivity growth.

[13] Note that our data only allow us to calculate a variable indicating whether there is pressure from customers, not whether these pressuring customers are multinationals. We only know whether a firm is intensively pressured by customers and at the same time whether it has multinational firms as customers. It is unlikely that the average domestic customer in emerging economies has access to international best practices and the resulting accumulated knowledge that they could impose upon their suppliers.

[14] The survey questions related to all variables are listed in Appendix 1.

Table 1
Countries in the sample.

Country	No. of observations
Albania	48
Armenia	37
Azerbaijan	46
Belarus	23
Bulgaria	69
Croatia	43
Czech Republic	29
Estonia	45
Former Yugoslav Republic of Macedonia	24
Georgia	36
Hungary	44
Kazakhstan	40
Kyrgyz Republic	27
Latvia	36
Lithuania	33
Moldova	26
Poland	58
Romania	50
Russia	26
Serbia and Montenegro	36
Slovak Republic	21
Slovenia	54
Tajikistan	13
Turkey	41
Ukraine	107
Total	1012

high pressure from competitors is related to more managerial effort provided by the supplying agent and thus improved productivity.[15]

Including p_i^{COMPET} and $(p_i^{COMPET} \times s_i^{MNE})$ shows whether our interpretation of the forced linkages holds or if pressure from competitors (external to the supplier–multinational relationship) potentially drives the measured forced linkage effect.

In a further extension to the baseline model we also include some other variables that are by their very nature closely related to a more benevolent relationship between customers and their suppliers. These variables are defined in Appendix 1. The first variable uses a question about whether a surveyed firm has acquired a new technology ($TECH_i$). Including this variable together with a variable about whether cooperation with customers resulted in these new technology acquirements ($COOPTECH_i$) permits us to control for a more cooperative learning mechanism.

Note that a potential problem with estimating Eq. (1) using OLS is that we assume that the suppliers' status is exogenous. This may be a problematic assumption, in particular because there may be self-selection of more productive firms as suppliers to multinationals (Javorcik and Spatareanu, 2009). However, this problem is likely to be less acute in our case as we define the supplier status in 2002, while productivity growth is calculated between 2002 and 2005. Also, our variable of most interest is the interaction of pressure from customers and the supplier status. There is no clear reason to suspect that among the suppliers of MNEs the most productive ones are also necessarily the most subjected to customers' pressure. Nevertheless, we check the assumption of exogeneity using an instrumental variables approach. Details are in the results section.

3. Data sources and summary statistics

This paper uses the 2002 and 2005 versions of the EBRD/World Bank Business Environment and Enterprise Performance Surveys (BEEPS) of firms in "transition countries". This dataset provides ample information on enterprises and their business environment in many emerging countries (see the list of countries in Table 1) in three rounds in 1999, 2002 and 2005. A limited number of firms can be linked in the 2002 and 2005 surveys.[16] In our analysis, we exclusively use the panel component of the BEEPS data. It includes more than 1000 firms that have been surveyed in the 2002 survey as well as in the 2005 survey. This allows us to measure the supplier status, as well as pressure from customers, in the 2002 survey, while productivity growth is calculated from the 2005 data.

The survey's main aim is to allow for a cross country comparison of business activities and, to that end, asks each firm more than 80 questions about their business, the institutional environment and their perceptions about the business environment.

[15] According to Javorcik et al. (2008) competition between suppliers is important for the diffusion of best practices among suppliers in the Mexican soap and detergents industry. They argue that Walmart brought its best standards and practices into Mexico and that those have been quickly adopted by their suppliersǐ competitors in this retail industry.

[16] Unfortunately there is no panel structure linked to the BEEPS 1999 survey.

Table 2
Summary statistics.

	p_i^{CUST}	p_i^{COMPET}	$TECH_i$	$COOPTECH_i$	ΔY_i	$share_i^{MNE}$	s_i^{MNE}
All firms							
Mean	0.376	0.302	0.298	0.015	0.105	0.033	0.144
Std. dev.	0.484	0.460	0.458	0.121	0.370	0.115	0.352
No. of obs.	1012	1012	1012	1012	1012	1012	1012
Non-suppliers of MNEs							
Mean	0.368	0.291	0.283	0.012	0.096	-	-
Std. dev.	0.482	0.454	0.451	0.107	0.369	-	-
No. of Obs.	866	866	866	866	866	-	-
All suppliers of MNEs							
Mean	0.418	0.370	0.390	0.034	0.153	0.228	-
Std. dev.	0.495	0.484	0.490	0.182	0.372	0.218	-
No. of Obs.	146	146	146	146	146	146	-
"Pressured" Suppliers of MNEs							
Mean	1	0.492	0.311	0.049	0.244	0.235	-
Std. dev.	0	0.504	0.467	0.218	0.407	0.220	-
No. of Obs.	61	61	61	61	61	61	-

All variables are defined in Appendix 1.

The survey sample in each country is stratified by firm size, sector and region. Sector stratification is undertaken to reflect the relative contribution of each sector to the region's GDP.[17]

Great care has been taken to train and advise interviewers in order to minimize potential distortions and irregularities between countries or during each interview. Interviews have been conducted face-to-face and anonymity has been guaranteed to all participants. Still, a typical concern when using survey data is that of individual perception bias, since it is common that responses of firms based on surveys are likely to be prejudiced by the general perception of firms (Kaufmann and Wei, 1999). Some firms may consistently provide positive or negative answers depending on their general perception of the environment in which they currently operate. In principle, assuming that the bias is uncorrelated among groups of respondents, individual perception bias contributes only to the standard error of estimates obtained from the survey responses. In cross-country surveys, such as the BEEPS, the group within which the bias is correlated is the particular country in which respondents operate. Perception bias at the country level could originate from different cultural norms and degrees of political freedom across countries, which may influence the choice of specific ratings and the willingness of business people to criticize state institutions for example. Fries et al. (2003) check for such perception bias in the BEEPS 2002 by statistically comparing qualitative measures to related objective measures and find no significant perception biases across the countries in the sample. Since the BEEPS 2005 follows a similar methodology, we may be reasonably confident that perception bias will not affect the results of the analysis. However, as a further control, the empirical model in Eq. (1) includes industry and country level fixed effects.

The BEEPS data provide crucial information for estimating productivity growth and unique information on the share of firms' sales to multinational clients as well as on whether firms feel pressured by their customers to reduce production costs or to create new products.

The survey provides information on changes in input use and output between 2002 and 2005. Specifically, the responding firm has to answer the following question in 2005 for each of the variables in brackets.

> "Over the last 36 months how have [**sales, fixed assets, material inputs**] changed and what is the percent of change for your company, in real terms (i.e. after allowing for inflation)"

A similar question is asked for changes in employment over the same 36 months in each firm and described in Appendix 1. We use answers to these questions as a base for our productivity growth estimation in Eq. (1). Such data enable us to construct a simple Cobb Douglas production function. We acknowledge that there is a potential simultaneity problem in input choices in the production function estimation, as described, for example, by Levinsohn and Petrin (2003). Unfortunately, we do not have sufficient data to implement the techniques suggested in their paper. However, this potential disadvantage has to be weighed against the advantages of having unique information on pressure from customers reported by their suppliers as well as detailed information on suppliers' sales to multinationals. Such information makes it possible, for the first time, to confront the forced linkages effect with a formal econometric analysis.

Table 2 presents some summary statistics relating to the variables included in the econometric analysis. We describe our whole sample in the top panel. The sample contains 1012 active firms during the study period. First, note that around

[17] To be precise, stratification by sector depends on the size of the economy. Very small economies (less than $15bn GNI) are stratified into manufacturing and non-agricultural sector; small economies ($15–$100bn GNI) into manufacturing, retail, and rest of non-agricultural sector; medium economies ($100–$500bn GNI) into five manufacturing sectors, retail and rest; large economies (more than $500bn GNI) into seven manufacturing sectors, retail and rest. This implies that for all economy sizes, the sample should be representative at least of total manufacturing and the non-agricultural economy. As the economy size increases, representativeness of other more narrowly defined sectors increases. Details of the sampling methodology are available at www.enterprisesurveys.org.

38% of our firms reported "very important" pressure from their customers (p_i^{CUST}). Furthermore, 30% of firms reported to have developed a new technology (*TECH$_i$*) while only 2% of them responded that customers help them develop their new technology (*COOPTECH$_i$*). Note also that the average firm in our sample had an increase in sales of about 11% between 2002 and 2005.[18] Finally, in the last columns of the upper panel we see that 14% of our firms are suppliers of multinationals and the average firm (including non-suppliers) sells 3% of their output to multinationals.

We distinguish suppliers from other firms that do not supply multinational customers in the lower panels of the table. We notice some differences in the mean values between both types of firms. First, suppliers of multinationals are more likely, on average, to report pressure from customers than firms that do not supply any multinational. Second, firms serving multinationals are on average more likely to introduce new technologies and especially, they are more likely to cooperate with their customers to obtain these new technologies. Suppliers of multinationals are also more often subject to pressure from competitors than firms that do not sell goods to multinational firms. Concerning economic performance over the period, we note that firms that supply goods or services to multinationals in 2002 seem to have a higher mean output growth over the subsequent three years. The average supplier sells roughly 23% of output to multinational customers.

We also distinguish "pressured" suppliers in the table. We have 61 of such firms in our data.[19] These are firms for which the interaction term ($p_i^{CUST} \times s_i^{MNE}$) equals one. We find that these firms are more likely to report pressure from competitors than other suppliers. They are also firms that experience higher output growth in the subsequent periods. However, there is no obvious difference in the share of output sold to multinationals when comparing "pressured" and "non-pressured" suppliers.

4. Empirical results

4.1. Baseline model

Table 3 presents the baseline regression results from estimating Eq. (1) using the supplier dummy s_i^{MNE}. Column (1) shows a simple estimation of a Cobb Douglas production function that is solely augmented by s_i^{MNE}. Note that Δx_i^M, Δx_i^L and Δx_i^K are all positive as expected. A dummy variable for firms that are larger than 250 employees (large size) is also significant and positive. By contrast, dummies for medium sized firms (50–249 employees) and foreign-owned firms are not statistically significant. Most importantly from our point of view, the variable s_i^{MNE} which measures whether or not a firm supplies goods or services to foreign multinational companies located in the host country is not statistically significant.[20] It indicates that in our data selling goods to multinationals is not necessarily automatically statistically related to higher gains in productivity.

In column (2) we turn to the estimation of Eq. (1) that includes s_i^{MNE}, p_i^{CUST} and ($p_i^{CUST} \times s_i^{MNE}$) jointly in our productivity specification. The supplier dummy remains statistically insignificant in this specification. The coefficient on p_i^{CUST} is, however, negative and significant. It suggests that firms that experience high pressure by their customers have lower productivity growth than firms that do not report such pressure. This negative sign is in line with our argument that p_i^{CUST} captures the underinvestment problem resulting from a weakened bargaining strength of the supplier when pressure is exerted by its customers. It reduces the incentives for this supplier and thus is related to less effort and lower productivity.

The coefficient of the interaction term ($p_i^{CUST} \times s_i^{MNE}$), our proxy for the "forced linkage effect" is positive and highly significant. Given that its absolute value is higher than the value of the coefficient of p_i^{PC}, it supports the forced linkage effect. Hence, suppliers of multinationals that are pressured by their customers to reduce production costs or create new products have higher productivity increase relative to all other firms, including other suppliers of multinationals. There is no productivity enhancing effect for suppliers that are not pressured by their customers, thus casting doubt on whether, on average, multinationals transfer technology to their suppliers unconditionally. The point estimate suggests that suppliers that experience pressure from their customers experience productivity growth that is about 11% higher than that of other firms.

We might ask whether our proxy for the forced linkage does not capture a mere competition effect through which suppliers of multinationals are forced to adopt their industry's best practices because their domestic competitors apply such practices as well. This could also result in a productivity enhancing effect, but not through the direct supplier–customer relationship (Horn et al., 1995). We consider this hypothesis by enlarging our baseline equation with a variable that considers "pressure from domestic competition to reduce production costs" p_i^{COMPET} and the interaction term ($p_i^{COMPET} \times s_i^{MNE}$).

Results are shown in column (3). First, neither p_i^{COMPET} nor ($p_i^{COMPET} \times s_i^{MNE}$) are statistically significant while ($p_i^{CUST} \times s_i^{MNE}$) is still positive and significant, with a magnitude similar to that found in column (2). This result suggests that the positive coefficient on ($p_i^{CUST} \times s_i^{MNE}$) is not merely driven by a general competition channel in our data.[21] Rather it gives

18 This growth rate is measured in real terms.
19 This relatively small number of firms should be kept in mind when interpreting results.
20 Gorodnichenko et al. (2007) find a similar result when using panel data for 2002 and 2005.
21 This finding does not mean that X-inefficiencies are not reduced through competition effects in the spirit of Horn et al. (1995), as such general equilibrium effects might take more time to materialize. Nevertheless, the forced linkage effect is not disrupted when controlling for such a possible channel.

Table 3
Baseline results using supplier dummy.

	(1)	(2)	(3)	(4)
s_i^{MNE}	0.020	−0.024	−0.014	−0.023
	(0.023)	(0.031)	(0.036)	(0.044)
p_i^{PC}		−0.036	−0.029	−0.039
		(0.017)**	(0.017)*	(0.017)**
$p_i^{PC} \times s_i^{MNE}$		0.109	0.112	0.115
		(0.049)**	(0.048)**	(0.052)**
Δx_i^M	0.910	0.907	0.903	0.904
	(0.045)***	(0.046)***	(0.046)***	(0.046)***
Δx_i^L	0.059	0.059	0.061	0.058
	(0.016)***	(0.017)***	(0.017)***	(0.017)***
Δx_i^K	0.046	0.048	0.049	0.045
	(0.037)	(0.037)	(0.037)	(0.038)
Medium size	0.020	0.018	0.018	0.016
	(0.019)	(0.019)	(0.019)	(0.019)
Large size	0.058	0.056	0.056	0.052
	(0.024)**	(0.024)**	(0.024)**	(0.023)**
Foreign$_i$	0.025	0.027	0.028	0.026
	(0.023)	(0.024)	(0.024)	(0.023)
p_i^{COMPET}			−0.022	
			(0.018)	
$p_i^{COMPET} \times s_i^{MNE}$			−0.028	
			(0.048)	
$TECH_i$				0.022
				(0.018)
$TECH_i \times s_i^{MNE}$				−0.007
				(0.047)
$COOPTECH_i$				0.092
				(0.064)
$COOPTECH_i \times s_i^{MNE}$				−0.142
				(0.121)
Observations	1012	1012	1012	1012
R^2	0.61	0.61	0.61	0.61

Dependent variable: (ΔY_i). Regression includes constant term and full sets of country and industry dummies. Robust standard errors in parentheses.
* Significant at 10%.
** Significant at 5%.
*** Significant at 1%.

further support that the benefit of the forced linkage effect and its coercive mechanism runs through the customer–supplier relationship.

In column (4), we enlarge our specification with qualitative variables closely related to a more cooperative mechanism that might channel productivity gains for suppliers because they sell their products to multinational firms. These variables are $TECH_i$, $COOPTECH_i$ and their respective interaction terms with s_i^{MNE}. The introduction of these variables jointly tests whether the beneficial productivity effect induced by the forced linkage is, as hypothesized, the result of tough demands by multinationals or whether it is the result of a more frictionless technology transfer between multinationals and their suppliers. Results show that neither the two variables nor their interaction terms are significant. At the same time, ($p_i^{CUST} \times s_i^{MNE}$) stays positive and significant as before. Thus controlling for collaboration between suppliers and customers in the development of new technologies does not affect the quantitative role of the forced linkage effect in the supplier–customer relationship thus far.

In the above estimations, we defined the supplier status of a firm using a binary yes/no variable. However, we also have information on the share of output that is sold to a multinational. We use this information in the results reported in Table 4. We re-estimate Eq. (1) but now using the share of output and its interaction as independent variables. Results are much in line with the results in Table 3. We find that the share of output sold to multinationals is only positively associated with productivity growth when it is accompanied by pressure from customers. This, hence, provides further support for our hypothesis of a forced linkage effect.

4.2. Exogeneity of supplier status

Before we move on to some further robustness checks, we consider the assumption of exogeneity of the supplier status. This assumption would not hold if there were self-selection, whereby the most productive firms might self-select to become suppliers of multinationals (Javorcik and Spatareanu, 2008). One way of alleviating this problem is our definition of the supplier status in the period before productivity growth is measured. Note also that our variable of most interest is the interaction of pressure from customers and the supplier status, not solely the supplier status. There is no reason to suspect

Table 4
Estimation results using share of output to multinationals.

	(1)	(2)	(3)	(4)
$share_i^{MNE}$	0.165	0.040	0.041	0.052
	(0.068)**	(0.067)	(0.072)	(0.085)
p_i^{PC}		−0.031	−0.022	−0.033
		(0.018)*	(0.017)	(0.018)*
$p_i^{PC} \times share_i^{MNE}$		0.296	0.284	0.304
		(0.129)**	(0.134)**	(0.129)**
Δx_i^M	0.913	0.912	0.908	0.908
	(0.045)***	(0.045)***	(0.046)***	(0.046)***
Δx_i^L	0.055	0.055	0.057	0.054
	(0.016)***	(0.017)***	(0.017)***	(0.017)***
Δx_i^K	0.046	0.047	0.048	0.043
	(0.037)	(0.037)	(0.037)	(0.038)
Medium size	0.021	0.020	0.019	0.018
	(0.019)	(0.019)	(0.019)	(0.019)
Large size	0.059	0.055	0.055	0.050
	(0.024)**	(0.024)**	(0.024)**	(0.023)**
$Foreign_i$	0.018	0.022	0.023	0.020
	(0.023)	(0.023)	(0.023)	(0.023)
p_i^{COMPET}			−0.025	
			(0.018)	
$p_i^{COMPET} \times s_i^{MNE}$			0.001	
			(0.130)	
$TECH_i$				0.021
				(0.017)
$TECH_i \times s_i^{MNE}$				−0.049
				(0.111)
$COOPTECH_i$				0.071
				(0.065)
$COOPTECH_i \times s_i^{MNE}$				−0.397
				(0.444)
Observations	1012	1012	1012	1012
R^2	0.61	0.61	0.61	0.61

Dependent variable: (ΔY_i). Regression includes constant term and full sets of country and industry dummies. Robust standard errors in parentheses.
* Significant at 10%.
** Significant at 5%.
*** Significant at 1%.

that among suppliers of MNEs, those suppliers that exhibit higher pressure from their multinational customers experience it because they have higher productivity growth.[22]

Nevertheless, we also test explicitly for exogeneity using an instrumental variables approach. The BEEPS data provides us with a number of potential instruments. We employ two instruments for the supplier status (either dummy variable or the share of output supplied to multinationals) which are based on two questions in the 2002 survey. The first is a dummy variable that indicates whether a firm ever had to resolve an overdue payment, the second a dummy indicating whether a firm is a member of a business association or chamber of commerce.

We consider the first to be a relevant instrument, as being a supplier necessarily implies the receipt of payment from the customer. However, there may be a difference in the speed and reliability of the payment depending on the nature of the customer. On the one hand, multinationals as opposed to domestic customers, may be more forthcoming with their payments as they are part of a large internationally operating enterprise which is likely to be a reliable debtor. On the other hand, a multinational is likely to be in a strong bargaining position and might optimize its timing of payment flows which could result in payment delays. In any case, the variable is likely to be correlated with the supplier status of a firm. There is, however, no reason to suppose that the receipt of an overdue payment is related to productivity growth of the firm.

The second instrument is also expected to be correlated with the supplier status as the membership of an association or chamber of commerce may make it easier for a local supplier to find customers. Again, however there is no reason to believe that such a membership may be more or less likely for firms with high vs low productivity growth.

Table 5 presents the first stage regression coefficients for the excluded instruments as well as the diagnostic tests. We re-estimate the models presented in columns (2) in Table 3 (supplier dummy) and Table 4 (share of output), respectively, using an IV estimator. Column (1) in Table 5 assumes the supplier dummy to be endogenous, column (2) uses the share of output supplied to multinationals.

[22] In fact, as a referee pointed out to us, the interaction of the supplier status and pressure shows how suppliers are persuaded to improve in light of multinationals' demands – and for this, in some sense, it does not matter whether the supplier status is exogenous or not.

402 O.N. Godart, H. Görg / Journal of Economic Behavior & Organization 94 (2013) 393–404

Table 5
Exogeneity test: first stage regression results.

	(1)	(2)
Dependent variable	s_i^{MNE}	$share_i^{MNE}$
Payment	−0.092	−0.023
	(0.018)***	(0.006)***
Business association	−0.041	−0.005
	(0.020)**	(0.06)
F test	15.18	10.37
(*p*-value)	(0.000)***	(0.000)***
Underidentification	29.72	20.81
(*p*-value)	(0.000)***	(0.000)**
Hansen J	0.023	0.000
(*p*-value)	(0.880)	(0.994)
Exogeneity	0.457	0.328
(*p*-value)	(0.499)	(0.567)

Table only reports coefficients and standard errors for excluded instruments in the first stage; regression includes all exogenous variables included in specifications in column (2) in Tables 3 and 4, respectively. Instruments are (i) dummy whether a firm ever had to resolve an overdue payment, (ii) dummy whether a firm is a member of a business association or chamber of commerce. Dummies defined as 1 = yes, 2 = no. Robust standard errors in parentheses.
* Significant at 10%.
** Significant at 5%.
*** Significant at 1%.

Note, firstly, that both instruments are individually significant in the regressions. Given the way these variables are defined, the negative coefficients imply that a firm is more likely to be a supplier (or supply a larger proportion of output to a multinational) if the firm either had to resolve an overdue payment or is a member of a business organization/chamber of commerce. The F-tests also suggest that the instruments are jointly relevant, and the F-statistics are above 10, the value generally considered to be high enough to reject the assumption of weak instruments (Staiger and Stock, 1997). The under-identification tests also suggest that we do not suffer from a weak instrument problem. The Hansen J statistics furthermore suggest that our overidentification restrictions are valid, suggesting instrument validity.

Based on these instruments, we then test for the assumption of exogeneity of the two alternative measures of the supplier status in Eq. (1). We are not able to reject this assumption. Hence, we are confident that our estimations based on the assumption of exogeneity allow us to identify an effect of the supplier status on productivity growth of firms.

Table 6
Robustness checks.

	(1) Pressure defined as fairly or very important	(2) Pressure defined as fairly or very important	(3) Only domestic firms	(4) Only domestic firms
s_i^{MNE}	0.005		−0.042	
	(0.040)		(0.035)	
$share_i^{MNE}$		−0.010		−0.004
		(0.098)		(0.071)
p_i^{PC}	0.007	0.002	−0.049	−0.042
	(0.020)	(0.019)	(0.019)***	(0.019)**
$p_i^{PC} \times s_i^{MNE}$	0.017		0.134	
	(0.048)		(0.055)**	
$p_i^{PC} \times share_i^{MNE}$		0.244		0.330
		(0.123)**		(0.147)**
Δx_i^M	0.910	0.913	0.895	0.898
	(0.045)***	(0.045)***	(0.052)***	(0.052)***
Δx_i^K	0.059	0.052	0.045	0.043
	(0.016)***	(0.016)***	(0.017)**	(0.018)**
Δx_i^L	0.046	0.044	0.052	0.051
	(0.037)	(0.037)	(0.038)	(0.039)
Medium size	0.019	0.020	0.019	0.020
	(0.019)	(0.019)	(0.020)	(0.021)
Large size	0.059	0.058	0.064	0.064
	(0.024)**	(0.024)**	(0.027)**	(0.027)**
$Foreign_i$	0.026	0.018		
	(0.023)	(0.022)		
Observations	1012	1012	910	910
R^2	0.61	0.61	0.59	0.59

Dependent variable: (ΔY_i). Regression includes constant term and full sets of country and industry dummies. Robust standard errors in parentheses.
* Significant at 10%.
** Significant at 5%.
*** Significant at 1%.

4.3. Further robustness checks

Table 6 presents the results of two further robustness checks. The first one, reported in columns (1) and (2) uses a slightly re-defined measure of pressure from customers. Recall that in the estimations thus far this is measured as a dummy equal to one if the firm reports that pressure from customers is "very important". We now redefine this variable as equal to one if the firm answers "very important" or "fairly important" to this question. This, of course, also implies that the interaction terms ($p_i^{CUST} \times s_i^{MNE}$) and ($p_i^{CUST} \times s_i^{MNE}$) are recalculated. The results in columns (1) and (2) are fairly similar to those reported in Tables 3 and 4, with one important exception. The coefficient on the interaction term ($p_i^{CUST} \times s_i^{MNE}$) is no longer statistically significant in column (1). This indicates that the supplier status per se (i.e. measured with a dummy) only has a positive effect on productivity growth if firms are subject to very important pressure from customers.

The analysis thus far includes both domestic and foreign firms. From the perspective of a host country policy maker it may, however, be particularly important to know how domestic firms are impacted upon by their linkages with multinationals. In order to consider this explicitly, we dropped all foreign firms from our sample and re-estimated Eq. (1) only for the sample of domestic firms. The results, which are very similar to those found in Tables 3 and 4, are reported in columns (3) and (4) of Table 6. They support our hypothesis of a forced linkage effect in the customer–supplier relationship between multinationals and domestic firms.

5. Conclusions

This paper presents the first empirical evidence of a forced linkage effect in the context of spillovers from FDI using a large sample of more than 1000 firms in 25 emerging economies. We find that productivity gains only materialize for suppliers of multinationals when they are pressured by their customers to reduce production costs or create new products. Suppliers of multinational firms appear to be forced by their multinational customers to adopt some tough demands on product features and business interaction procedures that have a positive productivity effect.

Such an effect of serving multinationals has largely been ignored by the recent literature on backward spillovers. We show that the forced linkage effect holds in various specifications, controlling for other factors that may impact the supplier–customer relationship.

This adds a new policy relevant angle to the spillovers literature. Most of the studies on spillovers through backward linkages at least implicitly, if not explicitly, seem to be based on the assumption of a benevolent multinational that is willing to share knowledge voluntarily and instruct willing suppliers. While our evidence does not indicate that this is not the case, our results suggest that the customer–supplier relationship may not always be so harmonious. Multinationals' accumulated experience allows them to put pressure on their suppliers to improve production costs or create new products – which also turns out to be to the benefit of the supplier, in terms of increased productivity growth.

Acknowledgements

We are grateful to Robert Feenstra, Lionel Fontagné, Gene Grossman, Aoife Hanley, Richard Kneller, Peter Neary, Horst Raff, Selin Sayek Böke, Eric Strobl, seminar participants at the Kiel Institute, the University of Granada and Bilkent University, and two anonymous referees for very helpful comments. All remaining errors are our own.

Appendix 1.

Description of the variables used.

Questions	Year of the survey	Answers used	Name of variable
*"Over the last 36 month how have [**sales, fixed assets, material inputs**] changed and what is the percent of change for your company, in real terms (i.e. after allowing for inflation)"*	2005	Sales	Δy_i
		Fixed assets	Δx_i^K
		Material inputs	Δx_i^M
Percentage change in fulltime employment between 2002 and 2005 (in decimals)	2005	Employment	Δx_i^L
"What percent of your domestic sales are to: . . .?" Dummy equal to one if answer is positive	2002	Multinationals located in your country	s_i^{MNE}
"What percent of your domestic sales are to: . . .?"	2002	Multinationals located in your country	$share_i^{MNE}$
"How would you rate the importance of each of the following factors *on key decisions about your business with respect to "Reducing the production costs of existing products and services"?"*	2002	Pressure from domestic competitors	p_i^{COMPET}
How would you rate the importance on key decisions about your business with respect to "*Reducing the production costs of existing products and services"?*" or "Developing new products or services and markets"	2002	Pressure from customers	p_i^{CUST}
"Has your firm acquired new production technology over the last 36 months?"	2005	Yes = 1; No = 0	$TECH_i$

Appendix 1 (*Continued*)

Questions	Year of the survey	Answers used	Name of variable
"What was the most important way your firm acquired this new technology, choosing from the list below?"	2005	In cooperation with customers	$COOPTECH_i$
Which of the following best describes the main chairholder(s) in your the firm...?	2005	Foreign company: Yes = 1; No = 0	*Foreign*
How many permanent, full time employees has your firm now...	2005	Dummy if 1–49 employees	Small size
How many permanent, full time employees has your firm now...	2005	Dummy if 50 – 249 employees	Medium size
How many permanent, full time employees has your firm now...	2005	Dummy if more than 249 employees	Large size
Industry	2005		μ_j

References

Aitken, B., Harrison, A., 1999. Do domestic firms benefit from direct foreign investment? Evidence from Venezuela. American Economic Review 89, 605–618.
Antràs, P., 2003. Firms, contracts, and trade structure. Quarterly Journal of Economics 118, 1375–1418.
Antràs, P., Helpman, E., 2004. Global sourcing. Journal of Political Economy 112, 552–580.
Antràs, P., Helpman, E., 2008. Contractual frictions and global sourcing. In: Helpman, E., Marin, D., Verdier, T. (Eds.), The Organization of Firms in a Global Economy. Harvard University Press, Cambridge, MA, pp. 9–54.
Barrios, S., Görg, H., Strobl, E., 2011. Spillovers through backward linkages from multinationals: measurement matters! European Economic Review 55, 862–875.
Blalock, G., Gertler, P.J., 2008. Welfare gains from foreign direct investment through technology transfer to local suppliers. Journal of International Economics 74, 402–421.
Blomström, M., Kokko, A., 1998. Multinational corporations and spillovers. Journal of Economic Surveys 12, 247–277.
Driffield, N., Munday, M., Roberts, A., 2002. Foreign direct investment, transactions linkages, and the performance of the domestic sector. International Journal of the Economics of Business 9, 335–351.
Fries, S., Lysenko, T., Polenac, S., 2003. The 2002 Business Environment and Enterprise Performance Survey: Results From a Survey of 6,100 Firms. EBRD, London.
Girma, S., Görg, H., Pisu, M., 2008. Exporting, linkages and productivity spillovers from foreign direct investment. Canadian Journal of Economics 41, 320–340.
Görg, H., Greenaway, D., 2004. Much ado about nothing? Do domestic firms really benefit from foreign direct investment? World Bank Research Observer 19, 171–197.
Gorodnichenko, Y., Svejnar, J., Terrell, K., 2007. When does FDI have positive spillovers? Evidence from 17 Emerging Market Economies. IZA Discussion Paper 3079.
Gorodnichenko, Y., Svejnar, J., Terrell, K., 2010. Globalization and innovation in emerging markets. American Economic Journal: Macroeconomics 2, 194–226.
Grossman, G.M., Helpman, E., 2002. Integration versus outsourcing in industry equilibrium. Quarterly Journal of Economics 117, 85–120.
Grossman, G.M., Helpman, E., 2004. Managerial incentives and the international organization of production. Journal of International Economics 63, 237–262.
Harrison, A., Rodriguez-Clare, A., 2009. Trade, foreign investment, and industrial policy for developing countries. NBER Working Paper 15261.
Haskel, J.E., Pereira, S.C., Slaughter, M.J., 2007. Does inward foreign direct investment boost the productivity of domestic firms? Review of Economics and Statistics 89, 482–496.
Havranek, T., Irsova, Z., 2011. Estimating vertical spillovers from FDI: why results vary and what the true effect is. Journal of International Economics 85, 234244.
Horn, H., Lang, H., Lundgren, S., 1995. Managerial effort incentives, X-inefficiency and international trade. European Economic Review 39, 117–138.
Javorcik, B.S., 2004. Does foreign direct investment increase the productivity of domestic firms? In search of spillovers through backward linkages. American Economic Review 94, 605–627.
Javorcik, B., 2008. Can survey evidence shed light on spillovers from foreign direct investment? World Bank Research Observer 23, 139–159.
Javorcik, B., Spatareanu, M., 2009. Tough love: do Czech suppliers learn from their relationships with multinationals. Scandinavian Journal of Economics 111, 811–833.
Javorcik, B., Keller, W., Tybout, J., 2008. Openness and industrial responses in a Wal-Mart world: a case study of Mexican soaps, detergents and surfactant producers. The World Economy 31, 1558–1580.
Kaufmann, D., Wei, S., 1999. Does Grease money speed up the wheels of commerce? NBER Working Papers 7093.
Keller, W., Yeaple, S.R., 2009. Multinational enterprises, international trade, and productivity growth: firm-level evidence from the United States. Review of Economics and Statistics 91, 821–831.
Levinsohn, J., Petrin, A., 2003. Estimating production functions using inputs to control for observables. Review of Economic Studies 70, 317–341.
Liker, J., Choi, T., 2004. Building deep supplier relationship. Harvard Business Review 32, 104–113.
Liu, Z., 2008. Foreign direct investment and technology spillovers: theory and evidence. Journal of Development Economics 85, 176–193.
Markusen, J., Venables, A., 1999. Foreign direct investment as a catalyst for industrial development. European Economic Review 43, 335–356.
Moran, T., 2001. Parental Supervision: The New Paradigm for Foreign Direct Investment and Development. Institute for International Economics, Washington, DC.
Rodriguez-Clare, A., 1996. Multinationals, linkages, and economic development. American Economic Review 86, 852–873.
Staiger, D., Stock, J.H., 1997. Instrumental variables regression with weak instruments. Econometrica 65, 557–586.

Chapter 16

Multinational Companies, Technology Spillovers and Plant Survival*

Holger Görg
University of Nottingham, Nottingham NG7 2RD, England
holger.gorg@nottingham.ac.uk

Eric Strobl
Université Catholique de Louvain, B-1348 Louvain-la-Neuve, Belgium
strobl@core.ucl.ac.be

Abstract

How does the presence of multinational companies affect plant survival in the host country? We postulate that multinational companies can impact positively on plant survival through technology spillovers. We examine the nature of the effect of multinationals using a Cox proportional hazard model, which we estimate using plant-level data for Irish manufacturing industries. Our results show that the presence of multinationals has a life-enhancing effect only on indigenous plants in high-tech industries, suggesting the presence of technology spillovers. In contrast, multinationals compete with each other in low-tech sectors in the host country.

Keywords: Multinational companies; technology spillovers; plant survival
JEL classification: *F*23; *L*60

I. Introduction

Multinational companies and their associated foreign direct investment (FDI) may have various effects on the host country over and above the inflow of physical capital. In particular, foreign direct investment can bring about the inflow of superior knowledge into the economy, which can be adapted by host country firms. Multinational companies (MNCs) find it profitable to invest abroad because they own firm-specific assets, one of which is the multinational's access to improved production technology; see Caves (1996).

Blomström and Kokko (1998) discuss a number of channels through which superior knowledge may spill over to other firms located in the host

*We are grateful to Salvador Barrios, Sourafel Girma, Richard Upward, two anonymous referees and seminar participants at Trinity College Dublin for helpful comments and suggestions. Thanks are also due to Gerry Brett and Elaine Lucey for help with the CSO data. All remaining errors are, of course, ours. This project was supported by the European Commission as part of a TMR programme on Foreign Direct Investment and the Multinational Corporation (contract no. ERBFMRXCT980215). Görg gratefully acknowledges additional financial support from the Leverhulme Trust under Programme Grant F114/BF.

country. For instance, arm's-length relationships between host country suppliers and MNCs may imply that domestic suppliers are not only exposed to new products and production techniques, but may also receive technical or managerial support from their multinational customers. Hence, suppliers learn new production technologies through contacts with MNC customers. Moreover, spillovers of technology may occur from MNCs to domestic firms through employees' moving from the former to the latter, taking their knowledge of production techniques with them and applying it in the domestic firm. Therefore, host country firms may benefit from technology spillovers from MNCs, and may be able to improve their productive efficiency as they learn from MNCs.

There are a number of empirical studies on the presence of technology spillovers between MNCs and host country firms; some of the more recent analyses include Blomström and Sjöholm (1999) for Indonesia, Aitken and Harrison (1999) for Venezuela, and Girma, Greenaway and Wakelin (2001) for the UK.[1] These studies usually regress productivity in host country firm *i*, measured as either labour or total factor productivity, on a number of firm and industry variables, using data for manufacturing industries at the firm or sectoral level. To check for technology spillovers, they also include a proxy for the extent of MNC investment in the sector in which firm *i* operates. The results are mixed, showing that the effects of FDI on technology vary for different countries and sectors.

These mixed results provide evidence for the claim that the absorptive capacity of host country firms is an important determinant of whether or not they benefit from FDI; see e.g. Kokko (1994) and Kokko, Tansini and Zejan (1996). That is, firms have to be able to utilise spillovers from multinationals in order to improve their productivity. Glass and Saggi (1998), for example, argue that the technology gap between the host and home country indicates the absorptive capacity of host country firms. The larger the gap, the less likely are host country firms to have the human capital and technological know-how to benefit from the technology transferred by multinationals.

Here, we offer an alternative approach to examining technology spillovers from MNCs, based on the following idea: an increase in productivity through technology spillovers will, all else equal, reduce a host country firm's average cost of production. This has obvious benefits for the firm and, in this paper, we are concerned with the benefit associated with firm survival. Audretsch (1991, 1995) argues that the probability of firm *i* remaining in industry *j* at time *t* is determined by a firm's price cost margin, i.e., the degree to which price exceeds a firm's average cost. According to this argument, a firm's ability to increase price and/or reduce average cost will have a positive effect on firm survival, *ceteris paribus*. In this

[1] See Görg and Strobl (2001) and Blomström and Kokko (1998) for recent surveys.

framework, technology spillovers from MNCs and the associated increase in productivity enable host country firms to produce at lower average cost for a given level of production, which increases their price–cost margins. All else equal, this leads to a higher probability of survival for host country firms.

The presence of multinationals can also have negative effects on the survival of host country firms, however. As argued by Aitken and Harrison (1999), multinationals producing at lower marginal costs than host country firms have an incentive to increase output and attract demand away from these firms. This will cause host country rivals to cut production which, if they face fixed costs of production, will raise their average cost, thereby reducing their probability of survival. In fact, regardless of cost structure, increased production by foreign rivals will generally lead to a reduction in output price (at least in the short run) which will reduce profitability and, thus, may have a negative effect on survival. In addition, to the extent that the presence of multinationals leads to higher wage demands in the economy, this will increase a firm's average costs. This, *ceteris paribus*, will also reduce its probability of survival. Whether the effect of MNCs on the survival of host country firms is, on average, positive or negative is therefore ambiguous and has to be determined empirically.[2]

We address the issue of the effects of MNCs on firm survival using the example of the Republic of Ireland, which appears to be a model illustration for studying this effect due to the importance of MNCs for its economy. Data from the Irish Central Statistics Office show that foreign multinationals in Ireland accounted for roughly 47 percent of manufacturing employment and 77 percent of net output in manufacturing in 1996. The corresponding figures in 1983 (the first year for which these data are available) were 38 and 58 percent, respectively, which illustrate the increasing importance of multinationals for Irish manufacturing. While indigenous manufacturing tended to be concentrated on traditional and food-sector activities, MNCs have invested primarily in modern high-tech sectors. This has led to a rapid increase in the significance of high-tech sectors for the Irish economy; see Barry and Bradley (1997). From the perspective of this paper, the increasing role of MNCs provides us not only with cross-sectional but also intertemporal variation in the degree of FDI.

Using plant-level data for the Irish manufacturing sector, we investigate whether the presence of multinational companies in sector j has any effect on the survival of plants in the same sector, *ceteris paribus*.[3] In examining the

[2] Unfortunately, with the data available to us, i.e., employment data, we are not able to distinguish empirically between the various positive and negative effects, only whether in total positive or negative effects dominate.

[3] In a related paper using the same dataset, Görg and Strobl (2002) find that the presence of MNCs fosters the entry of domestic plants in Irish manufacturing industries.

effect of MNCs on the survival of host country plants, we distinguish between the impact of MNCs on Irish-owned (indigenous) plants and on foreign-owned plants (i.e., subsidiaries of other MNCs) located in the host country, where the latter essentially serve as a natural control group. While there have been several studies of plant and firm survival for different countries, the effect of MNCs on survival has, to the best of our knowledge, not received any in-depth attention in the literature to date.[4]

At least two issues may be expected to impact on the nature of this effect. First, the effects of greenfield investment by multinationals and takeovers of existing domestic firms may differ. In the case of the former, increased capacity may lead to reductions in output price. Second, the market orientation of multinationals may matter. If they produce primarily for export markets, there should be more scope for expanding production without having to reduce the output price on the host country market. In contrast, if multinationals serve only domestic markets, the negative effects may outweigh any possible positive effects of spillovers. While we do not have plant-level data to account for these possibilities in any detail, aggregate data suggest that most of the FDI in Ireland has been greenfield investment (i.e., the setting up of new plants) with, on average, more than 85 percent of output produced by MNCs exported to world markets; see Barry and Bradley (1997).

The remainder of the paper is structured as follows. In Section II we briefly discuss the dataset used. Section III examines the effect of the presence of multinationals on plant survival by estimating hazard functions. Section IV summarises our results along with some concluding comments.

II. Dataset

We investigate the effect of the presence of multinationals on plant survival using data taken from the *Employment Survey* which is carried out annually by Forfás, the policy and advisory board for industrial development in Ireland. The survey has been undertaken since 1973 and data are available to us for the period 1973–1996. The main advantages of the survey are that it covers virtually all known active manufacturing plants, and that the response rate is generally over 99 percent, thus providing a sample of over 17,000 plants. For these plants we have data on employment, nationality of

[4] See, for example, Audretsch (1991) and Audretsch and Mahmood (1995) for the US, Mata and Portugal (1994) and Mata, Portugal and Guimaraes (1995) for Portugal, McCloughan and Stone (1998) for the UK and Kearns and Ruane (2001) for Ireland.

ownership, sector of location, and start-up year, among other information. A plant is classified as foreign-owned if 50 percent or more of its shares are held by foreign owners.

Given the nature of our dataset, the observed lifetimes of some of the plants in the sample are necessarily left censored while others are right censored, and these phenomena are appropriately dealt with in all estimations in the paper.[5] In total our sample covers 17,789 plants, of which 4,658 existed at the beginning and 6,667 at the end of our sample period. Of those that existed from the beginning, only 1,632 remained at the end of our sample period.

Table 1 provides summary measures of the foreign and indigenous sub-sectors of Irish manufacturing for the years 1973, 1984 and 1996. The indigenous sector has steadily decreased its share of manufacturing employment from roughly 67 to 55 percent, reflecting the growing importance of multinationals for the manufacturing sector. However, the share of indigenous plants has remained relatively constant around 87 percent over the period. This is due to a reduction in the average plant size for domestic plants, while the size of foreign-owned plants has remained fairly constant. It should also be noted that foreign plants are, on average, considerably larger than domestic plants.

We have also grouped the 68 sub-sector classifications used throughout this paper into two broader groups—high- and low-technology sectors—in order to provide and compare summary statistics for indigenous and foreign plants within sectors of different technology intensity.[6] The statistics show that indigenous high-tech plants are considerably smaller than foreign high-tech plants and, while their average size has fallen since 1973, the size of foreign plants has risen over the sampling period. Most notably, the employment share in indigenous plants in high-tech sectors has fallen over the period from 44 to 23 percent, indicating the dominance of foreign-owned plants in this technology group.

The low-tech sector, in contrast, is dominated by domestic plants. Their employment share has remained constant at about 70 percent of total employment. The average size of both foreign and indigenous plants in total manufacturing has fallen, although that of indigenous plants remains substantially smaller.

[5] All estimations were performed using STATA version 7.0, which can be used to control appropriately for left and right truncation.

[6] The classification of sectors into high tech and low tech is based on an OECD classification as used by Kearns and Ruane (2001). We aggregated the OECD's medium- and high-tech sectors to define our high-tech group. Accordingly, high-tech sectors are Aerospace, Computers & Office Machinery, Electronics & Communications, Pharmaceuticals, Scientific Instruments, Electrical Machinery, Motor Vehicles, Chemicals, and Non-electrical Machinery.

III. Modelling Plant Survival using a Hazard Function

The aim of this paper is to determine whether the presence of multinationals has an effect on the survival of both indigenous and foreign plants in Irish manufacturing. It has been established in the empirical IO literature (as cited above) that there are many factors which can possibly affect plant survival. In order to properly disentangle the impact of plant- and industry-specific factors from that of the presence of MNCs on the survivability of plants, we turn to semi-parametric modelling of plants' hazard rates.

Following the related empirical literature, for example, Audretsch and Mahmood (1995) and Mata and Portugal (1994), we utilise a Cox (1972) proportional hazard model as our equation to be estimated. The Cox proportional hazard model does not require any restrictive assumptions regarding the baseline hazard, such as a Weibull or log-normal specification. This is appropriate for our purposes, as our main interest is not in the estimation of the underlying baseline hazard but in the effect of the presence of MNCs on

Table 1. *Descriptive statistics by nationality*

Sample		1973	1984	1996
Total indigenous	employment	151,741	126,687	120,728
	plants	4,039	6,448	5,830
	size	38	20	21
Total foreign	employment	73,827	80,550	97,559
	plants	619	861	837
	size	119	94	117
of which				
Indigenous high tech	employment	11,492	12,452	16,726
	plants	313	651	805
	size	37	19	21
Foreign high tech	employment	14,924	30,767	54,519
	plants	137	328	377
	size	109	94	145
Indigenous low tech	employment	140,249	114,235	104,002
	plants	3,726	5,811	5,025
	size	38	20	21
Foreign low tech	employment	58,903	49,783	43,040
	plants	482	536	460
	size	122	93	94
Indigenous share of plants	Total	0.87	0.88	0.87
	High tech	0.70	0.66	0.68
	Low tech	0.88	0.92	0.92
Indigenous share of employment	Total	0.67	0.61	0.55
	High tech	0.44	0.29	0.23
	Low tech	0.70	0.70	0.71

plant survival. As pointed out in the literature on survival analysis, the semi-parametric modelling approach of the Cox proportional hazard model is advantageous if the parametric form of the underlying baseline hazard function is not known with certainty.

The Cox proportional hazard model specifies the hazard function $h(t)$ to be:

$$h(t) = h_0(t)e^{(X\beta)}, \tag{1}$$

where $h(t)$ is the rate at which plants exit at time t given that they have survived in $t-1$, h_0 is the baseline hazard function (the parametric form of which is not specified) when all of the covariates are set to zero, and X is a vector of plant and industry characteristics postulated to impact on a plant's hazard rate. The covariates included are described below.

SIZE is the plant's size in terms of employment at time t and is included because it can be considered a stylised fact that small plants generally have lower probabilities of survival than large plants; see, for example, Audretsch and Mahmood (1995) and Mata and Portugal (1994). Moreover, Mata *et al.* (1995) find that current plant size is a better predictor of plant failure than initial size. Hence we include size at time t in the regression.

The minimum efficient scale of the industry, *MES*, is measured as the log of median employment size in sector j, as in Sutton (1991).[7] Our *a priori* expectation as to the sign of the coefficient is ambiguous. On the one hand, plants entering industries with large minimum efficient scale may be expected to have lower probabilities of survival than plants entering other industries, as small entrants may find it difficult to attain the efficient level of production unless they experience sufficient growth in their infancy; see Audretsch (1991) and Mata and Portugal (1994). On the other hand, as Audretsch (1991) points out, industries with high MES are usually industries that also show high price–cost margins, which should increase plant survival.

HERF denotes the Herfindahl index of sector j, measured in terms of plants' employment shares. Again, expectations regarding the effect of market concentration on survival are not clear-cut. Higher market concentration may lead to higher price–cost margins in the industry which, *ceteris paribus*, should increase a plant's probability of survival. However, plants in highly concentrated markets may be subject to fiercely aggressive behaviour by rivals, thereby reducing chances of survival. Note that since we are not

[7] In an alternative specification we defined *MES* as (the log of) average plant size in the industry. These results, which are not reported here but can be obtained from the authors on request, yield results similar to those obtained using median size. We could not calculate any additional alternative measures of *MES* due to lack of appropriate data.

able to completely identify all plants belonging to the same firm, our *HERF* is based on plant rather than firm data and is thus an inferior (to that based on firm-level data) measure of industry concentration. However, this is likely to be less problematic in the Irish case as the size of the domestic market and the importance of the export market for foreign firms imply that most foreign and domestic firms are single plant firms.

GROWTH is the net sectoral (employment) growth rate. Audretsch (1991) argues that industry growth may elevate the price above the long-run average cost, i.e., increase firms' price–cost margin which would, all else equal, affect survival rates positively. The sectoral growth rate also allows us to control for other sector-specific cyclical effects which may impact on plant survival.

Most importantly from our point of view, *MNC* is a proxy for the presence of multinationals in a sector and is defined as the share of employment by MNCs in sector j at time t. This variable is supposed to capture the spillover effects of multinationals on plant survival. If positive spillover effects occur, the presence of MNCs should have a positive effect on plant survival.

All sector-specific variables are calculated for the 68 sub-sector classifications commonly used by the Irish Central Statistics Office. Table 2 provides some summary statistics on these sectoral variables. It is worth noting that there is substantial variation in these variables, not only cross-section but also over time.

The specification of equation (1) also includes a number of dummy variables. *TECH* is a dummy variable equal to one if the plant operates in a sector categorised as high tech. This should allow for taking into account differences in innovation potential in high- and low-tech industries, since a plant's ability to innovate has been found to be an important determinant of survival; see Audretsch (1991, 1995). *BEU* takes the value of one if the plant came into existence prior to Ireland's entry into the European Union (EU) in 1973 and is intended to control for different policy regimes at the time of start-up. A further dummy variable is *OWN* which takes on the value of one if the plant is foreign-owned and zero otherwise. We also include time dummies to control for year-specific macroeconomic effects.

Table 2. *Description of sectoral variables*

	Mean	Max.	Min.	Std. dev. (total)	Std. dev. (time)
MNC	0.10	1.00	0.25	0.25	0.03
GROWTH	0.01	0.96	−0.49	0.10	0.06
HERF	0.12	0.01	0.94	0.12	0.04
MES	2.25	94.5	1	7.42	0.55

The results of estimating different variations of the hazard model described in (1) using data for the total sample are shown in Table 3.[8] All estimations are stratified by sector, which allows for equal coefficients of the covariates across strata (sectors), but baseline hazards unique to each stratum (sector). As can be seen, the log-likelihood and Wald tests provide satisfactory support for our model specifications. In interpreting the results, it should be recalled that our dependent variable is the hazard rate, i.e., a negative coefficient on an independent variable implies that it reduces the rate of hazard, thus increasing chances of survival, *ceteris paribus*.

In the base specification in column (i) we find that a greater presence of MNCs, measured in terms of share of employment in foreign multinationals,

Table 3. *Results of the Cox hazard-rate regression*

	All sectors		High tech		Low tech	
	(i) All	(ii) All	(iii) Foreign	(iv) Indigenous	(v) Foreign	(vi) Indigenous
SIZE	−0.007**	−0.007**	−0.008**	−0.014**	−0.006**	−0.008**
	(0.001)	(0.001)	(0.002)	(0.004)	(0.001)	(0.001)
MNC	−0.340**	−0.444*	1.350	−1.794*	1.398**	−0.076
	(0.072)	(0.189)	(1.918)	(0.831)	(0.539)	(0.228)
OWN	0.240**	0.104	—	—	—	—
	(0.044)	(0.198)				
TECH	0.242	0.284	—	—	—	—
	(0.128)	(0.146)				
*OWN*MNC*	—	−0.115	—	—	—	—
		(0.205)				
*TECH*MNC*	—	0.310	—	—	—	—
		(0.400)				
MES	0.007	0.007	0.068	0.027	0.010	0.011
	(0.009)	(0.009)	(0.086)	(0.041)	(0.018)	(0.014)
HERF	0.001*	0.001*	−0.000	0.000	0.003	0.001
	(0.000)	(0.000)	(0.002)	(0.002)	(0.001)	(0.001)
GROWTH	−1.148**	−1.149**	−0.462	0.822	−1.478*	−1.310**
	(0.161)	(0.161)	(1.020)	(0.631)	(0.613)	(0.179)
BEU	0.121*	0.122**	0.660*	0.199	0.088	0.107*
	(0.047)	(0.047)	(0.271)	(0.164)	(0.151)	(0.054)
No. of obs.	149,555	149,555	6,771	14,641	11,803	116,340
No. of subj.	14,388	14,388	596	1,495	1,080	11,217
Log likelihood	−36,683	−36,682	−690	−3,025	−1,417	28,870
Wald test ($\beta_i=0$)	45,708**	45,711**	136**	235**	158**	1,519**

Notes. Heteroscedasticity-consistent standard error in parentheses. ** and * imply significant at 1 and at 5 percent level, respectively. Time dummies included in all regressions.

[8] The regression results reported here are based on the sample of plants described above which includes incumbents as well as new entrants. We also estimated the survival regressions using new entrants only. The results, which can be obtained from the authors on request, are qualitatively similar to the results in this paper.

acts to increase the survival of plants.[9] This result suggests that there may be technology spillovers from MNCs to other plants in the same industrial sector, as argued above. This would lead to a reduction in average cost for the benefiting plant, which, *ceteris paribus*, increases its probability of survival.

An alternative interpretation of this positive effect could be that multinationals locate in industries that have higher productivity, as argued by Aitken and Harrison (1999), and hence higher survival rates. In this case, of course, the positive result would not necessarily indicate spillovers. Aitken and Harrison (1999) suggest that sectoral dummies be included to control for such a possible bias. In our estimation, the baseline hazard is stratified by sector, which allows for different baseline hazards per sector. As with sectoral dummies, this should take account of possible productivity differences across sectors.

There are several possible reasons why we, in contrast to Aitken and Harrison (1999), find evidence of positive spillovers despite controlling for time-invariant sector-specific effects. First, it may be that unlike domestic firms in many developing countries, Irish plants have relatively more absorptive capacity to avail themselves of spillovers from multinationals. For instance, in their study of Spain, Barrios and Strobl (2002) find that only domestic firms that were likely to be more technologically advanced, as proxied by the incidence of R&D and/or exporting activity, benefited from foreign presence in Spain. Second, it may also be that because studies of direct productivity spillovers, like Aitken and Harrison (1999), only measure potential spillovers for continuing plants, they miss a substantial proportion of the impact, i.e., on plant exit. However, it should also be noted that under the argument presented here, the impact of foreign presence on the productivity of domestic plants is, in contrast to studies such as Aitken and Harrison (1999), assumed to act indirectly through its impact on a plant's price–cost margin.

In terms of our other results, we also discover that plant size turns out to affect survival positively, i.e., small plants face a higher hazard of exit than do large plants. As pointed out above, this is a fairly standard finding in studies of survival; our result is thus in line with a large body of other empirical studies. Not surprisingly, we find that benevolent economic sectoral conditions, as measured by the sectoral growth rate, decrease the hazard of plant exits. In other words, fast growing markets appear to increase plant survival. This finding is in line with Mata and Portugal (1994) who

[9] We also experimented with including up to two lags of the foreign presence variable in this and subsequent regressions. In none of the cases did the lagged variables prove to be significant determinants of domestic plant survival and hence we do not report these results (they are also available on request).

report that, for Portuguese firms, fast growing markets make survival easier for new entrants. Our results also suggest that the higher the level of industry concentration, the less likely a plant is to survive. The coefficient on minimum efficient scale, another variable which captures industry characteristics, is statistically insignificant.

Turning to the dummy variables, we find that when controlling for other factors, foreign plants have higher hazards of exiting than indigenous plants. We do not find a difference in the hazard rate for plants located in high- and low-tech sectors, as indicated by the statistically insignificant coefficient on *TECH* once other sector- and plant-specific factors are controlled for. Finally, we find that plants that started up before Ireland's entry into the EU have a lower rate of survival than those that were established after this change in policy regime. This may not be surprising given that many of these firms would have still enjoyed tariffs and other forms of protection until Ireland's EU entry. As argued by Walsh and Whelan (2000), many such firms failed to adapt to the new challenges when markets opened up and subsequently declined since then.

In estimating the hazard model using data for all manufacturing industries, we implicitly assume that the effect of the explanatory variables is uniform across different plant types. This is arguably quite a restrictive assumption, given that we pool plants of different nationalities operating in sectors with different technology intensities. For example, *a priori*, these two characteristics may be expected to impact on whether or not plants are positively or negatively affected by the presence of multinationals in the same sector. As regards nationality, foreign-owned and domestic plants have different market orientations; the former are mainly export oriented and the latter serve mainly domestic markets; see Barry and Bradley (1997). Therefore, foreign plants are more likely to be in competition with other multinationals located in the sector serving the same export or domestic markets and may thus be more likely to experience a negative competition effect. Indigenous plants, on the other hand, may be less likely to experience such negative effects. Similar arguments can easily be made with regard to the other explanatory variables and, while their impact may not be the explicit focus of this paper, restricting them to be similar across nationality types could feasibly bias our results on the foreign presence variable.

In terms of technology, we expect foreign-owned plants to have higher technology levels than domestic plants operating in the same sector, thereby reflecting their firm-specific assets; see Caves (1996). Domestic plants operating in high-tech sectors may then be more likely to benefit from positive spillovers as they can be assumed to have relatively high levels of technology themselves. Thus, they can be expected to have some level of absorptive capacity, i.e., the necessary stock of knowledge which allows them to utilise spillovers from multinationals. This may not be the case for domestic plants operating in low-tech sectors. As with nationality types, it may also be important to allow for variation across technology groups in the other explanatory variables so as to obtain an unbiased estimate of the impact of foreign presence.

In order to investigate these issues we first re-ran the hazard model including interaction terms of the ownership and high-tech dummies with the MNC variable, thus allowing the coefficients of the MNC variable to vary across these two firm types. The results are reported in the second column of Table 3 and, as can be seen, the interaction terms are insignificant. It is also noteworthy that including these interaction terms makes the coefficient on the ownership dummy insignificant, thus suggesting some correlation between these variables that would be difficult to disentangle.

Hence we proceeded to investigate whether all coefficients should (jointly) vary across ownership type by implementing a likelihood ratio test in order to compare such an unrestricted model with the previous restricted model without interaction terms. The resultant likelihood ratio test statistic (47.61) was highly statistically significant, allowing us to reject the hypothesis that the data can be pooled across these two plant types. We also experimented in a similar manner to see whether we could pool the data across the two broad sector groups—high- and low-tech sectors—for the indigenous and foreign samples separately. For the case of indigenous plants, the likelihood ratio test statistic (22.87) was significant at the 1 percent level, suggesting that even within the indigenous group sample our model needs to be estimated separately for the high- and low-tech sector groups. In contrast, the resultant likelihood ratio test statistic (5.60) for foreign plants was statistically insignificant, thus indicating that the coefficients on the covariates jointly did not differ significantly across the broad sector groups.[10]

These results suggest that it is sensible to split the total sample into indigenous and foreign sub-samples. Moreover, for the indigenous subsample, our test suggests that it is necessary to break it up into high- and low-tech sub-samples. For consistency, we also broke up the foreign subsample into the two broad sector samples. We then re-estimated the hazard model for these four groups. The results are reported in Table 3, columns (iii)–(vi).

We now focus our attention on *MNC* as the main variable of interest. For domestic plants, we find that the presence of multinationals has a positive effect on plant survival only for plants operating in high-tech sectors. The

[10] The results of these estimations are not reported here but can be obtained from the authors on request.

coefficient on this variable for the low-tech sub-sample is statistically insignificant, suggesting that survival for this group is not affected by multinational presence. This finding is in line with the idea that plants need to have some level of absorptive capacity in order to be able to benefit from spillovers. High-tech plants may be expected to have such capacity, while low-tech plants may not.

Turning to the foreign sub-sample, we find that our estimations turn out positive coefficients on the *MNC* variable, although the coefficient is statistically significant only for the low-tech sectors. This suggests that the presence of multinationals in the sector reduces the survival of other foreign-owned plants in low-tech sectors. This is consistent with the idea that foreign plants are in competition with other multinationals located in the same sector, thus exerting negative effects on plant survival. This effect may be expected to be relatively more prevalent in sectors where multinationals produce more for the domestic market, such as the low-tech sectors in Ireland.[11]

IV. Conclusions

We have examined the effects of the presence of multinational companies on plant survival in the host country. We postulated that MNCs can impact positively on plant survival through technology spillovers. If such technology spillovers take place, the receipt of a superior technology by the recipient plant will lower its average cost of production which, all else equal, will increase a plant's probability of survival. However, multinationals can also have negative effects on plant survival. This may occur either through a reduction in output price, forcing domestic firms to cut production and thus increasing their average costs of production, or through crowding out domestic rivals by increasing the wage rate in the economy.

We studied the nature of the effect of multinationals using data for the Irish economy, an economy with high levels of foreign MNC involvement. In our empirical analysis, using a Cox proportional hazard model, we find that when controlling for other plant- and sector-specific effects, the presence of multinationals has a life-enhancing effect only on domestic plants operating in high-tech sectors. This suggests the presence of technology spillovers. We do not find any evidence for such an effect on the survival of domestic low-tech plants. This perhaps indicates a lack of absorptive capacity in low-tech plants in terms of their inability to absorb relevant

[11] Data available from the *Irish Economy Expenditure Survey* database, also maintained by Forfás, indicate that in 1996 foreign plants in low-tech sectors exported around 69 percent of output compared to 93 percent in high-tech sectors.

knowledge from multinationals. If this is the case, there would clearly be scope for policy intervention targeted at assisting low-tech indigenous plants to increase their learning ability.

We also find evidence that the presence of multinationals has a negative effect on the survival of other foreign-owned plants in the low-tech sectors. This may reflect that a negative competition effect, emanating from the presence of multinationals in the sector in which the foreign plant operates, outweighs any potential positive spillovers.

References

Aitken, B. J. and Harrison, A. E. (1999), Do Domestic Firms Benefit from Direct Foreign Investment? Evidence from Venezuela, *American Economic Review 89*, 605–618.

Audretsch, D. B. (1991), New-firm Survival and the Technological Regime, *Review of Economics and Statistics 60*, 441–450.

Audretsch, D. B. (1995), *Innovation and Industry Evolution*, MIT Press, Cambridge, MA.

Audretsch, D. B. and Mahmood, T. (1995), New-firm Survival: New Results using a Hazard Function, *Review of Economics and Statistics 77*, 97–103.

Barrios, S. and Strobl, E. (2002), Foreign Direct Investment and Productivity Spillovers: Evidence from the Spanish Experience, *Weltwirtschaftliches Archiv 138*, 459–481.

Barry, F. and Bradley, J. (1997), FDI and Trade: The Irish Host-country Experience, *Economic Journal 107*, 1798–1811.

Blomström, M. and Kokko, A. (1998), Multinational Corporations and Spillovers, *Journal of Economic Surveys 12*, 247–277.

Blomström, M. and Sjöholm, F. (1999), Technology Transfer and Spillovers: Does Local Participation with Multinationals Matter?, *European Economic Review 43*, 915–923.

Caves, R. E. (1996), *Multinational Enterprise and Economic Analysis*, 2nd ed., Cambridge University Press, Cambridge.

Cox, D. R. (1972), Regression Models and Life Tables, *Journal of the Royal Statistical Society, Series B 34*, 187–220.

Girma, S., Greenaway, D. and Wakelin, K. (2001), Who Benefits from Foreign Direct Investment in the UK?, *Scottish Journal of Political Economy 48*, 119–133.

Glass, A. J. and Saggi, K. (1998), International Technology Transfer and the Technology Gap, *Journal of Development Economics 55*, 369–398.

Görg, H. and Strobl, E. (2001), Multinational Companies and Productivity Spillovers: A Meta-analysis, *Economic Journal 111*, F723–F739.

Görg, H. and Strobl, E. (2002), Multinational Companies and Indigenous Development: An Empirical Analysis, *European Economic Review 46*, 1305–1322.

Kearns, A. and Ruane, F. (2001), The Tangible Contribution of R&D Spending by Foreign-owned Plants to a Host Region: A Plant Level Study of the Irish Manufacturing Sector 1980–1996, *Research Policy 30*, 227–244.

Kokko, A. (1994), Technology, Market Characteristics, and Spillovers, *Journal of Development Economics 43*, 279–293.

Kokko, A., Tansini, R. and Zejan, M. C. (1996), Local Technological Capability and Productivity Spillovers from FDI in the Uruguayan Manufacturing Sector, *Journal of Development Studies 32*, 602–611.

Mata, J. and Portugal, P. (1994), Life Duration of New Firms, *Journal of Industrial Economics 42*, 227–245.

Mata, J., Portugal, P. and Guimaraes, P. (1995), The Survival of New Plants: Start-up Conditions and Post-entry Evolution, *International Journal of Industrial Organization 13*, 459–482.

McCloughan, P. and Stone, I. (1998), Life Duration of Foreign Multinational Subsidiaries: Evidence from UK Northern Manufacturing Industry 1970–93, *International Journal of Industrial Organization 16*, 719–747.

Sutton, J. (1991), *Sunk Costs and Market Structure*, MIT Press, Cambridge, MA.

Walsh, P. P. and Whelan, C. (2000), The Importance of Structural Change in Industry for Growth, *Journal of the Statistical and Social Inquiry Society of Ireland 29*, 1–32.

First version submitted November 2001;
final version received January 2003.

Chapter 17

Multinational companies and indigenous development: An empirical analysis

Holger Görg[a,*], Eric Strobl[b]

[a] *School of Economics, University of Nottingham, Nottingham NG7 2RD, UK*
[b] *Department of Economics, University College Dublin, Belfield, Dublin 4, Ireland*

Received 1 May 1999; accepted 1 February 2001

Abstract

This paper presents an empirical study of the effect of foreign multinational companies on the development of indigenous firms in the host country. Our starting point is a recent paper by Markusen and Venables (European Economic Review 43 (1999) 335–356) that shows formally that multinationals, through the creation of linkages with indigenous suppliers, can exert positive effects on the development of indigenous firms. Based on the literature on entry in industrial organisation, we estimate empirically a model describing the entry of indigenous firms using data for the Irish manufacturing sector. Our results indicate that there is a positive effect of multinational companies on the entry of indigenous firms for a variety of alternative specifications. © 2002 Elsevier Science B.V. All rights reserved.

JEL classification: F23; L60

Keywords: Multinational companies; Firm entry; Host country development

1. Introduction

In a recent paper, Markusen and Venables (1999) analyse the effects of multinational companies on the development of domestic firms in the host economy. They argue that multinationals can change the structure of imperfectly competitive industries in the host country by fostering the development of domestic intermediate good producing firms, which in turn may have positive effects on the development of domestic final good producing firms.

* Corresponding author.
E-mail address: holger.gorg@nottingham.ac.uk (H. Görg).

PII: S0014-2921(01)00146-5

In this paper, we set out to study the effect of multinationals on host country development empirically, complementing Markusen and Venables' theoretical analysis.

The Markusen–Venables model features two types of industries, intermediate and final consumer good producing, and three types of firms: domestic firms producing intermediate goods, domestic firms producing final consumer goods, and multinational firms producing final consumer goods. Both industries are assumed to be imperfectly competitive with increasing returns to scale of production. This assumption allows the possibility of external effects which drive the positive effects described in the model. [1]

According to the model the presence of multinationals has three effects on the host economy. First, there is a competition effect as multinationals compete with domestic final good producers. The increase in total output due to output produced by multinationals decreases the market price, which leads to the exit of some domestic firms. This, thus, leads to multinationals crowding out domestic firms. Second, multinationals create additional demand for domestically produced intermediate goods through linkages with indigenous suppliers. In an imperfectly competitive domestic supplier industry, this leads to decreasing average costs leading to increases in profits for intermediate good producers, which, in turn, may induce entry into the intermediate good producing sector. This entry causes the third effect, namely a fall in the price of intermediates which favours customer firms through lower input prices. Customer firms can be both domestic or multinational final good producing firms. Through these effects multinationals may induce the entry of domestic intermediate good producers as well as domestic final good producing firms. [2]

Although the Markusen–Venables model appears to provide a very intuitive tool to analyse the impact of the presence of multinationals on host country development, there has, to the best of our knowledge, not been any empirical study investigating the possible effects described in the model. In fact, most papers on the host country effects of multinationals seem to focus on measuring technological spillovers, which are posited to affect existing indigenous firms' productivity. See, for example, the recent study by Aitken and Harrison (1999) analysing the effect of MNCs on productivity in Venezuelan

[1] The structure of the model is similar to other models in the so-called 'new economic geography' literature, such as the models by Krugman and Venables (1995, 1996) and Puga (1999) which deal with the issue of industrial agglomerations. See, for example, Ottaviano and Puga (1998) for a survey of the 'new economic geography' literature.

[2] The latter two effects resemble the backward and forward linkage effects as discussed by Hirschman (1958). Rodríguez-Clare (1996) examines a similar mechanism in a more aggregate two-country model with countries specialising in the production of different goods. Multinationals can help develop domestic supplier industries which in turn leads to the development of indigenous final-good producers.

manufacturing industries, and a somewhat similar study by Blomström and Sjöholm (1999) using data for the Indonesian manufacturing sector.[3]

In this paper we, therefore, set out to provide empirical evidence on the effect of foreign multinationals on the development of indigenous firms in the host country. Our empirical 'case study' is the manufacturing sector of the Irish economy, as it provides a model example for such an analysis given that it is heavily dependent on multinational companies. This is evident from figures from the Central Statistics Office (1997), which show that foreign multinationals located in Ireland accounted for roughly 47 per cent of employment, 77 per cent of net output produced and 83 per cent of total exports in the Irish manufacturing sector in 1995. The presence of multinationals has arguably had profound effects on sectoral adjustment in the Irish manufacturing sector. While indigenous manufacturing industry tended to be concentrated on traditional and food-sector activities, MNCs have invested primarily in modern high-tech sectors, leading to a rapid increase in the significance of the high-tech sectors for the Irish economy (Barry and Bradley, 1997; Ruane and Görg, 1997).

In the context of the model developed by Markusen and Venables (1999) we estimate the factors that affect the entry of indigenous firms using plant level data for the Irish manufacturing sector. In particular, we use a simple entry model familiar from industrial organisation theory to investigate whether the presence of multinational companies in a sector helps to explain indigenous entry.[4] Our findings suggest that there is a positive effect of the presence of multinational companies on indigenous entry, which is consistent with the predictions of the Markusen–Venables model.

The paper is structured as follows. Section 2 provides a brief analysis of the competition effect and linkages in Irish manufacturing. In Section 3 we discuss the empirical model of firm entry used in the analysis, while Section 4 presents the results of our econometric analysis of the determinants of the indigenous entry rate for a number of alternative specifications. Section 5 presents a summary and concluding remarks.

2. Competition effect and linkages

The first effect of the presence of multinationals on indigenous development identified by Markusen and Venables is a competition effect, whereby multinationals crowd out indigenous firms. To investigate whether such crowding out seems likely to have happened in the Irish case we examine data

[3] See Blomström and Kokko (1998) and Görg and Strobl (2001) for reviews of the literature on productivity spillovers.

[4] See Caves (1998) and Geroski (1995) for recent surveys of the literature on firm entry.

available from the *Employment Survey*, an annual plant-level survey of all existing indigenous and foreign manufacturing firms in Ireland. [5]

It is of course difficult to directly disentangle the extent of the competition effect with simple employment data. Our approach is based on the insight that a decrease in the share of manufacturing employment in indigenous firms relative to foreign firms must be due to two reasons: Either due to losses of share of indigenous-intensive sectors in overall manufacturing (i.e., between sectors) and/or due to losses of employment shares of indigenous firms relative to foreign firms within the same sectors. It is the latter part that can be thought of as an indicator of the extent to which multinational companies located in Ireland have eroded existing or potential employment of indigenous firms or potential entrants in the same product market through the competition effect.

To isolate the importance of the loss of share within sectors we employ the following composition of a change in aggregate share of indigenous employment for $j = 1,\dots,J$ industries: [6]

$$\Delta S_i = \sum_j \Delta S_j \bar{S}_{ij} + \sum_j \Delta S_{ij} \bar{S}_j, \tag{1}$$

where S_{ij} is the share of indigenous employment in industry j, S_j is the proportion of industry j in aggregate employment and a bar over a term denotes a mean over time. The first term on the right-hand side of (1) represents the change in the aggregate proportion of indigenous employment due to shifts in the shares of employment between industries, whereas the second term is the change in the aggregate share attributable to changes in the share of indigenous employment within industries.

The results of employing (1) to our employment survey data set for the standard CSO sectoral breakdown, distinguishing 68 manufacturing sectors for the period 1974–1995, are reported in Table 1. Accordingly, over our sample period the indigenous sector lost 11.4 percentage points of its share of manufacturing employment. As our decomposition shows, over 76 per cent of this is attributable to shifts away from indigenous employment intensive sectors. Even if we break down our sample period into two sub-periods, 1974–1985 and 1985–1995, also shown in Table 1, a similar picture emerges. For

[5] Data for the *Employment Survey* are collected by Forfás, the policy and advisory board for industrial development in Ireland. The response rate to the survey is estimated by Forfás to be generally well over 90 per cent, i.e., our data can be seen as including virtually the whole population of manufacturing firms in Ireland. Forfás (1996) defines foreign firms as firms which are majority-owned by foreign shareholders, i.e., where 50 per cent or more of the shares are owned by foreign shareholders.

[6] See Berman et al. (1994) for a use of this decomposition to examine the change in the demand for skilled labour.

Table 1
Decomposition of the change in the indigenous share of manufacturing employment: 1974–1995[a]

	ΔShare	Between	Within
1974–1985	−0.064	−0.040	−0.024
1985–1995	−0.052	−0.051	−0.001
1974–1995	−0.114	−0.087	−0.027

[a]*Source*: Own estimations based on Forfás Employment Survey data.

Table 2
Linkages of foreign firms in manufacturing,[a] 1986–1995 (Irish raw materials as percentage of total raw material purchases)

	1986	1989	1992	1995
Non-food manufacturing (%)	16.2	16.5	19.2	19.8
£m (1996 prices)	353	546	734	1326

[a]Excluding food, drink and tobacco.
Source: Forfás (1998).

both sub-periods, the loss due to between sector shifts in shares of aggregate employment is substantially larger, particularly for the latter period.

Our results thus show that most of the loss of the share of the indigenous sector in manufacturing employment was not due to an erosion of share of employment by multinational companies operating in the same sectors, but because of the decline in importance of indigenous employment intensive sectors. They thus suggest that the competition effect, à la Markusen and Venables (1999), is unlikely to have been important for Irish manufacturing. This result may not be surprising, as multinational companies mainly located in Ireland in sectors which did not exist beforehand, i.e., predominantly high-tech sectors such as electronics and pharmaceuticals (see also Barry and Bradley, 1997).

The Markusen–Venables model predicts that, if linkages between multinationals and indigenous firms exist, indigenous intermediate and final good producing firms will benefit and the number of indigenous firms will increase. To investigate whether there may have been positive effects we, therefore, examine linkages between multinationals and indigenous firms as a first step. There have been a number of studies of linkages in Ireland which show that multinationals have backward linkages with indigenous firms and that they are likely to increase these linkages over time (McAleese and McDonald, 1978; Kennedy, 1991; Görg and Ruane, 2001).

Table 2 provides some aggregate statistics on the extent of linkages, defined as the percentage of intermediate inputs and raw materials purchased domestically, between foreign multinationals and domestic suppliers in manufacturing industries.[7] The table shows that foreign firms have increased their linkages between 1986 and 1995 by almost 4 percentage points. The data on linkages may be taken to indicate that the conduit for the positive development effect, as described by Markusen and Venables (1999), exists which, in turn, suggests that this effect may have taken place in Ireland.

3. The entry model

To investigate further the impact of multinationals on the development of indigenous firms we model the entry of indigenous firms as dependent on, amongst other factors, the presence of multinationals, and estimate this model empirically. To this end, we calculate two measures of entry: First, the net entry rate defined as the number of indigenous plant entries minus exits over the period t to $t+1$ divided by the total number of plants at time t in industry j, and, second, the gross entry rate which is calculated as only the number of indigenous plant entries over the total number of plants. While the Markusen–Venables model seems to be concerned solely with (changes in) firm numbers, which would point to analysing net entry, it may be of interest to study the effects of multinationals on gross entry as well since most studies of firm entry employ this latter measure (for example, Acs and Audretsch, 1989; Mata, 1993).[8]

Table 3 provides some aggregate data pertaining to the net and gross entry rates of indigenous plants and one measure of the presence of foreign multinationals, namely the share of employment in foreign multinationals as a percentage of total manufacturing employment. The data are calculated for the period 1974–1995 using plant-level data from the *Employment Survey*.

The gross entry rate of indigenous plants has fluctuated considerably over the years, as shown in the table. It reached a high of almost 14 per cent in 1983, while it has fluctuated around roughly 6–7 per cent in the late 1980s and early 1990s. The net entry rate has followed a similar pattern, reaching a

[7] The figures are derived from the *Irish Economy Expenditure Survey*, which is undertaken annually by Forfás. The survey includes output and employment data as well as detailed information on each firm's expenditure on labour, material and services inputs. It is sent out to firms with 30 or more employees. It is not compulsory for firms to take part in the survey, but response rates are generally good; firms responding to the survey account for around 60–80 per cent of employment of the target population each year (O'Malley, 1995).

[8] In the context of the model, one could arguably also expect effects of MNCs on other measures of domestic industrial activity, such as expansions of output or employment. An analysis of such effects would be beyond the scope of the present paper. Also, the main results of the Markusen–Venables model relate to firm numbers, and it therefore appears reasonable to focus on entry of indigenous firms.

Table 3
Indigenous entry rate and foreign presence[a]

Sector	1974	1978	1982	1986	1990	1992	1994	1995
Indigenous gross entry rate								
Chemicals	7.0	7.5	14.0	11.3	3.0	7.4	7.0	6.8
Clothing & textiles	4.8	9.3	9.7	13.3	7.2	7.8	6.4	4.6
Food, drink & tobacco	2.1	3.7	6.0	7.6	9.6	12.1	12.7	4.9
Furniture & timber	5.7	11.7	9.2	4.9	4.4	4.8	4.5	3.8
Metals & engineering	6.6	15.0	9.9	9.0	5.0	4.6	6.9	4.9
Non-metallic minerals	4.9	6.3	11.3	6.2	5.6	3.4	3.7	3.8
Paper & printing	5.1	4.9	6.0	6.4	5.3	2.9	5.0	3.1
Miscellaneous	4.3	16.6	15.1	13.7	16.0	13.9	11.2	4.7
Total	4.8	9.8	9.4	8.8	7.2	7.3	7.9	4.6
Indigenous net entry rate								
Chemicals	0.5	1.5	3.1	2.6	−2.1	−2.5	0.3	1.4
Clothing & textiles	−0.3	3.2	1.0	2.1	−6.7	−6.3	−5.0	−3.8
Food, drink & tobacco	−1.0	1.3	3.0	0.4	1.8	2.2	3.5	−3.9
Furniture & timber	2.4	8.8	3.8	−3.2	−3.4	−5.9	−2.5	−2.4
Metals & engineering	3.0	9.7	2.8	1.3	−2.3	−3.1	0.3	−1.1
Non-metallic minerals	0.8	4.3	5.4	1.1	−0.6	−5.5	−1.6	−2.4
Paper & printing	3.6	1.9	2.4	1.5	−0.2	−6.2	−0.4	−2.5
Miscellaneous	1.6	10.8	8.4	5.7	6.7	1.6	1.1	−4.0
Total	1.2	5.9	3.4	1.1	−1.1	−2.6	0.0	−2.5
Foreign employment share								
Chemicals	59.4	71.8	73.5	77.0	78.3	79.8	80.2	80.3
Clothing & textiles	29.7	36.4	39.8	41.9	43.7	44.2	43.7	43.1
Food, drink & tobacco	28.7	28.4	29.9	29.6	28.8	26.7	26.8	26.2
Furniture & timber	7.1	7.2	5.7	6.5	6.7	6.6	6.5	6.7
Metals & engineering	50.3	52.2	55.7	57.3	60.1	60.0	61.8	61.9
Non-metallic minerals	21.8	21.3	22.3	19.5	20.1	20.5	19.8	18.6
Paper & printing	14.8	13.3	13.2	14.4	14.1	13.1	14.5	15.0
Miscellaneous	41.3	45.0	45.6	42.2	42.2	40.9	41.2	40.0
Total	33.4	36.4	39.3	40.5	42.9	42.8	44.3	44.8

[a]*Source*: Own estimations based on Forfás Employment Survey data.

high of 6.6 per cent in the late 1970s and fluctuating between 0.0 and −2.6 per cent in the 1990s. The share of employment in foreign multinationals has constantly increased over the same period. Foreign multinationals accounted for some 34 per cent of manufacturing employment in 1975, and this share has risen to around 45 per cent in 1995. The data in the table show that there are considerable sectoral differences for both entry rates and foreign presence.

To model empirically the entry of indigenous manufacturing plants we follow Geroski (1991, Chapter 3) who shows that the rate of entry into a market is positively related to the level of expected post-entry profits which, in turn, depend on the level of existing barriers to entry and other structural and transitory factors. Combining this with the result by Markusen and Venables (1999), we may suggest that the entry rate of indigenous plants may be related to a number of barriers to entry, the presence of multinational companies, and other factors.[9]

Similar to other empirical studies of firm entry, such as, for example, Orr (1974) or Mata (1993), we postulate the following empirical model of the relationship between the entry rate and other factors:

$$E_{jt} = \beta_0 + \beta_1 GR_{jt} + \beta_2 MES_{jt} + \beta_3 SIZE_{jt} + \beta_4 AGE_{jt} + \beta_5 MNC_{jt} + \alpha_j + v_t + \varepsilon_{jt}, \qquad (2)$$

where α_j is a sector-specific term, v_t is a year-specific effect, and ε_{jt} is the remaining error term, assumed to be independent across sectors and over time. GR_{jt} denotes the growth rate of industry j, MES_{jt} represents the minimum efficient scale, $SIZE_{jt}$ is the size of the industry, AGE_{jt} denotes the average age of all existing plants in the industry, MNC_{jt} represents the presence of foreign multinational companies. The first three independent variables are widely accepted in the literature as having an effect on the rate of firm entry (Acs and Audretsch, 1989; Mata, 1993, 1991; Mata and Machado, 1996; Orr, 1974).

GR_{jt} is measured as the annual net employment growth rate of industry j. The industry growth rate is assumed to have a positive effect on the entry rate because a growing market offers a higher probability of survival for an entrant and makes entry, therefore, more likely. This follows from the possibility that incumbent firms may be able to maintain their relative position in a growing market even after the entry of the new firm, which reduces the likelihood of retaliation on part of the incumbent (Mata and Machado, 1996).

MES_{jt} is measured as the average plant size of existing plants in industry j.[10] Minimum efficient scale serves as a proxy for barriers to entry in the industry. When MES is high, new entrants may be deterred from entering the market because capital requirements may be too high. Thus, we would expect

[9] Empirical studies of firm entry frequently include past profitability as a proxy for expected profits, since the latter is an unobservable variable (Mata, 1991, 1993). The problem with such a measure is that it assumes that firms do not adjust their profit expectations following the entry of firms, but base their entry decision entirely on past profits. Firms, however, can be expected to take into account that firm entry affects the level of expected profits.

[10] We also experimented using median size as a proxy for MES but found that the results were qualitatively and quantitatively similar.

a negative relationship between MES and the rate of entry (see Geroski, 1991).

$SIZE_{jt}$ is defined as total employment in industry j as a measure of industry size. One rationale for including this variable is to control for the fact that a fraction of entry occurs simply to replace exiting firms. This replacement entry can be expected to depend on the size of the market, and therefore, industry size is included in the regression (Mata, 1991). Also, entry may be easier in a larger market as there may be a lower probability of retaliation by incumbents, all other things equal. We would hence expect a positive relationship between industry size and entry.

AGE_{jt} represents average age of all existing plants in industry j. We take this as a proxy to identify traditional industries in which long-established incumbents may be expected to have absolute cost advantages vis-à-vis entrants. This, thus, creates an additional barrier to entry for new firms and we would predict a negative relationship between this variable and the rate of entry of indigenous plants.

The *MNC* variable is intended to capture the effect of foreign multinational companies on the entry of new firms. As suggested by Markusen and Venables (1999), we would expect the presence of multinational companies to have a stimulating effect on firm entry, other things being equal, in the presence of linkage effects.[11] On the other hand, however, the competition effect may lead to foreign multinationals crowding out indigenous firms, which should, ceteris paribus, have a negative effect on the entry rate. As pointed out above, we would not expect the latter effect to dominate in the Irish manufacturing sector for the period analysed, however.

We employ different proxies for the *MNC* variable. First, we calculate $MNC1_{jt}$ as the share of manufacturing employment in foreign plants, i.e., employment in foreign plants divided by total employment in industry j at time t, while $MNC2_{jt}$ is defined as the ratio of foreign plants to the total number of plants in industry j. $MNC3_{jt}$ denotes the net entry rate of foreign plants into industry j, calculated as the number of foreign entries minus exits between t and $t+1$, divided by the total number of plants in time t in industry j.

All variables included in (2) are calculated from the *Employment Survey* for the 68 sector breakdown of Irish manufacturing for the period 1974–1995. Table 4 presents some summary statistics for these. One point to note is that, as indicated by the average of within sector standard deviation given in the last column, a substantial proportion of variation of our variables is due to their movement over time within sectors.

[11] Ideally, we would also want to include the extent of linkages between multinationals and indigenous firms for each sector. However, such dis-aggregated data on linkages were not available to us.

Table 4
Summary statistics for variables used for 68 sectors[a]

	Mean	Standard deviation	Minimum	Maximum	Standard deviation (within)
Gross entry rate	0.0881	0.1207	0.0000	1.3680	0.0470
Net entry rate	0.0195	0.0925	−0.3000	1.2380	0.0577
*MNC*1	0.4147	0.2909	0.0000	0.9958	0.0590
*MNC*2	0.2103	0.1766	0.0000	0.8750	0.0375
*MNC*3	0.004	0.0359	−0.2174	0.4375	0.0159
GR	0.0010	0.1056	−0.4909	0.9623	0.0638
SIZE	3113	3072	24	18981	569.7
MES	53.90	56.57	4.80	641.50	12.54
AGE	19.54	10.08	2.91	64.37	2.33

[a] *Source*: Own estimations based on Forfás Employment Survey data.

4. Econometric results

We estimate the model described in Eq. (2) using the fixed-effects panel data regression technique as described by Baltagi (1995), which was deemed preferable for the estimation of the sector-specific effects to a random-effects specification since our data set consists of essentially the population of manufacturing industries in Ireland. All specifications include time dummies to control for year specific effects. We apply (2) to a number of alternative specifications to determine whether the presence of multinationals has had a positive effect on the incidence of indigenous plant entry in Irish manufacturing.

4.1. Intra-industry effect

If our three foreign presence variable alternatives, as described in the previous section, are calculated for the same sector as the indigenous entry rate, then they may be considered to be proxies for measuring the *intra-industry* effects of MNCs, i.e., the coefficients on these variables should indicate whether the presence of multinationals in sector j has an impact on the entry of indigenous plants in the same sector. One may expect such intra-industry effects for two reasons. First, as pointed out above, there is an effect on indigenous final good producers which may be in the same sector as MNCs. Second, one may expect heterogeneities across firms even within our 68 sector definition, i.e., even within sectors there may be upstream (suppliers) and downstream (final good) firms. Multinationals can be assumed to be mainly downstream firms, thus an intra-industry effect may show that multinationals affect the entry of indigenous suppliers in the same sector.

Table 5
Fixed effects estimates-intra-industry effects[a]

	Net entry rate			Gross entry rate		
	(1)	(2)	(3)	(4)	(5)	(6)
*MNC*1	0.060**	—	—	0.061***	—	—
	(0.027)			(0.024)		
*MNC*2	—	0.206***	—	—	0.161***	—
		(0.054)			(0.047)	
*MNC*3	—	—	0.185**	—	—	0.310**
			(0.086)			(0.136)
$MNC3_{t-1}$	—	—	0.224**	—	—	0.248**
			(0.092)			(0.116)
$MNC3_{t-2}$	—	—	−0.092	—	—	0.041
			(0.099)			(0.110)
$MNC3_{t-3}$	—	—	−0.019	—	—	0.026
			(0.088)			(0.110)
GR	0.042	0.040	0.061*	0.034	0.034	0.046
	(0.034)	(0.033)	(0.036)	(0.030)	(0.029)	(0.029)
$SIZE/10^5$	−0.522**	−0.420*	−0.370	−0.602***	−0.506***	−0.048
	(0.275)	(0.252)	(0.240)	(0.194)	(0.181)	(0.228)
$MES/10^3$	0.254	0.197	0.028	0.245	0.201	−0.764
	(0.272)	(0.264)	(0.202)	(0.267)	(0.260)	(0.185)
$AGE/10^2$	−0.105	−0.156	−0.028	−0.198	−0.232*	−0.832
	(0.137)	(0.137)	(0.145)	(0.130)	(0.130)	(0.135)
Sectors, periods	68, 22	68, 22	68, 19	68, 22	68, 22	68, 19
Observations	1496	1496	1292	1496	1496	1292
R^2	0.14	0.15	0.16	0.18	0.19	0.20
$F\ (H_0{:}v_i = v_j)$	6.47	4.64	5.82	3.65	3.76	3.52
$F\ (H_0{:}\beta_i = 0)$	14.82	15.10	14.13	17.88	18.37	17.24
$F\ (H_0{:}\alpha_i = \alpha_k)$	2.06	2.15	1.78	3.15	3.19	3.52

[a]Heteroskedasticity consistent standard error in parentheses; *MNC*1: foreign employment share, *MNC*2: foreign plant share, *MNC*3: foreign entry rate in case of (1) through (3) and net foreign entry rate in case of (4) through (5).

*Significant at 10 per cent level.

**Significant at 5 per cent level.

***Significant at 1 per cent level.

The results of the analysis of intra-industry effects of MNCs on the entry of indigenous plants, using data for all manufacturing sectors are presented in Table 5. It is noteworthy from this and subsequent tables that the R^2s are fairly low for all our estimations. However, Geroski (1995) in his survey of the literature on entry concedes that: 'Virtually all of the regressions designed to explain variations in entry across industries and over time have reported very low R^2s' (p. 430), and thus we view our results as no exception to this apparent 'rule'. Despite the low explanatory power of our independent variables, the F-tests for the joint significance of the β's reject the hypothesis that all β's are equal to zero for these estimations.

Columns (1)–(3) of Table 5 show the results of the estimation using the net entry rate as dependent variable, while columns (4)–(6) were estimated with the gross entry rate. Inspection of the results shows that the results are qualitatively and quantitatively similar and thus all subsequent estimations were carried out using the net entry rate as this may be more appropriate for an analysis of the effects suggested by the Markusen and Venables (1999) model.[12] We proxy the presence of foreign firms using the three different measures as described above. The specifications in columns (1) and (4) include the foreign share of employment in sector j, columns (2) and (5) use the foreign share of plants in sector j while columns (3) and (6) utilise current and lagged values of the entry rate of foreign firms in sector j. In line with Geroski (1989), we have allowed for three years lags of the foreign entry rate.

For all specifications we find a positive and statistically significant effect of the presence of foreign multinationals on indigenous entry in the same sector. The interpretation of the coefficients is straightforward, as both dependent and independent variables are specified as percentages. In the case of the specification in column (1), for example, a one-percent increase in the employment share of foreign firms leads to an increase in the net entry rate of indigenous plants by 0.06 percentage points. These results indicate that there is evidence that, ceteris paribus, foreign firms have indeed had positive effects on the entry of indigenous firms.

While the coefficients for the age, minimum efficient scale and net growth rate variable are generally statistically insignificant in all specifications, the coefficient of the industry size variable shows a negative and statistically significant sign in four out of the six specifications. This is contrary to our expectations, as we would have predicted that a larger market size has a positive effect on the indigenous entry rate, all other things being equal. One possibility is that in larger sectors less firms enter relative to the total number of incumbent firms, but that these can afford to be of larger size due the lower probability of retaliation from incumbents. Running a simple fixed effects regression of the average/median size of indigenous entrants on industry size we find that these are positively related, thus suggesting that this may indeed be the case in Irish manufacturing.

[12] We, however, also tried all specifications presented here with the gross entry rate; the results were qualitatively and quantitatively similar and are available from the authors.

4.2. Long run effect

The definitions of the *MNC*1 and *MNC*2 variables as used above implicitly assume that increases in multinational presence in one year lead to entry in the industry in the same year, which is to say that all adjustments take place over the short run. To investigate whether there are long run effects of MNC presence as well, we calculated the three foreign presence variables as averages of their values at time t, $t-1$, $t-2$ and $t-3$ to get an average of the present and the previous three years for each year.

The results of including these averages instead of the single year values in the estimation are reported in columns (1)–(3) of Table 6. As can be seen, all three proxies of multinational presence turn out to have statistically significant and positive signs, which suggests that there are also long run positive effects of MNC presence on the indigenous entry rate.

4.3. Inter-industry effect

While our foreign presence proxies as defined above are likely to capture linkage effects within industries, some intermediate goods suppliers may of course be supplying industries outside of their own industry as defined above. We thus also examine further the prediction that multinational presence in one industry also leads to entry in upstream industries that are not necessarily in the same industrial group, i.e., we test for *inter-industry* linkages effects in addition to *intra-industry* linkages effects of multinationals. To do so we include three MNC proxies, *MNC*1(*DS*), *MNC*2(*DS*), and *MNC*3(*DS*), that are similar to the ones above, but that capture inter-industry linkages effects by foreign multinationals as follows. Based on the 1993 Input–Output Tables for the Irish economy, [13] which provide data on breakdown of manufacturing into twenty sectors, we are able to determine the destination of output produced by sector j, which can either go to final demand, or as an input into its own industrial group or other (downstream) industries. Using these data we calculate the three MNC proxies as an average of the foreign presence in the downstream sectors to which sector j supplies, other than its own, in each year, weighted by the importance of the downstream sector as a destination for output (in terms of output received) in 1993. [14] This allows us to investigate whether entry of indigenous firms into industry j is affected

[13] The Input–Output Tables are only published intermittently and the latest ones available are those of 1993. See Central Statistics Office (1999).

[14] This implicitly assumes that the importance of linkages between the 20 sectors is time invariant and that the 1993 data are representative of these relationships.

Table 6
Fixed effects estimates – long run and inter-industry effects (dependent variable: net entry rate)[a]

	Long run effects			Inter-industry effects		
	(1)	(2)	(3)	(4)	(5)	(6)
*MNC*1	0.126	—	—	0.127	—	—
	(0.029)***			(0.039)***		
*MNC*2	—	0.231	—	—	0.437	—
		(0.059)***	—	—	(0.058)***	
*MNC*3	—	—	0.517	—	—	0.046
			(0.189)***			(0.092)
$MNC3_{t-1}$	—	—	—	—	—	−0.023
						(0.089)
$MNC3_{t-2}$	—	—	—	—	—	0.120
						(0.080)
$MNC3_{t-3}$	—	—	—	—	—	0.229***
						(0.077)
*MNC*1(*DS*)	—	—	—	0.155	—	—
				(0.080)*		
*MNC*2(*DS*)	—	—	—	—	−0.076	—
					(0.108)	
*MNC*3(*DS*)	—	—	—	—	—	0.098
						(0.136)
$MNC3(DS)_{t-1}$	—	—	—	—	—	−0.103
						(0.130)
$MNC3(DS)_{t-2}$	—	—	—	—	—	−0.060
						(0.117)
$MNC3(DS)_{t-3}$	—	—	—	—	—	0.146
						(0.108)
GR	0.085	0.081	0.057	−0.041	−0.080*	−0.012
	(0.035)**	(0.035)**	(0.036)	(0.045)	(0.043)	(0.048)
$SIZE/10^5$	−0.746	−0.561	−0.267	−0.099	0.011	−0.030
	(0.204)***	(0.204)***	(0.249)***	(0.113)	(0.112)	(0.149)
$MES/10^3$	0.007	−0.015	−0.001	−0.014	0.019	−0.377
	(0.200)	(0.201)	(0.204)	(0.217)	(0.204)	(0.235)
$AGE/10^2$	−0.065	−0.091	0.004	−0.197	−0.192*	−0.028
	(0.414)	(0.146)	(0.141)	(0.129)	(0.116)	(0.127)
Sectors, periods	68, 20	68, 20	68, 20	20, 22	20, 22	20, 19
Observations	1360	1360	1360	440	440	380
Adjusted R^2	0.16	0.16	0.16	0.31	0.39	0.42
$F\ (H_0{:}v_i = v_j)$	6.11	4.50	4.74	5.99	4.59	5.99
$F\ (H_0{:}\beta_i = 0)$	16.22	16.23	15.75	6.68	9.12	6.93
$F\ (H_0{:}\alpha_i = \alpha_k)$	2.13	2.14	1.89	2.69	4.70	2.60

[a]Heteroskedasticity consistent standard error in parentheses. *MNC*1: foreign employment share, *MNC*2: foreign plant share, *MNC*3: foreign entry rate within a sector, except in the case of (1) through (3) where these are the average over the present and the three previous years within sectors; *MNC*1(*DS*), *MNC*2(*DS*), and *MNC*3(*DS*) are the corresponding foreign presence variables in the 'downstream' sectors. Columns (4)–(6) report results using data based on Input–Output Tables. These data cover the whole manufacturing sector albeit at a fairly high level of sectoral aggregation. The Input–Output Tables distinguish 20 manufacturing sub-sectors as opposed to the 68 sub-sectors as used in columns (1)–(3).

*Significant at 10 per cent level.

**Significant at 5 per cent level.

***Significant at 1 per cent level.

by the presence of multinationals in downstream sectors in other industrial groups.[15]

The results of the estimations are reported in columns (4)–(6) of Table 6. Accordingly, we still find statistically significant and positive results for all of the *intra-industry* foreign presence variables. As regards multinational presence in downstream industries, we find a positive and statistically significant effect for $MNC1(DS)$, i.e., where multinational presence is measured in terms of employment share. Given that Markusen (1998) argues that employment data may be the most appropriate for measuring the importance of MNCs, our results lend support to the notion that there are significant intra-industry and inter-industry linkages effects of multinational companies. In other words, the entry of indigenous firms in industry j is positively influenced by the presence of multinationals in industry j and in industries downstream of j.

4.4. Sensitivity analysis

Based on the specification and data used to analyse intra-industry effects of multinationals on indigenous entry we also estimated a number of alternative specifications to check the general robustness of our results.[16] First, we divided our total sample into high-tech and low-tech sectors based on an OECD classification as used by Kearns and Ruane (2001) and estimated the empirical model separately. We find statistically significant positive effects of MNC presence on the indigenous entry rate for both groups, although the magnitude of the positive effect of the foreign presence appears to be higher for high-tech sectors than for low-tech sectors. Second, we explored the possibility that the indigenous entry rate responds to changes in the explanatory variables over a number of years, rather than in only one year, by including the lagged indigenous entry rate as an explanatory variable. The results for a dynamic panel GMM estimation of our total sample using the foreign share of employment as our preferred measure of foreign presence show that the lagged dependent variable, although of the expected sign, is not significant, suggesting that our model does not involve a dynamic adjustment process. The coefficient on the foreign presence variable is positive and significant, however. Third, we estimated the entry equation calculating the industry growth, size, and minimum efficient scale variables using

[15] Note that the Input–Output Tables provide data on only 20 sectors which cover the whole manufacturing sector at a higher level of sectoral aggregation than above, where we were able to distinguish 68 manufacturing sub-sectors. This, of course, means that the extension of our analysis comes at the cost of a reduction in the level of sectoral disaggregation, implying that the 20 manufacturing sub-sector are likely to be less homogenous than the 68 sectors used above.

[16] The results of these estimations are not reported here but can be obtained from the authors upon request.

data for the UK. Given that the Irish market is small one may argue that characteristics of industries in Ireland do not matter for the entry decision of indigenous firms. By contrast, market conditions in the UK may be important determinants for the entry and performance of Irish firms (see Burke, 1996). While coefficients on UK sectoral characteristics were statistically insignificant, the results on the MNC variables remained essentially unchanged. Fourth, we tested whether improvements in Irish cost competitiveness, measured as the ratio of real wages per employee in Ireland relative to the UK, may have impacted on indigenous entry (as suggested by O'Malley, 1998). Again, the results for MNC presence were essentially unchanged, while the relative wage variable turned out to be insignificant.

Our results reported above thus suggest that there is a positive effect of multinational presence on the indigenous entry rate in the host country. This effect operates through two channels, namely, firstly, the presence of multinationals in the same industry and, secondly, the presence of multinationals in downstream industries. These results, particularly the first one, appear to be robust to different specifications of the empirical entry model.

5. Conclusions

In a recent paper, Markusen and Venables (1999) show theoretically that multinational companies, through the creation of linkages with indigenous suppliers, can exert positive effects on the development of indigenous firms in the host country. Our paper examines this issue for the first time from an empirical perspective, thus complementing the theoretical analysis by Markusen and Venables and adding to the empirical literature on the impact of multinationals on the host country. Using data for the Irish manufacturing sector we find that such positive effects have, indeed, taken place in the Irish economy. Specifically, we find that the presence of multinational companies has had a positive effect on the entry of indigenous firms.

Even though we find a positive effect from the presence of foreign multinationals on indigenous entry, we must be cautious to point out that we are only measuring the incidence of entry. To conclude on a lasting positive effect of multinationals on indigenous development, one would also need to investigate whether new indigenous firms are able to survive in the industry. Furthermore, it would also be of interest to examine not only the number of firms entering the industry but also the levels of employment associated with this entry.

Acknowledgements

We are grateful to Frank Barry, François Bourguignon (the editor), and two anonymous referees for helpful comments and suggestions. We also thank

H. Görg, E. Strobl / European Economic Review 46 (2002) 1305–1322 1321

Salvador Barrios and Noel Woods for help with the data. Earlier versions of the paper were presented at the Network of Industrial Economists Conference in Oxford, April 1999 and the Irish Economic Association Conference in Westport, April 1999. All remaining errors are, of course, our own. Financial support through the European Commission Fifth Framework Programme (Grant No. HPSE-CT-1999-00017) and the Leverhulme Trust (Grant No. F114/BF) is gratefully acknowledged.

References

Acs, Z.J., Audretsch, D.B., 1989. Small-firm entry in US manufacturing. Economica 56, 255–265.

Aitken, B.J., Harrison, A.E., 1999. Do domestic firms benefit from direct foreign investment? evidence from Venezuela. American Economic Review 89, 605–618.

Baltagi, B.H., 1995. Econometric Analysis of Panel Data. Wiley, Chichester.

Barry, F., Bradley, J., 1997. FDI and trade: The Irish host-country experience. Economic Journal 107, 1798–1811.

Berman, E., Bound, J., Griliches, Z., 1994. Changes in the demand for skilled labor within U.S. manufacturing: Evidence from the annual survey of manufacturers. Quarterly Journal of Economics 109, 367–397.

Blomström, M., Kokko, A., 1998. Multinational corporations and spillovers. Journal of Economic Surveys 12, 247–277.

Blomström, M., Sjöholm, F., 1999. Technology transfer and spillovers: Does local participation with multinationals matter? European Economic Review 43, 915–923.

Burke, A., 1996. Economic integration and new firm formation: Britain's impact on Irish enterprise. Review of Industrial Organization 11, 183–200.

Caves, R.E., 1998. Industrial organization and new findings on the turnover and mobility of firms. Journal of Economic Literature 36, 1947–1982.

Central Statistics Office, 1997. Census of Industrial Production 1995. Stationary Office, Dublin.

Central Statistics Office, 1999. Input–Output Tables 1993, Stationary Office, Dublin.

Forfás, 1996. 1995 Employment Survey. Forfás, Dublin.

Forfás, 1998. Annual Survey of Irish Economy Expenditures: Results for 1996. Forfás, Dublin.

Geroski, P.A., 1989. The interaction between domestic and foreign based entrants. In: Audretsch, D.B., Sleuwaegen, L., Yamawaki, H. (Eds.), The Convergence of International and Domestic Markets. North-Holland, Amsterdam, pp. 59–83.

Geroski, P.A., 1991. Market Dynamics and Entry. Blackwell, Oxford.

Geroski, P.A., 1995. What do we know about entry? International Journal of Industrial Organization 13, 421–440.

Görg, H., Ruane, F., 2001. Multinational companies and linkages: Panel-Data evidence for the Irish electronics sector. International Journal of the Economics of Business 8, 1–18.

Görg, H., Strobl, E., 2001. Multinational companies and productivity spillovers: A meta-analysis Economic Journal 111 (475), 723–739.

Hirschman, A.O., 1958. The Strategy of Economic Development. Yale University Press, New Haven, CT.

Kearns, A., Ruane, F., 2001. The tangible contribution of R&D spending by foreign-owned plants to a host region: A plant level study of the Irish manufacturing sector (1980–1996). Research Policy 30, 227–244.

Kennedy, K.A., 1991. Linkages and overseas industry. In: Foley, A., McAleese, D. (Eds.), Overseas Industry in Ireland. Gill and Macmillan, Dublin, pp. 82–105.

Krugman, P.R., Venables, A.J., 1995. Globalization and the inequality of nations. Quarterly Journal of Economics 110, 857–880.

Krugman, P.R., Venables, A.J., 1996. Integration, specialization, and adjustment. European Economic Review 40, 959–967.

Markusen, J.R., 1998. Multinational firms, location and trade. World Economy 21, 733–756.

Markusen, J.R., Venables, A.J., 1999. Foreign direct investment as a catalyst for industrial development. European Economic Review 43, 335–356.

Mata, J., 1991. Sunk costs and entry by small and large plants. In: Geroski, P.A., Schwalbach, J. (Eds.), Entry and Market Contestability: An International Comparison. Blackwell, Oxford, pp. 49–62.

Mata, J., 1993. Entry and type of entrant: Evidence from Portugal. International Journal of Industrial Organization 11, 101–122.

Mata, J., Machado, J.A.E., 1996. Firm start-up size: A conditional quantile approach. European Economic Review 40, 1305–1323.

McAleese, D., McDonald, D., 1978. Employment growth and the development of linkages in foreign-owned and domestic manufacturing enterprises. Oxford Bulletin of Economics and Statistics 40, 321–339.

O'Malley, E., 1995. An analysis of secondary employment associated with manufacturing industry, General Research Series Paper No. 167, Economic and Social Research Institute, Dublin.

O'Malley, E., 1998. The revival of Irish indigenous industry 1987–1997. In: Baker, T., Duffy, D., Shortall, F. (Eds.), Quarterly Economic Commentary: April 1998. Economic and Social Research Institute, Dublin.

Orr, D., 1974. The determinants of entry: A study of the Canadian manufacturing industries. Review of Economics and Statistics 56, 58–66.

Ottaviano, G.I.P., Puga, D., 1998. Agglomeration in the global economy: A survey of the new economic geography. World Economy 21, 707–731.

Puga, D., 1999. The rise and fall of regional inequalities. European Economic Review 43, 303–334.

Rodríguez-Clare, A., 1996. Multinationals, linkages, and economic development. American Economic Review 86, 852–873.

Ruane, F., Görg, H., 1997. The impact of foreign direct investment on sectoral adjustment in the Irish economy. National Institute Economic Review No. 160, pp. 76–86.

Chapter 18

Foreign direct investment, competition and industrial development in the host country

Salvador Barrios[a], Holger Görg[b], Eric Strobl[a,*]

[a] *CORE, Université Catholique de Louvain, 34 Voie du Roman Pays, 1348, Louvain-la-Neuve, Belgium*
[b] *University of Nottingham, Nottingham, UK*

Received 22 August 2003; accepted 24 May 2004
Available online 10 August 2004

Abstract

This paper analyses the impact of foreign direct investment (FDI) on the development of local firms. We focus on two likely effects of FDI: A competition effect which deters entry of domestic firms and positive market externalities which foster the development of local industry. Using a simple theoretical model to illustrate how these forces work we show that the number of domestic firms follows a u-shaped curve, where the competition effect first dominates but is gradually outweighed by positive externalities. Evidence for Ireland tends to support this result. Specifically, applying semi-parametric regression techniques on plant level panel data for the manufacturing sector we find that while the competition effect may have initially deterred local firms' entry, this initial effect has been outpaced by positive externalities making the overall impact of FDI largely positive for the domestic industry.

JEL classification: F2; L6; O1

Keywords: Foreign direct investment; Spillovers; Industrial development; Firm entry; Semi-parametric estimations

*Corresponding author. Tel.: +32-10-474328; fax: +32-10-474301
E-mail address: strobl@core.ucl.ac.be (E. Strobl).

0278-4319/$ - see front matter © 2004 Published by Elsevier Ltd.
doi:10.1016/j.euroecorev.2004.05.005

1. Introduction

It is a well-known fact that foreign direct investment (FDI) flows have increased dramatically over the last three decades or so. It is also undoubted that governments across the world, in developing and developed countries alike, are trying to attract multinational enterprises (MNEs) to locate in their country, using generous financial and fiscal incentives (see, for example, Hanson, 2001). The rationale for such enthusiasm displayed at attracting MNEs has been debated in the academic literature as well as in policy making circles. One argument is that multinationals bring with them some sort of superior technology and that this will "spill over" to domestic firms, thus assisting them in improving their efficiency and, hence, productivity. However, the vast evidence that has thus far been accumulated is less than conclusive on whether such spillovers do take place. In fact, there are a substantial number of studies arguing that there are actually negative spillover effects, i.e., the presence of multinationals harms productivity in domestic firms due to increased competition.[1]

Even disregarding the issue of knowledge spillovers, there are other ways in which the entry or presence of MNEs may assist the development of host country firms. In particular, multinationals' demand for intermediate inputs, some of which will be sourced on the domestic market, can induce changes in the domestic industrial structure and can kick-start the development of local industry. This is the issue with which we concern ourselves in this paper, analyzing the impact of FDI on the development of local firms.

In order to illustrate these arguments and motivate our subsequent empirical analysis we begin by presenting a simple theoretical framework in order to analyze the main mechanisms at hand. We build on the existing theoretical literature concerning the potential impact of FDI, in particular, Markusen and Venables (1999), Rodríguez-Clare (1996) and Rivera-Batiz and Rivera-Batiz (1991). The interaction between MNEs and domestic firms takes place through several channels. The first one is the factor market, as FDI represents a capital inflow and modifies the host country capital endowment. In addition, foreign affiliates use differentiated intermediate product which indirectly affects the production conditions for domestic firms. The second channel is a competition effect, where MNEs are competing with local producers on their product market as well as on the factor market. We show that the evolution of the number of local firms as a function of the presence of foreign firms can be depicted as a u-shaped relationship where the competition effect first dominates but is gradually outweighed by positive externality effects.

We then analyze empirically the impact of FDI on domestic start-ups using plant level panel data for the manufacturing sector in the Republic of Ireland over the period 1972 to 2000. The Irish economy provides arguably a model example for such an analysis given that it is heavily dependent on multinational companies, which

[1] See, for example, Aitken and Harrison (1999) and Konings (2001) for arguments to that extent. Recent studies finding positive spillover effects are, for example, Keller and Yeaple (2003) and Haskel et al. (2002). See Görg and Strobl (2001) and Lipsey (2002) for surveys of the literature.

accounted for roughly one half of manufacturing employment in 2000.[2] More importantly, the presence of multinationals has had profound effects on sectoral adjustment in the Irish manufacturing sector. While indigenous manufacturing industry tended to initially be concentrated in traditional and food-sector activities, MNEs have invested primarily in modern high-tech sectors, leading to an increase in the significance of the high-tech sectors for the Irish economy (Barry and Bradley, 1997).

Using the plant level data and applying semi-parametric regression techniques we find that the impact of FDI on domestic firms' entry follows a u-shaped curve. In other words, an increasing presence of multinationals may initially harm the development of domestic firms due to increasing competitive pressure. However, after reaching a certain threshold value, the positive benefits of FDI outweigh the negative factors, hence fostering the development of domestic firms.[3]

The rest of the paper is structured as follows. In the next section we describe our theoretical framework. Section 3 outlines our empirical specification in order to test these predications and contains a description of our data. Our empirical results are presented in Section A. Concluding remarks are provided in the last section.

2. Theoretical framework

In order to motivate our empirical analysis of the effects of FDI on local development this section builds a simple model to illustrate the main forces at hand. In order to do so we draw on the literature on imperfect competition and intermediate linkages between industries. One of the main analytical tools used here is a transformation of the Dixit–Stiglitz (1977) utility function into a production function. As pointed out by Romer (1987), this allows capturing a preference for variety in intermediate inputs and, as a consequence, to consider increasing returns due to specialization. In particular, Ethier (1982) used this tool in a model of international trade with external increasing returns to scale. This idea has also been applied by Rivera-Batiz and Rivera-Batiz (1991) to analyze the impact of FDI on host economies. Using a simple general equilibrium model, they show how foreign capital entry may induce more specialization in services, which in turn has a positive effect on efficiency in related industries.

The idea is fairly straightforward. Consider an economy with two sectors of activity, services and manufacturing, both of which employ capital as primary input. In addition, the manufacturing industry uses differentiated services as inputs. Since

[2] This is evident from our datasource, see also Table 1 below.

[3] There are a number of related empirical papers examining the effect of multinationals on the Irish economy. Ruane and Ugur (2002) find evidence for positive spillovers emanating from multinationals. Görg and Strobl (2003) show that the presence of multinationals enhances the survival probabilities of domestic firms in the same industry. The paper most closely related to ours is an earlier study by Görg and Strobl (2002) on the effect of multinationals on domestic firms. While they find a positive effect, their study is limited in that it is not directly based on a theoretical model and that they do not allow for a potential non-linear relationship.

there are increasing returns in services and competition is of the monopolistic type, an external entry of foreign capital makes available capital cheaper and average costs lower in the service sector. If the number of firms in equilibrium (and the variety of differentiated services) is determined by a zero profit condition in the service sector, then lowering the average cost through foreign capital entry causes an increase in services variety. This has, in turn, an indirect impact on the manufacturing sector as the number of services available in the economy increases the productive efficiency of manufacturing firms.

However, this model has some limitations. First, FDI is modeled only through foreign capital entry. Second, competition in the manufacturing sector within which FDI occurs is supposed to be perfect while the general theory of FDI postulates that multinationals are more likely to exist in imperfectly competitive markets, see Hymer (1976), and, more recently Markusen (1995, 2002). According to these latter contributions, multinationals own some advantages internalized through FDI against other possible strategies like exporting or licensing. Recent studies, in particular Rodríguez-Clare (1996) and Markusen and Venables (1999) considered these elements in an explicit way to analyze the effects of FDI on host economies.

In Rodríguez-Clare (1996) the impact of FDI on host economy industry depends on the input–output linkages multinationals generate compared to the linkages domestic firms would themselves generate. When a multinational has a higher linkage coefficient than domestic firms this leads to a higher equilibrium variety of specialized inputs and this is thus beneficial to the domestic economy as whole. However, in Rodríguez-Clare (1996) the relative strength of the competition and spillovers effects is left unclear. In fact, one can consider that the competition effect may condition the way FDI affect the local industry. Such a competition effect is explicitly analysed in the model by Markusen and Venables (1999).[4] Their results show that FDI may have two main effects on host economies: The linkage effect through intermediate demands as described above and the product competition effect through which multinationals may force domestic firms to exit the market. However, their model suggests that, while multinationals can act as a catalyst to stimulate local industry, local industry and multinationals do not coexist.[5] One can, however, consider this result as particular case. As noted by Markusen and Venables themselves, "this result comes from the relatively high degree of similarity between local and multinational firms, and it is easy to imagine circumstances which would permit coexistence" (1999, p. 351).

In what follows we build a simple model in which coexistence of domestic firms and foreign multinationals is possible. Such a scenario may arguably be more general than the specific case considered by Markusen and Venables (1999). In particular, this allows us to study the way competition and spillovers effects act successively

[4]Haaland and Wooton (1999) have a similar theoretical setting, though they focus on the rationale for financial incentives.

[5]The authors argue that this case corresponds to the experience of some countries in East Asia where multinationals have served as catalyst for industrial development and, after a certain period of time, have been wiped out because of the strong competition they ended-up facing on their own product market.

through the entry of FDI. We do not consider the conditions under which the coexistence between domestic and foreign firms is possible, as in Markusen and Venables (1999). Instead, we assume that FDI is determined exogenously and takes place both through the entry of new firms into the product market and of foreign capital entry as described by Rivera-Batiz and Rivera-Batiz (1991). This is made possible by considering that FDI occurs through foreign capital entry as long as the based on a theoretical model and that they do not allow for a potential non-linear relationship. return to capital in the host economy is higher than in the origin country. In doing so, we introduce a simple law of motion where FDI ceases when the returns to capital are equalized in both countries. This allows us to describe the way competition and positive externalities act successively and how they can possibly influence the development of a local industry in which both domestic and multinational firms coexist.

2.1. Structure of the model

We consider an economy with three sectors: agriculture, which produces a homogeneous good y, manufacturing and services which produce differentiated goods x and s, respectively. All sectors use a composite factor K which includes both labor and capital. Services are intermediate inputs in the production of the manufacturing good. Consumers own K and purchase x and y and have identical preferences described by a utility function defined on y and on a sub-utility function defined on x. The utility function of the representative consumer takes the form

$$U = X^{\delta} Y^{1-\delta}, \tag{1}$$

where $0<\delta<1$ and X is a sub-utility function of CES-type defined by

$$X = \left\{ \sum_j x_j^{\Gamma} \right\}^{1/\Gamma} \tag{2}$$

where $0<\Gamma<1$ and $j = 1 \ldots n_x$, with n_x being the number of varieties of the manufactured good.

We assume monopolistic competition in manufacturing so that each variety of the manufacturing good is produced by only one firm. Additionally, there are increasing returns to scale represented by decreasing average costs and manufacturers use K as a primary production factor and services as intermediate inputs. Given r, the unit price of K, q_s, the price index of services, and x_j, the production level of each producer taken individually the cost function of each manufacturing firm is defined by[6]

$$C_j(x_j) = q^{u}\, r1^{-\mu}(\alpha + \beta\, x_j) \tag{3}$$

with $0 < \mu < 1$.

[6]This is the cost function used by Venables (1996) and it can be easily derived from a Cobb–Douglas production function with a fixed component in terms of services and the composite factor.

The terms α and β are positive parameters and average costs are decreasing with production so that there are increasing returns to scale, specifically *internal returns to scale*. The price index of services is defined as follows:

$$q_s = \left\{ \sum_i p_i^{1-\sigma} \right\}^{1/(1-\sigma)} \tag{4}$$

where $i = 1, \ldots, n_s$ and n_s is the number of available varieties of differentiated services and σ is the constant elasticity of substitution between each pair of variety of differentiated services with $\sigma > 1$. Assuming that all varieties of the differentiated services enter symmetrically in the production function, expression (4) can be simplified to

$$qs = n_s 1/(1-\sigma) p_i. \tag{4′}$$

Eq. (4′) depicts the relationship between q_s and n_s. Since the expression $1/1 - \sigma$ is negative, an increase in n_s provokes a decrease in q_s. The direct consequence is that the cost function of manufacturing firms defined by (3) decreases with n_s for a given production level. This implies a potential external effect or *external returns to scale* of service sector activity on manufacturing because service variety, represented by n_s, plays a positive role for manufacturing firm efficiency per se. Given the specification of the utility function in (1) and (2), constant elasticity of substitution between each pair of differentiated manufactured products is equal to

$$\theta = \frac{1}{1-\Gamma} > 1. \tag{5}$$

It can be shown that, for a sufficiently large number of firms, θ is also the price elasticity of demand. We can then write the price index for manufactured products:

$$q_x = \left\{ \sum_j p_j^{1-\theta} \right\}^{1/(1-\theta)}. \tag{6}$$

Given θ, individual prices are determined by the equalization of marginal income to marginal costs. Prices are set above marginal cost and using (3) and (5) we can find the expression for the price of the manufactured good:

$$p_j = \frac{\theta}{\theta - 1} \beta q_s^{\mu} r^{1-\mu}. \tag{7}$$

There is free entry and exit in manufacturing implying zero profits. Using (3) and (7) one can find the expression for the quantity produced by each manufacturing firm as a constant term equal to

$$x_j = \frac{\alpha(\theta - 1)}{\beta}. \tag{8}$$

This represents the break-even level of production or, in other words, the production level to be reached by each manufacturing firms to cover fixed costs.

There is monopolistic competition also in the services sector so prices and quantities can be derived using the same assumptions as above. In addition, as in Markusen and Venables (1999), we assume that services are non-tradable. The cost function is the same for each service producer and is equal to

$$C_i(s_i) = r(\gamma + \rho\, s_i), \tag{9}$$

where s_i is the production level of each service firm i and γ and ρ are positive constant terms. Average costs decrease with s_i so that there are increasing returns in the service sector. Hence, firm behaviour is similar in the service and manufacturing sectors. Given σ, the constant demand elasticity between each pair of services, individual prices are set above marginal costs. Services are only used by manufacturing firms but not by consumers. With a sufficiently large number of service varieties, σ can be taken as the price elasticity of demand, so that using Eq. (9), the expression for service price is equal to

$$p_i = \frac{\sigma}{\sigma - 1}\rho r. \tag{10}$$

As in manufacturing, there is free entry and exit in the service market so that profits equal zero in equilibrium. Using Eqs. (9) and (10) we can derive the break-even level of output in services as

$$s_i = \frac{\gamma(\sigma - 1)}{\rho}. \tag{11}$$

Finally, equilibrium in the agricultural sector is quite simple. We assume that y is the production level of the agricultural good, which is also the numeraire. There is perfect competition in this sector, the production function for agriculture can then be represented by an aggregated function as

$$y = K_y, \tag{12}$$

where K_y is the total quantity of composite factor employed in agriculture. The price of the agricultural good is equal to marginal cost:

$$p_y = r. \tag{13}$$

The description of the model is completed with equilibrium in the composite factor market. Using Shephard's lemma to derive demand for capital by manufacturing and service firms from Eqs. (3) and (9), respectively, and from Eq. (12) for agriculture, it is possible to derive the equilibrium condition in the composite factor market as

$$n_x \frac{\partial C_j}{\partial r} + n_s \frac{\partial C_i}{\partial r} + K_y = K. \tag{14}$$

K is the total endowment in the composite factor of the economy and the second partial derivative of the left hand side is defined taking p_i as given and k_y is the total factor employed in agriculture.

One can now use the model to analyze the relationships between the service sector and the manufacturing industry. To simplify the analysis, we examine first the closed economy case and show afterwards how FDI may modify the picture and play an active role for the development of local firms.

2.2. The closed economy case

The interactions between service and manufacturing firms work through two channels, namely, the factor market and the upstream-downstream production structure. To consider interactions in the factor market, one has to bear in mind that all sectors use the same factor. The equilibrium number of firms in services and manufacturing is determined by the size of the market, i.e., the total endowment of K in the economy. Hence one can use Eq. (14) to derive the first relationship between the equilibrium number of firms of both sectors as follows.

Since the utility function depicted in Eq. (1) has a Cobb–Douglas form, the expenditure on the agriculture good equals

$$P_y\ y = (1-\delta)rK. \tag{15}$$

With full employment, the term rK is equal to the available income destined for consumption of agricultural and manufactured goods. Then $(1-\delta)rK$ is the value of income available for consumption of the agricultural good. Using Eq. (13) one can show that the demand for the composite factor in agriculture is equal to

$$K_y = (1-\delta)K. \tag{16}$$

The term δK represents the total quantity of the composite factor employed in the service and manufacturing sectors. We can then use Eq. (14) together with Eqs. (3) and (9) for the cost function, and Eqs. (4′), (8), (10), and (11), which gives the equilibrium values for prices and quantities, to determine the equilibrium number of manufacturing firms as a function of the parameters of the model, the number of services firms and the total capital endowment of the economy. This yields the following expression:

$$n_x = \frac{\delta K - n_s(\gamma\sigma)}{(\sigma/(\sigma-1)\rho)^{\mu}(\alpha\theta)n_s^{\mu/(1-\sigma)}}. \tag{17}$$

Eq. (17) shows that n_x is greater, the larger is K. Here the equilibrium number of firms in the service sector n_s, acts on n_x through two opposite effects. The first one is positive and plays through the externality effect since a larger number of varieties in the service sector implies a lower price index for such services as described in Eq. (4′) and increases manufacturing firms' efficiency. This is because the exponent $\mu/(1-\sigma)$ of n_s in the denominator is negative, a rise n_s provokes a rise of n_x. The second one is negative since a higher number of service firms implies also a higher demand for K which increases the price of capital *ceteris paribus*, playing against manufacturing firms efficiency. There is then competition on the factor market which limits the equilibrium number of firms in the two different industries as these firms use both K factor. The general relationship between n_x and n_s is thus ambiguous although one should note that both are affected positively by a larger endowment in K.

Finally, one can derive the number of service firms by using the equilibrium condition on the service market. We assume that each service enters the production function symmetrically. One can then use the cost function for manufacturing firms given by Eq. (3) to determine the total demand for intermediate services multiplying individual demands by the equilibrium number of manufacturing firms. We can use Shephard's lemma to derive individual demand for each service variety. Since the individual supply of each service is fixed at the break-even level of production given by Eq. (11), the demand for each service variety is equal to its supply which gives the following expression:

$$n_x \frac{\partial C_j}{\partial P_i} = s_i. \tag{18}$$

2.3. Multinationals in the model

In order to introduce MNEs into the model we need to make two important assumptions. First, we assume that there is a continuous entry of new firms in the market. Second, we assume that FDI is the only way to penetrate the local market. FDI occurs through firms located outside the host country ignoring the production and competition conditions in their home market. The entry of foreign firms is then determined by the differential in the price of r between the host market and the home market (r^*), namely, $\Delta n_m > 0$ if $r > r^*$ and $\Delta n_m = 0$ if $r \leqslant r^*$. That is, with $r > r^*$, foreign firms enter the market until $r = r^*$. The number of local firms is then endogenous in the model while the number of MNEs is directly determined by the relative value of r and r^*.[7]

It then follows that the entry of foreign firms in the local market is accompanied by an exogenous entry of the foreign composite factor K. The amount of K transferred by each multinational is represented by a constant term Φ. This entry of the additional factor exerts indirectly a positive effect on domestic firms since it increases K. As such, the potential negative impact of an increase in demand for production factors represented by a larger number of firms is lowered through a larger endowment in capital which increases the variety of services available in the economy. This also captures the positive macroeconomic effect of a larger capital endowment in the host economy, as in Rivera-Batiz and Rivera-Batiz (1991).

In addition we assume that MNEs have the same cost function compared to their local counterparts and we can use Eqs. (7) and (8) to determine the equilibrium level of prices and quantities as before.[8] The number of multinationals is represented by n_m and the number of local firms n_l, which are our two main variables of interest. Given that all firms within each type are identical, each variety of manufactured good enters the price index symmetrically and we can rewrite Eq. (6) as the price

[7]Note that in order to make the analysis more tractable we still assume that for MNEs, like domestic firms, output level is set in order to get zero profit. In addition, we assume that all services consumed by MNEs are produced locally by firms from the service sectors.

[8]Note that one could perfectly imagine cases where production cost differ between each firm-type, as in Markusen and Venables (1999), without changing the main results.

index for the manufacturing product including multinationals:

$$q_x = \{n_1 p_1^{1-\theta} + n_m p_m^{1-\theta}\}^{1(1-\theta)}. \tag{19}$$

This equation shows, as in Markusen and Venables (1999), that multinationals will exert a competitive pressure on domestic firms by lowering the price index of the final product. As a consequence, the entry of multinationals reduces domestic firms' sales and drives some to exit the market in order to fulfill the zero-profit condition.

Conditions remain equal in the service sector and conditions for equilibrium depicted in the previous section remain unchanged. We can then rewrite Eq. (14) and (18) by considering the entry of MNEs and the modification of K to represent the magnitude of FDI in order to determine the equilibrium number of local firms in manufacturing and service sectors. This leaves us with two expressions to determine: the equilibrium condition for full employment in the capital market and the equality between demand and supply of individual services. Both equations are derived taking as given the equilibrium values for prices and quantities as before. After some calculation, the equilibrium in the capital market is given by

$$\alpha\theta\left(\frac{\sigma}{\sigma-1}\rho\right)^{\mu} n_s\mu(1-\sigma)(n_l+n_m) + n_s\gamma\sigma = \delta K + \Phi n_m, \tag{20}$$

where Φn_m represents the proportional change in the capital endowment of the host economy due to FDI. The term Φ represents the variation rate at which K changes. Given that we assume that domestic firms and multinationals have the same cost functions, the equilibrium conditions in the service market is given by the following expression:

$$(n_l+n_m)\frac{\partial C_j}{\partial p_i} = s_i. \tag{21}$$

Using the expression of the cost function and the equilibrium level of each service production, the preceding expression can be rewritten as

$$\mu\theta\alpha\left(\frac{\sigma}{\sigma-1}\rho\right)^{\mu-1} n_s\mu/(1-\sigma)(n_l+n_m) = \frac{\gamma(\sigma-1)}{\rho}. \tag{22}$$

Eqs. (20) and (22) have no straightforward interpretation, however, and one has to rely on numerical simulation in order to analyze the mechanisms at hand. Before doing this, let us recall the main economic forces at work. The first mechanism is represented by the positive externality arising from the increase of K by an amount that we have supposed to be proportional to the number of MNEs. The second element is that an increase in the number of active firms in the market increases the demand for intermediates and provokes externality effects through the relationship between the equilibrium number of manufacturing and services firms. However, the last element can also play against the equilibrium number of local firms. An entry of MNEs increases competition and, *ceteris paribus*, provokes the exit of a determined number of local firms to restore zero-profit given the break-even level of output. There are thus several elements working simultaneously making the analysis quite difficult.

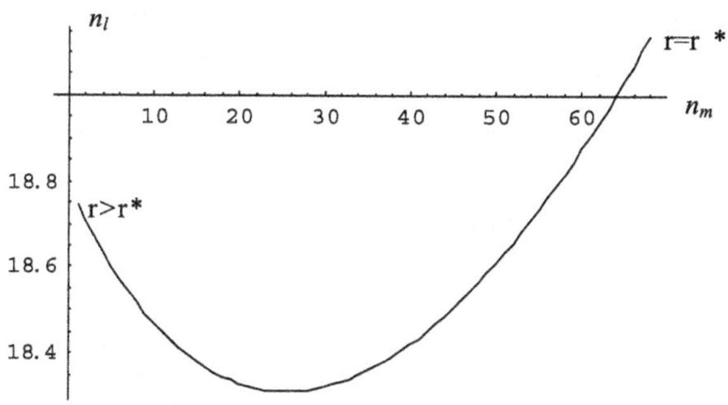

Fig. 1. Parameter values: $K=50$, $\delta=0.5$, $\alpha=0.4$, $\beta=1$, $\lambda=0.8$, $\mu=0.4$, $\theta=6$, $\rho=1$, $\sigma=1.38$, $\gamma=0.5$, $\Phi=1$.

The numerical simulations of (20) and (22) is represented in Fig. 1. The *u-curve* represented in this figure depicts the potential effect of FDI on the number of local firms in the host economy. This effect is first negative meaning that first the competition effect of FDI dominates. Entry of new foreign firms, although they have higher fixed costs than local firms, provokes the exit of a determined number of local firms. This is in part due to our hypothesis concerning the way in which FDI occurs. The entry of multinationals then forces some domestic firms out of the market through competitive pressure. However, for further increases of n_m, the equilibrium number of local firms starts to increase as a result of the dominance of the positive externalities effect. Moreover, since we have considered successive changes in the capital endowment of the economy, the competition effect begins to be less important relative to the larger market reflected by a larger factor market and, as a consequence, a larger market for intermediate products and final consumption.

It is important to mention the particularity of our hypothesis. Taking FDI as both an entry of new firms in the market and as a capital inflow it causes n_s to increase monotonously. Consequently, FDI always has a positive effect on intermediate services variety. The potential benefit for domestic firm then lies in the relative strength of this positive externality and of the competition effect as described earlier in the model. Perhaps more interestingly, Fig. 1 shows that the potential positive effect of FDI is more important than the negative one. When positive externalities from FDI dominate, the number of local firms ends up being higher than initially, in the equilibrium without FDI.[9]

Note finally that, in the model presented here, we make the hypothesis that FDI is the only way to penetrate the local market and that multinationals do not re-export

[9]Other numerical examples could have been considered here. For example, if local firms are relatively less efficient than MNEs (i.e. for a α sufficiently lower for multinationals than for domestic firms), FDI may provoke the exit of all the local firms. Efficiency is then a key determinant making local firms able to capture potential spillovers arising from FDI. A more complete model would also include the balance of payments equilibrium to determine the potential effect of FDI on local wages and welfare; however, this is not the focus of our analysis here and is therefore not pursued.

their production to third markets. The literature on MNEs suggests however that FDI and international trade may well be complementary rather than substitute see, for instance, Markusen (1995, 2002). This, in turn, means that the potential effect of MNEs entry could be large if FDI is export-oriented. One could imagine for instance that, in addition to the different effects of FDI considered in our model, another effect could be represented by the fact that FDI allows domestic firms in the intermediate product sector to expand their production via the exports of multinationals. While the data set used for our empirical analysis does not contain information on exports, studies by Ruane and Sutherland (2002) and Barry and Bradley (1997) find that foreign multinationals, in particular from non-EU countries, export over 90 percent of their total output in the 1990s. This picture was similar at the beginning of our sample period, with McAleese (1977) showing that US multinationals exported 95 percent of sales, while British and German owned affiliates had export ratios of 82 percent in 1974.[10] Hence, changes in the impact of FDI on the local industry are not likely to be due to changes in the propensity of foreign affiliates to export in our Irish case study.

3. Empirical specification and data

3.1. Empirical specification

We take the prediction of a u-shaped relationship between FDI and domestic firms as a guide for our empirical work. However, in order to provide empirical evidence we need to slightly depart from the theory in two main ways. Firstly, the theory considers the number of MNEs as the crucial variable. However, that does not take account of the empirical fact that multinationals are generally much larger than domestic firms (e.g., Barry and Bradley, 1997, for Ireland). Hence, in order to measure the importance of multinationals in an industry we measure the presence of MNEs by the share of employment in MNEs, as is commonly done in the related recent literature (see, e.g., Keller and Yeaple, 2003; Görg and Strobl, 2003). Nevertheless, we also experiment in our empirical analysis with using the share of total plant numbers as a proxy for foreign presence.

Secondly, the theory predicts a relationship between the number of MNEs and the number of domestic firms. However, rather than examining the absolute number our empirical approach is to look at the rate of entry of new domestic firms. This allows us to focus on the effect of fostering or discouraging new entry while at the same time scaling entry relative to the total number of firms in the industry. Furthermore, it places our paper firmly into the tradition of entry models in empirical industrial organisation (e.g., Acs and Audretsch, 1989; Mata, 1993).

[10]The current high export ratios are frequently attributed, at least in part, to Ireland's being an EU member. In the earlier years, multinationals locating in Ireland could benefit from an export tax holiday, explaining the high export ratios. See Ruane (1991) for a detailed discussion of Irish industrial policy.

Hence, our empirical implementation of the theoretical relationship amounts to estimating the following relationship:

$$E_{jt} = \alpha + g(FS_{jt}) + \gamma \mathbf{Z}_{jt} + u_j + v_t + \varepsilon_{jt}, \tag{23}$$

where the dependent variable is the net entry rate defined as the number of indigenous plant entries minus exits over the period t to $t+1$ divided by the total number of plants at time t in industry j, u_j is a sector (three digit NACE Rev 1) specific term, v_t is a year specific effect, and ε_{jt} is the remaining error term, assumed to be independent across sectors and over time. $\mathbf{Z}$ is a vector of time and industry varying covariates, namely the sectoral growth rate (SEGR), industry size (ISIZE), minimum efficient scale (MES—measured as average size), and average age of plants in the industry (AGE). The inclusion of these is motivated by empirical studies of firm entry (e.g., Mata, 1993; Mata and Machado, 1996; Görg and Strobl, 2002); detailed descriptions and definitions are included in the appendix.

FS is our proxy intended to capture the effect of foreign multinational companies on the entry of new firms. As discussed above, it is calculated as the share of employment in foreign-owned plants, i.e., employment in foreign plants divided by total employment in industry j at time t. One should note, that we do not restrict it to be linear, but to be of some function $g(\cdot)$. Our theoretical model suggests that it should be u-shaped.

3.2. Data

Our plant level data source is the annual Employment Survey collected since 1972 by Forfás, the policy and advisory board for industrial development in Ireland, and we have access to this data up until and including the year 2000. The response rate to this survey is estimated by Forfás to be generally well over 99 percent, i.e., our data can be seen as including virtually the whole population of manufacturing firms in Ireland. Information at the plant level include the nationality of ownership, level of employment, and the sector of production of each plant. Forfás defines foreign firms as firms which are majority-owned by foreign shareholders, i.e., where 50 percent or more of the shares are owned by foreign shareholders. While arguably, firms with lower foreign ownership should possibly still be considered foreign owned, this is not necessarily a problem for the case of Ireland since almost all foreign direct investment in Ireland has been greenfield investment rather than acquisition of local firms; see Barry and Bradley (1997).

Tables 1 and 2 provide some aggregate data averaged over several years pertaining to the net entry rate of indigenous plants and the share of employment in foreign multinationals as a percentage of total employment in the two digit (NACE Rev 1) industry, respectively. As can be seen, the net entry rate of indigenous plants has fluctuated considerably over the years. In aggregate, it reached a high of a little over 9 percent in the late 1970s, but has been steadily decreasing since the late 1980s. Examining individual sectors reveals considerable variability across these, where the high entry rates in the more high-tech sectors are particularly notable. The aggregate series concerning foreign presence in Table 2 reveals that multinationals have been

1774 S. Barrios et al. / European Economic Review 49 (2005) 1761–1784

Table 1
Domestic entry rate five year averages

Nace	Name	1972–1977	1977–1982	1982–1987	1987–1992	1992–1997	1997–2000
15	Food	5.3	3.8	6.8	5.9	5.3	4.5
16	Drink & tobacco	3.3	0.0	0.0	5.0	0.0	19.4
17	Textiles	5.6	8.8	15.4	9.1	5.5	2.6
18	Wood and wood products	5.2	6.6	10.3	11.7	5.3	3.1
19	Clothing	6.4	5.9	9.1	6.5	4.6	4.1
20	Leather products	8.1	9.1	6.4	4.2	3.8	2.6
21	Paper and paper products	6.4	9.8	7.4	7.2	5.1	3.3
22	Printing and publishing	7.1	5.7	3.9	3.6	3.4	3.2
23	Coke and petr. pr. & nuclear f.	0.0	6.7	17.6	4.7	0.0	0.0
24	Chemicals and chemical prod.	7.2	7.7	12.2	7.9	5.3	6.5
25	Rubber and plastic products	7.2	12.2	10.1	7.6	5.9	3.3
26	Other non-metallic minerals	7.0	7.9	9.2	5.2	3.6	2.8
27	Basic metals	8.5	13.4	11.2	8.5	10.8	4.6
28	Fabricated metal products	8.7	13.0	8.5	4.8	3.0	2.9
29	Machinery and equipment NEC	10.5	13.5	6.0	9.8	5.7	5.3
30	Office machines and computers	18.3	28.4	23.2	13.3	13.0	10.1
31	Electrical machinery	9.1	15.4	12.6	7.3	5.7	5.7
32	Electronic equipment	6.1	21.6	8.1	9.5	12.5	9.3
33	Medical and precision instr.	14.7	13.2	12.9	9.4	9.0	9.6
34	Automobile products	5.9	8.5	5.1	4.1	2.7	2.1
35	Other transport products NEC	7.3	6.8	10.0	5.6	5.3	5.1
36	Furniture	8.2	13.0	11.2	7.3	7.9	5.3
37	Other manufacturing NEC	—	—	—	50.0	0.0	—
All		7.0	9.1	8.9	6.7	5.3	4.3

steadily increasing their importance in the Irish manufacturing sector. More precisely, foreign multinationals accounted for some 33 percent of manufacturing employment in the early 1970s, and this share has risen to around 47 percent by the end of our sample period. Again, however, the data in the table show that there are considerable sectoral differences, where foreign presence has been generally lower in the traditional sectors.

4. Econometric results

4.1. OLS estimator

In order to estimate the impact of foreign presence on entry of domestic firms we first proceed using simple OLS and including foreign presence and its higher order values. Results of this using foreign presence defined in terms of share of employment are depicted in Table 3. Restricting FS to a linear impact we find it has a positive and statistically significant effect on the net indigenous entry rate, in line with the findings by Görg and Strobl (2002). However, estimating (23) without

Table 2
Foreign presence five year averages

NACE	NAME	1972–1977	1977–1982	1982–1987	1987–1992	1992–1997	1997–2000
15	Food	28.7	28.6	29.1	29.1	26.5	24.7
16	Drink & tobacco	64.1	57.7	59.4	61.0	75.5	75.5
17	Textiles	41.2	53.7	57.1	59.6	59.3	52.0
18	Wood and wood products	21.2	23.9	33.2	35.6	31.7	28.6
19	Clothing	27.1	31.0	25.5	7.9	13.1	13.8
20	Leather products	10.0	7.4	7.7	9.4	9.0	13.5
21	Paper and paper products	29.0	28.9	31.9	32.1	27.8	21.9
22	Printing and publishing	8.4	7.7	6.8	7.0	8.8	8.8
23	Coke and petr. pr. & nuclear f.	28.3	27.6	21.9	19.7	17.6	19.3
24	Chemicals and chemical prod.	58.0	70.5	75.7	79.0	81.5	82.4
25	Rubber and plastic products	42.2	47.4	45.7	44.9	42.5	40.8
26	Other non-metallic minerals	22.3	23.1	23.6	23.0	20.3	15.8
27	Basic metals	75.6	68.3	69.5	65.0	55.4	46.2
28	Fabricated metal products	33.4	27.2	23.8	26.9	26.6	25.5
29	Machinery and equipment NEC	51.0	55.6	57.7	55.7	50.1	48.5
30	Office machines and computers	86.9	97.0	94.4	90.1	90.6	92.7
31	Electrical machinery	33.0	50.4	62.2	67.4	69.4	66.9
32	Electronic equipment	44.5	56.1	72.7	77.9	82.5	82.4
33	Medical and precision instr.	81.4	86.3	86.9	86.4	86.2	85.1
34	Automobile products	70.9	69.5	69.2	78.1	77.0	71.0
35	Other transport products NEC	49.7	43.5	26.7	32.4	45.2	50.9
36	Furniture	13.9	16.9	15.5	16.8	19.6	16.5
37	Other manufacturing NEC	—	—	—	58.3	62.5	—
ALL		33.8	37.6	40.8	43.8	45.7	47.1

FS, regressing the subsequent residual on FS, and then employing a Ramsey test suggests that a simple linear effect may not be correctly capturing the required functional form. We thus proceed and include a quadratic term, but this renders the linear term insignificant and a Ramsey test still suggests that the specification is unsatisfactory. While including a third order term does result in all FS variables being significant, a Ramsey test still suggests misspecification. Moreover, the inclusion of fourth and fifth order terms, as shown in the last two columns, suggests that the relationship between the net indigenous entry rate and foreign presence is not easily modelled by the shape restrictions that come with using higher order terms. We also conduct a similar exercise using the share of foreign plants in total plant population within a sector as a foreign presence proxy, as shown in Table 4. Here, similarly, it is difficult to judge from the higher order terms and the Ramsey tests what proper functional form FS should take.

4.2. Semi-parametric kernel regression estimator

A more flexible and perhaps more attractive approach to further investigate the possible non-linearity of the relationship between E and FS in (23), while also

Table 3
OLS estimation using foreign share of employment

	(1)	(2)	(3)	(4)	(5)
FS	0.190***	−0.015	0.505***	−0.162	0.471
	(0.035)	(0.091)	(0.184)	(0.325)	(0.476)
FS2		0.233**	−1.326***	2.226	−3.375
		(0.095)	(0.489)	(1.510)	(3.420)
FS3			1.132***	−4.840**	11.874
			(0.349)	(2.426)	(9.473)
FS4				3.148**	−17.027
				(1.266)	(11.127)
FS5					8.495*
					(4.655)
MES	0.000*	0.000	0.000	0.000	0.000
	(0.000)	(0.000)	(0.000)	(0.000)	(0.000)
AGE	0.004**	0.004**	0.004**	0.004**	0.004**
	(0.002)	(0.002)	(0.002)	(0.002)	(0.002)
SEGR	0.150***	0.149***	0.150***	0.149***	0.149***
	(0.010)	(0.010)	(0.010)	(0.010)	(0.010)
ISIZE	−0.000***	−0.000***	−0.000***	−0.000**	−0.000**
	(0.000)	(0.000)	(0.000)	(0.000)	(0.000)
Constant	0.119	0.124	0.120	0.123	0.126
	(0.198)	(0.197)	(0.197)	(0.197)	(0.197)
Observations	2530	2530	2530	2530	2530
F-test	5.19***	5.21***	5.27***	5.29***	5.28***
Ramsey test	3.76***	5.00***	7.27***	7.22***	7.76***
R^2	0.22	0.22	0.22	0.23	0.23

Notes: (1) Time and Industry Dummies included. (2) Standard errors in parentheses. (3) ***, **, and * are 1, 5, and 10 percent significance levels.

allowing for the (linear) effect of other conditioning variables Z, follows the semi-parametric methodology proposed by Robinson (1988) using the Kernel regression estimator.[11] Specifically, this estimator does not, in contrast to including higher order terms, impose any restrictions on the relationship of interest. Accordingly, one can consider the following equation to be estimated:

$$Y = \alpha + g(X) + \delta Z, +\mu, \tag{24}$$

where Z is a set of explanatory variables that are assumed to have a linear effect on $\tilde{y}(= \Delta \log y)$, $g()$ is a smooth and continuous, possibly non-linear, unknown function of X, and u is a random error term. A commonly used non-parametric estimator of an unknown function like $g(X)$ without allowing for the effect of other conditioning

[11] See Blundell and Duncan (1998) for details and a helpful discussion of the implementation of this method.

Table 4
OLS estimation using foreign share of plant numbers

	(1)	(2)	(3)	(4)	(5)
FS	0.565***	−0.213	0.577**	0.016	−0.514
	(0.057)	(0.136)	(0.236)	(0.417)	(0.650)
FS2		1.280***	−2.054**	2.076	7.831
		(0.203)	(0.843)	(2.661)	(6.040)
FS3			3.398***	−5.985	−27.931
			(0.833)	(5.795)	(21.475)
FS4				6.561	40.867
				(4.010)	(32.571)
FS5					−18.723
					(17.641)
MES	0.000***	0.000***	0.000***	0.000***	0.000***
	(0.000)	(0.000)	(0.000)	(0.000)	(0.000)
AGE	0.001	0.002	0.003*	0.003	0.003
	(0.002)	(0.002)	(0.002)	(0.002)	(0.002)
SEGR	0.152***	0.149***	0.149***	0.149***	0.149***
	(0.010)	(0.010)	(0.010)	(0.010)	(0.010)
ISIZE	−0.000***	−0.000**	−0.000**	−0.000**	−0.000**
	(0.000)	(0.000)	(0.000)	(0.000)	(0.000)
Constant	0.067	0.090	0.094	0.090	0.089
	(0.195)	(0.193)	(0.193)	(0.193)	(0.193)
Observations	2530	2530	2530	2530	2530
F-test	5.86***	6.21***	6.33***	6.31***	6.27***
Ramsey test	8.41***	2.15**	1.96*	0.99	1.84*
R^2	0.24	0.25	0.26	0.26	0.26

Notes: (1) Time and Industry Dummies included. (2) Standard errors in parentheses. (3) ***, **, and * are 1, 5, and 10 percent significance levels.

variables is the Nadaraya–Watson estimator (see Nadaraya, 1964; Watson, 1964):

$$\hat{m}_h(X) = n^{-1} \frac{\sum_{i=1}^{n} K_h(X - X_i)\tilde{y}_i}{n^{-1}\sum_{i=1}^{n} K_h(X - X_i)} \tag{25}$$

such that $i = 1, \ldots, n$ are the n number of observations, $K_h()$ is the shape function, commonly referred to as the Kernel, that is a continuous, bounded and real function that integrates to one and acts as a weighting function of observations around X and depends on the choice of bandwidth h.

The appeal of this estimator lies in its very flexible approach to non-linearity by allowing the relationship of $\tilde{y}$ with respect to X to vary over all values of X. Specifically, this technique corresponds to estimating the regression function at a particular point by locally fitting constants to the data via weighted least squares, where those observations closer to the chosen point have more influence on the regression estimate than those further away, as determined by the choice of h and K.

An additional appeal of this sort of technique is that it avoids any parametric assumptions regarding the conditional mean function $m(X)$, and thus about its functional form or error structure.

Allowing for the linear effect of other explanatory variables only slightly complicates the estimation of $g(X)$. Specifically, Robinson (1988) showed that in controlling for other conditioning variables the (semi-parametric) Kernel regression estimator for $g(X)$ simply becomes[12]

$$\hat{g}(X) = \hat{m}_{\tilde{y}}(X) - \hat{\delta}\hat{m}_x(X), \tag{26}$$

where $\hat{m}_{\tilde{y}}(X)$ and $\hat{m}_x(X)$ are the (non-parametric) Kernel regression estimates of $E(\tilde{y}/X)$ and $E(Z/X)$, and $\hat{\delta}$ is the OLS estimator of

$$\tilde{y} - \hat{m}_{\tilde{y}}(X) = \delta(Z - \hat{m}_x(X)) + \varepsilon, \tag{27}$$

where ε is a random error term. Intuitively, $\hat{g}(X)$ is the estimate of $g(X)$ after the independent effect(s) of Z on Y has been removed.

Given that the estimate of $\hat{g}(X)$ is at least in part based on non-parametric estimation techniques, one cannot subject it to the standard statistical type tests (e.g. t-test) that economists have grown so accustomed to using in parametric regressions. One can, however, relatively easily calculate upper and lower pointwise confidence bands as[13]

$$CI = \hat{g}(X) + / - (c_\alpha c_\kappa)^{1/2}\hat{\eta}(x)/[h\; CI = \hat{g}(X)]$$
$$\pm(c_\alpha c_\kappa)^{1/2}\hat{\eta}(X)(X) \pm 0^{1/2} \Bigg/ \left[\sum_{i=1}^{n}(X - X_i)\right]^{1/2} \tag{28}$$

where $c_\alpha c_K$ is a kernel specific constant corresponding to the α quantile of the distribution and $\hat{\eta}^2(X)$ is defined as

$$\hat{\eta}(X) = n^{-1}\frac{\sum_{i=1}^{n} K_h(X - X_i)\tilde{y}_i}{n^{-1}\sum_{i=1}^{n} K_h(X - X_i)}. \tag{29}$$

One should note that (29) ignores the possible approximation error bias of $\hat{g}(X)$. Including this in (29) would complicate the expression considerably since the bias is a complicated function of the first and second derivatives of $g(X)$. This bias tends to be highest at sudden peaks of $\hat{g}(X)$ and at the necessarily truncated left and right boundaries of the data. However, if h is chosen proportional to $1/n^{(1/5)}$ times a sequence that tends slowly to zero then the bias vanishes asymptotically for the interior points.[14] For all our estimations we use a Gaussian kernel for K_h and an

[12]The fact that δ is in part estimated using OLS makes this a semi- rather than non-parametric estimator.

[13]See Haerdle (1990) for details.

[14]See Haerdle (1990) and Wand and Jones (1995) for a discussion of these aspects.

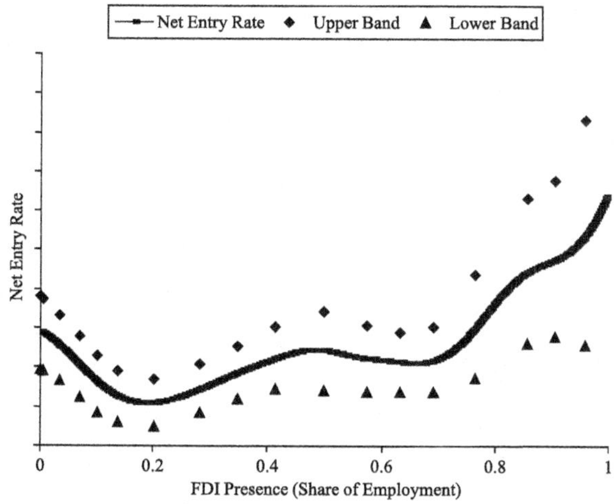

Fig. 2. Net domestic entry rate—share of total employment by foreign plants.

optimal bandwidth h such that:

$$h = \frac{0.9m}{n^{1/5}}. \tag{30}$$

where $m = (\hat{\sigma}^2(X) \times \text{(interquantile range)}_x / 1.349)$

One should also note that the size of $\hat{\sigma}^2(X)$ any point of X will depend proportionally on the marginal distribution of X. In other words the accuracy of the estimate of $g(X)$ at X is positively related to the density of other observations around that point. In order to visualize this effect we, as suggested by Haerdle (1990), calculate the pointwise confidence bands at points chosen according to the distribution of X. Specifically, we chose points so that five percent of the observations lie between them.[15]

Our semi-parametric kernel regression estimates of $g(x)$ along with pointwise confidence bands using the net entry rate as the dependent variable and foreign share of employment as the measure of FDI presence are given in Fig. 2.[16] One should also note that we do not report the actual estimates of $g(FS)$ on the vertical axes, just graph the relationship between FS and the dependent variable. Our primary reason for not reporting these is that our estimates of $g(FS)$ are predicted values from which the influence of the other control variables have been purged, and hence, cannot be directly linked to the actual range observed, the net indigenous entry rate. Instead, as is standard, one should use the figures to gauge the estimated slope of the

[15]From the endpoints we chose the 1 and 99 percentiles of the distribution.

[16]Given that values on the vertical axis for the net entry rate are based on predicted values and thus do not correspond necessarily to the actual observed entry rates, we have omitted labeling the axis rather than shifting the value by some constant to fall within the range of actual values.

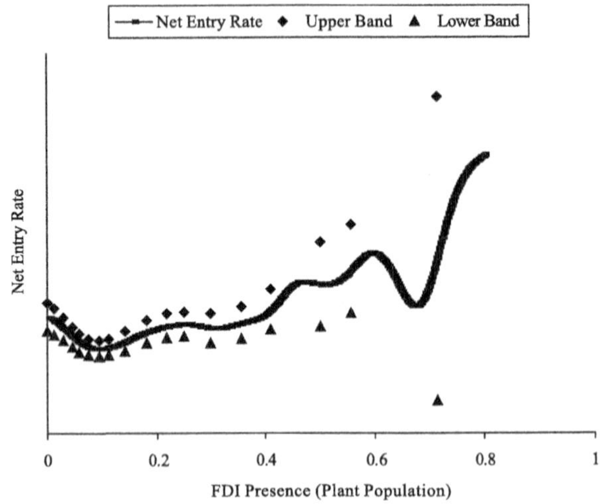

Fig. 3. Net domestic entry rate—share of total plant population by foreign plants.

relationship in question. Of course, it is this relationship that this paper is concerned with in any case.

As can be seen, we find a u-shaped relationship between the net entry rate and foreign presence within a sector, although this is not continuously smooth.[17] Nevertheless, the size of the confidence bands shows that the curve is estimated with considerable confidence, except for higher values of FDI presence where also the distribution of observations is relatively small, as indicated by the horizontal width between each confidence band. If our estimate of $g(FS)$ is taken at face value, then the minimum of the curve is found where FDI presence takes the value of 29 percent. Thus the competition effect of FDI outweighs any positive spillover effects on net indigenous plant entry up until this point, but once this threshold level is reached positive spillover effects dominate. This evidence, thus, is in line with the patterns suggested in the theoretical analysis in Section 2.

We also estimated the model using the share of multinationals in total plant population as a proxy for FDI presence and present the results in Fig. 3. First of all one should note that the observations near the maximum value of FDI in our data (0.8) are very sparsely distributed, so that estimates are likely to be poor. This is at least in part probably part of the reason for the curve's wide fluctuations near the right boundary. The rest of the curve is similar to that for foreign employment share, although the turning point is somewhat earlier, namely around 23 percent.

One should note that the semi-parametric Kernel regression estimator can be extremely sensitive to outliers given that it is roughly speaking simply a local

[17]Using a larger value of h could ensure greater smoothness, but the trade-off is a greater approximation bias.

S. Barrios et al. / European Economic Review 49 (2005) 1761–1784 1781

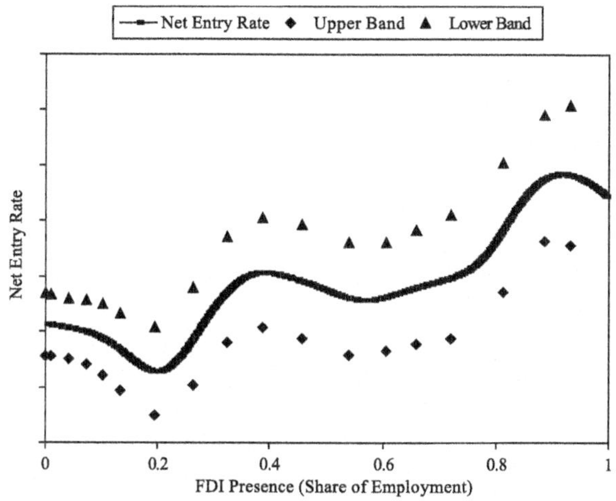

Fig. 4. Net domestic entry rate—share of total employment by foreign plants—without outliers.

weighted average of the response variable. This is already apparent from the greater width of the confidence bands around peaks and near the right hand side end points where there are fewer observations. In order to check for the robustness of the shapes implied by the overall sample we re-estimated our regressions excluding what may be 'outliers'. Specifically, we excluded all observations where the net entry rate was one standard deviation above or below the sample mean. For the foreign share of plant population regression we also excluded all observations where the share was above 0.6, since Fig. 3 seems to suggest a number of poorly estimated peaks to the right of this value. The kernel regression estimates for these sub-samples for foreign presence measured in terms of employment and in terms of plant population are given in Figs. 4 and 5, respectively.

Accordingly, in terms of employment share there still exists a general u-shaped relationship, although, given that a large part of the right hand side has been truncated, this is not as pronounced as for the unrestricted sample. Clearly, however, the depicted curve suggests that at low values of foreign presence there is a competition effect, while the overall trend beyond a value of 0.2 is upward sloping, indicating positive spillovers. For the plant population curve, as shown in Fig. 5, the u-shaped link between net indigenous entry and foreign presence similarly remains, although perhaps not as pronounced as for the full sample.

5. Conclusion

This paper examines the effect of FDI on the entry of local firms in host economies. In our theoretical framework we show that the impact of FDI on local development depends on two countervailing forces: first, a competition effect which

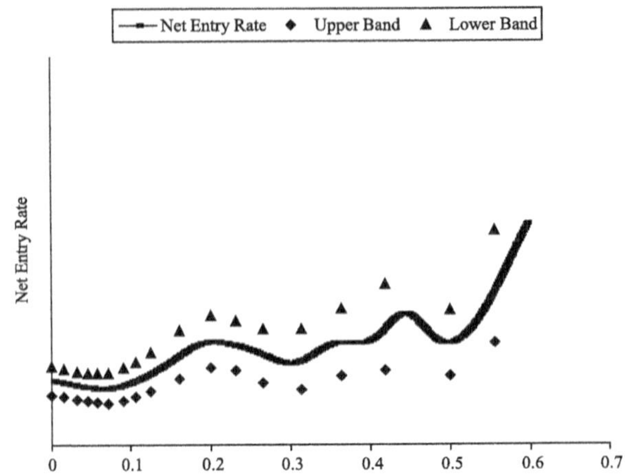

Fig. 5. Net domestic entry rate—share of total plant population by foreign plants.

provokes the exit of local firms; second, positive market externalities related with foreign presence which foster domestic firms' start-up. With a continuous flow of FDI, the evolution of the number of local firms can be depicted as a u-curve where the competition effect first dominates but is gradually outweighed by positive externalities effects. Taking this as a motivating framework for our empirical analysis and applying semi-parametric regression techniques on plant level panel data for the manufacturing sector in the Republic of Ireland, we find support for such a u-shape.

Our results have important implications for economic policies pursued in host countries. This concerns questions such as incentives for resources transfer with FDI. Our model shows how FDI can be positive for local firms expansion and that positive externalities are more likely to occur the larger is the amount of capital transferred through FDI and the greater is the efficiency of local firms. We also show that local firms need to adapt to new competitors since FDI represents a greater competition factor than imports due to the factor market size limitation. FDI may provoke the exit of a given number of local firms while the remaining firms will be able to capture the positive spillovers effects related to FDI. This implies a transition period in which the competition effect dominates. In this case policy may be aimed at shortening this period and smoothing the transition process by assisting domestic firms to improve their capacities in order to be able to compete with multinationals. Thus, policy could be aimed at increasing R&D and innovative activity, as well as training of workers.

Acknowledgements

We are grateful to Forfás for the provision of the data. We would also like to thank the participants at a research seminar organized by FEDEA (Madrid) and to the VI Jornadas de Economía Internacional at the University of Valencia for useful comments. We are especially grateful to Omar Licandro and Juan José de Lucio for very helpful suggestions. We also wish to thank Oscar Bajo, Lionel Fontagné, Jacques Mélitz, Patrick Messerlin and two anonymous referees for very useful comments on earlier versions of this work. Holger Görg gratefully acknowledges financial support from the Leverhulme Trust under Programme Grant F114/BF and the European Commission under Grant No. SERD-2002-00077. Eric Strobl is grateful for his Marie Curie Research Fellowship.

References

Acs, Z.J., Audretsch, D.B., 1989. Small-firm entry in US manufacturing. Economica 56, 255–265.

Aitken, B.J., Harrison, A.E., 1999. Do domestic firms benefit from direct foreign investment? Evidence from Venezuela. American Economic Review 89, 605–618.

Barry, F., Bradley, J., 1997. FDI and trade: the Irish host-country experience. Economic Journal 107, 1798–1811.

Blundell, R., Duncan, A., 1998. Kernel regression in empirical microeconomics. Journal of Human Resources 33 (1), 62–87.

Dixit, A.K., Stiglitz, J., 1977. Monopolistic competition and optimum product diversity. American Economic Review 67, 297–308.

Ethier, W.J., 1982. National and international returns to scale in the modern theory of international trade. American Economic Review 72, 389–405.

Görg, H., Strobl, E., 2001. Multinational companies and productivity spillovers: A meta-analysis. Economic Journal 111, F723–F739.

Görg, H., Strobl, E., 2002. Multinational companies and indigenous development: An empirical analysis. European Economic Review 46, 1305–1322.

Görg, H., Strobl, E., 2003. Multinational companies, technology spillovers and plant survival. Scandinavian. Journal of Economics 105, 581–595.

Haaland, J.I., Wooton, I., 1999. International competition for multinational investment. Scandinavian Journal of Economics 101, 631–649.

Haerdle, W., 1990. Applied Nonparametric Regression. Cambridge University Press, Cambridge.

Hanson, G.H., 2001. Should countries promote foreign direct investment. G-24 Discussion Paper No. 9, UNCTAD, Geneva.

Haskel, J.E., Pereira, S.C., Slaughter, M.J. 2002. Does inward foreign direct investment boost the productivity of domestic firms? NBER Working Paper 8724.

Hymer, S.H., 1976. The International Operations of Multinationals Firms: A Study of Direct Foreign Investment. MIT Press, Cambridge, MA.

Keller, W., Yeaple, S., 2003. Multinational enterprises, international trade, and productivity growth: Firm-level evidence from the US. NBER Working Paper 9504.

Konings, J., 2001. The effects of foreign direct investment on domestic firms: Evidence from firm level panel data in emerging economies. Economics of Transition 9, 619–633.

Lipsey, R.E., 2002. Home and host country effects of FDI. NBER Working Paper 9293.

Markusen, J.R., 1995. The boundaries of multinational enterprises and the theory of international trade. Journal of Economic Perspectives 9 (2), 169–189.

Markusen, J.R., 2002. Multinational Firms and the Theory of International Trade. MIT Press, Cambridge, MA.

Markusen, J.R., Venables, A., 1999. Foreign direct investment as a catalyst for industrial development. European Economic Review 43, 335–356.

Mata, J., 1993. Entry and type of entrant: Evidence from Portugal. International Journal of Industrial Organization 11, 101–122.

Mata, J., Machado, J.A.E., 1996. Firm start-up size: A conditional quantile approach. European Economic Review 40, 1305–1323.

McAleese, D. 1977. A Profile of Grant-Aided Industry in Ireland. IDA Publication Series No. 5, Dublin: The Industrial Development Authority.

Nadaraya, E., 1964. On estimating regression. Theory of Probability and its Applications 9, 141–142.

Rivera-Batiz, F.L., Rivera-Batiz, L.A., 1991. The effects of direct foreign investment in the presence of increasing returns due to specialization. Journal of Development Economics 34, 87–307.

Robinson, P., 1988. Root-N-consistent semiparametric regression. Econometrica 56, 931–954.

Rodríguez-Clare, A., 1996. Multinationals, linkages, and economic development. American Economic Review 86, 852–873.

Romer, P.M., 1987. Growth based on increasing returns due to specialization. American Economic Review 77 (2), 56–62.

Ruane, F., Sutherland, J., 2002. Globalization, Europeanization and trade in the 1990s: Export responses of foreign and indigenous manufacturing companies. In: Kierzkowski, H. (Ed.), Europe and Globalization. Palgrave Macmillan, London, pp. 207–228.

Ruane, F., Ugur, A., 2002. Foreign direct investment and productivity spillovers in Irish manufacturing industry: Evidence from firm level panel data, Trinity Economic Papers 02/06, Trinity College, Dublin.

Venables, A., 1996. Equilibrium location of vertically linked industries. International Economic Review 37, 341–359.

Wand, M.P., Jones, M.C., 1995. Kernel Smoothing. Chapman & Hall, London.

Watson, G.S., 1964. Smooth regression analysis. Sankhya Series A 26, 359–372.

CPSIA information can be obtained at www.ICGtesting.com
Printed in the USA
BVOW06*0604080716

454680BV00002B/4/P

9 789814 749220